R. Gupta's®

POPULAR MASTER GUIDE

Hotel Management

NCHMCT-JEE

National Council for Hotel Management & Catering Technology JOINT ENTRANCE EXAM

Conducted by
National Testing Agency (NTA)

by
RPH Editorial Board

2026
EDITION

RAMESH PUBLISHING HOUSE, NEW DELHI

Published by

O.P. Gupta *for* Ramesh Publishing House

Admin. Office

12-H, New Daryaganj Road, Opp. Officer' Mess,
New Delhi-110002 ✆ 23275224, 23245124

E-mail: info@rameshpublishinghouse.com
For Online Shopping: www.rameshpublishinghouse.com

Showroom

- Balaji Market, Nai Sarak, Delhi-6 ✆ 23282525 📱 9354373464
- 4457, Nai Sarak, Delhi-6, ✆ 23918938

Book Code: R-2651

ISBN: 978-93-5477-685-4

Price: ₹ 495

Printed at: Deepak Offset, Delhi

CONTENTS

SCHEME OF EXAMINATION

PATTERN OF EXAMINATION

Type of Questions (MCQ)	No. of Questions
Numerical Ability and Analytical Aptitude	30
Reasoning and Logical Deduction	30
General Knowledge & Current Affairs	30
English Language	60
Aptitude for Service Sector	50
Total	**200**

MEDIUM OF QUESTION PAPER

(i) The medium of Question Paper shall be in English & Hindi only.

(ii) Option of medium of Question Paper should be carefully chosen by the Candidate, while filling the Application Form online. The option once exercised cannot be changed.

(iii) In case of any ambiguity in translation/construction of a question in the exam, its English version shall be treated as final and the decision of NTA shall be final in this regard.

MARKING SCHEME

(i) Each Question carries 04 (four) marks.

(ii) For each correct response, Candidate will get 04 (four) marks.

(iii) For each incorrect response, 01 (one) mark will be deducted from the total score.

(iv) Un-answered/un-attempted will be given Zero (0) mark.

(v) To answer a question, the candidate needs to choose one option as correct option.

Previous Years' Paper

National Testing Agency (NTA)

NCHMCT-JEE—National Council for Hotel Management and Catering Technology Joint Entrance Exam, 2025

(Exam held on 27-04-2025)

NUMERICAL ABILITY

1. Find the value of: $\dfrac{\sqrt[3]{3375}+\sqrt{144}}{\sqrt[3]{729}+\sqrt[3]{1728}}$

1. $\dfrac{8}{7}$ 2. $\dfrac{9}{7}$
3. $\dfrac{5}{4}$ 4. $\dfrac{4}{3}$

2. A wooden cuboidal box with lid has external dimensions 80 cm × 49 cm × 30 cm. If thickness of the wood is 2 cm, then find the volume of the wood (in cm^3) used.

1. 28420 2. 28620
3. 28680 4. 29940

3. What is the area of an isosceles triangle whose perimeter is 11 cm and base is 5 cm?

1. 10 cm^2 2. $\dfrac{5}{4}\sqrt{11}$ cm^2
3. $20\sqrt{11}$ cm^2 4. $\dfrac{4}{5\sqrt{11}}$ cm^2

4. 22 solid metallic cubes of side 4 cm are melted and 16 equal solid cylinders of height 7 cm are formed. Find the radius (in cm) of the cylinders so formed. ($\pi = 22/7$)

1. 1.5 2. 2
3. 2.4 4. 2.5

5. If A : B = 2 : 3, A : C = 6 : 7, C : D = 14 : 15, then find A : B : C : D.

1. 6 : 9 : 7 : 15
2. 12 : 18 : 14 : 30
3. 12 : 18 : 14 : 15
4. 8 : 12 : 14 : 15

6. A vessel contains 100 liters of solution having 80 liters of spirit and the remaining is water. If 20 liters of the mixture is taken out from the vessel and replaced by water, then what will be the ratio of spirit to water in the new solution?

1. 15 : 8
2. 16 : 9
3. 17 : 8
4. 3 : 2

7. A shopkeeper sold two electric irons at ₹ 1344 each. He earned 12% profit on one iron and lost 4% on the other. Find his overall profit percentage (correct to 2 decimal places).

1. 8.22% 2. 3.38%
3. 4.35% 4. 2.66%

8. A shopkeeper allowed successive discounts of 12% and x% on every item. A customer paid ₹ 15048 for an item marked for ₹ 18000. Find the value of x.

1. 7 2. 5
3. 4 4. 6

9. Simplify: $(27)^{-\frac{1}{3}} \times (27)^{-\frac{1}{3}} \times \left(27^{\frac{1}{3}} - 27^{\frac{2}{3}}\right)$

1. $-\dfrac{2}{3}$ 2. 6
3. −2 4. 54

10. Find the value of $p^3 - 27q^3$ if $p - 3q = -7$ and $pq = -10$.

1. −133 2. 973
3. 287 4. −553

1. 2	**2.** 3	**3.** 2	**4.** 2	**5.** 3	**6.** 2	**7.** 2	**8.** 2	**9.** 1	**10.** 4

11. The value of $(2.3\overline{6} - 0.1\overline{4})$ expressed as fraction in lowest terms is:

1. $\frac{111}{50}$ 2. $\frac{24}{11}$
3. $\frac{20}{9}$ 4. $\frac{11}{5}$

12. If $P = \frac{1}{2} + \frac{1}{6} + \frac{1}{12} + \frac{1}{20} + \frac{1}{30}$, then find the value of $\sqrt{6(9-P)}$.

1. 5 2. 6
3. 7 4. 8

13. Which of the following is correct for a number to be divisible by 8?

1. Sum of the digits should be divisible by 8
2. Unit digit should be divisible by 8
3. Number formed by the last two digits should be divisible by 8
4. Number formed by the last three digits should be divisible by 8

14. If the mean of the observations k, $(k + 8)$, $(2k - 1)$, $(k + 12)$, 12 and 17 is 13, then find the median of these observations.

1. 11 2. 14.5
3. 12.5 4. 13

15. Aniket can row a boat, 21 km downstream in 1 hr 30 min and 20 km upstream in 2 hours. He can row the boat in still water at the speed of (in km/h).

1. 11 2. 11.6
3. 12 4. 12.5

16. To reduce the usual time taken to cover a distance of 300 km by 1 hour, the speed of a bus is increased by 10 km/h. The usual speed of the bus (in km/h) is:

1. 62 2. 60
3. 55 4. 50

17. In a class, there are 40 students. Their average marks in a test are 33. If the average marks of the boys are 30 and that of the girls are 35, then what is the number of boys in the class?

1. 15 2. 20
3. 16 4. 18

18. The average weight of 11 persons in a group of 12 persons is 64 kg. The weight of the 12th person is 22 kg more than the average weight of all the 12 persons. The weight of the 12th person (in kg) is:

1. 80 2. 84
3. 88 4. 90

19. Four men can do 60% of a work in 6 days, whereas 6 women can do 50% of the same work in 5 days. How many days will 2 men and 3 women take to do the work if they work together?

1. 9 2. 9½
3. 10 4. 12

20. 4 men can do a work in 5 days and 5 women can do it in 6 days. How many women should work with 2 men to complete the work in 5 days?

1. 4 2. 3
3. 2 4. 1

21. Aditya and Bipin entered into a partnership by investing ₹ 40,000 and ₹ 50,000, respectively. After 4 months, Aditya made additional investment equal to $\left(\frac{1}{4}\right)$th of his investment and Bipin withdrew $\left(\frac{1}{5}\right)$th of his investment. The share of Aditya in the profit of ₹ 16,200 at the end of the year is:

1. ₹ 8280 2. ₹ 8320
3. ₹ 8400 4. ₹ 8480

22. Two years ago, the ages of Rekha and Shruti were in the ratio 2 : 3. Three years hence, the ratio will become 3 : 4. How old will Shruti be after 8 years from now?

1. 25 years 2. 24 years
3. 23 years 4. 22 years

23. Simplify: $15 + 60 \div 15 \times 2 - 1$

1. 5 2. 9
3. 16 4. 22

24. What smallest number should be subtracted from 81025 to get a perfect square number?

1. 238 2. 0
3. 369 4. 25

25. If the adjacent sides of a rectangle are increased by 35% and 20%, respectively, then by what percent will its area increase?

1. 70% 2. 62%
3. 55% 4. 58%

11. 3	**12.** 3	**13.** 4	**14.** 4	**15.** 3	**16.** 4	**17.** 3	**18.** 3
19. 3	**20.** 2	**21.** 3	**22.** 1	**23.** 4	**24.** 3	**25.** 2	

26. In an election between two candidates, 12% votes did not cast their vote. $\left(\frac{1}{6}\right)$th of the votes casted were found to be invalid. The winner obtained 55% of the valid votes and won the election by 36542 votes. Find the total number of voters registered.

1. 499500
2. 498300
3. 48920
4. 47580

27. Find the LCM of the numbers: $\frac{4}{9}, \frac{8}{15}, \frac{6}{9}, \frac{12}{21}, \frac{14}{33}$

1. $\frac{160}{3}$ 2. $\frac{168}{3}$
3. 52 4. 56

28. The LCM of two numbers is 15 times their HCF. If the sum of their LCM and HCF is 160 and one of the numbers is 50, then what is the other number?

1. 20 2. 24
3. 30 4. 40

29. On simple interest a certain sum amounts to ₹ 14061 in 6 years and to ₹ 16023 in 8 years on the same rate of interest. The rate of interest per annum is:

1. 9% 2. 10%
3. 12% 4. 14%

30. A certain sum on compound interest becomes ₹ 19573 at 15% per annum in 2 years. Find the compound interest on the same sum at 10% per annum in 2 years.

1. ₹ 3078 2. ₹ 3094
3. ₹ 3108 4. ₹ 3206

REASONING AND LOGICAL DEDUCTION

31. If a 'girl' is called a 'boy', 'boy' is called a 'man', 'man' is called a 'waiter', 'waiter' is called a 'woman', 'woman' is called a 'teacher' and 'teacher' is called a 'girl', then who will serve food in a restaurant?

1. Man
2. Teacher
3. Woman
4. Boy

32. Varun wants to go to school, which is neither in direction of cinema hall nor in direction of market. He starts from his home which is in West and goes straight in East direction, where he finds a crossing. On the road to the left side is a cinema hall; straight ahead is a market. In which direction is the school?

1. East 2. West
3. South 4. North

33. A statement is followed by two conclusions (I) and (II). Assume the statement to be true, then consider the conclusions and decide which of them logically follow(s), from the information given in the statement?

Statement: Morning walks are good for health.

Conclusions:

I. Evening walks are harmful
II. All healthy people go for morning walks.

1. Only Conclusion (I) follows
2. Only Conclusion (II) follows
3. Neither (I) nor (II) follows
4. Both (I) and (II) follow

34. A statement is followed by two courses of action numbered (I) and (II). Assume the Statement to be true, then on the basis of the information given in the statement, decide which of the suggested courses of action logically follow(s) for pursuing?

Statement: Footpaths of a busy road are crowded with vendors selling their items, causing a great inconvenience for walkers.

Course of action:

I. The help of police/authority should be sought to drive them away.
II. Some space should be provided to them where they can earn their livelihood without blocking the footpaths.

1. Only (I) follows
2. Only (II) follows
3. Both (I) and (II) follow
4. Neither (I) nor (II) follows

35. A, B, C, D and E five boys are standing in a row facing North. C is sitting to the immediate right of D. A and B are at the ends. E is sitting to the immediate left of A. Who is sitting in the middle?

1. D 2. C
3. E 4. B

26. 2	**27.** 4, 2	**28.** 3	**29.** 3	**30.** 3	**31.** 3	**32.** 3	**33.** 3	**34.** 3	**35.** 2

36. A pair of words is given below which are related in a particular way. The same relationship exists among the words in one of the four given alternatives. Find the correct alternative.

Car : Road

1. Bus : Passengers
2. Track : Train
3. Ship : Sea
4. Aeroplane : Pilot

37. Go through the following information carefully and answer the given question.

(*i*) Sita and Rita are dancers
(*ii*) Gita, Meeta and Anita are singers
(*iii*) Sita and Anita are musicians
(*iv*) Sita, Rita and Anita are comedians

Which of the following is dancer, musician and comedian?

1. Rita 2. Sita
3. Anita 4. Meeta

38. Select a figure from the given alternatives which when placed in the blank space (?) of the given figure would complete the pattern.

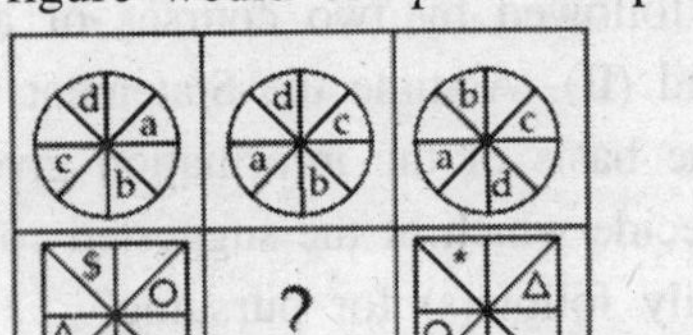

1.  2. 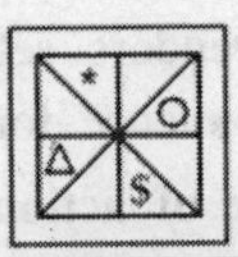
3. 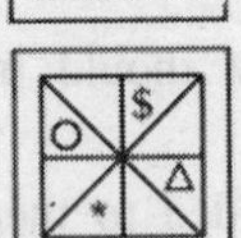 4. 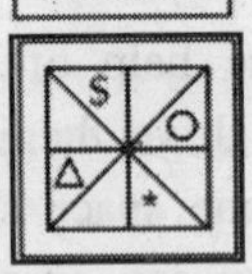

39. Choose the correct figure to complete the following figural series.

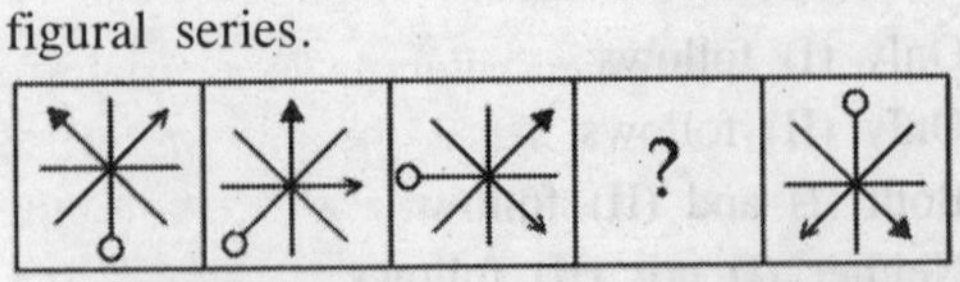

1.  2. 
3.  4. 

40. If the 1st and 26th, 2nd and 25th, 3rd and 24th, and so on letters of the English alphabet are paired, then which of the following pairs is wrong?

1. CX 2. LO
3. IS 4. MN

41. Arrange the following words in the sequence in which they occur in the dictionary and choose the correct sequence.

(*a*) Discount
(*b*) Disclose
(*c*) Discourage
(*d*) Disconnect

1. (*b*), (*d*), (*c*), (*a*) 2. (*d*), (*b*), (*a*), (*c*)
3. (*b*), (*a*), (*d*), (*c*) 4. (*b*), (*d*), (*a*), (*c*)

42. Observe the figures given below and answer the question.

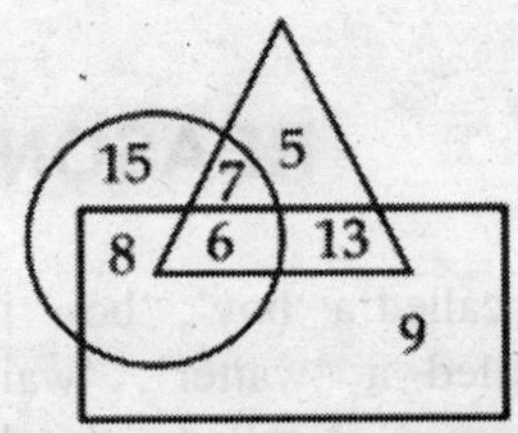

What is the sum of the numbers which belong to any two figures only?

1. 28 2. 26
3. 21 4. 13

43. Seven officers G, H, I, J, K, L and M reach office in a particular sequence. L reaches immediately before G but does not immediately follow J. I is the last one to reach office. K follows immediately after G and is immediately followed by M. Who reaches the office first?

1. J 2. H
3. L 4. G

44. P, Q, R, S, T, U and W are sitting in a circle facing towards the centre. T is neighbour of P and S. Q is between U and R. U is to the immediate right of P. Who is sitting to the immediate left of S?

1. Q 2. W
3. R 4. T

45. If 1st October in a year was on Monday, then what day was on 1st November of the same year?

1. Friday
2. Wednesday
3. Thursday
4. Tuesday

36. 3 **37.** 2 **38.** 1 **39.** 4 **40.** 3 **41.** 4 **42.** 1 **43.** 1 **44.** 2 **45.** 3

46. The number of triangles in the given figure is:

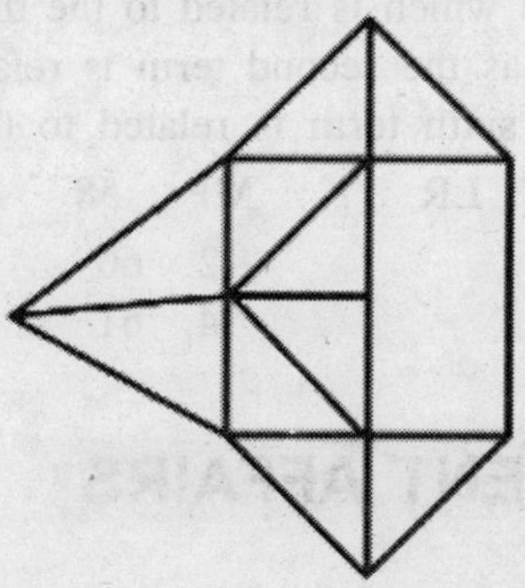

1. 16 2. 12
3. 14 4. 13

47. Which of the following Venn diagrams indicates the best relationship between Vegetables, Food and Potatoes?

1. 

2. 

3. 

4. 

48. Manoj has a brother Abhishek. Manoj is the son of Neeraj. Sunil is father of Neeraj. How is Abhishek related to Sunil?

1. Son 2. Brother
3. Grandfather 4. Grandson

49. If D is sister of E, F is sister of E and D is sister of G, then which of the following statements is definitely true?

1. E is sister of F 2. G is sister of F
3. E is sister of G 4. F is sister of D

50. Choose the odd number pair from the given alternatives:

1. (13 : 143) 2. (19 : 209)
3. (23 : 251) 4. (17 : 187)

51. 'Flower' is related to 'Petal' in the same way as 'Book' is related to:

1. Author 2. Library
3. Page 4. Editor

52. Find the wrong term in the following series:
K 7 D, P 9 G, V 11 J, Z 13 M, E 15 P

1. P 9 G 2. Z 13 M
3. V 11 J 4. E 15 P

53. Arrange the following body parts from top to bottom in a logical and meaningful sequence.

(*i*) Stomach (*ii*) Large intestines
(*iii*) Anus (*iv*) Oesophagus
(*v*) Small intestines (*vi*) Mouth

1. (*vi*), (*iv*), (*i*), (*ii*), (*iii*), (*v*)
2. (*vi*), (*iv*), (*i*), (*ii*), (*v*), (*iii*)
3. (*vi*), (*iv*), (*i*), (*v*), (*ii*), (*iii*)
4. (*vi*), (*i*), (*iv*), (*v*), (*ii*), (*iii*)

54. In a code language 'ALIGRAPH' is written as 'ZMFJVWA' and 'CALICUT' is written as 'BBILXZM' then how will 'AYODHYA' be written in the same code language?

1. ZZLGCDS 2. ZZLGDCT
3. ZZLGCDT 4. ZZLHCDT

55. In a code language 'RED' is written as 4-5-18 and 'GREEN' is written as 14-5-5-18-7 then how is 'PINK' written in the same code language?

1. 11-14-9-15 2. 11-14-8-16
3. 16-9-14-11 4. 11-14-9-16

56. Four groups of letters are given, three of them share a common relationship, while one is different. Choose the odd one out.

1. l g z 2. f a t
3. d y p 4. v q j

57. Four pairs of words are given below out of the words in three pairs bear a certain common relationship. Choose the odd pair of words.

1. Fresh : Stale
2. Initial : Create
3. Sink : Float
4. Cruel : Kind

58. A pair of words given below have a certain relationship to each other. Select the pair of words from the options that has the similar relationship as the following pair of words.

Court : Lawyer

1. Clerk : Office
2. University : Student
3. School : Teacher
4. Army : Soldier

46. 3	**47.** 4	**48.** 4	**49.** 4	**50.** 3	**51.** 3	**52.** 3
53. 3	**54.** *	**55.** 4	**56.** 3	**57.** 2	**58.** 3	

59. Choose the missing term (?) from the given alternatives which is related to the fifth term in the same way as the second term is related to the first term and fourth term is related to the third term.

10 : 95 :: 20 : 395 :: 25 : ?

1. 625
2. 620
3. 595
4. 610

60. Choose the missing terms (?) from the given alternatives which is related to the third term in the same way as the second term is related to the first terms and sixth term is related to the fifth term.

CG : 20 :: LR : ? :: MP : 58

1. 38
2. 60
3. 46
4. 61

GENERAL KNOWLEDGE AND CURRENT AFFAIRS

61. Who among the following Ramon Magsaysay awardees 2024 is a dedicated physician who has championed the fight against the devastating effects of Agent Orange?

1. Miyazaki, Hayao
2. Phuntsho, Karma
3. Farhan, Farviza
4. Nguyen Thi Ngoc Phyong

62. Match List-I with List-II regarding Major Dhyan Chand Khel Ratna Award 2024.

List-I (Sports person)	List-II (Discipline)
A. Shri Gukesh D	I. Hockey
B. Shri Harmanpreet Singh	II. Shooting
C. Shri Praveen Kumar	III. Para Athletics
D. Ms. Manu Bhaker	IV. Chess

Choose the ***correct*** answer from the options given below:

1. (A)-(IV), (B)-(II), (C)-(I), (D)-(III)
2. (A)-(I), (B)-(III), (C)-(IV), (D)-(II)
3. (A)-(II), (B)-(I), (C)-(III), (D)-(IV)
4. (A)-(IV), (B)-(I), (C)-(III), (D)-(II)

63. Which of the following countries became the newest member of NATO on March 7, 2024?

1. Turkey
2. Hungary
3. Sweden
4. Norway

64. Who among the following has been awarded with Pulitzer prize 2024 for fiction?

1. Jacqueline Jones
2. Jayne Anne Phillips (Knopf)
3. Eboni Booth
4. David E. Hoffman

65. Which of the following pairs of book and author is ***not*** correctly matched?

1. H is for Hope — Elizabeth Kolbert
2. Beautiful Days — Zach Williams
3. Martyr — Kaveh Akbar
4. Meditations for Mortals — Tom Baldwin

66. Arrange the following Mughal Emperors in the chronological order:

A. Shah Jahan
B. Babur
C. Jahangir
D. Akbar
E. Humayun

Choose the ***correct*** answer from the options given below:

1. (A), (C), (B), (D), (E)
2. (B), (E), (D), (C), (A)
3. (B), (E), (A), (D), (C)
4. (B), (E), (A), (C), (D)

67. The two upper chambers of the heart are called:

1. Ventricles
2. Capillaries
3. Vena Cava
4. Atria

68. Which of the following are Non-metallic minerals?

A. Bauxite
B. Gypsum
C. Limestone
D. Mica
E. Manganese

Choose the ***correct*** answer from the options given below:

1. (A), (B) and (D) Only
2. (B), (C) and (D) Only
3. (A), (C) and (E) Only
4. (C) and (E) Only

69. Arrange the following continents from the largest to the smallest in size:

A. Australia
B. Asia
C. North America
D. Africa
E. Europe

Choose the ***correct*** answer from the options given below:

1. (C), (B), (D), (E), (A)
2. (B), (D), (C), (E), (A)
3. (B), (D), (A), (C), (E)
4. (A), (D), (C), (B), (E)

59. 2	**60.** 2	**61.** 4	**62.** 4	**63.** 3	**64.** 2
65. 4	**66.** 2	**67.** 4	**68.** 2	**69.** 2	

70. Which of the following planets completes one orbit around Sun in 255 days?

1. Venus
2. Mercury
3. Saturn
4. Mars

71. The soil is classified on the basis of the proportion of particles of various sizes. If soil contains greater proportion of big particles, it is called:

1. Humus
2. Loamy
3. Sandy
4. Clayey

72. The earth worms breathe through their:

1. Lungs
2. Skin
3. Spiracles
4. Tracheae

73. Which of the following planets do not have rings around them?

A. Mercury
B. Venus
C. Jupiter
D. Uranus
E. Mars

Choose the ***correct*** answer from the options given below:

1. (A) and (B) Only
2. (A), (B) and (E) Only
3. (C) and (D) Only
4. (B), (D) and (E) Only

74. Match the following with respect to the French Revolution:

List-I	List-II
A. Nobility	I. 1st Estate
B. Clergy	II. Tax to be paid directly to the State
C. Taille	III. Unit of Currency in France, discontinued in 1794
D. Livre	IV. 2nd Estate

Choose the ***correct*** answer from the options given below:

1. (A)-(IV), (B)-(II), (C)-(I), (D)-(III)
2. (A)-(I), (B)-(III), (C)-(II), (D)-(IV)
3. (A)-(IV), (B)-(I), (C)-(II), (D)-(III)
4. (A)-(IV), (B)-(III), (C)-(II), (D)-(I)

75. Who amongst the following has been conferred with Sahitya Akademi award 2024 for Hindi?

1. Gagan Gill
2. Anamika
3. Mamta Kalia
4. Maitreyi Pushpa

76. Madhubani, an art form, belongs to which State of India?

1. Madhya Pradesh
2. Gujarat
3. Bihar
4. Rajasthan

77. Chola inscriptions deal with several categories of land. Match the categories with their descriptions.

List-I	List-II
A. Shalabhoga	I. land gifted to Brahmanas
B. Brahmadeya	II. land donated to Jaina institutions
C. Vellanvagai	III. land for the maintenance of a school
D. Pallichchhandam	IV. land of non-Brahmana peasant proprietors

Choose the ***correct*** answer from the options given below:

1. (A)-(III), (B)-(I), (C)-(II), (D)-(IV)
2. (A)-(I), (B)-(IV), (C)-(III), (D)-(II)
3. (A)-(II), (B)-(IV), (C)-(I), (D)-(III)
4. (A)-(III), (B)-(I), (C)-(IV), (D)-(II)

78. Who led the East India Company's army against Sirajuddaulah at Plassey in 1757?

1. Robert Clive
2. Lord Cornwallis
3. Tilly Kettle
4. Lord Hastings

79. Which of the following rivers drain into the Arabian Sea?

A. Narmada
B. Mahanadi
C. Tapi
D. Godavari
E. Krishna

Choose the ***correct*** answer from the options given below:

1. (A) and (B) Only
2. (B), (C) and (E) Only
3. (B), (C) and (D) Only
4. (A) and (C) Only

80. Which of the following are Ferrous minerals?

A. Iron ore
B. Gold
C. Copper
D. Manganese
E. Chromite

Choose the ***correct*** answer from the options given below:

1. (A), (D) and (E) Only
2. (A), (B) and (C) Only
3. (B) and (C) Only
4. (B), (D) and (E) Only

70. 1	**71.** 3	**72.** 2	**73.** 2	**74.** 3	**75.** 1
76. 3	**77.** 4	**78.** 1	**79.** 4	**80.** 1	

81. Which among the following are "Working Capital" of production?

A. Tools and Machines B. Buildings
C. Raw materials D. Money in hand

Choose the *correct* answer from the options given below:

1. (A) and (B) Only 2. (B) and (C) Only
3. (C) and (D) Only 4. (B) and (D) Only

82. Consider the following statements regarding the Minimum Support Price (MSP) for farmers?

Statement (A): Farmers are paid a pre-announced price for their crops declared by the Government every year before the sowing season.

Statement (B): Food grains are sold by the Government at a price lower than the market price.

Choose the *correct* answer from the options given below:

1. Both Statement (A) and (B) are correct
2. Both Statement (A) and (B) are incorrect
3. Statement (A) is correct, (B) is incorrect
4. Statement (A) is incorrect, (B) is correct

83. Who among the following went on to set up a Mission in Khedgaon near Pune to encourage widows and poor women to become literate and independent?

1. Tarabai Shinde
2. Pandita Ramabai
3. Rokeya Sakhawat Hossain
4. Rashsundari Devi

84. Consider the following statements regarding the "Read Only Memory" (ROM).

Statement (A): ROM is permanently built into the computer at the time of production.

Statement (B): The information stored in ROM disappears the very moment the machine is turned off.

Choose the *correct* answer from the options given below:

1. Both Statement (A) and (B) are correct
2. Both Statement (A) and (B) are incorrect
3. Statement (A) is correct, (B) is incorrect
4. Statement (A) is incorrect, (B) is correct

85. A program or hardware device that filters the information coming through an internet connection on a computer system is called:

1. Firewall 2. Malware
3. Denial of service 4. Cookies

86. The mode of nutrition used by a fungi is called:

1. Heterotropic mode 2. Saprotropic mode
3. Autotropic mode 4. Digestive mode

87. Which among the following are ***not*** present in an animal cell?

A. Cell membrane B. Cell wall
C. Cytoplasm D. Chloroplast

Choose the *correct* answer from the options given below:

1. (A) and (C) Only 2. (B) and (C) Only
3. (B) and (D) Only 4. (A) and (D) Only

88. Which of the following statements regarding the Parliament of India are correct?

A. Rajya Sabha does not have the power to pass "no confidence" motion.
B. The President of India is not a part of the Parliament.
C. Once passed by the Lok Sabha, the budget of the Government cannot be rejected by the Rajya Sabha.
D. Money related laws passed by both the houses of the Parliament do not need the assent of the President to come into force.

Choose the *correct* answer from the options given below:

1. (A) and (C) Only 2. (A) and (D) Only
3. (B) and (C) Only 4. (B) and (D) Only

89. Which among the following statements is ***not*** correct for a colloidal solution?

1. Heterogenous mixture
2. The particles of the suspension are too small to be individually seen by naked eyes
3. The solute particles settle down when the suspension is left undisturbed
4. Colloids are big enough to scatter a beam of light passing through it

90. Match List-I with List-II.

List-I	List-II
A. Bharatiya Janata Party (BJP)	I. Founded in 1925
B. Nationalist Congress Party (NCP)	II. Founded in 1980
C. Bahujan Samaj Party (BSP)	III. Founded in 1984
D. Communist Party of India (CPI)	IV. Founded in 1999

Choose the *correct* answer from the options given below:

1. (A)-(IV), (B)-(II), (C)-(III), (D)-(I)
2. (A)-(II), (B)-(IV), (C)-(III), (D)-(I)
3. (A)-(II), (B)-(IV), (C)-(I), (D)-(III)
4. (A)-(IV), (B)-(II), (C)-(I), (D)-(III)

81. 3	**82.** 3	**83.** 2	**84.** 3	**85.** 1	**86.** 2	**87.** 3	**88.** 1	**89.** 3	**90.** 2

ENGLISH LANGUAGE AND COMPREHENSION

Directions (Qs. No. 91 to 95): *Read the passage given below and answer the questions that follow:*

Sport helps children to develop both physically and mentally. Physical activity should be part of our daily life. Practicing any kind of sport from an early age helps children in many ways, for example, group activities improve interaction and social integration. It also improves the mental level and promotes a healthy lifestyle in adulthood, as the habits we acquire as children are often to stay. Sports have multiple healthy benefits. If we talk on a psychological or personality level, sports activities (especially those done in groups) help children to strengthen their social self-esteem, and allow them to understand the importance of having and respecting the rules. Another aspect to consider is what type of sport or activity will suit the child considering his/her conditions and abilities. A more timid and shy child is likely to get better at a sport where she/he has to relate to peers. To a more active one, an individual sport such as tennis can help better develop her/his ability to concentrate. Perhaps one of the most relevant issues is the importance of physical exercise, not only in children but also in young and old people, because moderate daily physical exercise helps prevent overweight and obesity. Taking into account the growth of the percentage of children and young people with obesity and overweight in the Western world, the inclusion of sport in the family routine becomes almost mandatory. Sport can also have the power to help us rest. For all those fathers and mothers of active children, try to get them to run every day playing soccer, or swimming or any other activity that keeps them physically active. They will fall asleep in bed in a matter of seconds and you, dads and moms, too.

91. Sport helps children develop both physically and mentally by:

1. developing their ability to concentrate
2. improving the mental level and promoting a healthy lifestyle
3. Stressing upon the importance of physical exercises
4. facilitating and improving group interaction and social integration

92. Choose the appropriate antonym of the word "dissociation" from the options given below:

1. strengthen
2. integration
3. interaction
4. growth

93. Choose the appropriate synonym of the word "reasonable" from the options given below:

1. mandatory
2. better
3. moderate
4. important

94. Choosing the sport best suited for someone depends on:

1. psychological or lifestyle benefits of the sport
2. physical benefits of the sport
3. economic benefits of the sport
4. conditions and abilities of the person

95. Sports should also be included as a part of the family routine mandatorily because:

1. It keeps the family together
2. Makes the adults more receptive to the needs of the old people in the family
3. Prevents the young people and children from getting lazy and becoming obese or overweight
4. It improves social interaction and social integration

Directions (Qs. No. 96 to 100): *Read the passage given below and answer the questions that follow:*

At its core, pollution occurs when ecosystems become overwhelmed and cannot effectively eliminate introduced substances, leading to a breakdown in their natural processes. This disruption often results in irreversible damage to the environment.

The sources of pollution are diverse and can stem from both natural events and human activities. Human-induced pollution, such as oil spills, chemical leaks, and nuclear accidents, can have catastrophic effects on ecosystems and communities. These events contribute to the destruction of biodiversity, increased mortality rates among humans and animals, habitat loss, and degradation of soil, water, and air quality.

Addressing pollution and safeguarding the environment requires the application of principles rooted in sustainable development. This entails meeting current needs without compromising the ability of future generations to meet their own needs. It is imperative to not only remediate existing pollution but also to proactively identify and prevent future sources of contamination.

Furthermore, there must be legal repercussions for environmental damage, with polluters held accountable for the harm they cause. Compensation should be mandated to mitigate the adverse effects on the environment and public health.

91. 2	**92.** 2	**93.** 3	**94.** 4	**95.** 3

96. Pollution control is only possible when:

1. ecosystems become overwhelmed
2. events contribute to the destruction of biodiversity
3. principles rooted in sustainable development are applied
4. compensation is mandated to mitigate pollution

97. Find the antonym of the given word from the passage:

'EXACERBATE'

1. overwhelmed 2. eliminate
3. catastrophic 4. mitigate

98. Pollution : Natural events and human activities :: Safeguarding environment : ______.

1. Safeguarding humans and animals
2. Principles rooted in sustainable development
3. Remediate existing pollution by compromising the future needs
4. Legal repercussions and compensation

99. Choose the sentence that uses the underlined phrase in the same sense as used in the passage.

1. The stems from the tree spread all around the garden
2. The stems from the drainage network are extensive
3. Her unhappiness stems from the realization of his betrayal
4. The stems from the Banyan tree move towards the soil as stilt roots

100. Choose the most appropriate word for the given phrase/group of words:

"an indirect and usually bad result of an action or event that may happen sometime afterwards".

1. disruption 2. pollution
3. repercussion 4. compensation

Directions (Qs. No. 101 to 105): *Pick out the adjective from the given words:*

101. 1. medicine 2. medicinal
3. medicate 4. medic

102. 1. minister 2. ministry
3. ministerial 4. administer

103. 1. table 2. tabular
3. tabloid 4. tablet

104. 1. study 2. studious
3. student 4. studiously

105. 1. Expect 2. Expectation
3. Expectancy 4. Expectant

Directions (Qs. No. 106 to 110): *Choose the word closest in meaning to the given word:*

106. REMISSION

1. Credit
2. Abatement
3. Remembrance
4. Execution

107. ALLITERATION

1. Reduction 2. Repercussion
3. Repartee 4. Repetition

108. REPREHENSION

1. Anxiety 2. Admonition
3. Acidity 4. Acrimony

109. REPUDIATE

1. Censure 2. Disavow
3. Distaste 4. Memorise

110. RETINUE

1. Avenge 2. Review
3. Entourage 4. Withdraw

Directions (Qs. No. 111 to 115): *Choose the correctly spelt word from the following:*

111. 1. Procastrinate 2. Procrastinate
3. Procrastrinate 4. Procastinate

112. 1. Psycosomatic 2. Psychosomatic
3. Psycosomattic 4. Psychosommatic

113. 1. Credebility 2. Credability
3. Credibility 4. Craedebility

114. 1. Cumulative 2. Cummulative
3. Cumullative 4. Cummullative

115. 1. Desicated 2. Dessicated
3. Desiccated 4. Dessiccated

Directions (Qs. No. 116 to 118): *A part of the sentence is underlined. Below are the alternatives which may improve the sentence. Choose the correct alternative.*

116. Two smart-dressed women came to blows on a train yesterday.

1. Smartly-dressed women came to blows
2. Smart-dressed women came to blow
3. Smartly-dressed women come to blow
4. Smart-dressed women come to blows

96. 3	**97.** 4	**98.** 2	**99.** 3	**100.** 3	**101.** 2	**102.** 3	**103.** 2	**104.** 2	**105.** 4	**106.** 2
107. 4	**108.** 2	**109.** 2	**110.** 3	**111.** 2	**112.** 2	**113.** 3	**114.** 1	**115.** 3	**116.** 1	

117. If you say something off the cuff, you say it spontaneously.

1. said something off of the cuff
2. said something off the cuff
3. say something off of the cuff
4. No improvement

118. My mother was in her element, organizing everything perfectly.

1. in her elementary, organizing everything perfect
2. in her elementary, organizing everything perfectly
3. at her elemental, organizing everything perfectly
4. No improvement

Directions (Qs. No. 119 to 123): *Choose the word opposite in meaning to the given word:*

119. EXPEDITE

1. Repudiate 2. Delay
3. Efficient 4. Dispense

120. OPTIMAL

1. Pessimist 2. Compulsory
3. Useful 4. Wasteful

121. CONGENIAL

1. Congested 2. Amiable
3. Confused 4. Rude

122. DEXTEROUS

1. Novice 2. Skilled
3. Expert 4. Apprentice

123. PARCHED

1. Dried 2. Documented
3. Soaked 4. Dissolved

Directions (Qs. No. 124 to 128): *Choose the appropriate word for the given group of words:*

124. 'Clever and funny comments and replies that are made quickly'.

1. banter 2. response
3. repartee 4. rhetoric

125. 'The process of becoming old and showing the effects of being old'.

1. growth 2. dementia
3. septicaemia 4. senescence

126. 'The fact of something interesting or pleasant happening by chance'.

1. accidental 2. sequestration
3. serendipity 4. happenchance

127. 'Being careful that every detail of something is correct'.

1. fastidious 2. contrarian
3. nonchalant 4. consistent

128. 'A long and serious piece of writing on a particular subject'.

1. essay 2. journal
3. epic 4. treatise

Directions (Qs. No. 129 to 137): *Fill in the blank with correct alternative:*

129. I am fed up _____ living with my parents, so I am looking for a place of my own.

1. of 2. since
3. about 4. with

130. New restaurants are appearing all _____ the place.

1. about 2. at
3. over 4. around

131. She's been offered a place _____ Bath to study business.

1. at 2. in
3. into 4. by

132. He is assured _____ his place in history.

1. of 2. for
3. from 4. at

133. The song was pitched too low _____ my voice.

1. of 2. for
3. with 4. on

134. The job doesn't pay _____ near enough for me.

1. anywhere 2. nowhere
3. somewhere 4. elsewhere

135. The two planes were _____ in a near miss.

1. associated 2. crashed
3. engaged 4. involved

136. Searching for one man in this city is like looking for a _____ in a hay sack.

1. bug 2. pearl
3. needle 4. fiddle

137. She made a _____ remark when she realised that her team was angry with her.

1. objectionable 2. firm
3. false 4. placatory

117. 4	**118.** 4	**119.** 2	**120.** 4	**121.** 4	**122.** 1	**123.** 3	**124.** 3	**125.** 4	**126.** 3	**127.** 1
128. 4	**129.** 1	**130.** 3	**131.** 1	**132.** 1	**133.** 2	**134.** 1	**135.** 4	**136.** 3	**137.** 4	

Directions (Qs. No. 138 to 142): *Choose the appropriate Passive Voice for the given sentence:*

138. He handed her a chair.
1. She was handing a chair
2. She was handed a chair
3. A chair was being handed to her by him
4. She was being handed a chair by him

139. He satisfied everybody.
1. Everybody felt satisfied by him
2. Everybody felt satisfied at him
3. Everybody was satisfied by him
4. Everybody was satisfied with him

140. Why have you broken the mirror?
1. Why was the mirror broken by you?
2. Why did you break the mirror?
3. Why was the mirror being broken by you?
4. Why has the mirror been broken by you?

141. Was he washing the clothes?
1. Were the clothes washed by him?
2. Were the clothes been washed by him?
3. Were the clothes being washed by him?
4. Had the clothes been washed by him?

142. Her behaviour annoyed him.
1. He was annoyed at her behaviour
2. He was annoyed with her behaviour
3. He was annoyed by her behaviour
4. He was annoyed on her behaviour

Directions (Qs. No. 143 to 147): *Spot the error in the given sentence:*

143. (A) Much students prefer/ (B) courses in classical/ (C) arts to courses in science unless/ (D) they are science majors.

144. (A) The driver as well as/ (B) the conductor are/ (C) responsible for/ (D) this accident.

145. (A) In colonial America/ (B) there has been very little/ (C) to read except for/ (D) the books sent from Britain.

146. (A) After listening to/ (B) much of songs/ (C) she switched/ (D) off the radio.

147. (A) She told/ (B) her mother/ (C) that she/ (D) were busy.

Directions (Qs. No. 148 to 150): *Choose the alternative which best expresses the meaning of the idiom/phrase.*

148. 'dot the i's and cross the t's'
1. to be very particular about writing the alphabets properly
2. to write in cursive handwriting
3. to add the final minor details to a plan or a piece of work
4. to edit the agreement document after final proof-reading

149. 'skate on thin ice'
1. to get oneself into a difficult situation
2. to take risk while skating
3. to take your chances while skating
4. to go for skating when the winter has just started

150. 'to lose heart'
1. to fall in love with someone
2. to fall out of love
3. to feel discouraged
4. to show kindness towards someone

APTITUDE FOR SERVICE SECTOR

151. While you leave your institute after attending all classes (in the evening). You are the last person exiting from the classroom. You will:
1. Tell the principal to direct any peon to switch off all lights and fans
2. Ask any of your classmate to ensure switching off all lights and fans
3. Not switch off any lights and fans since in the institute, these electrical equipments work 24 × 7
4. Personally see that all lights and fans are switched off

152. Your immediate neighbour urgently requests you to help him taking his own younger brother to a nearby hospital You will:
1. Give him a number for ambulance services due to your belief that 'work is priority' as you have some urgent work so you will not be able to accompany
2. Drive them to the hospital and offer necessary assistance
3. Talk to your fellow neighbour about modern hospital facilities these days which offers medical support at home therefore there arise no urgency to go to hospital these days
4. Start feeling restless and try to consult experienced people over the phone

138. 2	**139.** 3	**140.** 4	**141.** 3	**142.** 3	**143.** 1	**144.** 2	**145.** 2
146. 2	**147.** 4	**148.** 3	**149.** 1	**150.** 3	**151.** 4	**152.** 2	

153. Your classmate comes and tell you that your closer friends talk ill and also spread rumors about you. You will:

1. fight with your friends
2. follow 'tit for tat' and will start talking ill about your friends
3. not bother about the rumors of your closer friends
4. stop talking for 2 weeks

154. Which of the following statement best matches your opinion?

1. Hard working people are not successful most the times
2. The time to work hard has just came now
3. Only and only hard working people succeed
4. Hard working people can move ahead in life

155. While you are having a walk on the road with your pet (dog). All off a sudden your dog barks and injures an elderly man on the road. You will:

1. Convince the man that no one has control over pet (dog)
2. Apologize by repeatedly saying sorry
3. Console that man and offer him to take him to the nearby and good hospital
4. Try to run from that particular area immediately

156. Your newspaper hawker comes late every morning and therefore you go to college without reading the newspaper. You will:

1. Stop taking newspaper and also scold him nicely
2. Delay his payment to take aptful revenge
3. Apprise him about your problem
4. Stop taking newspaper and rather would be dependent on news bulletin through television

157. In the examination hall, you find that your question paper is very difficult to be answered by your end, the best thing you can do is:

1. lead the whole student by convincing them to walk out as question paper is out of syllabus
2. collect money from all students after the exam and submit to the examiner as a fine for not attempting the questions well and request to pass all students
3. always keep some written material to avoid such circumstances
4. try attempting questions first of which you know something and then proceed others by writing what you know

158. It is necessary to do exercise in the morning because:

1. It is a good way to meet different people of your age and pass lime
2. It keeps our body fit
3. It is generally a trend followed by many people
4. Ways of doing exercise is displayed over television. This helps in knowing the correct way of doing exercise without even actively doing it by own

159. You are feeling stressed out as exams are approaching, what is the best way to manage your stress?

1. Study continuously without taking any breaks
2. Panic for the exams
3. Take regular breaks and maintain a good study schedule with enough sleep
4. Study whole night and skip sleep entirely

160. In a group project, one of your team mate is not contributing in the group which is affecting the project. What would you do?

1. Ignore him and do your work
2. Blame him for not contributing
3. Talk to him personally and solve his problem
4. Complain about him to the teacher

161. Your monthly budget is ₹ 5000/- and you are spending on non-essential things. How would you manage expenses?

1. Spend freely and worry later
2. Ignore the budget and buy whatever you need
3. Save all your money and spend all the money next month
4. Allocate your expenses and save money for future

162. You overhear two co-workers discussing a security breach at your company. What should you do?

1. Report the information to your officer
2. Ignore it since it's not your concern
3. Confront the co-workers about what they know
4. Share the information with police

163. A stranger offers you a free drink at a party, what is the safest choice?

1. Accept it without hesitation
2. Take a small sip to check if it's okay
3. Accept and share it with friend
4. Politely decline

153. 3	**154.** 4	**155.** 3	**156.** 3	**157.** 4	**158.** 2
159. 3	**160.** 3	**161.** 4	**162.** 1	**163.** 4	

164. While driving, you notice a pedestrian suddenly crossing the road. What is your immediate action?
1. Speed up to pass before the pedestrian crosses the road
2. Honk continuously to warn them
3. Apply brake and let the pedestrian cross safely
4. Go to the other lane without checking/verifying

165. You are at a crowded train station, when you see a bag left unattended. What should you do?
1. Open the bag to check the items present inside
2. Walk away to a far away distance by ignoring it
3. Inform station security immediately
4. Move the bag to a safer place

166. You are at a bank when two masked individuals enter with weapons. What is the safest response in this situation?
1. Try to escape immediately
2. Remain calm and follow instructions without resistance
3. Record the event on your phone to enjoy later on
4. Confront the robbers and try to stop them

167. You are driving your car on the road when you hit against a fruit vendor's cart. You would:
1. Escape from that place by driving your car
2. Abuse the fruit vendor for putting his cart on the way
3. Pay the fruit vendor for the damage done to him
4. Insist that it was not your fault

168. Your parents do not agree with your career choice. What is the best way to handle this?
1. Disrespect their opinion and do what you want
2. Discuss your reasons calmly and would try to understand their concerns
3. Give up your dream and follow their decision
4. Stop speaking to them until they agree

169. Your friend has lost his wallet with your important documents in it. You would:
1. Understand the situation and would not react as anyone can make mistakes
2. Angrily would ask him (your friend) to replace/duplicate the documents
3. Blame him for being careless and stop talking to him
4. Tell everyone not to trust him in future

170. All the hard work done by you at your workplace is hijacked by one of your colleague, who is a good friend of yours. You will:
1. Start praising your work yourself
2. Leave the job
3. Criticise him in front of other colleagues
4. Continue hard work as hard work always pays

171. Why first aid box is important in any organisation?
1. Because it looks beautiful
2. No, it's not that important
3. Minor injury could be treated quickly
4. Only because it comes under guidelines

172. What is the most appropriate way to communicate with a customer?
1. By being rude
2. By being polite
3. By being aggressive
4. By being phlegmatic

173. You accidently break a classroom chair while playing, what should you do?
1. Inform the teacher honestly and apologize
2. Blame someone else
3. Hide the broken chair so no one notices
4. Leave the classroom before any one sees you

174. While using an ATM, you notice someone standing too close behind you. What shall you do?
1. Cancel your transaction and step away
2. Continue without worrying
3. Ask help from the people standing around
4. Call the police to help

175. You find a lost wallet with lots of cash inside. What you will take now as a best decision?
1. Take the money and throw away the wallet
2. Keep the money but leave the wallet where it is
3. Return it to the owner if possible or submit it to the police
4. Ask your friends if they want to share the money

176. You notice a wet floor in your hotel that could cause someone to slip. What should you do?
1. Walk away and ignore it
2. Inform cleaning department or clean it up if possible
3. Wait for someone else to report it
4. Warn only to your close colleagues

164. 3	**165.** 3	**166.** 2	**167.** 3	**168.** 2	**169.** 1	**170.** 4
171. 3	**172.** 2	**173.** 1	**174.** 1	**175.** 3	**176.** 2	

177. You are in a taxi and the driver is driving recklessly, you:
1. Ask the driver to slow down
2. Stay silent and hope nothing happens
3. Get out at the next stop, even it it's unsafe
4. Call the police immediately

178. You are riding a motor-bike, and the traffic light turns red. You:
1. Quickly cross before cars start moving
2. Ignore the light and keep going
3. Look for a short cut to avoid waiting
4. Stop, and wait for the green light

179. You accidently spill a drink on a fellow passenger. How should you handle it?
1. Apologize and offer to help for cleaning it up
2. Ignore your fellow passenger and pretend as if nothing has happened
3. Blame the crowd for the spill
4. Laugh and tell them it's just a small accident

180. A guest at your hotel is complaining his/her allocated room is too noisy due to the construction outside. What should you do?
1. Apologize and offer to move him/her a quieter room
2. Tell him/ her to deal with it because construction is necessary
3. Ignore the complaint and hope he/she stops mentioning it
4. Offer him/her earplugs and continue with your work

181. Your neighbour's pet dog keep coming to your yard and thereby making it a mess. You will:
1. Talk to your neighbour and would just ask to control his/her own pet dog
2. Throw things at the dog to scare it away
3. Call animal control immediately
4. Let it continue and complain later

182. You are waiting in a long billing queue at a store, and someone tries to come in between the line, what should you do?
1. Ignore to avoid conflict
2. Politely tell to wait for one's own turn
3. Let him go ahead to came in between the line
4. Argue with him loudly

183. You have invited your neighbour over for the coffee, but they've brought an unexpected guests without informing. You will:
1. Greet both, your neighbour and their guest warmly, making the best of the situation
2. Tell your neighbour it's not okay to bring unexpected guests
3. Ignore the situation and avoid interacting with the guest
4. Ask the neighbour to leave immediately

184. What would you do if you made a mistake at work and nobody noticed?
1. Blame it to your co-worker for the mistake
2. Accept the mistake and inform to your senior officer
3. Ignore the mistake, that it never happened
4. Resign from the job without informing the mistake to seniors

185. What would you do if your teacher blamed you for a mistake that you were not responsible for?
1. Be polite in situation where you felt blamed
2. Never speak with that teacher again
3. Start criticizing that teacher
4. Leave the school because of that teacher

186. Your neighbour has left a package at your door and accidently damaged your car parked by scratching it while moving the package, your reaction would be:
1. Ignore the situation as nothing happened
2. Confront aggressively with your neighbour
3. Demand payment for repairs immediately
4. Inform your neighbour and discuss about solution/s calmly

187. You have an assignment to complete but your friends are planning for a trip. How would you make decision?
1. Skip the assignment and go for trip
2. Complete your assignment and then go for a trip
3. Do half of the assignment and hope you can finish it later on
4. Let your friend decide without seeking your opinion

188. In case if you get any infection then what is the most suitable thing to do?
1. Show up at work to display your dedication
2. Take rest so that you don't spread the infection
3. Keep doing your work as if nothing happened
4. Resign from current job and look for new job

177. 1	**178.** 4	**179.** 1	**180.** 1	**181.** 1	**182.** 2
183. 1	**184.** 2	**185.** 1	**186.** 4	**187.** 2	**188.** 2

189. If any guest complains frequently then what is the best thing that can be done from your side?

1. Just resolve his/ her problems and stop interacting thereafter
2. Ask them to stop complaining
3. Resolve their problems and build a good image
4. Ignore their problems and avoid them

190. The flight experience sudden turbulence. What should you do?

1. Panic and scream
2. Fasten your seatbelt and stay calm
3. Run towards the flight attendant for help
4. Take off your seatbelt and move around

191. A customer is furious about a delayed order and is shouting at you. What is the best response?

1. Shout back and defend yourself
2. Apologize sincerely and offer a solution
3. Ignore the customer until they calm down
4. Tell them it's not your fault

192. You visit a zoo and see someone feeding animals despite the rules saying no to. You:

1. Report to zoo staff
2. Feed the animals yourself
3. Ignore it since it's not your problem
4. Tell the person to continue because animals love food

193. If a customer is being impatient because order hasn't arrived yet, then how will you handle him?

1. Ask him to leave
2. Apologize to him and tell him to wait
3. Serve him something else
4. Stop listening to him

194. A team mate gets injured in an important game. How should the team react?

1. Must panic and loose concentration
2. Curse the injured player for getting hurt
3. Stop playing and refuse for continuing the game
4. Adjust position and maintain focus

195. If you mistakenly occupy a wrong berth in the train, on arrival of the rightful passenger, you would:

1. Quietly vacate the berth
2. Tell the passengers that you would vacate the berth after you get a berth
3. Vacate but tell the passenger that nothing much has happened and he should not make a fuss
4. Apologize mid then vacate the berth

196. Independence day function is to be organised in your school, the responsibility of this has been assigned to you. You would:

1. Try to get rid of this responsibility
2. Try to organize it with the help of your batch mates
3. Avoid all your responsibilities
4. Delegate it to someone else

197. If two players of your team are openly having a flight, you will:

1. Support the player who plays well
2. Call the security on the ground and handover them
3. Do not get involved
4. Learn about the issue and try to end the conflict

198. At the hotel reception, one should:

1. Remain well grounded and smiling face
2. Remain confused and perplexed
3. Remain careless
4. Always busy on mobile phone

199. Due to some security issue, security services staffs have locked down the hall area of your workplace, you are inside and in a hurry to go back home as your daily work is over. What will you do?

1. Open the window and jump outside
2. Open the back door and leave
3. Remain calm and wait for the security to pass the instructions
4. Put some music on and enjoy songs

200. While travelling along, your phone battery dies, and your are lost. What should you do?

1. Ask any stranger to lend their phone
2. Look for a safe public place like a police station or cafe
3. Keep walking in random directions
4. Wait until someone approaches you for help

189. 3	**190.** 2	**191.** 2	**192.** 1	**193.** 2	**194.** 4
195. 4	**196.** 2	**197.** 4	**198.** 1	**199.** 3	**200.** 2

EXPLANATORY ANSWERS

1. (2): $\dfrac{\sqrt[3]{3375}+\sqrt{144}}{\sqrt[3]{729}+\sqrt[3]{1728}} = \dfrac{(15^3)^{1/3}+(12^2)^{1/2}}{(9^3)^{1/3}+(12^3)^{1/3}}$

$= \dfrac{15+12}{9+12} = \dfrac{27}{21} = \dfrac{9}{7}.$

2. (3): External volume of a wooden cuboidal box

$= l \times b \times h$

$= 80 \text{ cm} \times 49 \text{ cm} \times 30 \text{ cm}$

$= 117600 \text{ cm}^3$

and Internal volume of a wooden cuboidal box

$= (80 - 4) \text{ cm} \times (49 - 4) \text{ cm} \times (30 - 4) \text{ cm}$

$= 76 \text{ cm} \times 45 \text{ cm} \times 26 \text{ cm}$

$= 88920 \text{ cm}^3$

∴ The volume of the wood used

$= 117600 - 88920 = 28680 \text{ cm}^3.$

3. (2): Here, an isosceles triangle whose perimeter is 11 cm and base is 5 cm

∴ length of equal side $= \dfrac{11-5}{2} = 3$ cm

$2S = \text{Perimeter} = 11 \text{ cm}$

$\Rightarrow \quad S = \dfrac{11}{2}$

Let, $a = 3,\ b = 3$ and $c = 5$

∴ Area of an isosceles triangle

$= \sqrt{S(S-a)(S-b)(S-c)}$

$= \sqrt{\dfrac{11}{2}\left(\dfrac{11}{2}-3\right)\left(\dfrac{11}{2}-3\right)\left(\dfrac{11}{2}-5\right)}$

$= \sqrt{\dfrac{11}{2}\times\dfrac{5}{2}\times\dfrac{5}{2}\times\dfrac{1}{2}}$

$= \sqrt{\dfrac{11\times 25}{16}} = \dfrac{5}{4}\sqrt{11} \text{ cm}^2.$

4. (2): ∵ The volume of a cube = $(\text{side})^3$

∴ The volume of 22 solid metallic cubes

$= 22 \times (4)^3 \text{ cm}^3$

and the volume of cylinder $= \pi r^2 h$

∴ the volume of 16 solid cylinder

$= 16 \times \pi r^2 \times 7 \text{ cm}^3$

According to question

$22 \times (4)^3 = 16 \times \pi r^2 \times 7$

$\Rightarrow \quad 22 \times 64 = 16 \times \dfrac{22}{7} r^2 \times 7$

$\Rightarrow \quad 22 \times 64 = 16 \times 22 r^2$

$\Rightarrow \quad r^2 = \dfrac{22\times 64}{16\times 22}$

$\Rightarrow \quad r^2 = 4$

$\Rightarrow \quad r = 2 \text{ cm}$

∴ The radius of the cylinder.

5. (3): Given, $A : B = 2 : 3,\ A : C = 6 : 7,$
$C : D = 14 : 15$

$\Rightarrow \quad C : A = 7 : 6,\ A : B = 2 : 3$

$\Rightarrow \quad C : A = 7 : 6,\ A : B = 6 : 9$

$\Rightarrow \quad C : A : B = 7 : 6 : 9$

$\Rightarrow \quad A : B : C = 6 : 9 : 7$

$\Rightarrow \quad A : B : C = 12 : 18 : 14$

and $\quad C : D = 14 : 15$

$\Rightarrow \quad A : B : C : D = 12 : 18 : 14 : 15.$

6. (2): Given, A vessel contains 100 liters of solution

Spirit : Water $= 80 : (100 - 80)$

$= 80 : 20 = 4 : 1$

given, 20 litres of the mixture is taken out

∴ Remaining mixture $= 100 - 20 = 80$ litre

∴ Spirit in remaining mixture $= 80 \times \dfrac{4}{5} = 64$ litres

and Water $= 80 - 64 = 16$ litres

According to question

$\dfrac{64}{16+20} = \dfrac{64}{36} = \dfrac{16}{9} = 16 : 9$

∴ The ratio of spirit to water in the new solution $= 16 : 9.$

7. (2): Here, S.P. of two electric iron = 2 × ₹ 1344

= ₹ 2688

and C.P. of two electric iron

$= 1344\times\dfrac{100}{112} + 1344\times\dfrac{100}{96}$

$= 1344\times 100\left(\dfrac{1}{112}+\dfrac{1}{96}\right)$

$= 1344\times 100\left(\dfrac{6+7}{672}\right)$

= 2 × 100 × 13 = ₹ 2600

∴ Profit = S.P. – C.P. = 2688 – 2600 = ₹ 88

∴ His overall profit percentage

$= \dfrac{\text{Profit}\times 100}{\text{C.P.}}$

$= \dfrac{88\times 100}{2600} = \dfrac{44}{13} = 3.38\%.$

8. (2): $18000\times\dfrac{100-12}{100}\times\dfrac{100-x}{100} = 15048$

$\Rightarrow \quad 18000\times\dfrac{88}{100}\times\dfrac{100-x}{100} = 15048$

$\Rightarrow \quad \dfrac{18}{10}\times 88\times(100-x) = 15048$

$\Rightarrow \quad 100 - x = \dfrac{15048\times 10}{18\times 88}$

$\Rightarrow \quad 100 - x = \dfrac{171\times 10}{18}$

$\Rightarrow \quad 100 - x = \dfrac{19\times 10}{2}$

$\Rightarrow \quad 100 - x = 19 \times 5$
$\Rightarrow \quad x = 100 - 95$
$\Rightarrow \quad x = 5\%.$

9. (1): $(27)^{-1/3} \times (27)^{-1/3} \times (27^{1/3} - 27^{2/3})$

$$= (27)^{-2/3} \times [(3^3)^{1/3} - (3^3)^{2/3}]$$
$$= (3^3)^{-2/3} \times [3 - 3^2]$$
$$= 3^{-2} \times [3 - 9]$$
$$= \frac{1}{9} \times -6 = \frac{-2}{3}.$$

10. (4): Given, $p - 3q = -7$ and $pq = -10$

$\because \quad p^3 - 27q^3 = p^3 - (3q)^3$
$$= (p - 3q)(p^2 + 9q^2 + 3pq)$$
$$= (p - 3q)[(p - 3q)^2 - 6pq + 3pq]$$
$$= (p - 3q)[(p - 3q)^2 - 3pq]$$
$$= -7 \times [(-7)^2 - 3 \times 10]$$
$$= -7 \times [49 + 30]$$
$$= -7 \times 79 = -553.$$

11. (3): $2.3\bar{6} - 0.1\bar{4} = 2 + \frac{36-3}{90} - \frac{14-1}{90}$

$$= 2 + \frac{33}{90} - \frac{13}{90}$$
$$= 2 + \frac{20}{90} = 2 + \frac{2}{9} = \frac{20}{9}.$$

12. (3): Given, $P = \frac{1}{2} + \frac{1}{6} + \frac{1}{12} + \frac{1}{20} + \frac{1}{30}$

$$= \frac{30+10+5+3+2}{60} = \frac{50}{60} = \frac{5}{6}$$

$\therefore \quad 6(9 - P) = 6\left(9 - \frac{5}{6}\right) = 6\left(\frac{49}{6}\right) = 49$

$\therefore \quad \sqrt{6(9-P)} = \sqrt{49} = 7.$

14. (4): Given, the mean of the observation = 13

$\therefore \quad \frac{k + k + 8 + 2k - 1 + k + 12 + 12 + 17}{6} = 13$

$\Rightarrow \quad 5k + 48 = 13 \times 6$
$\Rightarrow \quad 5k + 48 = 78$
$\Rightarrow \quad 5k = 78 - 48$
$\Rightarrow \quad 5k = 30$
$\Rightarrow \quad k = 6$

$\therefore$ Observation : $k, (k + 8), (2k - 1), (k + 12), 12, 17$
: 6, 14, 11, 18, 12, 17

observation in ascending order
6, 11, 12, 14, 17, 18

Here, $n = 6$ (even number)

$\therefore \quad \text{Median} = \frac{1}{2}\left[\frac{n}{2}\text{th term} + \left(\frac{n}{2}+1\right)\text{th term}\right]$

$$= \frac{1}{2}[\text{3rd term} + \text{4th term}]$$
$$= \frac{1}{2}[12 + 14] = 13.$$

15. (3): Let the speed of the boat in still water be x km/h and the speed of stream be y km/h

Then, downstream speed = $(x + y)$ km/h
and upstream speed = $(x - y)$ km/h
According to question

$$\frac{21}{x+y} = 1\frac{1}{2} \Rightarrow \frac{21}{x+y} = \frac{3}{2}$$

$\Rightarrow \quad x + y = 14 \qquad ...(i)$

and $\quad \frac{20}{x-y} = 2$

$\Rightarrow \quad x - y = 10 \qquad ...(ii)$

from adding (*i*) and (*ii*), we get
$2x = 24$
$\Rightarrow \quad x = 12$ km/h

$\therefore$ The speed of the boat in still water be 12 km/h.

16. (4): Let the usual speed of the bus is x km/h

Then, $\quad \frac{300}{x} - \frac{300}{x+10} = 1$

$$300\left[\frac{1}{x} - \frac{1}{x+10}\right] = 1$$

$\Rightarrow \quad 300\left[\frac{x+10-x}{x(x+10)}\right] = 1$

$\Rightarrow \quad 300\left[\frac{10}{x(x+10)}\right] = 1$

$\Rightarrow \quad x(x + 10) = 3000$
$\Rightarrow \quad x^2 + 10x - 3000 = 0$
$\Rightarrow \quad x^2 + 60x - 50x - 3000 = 0$
$\Rightarrow \quad x(x + 60) - 50(x + 60) = 0$
$\Rightarrow \quad (x - 50)(x + 60) = 0$
$\Rightarrow \quad x = 50$ or $x = -60$

$\therefore$ The usual speed of the bus is 50 km/h.

17. (3): Given, in a class, there are 40 students.
Let the number of boys in the class be x
then the number of girls in the class be $(40 - x)$

$\therefore \quad 30x + 35(40 - x) = 33 \times 40$
$\Rightarrow \quad 30x + 1400 - 35x = 1320$
$\Rightarrow \quad 1400 - 5x = 1320$
$\Rightarrow \quad 5x = 1400 \quad 1320$
$\Rightarrow \quad x = \frac{80}{5} = 16$
$\Rightarrow \quad x = 16$

$\therefore$ the number of boys in the class = 16.

18. (3): The total weight of 11 persons
$= 11 \times 64$ kg $= 704$ kg

Let the weight of 12th person be x kg
Then, the average of all the 12 person

$$= \frac{704 + x}{12} \text{ kg}$$

According to question

$$x - \frac{704 + x}{12} = 22$$

$\Rightarrow \quad 12x - 704 - x = 12 \times 22$

$\Rightarrow \quad 11x - 704 = 264$

$\Rightarrow \quad 11x = 704 + 264$

$\Rightarrow \quad 11x = 968$

$\Rightarrow \quad x = 88$

$\therefore$ the weight of the 12th person is 88 kg.

19. (3): $\because$ 4 men can do 60% $= \frac{3}{5}$ of work in 6 days

$\therefore$ 4 men can do 1 work in $6 \times \frac{5}{3} = 10$ days

$\Rightarrow$ 1 man's 1 day's work $= \frac{1}{40}$

and 6 women can do 50% $= \left(\frac{1}{2}\right)$ of the same work in 5 days

$\therefore$ 6 women can do 1 work in $5 \times \frac{2}{1} = 10$ days

$\Rightarrow$ 1 woman's 1 day's work $= \frac{1}{60}$

$\therefore$ (2 Men + 3 Women)'s 1 day's work

$$= \frac{2}{40} + \frac{3}{60} = \frac{1}{20} + \frac{1}{20}$$

$$= \frac{1+1}{20} = \frac{2}{20} + \frac{1}{10}$$

$\therefore$ 2 men and 3 women will take 10 days to do the work if they work together.

20. (2): 1 man's 1 day's work $= \frac{1}{4 \times 5} = \frac{1}{20}$

and 1 woman's 1 day's work $= \frac{1}{5 \times 6} = \frac{1}{30}$

Let x women should work with 2 men to complete the work in 5 days

Then, $\frac{2}{20} + \frac{x}{30} = \frac{1}{5}$

$\Rightarrow \quad \frac{x}{30} = \frac{1}{5} - \frac{1}{10}$

$\Rightarrow \quad \frac{x}{30} = \frac{1}{10}$

$\Rightarrow \quad x = 3$

$\therefore$ Required women = 3.

21. (3): Ratio of investment

Aditya : Bipin = 40,000 × 4 + 50,000 × 8 : 50,000 × 4 + 40,000 × 8

= 1,60,000 + 4,00,000 : 2,00,000 + 3,20,000

= 5,60,000 : 520 = 56 : 52 = 14 : 13

Given, profit at the end of the year = ₹ 16,200

$\therefore$ The share of Aditya in the profit

$$= 16,200 \times \frac{14}{14+13}$$

$$= 16,200 \times \frac{14}{27}$$

= 600 × 14 = ₹ 8400.

22. (1): Let two years ago, the ages of Rekha and Shruti were $2x$ years and $3x$ years

Then, Rekha's present age = $(2x + 2)$ years

and Shruti's present age = $(3x + 2)$ years

Now, 3 years hence

$(2x + 2 + 3) : (3x + 2 + 3) = 3 : 4$

$\Rightarrow (2x + 5) : (3x + 5) = 3 : 4$

$\Rightarrow \quad 4(2x + 5) = 3(3x + 5)$

$\Rightarrow \quad 8x + 20 = 9x + 15$

$\Rightarrow \quad 9x - 8x = 20 - 15$

$\Rightarrow \quad x = 5$

$\therefore$ Shruti's age after 8 years from now

$= 3x + 2 + 8 = 3x + 10$

$= 3 \times 5 + 10 = 25$ years.

23. (4): $15 + 60 \div 15 \times 2 - 1$

$= 15 + 4 \times 2 - 1$

$= 15 + 8 - 1 = 23 - 1 = 22.$

24. (3): Let smallest number be x

then, $\quad 81025 - x = 80656 = (284)^2$

$\Rightarrow \quad x = 81025 - 80656$

$\Rightarrow \quad x = 369.$

25. (2): Given, the adjacent sides of a rectangle are increased by 35% and 20%

Its are increase $= 35 + 20 + \frac{35 \times 20}{100}$

$$= 55 + \frac{700}{100}$$

= 55 + 7 = 62%.

26. (2): Let the total number of votes be x

Then, the number of cast votes

$$= x \times \frac{100-12}{100} = \frac{88}{100}x$$

Now, The number of valid cast votes

$$= \frac{88}{100}x \times \left(1 - \frac{1}{6}\right)$$

$$= \frac{5}{6} \times \frac{88}{100}x = \frac{44}{3} \times \frac{1}{20}x = \frac{11}{15}x$$

According to question

$$\frac{11}{15}x\left(\frac{55}{100} - \frac{45}{100}\right) = 36542$$

$$\Rightarrow \quad \frac{11}{15}x \times \frac{10}{100} = 36542$$

$$\Rightarrow \quad x \times \frac{11}{10} \times \frac{1}{15} = 36542$$

$$\Rightarrow \quad x = 36542 \times 10 \times \frac{15}{11}$$

$$\Rightarrow \quad x = 3322 \times 150$$

$$\Rightarrow \quad x = 498300$$

Hence, the total number of votes registered = 498300.

27. (2): LCM of $\frac{4}{9}, \frac{8}{15}, \frac{6}{9}, \frac{12}{21}, \frac{14}{33}$

$$= \frac{\text{LCM of 4, 8, 6, 12 and 14}}{\text{HCF of 9, 15, 9, 21 and 33}} = \frac{168}{3}.$$

28. (3): Let HCF of two numbers be a

Then LCM of two numbers be $15a$

Given, LCM + HCF = 160

$$\Rightarrow \quad 15a + a = 160 \Rightarrow a = 10$$

Given, one of the number = 50

$\because$ LCM × HCF = one number × other number

$$\therefore \quad 15a \times a = 50 \times \text{other number}$$

$$\Rightarrow \quad \text{other number} = \frac{15a \times a}{50}$$

$$= \frac{15 \times 10 \times 10}{50} = 30$$

$\Rightarrow$ Other number = 30.

29. (3): Given, on simple interest

Amount to ₹ 14061 in 6 years

and amount to ₹ 16023 in 8 years

$\therefore$ Simple interest in (8 – 6) = 2 years

= 16023 – 14061 = ₹ 1962

$\Rightarrow$ Simple Interest in 6 years = 3 × ₹ 1962

= ₹ 5886

Sum = P = 14061 – 5886 = ₹ 8175

$$\because \quad r = \frac{\text{S.I.} \times 100}{\text{P} \times t}$$

$$\therefore \quad r = \frac{5886 \times 100}{8175 \times 6} = \frac{981 \times 4}{327}$$

$$= 3 \times 4 = 12\%.$$

Hence, the rate of interest per annum is 12%.

30. (3): Let a certain sum = P

$$\text{Then,} \quad A = P\left(1 + \frac{r}{100}\right)^n$$

$$\Rightarrow \quad ₹\ 19573 = P\left(1 + \frac{15}{100}\right)^2$$

$$\Rightarrow \quad 19573 = P\left(\frac{23}{20}\right)^2$$

$$\Rightarrow \quad 19573 = P\left(\frac{529}{400}\right)$$

$$\Rightarrow \quad P = \frac{19573 \times 400}{529} = 37 \times 400$$

$$\Rightarrow \quad P = ₹\ 14800$$

Now, compound interest on the same sum

$$= P\left(1 + \frac{r}{100}\right)^n - P$$

$$= P\left[\left(1 + \frac{r}{100}\right)^n - 1\right]$$

$$= 14800\left[\left(1 + \frac{10}{100}\right)^2 - 1\right]$$

$$= 14800\left[\left(\frac{11}{10}\right)^2 - 1\right]$$

$$= 14800\left[\frac{121}{100} - 1\right] = 14800 \times \frac{21}{100}$$

$$= 148 \times 21 = ₹\ 3108.$$

31. (3): Given,

Girl = Boy

Boy = Man

Man = Waiter

Waiter = Woman

Woman = Teacher

Teacher = Girl

Here, Woman will serve food in a restaurant.

32. (3):

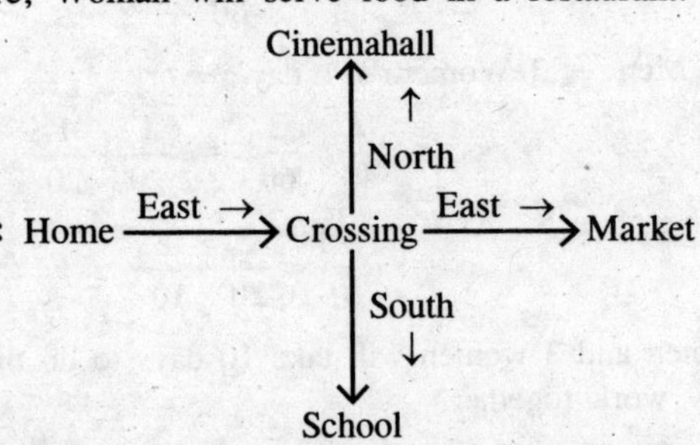

Here, School is in the South direction.

35. (2): Given, five boys are standing in a row facing North.

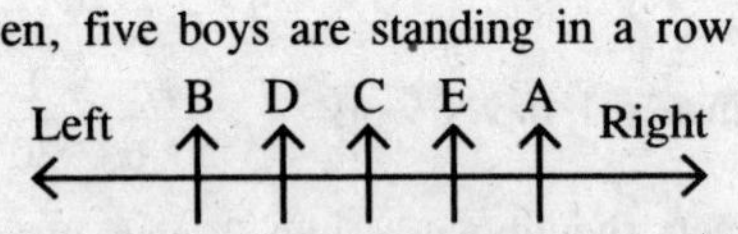

Here, C is sitting in the middle.

37. (2): From given information

(Sita) + Rita = Dancer

Gita + Meeta + Anita = Singers

(Sita) + Anita = Musicians

(Sita) + Rita + Anita = Comedian

Here, Sita is Dancer, Musician and Comedian.

40. (3): Given, 1 + 26 = 27, 2 + 25 = 27, 3 + 24 = 27

1. C, X ⇒ 3 + 24 = 27
2. L, O ⇒ 12 + 15 = 27
3. I, S ⇒ 9 + 19 = 28
4. M, N ⇒ 13 + 14 = 27

Here, Option (3) I, S pairs is wrong.

41. (4): Arranging the given words in dictionary order.
Disclose → Disconnect → Discount → Discourage
Here, Option (4) is the correct sequence.

42. (1): From given figure
The sum of the numbers which belong to any two figures only = 8 + 7 + 13 = 28.

43. (1): Given, 7 officers reach office in a particular sequence.

J > L > G > K > M > H > I

Here, J reaches the office first.

44. (2): Given, P, Q, R, S, T, U and W are sitting in a circle facing towards the centre.

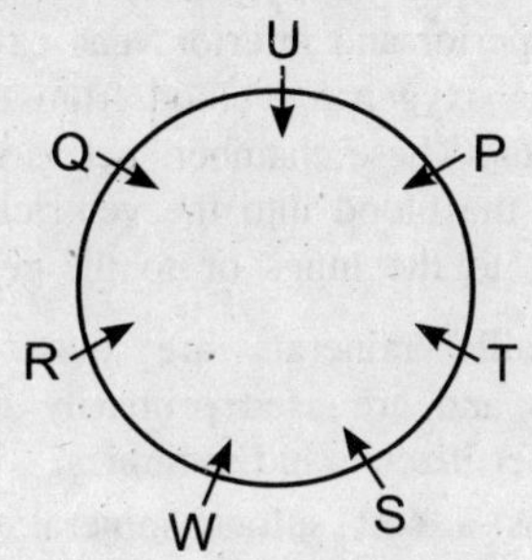

Here, W is sitting to the immediate left of S.

45. (3): Given, 1st October = Monday
= 8th October
= 15th October
= 22nd October
= 29th October
= Monday
∵ 1 November = 29 + 3 day
= Monday + 3 day
= Thursday

∴ Thursday was on 1st November of the same year.

47. (4): The best relationship between Vegetable, Food and Potatoes.

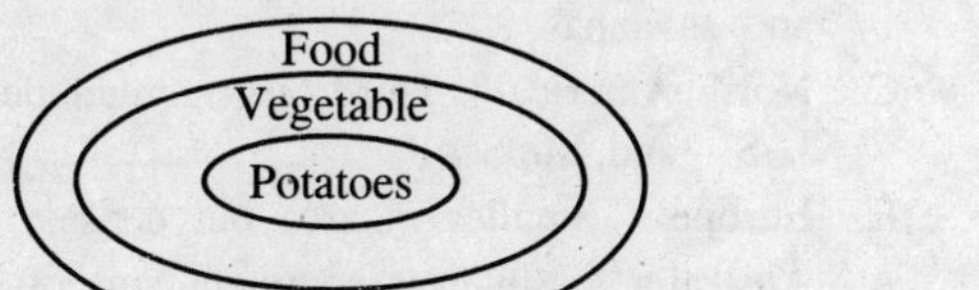

48. (4):

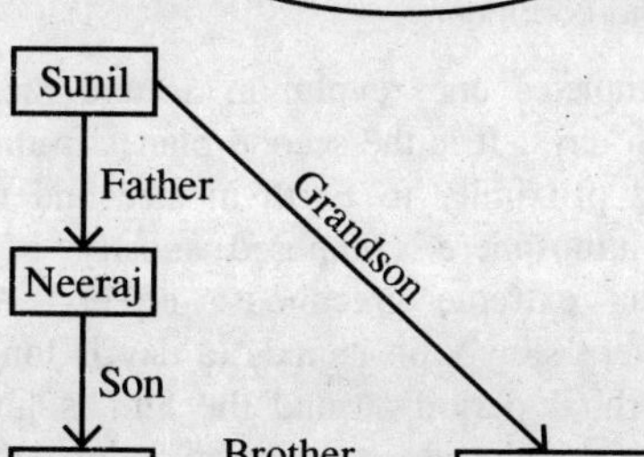

Here, Abhishek is the Grandson of Sunil.

49. (4): Given,

$G \xrightarrow{\text{Sister}} D \xrightarrow{\text{Sister}} E \xrightarrow{\text{Sister}} F$

Here, F is sister of D. Which is definitely true.

50. (3): 1. (13 : 143) ⇒ 13 × 11 = 143
2. (19 : 209) ⇒ 19 × 11 = 209
3. (23 : 251) ⇒ 23 × 11 = 253
4. (17 : 187) ⇒ 17 × 11 = 187

Here, Option (3) is the odd number pair from the given alternatives.

52. (3): Here, Place of V, it should be U

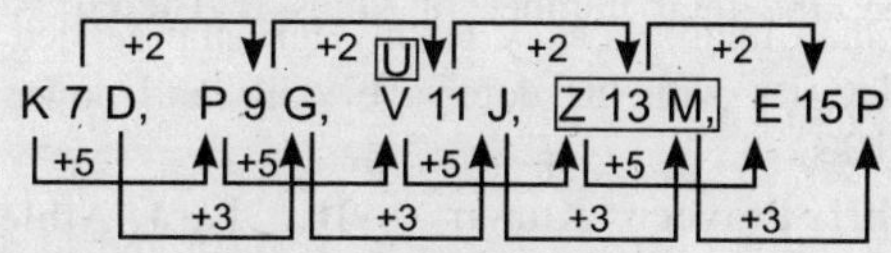

∴ The wrong term = V11J.

53. (3): Meaningfull sequence:
Mouth → Oesophagus → Stomach → Small Intestines → Large Intestines → Anus.

55. (4): Given,

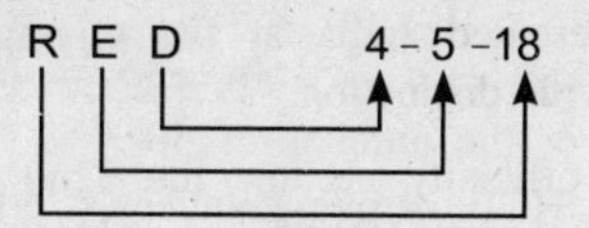

and

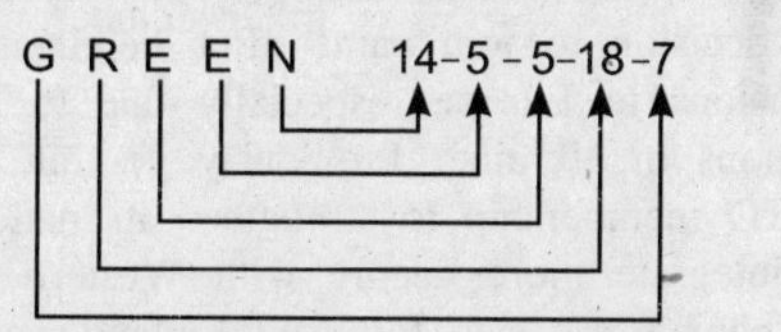

Similarly,

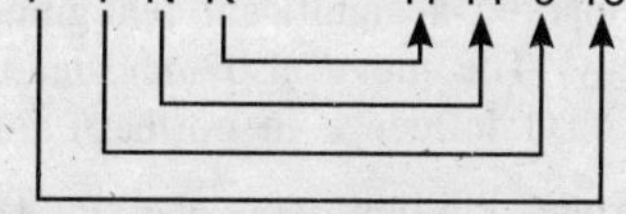

∴ PINK is written as 11-14-9-16.

59. (2): 10 : 95 :: 20 : 395 :: 25 : ?

Here, 10 : 95 ⇒ $(10)^2 - 5 = 100 - 5 = 95$,
20 : 395 ⇒ $(20)^2 - 5 = 400 - 5 = 395$,
25 : ? ⇒ $(25)^2 - 5 = 625 - 5 = \boxed{620}$

Hence, ? = 620.

60. (2): CG : 20 :: LR : ? :: MP : 58
Here, CG : 20 ⇒ (C + G) × 2 = (3 + 7) × 2 = 20
LR : ? ⇒ (L + R) × 2 = (12 + 18) × 2 = $\boxed{60}$
MP : 58 ⇒ (M + P) × 2 = (13 + 16) × 2 = 58
Hence, ? = 60.

61. (4): Nguyen Thi Ngoc Phyong is a Vietnamese physician and one of the 2024 Ramon Magsaysay Award winners. She has dedicated her life to addressing the long-term health consequences of Agent Orange, a chemical defoliant used by the U.S. military during the Vietnam War. This toxic compound caused severe birth defects, cancers, and other chronic illnesses in affected populations. Dr. Phyong provided crucial medical assistance, advocacy, and rehabilitation for the victims—especially poor and marginalized children suffering from congenital disabilities. Her decades-long commitment to public health and humanitarian service reflects the core ideals of the Ramon Magsaysay Award, often referred to as Asia's Nobel Prize.

62. (4): This matching pertains to the 2024 Major Dhyan Chand Khel Ratna Awards, India's highest sporting honour:

A. Shri Gukesh D – IV. Chess: A teenage chess prodigy from Chennai, Gukesh made history by becoming one of the youngest players to enter the Candidates Tournament and achieve a top-10 global FIDE ranking.

B. Shri Harmanpreet Singh – I. Hockey: Captain of the Indian men's hockey team, Harmanpreet led India to victories with his defensive skills and powerful drag flicks.

C. Shri Praveen Kumar – III. Para Athletics: A Paralympian who has won multiple international medals in high jump, Kumar's achievements exemplify excellence in para sports.

D. Ms. Manu Bhaker – II. Shooting: A consistent medal-winner in international shooting championships, Manu has represented India at the Olympics and Youth Games with distinction.

63. (3): Sweden officially became the 32nd member of the North Atlantic Treaty Organization (NATO) on March 7, 2024. The decision to join came after heightened geo-political tensions in Europe, especially due to Russia's military actions in Ukraine. Previously neutral, Sweden sought NATO membership to strengthen its national defense and integrate more deeply with Western military alliances. This historic step followed Finland's accession in 2023 and marked a significant realignment of Nordic defense strategy. The move also indicated a broader expansion of NATO influence in northern Europe.

64. (2): Jayne Anne Phillips won the Pulitzer Prize for Fiction in 2024 for her novel Night Watch, published by Knopf. The novel explores the emotional aftermath of the American Civil War and the establishment of one of the country's first asylums for women. Known for her evocative prose and psychological depth, Phillips paints a moving narrative about trauma, memory, and healing. The Pulitzer jury praised her for the lyrical quality of her writing and her ability to capture the historical and human dimensions of postwar America.

65. (4): This pair is incorrectly matched. While the first three pairs refer to genuine books and authors, Meditations for Mortals is not written by Tom Baldwin. Baldwin is known more for his political commentary and biographical works, not philosophical or reflective literature. The other options are correctly matched:

- H is for Hope is authored by Elizabeth Kolbert, who is renowned for her environmental writing.
- Beautiful Days is correctly linked to Zach Williams, who is a musician but not an author of this title (so 2 is also slightly doubtful).
- Martyr is a known poetry work by Kaveh Akbar.

Thus, while options 2 and 4 both raise concerns, Option 4 is clearly incorrect as per existing publication records.

66. (2): The correct chronological order of Mughal emperors is:

B. Babur (1526–1530): Founder of the Mughal Empire in India, after winning the Battle of Panipat.

E. Humayun (1530–1540 and 1555–1556): Babur's son who lost the empire briefly to Sher Shah Suri and later regained it.

D. Akbar (1556–1605): Humayun's son, known for consolidating and expanding the empire, introducing religious tolerance, and administrative reforms.

C. Jahangir (1605–1627): Akbar's son, known for his interest in justice and art.

A. Shah Jahan (1628–1658): Famous for monumental architecture, especially the Taj Mahal.

67. (4): The human heart has four chambers—two atria and two ventricles. The atria are the two upper chambers: the right atrium receives deoxygenated blood from the body through the superior and inferior vena cava, while the left atrium receives oxygenated blood from the lungs via the pulmonary veins. These chambers act as receiving stations that then pass the blood into the ventricles below, which pump it either to the lungs or to the rest of the body.

68. (2): Non-metallic minerals are those which do not contain metals and are used primarily in industries like construction, fertilizers, and ceramics.

B. Gypsum is a soft sulfate mineral used in plaster, fertilizer, and cement.

C. Limestone is used in construction and cement-making, composed mostly of calcium carbonate.

D. Mica is a silicate mineral used in electronics and insulation.

On the other hand,

A. Bauxite is the chief ore of aluminum (metallic),

E. Manganese is a metallic mineral used in steel production.

69. (2): In terms of land area, the continents from largest to smallest are:

B. Asia – Largest continent, covering about 30% of Earth's land surface.

D. Africa – Second largest, with vast deserts, forests, and savannas.

C. North America – Third largest, includes Canada, the U.S., and Mexico.

E. Europe – Smaller in area but densely populated.

A. Australia – Smallest continent and often referred to as an island-continent.

70. (1): Venus completes one revolution around the Sun in about 225 Earth days. It is the second planet from the Sun and, despite its proximity to Earth in size and distance, has a dense atmosphere composed mostly of carbon dioxide, causing extreme greenhouse effects. Although Venus rotates very slowly on its axis (a day is longer than its year), its orbital period around the Sun is just under 255 days, making it the closest correct option among the given choices.

71. (3): Soil is classified based on particle size—sand (large), silt (medium), and clay (fine). Sandy soil contains a higher proportion of large, coarse particles. Because of this, it feels gritty to touch and drains water quickly. This type of soil has larger air spaces, is light, and is easy to cultivate but does not retain water or nutrients well. It is suitable for root crops like carrots and potatoes but not ideal for water-demanding plants. In contrast, loamy soil is a balanced mix of sand, silt, and clay and is considered best for agriculture.

72. (2): Earthworms lack lungs, spiracles, or tracheae. Instead, they respire through their moist skin. Oxygen diffuses directly into their bloodstream through the skin and carbon dioxide is expelled the same way. For this reason, earthworms must remain in moist environments; if their skin dries out, respiration fails, and they can die. This unique method of gaseous exchange makes them highly sensitive to environmental changes in humidity and soil moisture.

73. (2): (A) Mercury, (B) Venus, and (E) Mars do not have planetary rings.

(C) Jupiter and (D) Uranus both have rings, though they are not as prominent as Saturn's.

Jupiter's faint ring system was discovered by Voyager 1, while Uranus has a more complex ring system discovered in 1977. Mercury and Venus are too close to the Sun, and their gravitational conditions are not conducive to maintaining rings.

74. (3):

A. Nobility – (IV) 2nd Estate: They were land-owning aristocrats in pre-revolutionary France, forming the second of the three estates.

B. Clergy – (I) 1st Estate: This estate included the church leaders and priests, wielding both spiritual and political power.

C. Taille – (II) Tax to be paid directly to the State: It was a direct land tax imposed mainly on the peasantry and commoners, exempting the first two estates.

D. Livre – (III) Unit of Currency in France, discontinued in 1794: The livre was the pre-revolutionary currency which was replaced by the franc after 1794.

75. (1): Gagan Gill received the Sahitya Akademi Award in 2024 for Hindi literature. She is known for her profound and introspective writing, often reflecting themes of existence, gender, and modern Indian society. Her literary style combines lyrical intensity with emotional depth. The Sahitya Akademi Award is a prestigious recognition conferred by India's National Academy of Letters for outstanding literary work in any of the 24 recognized Indian languages.

76. (3): Madhubani painting, also called Mithila painting, originates from the Mithila region in Bihar. This folk art form is known for its intricate patterns and symbolic motifs using natural colours and brushes made of twigs or fingers. Traditionally created by women on walls and floors during festivals and rituals, it has now gained global recognition and is also done on paper and canvas. The themes include mythology, nature, and daily life.

77. (4): Chola-era inscriptions mention land classifications as follows:

A. Shalabhoga – (III) Land for maintenance of a school: These lands were granted to educational institutions or for educational purposes.

B. Brahmadeya – (I) Land gifted to Brahmanas: This was a major form of land donation, often tax-free and hereditary.

C. Vellanvagai – (IV) Land of non-Brahmana peasant proprietors: Cultivated by peasants who were often taxed.

D. Pallichchhandam – (II) Land donated to Jaina institutions: "Palli" denotes Jain institutions, and this land supported Jain monasteries.

78. (1): Robert Clive led the East India Company's army at the Battle of Plassey in 1757 against Sirajuddaulah, the Nawab of Bengal. This decisive battle marked the beginning of British colonial dominance in India. Clive's strategic alliance with Mir Jafar and use of treachery turned the battle in favor of the British. His victory laid the foundation for British rule in Bengal, and eventually across India.

79. (4): Only the Narmada and Tapi rivers drain into the Arabian Sea.

- Narmada flows westward from Madhya Pradesh to the Arabian Sea.
- Tapi also flows westward, passing through Madhya Pradesh, Maharashtra, and Gujarat.
- Mahanadi, Godavari, and Krishna flow eastward and drain into the Bay of Bengal.

80. (1): Ferrous minerals contain iron and are magnetic in nature.

(A) Iron ore, (D) Manganese, and (E) Chromite are ferrous minerals as they contain iron or are used in steel making.

(B) Gold and (C) Copper are non-ferrous minerals as they don't contain iron and are used for conductivity and ornamentation.

81. (3): Working capital refers to the inputs used up during the production process. It includes those items that are consumed or used within one cycle of production.

C. Raw materials such as cotton, wheat, or minerals are essential consumables for producing goods.

D. Money in hand is needed to pay wages, buy inputs, and cover day-to-day expenses.

These are short-term resources, unlike tools, machines, and buildings which are considered fixed capital since they are used over a long period.

82. (3): Statement (A) is correct: Minimum Support Price (MSP) is a price fixed by the government before the sowing season to assure farmers of a guaranteed price for certain crops. It acts as a safety net to protect farmers from market price fluctuations.

Statement (B) is incorrect: This describes subsidized food grains sold under PDS, not MSP. MSP is about procurement from farmers, not to consumers. Hence, only (A) is true.

83. (2): Pandita Ramabai was a pioneer in women's education and social reform in India during the 19th century. She established a mission at Khedgaon near Pune, known as the Mukti Mission, which provided shelter, literacy, and vocational training to widows, orphans, and destitute women. She challenged traditional norms and worked for the upliftment of women, particularly those marginalized in society due to caste or widowhood.

84. (3): Statement (A) is correct: ROM (Read Only Memory) is non-volatile memory permanently embedded into a computer during manufacturing. It stores essential instructions like boot-up firmware.

Statement (B) is incorrect: ROM retains its data even when the system is powered off. In contrast, RAM loses its data when power is lost. Thus, ROM is a permanent memory type.

85. (1): A firewall is a program or hardware device that monitors and filters incoming and outgoing network traffic. It creates a barrier between a trusted internal network and untrusted external networks, such as the internet. It helps in preventing unauthorized access, hacking attempts, and malware infections. The other terms—malware, denial of service, and cookies—refer to other cyber concepts, not filtering tools.

86. (2): Fungi exhibit saprotrophic nutrition, meaning they derive nutrients from decaying organic matter. They release digestive enzymes into their surroundings, break down complex substances externally, and then absorb the simpler compounds. This method is distinct from autotrophic nutrition in plants and heterotrophic nutrition in animals.

87. (3): Animal cells lack:

B. Cell wall, which is found only in plant cells and provides rigidity and support.

D. Chloroplast, present in plant cells to conduct photosynthesis using chlorophyll.

Animal cells do have:

A. Cell membrane, which controls substance movement, and

C. Cytoplasm, the fluid in which organelles are suspended.

88. (1):

A. Correct: Rajya Sabha cannot pass a no-confidence motion; this is exclusive to Lok Sabha.

B. Incorrect: The President of India is a constitutional part of Parliament under Article 79.

C. Correct: If Lok Sabha passes the budget, Rajya Sabha can only discuss it; it cannot reject or amend it.

D. Incorrect: All money bills passed by both houses must receive Presidential assent to become law.

89. (3): This statement describes suspensions, not colloids.

- Colloidal solutions are heterogeneous, have particles invisible to the naked eye, and can scatter light (Tyndall effect).
- But colloid particles do not settle down upon standing, which is what separates them from suspensions. Thus, option 3 is not correct for colloids.

90. (2):

A. BJP – (II) Founded in 1980: Emerged from the Bharatiya Jana Sangh.

B. NCP – (IV) Founded in 1999: Formed by Sharad Pawar and others after splitting from the Indian National Congress.

C. BSP – (III) Founded in 1984: Founded by Kanshi Ram for the rights of Dalits and Bahujans.

D. CPI – (I) Founded in 1925: One of India's oldest leftist political parties.

91. (2): The passage clearly states that practicing sport from an early age promotes both mental development and a healthy lifestyle in adulthood. It highlights that the habits acquired during childhood—such as regular physical activity—tend to remain throughout life, positively impacting mental well-being and physical health. While interaction and concentration are mentioned, the most comprehensive reason aligning with both mental and physical development is the promotion of a healthy lifestyle combined with cognitive benefits.

92. (2): The word dissociation refers to separation or disconnection. The correct antonym from the passage context is integration, which means joining together or unifying. In the passage, sports are said to "improve interaction and social integration", implying the opposite of dissociation, where individuals come together rather than remain separate.

93. (3): The word reasonable generally means fair, sensible, or not extreme. In the passage, moderate daily physical exercise is recommended, suggesting something balanced—not excessive or inadequate. Hence, moderate is the correct synonym, as it conveys the same idea of being within reasonable or sensible limits.

94. (4): The passage explicitly mentions that when choosing a sport for a child, one should consider the child's conditions and abilities. For instance, a shy child may benefit from team sports that encourage interaction, while an active child may gain more from individual sports that improve focus. Therefore, the decision should be tailored to the child's temperament and physical or mental capacity.

95. (3): The passage stresses the increasing concern of obesity among children and emphasizes that including sports in the family routine helps prevent this issue. It specifically refers to the rise in childhood obesity in the Western world and claims that regular physical activity becomes essential to combat this trend. Therefore, the main reason for making sport a mandatory family habit is to prevent sedentary lifestyles and related health problems.

96. (3): The passage defines sustainable development as meeting present needs without compromising future generations. It clearly links pollution control with the adoption of sustainable practices, which include prevention, remediation, and legal accountability. Hence, applying sustainable development principles is essential to effectively address pollution.

97. (4): Exacerbate means to worsen or intensify a problem. The opposite, or antonym, is mitigate, which means to reduce the severity or seriousness of something. The passage uses "mitigate the adverse effects" in the context of reducing pollution damage, making mitigate the correct antonym of exacerbate.

98. (2): The analogy is based on cause and solution.
- Just as pollution arises from natural events and human activities,
- safeguarding the environment stems from applying principles rooted in sustainable development.

These principles aim to ensure ecological balance while meeting human needs, making this the most appropriate completion.

99. (3): In the passage, the phrase "stem from" means to originate from or arise due to. The correct sentence with the same meaning is option 3, where her unhappiness originates from his betrayal. All other options refer to physical stems of plants and don't match the figurative use of the phrase.

100. (3): The phrase "an indirect and usually bad result of an action or event that may happen sometime afterwards" best fits the word repercussion. The passage uses this term in the context of legal consequences for environmental damage. It suggests that such consequences are not immediate but follow after some time, aligning with the definition provided.

101. (2): Medicinal is the adjective form among the options. It describes something related to or having the properties of medicine (e.g., medicinal plants).
- Medicine (noun),
- Medicate (verb),
- Medic (noun, person).

102. (3): Ministerial is the adjective that relates to a minister or ministry (e.g., ministerial duties).
- Minister (noun),
- Ministry (noun),
- Administer (verb).

103. (2): Tabular is the adjective, meaning arranged in a table or flat form (e.g., tabular data).
- Table (noun),
- Tabloid (noun),
- Tablet (noun).

104. (2): Studious is the adjective, describing someone who studies diligently (e.g., a studious child).
- Study (verb/noun),
- Student (noun),
- Studiously (adverb).

105. (4): Expectant is the adjective form, meaning anticipating or awaiting (e.g., expectant mother).
- Expect (verb),
- Expectation and Expectancy (nouns).

106. (2): Remission means a decrease or reduction (especially of pain, punishment, or disease), which matches abatement—a reduction or decline.
- Credit and execution don't relate,
- Remembrance implies memory.

107. (4): Alliteration is the repetition of initial consonant sounds in closely connected words (e.g., Peter Piper picked). Thus, repetition is the closest synonym.
- Others are unrelated.

108. (2): Reprehension means criticism or disapproval, similar to admonition—a warning or reprimand.
- Anxiety is an emotional state,
- Acidity and Acrimony refer to bitterness but not in the same context.

109. (2): Repudiate means to reject or disown responsibility for something, aligning best with disavow.
- Censure means strong disapproval but not outright rejection,
- Distaste is dislike,
- Memorise is unrelated.

110. (3): Retinue refers to a group of attendants or followers accompanying an important person, just like entourage.
- Avenge, review, and withdraw do not fit.

111. (2): The correct spelling is Procrastinate, which means to delay or postpone doing something. The other spellings are incorrect variations.

112. (2): Psychosomatic refers to physical symptoms that are caused or worsened by mental factors such as stress. The correct spelling includes both "psycho" and "somatic."

113. (3): Credibility means the quality of being trusted or believed. This is the correct spelling; all other forms are incorrect or misspelled.

114. (1): Cumulative means increasing or growing by accumulation. It is correctly spelled here. The other options contain repeated or extra letters.

115. (3): Desiccated means dried out, especially by removing moisture. The other spellings are incorrect, containing extra or fewer "s" or "c" letters.

116. (1): "Smartly-dressed" is the correct adverbial phrase describing how the women were dressed. Also, "came to blows" (meaning fought physically) is correctly retained.

117. (4): The sentence is already correct. "If you say something off the cuff, you say it spontaneously" is a grammatically accurate and meaningful sentence using the idiom properly.

118. (4): The phrase "in her element" is correct and idiomatic, meaning someone is doing what they are naturally good at or comfortable with. No correction is needed.

119. (2): Expedite means to speed up a process. Its opposite is Delay, which means to slow down or postpone.

120. (4): Optimal means the best or most efficient condition or level. Its opposite is Wasteful, which implies inefficiency and poor use of resources.

121. (4): Congenial means friendly and pleasant. Rude is its opposite, meaning impolite or harsh.

122. (1): Dexterous means skillful, especially with hands. A novice is a beginner, making it the correct antonym here.

123. (3): Parched means extremely dry or thirsty. Its opposite is Soaked, meaning thoroughly wet or saturated.

124. (3): Repartee refers to witty, clever, and quick replies in conversation. It captures the idea of humorous and sharp exchanges.
- Banter is casual and playful talk, but repartee emphasizes speed and cleverness.

125. (4): Senescence is the biological process of aging or showing signs of old age.
- Dementia is a disease, not the general process,
- Septicaemia is blood poisoning,
- Growth is the opposite process.

126. (3): Serendipity refers to the occurrence of fortunate events by chance. It implies unexpected luck in finding something pleasant.
- Accidental is broader and not necessarily positive,
- Happenchance is outdated and less precise.

127. (1): Fastidious means being extremely attentive to accuracy and detail.
- Contrarian means someone who opposes the majority,
- Nonchalant implies indifference,
- Consistent means steady, not necessarily detail-oriented.

128. (4): A treatise is a formal and detailed written work on a specific subject, typically scholarly.
- Essay is shorter,
- Journal is periodical,
- Epic refers to long narrative poetry.

129. (1): The phrase is "fed up of" is incorrect in standard English. The correct usage is "fed up with."

130. (3): The idiomatic expression is "all over the place," meaning widely or everywhere.

131. (1): When referring to being accepted to study at a university, we use "at" (e.g., place at Bath).

132. (1): The correct phrase is "assured of something."

133. (2): "Too low for my voice" is the correct construction.

134. (1): The correct phrase is "doesn't pay anywhere near enough," meaning far too little.

135. (4): "Involved in a near miss" is the proper collocation.

136. (3): The idiom is "like looking for a needle in a haystack," meaning nearly impossible.

137. (4): A placatory remark is one intended to pacify or calm someone down, especially when they are upset.

138. (2): This sentence has two objects: "her" and "a chair." In passive voice, either object can become the subject. The most appropriate construction is "She was handed a chair." It is grammatically correct and keeps the sentence natural and clear.

139. (3): This is the correct passive voice transformation of "He satisfied everybody." It maintains the past tense and uses the passive construction correctly: subject + was + past participle + by agent.

140. (4): The active sentence is in present perfect tense ("have broken"), so the correct passive form is: has the mirror been broken. "By you" retains the agent, and "why" retains the interrogative structure.

141. (3): The original sentence is in past continuous tense: "Was he washing…?" The passive form of past continuous is was/were being + past participle, hence "Were the clothes being washed by him?"

142. (3): This is the grammatically correct passive voice form of the sentence. "By her behaviour" identifies the cause, and "was annoyed" retains the passive construction.

143. (1): Error: "Much" is used for uncountable nouns. "Students" is countable, so it should be "Many students prefer…"

144. (2): Error: The phrase "The driver as well as the conductor" is treated as singular. So the verb should be "is," not "are."

145. (2): Error: The sentence refers to a past time ("In colonial America"), so "has been" should be changed to "there was very little."

146. (2): Error: "Much" is used with uncountable nouns. "Songs" is plural and countable, so it should be "many songs" or simply "many of the songs."

147. (4): Error: "She" is singular, so the correct verb form is "was busy," not "were busy."

148. (3): The idiom "dot the i's and cross the t's" means to take care of all the small details, ensuring something is completely correct or finished.

149. (1): "Skate on thin ice" means to be in a risky or dangerous situation where a mistake can cause serious problems.

150. (3): "To lose heart" means to become demoralized or lose confidence, especially in the face of difficulty.

151. (4): This option reflects responsibility, accountability, and environmental awareness. As the last person leaving the classroom, it is your moral duty to ensure that no electricity is wasted.
- Option 1 passes responsibility to others.
- Option 2 is not valid as classmates have already left.
- Option 3 assumes irresponsibly that equipment runs 24 × 7, which is neither economical nor environmentally friendly.

152. (2): This option shows empathy, readiness to help, and quick decision-making in an emergency.
- Option 1 reflects indifference.
- Option 3 is impractical and unhelpful in a crisis.
- Option 4 shows confusion instead of action.

153. (3): This choice reflects maturity, emotional control, and focus. Reacting emotionally or seeking revenge only worsens relationships.
- Option 1 leads to conflict.
- Option 2 is petty and escalatory.
- Option 4 shows passive-aggressive behaviour.

The best way is to ignore rumors and not let them affect your peace.

154. (4): This is a balanced and realistic viewpoint. While hard work is important, success also depends on other factors like timing, opportunity, and adaptability.
- Option 1 is pessimistic.
- Option 2 is vague.
- Option 3 is an extreme generalization.

Option 4 acknowledges hard work as an important component of progress without overstatement.

155. (3): This is the most responsible, humane, and ethical response.
- Option 1 shows lack of accountability.
- Option 2 is superficial and insufficient.
- Option 4 is irresponsible and cowardly.

Offering medical help and taking responsibility is the right approach.

156. (3): If your newspaper hawker is regularly late, the best first step is to inform him politely. Communication is key.
- Option 1 and 2 are reactive and unkind.
- Option 4 is a personal choice, but avoids solving the actual issue.

By apprising the hawker, you give him a chance to improve.

157. (4): When facing a difficult paper, staying calm and doing your best is the mature choice.
- Option 1 (protest) disrupts everyone and has no merit.
- Option 2 is unethical and unrealistic.
- Option 3 promotes cheating.

Option 4 reflects a positive and solution-oriented attitude.

158. (2): The primary purpose of morning exercise is to maintain physical and mental fitness.
- Option 1 trivializes exercise.
- Option 3 follows trends without understanding purpose.
- Option 4 focuses on watching, not doing.

Thus, fitness remains the most accurate and beneficial reason.

159. (3): Managing stress during exams requires a balanced lifestyle.
- Option 1 and 4 promote overexertion and lack of sleep.
- Option 2 (panic) only worsens the situation.

A well-planned schedule with breaks and rest is the most healthy and effective strategy.

160. (3): Addressing issues in a group project starts with open communication.
- Option 1 and 2 ignore the root of the problem or create blame.
- Option 4 is a last resort after all dialogue fails.

Option 3 shows leadership, empathy, and teamwork.

161. (4): This option reflects financial discipline and planning. Allocating funds helps avoid overspending and ensures money is available for essential needs and emergencies.
- Option 1 and 2 are reckless.
- Option 3 delays the issue without resolving the problem of budgeting.

162. (1): When you overhear a security breach, it is your responsibility to alert an authority figure within the company.
- Option 2 shows negligence.
- Option 3 is confrontational and may escalate issues without proper action.
- Option 4 (police) may be premature unless advised by your officer.

163. (4): Accepting drinks from strangers is risky, especially in unknown or party environments.
- Options 1, 2, and 3 can expose you to spiking or harmful substances.

Declining politely is the safest and smartest choice.

164. (3): This shows responsible driving behaviour. Safety of pedestrians is a priority under traffic rules.
- Option 1 is dangerous.
- Option 2 may alert them but does not ensure safety.
- Option 4 is highly reckless.

165. (3): An unattended bag in a crowded area could be a security threat (e.g., explosive). Reporting to authorities ensures safety.
- Option 1 and 4 are risky and can be unsafe.
- Option 2 is negligent.

Only trained personnel should handle such objects.

166. (2): In an armed robbery, your safety is the top priority. Remaining calm and not provoking the attackers is the safest response.
- Option 1 may draw attention and increase risk.
- Option 3 is extremely irresponsible and dangerous.
- Option 4 could escalate the situation and endanger everyone.

167. (3): This reflects accountability and empathy. Even if it was unintentional, taking responsibility and compensating the vendor shows good character.
- Option 1 is unethical and cowardly.
- Option 2 and 4 shift blame unnecessarily.

168. (2): Respectful dialogue is key in family decisions. Sharing your views while listening to theirs fosters mutual understanding.
- Option 1 and 4 are disrespectful.
- Option 3 sacrifices your ambition without exploring resolution.

169. (1): Responding with empathy and maturity helps maintain the friendship and reduces tension.
- Option 2 may seem fair but can come across as harsh.
- Option 3 and 4 are emotionally reactive and harm relationships.

170. (4): Maintaining professionalism and commitment is the best long-term response.
- Option 1 looks boastful.
- Option 2 is an extreme decision.
- Option 3 creates negativity in the workplace.

171. (3): A first aid box is essential in any organization to provide immediate treatment for minor injuries. This can prevent complications, reduce pain, and stabilize the injured person before professional help arrives.
- Option 1 is irrelevant,
- Option 2 is incorrect, and
- Option 4 is incomplete as compliance isn't the only reason for its necessity.

172. (2): Politeness is the most effective way to communicate with customers. It builds trust, maintains professionalism, and promotes a positive reputation.
- Rudeness and aggression drive customers away,
- Being phlegmatic (unemotional or sluggish) is also unhelpful in service interactions.

173. (1): Owning up to mistakes shows integrity and responsibility. Reporting the damage helps the authorities take appropriate action and prevents false blame.
- Options 2, 3, and 4 involve dishonesty or avoidance.

174. (1): If someone stands too close at an ATM, your privacy and safety could be at risk. Stepping away avoids potential fraud or theft.
- Continuing the transaction (option 2) is unsafe,
- Option 3 may escalate things unnecessarily,
- Option 4 is too extreme unless there's a clear threat.

175. (3): This is the most honest and socially responsible action. It shows integrity and respect for others' property.
- Keeping the money in any form is theft.
- Option 4 promotes unethical behaviour.

176. (2): This reflects responsibility and concern for others' safety. If you can't clean it yourself, informing the right staff prevents accidents.
- Option 1 and 3 show negligence.
- Option 4 limits action to a small group and is not effective.

177. (1): Immediate verbal communication is the safest and most direct way to address reckless driving.
- Option 2 ignores the risk.
- Option 3 might place you in a worse situation.
- Option 4 is too extreme unless the driver becomes threatening or refuses to stop.

178. (4): Obeying traffic signals is essential for road safety.
- All other options reflect dangerous and illegal behaviour.

179. (1): Taking responsibility and offering assistance shows politeness and maturity.
- Options 2, 3, and 4 are dismissive, disrespectful, or immature.

180. (1): This shows empathy and good customer service. Addressing the issue directly improves guest satisfaction.
- Option 2 is dismissive,
- Option 3 is unprofessional,
- Option 4 shows minimal concern.

181. (1): This is the most civil and effective solution. Calm communication often resolves such issues peacefully.
- Option 2 is cruel and inappropriate.
- Option 3 is excessive for a first occurrence.
- Option 4 delays resolution unnecessarily.

182. (2): Handling line-cutting with politeness and assertiveness maintains order without creating conflict.
- Option 1 and 3 promote avoidance or passive behaviour.
- Option 4 escalates the situation unnecessarily.

183. (1): This reflects hospitality, flexibility, and maturity. Making guests feel welcome, even if unexpected, is a sign of emotional intelligence.
- Options 2 and 4 are blunt and may damage relations.
- Option 3 is impolite and creates discomfort.

184. (2): Taking ownership of your error, even if unnoticed, shows integrity, accountability, and professionalism.
- Option 1 is dishonest.
- Option 3 reflects negligence.
- Option 4 is extreme and irrational.

185. (1): Maintaining respect and composure even when wrongly accused is a mature way to handle misunderstandings.
- Options 2, 3, and 4 are emotionally reactive and damage relationships without resolution.

186. (4): This response shows maturity, communication, and problem-solving skills. Discussing the issue directly and politely helps maintain good relations while addressing the damage.
- Option 1 ignores the problem.
- Option 2 escalates conflict.
- Option 3 may seem demanding without discussion.

187. (2): This reflects prioritization and time management. Responsibilities should be fulfilled before leisure.
- Option 1 neglects duties.
- Option 3 risks incomplete work.
- Option 4 surrenders your responsibility to others.

188. (2): This is the most socially responsible and health-conscious choice. It prevents worsening your condition and protects others.
- Option 1 and 3 show disregard for health.
- Option 4 is extreme and unnecessary.

189. (3): Even frequent complaints should be handled with patience and professionalism, especially in customer-facing roles.
- Option 1 cuts off future interaction.
- Option 2 is defensive.
- Option 4 is negligent.

190. (2): This is the standard safety protocol during turbulence.
- Option 1 creates panic.
- Option 3 could endanger you and others.
- Option 4 is dangerous during turbulence.

191. (2): This shows professionalism, emotional control, and problem-solving. A calm and empathetic response can de-escalate anger and rebuild trust.
- Option 1 escalates the situation,
- Option 3 avoids responsibility,
- Option 4 deflects blame instead of solving the issue.

192. (1): Feeding animals in a zoo violates safety and health regulations. The responsible action is to inform the authorities.
- Option 2 breaks rules,
- Option 3 is negligent,
- Option 4 encourages wrong behaviour.

193. (2): Acknowledging the delay and requesting patience shows courtesy and service-oriented behaviour.
- Option 1 is disrespectful,
- Option 3 may not match the order,
- Option 4 is dismissive and unprofessional.

194. (4): Team spirit means adapting to challenges. Staying focused and reorganizing ensures continuity and shows resilience.
- Option 1, 2, and 3 reflect panic, blame, or quitting—none of which are constructive.

195. (4): Admitting your mistake and responding politely demonstrates maturity and courtesy.
- Option 1 lacks acknowledgment,
- Option 2 delays rightful resolution,
- Option 3 dismisses the other person's discomfort.

196. (2): Taking initiative and involving others reflects leadership, teamwork, and responsibility.
- Option 1 and 3 show irresponsibility.
- Option 4 shows avoidance of duty.

197. (4): This promotes team harmony and conflict resolution. Understanding the problem helps calm tensions constructively.
- Option 1 shows bias,
- Option 2 is too extreme unless violence occurs,
- Option 3 reflects indifference.

198. (1): Reception staff should maintain courtesy, professionalism, and a welcoming demeanor.
- Options 2, 3, and 4 reflect poor behaviour unfit for customer service roles.

199. (3): In security-related lockdowns, safety and patience are most important. Wait for official directions.
- Option 1 and 2 are unsafe and may violate protocols.
- Option 4 is unproductive and ignores seriousness.

200. (2): This shows presence of mind and safety awareness. Safe, public, and official spaces offer help without risk.
- Option 1 may be risky,
- Option 3 wastes time and energy,
- Option 4 is passive and may delay help.

Previous Years' Paper

National Testing Agency (NTA)

NCHMCT-JEE—National Council for Hotel Management and Catering Technology Joint Entrance Exam, 2024

(Exam held on 11-05-2024)

NUMERICAL ABILITY

1. The area of a rectangle having sides in the ratio 1 : 4 is equal to the area of a square of side 8 cm. The perimeter of the rectangle (in cm) is:

A. 32 B. 36
C. 40 D. 44

2. If mean of the observations 6, 16, (K + 26), (2K – 3) and 10 is 14, then the value of $\frac{K^2+1}{2}$ is:

A. 25 B. 18.5
C. 13 D. 8.5

3. If the length of the diagonal and the area of a rectangle are 25 m and 168 m^2, respectively, then the longer side of the rectangle is:

A. 21 m B. 22 m
C. 24 m D. 20 m

4. A and B, working together can do a work in 8 days. If A alone can do the work in 12 days, then in how many days can B alone do 25% of the work?

A. 5 B. 6
C. 7 D. 4

5. The sum of all possible values of K such that a 5-digit number 9 0 K 6 8 is divisible by 8 will be:

A. 21 B. 23
C. 25 D. 26

6. In a clearance sale, goods were sold at a reduction of 20%. Sarika purchased a saree for ₹ 984 in the clearance sale. The usual price of the saree was:

A. ₹ 1184 B. ₹ 1066
C. ₹ 1148 D. ₹ 1230

7. Two trains having lengths 680 m and 570 m are running towards each other on parallel tracks with speeds of 80 km/h and 70 km/h, respectively. In how many seconds will they be able to cross each other?

A. 20 B. 25
C. 30 D. 36

8. What is the HCF of $\frac{8}{5}, \frac{6}{8}, \frac{4}{25}$?

A. $\frac{1}{5}$ B. $\frac{1}{50}$
C. $\frac{1}{100}$ D. $\frac{1}{200}$

9. In a class of 60 students, 60% are boys. The average of marks of the boys is 68 and that of the girls is 72. What are the average marks of the whole class?

A. 68.8 B. 69.3
C. 69.6 D. 70.1

10. $\sqrt{\sqrt[3]{13824}+\sqrt[3]{15625}} =$

A. 6 B. 7
C. 8 D. 9

11. If $a^4 + \frac{1}{a^4} = 322,$ then the value of $a - \frac{1}{a}$ is:

A. $\frac{3}{2}$ B. 2
C. $\frac{8}{27}$ D. 4

12. In an election between two candidates, one of them got 62% of the total votes polled and won by 432 votes. What is the total number of votes polled?

A. 1500 B. 1600
C. 1800 D. 1900

1. C	2. C	3. C	4. B	5. C	6. D
7. C	8. C	9. C	10. B	11. D	12. C

13. If the difference between 58% and 76% of a number is 198, then the difference between 82% and 46% of the same number will be:

A. 286 B. 396
C. 432 D. 506

14. ₹ 10000 is invested for 1½ years at 10% p.a. What is the difference between the compound interests when the sum is compounded half yearly and when it is compounded annually?

A. ₹ 24.50 B. ₹ 25.25
C. ₹ 25.75 D. ₹ 26.25

15. Joseph started a business by investing ₹ 100000. After 2 months, B joined him by investing ₹ 90000. After 4 more months, C joined them by investing ₹ 100000. The ratio of their shares in the profit at the end of the year is:

A. 10 : 9 : 10 B. 10 : 9 : 5
C. 6 : 5 : 3 D. 4 : 3 : 2

16. The ratio of present ages of A, B and C is 3 : 4 : 5. After 6 years, the average age of all the three will be 26 years. What was the difference between the ages of B and C, 4 years ago?

A. 4 years B. 5 years
C. 6 years D. 8 years

17. A and B can do a work in 120 days, B and C can do it in 72 days while A and C can do it in 90 days. In how many days can C alone do the work?

A. 30 B. 60
C. 40 D. 120

18. A man sold two articles for ₹ 4000 each with no profit no loss in the whole transaction. If he sold one article at a gain of 25%, then the other article has been sold at a loss of:

A. $20\frac{2}{3}\%$ B. 25%
C. $18\frac{1}{2}\%$ D. $16\frac{2}{3}\%$

19. In a journey of total 24 km, a man noticed that after cycling for 1 hour 40 minutes, the distance covered by him was $\frac{5}{7}$ of the remaining distance. What was his speed in meters per second?

A. $1\frac{1}{3}$ B. $1\frac{2}{3}$
C. $1\frac{1}{2}$ D. $1\frac{1}{4}$

20. The sum of two numbers is 240. If the numbers are in the ratio 3 : 5, then the sum of their LCM and HCF is:

A. 450 B. 460
C. 480 D. 496

21. What is the average of first 16 multiples of 9?

A. 72 B. 76.5
C. 77.25 D. 79.75

22. What is the least number that must be added to 6412 to get a perfect square?

A. 12 B. 120
C. 149 D. 161

23. 2.8 − (7.4 ÷ 3.7 × 5) ÷ 5 × 2 =

A. 2.76 B. −2.64
C. 6.8 D. −1.2

24. The monthly salaries of A and B together amount to ₹ 40000. A spends 82% of his salary and B, 94% of his salary. If their savings are the same, then the salary of A is:

A. ₹ 10000 B. ₹ 18000
C. ₹ 22000 D. ₹ 30000

25. The simple interest on a certain sum at the rate of 7% for 6 years is ₹ 3024. The sum is:

A. ₹ 7000 B. ₹ 7150
C. ₹ 7200 D. ₹ 7280

26. If $(a + b) : (b + c) : (a + c) = 6 : 7 : 8$ and $a + b + c = 14$, then the value of a is:

A. $\frac{2}{7}$ B. 4
C. $\frac{11}{3}$ D. $\frac{14}{3}$

27. In what ratio should two varieties of sugar costing ₹ 52/kg and ₹ 42/kg, respectively, be mixed to get a variety of sugar costing ₹ 45/kg?

A. 21 : 26 B. 3 : 5
C. 3 : 7 D. 7 : 9

28. A solid metallic cube having surface area 864 cm^2 is melted to form 64 small solid cubes of same size. The sum of the surface areas of all the small cubes so formed (in cm^2) is:

A. 3200
B. 3328
C. 3456
D. 3584

13. B	14. D	15. D	16. B	17. D	18. D	19. B	20. C
21. B	22. C	23. D	24. A	25. C	26. D	27. C	28. C

29. A is three years older than B who is twice as old as C. If the sum of the ages of A, B and C be 28 years, then how old is B?

A. 7 years
B. 8 years
C. 9 years
D. 10 years

30. A number when multiplied by 18, increased by 357. The number is:

A. 19
B. 20
C. 21
D. 23

REASONING AND LOGICAL DEDUCTION

31. Select a word from the given options which is related to the third term in the same way as second term is related to the first term.

Professor : Teaching :: Physician : ?

A. Doctor
B. Patient
C. Treatment
D. Surgery

32. Arrange the given words in a meaningful sequence and choose the most appropriate sequence from the given alternatives.

(*a*) Book
(*b*) Pulp
(*c*) Tree
(*d*) Forest
(*e*) Paper

A. (*d*), (*c*), (*b*), (*a*), (*e*)
B. (*d*), (*c*), (*b*), (*e*), (*a*)
C. (*d*), (*b*), (*c*), (*e*), (*a*)
D. (*c*), (*d*), (*b*), (*e*), (*a*)

33. Choose the odd one out from the given alternatives.

A. NTP : PGR
B. RSB : THD
C. KGN : MTP
D. QDL : SWP

34. Six friends G, H, I, P, Q and R are sitting in a circle facing the centre. H is between P and I. G is between Q and I. R is to the right of P. Who is between G and H?

A. P
B. Q
C. I
D. R

35. Find the missing term in the following series,

ab, abbc, __?__, abbccdde, abbccddeef

A. abccd
B. abbccd
C. abbcd
D. abbccdd

36. Choose the odd number pair from the given alternatives.

A. 18 : 306
B. 16 : 272
C. 15 : 255
D. 19 : 313

37. 'X' is the husband of 'M'. 'N' is the only grandson of 'Z', who is the wife of 'Y' and mother-in-law of 'M'. How is 'X' related to 'Y'?

A. Nephew
B. Son
C. Son-in-law
D. Brother-in-law

38. Observe the figure given below and answer the question.

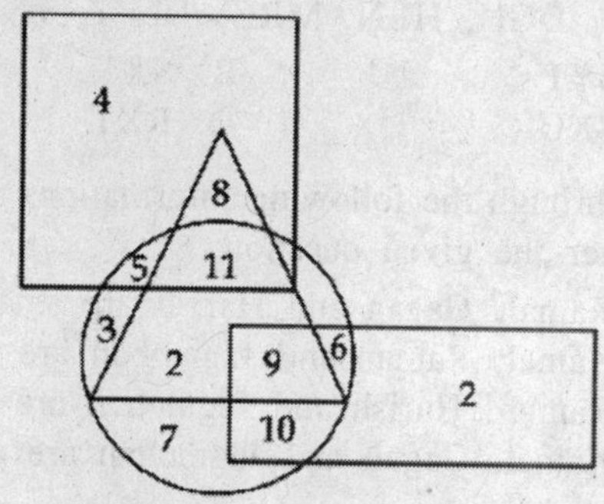

What is the sum of the numbers which belong to any two figures only?

A. 22
B. 34
C. 29
D. 31

39. 'G', 'H', 'I' and 'J' are playing carrom, 'G', 'I', 'J' and 'H' are partners. 'J' is to the right of 'I', who is facing West. Then 'H' is facing:

A. South
B. East
C. West
D. North

40. Some words are given below which are related in some way. The same relationship obtains among the words in one of the four alternatives given under it. Find the correct alternative.

Grass : Garden : Flowers

A. Quilt : Bed : Pillow
B. Road : Footpath : Traffic
C. Picture : Wall : Building
D. Pen : Book : Pencil

41. If in a code languages, 'JIYA' is coded as 180 and 'NAVAL' is coded as 250, then how will 'TANISHA' be coded in the same code language?

A. 288
B. 360
C. 432
D. 504

29. D	**30.** C	**31.** C	**32.** B	**33.** D	**34.** C	**35.** B
36. D	**37.** B	**38.** D	**39.** D	**40.** A	**41.** D	

42. Choose the missing term of the series from the given alternatives.

H20L, K19H, N19E, Q20C, ?

A. T21B B. S21B
C. T22B D. T22A

43. A 'Mechanic' is related to 'Garage' in the same way as 'Lawyer' is related to:

A. Criminal B. Judge
C. Court D. Client

44. Complete the series by replacing the question mark (?).

ACZ, DGU, HLN, MRE, ?

A. SYT B. SXT
C. SXU D. RXT

45. Go through the following informations carefully and answer the given question:

(*i*) Kamal, Gagan and Harish are smart.
(*ii*) Kamal, Raman and Jagmohan are sincere.
(*iii*) Raman, Harish and Jagmohan are loyal.
(*iv*) Kamal, Gagan and Jagmohan are ambitious.

Which of the following person is neither sincere nor ambitious?

A. Gagan B. Kamal
C. Raman D. Harish

46. In the given question certain pairs of words are given, out of which the words in all pairs except one bear a certain common relationship. Choose the pair in which the words are differently related.

A. Moon : Satellite B. Venus : Planet
C. Rocket : Space D. Sun : Star

47. If 'green' means 'blue', 'blue' means 'white', 'white' means 'red', 'red' means 'black', 'black' means 'brown' and 'brown' means 'yellow' then the colour of blood is:

A. blue B. brown
C. black D. white

48. Jaya and Kishore are a married couple having two sons Mohit and Naval. Binita is daughter of Mahesh and daughter-in-law of Kishore. Priyanka is daughter of Naval and Gauri. How is Mohit related to Mahesh?

A. Father
B. Son-in-law
C. Brother
D. Uncle

49. If in a certain code language 'NOTE' is coded as 'XOJE', 'ROSE' is coded as 'BOIE', then how will you code 'LOVE' in the same language?

A. VOME B. VOLE
C. WOLE D. VOKE

50. Arrange the words in the sequence in which they occur in the dictionary and then choose the correct sequence.

(*a*) Introduce (*b*) Intrude
(*c*) Introvert (*d*) Internal

A. (*a*), (*d*), (*b*), (*c*) B. (*a*), (*d*), (*c*), (*b*)
C. (*d*), (*a*), (*c*), (*b*) D. (*d*), (*c*), (*a*), (*b*)

51. Choose that set of numbers from the alternatives that is similar to the given set.

(9, 27, 81)

A. (15, 52, 125)
B. (12, 60, 98)
C. (3, 12, 31)
D. (12, 36, 108)

52. Which of the following Venn diagrams indicates the best relationship between Children, Naughty and studious?

A.  B. 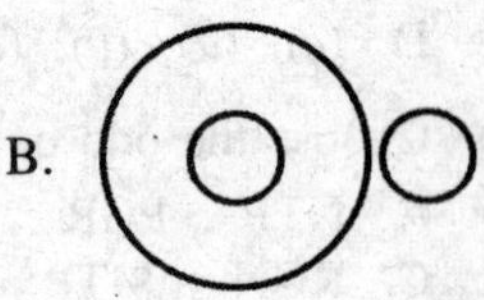

C. 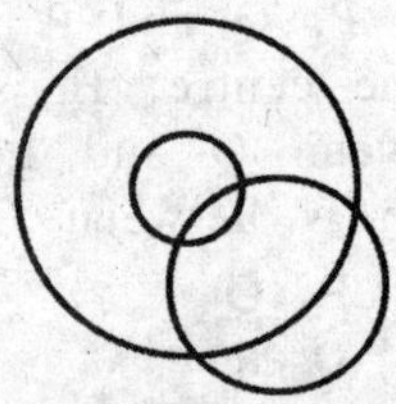 D. 

53. The number of triangles in the given figure is:

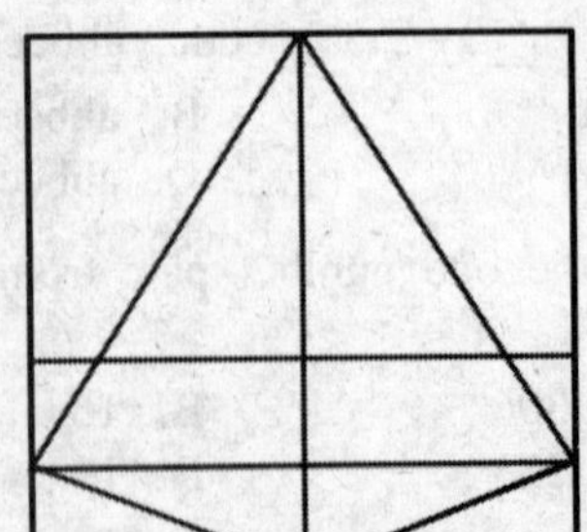

A. 13 B. 15
C. 17 D. 14

42. C	**43.** C	**44.** A	**45.** D	**46.** C	**47.** D
48. B	**49.** B	**50.** C	**51.** D	**52.** D	**53.** C

54. Select the option that is related to the third letter cluster in the same way as second letter cluster is related to the first letter cluster.

PQL : OJK :: FTS : ?

A. GYT B. HGX
C. GZU D. HGU

55. Select a figure from the given four alternatives which when placed in the blank space of the given figure would complete the pattern.

A.  B. 

C.  D. 

56. A statement is given below, followed by four arguments numbered (I), (II), (III) and (IV). Decide which of the following arguments is/are 'strong' arguments. Choose answer from the alternatives given below:

Statement: Should 'literacy' be the minimum criterion for becoming a voter in India?

Arguments:

I. No, more literacy is no guarantee of political maturity of an individual.
II. Yes, it will reduce corruption in the system.
III. No, voting is the constitutional right of every citizen.
IV. Yes, Illiterate people are less likely to make politically wiser decisions of voting for a right candidate or party.

A. Only (I) and (II) are strong.
B. Only (I), (II) and (IV) are strong.
C. Only (I), (III) and (IV) are strong.
D. Only (II) and (IV) are strong.

57. Find out the alternative which will replace the question mark.

January : November :: Monday : ?

A. Thursday B. Sunday
C. Tuesday D. Saturday

Directions (Qs. No. 58 to 60): *Study the following information carefully and answer the questions:*

Seven friends G, H, I, J, K, L and M live in three different buildings Ashiana, Gharonda and Basera. Each of them is wearing different colour shirts i.e. red, green, blue, white, black, yellow and pink not necessarily in that order. Not more than three or less than two stay in any of the buildings. L is wearing pink shirt and lives in the same building as only M, i.e. Ashiana. I is wearing a black shirt and does not live in Basera. J does not live in the same building as G or K and is wearing a yellow coloured shirt. H lives in Basera with only one more person and is wearing a green shirt. None in the Gharonda building wears a white shirt. K does not wear a blue shirt.

58. Who is wearing a blue shirt?

A. G B. J
C. M D. H

59. Who stay in Gharonda building?

A. K, H B. G, I, K
C. I, J, L D. G, M, H

60. What coloured shirt M is wearing?

A. Black B. Red
C. White D. Blue

GENERAL KNOWLEDGE AND CURRENT AFFAIRS

61. Arrange the five layers of our atmosphere in correct order starting from the earth's surface.

(*a*) Stratosphere (*b*) Troposphere
(*c*) Exosphere (*d*) Mesosphere
(*e*) Thermosphere

Choose the ***correct*** answer from the options given below:

A. (*b*), (*a*), (*d*), (*e*), (*c*)
B. (*b*), (*a*), (*d*), (*c*), (*e*)
C. (*a*), (*c*), (*d*), (*b*), (*e*)
D. (*a*), (*e*), (*b*), (*d*), (*c*)

62. Which river makes the second biggest waterfall in India, known as Shivasamudram Falls?

A. Mahanadi B. Kaveri
C. Krishna D. Narmada

54. D	**55.** C	**56.** C	**57.** D	**58.** A	**59.** B	**60.** C	**61.** A	**62.** B

63. **Statement (A):** Removing barriers or restrictions set by the government is known as liberalisation.
Statement (B): This meant that goods can be imported and exported easily.

Choose the *correct* answer from the options given below:
A. Both Statement (A) and (B) are correct.
B. Both Statement (A) and (B) are incorrect.
C. Statement (A) is correct, (B) is incorrect.
D. Statement (A) is incorrect, (B) is correct.

64. Which of the following is not included in terms of credit?
A. Interest rate
B. Collateral and documentation
C. Mode of repayment
D. History of the money lender

65. Which writ is issued when the court finds that a particular office holder is not doing legal duty and thereby is infringing on the right of an individual?
A. Mandamus B. Prohibition
C. Certiorari D. Habeas Corpus

66. Under Which writ, the court orders a lower court or another authority to transfer a matter pending before it to the higher authority or court?
A. Habeas Corpus B. Mandamus
C. Quo Warranto D. Certiorari

67. In which year was the Scheduled Castes and the Scheduled Tribes (Prevention of Atrocities) Act framed?
A. 1974 B. 1999
C. 1989 D. 1979

68. Who wrote the book titled 'Freedom from Fear'?
A. Aung San Suu Kyi B. Nelson Mandela
C. Karl Marx D. Mahatma Gandhi

69. Which of the following is known as 'Adi Kavya'?
A. Bhagavad Gita B. The Ramayana
C. The Mahabharata D. Matsya Purana

70. Match the Rigvedic names of the rivers (List-I) with their modern names (List-II).

List-I	List-II
(*a*) Vitasta	I. Beas
(*b*) Vipas	II. Chenab
(*c*) Asikani	III. Sutlej
(*d*) Sutudri	IV. Jhelum

Choose the *correct* answer from the options given below:

	(*a*)	(*b*)	(*c*)	(*d*)
A.	IV	I	II	III
B.	I	IV	II	III
C.	I	IV	III	II
D.	IV	I	III	II

71. Who said, "Jai Jawan, Jai Kisan, Jai Vigyan"?
A. Lal Bahadur Shastri
B. Jawahar Lal Nehru
C. Atal Bihari Vajpayee
D. Narendra Modi

72. Which of the following metals is most reactive?
A. Sodium B. Aluminium
C. Copper D. Zinc

73. Match List-I with List-II.

List-I (Agents)	List-II (Name of Disease)
(*a*) Virus	I. Ring Worm
(*b*) Protozoa	II. Tuberculosis
(*c*) Fungus	III. Malaria
(*d*) Bacteria	IV. Influenza

Choose the *correct* answer from the options given below:

	(*a*)	(*b*)	(*c*)	(*d*)
A.	III	IV	I	II
B.	IV	III	I	II
C.	IV	III	II	I
D.	III	IV	II	I

74. The headquarters of ISRO (Indian Space Research Organisation) is at:
A. Ahmedabad B. Hyderabad
C. Bengaluru D. Sriharikota

75. The twinkling of stars is because of which phenomenon of light?
A. Reflection of light
B. Atmospheric Scattering of light
C. Atmospheric Refraction of Star light
D. Total Internal Reflection of light

76. Who is the founder of ISRO (Indian Space Research Organisation)?
A. Dr. A.P.J. Abdul Kalam
B. Dr. Meghnad Saha
C. Dr. Homi. J. Bhabha
D. Dr. Vikram Sarabhai

63. A	**64.** D	**65.** A	**66.** D	**67.** C	**68.** A	**69.** B
70. A	**71.** C	**72.** A	**73.** B	**74.** C	**75.** C	**76.** D

77. Match List-I with List-II.

List-I (Olympic Medal Winner)	List-II (Sport in which they received)
(*a*) Gagan Narang	I. Badminton
(*b*) P.V. Sindhu	II. Lawn Tennis
(*c*) Vijender Singh	III. Shooting
(*d*) Leander Paes	IV. Boxing

Choose the ***correct*** answer from the options given below:

	(*a*)	(*b*)	(*c*)	(*d*)
A.	III	IV	I	II
B.	I	III	II	IV
C.	III	I	IV	II
D.	III	I	II	IV

78. When is the International Yoga Day celebrated every year?

A. 21st June B. 17th May
C. 1st July D. 22nd April

79. Match List-I with List-II.

List-I	List-II
(*a*) Kathak	I. Kerala
(*b*) Bharat Natyam	II. Andhra Pradesh
(*c*) Kuchipudi	III. Tamil Nadu
(*d*) Kathakali	IV. North India

Choose the ***correct*** answer from the options given below:

	(*a*)	(*b*)	(*c*)	(*d*)
A.	IV	III	II	I
B.	III	IV	II	I
C.	IV	III	I	II
D.	III	IV	I	II

80. Jagannath Temple is located in which state of India?

A. Tamil Nadu
B. Uttar Pradesh
C. Madhya Pradesh
D. Odisha

81. Palk Strait is the border line between:

A. India and Afghanistan
B. India and Sri Lanka
C. China and Pakistan
D. India and Nepal

82. Which of the following is wrongly matched?

A. Bit – Short form of Binary digit
B. Cell – Boxes created by the intersection of rows and columns in MS Excel sheet
C. Data – Raw facts and figures
D. MU – Short form of Modern Unit

83. Who amongst the following received the first Jnanpith Award?

A. Ranganath Misra B. G. Sankara Kurup
C. Damodar Mauzo D. Nilmani Phookan

84. Who amongst the following is the first women in the world to go into space?

A. Valentina Tereshkova
B. Kalpana Chawla
C. Caroline Mikkelsen
D. Marma Estela

85. Match List-I with List-II.

List-I (Book)	List-II (Author)
(*a*) A Tale of Two Cities	I. Emily Bronte
(*b*) Midnight's Children	II. Charles Dickens
(*c*) War and Peace	III. Salman Rushdie
(*d*) Wuthering Heights	IV. Leo Tolstoy

Choose the ***correct*** answer from the options given below:

	(*a*)	(*b*)	(*c*)	(*d*)
A.	III	II	I	IV
B.	II	III	I	IV
C.	III	II	IV	I
D.	II	III	IV	I

86. The Headquarters of United Nations is at:

A. New York B. Geneva
C. Paris D. London

87. Who is the first Sikh Guru and founder of Sikhism?

A. Guru Tegbahadur B. Guru Gobind Singh
C. Guru Arjan D. Guru Nanak

88. Who amongst the following is the first scientist to get the Nobel Prize for India?

A. Dr. Hargobind Khorana
B. Dr. C.V. Raman
C. Dr. Vikram Sarabhai
D. Dr. Homi Jehangir Bhabha

89. The first Commonwealth Games were held in the year 1930 at ______.

A. London B. Sydney
C. Hamilton D. Perth

90. 'Durand Cup' is associated with which sport?

A. Football B. Table Tennis
C. Cricket D. Polo

77. C	**78.** A	**79.** A	**80.** D	**81.** B	**82.** D	**83.** B
84. A	**85.** D	**86.** A	**87.** D	**88.** B	**89.** C	**90.** A

ENGLISH LANGUAGE AND COMPREHENSION

Directions (Qs. No. 91 to 95): *Study the following information carefully and answer the questions:*

As British rule expanded from Bengal to other parts of India, new systems of revenue were imposed. The Permanent Settlement was rarely extended to any region beyond Bengal.

Why was this so? One reason was that after 1810, agricultural prices rose, increasing the value of harvest produce, and enlarging the income of the Bengal zamindars. Since the revenue demand was fixed under the Permanent Settlement, the colonial state could not claim any share of this enhanced income. Keen on expanding its financial resources, the colonial government had to think of ways to maximise its land revenue. So in territories annexed in the nineteenth century, temporary revenue settlements were made.

There were other reasons too. When officials devise policies, their thinking is deeply shaped by economic theories they are familiar with. By the 1820s, the economist David Ricardo was a celebrated figure in England. Colonial officials had learnt Ricardian ideas during their college years. In Maharashtra when British officials set about formulating the terms of the early settlement in the 1820s, they operated with some of these ideas.

According to Ricardian ideas, a landowner should have a claim only to the "average rent" that prevailed at a given time. When the land yielded more than this "average rent", the landowner had a surplus that the state needed to tax. If tax was not levied, cultivators were likely to turn into rentiers, and their surplus income was unlikely to be productively invested in the improvement of the land. Many British officials in India thought that the history of Bengal confirmed Ricardo's theory.

91. Choose the correct statement.

A. The Permanent Settlement system was extended to Bombay Deccan beyond Bengal.
B. The income of the Bengal zamindars enlarged due to the increased value of harvest produce.
C. In territories annexed after 1900, temporary revenue settlements were made by the colonial government.
D. According to Ricardian ideas, the government should have a claim only to the average rent that the state needed to tax.

92. Choose the correct statement.

The landowners were likely to turn into rentiers if:

A. agricultural prices rose.
B. they had a surplus income yield.
C. they minimized their land revenue.
D. they collected the 'average rent'.

93. The colonial state could not claim any share of the enhanced income of the Bengal zamindars because:

A. the British rule had expanded from Bengal to other parts of India.
B. the rise of agricultural prices increased the value of the harvest produce.
C. the revenue demand was fixed under the Permanent Settlement.
D. the Permanent Settlement was not extended to any other region.

94. The meaning of the word 'celebrated' as it appears in the passage (para-3) is:

A. commemorated B. gala
C. reputed D. solemnized

95. According to the passage, the colonial government made temporary revenue settlements because:

A. they wanted to enhance the income of the Bengal zamindars.
B. they wanted to control the rising agricultural prices.
C. they wanted to expand their financial resources.
D. they wanted to decrease the value of harvest produce.

96. Spot the error in the given sentence:

(*a*) According to a survey/ (*b*) only those forests which were/ (*c*) not under village management/ (*d*) succumbed from fires recently.

A. (*a*) B. (*b*)
C. (*c*) D. (*d*)

97. Choose the correctly spelt word from the following options:

A. Hulaballoo B. Hypoteneuse
C. Humdrum D. Humourus

98. Choose the word which best expresses the meaning of the given word:

Humble

A. Wicked B. Demeanour
C. Reprove D. Ignoble

91. B	92. B	93. C	94. C	95. C	96. D	97. C	98. D

99. A part of the sentence is underlined. Below are the alternatives which may improve the sentence. Choose the correct alternative.

Sustainable development goals focus on adeptation and migration of climate change in agriculture too.

A. focuses on adeptation and migration
B. focus on adaptation and mitigation
C. focuses on adoption and migration
D. focus on adoption and mitigation

100. Fill in the blank with suitable alternative.

She has assured that she will comply ______ the latest directions.

A. for B. of
C. within D. with

101. Choose the word opposite in meaning to the given word.

RETAIN

A. Impose B. Renounce
C. Conserve D. Reserve

102. Choose the word which best expresses the meaning of the given word:

Succinctly

A. Rudely B. Viciously
C. Timidly D. Briefly

103. Fill in the blank with correct alternative.

After a long heated argument, she has given ______ the matter.

A. in B. for
C. to D. up

104. A part of the sentence is underlined. Below are alternatives which may improve the sentence. Choose the correct alternative.

I prefer to ride than to walk.

A. ride to walked B. walks to ride
C. riding than walking D. riding to walking

105. Choose the alternative which best expresses the meaning of the idiom/phrase.

Eat humble pie

A. To yield
B. To urge somebody
C. To apologize
D. To win approval

106. Pick out the noun form of 'leave'.

A. leaving B. lively
C. leave D. left

107. Choose the word nearest in meaning to the given word.

EXCULPATE

A. Absolve B. Relate
C. Subjugate D. Associate

108. Spot the error in the given sentence:

(*a*) The visitors/ (*b*) complained at/ (*c*) the poor accommodation/ (*d*) they were given.

A. (*a*) B. (*b*)
C. (*c*) D. (*d*)

109. Choose the correctly spelt word from the following options:

A. Imperterbable B. Impetous
C. Impetuous D. Apostacy

110. Choose the alternative which best expresses the meaning of the idiom/phrase.

Die in harness

A. Die while working
B. To die suddenly
C. To commit suicide
D. Die in poverty

111. Fill in the blank:

He has ______ this philosophy as being too oblique.

A. praised B. criticized
C. lauded D. hailed

112. Choose the word which best expresses the meaning of the given word:

Abundant

A. Diligent B. Apex
C. Copious D. Existant

113. Choose the correctly spelt word from the following options:

A. Dilletent B. Diletant
C. Dillettant D. Dilettante

114. Spot the error in the given sentence:

(*a*) I was pretty sure that/ (*b*) he would support me/ (*c*) to changing the age-old/ (*d*) and static structure of our organization.

A. (*a*) B. (*b*)
C. (*c*) D. (*d*)

99. B	**100.** D	**101.** B	**102.** D	**103.** D	**104.** D	**105.** C	**106.** C
107. A	**108.** B	**109.** C	**110.** A	**111.** B	**112.** C	**113.** D	**114.** C

115. Choose the word nearest in meaning to the given word.

UMBRAGE

A. annoyance B. Distracted
C. Reserved D. Contaminated

116. Choose the word opposite in meaning to the given word.

FOSTER

A. Abet B. Stake
C. Frustrate D. Endorse

117. Fill in the blank:

The details of the ______ are not known to me.

A. indent B. incident
C. antecedent D. abscondant

118. A part of the sentence is underlined. Below are the alternatives which may improve the sentence. Choose the correct alternative.

With this realisation, she finds himself loose.

A. found himself in the loss.
B. found herself loosened.
C. find herself lost.
D. found herself lost.

119. Choose the word opposite in meaning to the given word.

INAPPROPRIATE

A. Inapposite B. Uncouth
C. Amiss D. Acceptable

120. A part of the sentence is underlined. Below are the alternatives which may improve the sentence. Choose the correct alternative.

The company said to pay in cash or kind both.

A. inclined in paying B. suggested that pay
C. has offered to pay D. requested to pay

121. Choose the word opposite in meaning to the given word.

Narrow-minded

A. Broad-minded B. Broad scale
C. Intolerant D. Brooding

122. Choose the word nearest in meaning to the given word.

COUP

A. Degrade B. Encroach
C. Reinstate D. Compensate

123. Choose the alternative which best expresses the meaning of the idiom/phrase.

Flog a dead horse

A. To loose one's temper
B. To revive interest in old matters
C. To quarrel
D. To avoid something

124. Choose the word which best expresses the meaning of the given word.

Emulate

A. Imitate B. Eradicate
C. Annihilate D. Obstinate

125. A part of the sentence is underlined. Below are the alternatives (A), (B), (C) which may improve the sentence. Choose the correct alternative. Choose (D) if no improvement is required.

The central government were asked the states to end the discrimination on grounds of education.

A. has requested the states
B. had been ask the states
C. ask the states
D. No improvement

126. Choose the word opposite in meaning to the given word.

Wild

A. Cultured B. Ingenious
C. Rude D. Declassified

127. Fill in the blank.

Someone has defined genius as an infinite capacity ______ learning.

A. off B. from
C. for D. to

128. A part of the sentence is underlined. Below are the alternatives which may improve the sentence. Choose the correct alternative.

The machines stopped to work an hour ago.

A. stop working
B. stopped working
C. stops work
D. stopped the work

115. A	116. C	117. B	118. D	119. D	120. C	121. A
122. B	123. B	124. A	125. A	126. A	127. C	128. B

129. Choose the alternatives which best expresses the meaning of idiom/phrase.

Ill at ease

A. Hopeful B. Angry
C. In a dilemma D. Uncomfortable

130. Pick out the verb form of 'poison'.

A. poisonous B. imprison
C. poisonus D. poison

131. Choose the correctly spelt word from the following options:

A. Reminiscences B. Reminiscenses
C. Reminisenses D. Remenescenses

132. Spot the error in the given sentence:

(*a*) They took to/ (*b*) reading 'Times'/ (*c*) for the better knowledge/ (*d*) in the facts.

A. (*a*) B. (*b*)
C. (*c*) D. (*d*)

133. Pick out the verb form of 'troublesome'.

A. trouble-creator B. comfortable
C. trouble D. discomfort

134. Choose the word nearest in meaning to the given word.

CORPULENT

A. Palatable B. Flourishing
C. Bulky D. Affectionate

135. Fill in the blank with correct alternative.

You should not rely ______ the assurance of your friends.

A. on B. the
C. to D. with

136. Fill in the blank with correct alternative.

He will hand ______ the charge next week.

A. out B. fill
C. in D. over

137. Choose the alternative which best expresses the meaning of the idiom/phrase.

Plough the sands

A. Futile labour
B. To be suspicious
C. To show false sorrow
D. Fight meanly

138. Pick out adjective form of 'depress'.

A. depression B. desperate
C. depressed D. desperation

139. Choose the word opposite in meaning to the given word.

FARCICAL

A. Hysterical B. Terrible
C. Facetious D. Serious

140. Fill in the blank:

The ______ of these flowers is enchanting.

A. stench B. fragrance
C. smell D. odour

141. Choose the word opposite in meaning to the given word.

AGGRAVATE

A. Affront B. Abbreviate
C. Alleviate D. Irritate

142. Spot the error in the given sentence:

(*a*) All the doctors/ (*b*) were puzzled on the/ (*c*) strange symptoms/ (*d*) reported by the patient.

A. (*a*) B. (*b*)
C. (*c*) D. (*d*)

143. Choose the correctly spelt word from the following options:

A. Resplaindent B. Resplandant
C. Resplendent D. Resplandent

144. Spot the error in the given sentence:

(*a*) Either of the plans/ (*b*) suits him and therefore/ (*c*) he decided not to/ (*d*) go out yesterday.

A. (*a*) B. (*b*)
C. (*c*) D. (*d*)

145. Choose the word which best expresses the meaning of the given word.

Celestial

A. Perilous B. Perpetual
C. Enormous D. Divine

146. Pick out adjective form of the word 'command'.

A. commanding
B. commander
C. commanded
D. commanders

129. D	**130.** D	**131.** A	**132.** D	**133.** C	**134.** C	**135.** A	**136.** D	**137.** A
138. C	**139.** D	**140.** B	**141.** C	**142.** B	**143.** C	**144.** B	**145.** D	**146.** A

147. Choose the word which best expresses the meaning of the given word:

Mesmerize

A. Illusionary B. Enchant
C. Luxuriate D. Decoy

148. Choose the word opposite in meaning to the given word:

DELEGATE

A. Bequeath
B. Retain
C. Dispense
D. Relinquish

149. Choose the alternative which best expresses the meaning of the idiom/phrase.

At the beck and call

A. To look for power
B. At the service
C. In the centre
D. Run away from responsibilities

150. A part of the sentence is underlined. Below are the alternatives which may improve the sentence. Choose the correct alternative.

The world economy is <u>into the recession</u>.

A. of a recession B. on in recession
C. for recession D. in a recession

APTITUDE FOR SERVICE SECTOR

151. Suppose you are working in an organization where you require help from one of your colleague (with whom you don't get along well). Her help is needed to finish one crucial project, you will:

A. approach her and ask for help.
B. approach someone else.
C. approach her indirectly through another colleague.
D. try finishing this project single handedly.

152. You have a birthday party at your home. However, your maid due to her sudden ill-health, sends her 10 years old son instead to support you. You would:

A. Politely ask your maid to come even if she is sick
B. Send the little boy back to home and handle the arrangement work by your own skills
C. Start the work after giving work based instructions to the little boy
D. Take the little boy's help only for easier tasks

153. While handling a very angry guest in a hotel where you are working, you will:

A. Just ignore that guest as presently you are not working as a team leader
B. Raise your voice little loud to control the situation
C. Ask that guest to meet with your team leader and refuse to talk to him
D. Consult your team leader and try to resolve the issue at earliest

154. While you are out of your house, you realised that there has been a theft in your house where some cash and number of expensive items have been stolen. You will:

A. Feel really very disappointed and will curse your luck
B. Start meeting property dealers for buying a new house to shift there
C. Try to forget the incident and be more careful in future times
D. Talk to your neighbours and try to hold them responsible for the incident

155. When you are paying money (fare) to the old rickshaw puller, he urges you for some extra money apart from the standard (normal) fare, you will:

A. Scold him to teach him a lesson as these things are not good for society
B. Give him little extra money without making any hue and cry
C. Bluntly refuse to give him any money as asking extra money is an act of cheating
D. Tell him that you will give him only the normal fare at that moment and extra money he can take from you, the next day

156. In the boys hostel after taking a bath, you suddenly remember that you left the electrical geyser ON. You will:

A. Ignore thinking that this was your first incident and you will not repeat it again
B. Go back immediately to the hostel to turn it OFF
C. Ask your friends in the hostel to switch it OFF
D. Do it again since you regularly pay your hostel charges

147. B	148. B	149. B	150. D	151. A	152. B	153. D	154. C	155. B	156. C

157. The medicine you bought from nearby pharmacy store is not able to cure your disease. You suspect the medicine to be spurious and not genuine. You will:

A. Try to ignore the incident and purchase from another pharmacy store
B. Ask neighbours if they had similar experience while consuming same medicine and if yes, take up the matter to consumer court/other agencies
C. Tell the pharmacy store to change the medicine
D. Ask others to take up the matter in most genuine manner

158. Whenever I take any decision, then I:

A. Feel there can always be a possibility of even more better solutions and change it
B. Do not change it
C. Sometimes curse myself for taking that decision
D. Never change it

159. All Industrial units must be away from the residential units because:

A. The workers will go to the home frequently and work will suffer
B. Industry's expansion can easily take place
C. The smoke emitted from industrial units is bad for health
D. The town-planners are more concerned about standard rules so that votes can be increased during the time of election

160. A Fresher's welcome party is to be organized in your Institute. As a student, you will:

A. Try to organize single handedly on your own
B. Take the help of your fellow batchmates
C. Volunteer but let some other group of students take the lead
D. Try as far as possible organizing as less number of events as possible

161. Your friend has not invited you to her birthday party. You will:

A. Just ignore the whole affair
B. Attend the party
C. Send her your best wishes
D. Hold grudges against her

162. You came to know that your boss is writing a false report to the senior most authority of your organisation. You will:

A. Meet your boss and directly protest against his actions
B. Discuss with your colleagues and then further take any step, together
C. Somehow ignore the whole situation
D. Keep quiet as talent can never be kept hidden for long. Another opportunities will come.

163. You have just broken up with a long term friend whom you really cared and loved and are totally distraught. You:

A. Cry out when you are alone.
B. Resort to addictives for some time till the situation is not in control
C. Share your sorrow with someone
D. Try to forget about it by going out with friends

164. A metro train is coming and you are standing at the metro station. All of a sudden you notice that the track is broken. You will:

A. Immediately leave the metro station
B. Go and inform the authority of metro for taking suitable action
C. Use some means to stop the metro train immediately
D. Do not worry at all because metro station has all necessary infrastructure to tackle such situations

165. To be an ideal manager, you should:

A. Stick to your rules
B. Be authoritarian in your approach
C. Organise conferences and seminars for your subordinates
D. Present yourself as an example

166. A local Rowdy (bad element) has started illegal construction on your vacant plot. He has refused your request to vacate and has also threatened you with severe consequences in case you do not sell the plot at a throwaway price to him. You would:

A. Sell the property at cheaper price to him as unnecessarily we must avoid creating tensed situations
B. Ask help of local rowdy (bad elements) who is known to him
C. Inform the police for necessary action
D. Negotiate with the Rowdy to get a higher price

167. You do not like few habits of one of your close friends, you would:

A. Accept him as he is as this is the act of true friendship
B. Tell him indirectly that you do not like those habits
C. Start ignoring him since no one can change a grown up young mind
D. Tell him so and ask him to change his habits

157. B	**158.** D	**159.** C	**160.** B	**161.** C	**162.** A
163. D	**164.** C	**165.** D	**166.** C	**167.** D	

168. If you want to computerise your office to make it more efficient and upgraded, you would:

A. Ask old and less technical staffs to resign by themselves

B. Adjust the surplus workers at some other place as per their qualification and skills

C. Expel some of the employees due to surplus working staffs

D. Get the whole staff trained accordingly

169. You are store manager of a Retail outlet. You have thought of an innovative procedure that you consider would enhance the effectiveness of work process. Some employees including the senior staffs do not agree on this change. One senior staff openly criticized the innovative idea suggested by you to the CEO of your organization. You will:

A. Decide not to respond to the critics

B. Scold the senior staff who has complained to the CEO

C. Meet the employee for a talk and also explain the benefits of that innovative procedure

D. Decide not to go ahead with your plan as "employee satisfaction' is nowadays given a priority

170. In the hotel where you are working, a colleague asks for your views/opinion on specific matter that is not directly concerned with you. Therefore you will:

A. Show no interest in that conversation as the matter is not directly concerned with you

B. Give your opinion in a straight forward manner

C. Avoid your colleague since we must always mind our business

D. Revert in a diplomatic manner to please everybody

171. You are studying in class 10th. Your friends who are studying with you in the same class like consuming (drinking) beer. One evening after the completion of your tuition class your friends influence you to drink small glass filled with beer. You will:

A. Drink as once you heard somewhere by a doctor that consuming bear removes toxin from your body

B. Drink plenty of fruit juice first before consuming the beer

C. Refuse and lie to them (friends) that you have kidney problem

D. Refuse to drink (consume)

172. An angry guest in the hotel wants to meet the senior manager for grievance reporting. As an Assistant manager, you will:

A. Be patient and try to cool him down

B. Talk to him after consulting seniors

C. Tell him politely that senior manager is not available at the moment

D. Try to engage him in a long conversation

173. In the present context of Digitalization/Social media usage, listening to the news on television is a:

A. wastage of our time

B. way to know about happenings around

C. activity that has no practical relevance

D. tool for our gossips throughout that particular day

174. If two persons are openly having a fierce fight, you will:

A. Support one person who stays in your locality

B. Inform the police, next day

C. Do not get involved

D. Learn about the issue and try to end the conflict

175. You wish to have your own start up business in a new city. You will:

A. Start your business immediately and will come to know about market and consumer's choices

B. You will survey the entire state before investing your money

C. You will inquire your family, friends and relationship and relatives, about their choices and preferences and decide thereafter

D. You will select a sample area and sample size of people for survey and take decision accordingly

176. You and your father were about to enter one of the 5 star hotel of Delhi, suddenly you heard an intense sound of blast very close by you. You would:

A. Start screaming for help at the same time try calling to local police station.

B. Run towards the side of your father and hold him tightly. Start conversation with him to make him relaxed.

C. Start praying while controlling your anger.

D. Start locating the source of noise.

177. To be an ideal 'Team leader' I must possess:

A. Full support

B. Huge trust

C. Supervisory skills

D. Decision making ability

168. D	**169.** C	**170.** B	**171.** D	**172.** A	**173.** B	**174.** D	**175.** D	**176.** D	**177.** D

178. Preservation of the petroleum products is very important as:

A. Indian government has recently passed such law.

B. The Gulf countries are slowly exporting less oil than our requirement.

C. The preservation of petroleum products leads to better quality.

D. Improper usage will exhaust the resources.

179. While you are locking your flat to go somewhere, you will:

A. Expect your elder member of the family to switch off all lights and fans.

B. Ask any of your family member to switch off all lights except one to make an impression that someone is still staying inside the flat.

C. Personally ensure that it is done.

D. Think that being a younger family member it is none of your concern.

180. Do you agree with a opinion that one should ideally change his or her job and face new situations?

A. Never, as the new situation may or may not suit you.

B. No, as it takes lot of time making an impression in a company.

C. Yes, only when you are compelled to do so.

D. Yes, one should accept the challenge.

181. Give your honest opinion:

One morning after waking up you feel having a mild sore throat problem. Then you feel:

A. Not necessary attending office

B. Not required to go office whenever any one not feels well

C. Unnecessary to even think about any duty

D. Necessary to attend work to complete urgent work

182. In the Corporate Sector, people consider 'pleasing' as an important art for self growth. My view suggests:

A. It is very essential for making progress in one's life

B. It is an art which everyone can't do it

C. It is absolutely futile

D. I don't know since I am not experienced else I would have done it

183. If few students of a school fail in the mid term exam, it is the fault of:

A. The Administrator

B. The subject teacher

C. Students themselves

D. It cannot be generalized

184. 'Service aptitude' implies to you as:

A. Hard work and pain involved in providing services

B. Strong dedication in providing back office type of work assignments

C. Strong metal capabilities in handling pressure while offering services

D. Strong desire to provide services

185. Ideally while working in a group, I personally tend to be:

A. co-operative with others

B. a bit more assertive to be listened by others

C. more adjustable but also depends on situations

D. not involved as doing work alone is the best way recommended by many

186. Whenever you see water running from a tap in your school, while no one is using it. You consider:

A. Walking away as your job is not to take care of administration

B. Before closing the tap, drawing attention of other students and school staffs towards it

C. Closing the tap to ensure no water is wasted

D. Leave the water running, as practically it is impossible to close the tap perfectly

187. You are sitting inside your flat to prepare a project report for next day's presentation in the classroom, suddenly a procession comes in front of your flat. This acts like:

A. An input for your preparation as procession gives you valid inputs for making projects

B. A very normal incident in any urban locality

C. A barrier to your communication process

D. A distracter to your preparation

188. Which trait is considered to be the most desirable one for a person who wants to join any service sector?

A. Team work

B. Patience

C. Good Height

D. Helping attitude

178. D	**179.** C	**180.** D	**181.** D	**182.** C	**183.** D
184. D	**185.** A	**186.** C	**187.** D	**188.** D	

189. Assume a situation of a midnight when you are passing alone in an utterly secluded place, away from the main part of city. Few criminals with local pistol appears in front of you and softly asks you to cast off your gold chain and mobile phone. What will you do?

A. Politely tell them that you are new in that area so they must not behave like that
B. You will offer your gold chain and mobile phone
C. You will scold them badly and guide them how they can be successful if they study hard
D. You would run away as fast as you can

190. After joining the management trainee program of a hotel. You are paid your first month stipend. After your shift gets over you went to a mall for purchasing cloth for yourself. What factor is most important for your purchase?

A. The cloth must be suitable for you
B. The cloth must always be bought as suggested by shopkeepers or others
C. The costliest cloth
D. The unique design even if it is causing slight of discomfort to you

191. As per your temperament is concerned, you:

A. Won't criticize anybody unless you are sure about his/her fault
B. Would never criticize anybody
C. Do not like criticizing people
D. Criticize people, the moment you find any fault

192. Describing your personality, you are:

A. Optimistic
B. Pessimistic
C. In between
D. Apathetic

193. When I look at my past, I often regret of my past decisions?

A. Strongly agree
B. Agree
C. Disagree
D. Strongly disagree

194. While dealing with a customer who is very upset about some services provided by your hotel, which of the following you need most?

A. Cleverness
B. Politeness
C. Logic
D. Patience

195. As a reward to your service performance, your company has nominated you for a performance Improvement training program. The problem is that you are not interested in going there. You will:

A. Proceed for joining the training program, keeping your interest aside
B. Inform your supervisor (Boss) to send someone else
C. Go for the training but will participate only few sessions of the training program
D. Try to find some excuse to avoid the training

196. Who is mostly responsible for solving the problems of any business organisation?

A. Employees
B. Supplier
C. Management
D. Luck

197. Consider yourself as a parent of an adolescent son. Towards your son, your attitude is best reflected with which of the following statement?

A. I shall allow him full freedom to do whatever he thinks is good for him
B. I shall decide everything for him
C. I shall conduct an open discussion with him and let him make his own decision
D. I shall ask him to talk to his friends. The majority of his friend's decision should ideally be his

198. Effectiveness of classroom teaching in school has to be judged in terms of:

A. Course coverage
B. Student's interest
C. Learning outcomes of students of the class
D. Usage of strict discipline through punishments

199. One of your childhood friend wants to borrow some amount of money (that you have personally saved for yourself) what will you do?

A. Tell him that you will lend money provided he pays with some interest along with the principal amount
B. Say him 'NO' and teach him the ill effects of borrowing money from anyone
C. Suggest him to take money from another friend who is from a very rich background
D. Spare the money he wants and helps him out

200. Whenever you start doing any new activity, you:

A. Are hesitant
B. Start it with much enthusiasm but feel low in energy afterwards
C. Commence it after careful planning
D. Watch movies to divert your mind

189. B	**190.** A	**191.** A	**192.** A	**193.** D	**194.** B
195. B	**196.** C	**197.** C	**198.** C	**199.** D	**200.** C

EXPLANATORY ANSWERS

1. (C): Let length of rectangle = $4x$ and breadth = $1x$

Area of rectangle = Area of square

$\Rightarrow \quad 4x \times x = (8)^2$

$\Rightarrow \quad 4x^2 = 64 \Rightarrow x^2 = 16$

$\Rightarrow \quad x = 4$

Length of rectangle = $4 \times 4 = 16$ cm

Breadth of rectangle = $1 \times 4 = 4$ cm

Perimenter of rectangle = $2(l + b)$

$= 2(16 + 4) = 40$ cm.

2. (C): $\text{Mean} = \dfrac{6+16+(K+26)+(2K-3)+10}{5}$

$\Rightarrow \quad 14 = \dfrac{3K+55}{5}$

$\Rightarrow \quad 3K + 55 = 70$

$\Rightarrow \quad 3K = 15 \Rightarrow K = 5$

$\therefore$ Value of $\dfrac{K^2+1}{2} = \dfrac{25+1}{2} = 13.$

3. (C): According to the question,

$l^2 + b^2 = (25)^2 \Rightarrow l^2 + b^2 = 625$

$l \times b = 168$

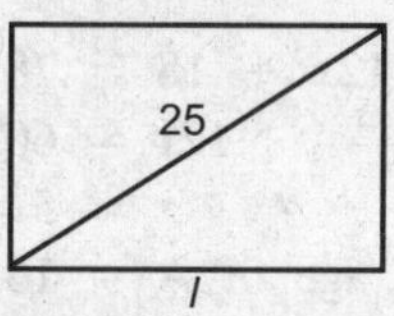

$\therefore \quad (l + b)^2 = l^2 + b^2 + 2lb$

$= 625 + 2(168)$

$\Rightarrow \quad (l + b^2) = 625 + 336 = 961$

$\Rightarrow \quad l + b = 31 \quad \ldots(i)$

$(l - b)^2 = l^2 + b^2 - 2lb = 625 - 2(168)$

$\Rightarrow \quad (l - b)^2 = 625 - 336 = 289$

$\Rightarrow \quad (l - b) = 17 \quad \ldots(ii)$

From (i) and (ii)

$l = 24, b = 7$

Hence, longer side of the rectangle = 24 m.

4. (B): (A + B)'s 1 day work = $\dfrac{1}{8}$

A's 1 day work = $\dfrac{1}{12}$

$\therefore$ B's 1 day work = $\dfrac{1}{8} - \dfrac{1}{12} = \dfrac{3-2}{24} = \dfrac{1}{24}$

B alone can do whole work in 24 days.

25% of this work = $1 \times \dfrac{25}{100} = \dfrac{1}{4}$

$\because$ B can do whole work in 24 days

$\therefore$ B can do $\dfrac{1}{4}$ work in $\dfrac{24}{4} = 6$ days.

5. (C): 9 0 K 6 8 is divisible by 8

Put K = 1, 3, 5, 7, 9

$\therefore$ 168 is divisible by 8

368 is divisible by 8

568 is divisible by 8

768 is divisible by 8

968 is divisible by 8

$\therefore$ Sum of $1 + 3 + 5 + 7 + 9 = 25$.

6. (D): Usual price of saree = $\dfrac{100}{80} \times 984$

$= 5 \times 246 = ₹\ 1230.$

7. (C): Total distance = 680 m + 570 m = 1250 m

Relative Speed = (80 + 70) km/hr.

= 150 km/hr

$= 150 \times \dfrac{5}{18}$ m/s $= \dfrac{125}{3}$ m/s

Time taken to cross each other

$= \dfrac{1250 \times 3}{125}$

$= 10 \times 3 = 30$ seconds.

8. (C): HCF of $\dfrac{8}{5}, \dfrac{6}{8}, \dfrac{4}{25}$

$\text{HCF} = \dfrac{\text{HCF of 8, 6, 4}}{\text{LCM of 5, 8, 25}}$

$= \dfrac{2}{200} = \dfrac{1}{100}.$

9. (C): No. of boys = $\dfrac{60}{100} \times 60 = 36$

$\therefore$ No. of girls = $60 - 36 = 24$

Total marks obtained by boys = $36 \times 68 = 2448$

Total marks obtained by girls = $24 \times 72 = 1728$

Hence, average marks of the whole class

$= \dfrac{2448 + 1728}{60}$

$= \dfrac{4176}{60} = 69.6.$

10. (B): $\sqrt{\sqrt[3]{13824}+\sqrt[3]{15625}} = \sqrt{24+25} = \sqrt{49} = 7.$

11. (D): $\because \quad a^4 + \frac{1}{a^4} = 322$

$$(a^2)^2 + \left(\frac{1}{a^2}\right)^2 = \left(a^2 + \frac{1}{a^2}\right)^2 - 2\cdot a^2 \cdot \frac{1}{a^2} = 322$$

$$\Rightarrow \left(a^2 + \frac{1}{a^2}\right)^2 = 324$$

$$\Rightarrow a^2 + \frac{1}{a^2} = 18$$

$$\Rightarrow \left(a - \frac{1}{a}\right)^2 + 2\cdot a \cdot \frac{1}{a} = 18$$

$$\Rightarrow \left(a - \frac{1}{a}\right)^2 = 18 - 2 = 16 = (4)^2$$

Hence, $a - \frac{1}{a} = 4.$

12. (C): Let total votes polled $= x$

(62% of x – 38% of x) = 432

$\Rightarrow$ 24% of x = 432

$$\Rightarrow \frac{24}{100}\times x = 432$$

$$\Rightarrow x = \frac{432\times 100}{24} = 1800$$

Hence, total number of votes polled = 1800.

13. (B): Let number $= x$

(76 – 58)% of x = 198

$\Rightarrow$ 18% of x = 198

$$\Rightarrow \frac{18}{100}\times x = 198$$

$$\Rightarrow x = \frac{198\times 100}{18} = 1100$$

$$(82 - 46)\% \text{ of } 1100 = \frac{36}{100}\times 1100 = 396.$$

14. (D): For half yearly,

$$A = P\left(1+\frac{r}{100}\right)^t$$

$$= 10000\left(1+\frac{5}{100}\right)^3$$

$$= 10000\times\frac{21\times 21\times 21}{20\times 20\times 20}$$

$$= 9261 \times 1.25$$

$$= 11576.25$$

C.I. = 11576.25 – 10000

= ₹ 1576.25

For annually

Again, $A = 10000\left(1+\frac{10}{100}\right)^1$

$$= 10000\times\frac{11}{10} = 11000$$

C.I. = 11000 – 10000 = ₹ 1000

and $\frac{11000\times 10\times 1}{2\times 100} = 550$

Total C.I. = 1000 + 550 = ₹ 1550

Required difference = 1576.25 – 1550

= ₹ 26.25.

15. (D): Ratio of their capitals

= 100000 × 12 : 90000 × 10 : 100000 × 6

= 1200000 : 900000 : 600000

= 12 : 9 : 6 = 4 : 3 : 2

Hence, ratio of their profit = 4 : 3 : 2.

16. (B): Let present age of A, B, C is $3x$, $4x$, $5x$ years.

After 6 years

$$\frac{3x+6+4x+6+5x+6}{3} = 26$$

$$12x + 18 = 78$$

$$\Rightarrow 12x = 60$$

$$\Rightarrow x = 5$$

Present age of A = 15 years

Present age of B = 20 years

Present age of C = 25 years

y years ago,

B's age = 20 – 4 = 16 years

C's age = 25 – 4 = 21 years

Required difference = (21 – 16) = 5 years.

17. (D): (A + B)'s 1 day work $= \frac{1}{120}$

(B + C)'s 1 day work $= \frac{1}{72}$

(A + C)'s 1 day work $= \frac{1}{90}$

Adding above,

2(A + B + C)'s 1 day work

$$= \frac{1}{120}+\frac{1}{72}+\frac{1}{90}$$

$$= \frac{3+5+4}{360} = \frac{12}{360} = \frac{1}{30}$$

$(A + B + C)$'s 1 day work

$$= \frac{1}{30 \times 2} = \frac{1}{60}$$

$\therefore$ C's 1 day work $= \frac{1}{60} - \frac{1}{120} = \frac{2-1}{120} = \frac{1}{120}$

C can do alone this work in 120 days.

18. (D):

I	II
SP = ₹ 4000	SP = ₹ 4000
Profit = 25%	Loss = x%
CP = $\frac{100 \times 4000}{125}$	CP = $\frac{100 \times 4000}{(100 - x)}$
= ₹ 3200	

Total SP = 4000 + 4000 = ₹ 8000

$$\text{Total CP} = 3200 + \frac{400000}{100 - x}$$

According to the question,

$$8000 = \frac{3200(100 - x) + 400000}{100 - x}$$

$\Rightarrow \quad 800000 - 8000x = 320000 - 3200x + 400000$

$\Rightarrow \quad 800000 - 720000 = 8000x - 3200x$

$\Rightarrow \quad 80000 = 4800x$

$\Rightarrow \quad x = \frac{80000}{4800} = \frac{50}{3}\% = 16\frac{2}{3}\%.$

19. (B): Let the speed be x km/hr.

Then, distance covered in 1 hr. 40 min.

= Time × Speed

$$1\frac{2}{3} \text{ hrs.} \times x = \frac{5x}{3} \text{ km}$$

$$\text{Remaining distance} = \left(24 - \frac{5x}{3}\right) \text{km}$$

$$\therefore \quad \frac{5x}{3} = \frac{5}{7}\left(24 - \frac{5x}{3}\right)$$

$\Rightarrow \quad 7x = 72 - 5x$

$\Rightarrow \quad 12x = 72 \Rightarrow x = 6$

Hence, speed = 6 km/hr.

$$= 6 \times \frac{5}{18} \text{ m/s}$$

$$= \frac{5}{3} \text{ m/s} = 1\frac{2}{3} \text{ m/s}.$$

20. (C): Let numbers are $3x$ and $5x$

$3x + 5x = 240$

$\Rightarrow \quad 8x = 240$

$\Rightarrow \quad x = 30$

Numbers are 90 and 150

LCM of 90 and 150 = 450

HCF of 90 and 150 = 30

Sum of their LCM and HCF = 450 + 30 = 480.

21. (B): Sum of 16 multiples of 9

$= 9(1 + 2 + 3 + 4 + 5 + 6 + 7 + 8 + 9 + \ldots + 16)$

$= 9 \times \frac{16 \times 17}{2}$

$= 72 \times 17 = 1224$

$$\text{Average} = \frac{1224}{16} = 76.5.$$

22. (C): Let adding x in 6412 then it becomes a perfect square.

$6412 + x = (81)^2 = 6561$

$\Rightarrow \quad x = 6561 - 6412 = 149$

Hence, 149 must be added to 6412 to get a perfect square.

23. (D): $2.8 - (7.4 \div 3.7 \times 5) \div 5 \times 2$

$= 2.8 - (2 \times 5) \div 5 \times 2$

$= 2.8 - 10 \div 5 \times 2$

$= 2.8 - 4 = -1.2.$

24. (A): Let monthly salary of A = ₹ x

$\therefore$ Monthly salary of B = ₹ $(40000 - x)$

Saving of A = 18% of x

Saving of B = 6% of $(40000 - x)$

According to the question,

$\because$ Saving of A = Saving of B

$\Rightarrow \quad 18\%$ of x = 6% of $(40000 - x)$

$\Rightarrow \quad \frac{18}{100}x = \frac{6}{100}(40000 - x)$

$\Rightarrow \quad 18x + 6x = 240000$

$\Rightarrow \quad 24x = 240000$

$\Rightarrow \quad x = 10000$

Hence, monthly salary of A = ₹ 10000.

25. (C):

$$P = \frac{SI \times 100}{r \times t}$$

$$= \frac{3024 \times 100}{7 \times 6}$$

$$= \frac{504 \times 100}{7} = 7200$$

Hence, Sum = ₹ 7200.

26. (D): Let $a + b = 6K$

$b + c = 7K$

$a + c = 8K$

$[\because A + B + C = 14 \text{ Given}]$

Then, $2(a + b + c) = 21K$

$\Rightarrow \quad 2 \times 14 = 21K$

$\Rightarrow \quad K = \frac{28}{21} = \frac{4}{3}$

$\therefore \quad b + c = 7K = 7 \times \frac{4}{3} = \frac{28}{3}$.

Hence, $\quad a = 14 - \frac{28}{3} = \frac{42 - 28}{3} = \frac{14}{3}$.

27. (C):

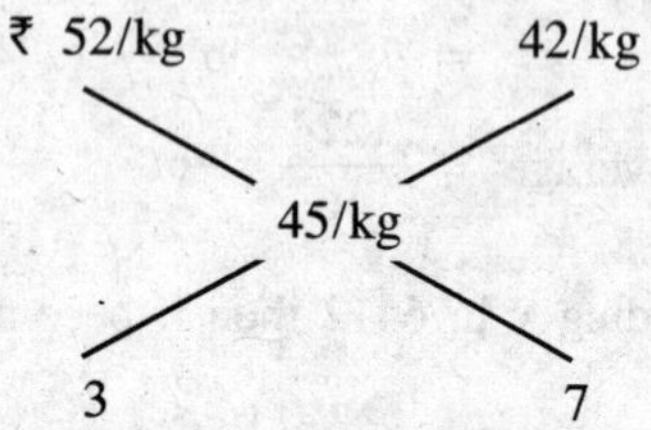

Required ratio = 3 : 7.

28. (C): $\quad 6a^2 = 864$

$\Rightarrow \quad a^2 = \frac{864}{6} = 144$

$\Rightarrow \quad a = 12$ cm

Volume of Cube = $12 \times 12 \times 12$ cm^3

According to the question

$$\frac{12 \times 12 \times 12}{x^3} = 64$$

$\Rightarrow \quad x^3 = \frac{12 \times 12 \times 12}{64} = 27$

$\Rightarrow \quad x = 3$

Sum of the surface area of all small cubes

$= 64 \times 6 \times 9$

$= 64 \times 54 = 3456$ cm^2.

29. (D): Let, age of C = x years

age of B = $2x$ years

age of A = $(2x + 3)$ years

A + B + C = 28

$\Rightarrow 2x + 3 + 2x + x = 28$

$\Rightarrow \quad 5x = 28 - 3$

$\Rightarrow \quad 5x = 25$

$\Rightarrow \quad x = \frac{25}{5} = 5$

Hence, the age of B = 2×5 = 10 years.

30. (C): Let the number = x

According to the question,

$18x = x + 357$

$\Rightarrow \quad 17x = 357$

$\Rightarrow \quad x = \frac{357}{17} = 21$

Hence, the number = 21.

31. (C): Professor is related to teaching. Similarly, Physician is related to treatment.

32. (B): Meaningful sequence.

Forest → Three → Pulp → Paper → Book.

33. (D): Alphabet in natural series and Alphabet in reverse series:

A B C D : S T U V W X Y Z
↓ ↓ ↓ ↓   ↓ ↓ ↓ ↓ ↓ ↓ ↓ ↓
Z Y X W   H G F E D C B A

A. N →(+2) P, T → G, P →(+2) R
B. R →(+2) T, S → H, B →(+2) D
C. K →(+2) M, G → T, N →(+2) P
D. Q →(+2) S, D → W, L →(+4) P

Here, Option (D) is the odd.

34. (C): Given, 6 friends are sitting in a circle facing the centre.

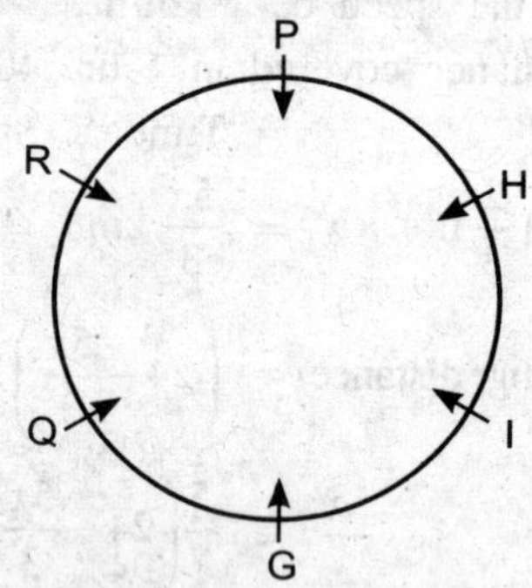

Here, I is between G and H.

35. (B): abbccd

∴ ab, abbc, abbccd, abbccdde, abbccddeef

Here, two letters are increasing in each term from second term.

∴ the Missing term = abbccd.

36. (D): A. $18 : 306 \Rightarrow \frac{306}{18} = 17$

B. $16 : 272 \Rightarrow \frac{272}{16} = 17$

C. $15 : 255 \Rightarrow \frac{255}{15} = 17$

D. $19 : 313 \Rightarrow \frac{313}{19}$

Here Option (D) is the odd number pair.

37. (B):

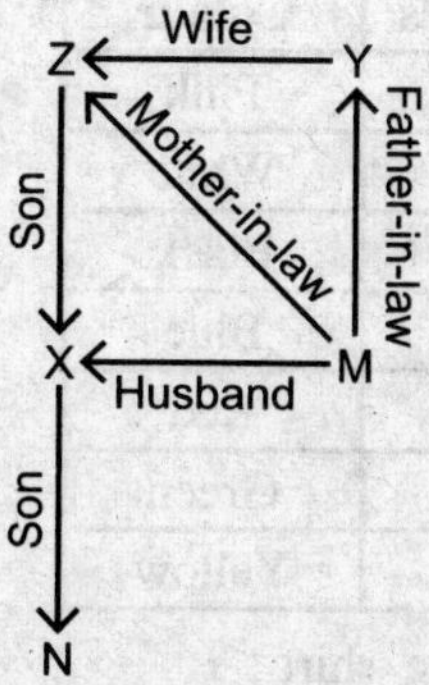

Here, X is the son of Y.

38. (D): From given figure

The sum of the numbers which belong to any two figures only

$= 5 + 8 + 2 + 6 + 10 = 31.$

39. (D): G, H, I and J are playing carrom.

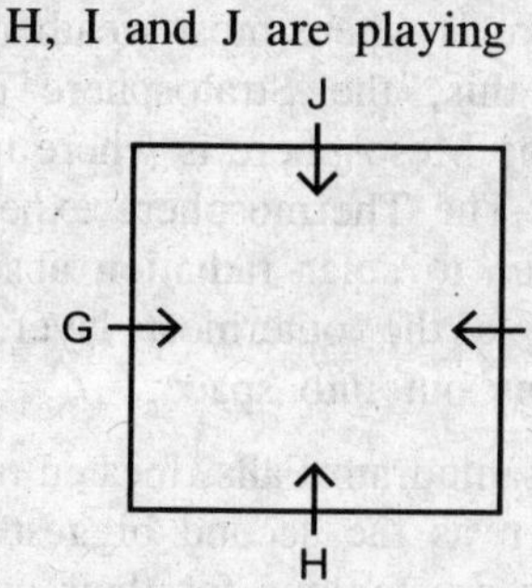

Here, H is facing North.

40. (A): Grass : Garden : Flowers

Similarly, Quilt : Bed : Pillow.

41. (D): Given, JIYA = 180

$\Rightarrow (10 + 9 + 25 + 1) \times 4 = 45 \times 4 = 180$

NAVAL = 250

$\Rightarrow (14 + 1 + 22 + 1 + 12) \times 5$

$= 50 \times 5 = 250$

Similarly,

TANISHA $= (20 + 1 + 14 + 9 + 19 + 8 + 1) \times 7$

$= 72 \times 7 = 504$

$\Rightarrow$ TANISHA = 504

$\therefore$ In given code language 'TANISHA' will be written as 504.

42. (C):

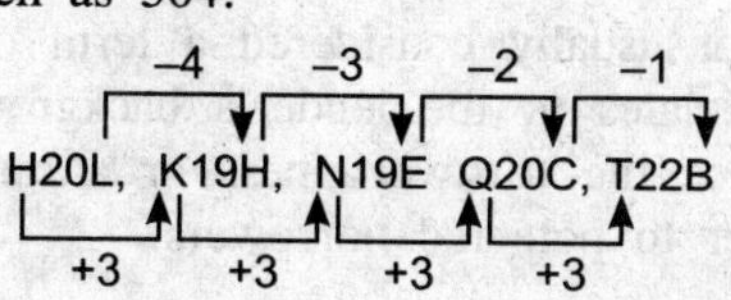

H + L = 8 + 12 = 20

K + H = 11 + 8 = 19

N + E = 14 + 5 = 19

Q + C = 17 + 3 = 20

T + B = 20 + 2 = 22

Here, ? = the missing term T22B.

43. (C): A 'Mechanic' is related to 'Garage'

Similarly, 'Lawyer' is related to 'Court'.

44. (A):

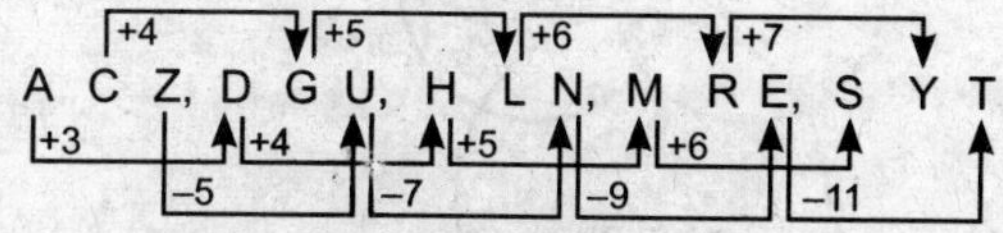

$\therefore$? = the next term = SYT.

45. (D): From given information.

Harish is neither sincere nor ambitious.

47. (D): Given, green = blue,

blue = white.

white = red,

red = black,

black = brown,

brown = yellow

$\therefore$ the colour of blood is black.

48. (B):

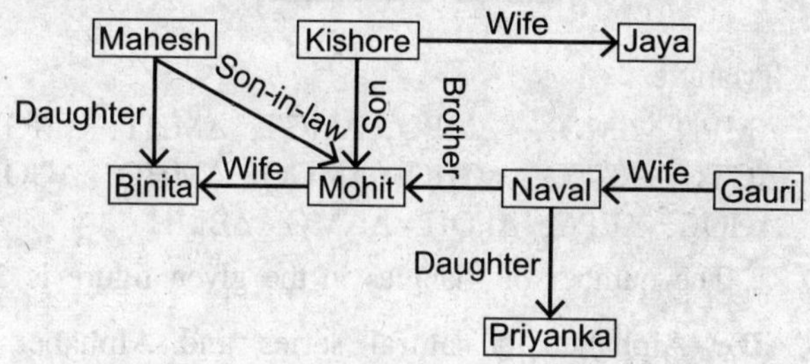

Here, Mohit is the son-in-low of Mahesh.

49. (B): Given,

N O T E

(N +10 → X, O → O, T –10 → J, E → E)

X O J E

and

R O S E

(R +10 → B, O → O, S –10 → I, E → E)

B O I E

[Vowels are not change]

Similarly,

L O V E

(L +10 → V, O → O, V –10 → L, E → E)

V O L E

$\therefore$ 'LOVE' will be coded as 'VOLE'.

50. (C): According to English dictionary,

Internal → Inroduce → Introvert → Intrude

$\therefore$ Option (C) is the correct sequence.

51. (D): (9, 27, 81) $\Rightarrow 9 \times 3 = 27,$
$27 \times 3 = 81$
Similarly, (12, 36, 108) $\Rightarrow 12 \times 3 = 36,$
$36 \times 3 = 108$
$\therefore$ Option (D) is similar to the given set.

52. (D):

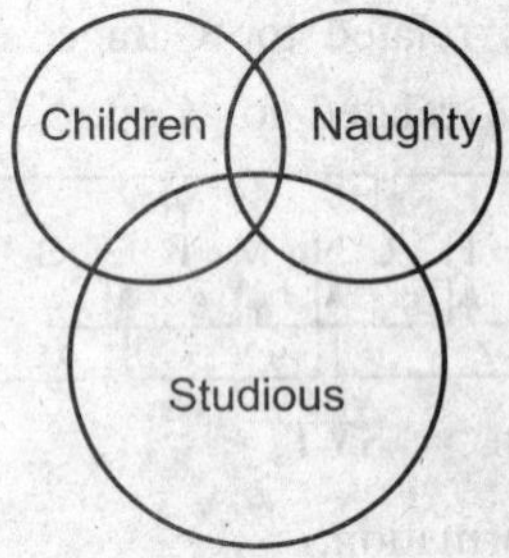

Here, option (D) is correct.

53. (C): Let from given figure:

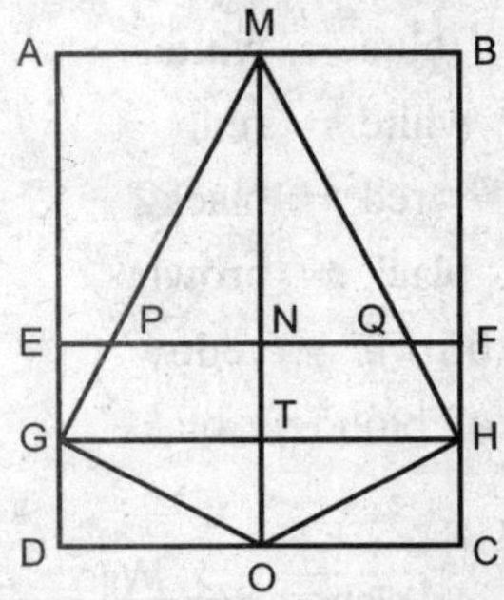

Triangles:
ΔMPN, ΔMQN, ΔMPQ, ΔMGT, ΔMHT, ΔMGH, ΔGTO, ΔHTO, ΔGHO, ΔMGO, ΔMHO, ΔGOD, ΔHOC, ΔEPG, ΔFQH, ΔAMG, ΔBMH
$\therefore$ The number of triangles in the given figure is 17.

54. (D): Alphabet in natural series and Alphabet in reverse series:

A B C D E … S T U V W X Y Z
↓ ↓ ↓ ↓ ↓   ↓ ↓ ↓ ↓ ↓ ↓ ↓ ↓
Z Y X W V … H G F E D C B A

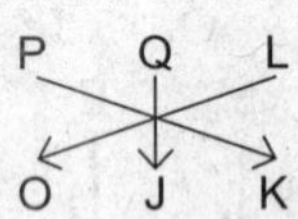

Similaly,

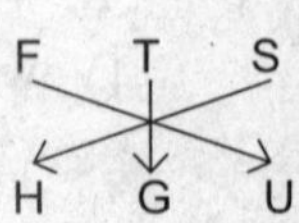

$\therefore$ PQL : OJK :: FTS : HGU.

57. (D): January : November $\Rightarrow$ January – 2 Months
= November
Similarly, Monday = ?
$\Rightarrow$ Monday – 2 days = Saturday
$\Rightarrow$ Monday : Saturday
$\therefore$? = Saturday.

For Qs. No. 58 to 60:

From given information
7 friends live in 3 different building.

Building	Friends	Colour
Ashina	L	Pink
	M	White
Gharonda	I	Black
	G	Blue
	K	Red
Basera	H	Green
	J	Yellow

58. (A): G is wearing a blue shirt.

59. (B): G, I, K stay in Gharonda buliding.

60. (C): M is wearing white colour shirt.

61. (A): The correct order of the atmospheric layers from the Earth's surface upwards is: Troposphere, Stratosphere, Mesosphere, Thermosphere, Exosphere. The Troposphere is where most weather phenomena occur. Above this, the Stratosphere contains the ozone layer. The Mesosphere is where meteors burn up upon entry. The Thermosphere experiences high temperatures due to solar radiation absorption, and the Exosphere is the outermost layer, where the atmosphere thins out into space.

62. (B): The Shivasamudram Falls, located on the Kaveri River, is known as the second biggest waterfall in India. The falls are famous for their natural beauty and are a significant source of hydroelectric power in the region. The Kaveri River itself is an important water source for agriculture in Karnataka and Tamil Nadu.

63. (A): Liberalisation refers to the removal of government controls and restrictions in the economy, particularly those that affect business and industry. This process facilitates easier import and export of goods, encouraging global trade and investment. Liberalisation aims to make economies more competitive and efficient by reducing government intervention in business operations.

64. (D): Credit terms typically include the interest rate, which dictates the cost of borrowing, collateral and documentation requirements for securing a loan, and the mode of repayment. The history of the money lender is not usually considered a term of credit but rather relates to the lender's background and may influence the trustworthiness or attractiveness of the lender to potential borrowers.

65. (A): The writ of Mandamus is issued by a court to compel an officer or governmental body to perform a mandatory or purely ministerial duty they are legally obligated to perform but have failed to do so. This writ ensures that public officials adhere to their duties and uphold the rights of individuals.

66. (D): A writ of Certiorari is issued by a higher court to a lower court or some other authority to transfer the record of a proceeding to it for review. The higher court then reviews the lower court's decision to ensure it was made in compliance with the law. This writ helps maintain the judicial system's checks and balances by allowing appellate review of lower court decisions.

67. (C): The Scheduled Castes and Scheduled Tribes (Prevention of Atrocities) Act was enacted in 1989 to prevent atrocities against members of Scheduled Castes and Scheduled Tribes. The act provides for specific offences which are considered atrocities and affords special courts for the trial of such offences and the rehabilitation of victims.

68. (A): Aung San Suu Kyi wrote "Freedom from Fear," which is a collection of writings that reflect her thoughts on democracy, human rights, and the struggle for freedom in Myanmar. The book is an important text in the field of political literature, offering insight into the challenges faced by those fighting for democratic reform in oppressive regimes.

69. (B): The Ramayana, attributed to the sage Valmiki, is known as the 'Adi Kavya' or the first poem. It narrates the life and adventures of Lord Rama, his wife Sita, and his loyal companion Hanuman. This ancient Indian epic has had a profound impact on art, culture, and religion in India and other parts of Asia.

70. (A): Matching the ancient names of rivers with their modern counterparts involves knowing their historical context and geographical details:

(*a*) Vitasta is the ancient name for the modern Jhelum River (IV).

(*b*) Vipas corresponds to the Beas River (I).

(*c*) Asikani is now known as the Chenab River (II).

(*d*) Sutudri refers to the Sutlej River (III).

This alignment helps in understanding the geographical and historical continuity of these river systems in the Indian subcontinent.

71. (C): The slogan "Jai Jawan, Jai Kisan, Jai Vigyan" was popularized by Atal Bihari Vajpayee, the former Prime Minister of India. Initially coined as "Jai Jawan, Jai Kisan" by Lal Bahadur Shastri during the 1965 Indo-Pak war, Vajpayee later added "Jai Vigyan" to this slogan to honor the Indian scientists after India's successful nuclear tests in 1998.

72. (A): Sodium is the most reactive metal among the options listed. It is highly reactive, particularly with water, to which it responds explosively. Sodium's reactivity is due to its single electron in its outermost shell, which it readily loses to form a stable ion, making it a highly reactive alkali metal.

73. (B): The correct matches for the agents and diseases are:

(*a*) Virus causes Influenza (IV).

(*b*) Protozoa cause Malaria (III).

(*c*) Fungus causes Ringworm (I).

(*d*) Bacteria cause Tuberculosis (II).

These matches are based on the pathogens that typically cause these diseases, correlating the biological nature of the agent with the disease it induces.

74. (C): The headquarters of the Indian Space Research Organisation (ISRO) is located in Bengaluru, Karnataka, India. Bengaluru, often called the Silicon Valley of India, hosts several key scientific and high-tech institutions, including ISRO, which coordinates India's space exploration and satellite programs.

75. (C): The twinkling of stars is caused by the atmospheric refraction of starlight. As starlight passes through the Earth's atmosphere, it is bent (refracted) by varying atmospheric layers with different densities and temperatures, causing the stars to appear as though they are twinkling.

76. (D): Dr. Vikram Sarabhai is recognized as the founder of the Indian Space Research Organisation (ISRO). He was instrumental in establishing the Physical Research Laboratory (PRL) in Ahmedabad in 1947, which later evolved into ISRO under his guidance, marking the beginning of India's space program.

77. (C): The correct matching of Olympic medal winners and the sports they received medals in are:

(*a*) Gagan Narang in Shooting (III).

(*b*) P.V. Sindhu in Badminton (I).

(*c*) Vijender Singh in Boxing (IV).

(*d*) Leander Paes in Lawn Tennis (II).

This matching is based on the sports disciplines for which these athletes are renowned and have received Olympic recognition.

78. (A): International Yoga Day is celebrated every year on June 21st. This day was designated by the United Nations General Assembly in 2014, recognizing the universal appeal of yoga. June 21st was suggested by India's Prime Minister, Narendra Modi, as it is the longest day of the year in the Northern Hemisphere.

79. (A): The correct association of the dance forms with their regions in India are:

(*a*) Kathak from North India (IV).

(*b*) Bharat Natyam from Tamil Nadu (III).

(*c*) Kuchipudi from Andhra Pradesh (II).

(*d*) Kathakali from Kerala (I).

These dance forms are classical styles that are deeply rooted in the cultural traditions of their respective regions.

80. (D): The Jagannath Temple is located in Puri, Odisha, India. This temple is a significant Hindu temple dedicated to Lord Jagannath, a form of Vishnu. It is famous for its annual Rath Yatra or Chariot Festival, which attracts thousands of pilgrims and visitors from all over the world.

81. (B): The Palk Strait is a narrow strip of water located between the Tamil Nadu state of India and the Jaffna District of the northern province of Sri Lanka. This strait connects the Bay of Bengal to the northeast with the Palk Bay to the southwest and is an important geographical feature in the maritime boundary and navigation between these two countries.

82. (D): The option "MU – Short form of Modern Unit" is incorrectly matched. "MU" does not commonly stand for "Modern Unit" in any standard academic or professional context. Instead, "MU" can stand for various terms depending on the context, such as Million Units in power sectors or Manipal University in educational contexts. The other options correctly define their respective terms.

83. (B): G. Sankara Kurup was the recipient of the first Jnanpith Award in 1965 for his contributions to Indian literature, particularly in Malayalam. The Jnanpith Award is one of the highest literary honours in India, awarded annually by the Bharatiya Jnanpith to an author for their outstanding contribution towards literature.

84. (A): Valentina Tereshkova, a Soviet cosmonaut, became the first woman to fly in space aboard Vostok 6 on June 16, 1963. Her solo mission made her the first and youngest woman to have flown in space and she remains the only woman to have been on a solo space mission. This milestone marked a significant achievement in the history of space exploration.

85. (D): The correct matches for the books and their authors are:

(*a*) A Tale of Two Cities by Charles Dickens (II).

(*b*) Midnight's Children by Salman Rushdie (III).

(*c*) War and Peace by Leo Tolstoy (IV).

(*d*) Wuthering Heights by Emily Bronte (I).

This arrangement is based on well-known literary works and their respective authors who have made significant contributions to English literature.

86. (A): The headquarters of the United Nations is located in New York City, USA. Established in 1945, the UN headquarters in New York is a complex designed by an international team of architects and holds extraterritorial status, serving as the venue for major international diplomacy efforts and meetings of its member states.

87. (D): Guru Nanak is the founder of Sikhism and the first of the ten Sikh Gurus. His teachings, which emphasize universal equality, justice, faith, and devotion to God, laid the foundation for Sikhism. He was born in 1469 in what is now Pakistan and travelled extensively to spread his spiritual teachings.

88. (B): Dr. C.V. Raman was the first Indian scientist to win the Nobel Prize in Physics in 1930 for his work on the scattering of light and for the discovery of the effect named after him, the Raman Effect. This groundbreaking work established important principles in the field of light scattering, which have applications in various scientific fields.

89. (C): The first Commonwealth Games were held in 1930 in Hamilton, Ontario, Canada. Originally known as the British Empire Games, the event featured 400 athletes from 11 different countries competing in six sports. This event marks the beginning of what is now known as the Commonwealth Games, held every four years with participants from Commonwealth nations.

90. (A): The Durand Cup is associated with football and is one of the oldest football tournaments in Asia, having been founded in 1888 by Sir Mortimer Durand in Shimla, India. The tournament was originally a competition for British troops but has since become an important domestic football competition in India, featuring clubs and military teams.

91. (B): The Permanent Settlement fixed the revenue that zamindars had to pay to the colonial government, which did not change even if the value of agricultural produce increased. Thus, during periods of agricultural price increases, like after 1810, the income of the Bengal zamindars grew significantly because they were able to retain the surplus that resulted from higher prices without an increase in the revenue they owed to the government.

92. (B): According to Ricardian economic theories adopted by the British colonial officials, landowners were likely to become rentiers (individuals who live off rental income) if they continued to earn surplus income beyond the 'average rent'. The concern was that these surplus earnings would not be reinvested into productive activities or the improvement of the land, hence justifying the need for the state to tax such surplus.

93. (C): Under the Permanent Settlement system, implemented in Bengal in 1793, the revenue that zamindars were required to pay to the colonial government was permanently fixed. This meant that even as agricultural prices rose, increasing the value of the harvest and consequently the income of the zamindars, the state could not claim any portion of this additional income because the revenue amounts were unchangeable.

94. (C): In the context of the passage, the word "celebrated" refers to David Ricardo being highly respected and well-known. The passage highlights that Ricardo was a celebrated economist, meaning he had a significant reputation in his field, which influenced the colonial officials who had studied his economic theories during their education.

95. (C): The colonial government opted for temporary revenue settlements in newly annexed territories during the 19th century to maximize land revenue. As agricultural prices rose, fixing the revenue under Permanent Settlement, like in Bengal, would limit the government's share of enhanced incomes. Therefore, to expand its financial resources, the government chose to implement temporary settlements that allowed periodic revisions based on the land's productivity.

96. (D): The error in the sentence is in part (*d*) "succumbed from fires recently". The correct preposition to be used with "succumbed" in this context is "to", not "from". The correct phrase should be "succumbed to fires recently", which means to have been destroyed or severely damaged by fires.

97. (C): The correctly spelled word among the options given is "Humdrum", which means lacking excitement or variety; boringly monotonous. The other options contain misspellings: "Hulaballoo" should be "Hullabaloo", "Hypoteneuse" should be "Hypotenuse" and "Humourus" should be "Humorous".

98. (D): The word "humble" has several nuances, but when seeking a word that expresses a similar meaning in a negative form, "ignoble" is the most appropriate among the options. While "humble" often connotes modesty or a lack of pretense, "ignoble" suggests a lack of honour or low character, which can be seen as a negative reflection of humility.

99. (B): The correct phrase for addressing strategies in sustainable development related to climate change should involve both adaptation and mitigation. "Adaptation" refers to adjustments in practices, processes, or structures to mitigate potential damage or to benefit from opportunities associated with climate change. "Mitigation" refers to efforts to reduce or prevent the emission of greenhouse gases. "Migration" is incorrect in this context.

100. (D): The correct preposition to use with "comply" in this sentence is "with". The sentence "She has assured that she will comply with the latest directions" correctly uses "with" to indicate conformity or adherence to the directions given.

101. (B): "Retain" means to keep or hold on to something. The opposite of retaining is to give up or renounce, which means to formally declare one's abandonment of a claim, right, or possession. "Renounce" is the correct choice as it directly contrasts with the idea of keeping or holding something.

102. (D): "Succinctly" means in a brief and clearly expressed manner. The word that best expresses this meaning is "Briefly", which directly refers to expressing something concisely and without unnecessary words. "Briefly" is the perfect synonym for "succinctly", as both imply a short and clear expression.

103. (D): The phrase "give up" means to cease making an effort; to surrender. This fits correctly into the sentence describing someone ending their involvement or quitting in an argument. "She has given up the matter" suggests that she has stopped arguing or has resigned herself to the outcome of the matter.

104. (D): The original sentence "I prefer to ride than to walk" is grammatically incorrect. The correct comparative form should maintain parallel structure. "Riding to walking" correctly uses the gerund form for both verbs, making the sentence both grammatically correct and smoother: "I prefer riding to walking."

105. (C): "Eat humble pie" is an idiom that means to apologize and face humiliation for a mistake. It comes from the phrase "umble pie", which historically referred to a pie made of the less appealing parts of an animal, eaten by lower-class people. Apologizing, especially after being wrong or arrogant, is akin to a humbling experience, thus aligning with the idiom's meaning.

106. (C): The noun form of the verb "leave" is also "leave", which refers to permission or the act of departing. It can be used in contexts like taking a leave from work or school, representing a period of absence. "Leave" as a noun is the only correct choice among the given options.

107. (A): To "exculpate" means to show or declare that someone is not guilty of wrongdoing. "Absolve" directly aligns with this as it means to free someone from blame, guilt, or responsibility. Both terms involve the clearing of any charges or accusations, making "absolve" the nearest in meaning.

108. (B): The error in the sentence is in part (*b*), "complained at".. The correct preposition to use with "complained" when referring to an object of dissatisfaction is "about", not "at". Thus, the corrected phrase should be "complained about the poor accommodation".

109. (C): "Impetuous" is the only correctly spelled word among the options. It means acting or done quickly and without thought or care. The other words contain spelling errors: "Imperterbable" should be "Imperturbable", "Impetous" is a misspelling, and "Apostacy" should be "Apostasy".

110. (A): "To die in harness" is an idiom meaning to die while still actively working or involved in one's work duties, typically implying dying while still employed or engaged in one's usual activities. It metaphorically refers to a workhorse dying while still in its harness, thus being active until the end.

111. (B): He has criticized this philosophy as being too oblique. When someone deems a philosophy as "too oblique," it implies that it is too indirect or obscure to be readily understood or straightforward. "Criticized" is appropriate here as it denotes disapproval or finding fault with the philosophy's lack of clarity or directness.

112. (C): "Abundant" means existing or available in large quantities; plentiful. "Copious" is synonymous with abundant and conveys the idea of a large amount, extensive quantity, or profuse. It is the best choice among the options as it directly reflects the concept of abundance.

113. (D): The correctly spelled word is "Dilettante," which refers to a person who cultivates an area of interest, such as the arts, without real commitment or knowledge. This spelling matches the recognized form of the word used to describe an amateur or someone with a superficial interest in the arts or a branch of knowledge.

114. (C): The error in the sentence is in part (*c*), "to changing the age-old." The correct phrase should use the infinitive form "to change" rather than "to changing" to match the intended meaning of proposing or intending to change something. It should read: "to change the age-old and static structure of our organization".

115. (A): "Umbrage" refers to offense or annoyance prompted by what one perceives as unfair treatment. "Annoyance" is the best fit as it directly corresponds to the feeling of being upset or irritated, which is what taking umbrage implies.

116. (C): "Foster" means to encourage the development or growth of ideas or feelings. The opposite of fostering something would be to hinder or frustrate its progress. "Frustrate" means to prevent the progress, success, or fulfillment of something, thereby directly opposing the act of fostering.

117. (B): The phrase "The details of the incident are not known to me" correctly fits into the sentence. An "incident" refers to an event or occurrence, especially one that is noteworthy or disruptive. This choice aligns with the context that there is specific information unknown to the speaker regarding an event.

118. (D): In the sentence "With this realization, she finds himself loose," the correct grammatical and contextual form is "found herself lost". This implies that upon realizing something, she felt disoriented or unable to understand her situation fully. The correction maintains proper subject-verb agreement and reflects a state of confusion appropriate to the context.

119. (D): The word "inappropriate" means not suitable or proper in the circumstances. The opposite of inappropriate would be something that is suitable, proper, or "Acceptable". This word signifies approval and fittingness to the context, making it the correct antonym.

120. (C): The original phrase "The company said to pay" lacks clarity and grammatical correctness. The corrected version "The company has offered to pay in cash or kind both" provides a clear, specific, and grammatically correct alternative that accurately reflects a formal proposal or offer by the company.

121. (A): "Narrow-minded" refers to someone who is not willing to listen to or tolerate other people's views. "Broad-minded," on the other hand, describes a person who is open to different opinions and tolerant of differing views. This term is the direct opposite of being narrow-minded, highlighting an accepting and comprehensive attitude.

122. (B): A "coup" generally refers to a sudden, violent, and illegal seizure of power from a government. Among the given options, "encroach" is the nearest in meaning as it also suggests an aggressive or forceful intrusion, albeit less violent than a coup. It conveys a sense of moving onto someone else's territory or rights, similar to how a coup intrudes upon the established order.

123. (B): The phrase "flog a dead horse" means to continue a particular endeavour is a waste of time as the outcome will not change. This often involves revisiting or reviving interest in matters that are already concluded and cannot be altered, making the effort pointless and redundant.

124. (A): To "emulate" means to match or surpass, typically by imitation. It is about striving to equal or excel, especially through imitation. Thus, "imitate" is the best choice as it encompasses the essence of emulation, where the effort to imitate someone or something is driven by a desire to reach or exceed a standard.

125. (A): The phrase "were asked the states" is grammatically incorrect and awkward. The correct form should be "has requested the states", which correctly aligns with the subject-verb agreement and more accurately conveys a formal request made by the central government to the states.

126. (A): "Wild" typically describes something natural, untamed, or uncultivated. The antonym would be "cultured", which refers to being enlightened, educated, or refined, especially in arts and manners. This represents characteristics developed opposite to wild or natural states.

127. (C): The phrase "an infinite capacity for learning" uses "for" to indicate a capability or potential. The preposition "for" is appropriate here as it expresses the function or intended purpose of the genius's capacity, which is geared towards the acquisition of knowledge or learning.

128. (B): The phrase "stopped to work" suggests pausing to start working, which contradicts the intended meaning. "Stopped working" correctly indicates that the machines ceased functioning an hour ago, conveying a complete halt in operation rather than a commencement.

129. (D): "Ill at ease" means feeling uneasy or uncomfortable. The idiom suggests a sense of discomfort or anxiety, rather than anger or being hopeful. Therefore, "uncomfortable" is the precise expression that matches the meaning of being ill at ease.

130. (D): The verb form of "poison" is simply "poison," which means to administer or expose someone or something to a substance that can cause death or injury. "Poison" used as a verb aligns with actions of contaminating or harming, thus it correctly maintains its form from noun to verb without change.

131. (A): The correctly spelled word is "Reminiscences", which refers to a recollection of past experiences or events. The other options contain incorrect formations and misspellings of the word.

132. (D): The error in the sentence "They took to reading 'Times' for the better knowledge in the facts" occurs in part (*d*). The correct phrase should be "for the better knowledge of the facts." This correction provides proper prepositional use, enhancing the clarity and correctness of the expression.

133. (C): The verb form of "troublesome" is "trouble". "Troublesome" describes something that causes difficulty or distress, and "trouble" as a verb means to cause distress or anxiety to someone, fitting as the action form of the adjective.

134. (C): "Corpulent" means having a large, bulky body; overweight. The word "Bulky" directly relates to this as it describes something large and of considerable size, which aligns perfectly with the meaning of corpulent.

135. (A): The phrase "You should not rely on the assurance of your friends" correctly uses "on" to express dependence or trust in something or someone. "On" is the appropriate preposition to use when indicating reliance or dependence.

136. (D): In the phrase "He will hand over the charge next week", "over" is the correct choice. This expression is used when someone is transferring responsibility, control, or possession of something to someone else.

137. (A): The phrase "Plough the sands" metaphorically means to engage in a futile labour or effort. It refers to the fruitlessness of plowing sandy soil, where no worthwhile outcome can be expected, analogous to doing any laborious task that yields no results.

138. (C): "Depressed" is the adjective form of the verb "depress." It describes a state of general unhappiness or despondency, aligning with the effect of the verb "depress", which means to lower someone's spirits or to cause someone to feel sad or discouraged.

139. (D): "Farcical" refers to something absurd, ludicrous, or laughable. The opposite of farcical, which involves triviality and ridicule, would be "Serious". Serious describes a manner that is sincere, earnest, or not joking, thus directly contrasting with the nature of something farcical.

140. (B): The phrase "The fragrance of these flowers is enchanting" uses "fragrance" to denote a pleasant, sweet smell. "Fragrance" specifically refers to a pleasant, often sweet scent, making it a more suitable choice for describing the delightful aroma of flowers, as opposed to stench, smell, or odour which could refer to any scent, not necessarily a pleasant one.

141. (C): "Aggravate" means to make a situation worse or more severe. The opposite of aggravating something is to alleviate it, which means to make less severe or to relieve pain or tension. Thus, "alleviate" is the correct antonym as it directly contrasts with the notion of worsening a condition.

142. (B): The error in the sentence "All the doctors were puzzled on the strange symptoms reported by the patient" is in part (*b*). The correct preposition to use with "puzzled" in this context is "by," not "on." The sentence should read "All the doctors were puzzled by the strange symptoms reported by the patient," which correctly indicates that the symptoms caused confusion among the doctors.

143. (C): The correctly spelled word is "Resplendent," which means attractive and impressive through being richly colorful or sumptuous. It is often used to describe something that shines brightly and appears dazzling or magnificent.

144. (B): The error in the sentence "Either of the plans suits him and therefore he decided not to go out yesterday" is in part (*b*). The correct conjunction for the phrase would be "nor" instead of "and" when using "either...or" construction. Thus, it should be "Either of the plans suits him nor therefore he decided not to go out yesterday," indicating that none of the plans were suitable.

145. (D): "Celestial" refers to something that is heavenly or related to the sky. The word "Divine" best expresses this meaning as it pertains to god, godly or coming from heaven, aligning with the ethereal or heavenly nature suggested by celestial.

146. (A): The adjective form of "command" is "commanding," which means having an air of authority, capable of demanding attention. It is used to describe someone or something that expresses confidence or authority, which is a quality derived from the verb command.

147. (B): To "mesmerize" means to hold the attention of (someone) to the exclusion of all else or so as to transfix them. "Enchant" closely captures this meaning, implying to attract and hold the attention through charm or beauty, making it synonymous with mesmerize.

148. (B): "Delegate" means to entrust (a task or responsibility) to another person, typically one who is less senior than oneself. The opposite of delegating would be to retain, which means to keep possession of or continue to have responsibility instead of passing it on.

149. (B): "At the beck and call" means to be always ready to serve or be available to obey someone's orders immediately. "At the service" directly reflects this readiness to assist or be available for someone, indicating being responsive to someone's requests or commands.

150. (D): The phrase "into the recession" is grammatically incorrect and awkward in the context of the global economy. "In a recession" is the correct expression, indicating the current state of the world economy being within a period of economic downturn.

151. (A): In a professional setting, it is crucial to prioritize the success of important projects over personal disagreements. Approaching a colleague directly and asking for help demonstrates professionalism and a commitment to the organization's objectives. It is the most straightforward and effective way to ensure the project's timely and successful completion.

152. (B): It is inappropriate and against labour laws to allow a child, especially one as young as 10 years old, to work in place of an adult. The ethical response is to send the child back home for his safety and well-being, and manage the arrangements yourself or seek alternative adult help.

153. (D): Handling an angry guest effectively is essential in maintaining the reputation and service quality of a hotel. Ignoring the guest or escalating the situation by refusing to communicate or raising your voice could worsen the situation. Consulting with a team leader for guidance and working together to address the guest's concerns promptly is a professional and constructive approach.

154. (C): While it's natural to feel disappointed after a theft, dwelling on misfortune is not productive. The practical and forward-looking response is to focus on being more vigilant in the future and taking steps to prevent such incidents, rather than dwelling on the past or making drastic decisions like moving house without careful consideration.

155. (B): Recognizing the hard work and perhaps the financial need of an old rickshaw puller, and responding with empathy by giving a little extra money can be a kind gesture. It supports the puller without creating any unnecessary fuss, reflecting kindness and understanding of his situation.

156. (C): If you're away from the hostel and remember that you left the electrical geyser on, the most immediate and practical solution is to ask friends who are still at the hostel to turn it off. This action prevents waste and potential hazards without requiring you to return to the hostel, which might not be feasible.

157. (B): If you suspect that the medicine is spurious, it is important to verify if others have had similar experiences. Gathering more information and evidence can help in making a strong case to be taken to consumer protection bodies to address potential public safety issues effectively.

158. (D): Confidence in decision-making is crucial. If you continually doubt your decisions or regret them, it can undermine your ability to make future decisions. Sticking to your decisions unless there's a compelling reason to change shows determination and conviction in your choices.

159. (C): Placing industrial units away from residential areas is primarily for health and safety reasons. Industrial smoke and other emissions can be harmful to residents, impacting air quality and overall health. This reason aligns with environmental and public health policies.

160. (B): Organizing an event like a Fresher's welcome party typically requires collaboration and teamwork. Taking the help of fellow batchmates not only distributes the workload but also fosters a sense of community and inclusion, making the event planning more efficient and enjoyable for everyone involved.

161. (C): If you are not invited to a friend's birthday party, a gracious and positive response would be to send your best wishes. This approach maintains friendly relations and shows maturity, avoiding potential awkwardness or conflict that could arise from expressing dissatisfaction or holding grudges.

162. (A): If your boss is writing a false report, it is important to address the issue directly and ethically. Meeting with your boss to express your concerns allows for open communication and gives your boss the opportunity to explain or reconsider the actions. This direct approach promotes transparency and integrity in the workplace.

163. (D): Dealing with a breakup from a long-term friendship can be emotionally draining. Seeking distraction and support by spending time with other friends can help you move past the hurt and start healing, providing a healthier alternative to staying alone or resorting to negative coping mechanisms.

164. (C): If you notice a broken track and a metro train approaching, the immediate priority is to prevent an accident. Using any available means to alert and stop the train is crucial, as it directly addresses the imminent danger and can save lives, relying on the station's infrastructure alone in such a critical situation may not be sufficient.

165. (D): To be an ideal manager, it is effective to lead by example. This approach not only establishes credibility but also inspires your team to emulate positive behaviours and attitudes. Demonstrating the standards you expect from others through your own actions reinforces leadership qualities and encourages a positive work culture.

166. (C): When faced with illegal construction and threats by a local rowdy, the most appropriate and safe response is to involve the police. This ensures that the matter is handled legally and helps avoid any potential harm that could arise from trying to deal with the situation personally or through informal channels.

167. (D): If a close friend has habits you find disagreeable, directly communicating your feelings and requesting a change is a forthright and honest approach. This response respects the friendship by addressing issues openly rather than ignoring them or being indirect, which can lead to misunderstandings and resentment over time.

168. (D): If you wish to computerize your office to enhance efficiency, training the entire staff is a constructive and inclusive approach. This ensures that all employees are equipped with the necessary skills to adapt to the new systems, thereby minimizing disruption and resistance to change.

169. (C): When facing criticism from senior staff about an innovative idea, it's beneficial to engage directly with the critics. Meeting to discuss their concerns and explaining the benefits of the new procedure can help alleviate doubts and garner support, fostering a collaborative and innovative workplace culture.

170. (B): When asked for your opinion on a matter at work, even if it's not directly related to your responsibilities, providing a straightforward response is helpful. This shows you are engaged and willing to contribute to discussions, enhancing collaboration and respect among colleagues.

171. (D): As a student in class 10th, the responsible decision when faced with peer pressure to drink beer is to refuse outright. Consuming alcohol at a young age is illegal and can have harmful effects on your health and academic performance. Refusing helps maintain personal integrity and promotes healthy, lawful behaviour.

172. (A): As an Assistant Manager in a hotel, dealing directly with an angry guest by being patient and attempting to calm him down is a proactive and responsible approach. It shows professionalism and dedication to customer service, aiming to resolve issues before they escalate, possibly satisfying the guest without needing to involve senior management.

173. (B): Listening to the news on television remains a valuable source for keeping informed about current events and happenings around the world. Despite the rise of digital and social media, television news can provide more in-depth coverage and expert analysis which are essential for a comprehensive understanding of global issues.

174. (D): If witnessing a fierce fight, the constructive approach is to understand the issue first and attempt to mediate and resolve the conflict. This promotes peace and safety in the community. Immediate intervention, especially informed, can prevent potential harm and help resolve underlying issues.

175. (D): Before starting a new business in a new city, it's prudent to conduct thorough market research to understand consumer preferences and market conditions. Selecting a representative sample area and size for the survey ensures that the data collected will inform effective business decisions, minimizing risk and maximizing potential for success.

176. (D): Upon hearing a blast sound near a five-star hotel, the appropriate response is to try to determine the source of the noise. This can help in assessing the situation accurately and aid in deciding the next steps, whether it's to evacuate, assist, or alert authorities.

177. (D): Being an ideal team leader requires strong decision-making abilities. This skill ensures that a leader can effectively assess situations, weigh options, and make choices that guide the team towards achieving their objectives efficiently and effectively.

178. (D): The preservation of petroleum products is crucial because their wasteful or improper usage can lead to rapid depletion of these non-renewable resources. By conserving petroleum, we ensure that these resources are available for longer periods and for future generations, supporting sustainable development.

179. (C): When locking your flat, it's important to personally ensure that all necessary precautions, such as switching off lights and appliances, are taken. This direct action prevents potential accidents, conserves energy, and ensures security, demonstrating responsibility and proactive household management.

180. (D): Changing jobs and facing new situations can lead to personal and professional growth. Accepting such challenges encourages adaptability and learning, opening up opportunities for career advancement and enrichment. This mindset supports a dynamic and progressive career path.

181. (D): If you wake up with a mild sore throat but have urgent work to complete, attending work can be necessary. It's important to assess whether your condition might worsen or be contagious. If it's just a mild sore throat and not symptomatic of a more serious condition, and you can manage your health without risking others, it is responsible to fulfill your obligations, especially if the work is time-sensitive.

182. (C): Pleasing in the corporate sector can sometimes be viewed as a strategy for career advancement. However, if one perceives this approach as being inauthentic or manipulative, it could be regarded as futile. Focusing on genuine performance and maintaining integrity might be more fulfilling and sustainable for personal growth and professional relationships.

183. (D): If a few students fail their mid-term exam, blaming one party (like the teacher or the students) solely is not justifiable without knowing all contributing factors. Many elements could lead to their failure, including personal issues, teaching methods, or external circumstances. Therefore, it cannot be generalized as solely the fault of the teacher or the students.

184. (D): "Service aptitude" implies having a strong desire and motivation to provide services. This involves a commitment to helping and serving others effectively and efficiently, which is crucial in any service-oriented role to ensure customer satisfaction and positive interactions.

185. (A): While working in a group, being cooperative is key to harmonious and productive group dynamics. This approach facilitates effective teamwork, promotes the exchange of ideas, enhances problem-solving capabilities, and generally leads to better outcomes for group tasks.

186. (C): Seeing water running from a tap unnecessarily prompts an immediate response to conserve resources. Closing the tap not only prevents wastage of water but also reflects personal responsibility and environmental awareness, qualities important in every community setting.

187. (D): A procession in front of your flat while you are preparing a project report can be a significant distraction. Such noise and activity could disrupt your concentration, affecting your ability to focus on your work. Recognizing it as a distraction helps in finding ways to minimize its impact, like closing windows or using noise-canceling headphones.

188. (D): In service sectors, having a helping attitude is essential. This trait involves a readiness to assist and address the needs of others, which is fundamental to service roles. Whether in customer service, healthcare, or hospitality, a helpful demeanor can significantly enhance the quality of service provided.

189. (B): In a dangerous situation like facing criminals asking for your possessions, prioritizing personal safety over material items is crucial. Offering the demanded items without resistance minimizes the risk of harm, as the safety of life is more important than material losses, which can be recovered or replaced.

190. (A): When purchasing clothing, especially with your first stipend, the most important factor is that the cloth must be suitable for you. This means it should fit well, be appropriate for the intended use, and make you feel confident. Comfort and suitability should always take precedence over fashion statements or price.

191. (A): This choice indicates a cautious approach to criticism, emphasizing the importance of having substantial evidence or certainty before pointing out someone's mistakes. It reflects a responsible and considerate temperament that values fairness and accuracy in judgments.

192. (A): Describing yourself as optimistic means you generally expect the best possible outcome from any situation. This trait is beneficial as it enhances resilience, promotes a positive working environment, and can lead to better health and stress management.

193. (D): If you strongly disagree with regretting past decisions often, it suggests a positive outlook on past choices and a belief that each decision has contributed to growth and learning. This mindset can lead to greater self-confidence and a forward-thinking approach in life.

194. (B): When dealing with an upset customer, maintaining politeness is crucial. It helps to calm the situation and convey respect and understanding towards the customer's concerns. Politeness can prevent the situation from escalating and create an environment where a resolution can be more easily achieved.

195. (B): If nominated for a training program that you are not interested in attending, informing your supervisor and suggesting that someone else who might benefit more be sent in your place is a practical approach. This keeps your professional integrity intact while ensuring that the opportunity is not wasted and could be more valuable to another employee more willing or needing of the development.

196. (C): Management is primarily responsible for solving problems in any business organization. They are tasked with decision-making, strategizing, and resource allocation, which are crucial for addressing challenges and guiding the organization towards achieving its goals.

197. (C): Encouraging open discussion and allowing your adolescent son to make his own decisions fosters independence and critical thinking. It supports his development into a responsible adult capable of making thoughtful decisions.

198. (C): The effectiveness of classroom teaching should be judged based on the learning outcomes of the students. This includes their understanding of the material, ability to apply what they've learned, and overall academic progress, which are direct indicators of teaching effectiveness.

199. (D): Choosing to lend money to a childhood friend without expecting interest shows generosity and a strong sense of loyalty and support. This decision prioritizes the friend's immediate needs and the value of the friendship over personal financial gain.

200. (C): Starting a new activity after careful planning indicates a methodical and thoughtful approach. It suggests that you prefer to be well-prepared and organized, which can lead to higher success rates and a better handling of potential challenges.

YOUR SPACE

Previous Paper (Solved)

National Testing Agency (NTA)

National Council for Hotel Management & Catering Technology

Joint Entrance Exam (NCHMCT-JEE), 2023*

NUMERICAL ABILITY

1. If the ratio of two numbers is 11 : 12 and their LCM is 528. Then their HCF is:

A. 4 B. 2
C. 8 D. 16

2. The HCF and LCM of two numbers are 12 and 336 respectively. If one of the numbers is 48, the other is:

A. 56 B. 84
C. 168 D. 96

3. The HCF of 3556 and 3444 is:

A. 14 B. 84
C. 56 D. 28

4. Which of the following is a pair of co-primes?

A. (16, 62) B. (23, 92)
C. (18, 25) D. (21, 35)

5. A number less than 100, when divided by 4, 5 and 6 leaves remainder 2 in each case. The number is:

A. 62 B. 54
C. 38 D. 44

6. The average of the first 100 positive integers is:

A. 50.5 B. 51
C. 51.5 D. 49.5

7. The average of 7 consecutive numbers is 20. The largest of these numbers is:

A. 24 B. 23
C. 20 D. 19

8. Simplify: $\dfrac{\frac{7}{8}\times\frac{7}{8}+\frac{5}{6}\times\frac{5}{6}+\frac{7}{8}\times\frac{5}{3}}{\frac{7}{8}\times\frac{7}{8}-\frac{5}{6}\times\frac{5}{6}}$

A. 41 B. 40
C. 38 D. 35

9. If $\sqrt{218+\sqrt{37+\sqrt{144}}} = K$, then value of K is:

A. 35 B. 25
C. 20 D. 15

10. If $\sqrt{x}+14=\sqrt{2601}$, then x is equal to:

A. 1359 B. 1379
C. 1369 D. 1309

11. The fraction equivalent to $\frac{2}{7}\%$ is:

A. $\frac{1}{350}$ B. $\frac{1}{700}$
C. $\frac{1}{750}$ D. $\frac{2}{350}$

12. In how many years will a sum of money double itself at $6\frac{1}{4}\%$ simple interest per annum?

A. 2 years B. 4 years
C. 8 years D. 16 years

13. The simple interest on a sum of money is $\frac{4}{9}$ of the principal. If rate percent and time are numerically equal then find the rate percent:

A. $5\frac{2}{3}\%$ B. $9\frac{2}{3}\%$
C. $8\frac{2}{3}\%$ D. $6\frac{2}{3}\%$

14. The ages of two persons differ by 16 years. If 6 years ago, the elder one was three times as old as the younger one, then present age of elder one is:

A. 14 years B. 30 years
C. 20 years D. 15 years

1. A	**2.** B	**3.** D	**4.** C	**5.** A	**6.** A	**7.** B	**8.** A	**9.** D	**10.** C
11. A	**12.** D	**13.** D	**14.** B						

* **Exam held on 14 May, 2023.**

15. 6 years ago, the ratio of the ages of Ram and Ravi was 6 : 5. Four years hence, the ratio of their ages will be 11 : 10. What is Ravi's age at present?
A. 18 years B. 20 years
C. 15 years D. 16 years

16. The ages of A and B are in the ratio 6 : 5 and the sum of their ages is 44 years. What will be the ratio of their ages after 8 years?
A. 8 : 7 B. 7 : 8
C. 8 : 9 D. 9 : 8

17. A 160 m long train crosses a 160 m long platform in 16 seconds, then the speed of the train is:
A. 55 km/hr
B. 60 km/hr
C. 72 km/hr
D. 75 km/hr

18. If a boat goes 7 km upstream in 42 minutes and the speed of the stream is 3 kmph, then, the speed of the boat in still water is:
A. 12 km/hr B. 15 km/hr
C. 14 km/hr D. 13 km/hr

19. The difference between the value of a number increased by 25% and the value of the original number decreased by 30% is 22. What is the original number?
A. 40 B. 35
C. 45 D. 50

20. In an examination, 35% of total students failed only in Hindi, 45% of students failed only in English and 20% failed in both, then the percentage of students who passed in both the subjects is:
A. 60% B. 40%
C. 30% D. 35%

21. The selling price of 30 items is equal to the purchase price of 25 items, then the profit or loss percent is:
A. $16\frac{2}{3}$ B. $18\frac{2}{3}$
C. $14\frac{2}{3}$ D. $15\frac{2}{3}$

22. The difference between the cost price and sale price of an article is ₹ 240. If the profit is 20%, the selling price is:
A. ₹ 1240 B. ₹ 1340
C. ₹ 1400 D. ₹ 1440

23. How much water must be added to 60 litres of milk, whose cost is ₹ 20 per $1\frac{1}{2}$ litres so as to have a mixture worth ₹ $10\frac{2}{3}$ a litre?
A. 15 litres B. 20 litres
C. 25 litres D. 10 litres

24. A can do a piece of work in 10 days and B in 20 days. They work together but 2 days before the completion of the work, A leaves. In how many days was the work completed?
A. 2 days B. 6 days
C. 8 days D. 10 days

25. Kavya is 40 years old and Neetu is 60 years old. How many years ago was the ratio of their ages 3 : 5?
A. 37 years B. 20 years
C. 10 years D. 15 years

26. A person reaches his destination 40 minutes late if his speed is 3 km/hr and reaches 30 minutes before time if his speed is 4 km/hr, then the distance of his destination from his starting point is:
A. 20 km B. 14 km
C. 24 km D. 12 km

27. A number when divided by 195 leaves a remainder 47. If the same number is divided by 15, the remainder will be:
A. 4 B. 3
C. 2 D. 1

28. Two pipes, A and B can fill a tank in 20 and 30 minutes respectively. If both the pipes are used together, how long will it take to fill the tank?
A. 10 minutes B. 12 minutes
C. 14 minutes D. 16 minutes

29. The total number of digits used in numbering the pages of a book having 366 pages, is:
A. 980 B. 990
C. 950 D. 1000

30. The value of
$$\left[35.7 - \left(3 + \frac{1}{3 + \frac{1}{3}}\right) - \left(2 + \frac{1}{2 + \frac{1}{2}}\right)\right]$$ is:
A. 30 B. 34.8
C. 36.6 D. 41.4

15. D	16. A	17. C	18. D	19. A	20. B	21. A	22. D	23. A	24. C
25. C	26. B	27. C	28. B	29. B	30. A				

REASONING AND LOGICAL DEDUCTION

31. Directions: Three words are given in the question given below, which have something in common among themselves. Choose one out of the given alternatives which mentions the quality common to the three given words:

Spain : Canada : India

A. Russia B. Paris
C. London D. Chicago

32. 'Tennis' is related to 'Court' in the same way as 'Boxing' is related to:

A. Pool B. Ring
C. Arena D. Course

33. Below given question consists of two words each that have a relationship to each other followed by four lettered pair of words. Select the lettered pair that has the same relationship as original pair of words.

Signal : Traffic

A. Dam : River B. Lens : Light
C. Door : House D. Operation : Doctor

34. What will come in place of question mark?

Clock : Time :: Thermometer : ?

A. Heat B. Energy
C. Radiation D. Temperature

35. Directions : Complete the series by replacing question mark?

ABD, DGK, HMS, MTB, '?'

A. RAM B. SBL
C. RBL D. TBL

36. 'College' is related to 'Student' in the same way as 'Hospital' is related to:

A. Musician B. Treatment
C. Nurse D. Patient

37. In the given question, a group of three inter related words is given. Choose a word from the given alternatives that is similar to the given words, hence belong to the group.

Grandfather : Father : Brother

A. Son-in-law B. Father-in-law
C. Son D. Servant

38. Choose the odd pair of words:

A. Mason : Wall B. Cobbler : Shoe
C. Farmer : Crop D. Chef : Cook

39. In the following question, four words have been given, out of which three are like in some manner and fourth one is different. Choose the odd one out.

A. Triangle B. Rectangle
C. Circle D. Square

40. In a certain code PUPIL is written as RWRKN. How ROAST is written in that code?

A. TQCUV B. TQCUW
C. TQCVW D. TQCUZ

41. The number of triangles in the given figure is:

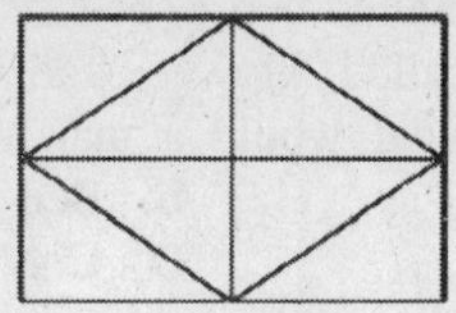

A. 8 B. 10
C. 12 D. 14

42. Which of the following shows the relationship among Rose, Flower and Lotus?

A. 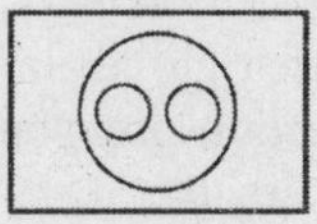

B. 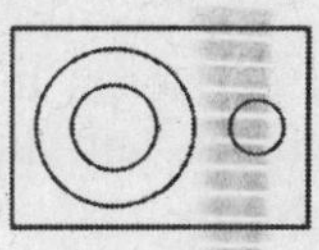

C. 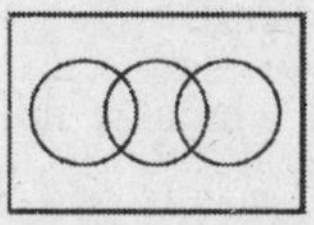

D. 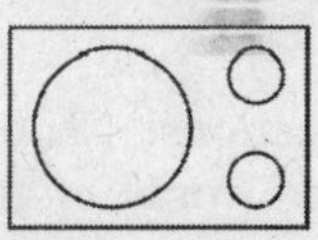

43. See the figure given below, and answer the question:

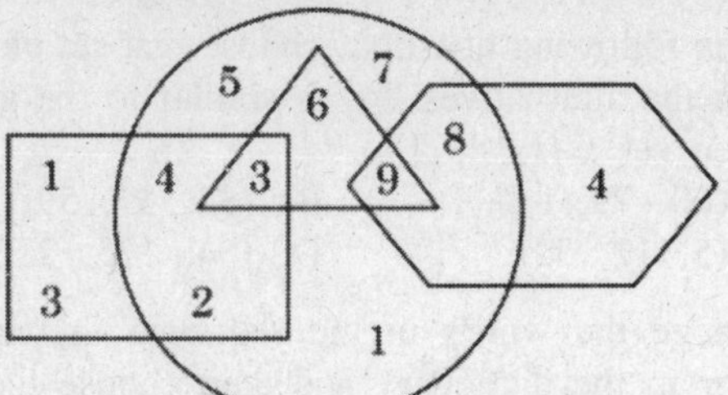

What is the sum of the numbers which belong to one figure only?

A. 5 B. 16
C. 21 D. 24

31. A	**32.** B	**33.** A	**34.** D	**35.** B	**36.** D	**37.** C	**38.** D	**39.** C	**40.** A
41. C	**42.** A	**43.** C							

44. Select a figure from amongst the four alternatives, which when placed in the blank space of given figure would complete the pattern:

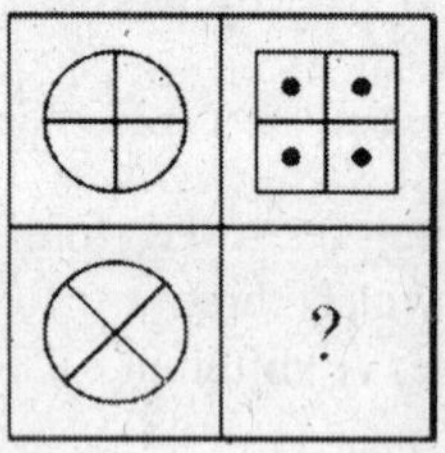

A. 
B. 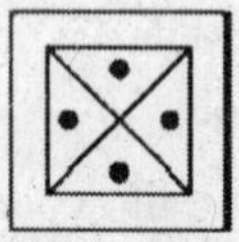
C. 
D. 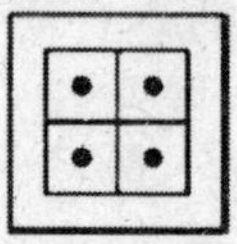

45. If 'room' is called 'bed', 'bed' is called 'window', 'window' is called 'flower' and 'flower' is called 'cooler', on what would a man sleep?

A. Window B. Bed
C. Flower D. Cooler

46. Pointing towards a boy, Veena said, "He is the son of only son of my grandfather". How is that boy related to Veena?

A. Uncle B. Brother
C. Cousin D. Husband

47. You go North, turn right, then right again and then go to the left. In which direction are you now?

A. North B. South
C. East D. West

48. **Directions:** Choose the word which is not like the other words in the group.

A. Apple B. Lotus
C. Rose D. Lily

49. In the following question, choose that set of numbers from the alternatives that is similar to the given set.
Given set : (1, 8, 27)

A. (60, 79, 86) B. (32, 39, 59)
C. (5, 12, 32) D. (64, 125, 216)

50. Arrange the words in the sequence in which they occur in the dictionary and then choose the correct sequence.

(*a*) Orange (*b*) Strike
(*c*) Effect (*d*) Wife

A. (*c*), (*b*), (*a*), (*d*) B. (*b*), (*c*), (*a*), (*d*)
C. (*c*), (*a*), (*b*), (*d*) D. (*a*), (*b*), (*c*), (*d*)

51. Find out the alternative which will replace the question mark.
White : Peace : : Red : ?

A. Violence B. Roses
C. Blackboard D. Cleanliness

52. Find the missing term of the series AI, BJ, CK, ?

A. DL B. DM
C. GH D. LM

53. Choose the missing term out of the given alternatives
C 4 X, F 9 U, I 16 R, ?

A. K 25 P B. L 25 P
C. L 25 O D. L 27 P

54. 'Thick' is related to 'Thin' in the same way as 'Idle' is related to:

A. Business B. Industrious
C. Activity D. Virtuous

55. Below is a question consisting of a statement, followed by 4 arguments numbered I, II, III, IV. Decide which of the following arguments is/are 'strong' arguments and which are 'weak' arguments and accordingly choose answer from the alternatives given below.
Statement: Should there be a complete ban on manufacture and use of fire crackers?
Arguments:

I. No, this wall render thousands of workers jobless.
II. Yes, the firecracker manufacturers use child labour to a great extent.
III. Yes, this will be a concrete step to reduce noise and air pollution.
IV. No, the use of firecrackers makes certain special occasions more lively and joyful.

A. Only I and II are strong
B. Only I and III are strong
C. Only III and IV are strong
D. Only I, II and III are strong

Directions (Qs. No. 56-60): *Go through the following information carefully and answer the given questions.*

(*i*) There is a group of five persons—A, B, C, D and E.
(*ii*) One of them is a horticulturist, one is a physicist, one is a journalist, one is an industrialist and one is an advocate.
(*iii*) Three of them—A, C and advocate prefer tea to coffee and two of them—B and the journalist prefer coffee to tea.
(*iv*) The industrialist and D and A are friends to one another but two of them prefer coffee to tea.
(*v*) The horticulturist is C's brother.

44. A **45.** A **46.** B **47.** C **48.** A **49.** D **50.** C **51.** A **52.** A **53.** C
54. B **55.** B

56. Who is the horticulturist?
A. A B. B
C. C D. D

57. Who is the industrialist?
A. C B. B
C. D D. E

58. Which of the following groups includes a person who likes tea but is not an advocate?
A. AC B. AD
C. BD D. CB

59. Who is a Physicist?
A. A B. B
C. C D. D

60. Which of the following group likes coffee only?
A. AB B. CD
C. BE D. BD

GENERAL KNOWLEDGE AND CURRENT AFFAIRS

61. Which of the following is the National Aquatic animal of India?
A. Whale B. Dolphin
C. Shark D. Tiger

62. Which award is given for lifetime achievement in Sports and Games?
A. Arjuna Award
B. Dhyan Chand Award
C. Rajiv Gandhi Khel Ratna
D. Dronacharya Award

63. Which of the following is the "highest honour" given by France?
A. Presidential Medal of freedom
B. Legend of Honour
C. Victoria Cross-member of British Empire
D. The Order of the Golden Star

64. Which is the correct order of precedence in our country?
A. Chief Justice of India, President, Prime Minister, Governor
B. President, Vice President, Prime Minister, Governor
C. President, Chief Justice of India, Deputy Prime Minister, Governor
D. Prime Minister, Governor, Chief Justice of India, Former Presidents

65. Who is the author of the book TOM SAWYER?
A. Leo Tolstoy B. Jane Austen
C. H.G. Wells D. Mark Twain

66. Who was the first Indian to win a Nobel Prize for literature?
A. C.V. Raman B. Mother Teresa
C. Amartya Sen D. R.N. Tagore

67. Amjad Ali Khan is associated with which of the following musical instruments?
A. Flute B. Sarod
C. Sitar D. Shehnai

68. In which city were 2016 Olympic Games held?
A. Rio de Janeiro B. Beijing
C. Sydney D. Tokyo

69. Ligaments and Tendons in the body are made up of:
A. Skeletal Tissue B. Muscular Tissue
C. Connective Tissue D. Epithelial Tissue

70. Which place is referred to as "Land of Midnight Sun"?
A. Japan B. Korea
C. Norway D. Finland

71. Who among the following was known as "Punjab Kesari" ?
A. Lala Lajpat Rai
B. Bal Gangadhar Tilak
C. Sardar Patel
D. Pt. Madan Mohan Malviya

72. India's National Academy of Literature is called:
A. Lalit Kala Akademi B. Kalakshetra Foundation
C. Sahitya Akademi D. Swadesh Darshan

73. In which of the following years was the first Battle of Panipat fought?
A. 1526 AD B. 1527 AD
C. 1539 AD D. 1556 AD

74. Who gave us these famous lines—*"Sarfaroshi ki Tamanna, Ab hamare dil mein hai"*?
A. Ram Prasad Bismil B. Bhagat Singh
C. Bal Gangadhar Tilak D. Dr. Mohammed Iqbal

56. A	**57.** B	**58.** A	**59.** C	**60.** D	**61.** B	**62.** B	**63.** B	**64.** B	**65.** D
66. D	**67.** B	**68.** A	**69.** C	**70.** C	**71.** A	**72.** C	**73.** A	**74.** A	

75. In which year did Rakesh Sharma, the first Indian go to space?
A. 1969 B. 1973
C. 1984 D. 1997

76. Which of the following is not a disease of bones?
A. Arthritis B. Gout
C. Rickets D. Leukemia

77. Which of the following is used to measure Atmospheric Pressure?
A. Altimeter B. Barometer
C. Hydrometer D. Thermometer

78. Who is associated with the invention of Aeroplane?
A. Sir Frank Whittle B. G. Daimler
C. Etienne Oehmichen D. Wilbur Wright

79. In which year was NITI Aayog established?
A. 2012 B. 2015
C. 2017 D. 2018

80. Who is the present Chief Justice of India?
A. Justice Dipak Mishra
B. Justice T.S. Thakur
C. Justice H.L. Lahoti
D. Justice Chandra Chud

81. Which of the following is not our fundamental right as per our Constitution?
A. Right to Equality
B. Right to Freedom of Religion
C. Right to Freedom
D. Right for Exploitation

82. Which is the local regional language of Bihar State?
A. Bhojpuri B. Bundeli
C. Bihari D. Khasi

83. Japanese art of flower arrangement is known as:
A. Ikebana B. Bonsai
C. Ongami D. Moribana

84. Solar eclipse occurs when:
A. Earth comes between Sun and Moon.
B. Moon is at right angle to the Earth.
C. Moon comes between Sun and Earth.
D. Sun comes between Moon and Earth.

85. Acid Rain is caused due to:
A. Deforestation
B. Carbon dioxide
C. Carbon monoxide
D. Oxides of Sulphur and Nitrogen

86. Which country has the largest rail network in the world?
A. India B. UK
C. China D. USA

87. Which of these major International Lawn Tennis Event is played on Grass Court?
A. US open B. Wimbledon
C. Australian open D. French open

88. Super computer "PARAM" was developed by:
A. TATA B. IIT Kharagpur
C. IIT Kanpur D. C–DAC

89. Which of the following Vitamin is excreted by humans in urine?
A. Vitamin A B. Vitamin D
C. Vitamin C D. Vitamin E

90. In which field, did Professor Amartya Sen receive the Nobel Prize?
A. Literature B. Sports
C. Economics D. Music

ENGLISH LANGUAGE AND COMPREHENSION

Directions (Qs. No. 91-96): *Fill in the blank with suitable alternatives given:*

91. She _______ silver medal in the race.
A. have got
B. has got
C. did not got
D. does not gets

92. Once she has signed the deal papers, she won't be able to _______ .
A. Backup B. Back in
C. Back it D. Back out

93. The crew was afraid, but the captain _______ them that there was no danger.
A. promised B. advised
C. assured D. commented

94. The two groups have been engaged in a bitter _______ for the past three decades.
A. fight B. intent
C. arrangement D. event

95. My house help _______ with all my money.
A. Have escape B. Has run away
C. Was run away D. Running away

75. C	**76.** D	**77.** B	**78.** D	**79.** B	**80.** D	**81.** D	**82.** A	**83.** A	**84.** C	**85.** D
86. D	**87.** B	**88.** D	**89.** C	**90.** C	**91.** B	**92.** D	**93.** C	**94.** B	**95.** B	

96. The audience listened to the artist with ________ attention.

A. Rapt B. Wrapped
C. Roped D. Rapped

Directions (Qs. No. 97-102): *Find out which part of the sentence has an error and choose that part as your answer out of (A), (B) and (C). If the sentence is free from any error, then choose your answer as choice (D).*

97. A. I was taken with surprise
B. When I saw
C. The beautiful building of Red Fort
D. No error

98. A. Freedom Fighters laboured
B. To the good of
C. The poor enslaved masses
D. No error

99. A. I was shocked to hear
B. That her son
C. died of an accident
D. No error

100. A. No one wants to drive to work anymore
B. Because of the rally
C. At such an hour
D. No error

101. A. Essay writing is an art
B. That requires many planning
C. On the part of the writer
D. No error

102. A. He seldom or ever
B. Goes to meet
C. His parents
D. No error

Directions (Qs. No. 103-108): *Four alternatives are given for the Idiom/Phrase given below. Choose the alternative which best expresses the meaning of the Idiom/Phrase.*

103. To turn a deaf ear
A. To show one's deaf ear to a Doctor
B. To disregard totally
C. To pay attention to
D. Not to come to the point

104. He surprised everyone by his performance and proved to be a dark horse.
A. A pedigree horse B. Favourite in race
C. Unexpected winner D. A difficult player

105. To break the ice
A. To keep cool
B. To break silence by speaking first
C. To start work
D. To break the idea

106. A red letter day
A. An unimportant Day
B. A festive occasion
C. An insignificant Day
D. An important Day

107. To be at sixes and sevens
A. To be Burdened
B. To be a great success
C. To be uncertain
D. To be extravagant

108. Bag of Bones
A. A very thin person
B. A bag full of Bones
C. A dead person
D. A carcass

Directions (Qs. No. 109-115): *Out of the four alternatives, choose the word which best expresses the meaning of the given word:*

109. METICULOUS
A. FALSE B. CAREFUL
C. CASUAL D. CAREFREE

110. BARTER
A. SEIZE B. REMOVE
C. STEAL D. EXCHANGE

111. ACCOLADE
A. CLUMSY B. PRAISE
C. INACTIVE D. ORTHODOX

112. YARD STICK
A. STANDARD B. STATISTICS
C. MARK D. SIZE

113. TEDIOUS
A. PAINFUL B. TIRESOME
C. TROUBLESOME D. LENGTHY

114. DEPLETE
A. DESTROY B. JOY
C. EXHAUST D. FINISH

115. RECTIFY
A. CORRECT B. TO COMMAND
C. DESTROY D. TO BUILD

96. A	**97.** A	**98.** B	**99.** C	**100.** D	**101.** B	**102.** A	**103.** B	**104.** C	**105.** B
106. D	**107.** C	**108.** A	**109.** B	**110.** D	**111.** B	**112.** A	**113.** B	**114.** C	**115.** A

Directions (Qs. No. 116-121): *Choose the word opposite in meaning to the given word:*

116. AUTHENTIC
A. GENUINE B. RELIABLE
C. VALID D. FICTITIOUS

117. BRITTLE
A. STRONG B. FRAIL
C. FRAGILE D. DISMAL

118. COMPASSION
A. KINDNESS B. SYMPATHY
C. CRUELTY D. EMPATHY

119. DISASTER
A. CALAMITY B. PROSPERITY
C. MISFORTUNE D. MISHAP

120. FATIGUE
A. VIGOUR B. EXHAUSTED
C. TIREDNESS D. WEAKNESS

121. MODERATE
A. LIMITED B. REASONABLE
C. LENIENT D. EXCESSIVE

Directions (Qs. No. 122-127): *Four words are given, out of which one word is spelt correctly. Choose the correctly spelt word:*

122. A. LAIESON B. LASION
C. LASSION D. LIAISON

123. A. IMMENCE B. IMMENSE
C. IMENCE D. IMMENZE

124. A. HOLISTIC B. HOLEISTIC
C. HOLESSTICE D. WHOLISTIC

125. A. PROPIRTY B. PROPERTY
C. PROPRITARY D. PROPORITY

126. A. PREMMISES B. PREMIISES
C. PREMISES D. PREEMISES

127. A. ASSIMILATED B. ASSIIMILATED
C. ASCIMILATED D. ASCEIMILATED

Directions (Qs. No. 128-135): *A part of the sentence is underlined, below are alternatives (A), (B), (C) which may improve the sentence. Choose the correct alternative. Choose (D) if no improvement is required.*

128. Ram is wearing his hat as it is getting very cold.
A. getting on B. putting on
C. taking on D. no improvement

129. The Host offered the coffee but I denied it.
A. said no B. rejected
C. refused D. no improvement

130. The teacher gave the students some advice.
A. Advices B. Advise
C. Advises D. No improvement

131. Few men were knocked down by a speeding car.
A. Turned down B. Pulled down
C. Brought down D. No improvement

132. Seema was working overtime for the last few weeks.
A. working B. Is being working
C. Has been working D. No improvement

133. The floor of the hall was covered by a carpet.
A. Covered in B. Covered with
C. Covered upon D. No improvement

134. This house is belonging to me for two years.
A. Had been belonging B. Is belongs
C. Has belonged D. No improvement

135. He has a very good command on Mathematics.
A. to B. of
C. in D. no improvement

Directions (Qs. No. 136-139): *Fill in the blank:*

136. I ________ him since my childhood
A. know B. has been knowing
C. have known D. had been known

137. It ________ raining here for two hours.
A. have been raining B. has been raining
C. have has been D. had has been

138. The army has been ________ to be ready to control the floods.
A. Awakened B. Alerted
C. Warned D. Wanted

139. I see certain problems in ________ execution of this plan.
A. the B. a
C. an D. on

Directions (Qs. No. 140-145): *Find out which part of the sentence has an error and choose that part as your answer out of (A), (B), and (C). If the sentence is free from any error, then choose your answer as choice (D).*

140. A. We know where it begins
B. But we don't know
C. That where it ends
D. No error

116. D	**117.** A	**118.** C	**119.** B	**120.** A	**121.** D	**122.** D	**123.** B	**124.** A	**125.** B
126. C	**127.** A	**128.** B	**129.** C	**130.** B	**131.** D	**132.** C	**133.** B	**134.** A	**135.** B
136. C	**137.** B	**138.** B	**139.** A	**140.** C					

141. A. Beware of
B. A fair weather friend
C. Who is neither a friend in a need nor a friend in deed
D. No error

142. A. Seldom we have been treated
B. In such a rude manner
C. By the police personnel
D. No error

143. A. The property
B. Was divided
C. Among the two brothers
D. No error

144. A. Long life is good
B. If one be happy
C. and has friends
D. No error

145. A. His assistants have
B. And are still doing
C. Excellent work for the organisation
D. No error

Directions (Qs. No. 146-150): *Based on your understanding of the passage, answer the questions given below:*

India is home to an estimated 10% of the global Snow Leopard population spread across five Himalayan states of Jammu and Kashmir, Himachal Pradesh, Uttarakhand, Sikkim and Arunachal Pradesh which is only 5% of the available global habitat for the animal.

Project Snow Leopard was introduced in India by the Project Snow Leopard Committee instituted by the Ministry of Environment and Forests, Government of India, in the year 2009 to safeguard and conserve India's unique natural heritage of high-altitude wildlife populations and their habitats by promoting conservation through participatory policies and actions.

Project Tiger and Project Elephant are prevalent in India with the former introduced in 1973 garnering worldwide attention.

The Snow Leopard usually occurs at an altitude of >2700 m above sea level and is the apex predator in the Himalayan Region along with the Tibetan Wolf. The project is not only to protect the Snow Leopard, but as with Project Tiger, it is considered an umbrella species and with its protection, comes the protection of other species and the habitat which they are all a part of.

Top 3 National Parks in India where the Snow Leopard can likely be seen:

Kibber Wildlife Sanctuary—Himachal Pradesh

Ulley Valley—Ladakh

Hemis National Park—Himachal Pradesh

The reasons for introduction of Project Snow-Leopard are as follows:

(*i*) High altitudes of India >3000 m including the Himalayan & Trans-Himalayan biogeographic zones support a unique wildlife assemblage of global conservation.

(*ii*) There has been relatively less attention on the region from the viewpoint of wildlife conservation.

(*iii*) The region represents a vast rangeland system supporting important traditional pastoral economic and lifestyles.

(*iv*) The region provides essential ecosystem services and harbours river systems vital for the nation's food security.

(*v*) India has ratified international agreements promoting the conservation of high-altitude wildlife species such as the snow leopard.

(*vi*) The region is important for the country's national security as well as international relations.

(*vii*) The high-altitude wildlife in India today faces a variety of threats.

(*viii*) The existing high altitude protected areas in India require considerable strengthening.

(*ix*) Wildlife Management in the region needs to be made participatory.

146. What is the purpose of the above passage/study?
A. Snow Leopards are vulnerable species and must be protected.
B. Are dangerous and must be left to die
C. Are aggressive
D. Are rigid species

147. What do you mean by the phrase "Snow Leopard is considered an umbrella species"?
A. They mate under the umbrella.
B. Species whose protection will insure protection of other species.
C. They live under the umbrella
D. They sleep under the umbrella

141. D **142.** A **143.** C **144.** B **145.** A **146.** A **147.** B

148. According to the passage high altitude regions should be protected. Why?
A. As they are cold and beautiful
B. As they are at a height
C. As they support unique wildlife of global significance
D. As it is a dynamic region

149. According to the passage what is integral to the nation's food security?
A. Wildlife
B. Population
C. Fresh air
D. River systems

150. Which Himalayan States comes under the Himalayan Region?
A. J & K, Himachal, Uttarakhand, Sikkim, Arunachal Pradesh
B. Delhi
C. Rajasthan
D. Raipur

APTITUDE FOR SERVICE SECTOR

151. Your friend shouts at you due to some misunderstanding. She thinks that you have been creating problems in her personal life, you would:
A. Shout back to her
B. Tell others that she is in a habit of doing it
C. Leave her and not talk to her
D. Make the first move to clear the misunderstanding

152. While returning home, after watching a late night movie show you found two people arguing loudly on the way, you will:
A. Ignore them and go your way
B. Ask them not to shout in the midnight
C. Inform the Police
D. Intervene between them, settle the argument amicably and proceed to your home

153. You have joined a company. People around you are quite friendly and helpful. What would you do to start a conversation with them?
A. Smile at everyone and say hello.
B. Go right up to everyone who seems approachable and start talking positively.
C. Take part in discussion that deal with work only.
D. Behave very formally.

154. Your best friend has invited you for a lunch but the same day you came to know about the interviews in the 'Job Placement Cell' of your college.
A. Enjoy with your friend and you will attend such interviews next time.
B. Ring up your friend and explain the whole situation.
C. You miss the interviews and leave for lunch.
D. You keep grumbling and you are confused.

155. While travelling in your car, certain persons stop you on the way and asks you to take an injured child to the hospital. You would:
A. Ask them to leave your way and then drive away.
B. Ask them to first call the police.
C. Immediately take the child to the hospital.
D. Get out of the car and ask some other person for help and will request him for taking the child to hospital.

156. When somebody asks your views regarding an issue:
A. You fail to give a realistic and precise answer.
B. Your views are dependent on other's views.
C. You diplomatically answer in a very realistic and straight forward manner.
D. Say anything that comes to your mind.

157. You are a member of a leading music group. During the performance, a judge asks you to step forward and sing alone as you are the main singer of the group.
A. You get distracted as the rest of the group is not with you.
B. You concentrate on your singing to perform your level best.
C. You form the opinion that you are going to be thrown out of the group.
D. You keep thinking why you were asked to sing alone and remain confused throughout.

158. Whenever Aman is free he likes to do painting, what type of Aptitude Aman has?
A. Ability
B. Interest
C. Weakness
D. None of the above

159. An Epidemic spread in your village due to poor hygiene conditions, you will:
A. Try to educate people about hygiene.
B. Ignore as it is the job of Government.
C. Intervene only if your family member get suffered.
D. Shift to the other village.

148. C **149.** D **150.** A **151.** D **152.** C, D **153.** A **154.** B **155.** C **156.** C **157.** B **158.** B **159.** A

160. You went, out of India, for higher studies. Due to financial conditions your parents are unable to send you money. You will:
A. Leave your studies and come back to India.
B. Do a part time job and complete your studies.
C. Leave the studies and do full time job.
D. Build a pressure on your parents to send you money.

161. While talking to your friend on the phone, you realize some one from the back is playing your favourite song. Then in this situation:
A. Tell your friend that you are listening to the song.
B. You are able to understand what your friend is saying and keep listening to the song along with the conversation.
C. Try to do both things together but cannot do either.
D. Forget about the song and concentrate on your friend's voice.

162. You are going to school on Bike and all of a sudden the Bike breaks down. You ring up to your father and he says that he will be there in half an hour. You cannot do anything except waiting for him. You:
A. Continue to sit patiently and keep waiting for your father.
B. Feel a bit scared.
C. Experience extreme panic as the waiting period increases
D. Decide to go to any house nearby as it is getting more scary.

163. You are alone at home when one of your niece gets badly hurt:
A. You start feeling panicky.
B. You ask for your neighbour's help
C. You call up your parents and ask them to come fast.
D. You call the family doctor immediately and go and sit beside her to keep watch in the meantime.

164. Your maid has invited you to her daughter's wedding. You would:
A. Completely ignore her.
B. Attend the wedding.
C. Buy a gift for her daughter and help in wedding.
D. Congratulate her and make up some excuse for not being able to attend.

165. You were discussing some important issue with one of your colleague and you end up having a fight. You would:
A. Ignore the whole situation and start chatting with others.
B. Blame her and move ahead.
C. Sit with her, and try to clarify things to sort out the matter.
D. Promise to your self that you will never talk to her in future.

166. If you have to prepare for your exam and at the same time prepare your project report, you will:
A. Do one thing at a time and plan out a Time Table and work accordingly.
B. Become anxious and impulsively do the tasks just for the sake of getting over with them.
C. Try to do all the tasks at the same time.
D. Keep crying without being able to work effectively at any tasks.

167. You have been asked to complete your work but others plan to leave the work and enjoy themselves at the Carnival.
A. You also start thinking the same way.
B. You do your work as there is no fun in taking chances for such an important work.
C. Ask your friends as well to do the work.
D. Leave your friends thinking they have a non-serious attitude towards work.

168. You are in a cinema hall watching a movie, you see a snake in front of your leg, you will:
A. Remain cool, warn others, notify the hall authorities.
B. Start shouting that no one should move.
C. Shout to switch on lights.
D. Take snake and place it outside.

169. You are very tired and have to do some important work. You:
A. Keep thinking that you are tired and won't be able to work.
B. Do the work whole heartedly.
C. Would do it without thinking that you can make errors.
D. Finish it off.

170. Your teacher tells you in advance that a certain project needs to be completed within two weeks time. You would:
A. Do the work patiently and complete it within the given time.
B. Leave the work for a while thinking that it will be done later.
C. Feel panicky and start devoting all your time to it.
D. Ignore the work thinking that its just a day's job.

160. B **161.** D **162.** A **163.** D **164.** C **165.** C **166.** A **167.** B **168.** A **169.** B **170.** A

171. You work in a Call center and a customer is angry and yelling at you on the phone. What is the best course of action?
A. Yell back at the customer
B. Apologize and try to calm down the customer
C. Argue with the customer
D. Ignore the complaint of customer

172. You work in a hotel and some guests complain about the noise level in their room. What is the best course of action?
A. Offer them earplugs.
B. Ignore their complaint.
C. Apologize and move them to a different room.
D. Tell them there's nothing you can do.

173. You are staying in a hostel, every day in the night seniors comes to your room and disturb you, first person whom you will inform would be:
A. Local Police Station
B. Principal of the college
C. Hostel Warden
D. Help Line Number

174. While dining at a reputed Restaurant you ordered vegetarian soup but you have been served with non-vegetarian soup. You will:
A. Call the server shout at him/her.
B. Forget the incident and do nothing about it.
C. Leave the restaurant immediately.
D. Call the manager and complain to him/her.

175. A Food Festival is to be organized at your college by group of students. You:
A. Volunteer for the group
B. Plan how to stop Food Festival
C. Not to bothered about it
D. Try to make another group and challenge the same

176. You are a telephone operator in a hotel, there is no call in waiting. You will:
A. Go and help in other department
B. Quit your seat and relax in the locker room
C. Be attentive on your given job only
D. Listen music through a pair of ear-phones

177. You have been sent to a monument for cleanliness project, as a group leader, your job is:
A. Only to supervise
B. Work with Team
C. Go away after giving task
D. Ask them to work only for photos

178. Light bulbs of the Park in your locality are not working, you will:
A. Pool money and get it repaired
B. Inform the Local Authorities
C. Ignore the situation
D. Ask people not to go to the Park

179. Your team has failed to achieve the given targets; As the captain of team:
A. Take all blame on yourself for the defeat.
B. Blame your team for the same.
C. Try to find out the reasons for not achieving the targets.
D. Resign from the organization.

180. A fight takes place between two employees at the hotel. As a Manager, what will you do?
A. Try to convince both to stop fighting and find a solution of the problem.
B. Handover the situation to your Junior.
C. Call Police and handover both employees to the police.
D. You also involve yourself in fighting.

181. While working in a group, you will:
A. Never participate in activity.
B. Share your ideas with others.
C. Based on listening others, you agree with them.
D. Dominate with your ideas over the others.

182. You have been given the responsibility of Class Monitor, you would:
A. Request your teacher not to give this responsibility
B. Request your friend to take this responsibility.
C. Gracefully take this responsibility as a new learning.
D. Ask you parents to talk to Principal for not giving this responsibility.

183. What do you do when you reach in meeting without preparation?
A. Make excuses to convince other members.
B. Admit your reason for being not prepared.
C. Try to escape from meeting
D. Do not attend the meeting only

184. In a class room, you find a topic which is very tough. The best thing you can do is :
A. Leave the class.
B. Ask your friend to teach you after the class.
C. In the class itself ask your teacher to repeat the topic.
D. Nothing can be done about it.

171. B	**172.** C	**173.** C	**174.** D	**175.** A	**176.** C	**177.** B	**178.** B	**179.** C	**180.** A
181. B	**182.** C	**183.** B	**184.** C						

185. You are transferred in a department which is not of your interest, you will?
A. Make mistakes so that you are transferred back to your interested department.
B. Give time limit to the management for transferring back.
C. Resign from the company.
D. Work hard and try to prove yourself in new department.

186. You find a person entering your restaurant on a wheel chair, you will:
A. Rush to open the door.
B. Not bother about the same.
C. Be agitated due to shortage of space in restaurant.
D. Ask the person that his food will be served in the room.

187. As a manager, you notice there has been repeated customer complaints against the smell of carpet of a particular room, you will:
A. Permanently block the room.
B. Ignore the complaint.
C. Remove the carpet from the room.
D. Replace the carpet with a new one.

188. Discipline, Hard work and Dedication are the essential requirements to be a successful hotel operator, upon getting this information:
A. Vouch never to become an hotel operator.
B. You ignore as you are not interested in Hotel Jobs.
C. You take this as a challenge to be a successful hotel operator.
D. You start wondering about the work pressure.

189. As a teacher, you have asked to select a team for Annual Day Celebration. You would select students:
A. Only those who are close to you.
B. Only those who would do whatever you ask.
C. Only those who are ready to adopt to any situation they may come across.
D. Those who are close to you; those who would do anything when asked and those who are ready to adopt to any situation they may come across.

190. You are working in a hotel, a fire breaks out. You would
A. Come back home and relax.
B. Go to a safe distance and watch.
C. Secure the children and the aged people first before you try to help others.
D. Panic and run away.

191. You were going through with a guest bill which was prepared and checked by your staff. You noticed a mistake. You would:
A. Take him to General Manager of hotel.
B. Go and speak to the concerned staff yourself without creating a fuss.
C. Transfer the concerned staff.
D. Permanently remove the concerned staff.

192. You have received a demanding customer in your hotel, you will:
A. Inform him that he should not behave like this.
B. Shout back and tell that you are not in a position to help.
C. Tactfully tell that his behaviour is not appropriate.
D. Make efforts to resolve the issue.

193. After receiving a Negative Feedback of your hotel, as a Manager, you would:
A. Shout on the staff.
B. Fight with the guest who has given Negative Comments.
C. Ignore the Negative Comments.
D. Take them in a positive manner and improve the standards of services.

194. In a College Mess, you are not getting food of your choice, you would:
A. Stop eating from Mess.
B. Ask Management to return back the money against the Mess Fee.
C. Speak with the Mess Incharge to add items on rotation basis of your choices.
D. Tell everyone to stop using the Mess Facility.

195. A Drunken Guest is creating problem in the lobby of hotel, as a Manager, you will:
A. Handover him to the Police.
B. Handover him to the Hotel Security.
C. Do not speak with him as he is Drunk.
D. Take him to his room and ask him to relax.

196. A delivery Boy takes more than usual time to deliver your food, you will:
A. Not take food from him
B. Not pay any amount to him
C. Stop ordering in future from that company
D. Write complaint to company about the incident

185. D **186.** A **187.** D **188.** C **189.** D **190.** C **191.** B **192.** D **193.** D **194.** C
195. D **196.** D

197. On a famous monument you see some people are writing something on walls, you will:
A. Educate them for not to write on walls
B. Ignore the situation
C. Start writing with them
D. Take photos and viral on social media

198. You have been recently promoted by the management, you would:
A. Stop performing as now you have already been promoted
B. Work hard as now you have more responsibilities
C. Start talking with every one that how you have been promoted
D. Move to the new Company

199. Eye contact with the guests represents towards:
A. Honesty and Respect
B. Disrespect and Dishonesty
C. Arrogance
D. Negative Attitude

200. Aviation, Cruise, Hotels, Travel, all these industries come under:
A. Manufacturing Industry B. Hospitality Industry
C. Cargo Industry D. Telecom Industry

EXPLANATORY ANSWERS

1. (A): Let the two numbers be $11x$ and $12x$

Then, $\text{LCM} = 11 \times 12x$

$\Rightarrow 528 = 11 \times 12x$

$\Rightarrow x = \frac{528}{11 \times 12} = \frac{44}{11} = 4$

$\therefore$ Two numbers be 11×4 and 12×4

Hence, HCF $= 4$.

2. (B): Let the two numbers are $12x$ and $12y$

Then, $\text{LCM} = 12xy$

$\Rightarrow 336 = 12xy$

$\Rightarrow xy = 28$ ...(*i*)

Given, one of the number is 48

$\Rightarrow 12x = 48 \Rightarrow x = 4$ ...(*ii*)

From (*i*) and (*ii*), we get, $y = 7$

Hence, the other number is $12y$

$= 12 \times 7 = 84$.

3. (D): $3556 = 4 \times 7 \times 127$

and $3444 = 4 \times 7 \times 123$

HCF of 3556 and 3444 $= 4 \times 7 = 28$.

4. (C): (A) HCF (16, 62) = 2

(B) HCF (23, 92) = 23

(C) HCF (18, 25) = 1

(D) HCF (21, 35) = 7

Here, (C) (18, 25) is a pair of co-primes.

5. (A): LCM of 4, 5 and 6 = 60

According to question,

$\therefore$ Required number $= 60 + 2 = 62$

(which is less than 100).

6. (A): $\because$ The sum of the first n positive integer

$= \frac{n(n+1)}{2}$

$\therefore$ The average of the first 100 positive integers

$= \frac{100(100+1)}{2 \times 100} = \frac{101}{2} = 50.5$

7. (B): Let the 7 consecutive numbers are

$x, x + 1, x + 2, x + 3, x + 4, x + 5, x + 6$

$\Rightarrow 7 \times 20 = 7x + 21$

$\Rightarrow 140 = 7x + 21$

$\Rightarrow 7x = 140 - 21$

$\Rightarrow 7x = 119 \Rightarrow x = 17$

Hence, the largest of these numbers is

$x + 6 = 17 + 6 = 23$.

8. (A): $\dfrac{\frac{7}{8}\times\frac{7}{8}+\frac{5}{6}\times\frac{5}{6}+\frac{7}{8}\times\frac{5}{3}}{\frac{7}{8}\times\frac{7}{8}-\frac{5}{6}\times\frac{5}{6}}$

$= \dfrac{\left(\frac{7}{8}\right)^2+\left(\frac{5}{6}\right)^2+2\times\frac{7}{8}\times\frac{5}{6}}{\left(\frac{7}{8}\right)^2-\left(\frac{5}{6}\right)^2}$

$= \dfrac{\left(\frac{7}{8}+\frac{5}{6}\right)^2}{\left(\frac{7}{8}+\frac{5}{6}\right)\left(\frac{7}{8}-\frac{5}{6}\right)} = \dfrac{\frac{7}{8}+\frac{5}{6}}{\frac{7}{8}-\frac{5}{6}}$

$= \dfrac{\frac{21+20}{24}}{\frac{21-20}{24}} = \frac{41}{24} \times \frac{24}{1} = 41.$

197. A	**198.** B	**199.** A	**200.** B

9. (D): $\sqrt{218+\sqrt{37+\sqrt{144}}} = k$

$\Rightarrow \sqrt{218+\sqrt{37+12}} = k$

$\Rightarrow \sqrt{218+\sqrt{49}} = k$

$\Rightarrow \sqrt{218+7} = k$

$\Rightarrow \sqrt{225} = k$

$\Rightarrow k = 15.$

10. (C): Given, $\sqrt{x}+14 = \sqrt{2601}$

$\Rightarrow \sqrt{x}+14 = 51$

$\Rightarrow \sqrt{x} = 51 - 14 = 37$

$\Rightarrow \sqrt{x} = 37$

$\Rightarrow x = 1369.$

11. (A): $\frac{2}{7}\% = \frac{\frac{2}{7}}{100} = \frac{2}{700} = \frac{1}{350}.$

12. (D): $t = \frac{(n-1)\times 100}{r}$

$= \frac{(2-1)\times 100}{\frac{25}{4}} = 100\times\frac{4}{25}$

$= 4 \times 4 = 16$ years.

13. (D): Let sum of money = P

then, Simple interest $= \frac{4}{9}P$

Given, $t = r$

$\because$ S.I. $= \frac{Prt}{100}$

$\therefore \frac{4}{9}P = \frac{P\times r\times r}{100}$

$\Rightarrow \frac{4}{9} = \frac{r^2}{100}$

$\Rightarrow r^2 = \frac{400}{9}$

$\Rightarrow r = \frac{20}{3} = 6\frac{2}{3}\%.$

14. (B): Let the present age of elder and younger person be x years and y years

Then, $x - y = 16$ ...(*i*)

Given, 6 years ago,

$x - 6 = 3(y - 6)$

$\Rightarrow x - 6 = 3y - 18$

$\Rightarrow x - 3y = -12$ ...(*ii*)

From solving (*i*) and (*ii*), we get,

$2y = 28$

$\Rightarrow y = 14$ and $x = 30$

Here, present age of elder one is

$x = 30$ years.

15. (D): Let 6 years ago, the ages of Ram and Ravi was $6x$ years and $5x$ years

Then, the present ages of Ram and Ravi be $(6x + 6)$ years and $(5x + 6)$ years

Now, 4 years hence,

$(6x + 6 + 4) : (5x + 6 + 4) = 11 : 10$

$\Rightarrow (6x + 10) \times 10 = (5x + 10) \times 11$

$\Rightarrow 60x + 100 = 55x + 110$

$\Rightarrow 60x - 55x = 110 - 100$

$\Rightarrow 5x = 10 \Rightarrow x = 2$

$\therefore$ Ravi's age of present $= 5x + 6$

$= 5 \times 2 + 6 = 16$ years.

16. (A): Let the ages of A and B are $6x$ years and $5x$ years

Then, $6x + 5x = 44$

$\Rightarrow 11x = 44 \Rightarrow x = 4$

$\therefore$ The ratio of their ages after 8 years

$= (6x + 8) : (5x + 8)$

$= (6 \times 4 + 8) : (5 \times 4 + 8)$

$= 32 : 28 = 8 : 7.$

17. (C): The Speed of the train

$= \frac{\text{Distance}}{\text{Time}}$

$= \frac{160+160}{16} = \frac{320}{16} = 20$ m/s

$= 20\times\frac{18}{5}$ km/h = 72 km/h.

18. (D): Let the speed of the boat in still water is x km/hr

Then, Speed of boat upstream $= x - 3$

$\Rightarrow \frac{7}{\frac{42}{60}} = x - 3$

$\Rightarrow \frac{7}{42}\times 60 = x - 3$

$\Rightarrow 10 = x - 3$

$\Rightarrow x = 10 + 3$

$\Rightarrow x = 13$ km/h.

19. (A): Let the original number be x

Then, $x \times \frac{125}{100} - x \times \frac{70}{100} = 22$

$\Rightarrow \quad \frac{5}{4}x - \frac{7}{10}x = 22$

$\Rightarrow \quad \frac{25x - 14x}{20} = 22$

$\Rightarrow \quad 11x = 22 \times 20$

$\Rightarrow \quad x = 40.$

20. (B): Let A and B be the sets of students who failed in Hindi and English respectively.

Then, $n(A) = 35$, $n(B) = 45$

$n(A \cap B) = 20$

So, $n(A \cup B) = n(A) + n(B) - n(A \cap B)$

$\Rightarrow n(A \cup B) = 35 + 45 - 20$

$\Rightarrow n(A \cup B) = 60$

$\therefore$ Percentage failed in Hindi or English or both $= 60\%$

Hence, percentage passed

$= 100 - 60$

$= 40\%$ in both the subjects.

21. (A): Let the S.P. of item = ₹ 1

Then, S.P. of 25 items = ₹ 25

C.P. of 25 items = S.P. of 30 items

= ₹ 30

$\because$ Loss = C.P. − S.P.

= 30 − 25 = ₹ 5

$\therefore$ Loss per cent $= \frac{\text{Loss} \times 100}{\text{C.P.}}$

$= \frac{5 \times 100}{30}$

$= \frac{100}{6} = \frac{50}{3} = 16\frac{2}{3}\%.$

22. (D): Given, S.P. − C.P. = ₹ 240 ...(*i*)

$\Rightarrow$ Profit = ₹ 240

and profit % = 20%

$\Rightarrow$ Profit % $= \frac{\text{Profit} \times 100}{\text{C.P.}}$

$\Rightarrow \quad 20 = \frac{240 \times 100}{\text{C.P.}}$

$\Rightarrow$ C.P. $= \frac{240 \times 100}{40}$

= ₹ 1200

From (*i*),

$\because$ S.P. − 1200 = 240

$\therefore$ S.P. = 240 + 1200

$\Rightarrow$ Selling price = ₹ 1440.

23. (A): Cost of $1\frac{1}{2} = \frac{3}{2}$ litres milk = ₹ 20

$\Rightarrow$ Cost of 1 litre milk $= 20 \times \frac{2}{3} = \frac{40}{3}$

Let x litres of water must be added to 60 litres of milk

Then, $(60 + x) \times \frac{32}{3} = 60 \times \frac{40}{3}$

$\Rightarrow \quad 60 \times 32 + 32x = 60 \times 40$

$\Rightarrow \quad 32x = 60 \times 40 - 60 \times 32$

$\Rightarrow \quad 32x = 60(40 - 32)$

$= 60 \times 8$

$\Rightarrow \quad x = \frac{60 \times 8}{32} = 15$

Hence, $x = 15$ litres.

24. (C): Let the work was completed in x days

Then, $\frac{x-2}{10} + \frac{x}{20} = 1$

$\Rightarrow \quad \frac{2(x-2) + x}{20} = 1$

$\Rightarrow \quad 2x - 4 + x = 20$

$\Rightarrow \quad 3x - 4 = 20$

$\Rightarrow \quad 3x = 24 \Rightarrow x = 8$

$\therefore$ Required days $= x = 8.$

25. (C): Let x years ago was the ratio of their ages 3 : 5

Then, $(40 - x) : (60 - x) = 3 : 5$

$\Rightarrow (40 - x) \times 5 = (60 - x) \times 3$

$\Rightarrow \quad 200 - 5x = 180 - 3x$

$\Rightarrow \quad 200 - 180 = 5x - 3x$

$\Rightarrow \quad 2x = 20$

$\Rightarrow \quad x = 10$ years.

26. (B): Let the distance of his destination from his starting point is x km

Then, $\frac{x}{3} - \frac{40}{60} = \frac{x}{4} + \frac{30}{60}$

$\Rightarrow \quad \frac{x}{3} - \frac{x}{4} = \frac{30}{60} + \frac{40}{60}$

$\Rightarrow \quad \frac{4x - 3x}{12} = \frac{70}{60}$

$\Rightarrow \quad \frac{x}{12} = \frac{7}{6}$

$\Rightarrow \quad x = 14$ km

Hence, the distance of destination $= x$

$= 14$ km.

27. (C): Let a number be x and Quotient be y

Then, $x = 195 \times y + 47$

$= 15 \times 13y + 15 \times 3 + 2$

$= 15(13y + 3) + 2$

Hence, the remainder will be 2.

28. (B): Part filled by (A + B) in 1 minute

$= \frac{1}{20} + \frac{1}{30} = \frac{3+2}{60} = \frac{5}{60} = \frac{1}{12}$

Hence, it (two pipes) will take 12 minutes to fill the tank.

29. (B): Given, Total number of digits = 366 pages

Total number of digits = Number of digits in 1-digit page numbers + Number of digits in 2-digit page numbers + Number of digits in 3-digit page numbers

$= 1 \times 9 + 2 \times 90 + 3 \times (366 - 99)$

$= 9 + 180 + 3(267)$

$= 189 + 801$

$= 990.$

30. (A): $\left[35.7 - \left(3 + \frac{1}{3 + \frac{1}{3}}\right) - \left(2 + \frac{1}{2 + \frac{1}{2}}\right)\right]$

$= \left[35.7 - \left(3 + \frac{1}{\frac{10}{3}}\right) - \left(2 + \frac{1}{\frac{5}{2}}\right)\right]$

$= \left[35.7 - \left(3 + \frac{3}{10}\right) - \left(2 + \frac{2}{5}\right)\right]$

$= [35.7 - 3.3 - 2.4]$

$= [35.7 - 5.7] = 30.$

35. (B):

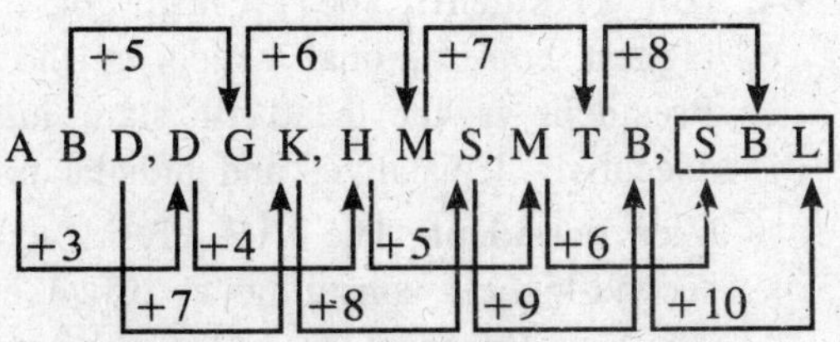

Here, ? = SBL.

40. (A): Given, P U P I L

+2 +2 +2 +2 +2

R W R K N

Similarly, R O A S T

+2 +2 +2 +2 +2

T Q C U V

Hence, ROAST is written in that code as TQCUV.

41. (C): Triangles in the given figure are:

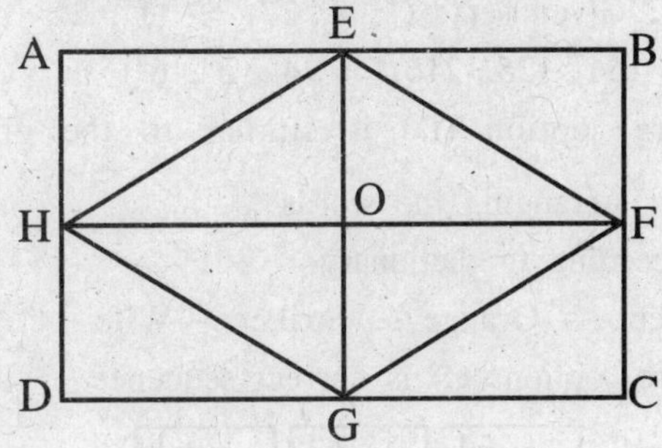

ΔAEH, ΔEOH, ΔBEF, ΔEOF, ΔHOG, ΔHDG, ΔOFG, ΔFGC, ΔEHF, ΔEHG, ΔHGF, ΔGFE

Here, the number of triangles in the given figure is 12.

43. (C): From given figure,

The sum of the numbers which belong to one figure-only

$= 1 + 3 + 1 + 4 + 7 + 5$

$= 21.$

45. (A): Given, room = bed

bed = window

window = flower

flower = cooler

Here, A man would sleep on window.

46. (B): From given figure,

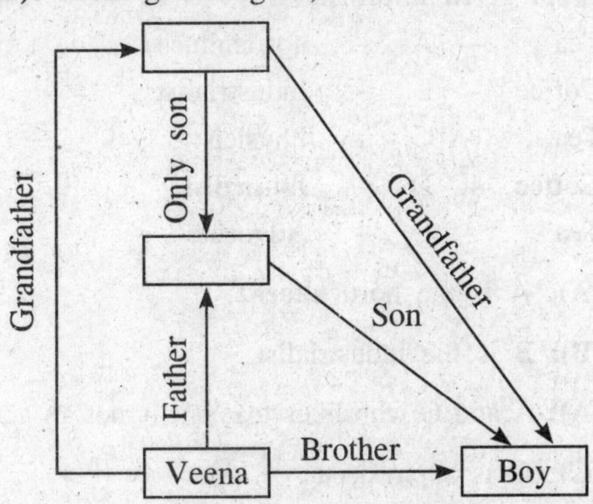

Here, Boy is the brother of Veena.

47. (C): From given figure,

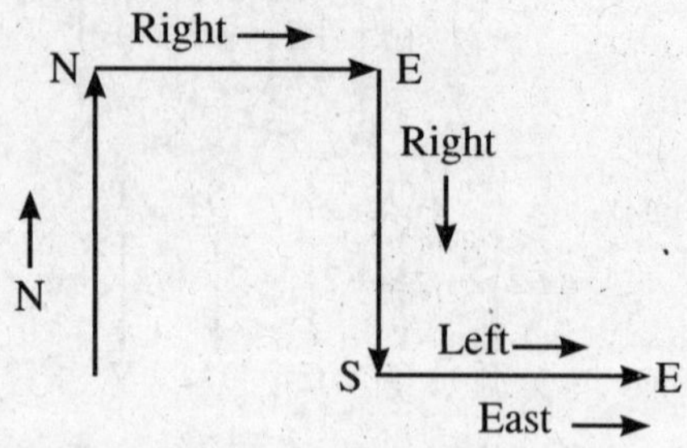

Here, you are now in East direction.

49. (D): Given set : (1, 8, 27) ⇒ $(1^3, 2^3, 3^3)$

(D) (64, 125, 216) ⇒ $(4^3, 5^3, 6^3)$

Here, option (D) is similar to the given set.

50. (C): Arranging the words:

According to dictionary

Effect → Orange → Strike → Wife

Here, option (C) is correct sequence.

52. (A):

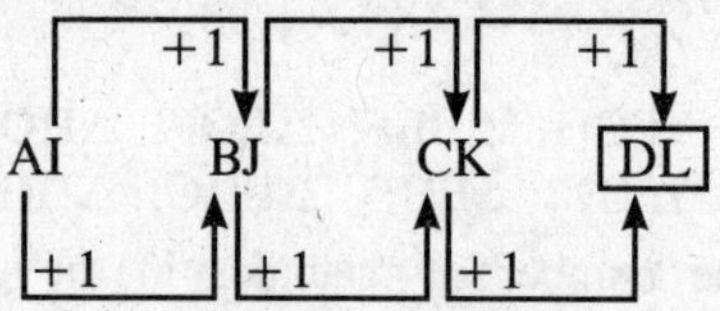

Here, ? = the missing term = DL.

53. (C): C4X, F9U, I16R, L25O

⇒ $C2^2X$, $F3^2U$, $I4^2R$, $L5^2O$

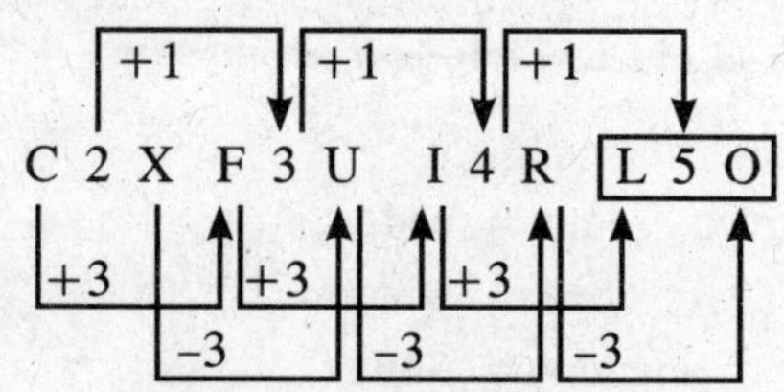

Here, ? = the missing term = L25O.

For Qs. No. 56-60:

From given information,

Tea	–	A	–	horticulturist
Coffee	–	B	–	Industrialist
Tea	–	C	–	Physicist
Coffee	–	D	–	Journalist
Tea	–	E	–	Advocate

56. (A): A is the horticulturist.

57. (B): B is the industrialist.

58. (A): A and C who likes tea, but is not an advocate.

59. (C): C is a physicist.

60. (D): Group BD likes only Coffee.

61. (B): The Gangetic Dolphin, scientifically known as *Platanista gangetica*, is the National Aquatic Animal of India. It is primarily found in the Ganges and Brahmaputra river systems, as well as their tributaries. This species is revered in Indian culture and mythology and holds significant ecological importance as an indicator of the health of river ecosystems. Due to various threats such as pollution, habitat destruction, and overfishing, Gangetic Dolphins are considered endangered, and their conservation is essential for maintaining the health of riverine environments in India. As a result of its cultural significance and ecological importance, the Gangetic Dolphin was designated as the National Aquatic Animal of India.

62. (B): The Dhyan Chand Award is bestowed upon individuals who have contributed significantly to sports and games throughout their lifetime. It is named after Major Dhyan Chand, one of India's greatest field hockey players, renowned for his exceptional skills and achievements in the sport. The award recognizes outstanding athletes who have consistently demonstrated excellence, sportsmanship, and leadership both on and off the field over an extended period. Recipients of the Dhyan Chand Award are honored for their lifetime achievements and contributions to the promotion and development of sports in India. It is one of the highest honors conferred by the Government of India in the field of sports.

63. (B): The "Legend of Honour" is the highest civilian award bestowed by France. Established by Napoleon Bonaparte in 1802, it is awarded to individuals for outstanding achievements in various fields, including arts, sciences, literature, military, and public service. The Legend of Honour is a prestigious recognition of merit and is considered one of the most esteemed distinctions in France. Recipients of this award are recognized for their exceptional contributions to society and their significant impact on French culture, society, or the nation as a whole. The Legend of Honour is presented by the President of France on behalf of the French government.

64. (B): President: The President of India holds the highest constitutional office in the country. The President is the head of state and has certain executive, legislative, and judicial powers.

Vice President: The Vice President of India is the second-highest constitutional office in the country. The Vice President serves as the ex-officio Chairman of the Rajya Sabha, the upper house of Parliament.

Prime Minister: The Prime Minister of India is the head of government and holds the highest executive office. The Prime Minister is appointed by the President and is usually the leader of the majority party or coalition in the Lok Sabha, the lower house of Parliament.

Governor: Governors are the ceremonial heads of the states in India. Each state has its own Governor appointed by the President of India. While their powers are limited compared to the President or Prime Minister, they play an important role in state administration.

65. (D): "Tom Sawyer" is a novel written by the renowned American author Mark Twain, who was born Samuel Langhorne Clemens. The book was first published in 1876 and is considered one of Twain's most famous works, alongside "Adventures of Huckleberry Finn". The story follows the adventures of a young boy named Tom Sawyer, set in the fictional town of St. Petersburg, inspired by Twain's own childhood experiences in Hannibal, Missouri. Tom is mischievous, adventurous, and imaginative, often getting into trouble with his friends, including Huckleberry Finn and Joe Harper. Throughout the novel, Tom engages in various escapades, from playing pirates on Jackson's Island to attending his own funeral after faking his own death. The narrative captures the essence of boyhood and the joys, challenges, and moral dilemmas faced by young people growing up in a small town along the Mississippi River in the mid-19th century.

66. (D): Rabindranath Tagore, a towering figure in Indian literature, became the first Indian to win the Nobel Prize for Literature in 1913 for his work "Gitanjali," a collection of poems originally written in Bengali and later translated into English. Tagore's writing reflects a deep spiritual and philosophical resonance, exploring themes of love, nature, and the human condition with profound simplicity and elegance. His lyrical poetry and prose transcend cultural boundaries, resonating with readers worldwide and earning him international acclaim. Beyond his literary contributions, Tagore was a multifaceted figure, also known for his work as a philosopher, educator, and social reformer, leaving an indelible mark on India's cultural and intellectual landscape.

67. (B): Amjad Ali Khan is a legendary Indian classical musician known for his mastery of the sarod, a stringed instrument central to the Hindustani classical music tradition. Born into a prestigious musical lineage, Khan inherited a rich musical heritage and began training on the sarod at an early age under the guidance of his father, Ustad Hafiz Ali Khan. Over the years, he has honed his skills and developed a distinctive style characterized by intricate melodies, intricate ornamentation, and emotive expression. Khan's performances are celebrated for their technical brilliance, depth of emotion, and improvisational prowess, captivating audiences worldwide and earning him acclaim as one of the greatest sarod players of his generation. He has dedicated his life to preserving and promoting Indian classical music, collaborating with musicians from diverse cultural backgrounds and inspiring countless aspiring artists with his virtuosity and artistry.

68. (A): The 2016 Summer Olympic Games, officially known as the Games of the XXXI Olympiad, took place in Rio de Janeiro, Brazil. This marked the first time the Olympics were held in South America. Rio de Janeiro, known for its stunning natural beauty and vibrant culture, provided a picturesque backdrop for the world's top athletes to compete across various sports disciplines. Despite facing challenges such as concerns over infrastructure, security, and environmental issues, the Games showcased the spirit of unity and athleticism, with athletes from around the globe coming together to celebrate the Olympic values of friendship, respect, and excellence. The Rio Olympics left a lasting legacy for Brazil, highlighting the country's ability to host a major international sporting event and inspiring future generations of athletes and spectators alike.

69. (C): Ligaments and tendons, both composed of connective tissue, play crucial roles in the musculoskeletal system. Ligaments are strong bands of fibrous tissue that connect bones to each other within joints, providing stability and limiting excessive movement. They help prevent dislocation and control the range of motion in joints. Tendons, on the other hand, are tough, flexible cords that attach muscles to bones, transmitting the force generated by muscle contraction to produce movement. They act as a bridge between muscles and bones, enabling coordinated movement and facilitating activities such as walking, running, and lifting. Together, ligaments and tendons contribute to the overall structural integrity and functionality of the body, supporting movement, stability, and joint function.

70. (C): The "Land of the Midnight Sun" refers to regions located within or near the Arctic Circle where, during the summer months, the sun remains visible for a continuous period of 24 hours or more, leading to extended daylight hours. In Norway, particularly in the northern regions such as Tromsø and Svalbard, this phenomenon occurs due to the tilt of the Earth's axis relative to its orbit around the sun. During the summer solstice, around June 21st, the sun does not set below the horizon, resulting in a surreal experience where daylight persists throughout the night. This unique natural occurrence has captivated travelers and locals alike, offering opportunities for activities such as midnight sun hikes, wildlife viewing, and cultural festivals that celebrate the enduring sunlight of the Arctic summer.

71. (A): Lala Lajpat Rai, widely known as "Punjab Kesari" or the "Lion of Punjab," was a towering figure in India's struggle for independence from British rule. He was a key member of the Lal Bal Pal triumvirate, along with Bal Gangadhar Tilak and Bipin Chandra Pal, who advocated for Swaraj or self-rule. Rai was renowned for his fiery oratory, staunch nationalism, and unwavering dedication to the cause of Indian freedom. He played pivotal roles in various movements, including the non-cooperation movement and the Swadeshi movement, mobilizing masses against British oppression. Despite facing imprisonment and physical assaults, Rai remained undeterred in his pursuit of liberty and justice for his fellow countrymen. His legacy as a fearless leader and champion of Indian nationalism continues to inspire generations of Indians.

72. (C): India's National Academy of Literature is called Sahitya Akademi. Established in 1954, Sahitya Akademi is an autonomous organization under the Ministry of Culture, Government of India. It is responsible for promoting and preserving literature in various Indian languages and recognizing outstanding literary works through awards such as the Sahitya Akademi Award. Its mission extends beyond mere recognition; it actively fosters literary activities, supports writers and poets, organizes literary festivals, seminars, and workshops, and publishes literary works of merit. Sahitya Akademi serves as a platform for fostering cross-cultural dialogue and understanding, celebrating the rich tapestry of India's literary heritage, and nurturing the growth of contemporary literature in all its vibrant forms and expressions.

73. (A): The first Battle of Panipat, fought in 1526 AD, was a momentous event that shaped the course of Indian history. It marked the establishment of the Mughal Empire in India under the leadership of Babur, a descendant of Timur and Genghis Khan. In this battle, Babur's relatively small but disciplined army, equipped with firearms and artillery, decisively defeated the larger forces of Ibrahim Lodhi, the Sultan of Delhi, who relied mainly on traditional cavalry and infantry tactics. Babur's victory heralded the beginning of Mughal rule in India, initiating a new era characterized by cultural syncretism, architectural splendor, and administrative innovations. The Battle of Panipat demonstrated the effectiveness of gunpowder weapons in warfare and established the Mughals as a dominant force in the Indian subcontinent for centuries to come.

74. (A): The stirring lines "Sarfaroshi ki Tamanna, Ab hamare dil mein hai" were penned by Ram Prasad Bismil, a prominent revolutionary and poet of the Indian independence movement. These words encapsulate the fervent desire for sacrifice and bravery in the pursuit of freedom from British colonial rule. Bismil, along with other revolutionary leaders like Ashfaqulla Khan and Bhagat Singh, embraced the spirit of selflessness and courage, inspiring countless others to join the struggle for independence. These lines served as a powerful anthem, igniting the passion and determination of freedom fighters across the nation, who was willing to lay down their lives for the cause of liberation. Bismil's poetic expression resonated deeply with the aspirations of a nation yearning for freedom, symbolizing the indomitable spirit of the Indian people in their quest for self-rule and dignity.

75. (C): Rakesh Sharma made history in 1984 by becoming the first Indian to travel to space. Selected as part of the joint space mission between the Indian Space Research Organisation (ISRO) and the Soviet space program, Sharma embarked on his journey aboard the Soviet spacecraft Soyuz T-11. His mission was a significant milestone not only for India but also for international cooperation in space exploration. During his 8-day spaceflight, Sharma conducted scientific experiments and observations, contributing to our understanding of space and its effects on the human body. His achievement inspired generations of Indians and symbolized the country's growing capabilities in space exploration and technology. Rakesh Sharma's pioneering journey remains a source of pride and inspiration for the nation.

76. (D): The disease that is not related to bones is Leukemia. Leukemia is a cancer of the blood and bone marrow, not specifically a disease of the bones themselves. It originates in the bone marrow, where blood cells are produced, and involves the abnormal production of white blood cells. In leukemia, the bone marrow produces large numbers of abnormal white blood cells, which interfere with the normal function of healthy blood cells. On the other hand, Arthritis, Gout and Rickets all involve issues directly related to bones or bone health. Arthritis is inflammation of the joints, Gout is a form of arthritis caused by excess uric acid in the bloodstream, and Rickets is a condition caused by a deficiency of vitamin D, calcium, or phosphate, leading to weak or soft bones in children.

77. (B): A barometer is an instrument used to measure atmospheric pressure, which is the force exerted by the weight of air molecules in the Earth's atmosphere. There are different types of barometers, but the most common is the mercury barometer, invented by Evangelista Torricelli in the 17th century. It consists of a long glass tube filled with mercury and inverted in a container of mercury. The height of the mercury column in the tube changes in response to variations in atmospheric pressure. High atmospheric pressure pushes the mercury column higher, while low pressure allows it to fall. By measuring the height of the mercury column, meteorologists can determine changes in atmospheric pressure, which are crucial for predicting weather patterns and forecasting changes in the atmosphere.

78. (D): The invention of the airplane is credited to the Wright brothers, Wilbur Wright and Orville Wright. In December 1903, near Kitty Hawk, North Carolina, the Wright brothers achieved the first controlled, sustained flight of a powered, heavier-than-air aircraft. Their aircraft, the Wright Flyer, was a biplane powered by a gasoline engine designed and built by the Wright brothers themselves. Wilbur and Orville's successful flight, which lasted for 12 seconds and covered a distance of 120 feet, marked a monumental breakthrough in human history, ushering in the era of powered flight. Their pioneering work laid the foundation for modern aviation and revolutionized transportation, communication, and commerce on a global scale. The Wright brothers' achievement remains one of the most iconic and celebrated milestones in the history of technology and innovation.

79. (B): NITI Aayog, or the National Institution for Transforming India, was established in 2015 to serve as the government of India's premier policy think tank and to provide strategic and technical advice across various sectors. It replaced the Planning Commission, reflecting a shift towards a more decentralized and participative approach to policymaking. NITI Aayog's mandate includes formulating long-term strategic plans and policies for sustainable development, fostering cooperative federalism by engaging with state governments, and promoting innovation and entrepreneurship to drive economic growth and social development. By bringing together experts from different fields and leveraging data-driven analysis, NITI Aayog aims to facilitate evidence-based policymaking and catalyze transformative change to realize India's full potential as a vibrant and inclusive democracy.

80. (D): The present Chief Justice of India is Justice Dhananjaya Y. Chandrachud. Justice Chandrachud assumed the position on November 9, 2022, becoming the 50th Chief Justice in the country's history. He brings a wealth of experience to the role, having served as a judge in both the Bombay High Court and the Supreme Court of India before his elevation. Justice Chandrachud is known for his progressive and liberal views, having championed issues like women's rights, environmental protection, and access to justice. He has also authored landmark judgments on various social and constitutional matters. His tenure as Chief Justice is expected to be marked by significant contributions to the Indian judiciary's evolution.

81. (D): The fundamental rights enshrined in the Constitution of India are the cornerstone of Indian democracy, safeguarding the freedoms and dignity of its citizens. The Right to Equality ensures equal treatment before the law and prohibits discrimination on various grounds. The Right to Freedom grants citizens essential liberties such as freedom of speech, expression, assembly, association, and movement, allowing them to participate actively in the democratic process. The Right to Freedom of Religion guarantees individuals the freedom to practice and propagate their religion of choice, fostering a secular and inclusive society. However, there is no provision in the Constitution that grants a right to exploitation. Instead, the Constitution explicitly prohibits exploitation and mandates the state to ensure social justice and protect vulnerable sections of society from exploitation, ensuring that all citizens can live with dignity and without fear of oppression.

82. (A): Bhojpuri is the local regional language of Bihar State, India, and is spoken by a significant portion of the population in the region. It belongs to the Bihari subgroup of the Indo-Aryan language family and has its roots deeply embedded in the cultural fabric of Bihar. Bhojpuri is characterized by its rich literary tradition, with a wealth of poetry, songs, and folk tales passed down through generations. It is widely used in various domains of daily life, including communication, literature, music, and cinema. Bhojpuri cinema, in particular, has gained popularity not only in Bihar but also in other parts of India and among Bhojpuri-speaking diaspora communities around the world. Overall, Bhojpuri serves as a vital link to the cultural heritage and identity of the people of Bihar, fostering a sense of belonging and pride among its speakers.

83. (A): Ikebana, the Japanese art of flower arrangement, is a highly refined and contemplative practice that dates back centuries. Unlike traditional Western floral arrangements, which often strive for symmetry and fullness, Ikebana focuses on simplicity, balance, and the use of negative space to evoke a sense of harmony and natural beauty. Each arrangement, known as a "kado" or "way of flowers," is carefully composed to reflect the changing seasons, the inherent qualities of the materials used, and the aesthetic sensibilities of the artist. Ikebana practitioners, known as "ikebanists," adhere to specific principles and techniques passed down through generations, but also value individual expression and creativity within the framework of tradition. Ikebana is not simply about arranging flowers; it is a meditative practice that encourages mindfulness, connection to nature, and appreciation for the fleeting beauty of life.

84. (C): A solar eclipse occurs when the Moon moves between the Sun and the Earth, casting its shadow on the Earth's surface. This happens only during the new moon phase when the Sun, Moon, and Earth align in a straight line, with the Moon positioned directly between the Sun and Earth. From the perspective of an observer on Earth, the Moon appears to block out or partially obscure the Sun, leading to a temporary decrease in sunlight or even total darkness in the path of the Moon's shadow, known as the umbra. Solar eclipses can be partial, where only a portion of the Sun is obscured, or total, where the Sun is completely covered by the Moon's shadow. These celestial events are awe-inspiring phenomena that captivate observers around the world, offering a rare glimpse of the cosmic dance between the Sun, Moon, and Earth.

85. (D): Acid rain is caused due to Oxides of Sulphur and Nitrogen. When sulphur dioxide (SO_2) and nitrogen oxides (NO_x) primarily emitted from industrial processes, vehicle emissions, and burning fossil fuels, react with water vapor and other atmospheric components, they form sulphuric acid (H_2SO_4) and nitric acid (HNO_3), respectively. These acids then combine with precipitation (rain, snow, fog) and fall to the ground as acid rain, which can have harmful effects on the environment, ecosystems, and human health.

86. (D): The United States boasts the world's most extensive rail network, spanning an impressive 223,508 kilometers. This network serves as a critical infrastructure backbone for the country's economy, with approximately 80% of its capacity dedicated to freight transportation. Major freight carriers such as Union Pacific, BNSF Railway, and CSX Transportation operate on this extensive network, facilitating the efficient movement of essential commodities including coal, grain, automobiles, and chemicals. The network's broad coverage and substantial capacity make it an indispensable component of the US supply chain, supporting diverse industries and economic activities across the nation. While freight transportation dominates the network, it also accommodates passenger travel, particularly in major metropolitan areas, underscoring its multifaceted role in facilitating both economic growth and mobility within the United States.

87. (B): Wimbledon, widely regarded as the most prestigious tennis tournament in the world, is unique for its traditional grass courts, which provide a distinctive playing surface compared to the hard courts or clay courts used in other Grand Slam events. The tournament's history dates back to 1877, making it the oldest tennis tournament in the world. The lush green grass of Wimbledon's courts adds a level of unpredictability to matches, as the surface tends to be faster, encouraging serve-and-volley play and rewarding players with precise shot-making skills. Wimbledon's grass courts evoke a sense of tradition and nostalgia, attracting top players and passionate fans from around the globe to witness thrilling matches and iconic moments on the hallowed lawns of the All England Club.

88. (D): The supercomputer "PARAM" was developed by the Centre for Development of Advanced Computing (C-DAC), an organization based in India that specializes in the research and development of advanced computing technologies. The PARAM series of supercomputers represents a significant milestone in India's pursuit of indigenous high-performance computing capabilities. These supercomputers have been instrumental in various scientific and technological endeavors, including weather forecasting, climate modeling, molecular modeling, and aerospace simulations. C-DAC's efforts in developing the PARAM series have not only advanced India's capabilities in the field of supercomputing but also contributed to the country's self-reliance in critical technological domains.

89. (C): Vitamin C, also known as ascorbic acid, is a water-soluble vitamin that plays a crucial role in various bodily functions, including collagen synthesis, immune function, and antioxidant defense. Unlike fat-soluble vitamins such as Vitamin A and Vitamin E, which can be stored in the body's fatty tissues for later use, Vitamin C is not stored in large amounts. Instead, any excess Vitamin C that the body does not need is excreted primarily through urine. This means that maintaining adequate levels of Vitamin C in the body requires regular dietary intake, as the body does not have the capacity to store it for prolonged periods. While Vitamin C is essential for health, it is important to consume it in appropriate amounts, as excessive intake can lead to adverse effects such as gastrointestinal discomfort or kidney stones.

90. (C): Professor Amartya Sen was awarded the Nobel Prize in Economics in 1998 for his groundbreaking contributions to welfare economics and social choice theory. His work has focused on advancing our understanding of poverty, inequality, and human development, fundamentally reshaping how economists approach these complex issues. Sen's research has emphasized the importance of considering not only economic indicators but also broader measures of well-being and social justice, such as freedom, capability, and functioning's. His insights have had profound implications for policy-making, advocating for policies that prioritize the enhancement of individuals' capabilities and opportunities, rather than merely focusing on economic growth or income redistribution. Through his pioneering work, Sen has profoundly influenced the field of economics and has inspired new approaches to addressing the most pressing challenges of global development.

91. (B): The correct sentence would be: "She has got a silver medal in the race." In this sentence, "has got" is used to indicate possession or acquisition of the silver medal. "Has got" is the present perfect tense of the verb "to get." It implies that the action of obtaining the silver medal occurred in the past and has relevance to the present moment. The use of "has" indicates that the subject ("She") is a singular third-person pronoun, and "got" is the past participle form of the verb "to get."

92. (D): The most suitable option to fill in the blank is Back out. So, the complete sentence would be: "Once she has signed the deal papers, she won't be able to back out." This sentence means that once she has signed the deal papers, she won't be able to withdraw or cancel her agreement to the deal. "Backing out" refers to retracting from a commitment or agreement.

93. (C): The most appropriate word to fill in the blank is assured. So, the complete sentence would be: "The crew was afraid, but the captain assured them that there was no danger." In this sentence, "assured" means to give confidence or certainty to someone by dispelling doubts or fears. The captain reassures the crew by confirming that there is no danger, thereby alleviating their fears and concerns.

94. (B): "The two groups have been engaged in a bitter intent for the past three decades." In this context, "intent" would suggest that the two groups have harbored bitter intentions or motives towards each other for the past three decades. It implies a longstanding animosity or hostility between the groups, driven by underlying motivations or agendas.

95. (B): The most appropriate option to fill in the blank is Has run away. So, the complete sentence would be: "My house help has run away with all my money." This sentence indicates that the house help has absconded or fled with all the money belonging to the speaker. The phrase "has run away" is in the present perfect tense, indicating that the action of running away occurred recently and has relevance to the present moment.

96. (A): The correct word to fill in the blank is Rapt. So, the complete sentence would be: "The audience listened to the artist with rapt attention." In this sentence, "rapt" means deeply engrossed or completely absorbed. It indicates that the audience was intensely focused on the artist's performance, giving their full attention and showing keen interest in what was being presented.

97. (A): The phrase "taken by surprise" is a common English idiom used to describe the state of being unexpectedly or suddenly surprised by something. It implies that the person did not anticipate or foresee the event or situation that caused the surprise. The corrected sentence would be: I was taken by surprise When I saw the beautiful building of Red Fort

98. (B): In the original sentence, the phrase "to the good of" is not incorrect grammatically, but it's less commonly used in this context. The phrase "to the benefit of" is more idiomatic and commonly used to express that someone is working or acting for the advantage or welfare of someone or something else. So, the corrected phrase "to the benefit of" in part B of the sentence conveys the intended meaning more effectively and aligns better with standard English usage.

99. (C): The phrase "died of an accident" is not the most appropriate usage in this context. It's more common to use "died in an accident" or simply "died" when referring to a death resulting from an accident.

Therefore, the corrected sentence would be died in an accident

100. (D): The given sentence seems to be grammatically correct. It conveys a complete thought and there is no apparent error in the structure or usage of the sentence.

101. (B): The error is in part B of the sentence. The word "many" should be replaced with "much" to make the sentence grammatically correct.

So, the corrected sentence would be: That requires much planning. The corrected sentence reads: "Essay writing is an art that requires much planning." This adjustment ensures that the sentence follows proper English grammar.

102. (A): The error is in part A of the sentence. The phrase "seldom or ever" is redundant as "seldom" already conveys the idea of rarity or infrequency. The correct expression should be "seldom or never."

So, the corrected sentence would be: He seldom or never. The corrected sentence reads: "He seldom or never goes to meet his parents." This adjustment removes the redundancy and ensures clarity in the expression.

103. (B): "To turn a deaf ear" is an idiom that figuratively describes the act of deliberately ignoring or refusing to listen to someone or something. It implies a willful disregard or indifference towards what is being said, often due to a lack of interest, disagreement, or stubbornness. When someone turns a deaf ear, they choose not to pay attention to the information, advice, or requests being presented to them. This idiom suggests a deliberate act of shutting out communication or disregarding input, even when it may be important or relevant.

104. (C): The phrase "dark horse" refers to someone or something that is relatively unknown or not widely considered to be a contender, but unexpectedly achieves success or victory. So, "unexpected winner," aligns with this meaning, indicating that the person surprised everyone by performing well and emerging as a winner despite not being the favorite or expected to win.

105. (B): "To break the ice" is an idiomatic expression that means to initiate conversation or alleviate tension in a social situation, especially when there is awkwardness or discomfort. It refers to taking the first step to establish rapport or create a friendly atmosphere, typically by saying something to start a conversation and make others feel more comfortable. So, "to break silence by speaking first," aligns with this meaning.

106. (D): "A red letter day" is an idiomatic expression used to denote a particularly memorable or significant day. The term originates from the practice of marking special dates on calendars with red ink to make them stand out. Therefore, a red letter day is one that is distinguished from ordinary days by its importance, whether due to personal milestones, notable achievements, or significant events. It is a day that holds special meaning or significance, often celebrated or remembered with particular fondness. The expression conveys a sense of excitement, joy, or significance attached to the day, making it stand out as a memorable occasion amidst the routine of everyday life. Overall, "a red letter day" signifies an important and memorable moment in time.

107. (C): "To be at sixes and sevens" is an idiom used to describe a state of confusion or disorder. The origin of the phrase is uncertain, but it likely comes from medieval gambling games where the numbers six and seven were considered unlucky or unpredictable. Therefore, being "at sixes and sevens" implies a sense of uncertainty or disarray, where things are not in their usual order or arrangement. It suggests a state of confusion or disorderliness, where one may feel unsure about what to do or how to proceed. This idiom is often used to describe situations where there is a lack of clarity or organization, leading to a sense of chaos or uncertainty. Overall, "to be at sixes and sevens" conveys the idea of being in a state of confusion or disorderliness.

108. (A): "Bag of bones" is an idiomatic expression used to describe a person who is extremely thin or emaciated, often to the point where their bones are prominently visible. It emphasizes the gaunt or skeletal appearance of the person due to extreme thinness or malnutrition. So, "a very thin person," aligns with this meaning.

109. (B): "Meticulous" is an adjective that describes someone who is extremely careful and precise in their work or actions, paying great attention to detail and ensuring thoroughness in everything they do. A meticulous person is diligent and methodical, leaving no room for errors or oversights. They take the time to thoroughly examine and scrutinize every aspect of a task or project, aiming for perfection in execution. This level of meticulousness often results in high-quality outcomes and reliable results, as the individual invests significant effort into ensuring accuracy and completeness.

110. (D): Barter is a method of trading goods or services directly for other goods or services without using money as a medium of exchange. In a barter transaction, individuals or parties exchange items that they possess for items that they need, based on mutual agreement and perceived value. This practice has been historically significant, predating the use of currency, and has been utilized in various societies and cultures around the world. Bartering relies on the principle of reciprocity, where both parties benefit from the exchange by acquiring goods or services that fulfill their needs or desires. It fosters a sense of community and cooperation, as individuals engage in negotiations to reach agreements that satisfy both parties.

111. (B): "Accolade" commonly refers to a mark of recognition or honor bestowed upon someone for their achievements, accomplishments, or contributions. It is often used to describe high praise, admiration, or approval given to individuals, groups, or works of art or literature. The term originates from the gesture of knighthood, where a blow with the flat side of a sword on the shoulders was considered a sign of honor. Today, accolades can take various forms, such as awards, commendations, or public recognition, and they serve to highlight and celebrate outstanding performance or merit.

112. (A): "Yard stick" is a metaphorical expression used to describe a standard or criterion against which other things are compared, evaluated, or measured. Originating from the literal yardstick, a long, slender ruler used for measuring length, the phrase implies a fixed reference point or measurement tool used for assessing quality, performance, or value. In a figurative sense, a yardstick serves as a benchmark or standard by which the characteristics or attributes of something else are judged or evaluated. It provides a basis for comparison and helps establish parameters for determining success, excellence, or adequacy in various contexts.

113. (B): "Tedious" describes something that is dull, monotonous, or repetitive, often causing boredom or weariness. It refers to tasks, activities, or situations that lack variety or excitement, making them feel prolonged or tiresome. A tedious task may require repeated or routine actions, leading to a sense of monotony and mental fatigue. This adjective is commonly used to characterize activities that demand sustained attention or effort without providing much stimulation or interest in return. Whether it's a tedious job, a tedious journey, or a tedious conversation, the term conveys a sense of drudgery or tedium, suggesting that the experience is tiresome and lacking in enjoyment or satisfaction.

114. (C): "Deplete" signifies the reduction or exhaustion of a resource, supply, or reserve to a point where it is significantly diminished or nearly exhausted. It implies a gradual or systematic reduction in the quantity or availability of something, often due to extensive use, consumption, or depletion over time. The term is commonly used to describe the diminishing of natural resources, such as water, oil, or forests, as well as the depletion of energy, funds, or other tangible or intangible assets. When something is depleted, it means that its original abundance or fullness has been substantially reduced, leaving it in a state of scarcity or inadequacy. Therefore, "deplete" conveys the idea of gradual consumption or exhaustion, resulting in a diminished state of availability or abundance.

115. (A): "Rectify" refers to the act of correcting or remedying a mistake, error, or problem to bring it into conformity with what is right, proper, or acceptable. When something needs to be rectified, it means that there is an identified flaw, discrepancy, or issue that requires attention and action to resolve. The process of rectification involves identifying the problem, determining the appropriate solution, and implementing corrective measures to ensure that the mistake is corrected and its effects mitigated. Whether it's fixing errors in data, addressing misunderstandings in communication, or resolving issues in a process or system, rectification aims to restore accuracy, integrity, or functionality.

116. (D): "Authentic" refers to something that is genuine, real, or true, possessing qualities or characteristics that are original and not counterfeit or fabricated. It conveys a sense of sincerity, reliability, and trustworthiness, indicating that the object, experience, or person in question is legitimate and conforms to its claimed identity or origin. On the other hand, "fictitious" denotes something that is imaginary, invented, or not based on reality. It implies a lack of authenticity or truthfulness, suggesting that the subject matter is fabricated or created for the purpose of deception or entertainment. Therefore, while "authentic" emphasizes genuineness and truth, "fictitious" represents the opposite by portraying something that is not real or genuine.

117. (A): "Brittle" describes something that is fragile and easily broken, typically lacking flexibility or resilience. It implies a tendency to crack, snap, or shatter under pressure or impact. This characteristic is often associated with materials like glass, ceramics, or certain types of metals that lack elasticity or toughness. Objects or substances that are brittle are vulnerable to damage or breakage when subjected to stress or force, making them less durable or reliable in certain applications. In contrast, the opposite of "brittle" would be something that is strong, robust, or flexible, able to withstand pressure or deformation without breaking or fracturing easily. Therefore, while "brittle" conveys a sense of fragility and susceptibility to damage, its opposite, "strong," suggests resilience, durability, and resistance to breaking or deformation.

118. (C): "Cruelty" represents the opposite of "compassion" in that it involves a deliberate and malicious disregard for the well-being of others. While compassion entails empathy and a desire to alleviate suffering, cruelty manifests as intentional harm or infliction of pain on others. Cruel actions are motivated by indifference, malice, or a lack of empathy towards the suffering of others. Unlike compassion, which seeks to alleviate suffering and promote kindness, cruelty perpetuates harm and suffering.

Therefore, while compassion fosters connection and empathy, cruelty severs these bonds and perpetuates harm, making it the antithesis of compassion.

119. (B): "Disaster" refers to a significant and often catastrophic event that brings about widespread damage, destruction, or adversity, resulting in distress, suffering, or loss. It encompasses various types of emergencies, crises, or calamities, such as natural disasters like earthquakes, floods, or hurricanes, as well as human-made disasters like accidents, conflicts, or economic downturns. In contrast, "prosperity" represents a state of flourishing, success, and well-being, characterized by economic growth, abundance, and favorable conditions.

It signifies a period of thriving and advancement, where individuals, communities, or societies experience positive outcomes, opportunities, and achievements.

Therefore, while "disaster" signifies hardship and adversity, "prosperity" denotes prosperity and flourishing, making them antonyms that represent contrasting states of circumstances and outcomes.

120. (A): "Fatigue" describes a feeling of extreme tiredness or exhaustion, typically resulting from physical or mental exertion, prolonged stress, or lack of sleep. It manifests as a decline in energy levels, motivation, and alertness, often accompanied by physical symptoms such as muscle weakness, lethargy, or difficulty concentrating. In contrast, "vigour" signifies robustness, vitality, and strength, representing a state of physical or mental vigor and resilience. Individuals experiencing vigour feel energetic, lively, and capable of taking on challenges with enthusiasm and determination.

Therefore, while fatigue denotes a state of depletion and weariness, vigour conveys a sense of vitality and strength, making them antonyms that represent contrasting states of energy and well-being.

121. (D): "Moderate" refers to maintaining a balance or staying within reasonable limits, often implying a degree of restraint or temperance. It suggests avoiding extremes and finding a middle ground that is neither excessive nor insufficient. A moderate approach involves exercising discretion and judiciousness, considering various factors before making decisions or taking actions. On the other hand, "excessive" conveys the idea of going beyond what is necessary or appropriate, indicating an abundance or surplus that may lead to negative consequences.

Therefore, while moderation implies prudence and moderation, excessiveness suggests immoderation and extravagance, making them antonyms that represent opposing ends of a spectrum.

128. (B): putting on: The sentence describes Ram's action of wearing his hat in response to the cold weather. The phrasal verb "putting on" accurately conveys this action, indicating that Ram is placing his hat on his head to protect himself from the cold.

Therefore, option B provides a more appropriate and clearer expression compared to the original sentence.

129. (C): refused: While "rejected" in option B is a suitable synonym for "denied," "refused" in option C provides a more precise and idiomatic expression in this context. "Refused" conveys the idea of actively declining or declining something offered, which aligns well with the meaning conveyed in the sentence.

Therefore, option C offers a more appropriate and clearer choice compared to the original sentence.

130. (B): It would indicate a change from the noun "advice" to the verb "advise." This change would be appropriate in the context of the sentence "The teacher gave the students some advise". "Advise" is a verb that means to give an opinion or suggestion to someone. It can also mean to caution or warn.

131. (D): No improvement: In the given sentence, "knocked down" is already in its correct form. It is a phrasal verb used to describe the action of someone or something being hit or struck to the ground by a speeding car.

Therefore, the sentence does not require any improvement, and option D is the correct choice.

132. (C): Has been working: The sentence "Seema was working overtime for the last few weeks" is in the past continuous tense, indicating an action that was ongoing in the past. However, the use of "was" suggests past continuous, while the context of the sentence suggests duration of time extending from the past up to the present.

Therefore, the most appropriate tense to use here is the present perfect continuous tense, which indicates an action that started in the past and is still ongoing. "Has been working" accurately conveys this meaning, making option C the correct choice for improvement.

133. (B): Covered with: In this sentence, "covered with" is the correct prepositional phrase to describe the relationship between the floor and the carpet. "Covered with" is used to indicate that the floor has something lying on its surface.

Therefore, option B, "covered with," is the most appropriate choice for improvement.

134. (A): "Had been belonging," is correct as it suggests the past perfect continuous tense, indicating an action that started in the past and continued for duration up to another point in the past. In this case, the sentence would imply that the ownership of the house had started in the past and continued up to a specific point in the past.

Therefore, the sentence would convey the idea that the speaker owned the house for duration of two years in the past.

135. (B): of: In the sentence "He has a very good command of Mathematics," the preposition "of" is the correct choice. When talking about someone's proficiency or mastery in a particular subject or field, we use the preposition "of" to indicate possession or knowledge in that area.

Therefore, option B, "of;" is the most appropriate choice for improvement in this sentence.

136. (C): have known: The sentence "I have known him since my childhood" is in the present perfect tense, which is used to indicate an action that started in the past and continues into the present. In this case, the action of knowing the person started in the past (childhood) and continues up to the present moment.

137. (B): has been raining: The sentence "It has been raining here for two hours" is in the present perfect continuous tense, indicating an action that started in the past and is still ongoing. In this case, the action of raining started in the past and continues up to the present moment. The correct form of the verb "to be" for the third person singular subject "It" is "has been".

138. (B): Alerted: In this context, the word "alerted" is the most suitable choice. When someone is "alerted" in the context of the army, it means that they have been informed or notified about a particular situation and are ready to respond to it.

Therefore, the sentence "The army has been alerted to be ready to control the floods" indicates that the army has been informed and is prepared to take action to control the floods.

139. (A): the: In this sentence, the word "execution" refers to the implementation or carrying out of a specific plan. Since "execution" is a singular countable noun, it requires an article before it. In this context, "the" is the appropriate article to use because it refers to a specific execution, indicating that the speaker is referring to particular problems observed in the execution of the mentioned plan.

140. (C): That where it ends: The phrase "That is where it ends" is grammatically correct. The word "that" functions as a conjunction here, introducing the dependent clause "where it ends".

Therefore, the corrected sentence would read: "We know where it begins, but we don't know that is where it ends".

141. (D): The given sentence appears to be grammatically correct with no error. It effectively conveys the idea of cautioning against fair-weather friends, who are not supportive or reliable in times of need.

142. (A): Seldom we have been treated: In English syntax, the adverb "seldom" is often placed at the beginning of a sentence for emphasis. When this occurs, the subject and the auxiliary verb must be inverted.

Therefore, the correct order is "seldom have" instead of "seldom we." The corrected sentence reads: "Seldom have we been treated in such a rude manner by the police personnel".

143. (C): Among the two brothers: When dividing something between two people or entities, the correct preposition to use is "between." "Among" is used for three or more entities.

Therefore, the correct preposition in this context is "between," as the sentence refers to the division of property between two brothers. The corrected sentence reads: "The property was divided between the two brothers".

144. (B): If one be happy: The phrase "If one be happy" uses the subjunctive mood incorrectly. In modern English, we typically use the indicative mood instead of the subjunctive mood in conditional clauses. Therefore, the correct form should be "If one is happy". The corrected sentence reads: "Long life is good if one is happy and has friends".

145. (A): His assistants have: While "His assistants have" is grammatically correct, it doesn't accurately convey the intended meaning in this context. The sentence implies that the assistants started their excellent work in the past and continue to do so in the present. To reflect this ongoing action, we need to use the present perfect tense.

Therefore, the corrected sentence should be: His assistants have done and are still doing excellent work for the organisation.

146. (A): The purpose of the passage/study is to highlight the importance of conservation efforts for the Snow Leopard population in India. It provides information about the establishment of Project Snow Leopard, which aims to safeguard and conserve India's unique high-altitude wildlife populations and their habitats. The passage emphasizes the significance of protecting the Snow Leopard, which serves as an umbrella species, indicating that with its protection, other species and their habitats are also preserved. Additionally, the passage discusses the reasons for introducing Project Snow Leopard, including the unique wildlife assemblage in high-altitude regions, the need for attention to wildlife conservation in these areas, and the importance of the region for national security and international relations.

147. (B): In conservation biology, an umbrella species is one whose conservation also protects a wide range of other species that share its habitat. By focusing conservation efforts on umbrella species like the Snow Leopard, which require large and intact habitats, the protection of their habitat indirectly benefits many other species that inhabit the same ecosystem. Therefore, protecting umbrella species serves as a way to conserve biodiversity on a broader scale.

148. (C): The passage highlights that high altitude regions, specifically those above 3000 meters, support a unique wildlife assemblage of global conservation significance. These regions are home to species like the Snow Leopard and other high-altitude wildlife, making them important for biodiversity conservation efforts. Therefore, protecting these regions helps safeguard not only the species living there but also the ecosystem as a whole.

149. (D): In the context of the passage, river systems are highlighted as crucial components of the high-altitude regions that are integral to the nation's food security. These river systems provide essential ecosystem services vital for sustaining agricultural activities and ensuring food production. They contribute to irrigation for crops, support hydroelectric power generation, and facilitate transportation of goods, all of which are fundamental aspects of agricultural productivity and food distribution. Furthermore, the passage underscores the importance of conserving these river systems, as they not only support human livelihoods but also play a significant role in maintaining the overall health and balance of the ecosystem. Therefore, safeguarding river systems is essential for ensuring the nation's food security and promoting sustainable development in these regions.

150. (A): The Himalayan region comprises several states that are characterized by their proximity to the Himalayan mountain range. These states include Jammu and Kashmir, Himachal Pradesh, Uttarakhand, Sikkim, and Arunachal Pradesh. Each of these states is nestled within the majestic Himalayas, boasting stunning landscapes, diverse ecosystems, and unique biodiversity. The Himalayan states are known for their rich cultural heritage, vibrant traditions, and significant contributions to India's natural and cultural diversity. Moreover, these regions play a crucial role in supporting the livelihoods of millions of people, providing essential ecosystem services such as freshwater resources, fertile soils for agriculture, and habitats for a wide range of flora and fauna. Therefore, the Himalayan states are not only geographically significant but also culturally, ecologically, and economically vital to India.

151. (D): Communication is key in resolving conflicts, especially with friends. Rather than escalating the situation by shouting back or spreading negative rumors about her, it's important to address the misunderstanding directly. By initiating a calm and honest conversation, you can clarify any misconceptions and work towards resolving the issue in a mature and respectful manner.

152. (C) and (D):

(C) Choosing to inform the police can indeed be a prudent decision, especially if the argument seems to be escalating or if there's a potential threat of violence. It's essential to prioritize safety for yourself and others in such situations. Informing the authorities ensures that trained professionals can handle the situation appropriately and prevent any further escalation or harm.

(D) Intervening between two people arguing loudly on the way home after a late-night movie can be a proactive approach to diffuse the situation and promote peace. By calmly stepping in and addressing both parties, you have the opportunity to de-escalate tensions and encourage open communication. Offering a listening ear, providing perspective, and facilitating a resolution can help the individuals involved find common ground and settle their argument amicably. This intervention not only fosters a sense of community responsibility but also contributes to a safer and more harmonious environment for everyone involved.

153. (A): Initiating conversation in a new workplace by smiling at everyone and saying hello is an effective way to break the ice and create a welcoming atmosphere. A smile communicates warmth and approachability, making it easier for colleagues to feel comfortable engaging in conversation or approaching you for assistance. This simple yet genuine gesture sets a positive tone for interactions and fosters a sense of camaraderie among coworkers, ultimately contributing to a supportive and inclusive work environment where collaboration thrives.

154. (B): Communicating openly and honestly with your friend about the conflicting situation demonstrates respect for their invitation and allows you to explain the circumstances preventing you from attending. This approach maintains the integrity of your friendship while also prioritizing your academic and career-related commitments. By discussing the situation with your friend, you can potentially reschedule the lunch or find an alternative way to spend time together that accommodates both your needs and responsibilities.

155. (C): In such a critical situation where an injured child's life may be in jeopardy, the most urgent and responsible course of action is to immediately take the child to the hospital. Prioritizing the well-being and safety of the child is paramount, and any delay in seeking medical attention could have severe consequences. By swiftly transporting the child to the hospital, you can ensure that they receive the necessary medical care and increase the chances of a positive outcome. In emergencies like this, every moment counts and taking prompt action can make a significant difference in saving a life or minimizing further injury.

156. (C): When asked for your views on an issue, it's important to provide a response that is both respectful and truthful. Diplomatically addressing the question allows you to express your perspective in a manner that acknowledges differing viewpoints while also staying true to your beliefs. This approach fosters constructive dialogue and promotes understanding, even in situations where opinions may differ. By being realistic and straightforward, you contribute to meaningful discussions and demonstrate integrity in expressing your thoughts.

157. (B): In such a scenario, it's crucial to maintain focus and professionalism despite the unexpected request. By concentrating on delivering your best performance as the main singer, you uphold the standards of the group and showcase your individual talent. Dwelling on distractions or negative thoughts about being singled out could detract from your performance and potentially undermine the group's overall presentation. Therefore, channeling your energy into singing confidently and skillfully demonstrates your ability to handle unexpected situations with poise and professionalism.

158. (B): Aptitude generally refers to a natural ability or talent for a particular activity or subject. In this case, Aman's enjoyment of painting when he is free indicates a strong interest in the activity. While interest and aptitude can be related, aptitude specifically pertains to inherent abilities or skills, whereas interest reflects personal preferences and passions. Therefore, Aman's inclination towards painting suggests a keen interest in the art form rather than necessarily an aptitude for it, although the two can certainly overlap.

159. **(A):** In a situation where an epidemic is spreading due to poor hygiene conditions in your village, it's essential to take proactive steps to address the issue. Educating people about hygiene practices can help prevent the spread of disease and improve overall community health. Waiting for the government to address the problem may not be timely or effective, and ignoring the issue or shifting to another village does not address the root cause of the problem. By actively engaging with the community to promote better hygiene practices, you can contribute to protecting the health and well-being of yourself and others in the village.

160. **(B):** Choosing to do a part-time job while pursuing higher studies abroad, especially when facing financial constraints, demonstrates resilience, determination, and responsibility. By taking on employment alongside academic commitments, you proactively address financial challenges without compromising the pursuit of your educational goals. This approach allows you to gain practical work experience, develop time management skills, and build a sense of independence. Additionally, working part-time can alleviate financial burdens, enabling you to cover living expenses and tuition fees while continuing to invest in your education and future prospects. Despite the challenges, balancing work and studies illustrates your commitment to personal growth and academic achievement.

161. **(D):** In this scenario, opting to forget about the song playing in the background and concentrating solely on your friend's voice is a considerate and focused approach to the conversation. By prioritizing active listening and engagement with your friend, you demonstrate respect for their communication and the importance of the interaction. Ignoring the distraction allows you to maintain clear communication and effectively participate in the conversation without being sidetracked by external stimuli. This ensures that your friend feels valued and heard during the conversation, fostering a meaningful and enjoyable exchange between the two of you.

162. **(A):** In this scenario, choosing to sit patiently and wait for your father is a prudent and responsible decision. By remaining calm and composed, you maintain control of the situation and prioritize safety. Waiting for your father's arrival as instructed ensures that you stay in a familiar and relatively safe environment until help arrives. This approach also minimizes the risk of encountering potential dangers or making impulsive decisions that could escalate the situation. Patience and trust in your father's ability to assist you contribute to a sense of security and allow for a smoother resolution to the unexpected breakdown.

163. **(D):** In an emergency situation where a family member gets badly hurt while you're alone at home, it's crucial to remain calm and take prompt action to ensure their well-being. Contacting the family doctor immediately allows for professional medical assistance to be provided swiftly. While waiting for the doctor's arrival, staying by your niece's side to provide comfort and monitor her condition is essential. This approach combines both seeking medical help and offering immediate support, prioritizing the health and safety of your niece.

164. **(C):** Attending the wedding of your maid's daughter while also offering a gift and assistance demonstrates both respect and kindness towards your maid and her family. By purchasing a gift, you show thoughtfulness and generosity, contributing to the celebration of the special occasion. Additionally, offering to help in the wedding, whether it's assisting with preparations or participating in the festivities, further strengthens your relationship with your maid and her family, fostering a sense of camaraderie and mutual support. This approach not only shows appreciation for the invitation but also demonstrates a genuine willingness to be involved and supportive during important moments in their lives.

165. **(C):** In the event of a disagreement or conflict with a colleague, choosing to sit down together and clarify things demonstrates a willingness to address issues openly and constructively. By engaging in a calm and respectful discussion, both parties have the opportunity to share their perspectives, clarify misunderstandings, and work towards finding a resolution. This approach fosters effective communication and problem-solving, ultimately strengthening the working relationship and promoting a more positive and productive work environment. Taking the initiative to sort out the matter through discussion reflects professionalism, maturity, and a commitment to maintaining healthy interpersonal dynamics in the workplace.

166. **(A):** In situations where you have multiple tasks to complete, such as preparing for an exam and working on a project report simultaneously, it's essential to approach the situation methodically and strategically. Creating a timetable that allocates specific time slots for each task allows you to focus on one thing at a time, ensuring that you can dedicate adequate attention and effort to each task without feeling

overwhelmed. This approach promotes effective time management, reduces stress, and increases productivity by providing structure and clarity to your workload.

167. (B): In this scenario, it's important to prioritize completing your work responsibly, especially if it's important and time-sensitive. While it may be tempting to join your friends at the carnival, neglecting your responsibilities could have negative consequences, such as missing deadlines or compromising the quality of your work. Choosing to stay focused and complete your tasks demonstrates professionalism, reliability, and a commitment to meeting your obligations.

168. (A): Encountering a snake in a cinema hall can be alarming, but it's important to remain calm and handle the situation responsibly. By staying composed, you can warn others discreetly to prevent panic and notify the hall authorities or staff immediately. This ensures that appropriate measures can be taken to safely remove the snake and prevent any potential harm to moviegoers. Acting swiftly and calmly in such a situation helps to maintain order and ensure the safety of everyone in the cinema hall. Maintaining a calm demeanor, warning others discreetly, and promptly notifying authorities are key steps in effectively managing a snake encounter in a cinema hall, prioritizing the safety and well-being of all individuals involved.

169. (B): Choosing to do the work wholeheartedly, despite feeling tired, demonstrates dedication and commitment to the task at hand. By approaching the work with enthusiasm and giving it your full effort, you increase the likelihood of completing it successfully and achieving desired outcomes. While tiredness may present challenges, maintaining a positive attitude and engaging with the work wholeheartedly can help overcome obstacles and maintain productivity. This approach also fosters a sense of accomplishment and satisfaction upon completing the task, reinforcing the value of perseverance and diligence even in challenging circumstances.

170. (A): When a teacher provides a clear deadline for a project with a two-week timeframe, the best approach is to plan and execute the work diligently within the allotted time. By approaching the project with patience and commitment, you can manage your time effectively, break down the tasks into manageable steps, and make steady progress towards completion. Procrastination or panicking can lead to unnecessary stress and compromise the quality of the work, while ignoring the project disregards the teacher's instructions and undermines your own learning and responsibility. Therefore, choosing to work patiently and complete the project within the given timeframe is the most responsible and effective option.

171. (B): In a call center environment, encountering an angry and yelling customer requires a calm and empathetic response. Apologizing and attempting to calm down the customer, is the most effective course of action. By acknowledging the customer's frustration and offering a sincere apology, you demonstrate empathy and validate their concerns. Furthermore, actively listening to the customer's grievances and showing a willingness to address their issues can help to de-escalate the situation and reassure the customer that their concerns are being taken seriously. Through patience, understanding, and a proactive approach to finding a resolution, you can work towards diffusing tension and ultimately improving the customer's experience.

172. (C): In a hotel setting, it's essential to address guest complaints promptly and effectively to ensure a positive experience. Apologizing to the guests for the noise level and offering to move them to a different room, is the best course of action. By acknowledging the issue and taking proactive steps to resolve it, you demonstrate a commitment to guest satisfaction and comfort. This approach not only addresses the immediate concern but also shows responsiveness and attentiveness to guest needs, enhancing their overall experience at the hotel.

173. (C): The first person to inform about the disturbance caused by seniors in a hostel would typically be the Hostel Warden. The Warden is responsible for maintaining discipline and ensuring the well-being of students residing in the hostel. By informing the Warden, you can seek immediate assistance and address the issue within the institutional framework, potentially leading to a resolution or appropriate action being taken against the seniors responsible for the disturbance. If the issue persists or escalates, further steps such as informing the college Principal may be necessary. In extreme cases where immediate assistance is required, contacting the local Police Station or a Help Line Number could also be considered. However, involving the hostel authorities initially is often the most appropriate and effective approach to addressing such matters.

174. (D): In the scenario where you have been served non-vegetarian soup instead of the vegetarian soup you ordered at a reputed restaurant, the appropriate course of action would be to call the manager and politely bring the issue to their attention. It's important to communicate the mistake calmly and professionally, without resorting to shouting or aggression towards the server. By notifying the manager, you give the restaurant an opportunity to rectify the mistake and ensure that your dietary preferences are accommodated. This approach allows for a resolution to be reached while also providing valuable feedback to the restaurant to prevent similar errors in the future.

175. (A): Volunteering to participate in organizing the food festival at your college reflects a proactive and collaborative approach to contributing to the campus community. By joining the group of students working on the event, you have the opportunity to play a direct role in its planning, organization, and execution. Your involvement can bring fresh ideas, creativity, and enthusiasm to the table, enriching the overall experience for participants and attendees. Additionally, volunteering allows you to develop valuable skills such as teamwork, communication, and event management, which are beneficial for personal growth and future endeavors. By actively engaging in the food festival's organization, you not only support your peers but also contribute to fostering a vibrant and inclusive campus environment where students can come together to celebrate and enjoy shared experiences.

176. (C): Remaining attentive to your given job as a telephone operator in a hotel, even when there are no calls waiting, is essential for ensuring efficient and responsive service. While it may be tempting to engage in other activities or relax during downtime, staying attentive allows you to quickly and effectively handle any incoming calls that may come through. By remaining focused on your responsibilities, you uphold the standard of professionalism expected in the hospitality industry, ensuring that guests receive prompt assistance and support whenever they require it. This proactive approach not only enhances guest satisfaction but also contributes to the smooth operation of the hotel's communication systems.

177. (B): Actively working alongside your team members as a leader in the cleanliness project at the monument. This involves collaborating with the team to accomplish the tasks at hand, whether it be picking up trash, cleaning surfaces, or organizing materials. By actively participating in the cleanup efforts, you demonstrate solidarity with your team, foster a sense of teamwork, and set a positive example for others to follow. Additionally, working together allows you to provide immediate support, guidance, and feedback to team members, ensuring that tasks are completed efficiently and effectively. This hands-on approach not only strengthens team cohesion but also enhances the overall success of the project by maximizing productivity and encouraging a shared sense of responsibility towards achieving the common goal of cleanliness at the monument.

178. (B): Informing the Local Authorities, involves reaching out to the appropriate government or municipal department responsible for the maintenance and management of public parks. This can typically be done by contacting the local municipality, parks and recreation department, or relevant government office through phone, email, or in person. By reporting the issue to the authorities, you provide them with essential information about the problem, such as the location of the park and details regarding the malfunctioning light bulbs. This allows them to prioritize the issue and dispatch maintenance personnel to address it promptly. Additionally, informing the authorities ensures that the problem is documented and tracked for follow-up and resolution, contributing to the overall maintenance and improvement of public amenities in the community.

179. (C): As the captain of the team, it is essential to take a proactive and constructive approach when faced with failure to achieve given targets. Examining the situation objectively and identifying the underlying reasons for the team's inability to meet the targets. By conducting a thorough analysis, you can pinpoint any deficiencies in strategy, execution, resources, or external factors that may have contributed to the shortfall. This allows for targeted improvements to be made, whether through adjusting tactics, providing additional support or resources, or addressing any challenges faced by team members.

180. (A): As a manager, it's crucial to intervene in a professional and constructive manner when a fight occurs between employees at the hotel. Upon witnessing the altercation, the manager intervenes to calm the situation and prevent further escalation of conflict. This may include physically separating the employees, maintaining a calm demeanor, and actively listening to understand the root cause of the dispute. The manager then works to facilitate open communication between the employees, encouraging them to express their grievances and concerns in a constructive manner. Through effective mediation and conflict resolution techniques, such as negotiation and compromise, the manager aims to find a mutually acceptable solution to the problem. By actively engaging in de-escalation and mediation efforts, the manager demonstrates leadership, professionalism, and a commitment to fostering a harmonious work environment conducive to productivity and collaboration.

181. (B): This involves contributing your thoughts, insights, and perspectives to the discussion, fostering collaboration and creativity within the group. By sharing your ideas, you not only contribute to the collective pool of knowledge and expertise but also encourage open communication and dialogue among group members. This allows for the exploration of diverse viewpoints and the generation of innovative solutions to the tasks or challenges at hand. Furthermore, sharing your ideas demonstrates your willingness to actively participate in the group's efforts and contribute to its overall success, promoting a sense of ownership and teamwork among all members.

182. (C): As the Class Monitor, embracing the responsibility as a new learning opportunity is the most constructive approach. This role offers valuable experiences in leadership, organization, and communication, which can contribute to personal growth and development. Rather than shying away from the responsibility or attempting to delegate it to someone else, taking on the role with grace and enthusiasm allows you to make a positive impact within the classroom and foster a supportive and productive learning environment.

This mindset encourages proactive participation, effective communication, and the cultivation of essential leadership skills such as organization, decision-making, and conflict resolution. Viewing the role as a learning experience enables you to approach it with enthusiasm and motivation, maximizing your potential for growth and success both as a student and as a leader within the classroom setting.

183. (B): This approach emphasizes honesty, accountability, and transparency, which are essential for maintaining trust and fostering effective communication within the team. By openly acknowledging your unpreparedness, you demonstrate integrity and a willingness to take ownership of your actions, rather than attempting to deflect responsibility or make excuses. Additionally, admitting your lack of preparation allows you to set a positive example of accountability for other team members, encouraging a culture of honesty and mutual respect. Furthermore, by being upfront about your situation, you can collaborate with the team to find solutions or adjust expectations as needed, ensuring that the meeting can still proceed productively despite the setback. Overall, this option promotes a constructive and mature approach to handling the situation, ultimately contributing to a more positive and supportive team dynamic.

184. (C): When encountering a tough topic in the classroom, the best course of action is to seek clarification and assistance from the teacher directly. When encountering difficulty understanding a concept, it's essential to utilize the resources available, and the teacher is the primary source of guidance and clarification in the classroom setting.

By requesting the teacher to repeat or further explain the topic, you demonstrate a commitment to understanding the material thoroughly and taking responsibility for your learning. This approach not only allows you to seek immediate clarification on specific points of confusion but also creates an opportunity for interactive learning and active participation in the classroom. Additionally, asking questions in class can benefit other students who may have similar uncertainties, contributing to a collaborative and supportive learning environment.

185. (D): When transferred to a department that is not of your interest, the most constructive approach is to embrace the opportunity and work diligently to excel in your new role. Instead of dwelling on personal preferences, it is crucial to embrace the opportunity for growth and development in the new role. By committing to working hard and proving yourself in the new department, you demonstrate resilience, adaptability, and professionalism. This approach enables you to focus on acquiring new skills, gaining valuable experience, and contributing positively to the team and the organization as a whole. Through dedication and perseverance, you have the potential to excel in your new role, build strong relationships with colleagues, and uncover unforeseen opportunities for career advancement. Ultimately, by embracing the challenge and investing your efforts wholeheartedly, you can transform a seemingly unfavorable situation into a rewarding and fulfilling professional experience.

186. (A): When you observe a person entering your restaurant in a wheelchair, the appropriate response is to rush to open the door for them. This proactive gesture demonstrates respect, consideration, and inclusivity towards individuals with mobility challenges, ensuring they have easy access to the establishment. By taking the initiative to assist with the door, you acknowledge and accommodate their needs, creating a welcoming and supportive environment. This small act of kindness not only facilitates the individual's entry into the restaurant but also communicates a message of hospitality and attentiveness to their comfort and convenience. Additionally, opening the door for them can help alleviate any potential difficulties or obstacles they may encounter, fostering a positive and inclusive dining experience for all patrons. Overall, option (A) exemplifies a proactive and compassionate approach to customer service, enhancing the overall atmosphere and reputation of the restaurant.

187. (D): As a manager, the most appropriate action in response to repeated customer complaints about the smell of the carpet in a particular room would be to replace the carpet with a new one. This proactive approach addresses the root cause of the issue by eliminating the source of the unpleasant odor and ensuring a fresh and pleasant environment for future guests. By investing in a new carpet, the manager demonstrates a commitment to maintaining high standards of cleanliness and guest satisfaction within the establishment. This action not only resolves the immediate problem but also prevents potential negative experiences for customers in the future, thereby enhancing the overall reputation and ambiance of the room. Ultimately, replacing the carpet with a new one exemplifies a proactive and customer-centric approach to resolving the issue and ensuring a positive guest experience.

188. (C): Embracing the qualities of discipline, hard work, and dedication as essential requirements for success in the role of a hotel operator. Rather than viewing this information as daunting or discouraging chooses to take it as a challenge reflects a proactive and determined attitude towards achieving professional goals. By accepting the challenge, individuals demonstrate a willingness to cultivate these qualities within themselves and apply them to their work in the hospitality industry. This mindset fosters a sense of ambition, resilience, and personal growth, driving individuals to strive for excellence and overcome obstacles along the path to success. Embracing the challenge as an opportunity to develop and excel as a hotel operator can inspire motivation, perseverance, and a commitment to delivering exceptional service and performance within the field. Therefore, this option represents a proactive and optimistic approach to leveraging the essential qualities required for success in the hospitality industry

189. (D): As a teacher tasked with selecting a team for the Annual Day Celebration, represents the most comprehensive approach. By selecting students who are close to you, you ensure a sense of familiarity and trust within the team, which can facilitate effective communication and collaboration. Additionally, choosing students who are willing to do whatever is asked demonstrates a readiness to take on responsibilities and contribute actively to the success of the event. Moreover, prioritizing students who are ready to adapt to any situation reflects flexibility and resilience, qualities that are crucial for handling unexpected challenges or changes that may arise during the preparation and execution of the Annual Day Celebration. Therefore, this option encompasses a diverse range of qualities and characteristics that are essential for building a strong and capable team for the event.

190. (C): Prioritizing the safety of vulnerable individuals, such as children and the elderly, in the event of a fire outbreak in a hotel. By securing them first before attempting to help others, you demonstrate compassion, responsibility, and a commitment to protecting lives. Children and the elderly may face difficulties evacuating on their own due to physical limitations or cognitive impairments, making them more vulnerable in emergency situations. Therefore, by ensuring their safety as a priority, you mitigate the risk of harm and provide them with the best chance of escaping the fire unharmed. Once they are secure, you can then proceed to assist other guests and staff members, contributing to the overall efforts to evacuate the premises safely and effectively. This approach reflects a proactive and caring response to emergencies, emphasizing the importance of prioritizing the well-being of all individuals, especially those who may need extra assistance.

191. (B): When noticing a mistake in a guest bill prepared and checked by your staff, go and speak to the concerned staff yourself without creating a fuss. This approach allows for direct communication with the staff member responsible for the error, providing an opportunity to address the issue calmly and professionally. By discussing the mistake with the staff member directly, you can clarify the situation, identify the cause of the error, and work together to rectify it promptly. Additionally, handling the matter discreetly without creating a fuss helps maintain a positive working environment and fosters constructive communication and problem-solving within the team.

192. (D): Prioritizing efforts to resolve the issue when dealing with a demanding customer in a hotel. This approach involves actively engaging with the customer to understand their concerns fully and identify potential solutions to address their needs or grievances. By demonstrating a willingness to listen, empathize, and take proactive steps to rectify any issues, hotel staff can effectively mitigate the customer's dissatisfaction and restore their confidence in the hotel's services. This may involve offering apologies, providing alternative solutions, offering compensation or refunds if appropriate, and ensuring that the customer's overall experience is positive and satisfactory. By prioritizing resolution and excellent customer service, hotel staff can turn a potentially negative situation into an opportunity to build trust, loyalty, and positive relationships with customers, ultimately enhancing the hotel's reputation and success.

193. (D): As a manager, receiving negative feedback about your hotel should be viewed as an opportunity for improvement rather than a reason for confrontation or dismissal. Option (D) involves acknowledging the criticism constructively, analyzing the areas highlighted for improvement, and taking proactive steps to enhance the standards of service. This approach demonstrates a commitment to continuous improvement and customer satisfaction. By addressing the concerns raised in the feedback and implementing necessary changes, the hotel can strive to provide better experiences for its guests in the future.

194. (C): Initiating a conversation with the Mess Incharge to propose the addition of items on a rotation basis that cater to your choice, by engaging in constructive dialogue, you communicate your concerns regarding the current food options while also presenting a proactive solution. This approach fosters open communication and collaboration between students and the mess management, creating an opportunity to address diverse dietary preferences and enhance overall satisfaction. Additionally, suggesting a rotation of menu items demonstrates flexibility and willingness to compromise, as it allows for variety without requiring permanent changes to the menu. By working together to find a mutually beneficial solution, both students and the mess management can contribute to improving the dining experience and fostering a positive atmosphere within the college community.

195. (D): "Take him to his room and ask him to relax," involves a more hands-on and empathetic approach to managing the situation with a drunken guest in the hotel lobby. By escorting the guest to their room, the manager aims to remove them from the public area where they may be causing a disturbance. Additionally, asking them to relax may help calm the guest down and mitigate any further disruptions. However, it's important to note that this approach should only be taken if the guest is cooperative and not posing a threat to themselves or others. If the guest continues to be disruptive or refuses to comply, it may be necessary to involve hotel security or local authorities for assistance. This option prioritizes de-escalation and resolving the situation with minimal confrontation, while also ensuring the safety and comfort of other guests in the hotel.

196. (D): Writing a complaint to the company about the incident, is a constructive and proactive approach to addressing a delivery taking more time than usual. By documenting your concerns and communicating them directly to the company, you provide them with valuable feedback that can help identify areas for improvement in their service. This action not only allows the company to investigate the specific incident but also enables them to take corrective measures to prevent similar occurrences in the future, ultimately enhancing their overall service quality. Additionally, writing a complaint allows you to express your dissatisfaction in a professional manner and seek appropriate resolution, such as a refund or compensation for the inconvenience caused. Overall, this approach promotes accountability, transparency, and continuous improvement within the company's delivery operations, benefiting both you as a customer and future patrons.

197. (A): When witnessing individuals writing on walls of a famous monument, the most responsible course of action is to educate them about the importance of preserving cultural heritage and the negative impact of defacing public property. Engaging in a constructive conversation with the individuals allows for the opportunity to explain the significance of the monument and the consequences of their actions, such as damaging historical artifacts and diminishing the beauty of the site for future visitors. By raising awareness and promoting respectful behavior, there is a greater chance of discouraging such actions and fostering a culture of preservation and appreciation for cultural landmarks.

198. (B): Upon being promoted by the management, the most appropriate response is to work harder and demonstrate dedication to your new role and increased responsibilities. Promotion typically signifies recognition of one's abilities and potential for greater contributions to the organization. Therefore, it is essential to approach the new position with enthusiasm, commitment, and a determination to excel. Embracing the additional responsibilities and challenges associated with the promotion showcases professionalism, ambition, and a proactive attitude towards personal and professional growth within the company.

199. **(A):** Eye contact with guests in hospitality settings is a fundamental aspect of communication that symbolizes honesty and respect. It serves as a nonverbal cue conveying attentiveness, sincerity, and a genuine interest in engaging with the individual. By making eye contact, hospitality professionals demonstrate their willingness to listen, understand, and address the needs and preferences of guests. It creates a connection that fosters trust, comfort, and positive rapport, enhancing the overall guest experience. Additionally, maintaining eye contact can help ensure effective communication, clarify messages, and convey warmth and sincerity, all of which contribute to a welcoming and hospitable atmosphere. Overall, eye contact plays a crucial role in building strong relationships with guests and promoting a culture of hospitality characterized by genuine care and respect.

200. **(B):** The aviation, cruise, hotels, and travel sectors all fall under the umbrella of the hospitality industry. This industry encompasses various businesses and services that focus on accommodating and catering to the needs of travelers and guests. Aviation involves air travel services, including airlines and airports; cruise refers to the cruise line industry, which provides leisure voyages on ships; hotels provide accommodation services for travelers; and travel involves agencies and companies that facilitate and organize trips and vacations. Collectively, these sectors contribute to the hospitality industry by offering services related to transportation, accommodation, and leisure activities for travelers and tourists.

Previous Paper (Solved)

National Testing Agency (NTA)

National Council for Hotel Management & Catering Technology

Joint Entrance Exam (NCHMCT-JEE), 2021*

APTITUDE FOR SERVICE SECTOR

1. Your Boss is short tempered and always shouts at everybody, you will:

Your boss is angry and always yells at all look like you?

A. Take sportingly and look for some ways to control his temper.
Don't take it too seriously and find some ways to keep his anger under control.

B. Feel that Boss can have short temper, as he has a right to shout at everybody.
Bosses are angry, so it is normal for him to get angry with someone.

C. Tell him that he is wrong as he has no right to shout at everyone.
Tell him that he is making a mistake and he has no right to be angry with anyone.

D. Tell your boss how you feel and that this situation is not acceptable to you.
Tell your boss how we feel and we don't accept this situation.

2. While going to your Office, one day your neighbour asks for lift, for going to his office which is in opposite direction, you will:

Have a day at the office while your neighbour is opposite asks you lift towards you:

A. Tell him that it may not be possible.
Tell him it is not possible.

B. Tell him that you are not there for these kinds of jobs.
Tell him that you don't do such things.

C. Shout at him that you are getting late.
Shout at him that you are late.

D. Politely refuse him that his office is just in the opposite direction and that you have to reach office on time.
Refuse politely that his office is on the opposite side and that he has to reach office on time.

3. Your driver's daughter is getting married and he needs some money, you will:

A. Ask him to take a loan from Bank
B. Give him some money which is in your capacity & ask him to refund
C. Straight away refuse him as you have nothing to do with that matter
D. Raise a fund from your friends and help him.

4. In your Society, you have people throwing garbage here & there, you will:

A. Try to educate people and keep a dustbin in Society
B. Forget as it is not only your job
C. Penalise the person who is throwing the garbage
D. Nothing can be done

5. After studying hard for your exams, you did not score well, you will:

A. Stop studying hard
B. Start blaming the teacher, that he is unfair
C. Continue to work hard and perform your duty to show better results
D. Ask your friends not to study hard as they will also not get good marks

6. Due to your mistake your car has hit an old man who was riding a cycle. You will:

A. Run away from the place
B. Start shouting and blaming the old man
C. Ask your friend to get his cycle repaired
D. Feel sorry, pay some money to get his cycle repaired and arrange Medical Aid.

7. While you are about to cross a major crossing, you notice a blind man struggling to cross the road. You will:

A. Ask a young boy to help him cross the road
B. Go and catch his hand and help him cross the road
C. Curse the blind man and say why he should come to such busy roads
D. Continue to go your way and ignore him

1. A	**2.** D	**3.** B	**4.** A	**5.** C	**6.** D	**7.** B

*** Exam held on 10-08-2021. (Conducted by NTA)**

8. At the Airport, Security asks you to remove your shoes, belt etc. You will:
A. Do it as per instructions
B. Refuse, as they are your personal property
C. You will call the Police for help
D. First you will fight with Security. After that you will remove it.

9. Your Classmate is very rude with the Teacher. You have seen him talking rudely many times. You will:
A. Ignore as this issue is between him and the Teacher
B. Talk to his parents and try to find out why is he behaving like this
C. Ask your teacher to cut his name from the Class as it is disturbing to entire Class
D. Talk to your friend reminding him that Teacher is to be respected.

10. Your Boss has shared with you a new plan for the Company, You will:
A. Leak the plan to the Competitors
B. Share the plan with Colleagues immediately
C. Keep it confidential as it is a new plan
D. Share only with your best friend

11. After reaching the destination, you come to know that the Airline Company has forgotten to load your luggage. You will:
A. Start shouting at the airport as it is not your mistake
B. Complain to the Police Station about the incident
C. Give in the Print Media about the incident
D. Forgive them as this happens very rarely

12. Everyone in your Class has received new uniforms except you. What would you do?
A. Ask your Uniform In charge and question him why you have not got a new set of uniform
B. Complain to the Principal
C. Purchase from the market & submit bill to the School
D. Keep on coming to the School without uniform as you have not been provided the same

13. Your Office has gifted you a Diwali present, which you did not like much. You will:
A. Return it
B. Exchange with friends
C. Sell in the market and get money
D. Accept gracefully

14. Even after taking coaching from an Institute, you failed to get admission through competitive exam. You will:
A. Ask the Coaching Institute to return money
B. Ask your friends not to join that Institute
C. Try sincerely this time
D. Ask for 1 year free coaching

15. You are the Principal of a School. One of your teachers always comes late. You will:
A. Terminate him immediately
B. Initiate disciplinary action
C. Call him and counsel him
D. Ignore his mistakes

16. While staying in a Hotel you have given a shirt for laundry. Upon receiving, you found that shirt is damaged. You will:
A. Vacate the room immediately
B. Ask for the money against the damage
C. Call the laundry manager and lodge a complaint
D. Inform the person who is giving the shirt to you and advise him not to repeat it

17. In your opinion, how the poor should become rich:
A. The Poor should not dream to become rich
B. The Poor should be given good education, to help them find a job
C. Nothing can be done
D. Govt. should give money every month to the Poor

18. In a city, a large number of clubs organize Blood Donation Camps. You feel:
A. Some clubs are really doing a very good job to serve the society
B. Most clubs are making money, selling blood in market
C. The concept of club itself is useless concept
D. Clubs are doing just to get money from the Government

19. During your final examination D. J. party is going on next to your house. You will:
A. Try and ignore the issue
B. Politely request him to play music softly
C. Go and pick up a fight with him to stop the music
D. Go to friend's house and study there for exams

8. A **9.** D **10.** C **11.** D **12.** A **13.** D **14.** C **15.** C **16.** D **17.** B
18. A **19.** B

20. Near your Colony, some people are cutting trees, you will:
A. Ask your friends to do something about this matter
B. Think that this to be dealt by the Government only
C. Go and talk to the people who are cutting trees and make them understand the benefits of trees
D. Straight away file a complaint in Police Station

21. In your Class one boy is differently abled and most of your friends avoid interactions with him. You will:
A. Try and ignore that boy, like many others
B. Request all the students to help him
C. Always be in touch with him, and provide assistance as needed
D. Give him money as and when he requires

22. Your boss criticizes you in front of your colleagues. He does it repeatedly and this makes you feel insulted. You will:
A. Complain to seniors
B. Ignore the situation
C. Talk to him openly about the way you feel and request him not to do it any more
D. Go to other staff members, discuss with them and talk to him jointly

23. A classmate of yours tells you in confidence that he plans to report sick, while he is actually going for a movie, what will you do?
A. Inform the class Teacher
B. Not do anything & let him go
C. Tell him to be cautious and ask if he needs some cash
D. Advise him to be honest with his class

24. The work of a subordinate or a Team Member of yours is not up to expectations. What will you do?
A. Report to higher Authority
B. Insult him for not doing his work properly
C. Ignore the issue as it is not improvable
D. Talk to him in person about the issue and provide all assistance required by him to improve.

25. What would be your course of action if management changes priorities of a Project suddenly?
A. Immediately leave that Project
B. Notify everyone working on the Project of the changes
C. Ask all the members to leave the Project
D. Register your grievance as you don't like it at all

26. You see some persons are trying to rob an old woman by snatching her purse. You will:
A. Start shouting & try to save her
B. Go away from the place
C. Call the Police and wait there
D. Ask the woman to leave her purse

27. In case your school switches over to new Technology for modernization, as a Principal you would:
A. Make arrangements to train staff as per the new Technology
B. Remove all the staff who are not familiar with the new Technology
C. Forget about the implementation of new Technology
D. Get rid of the employees whom you think are surplus

28. In your opinion, you consider a person as a good human being if:
A. He praises everyone all the time
B. He lends money to everyone all the time
C. He always helps everyone when they are in trouble
D. He remains with everyone all the time

29. If your elder brother does not look after your old parents well, you would:
A. Like to talk to your brother about this issue
B. Feel that the old parents have got to live like this only
C. Feel that it may not be possible for your brother to do the needful due to some problem
D. Tell your parents to adjust with the situation

30. While working in a Hotel if you came across a Guest who is unhappy with the services and starts misbehaving at the Reception with you, you would:
A. Keep yourself cool and tell him/her that you would do your best to help him/her
B. Tell him/her that he/she has no business to misbehave at the Reception
C. Inform your Manager & and wait for their instructions
D. Call the Police & handover the Guest

31. Describe how you would handle a situation where your Company is resisting a new idea or policy
A. Tell them you already know everything
B. Tell them that you are already qualified and trained
C. Understand the benefits and implement the new idea or policy
D. Understand the new policy but stick to old policy only

20. C **21.** C **22.** C **23.** D **24.** D **25.** B **26.** A **27.** A **28.** C **29.** A
30. A **31.** C

32. In a class, you find that the Teacher has a thick accent and you can't understand, what's being said, what would you do?
A. Point it out to the Teacher about it
B. Ask someone to translate everything that what the Teacher is saying
C. Try your best to understand what the Teacher is saying
D. Don't attend the class and ask your friend to teach you later

33. As per you, which is the best quality one leader should have:
A. Function according to his/her own style & need not bother about others' opinion
B. Listen to others and then accordingly tackle the situation
C. Go always by what others say or suggest
D. Wait for others to take decision

34. A group of people were beating a thief on the roadside who has been caught red handed. Your reaction:
A. Will inform the Police and hand him over to them
B. Will allow people to keep on beating
C. Let him go after advising him not to repeat
D. Will myself start beating him until he bleeds

35. According to you, in Election you should vote:
A. Who happens to be rich
B. Who is well educated and also a man of good character
C. Who just happens to be known to your family
D. Who just simply belongs to a political family

36. You are working at the Reception of a Hotel. Presently there is no guest at the Reception. You will:
A. Be attentive & remain present at the Reception only
B. Start watching videos on mobile
C. Go to Cafeteria & relax
D. Start talking with your family and friends over mobile phone

37. A teacher of yours, always make fun of you in class. You will:
A. Ignore and focus on your studies
B. Complain to the chairman of the school
C. Never attend his/her class
D. Change the school

38. Due to security reasons, Security Services have locked down the Hotel. You are inside and in a hurry to get back home, what will you do?
A. Check for any sign of immediate danger and open to leave
B. You are sure that it is just a drill, so you will open the back door, which is locked from inside
C. Remain calm and wait for Security to give instructions
D. Put some music on mobile and enjoy your favourite songs

39. You have promised your friend to go with him for a movie on Saturday. Your sister falls sick on Saturday and would like to stay at home. What would you do?
A. Tell your friend that you have changed your mind
B. Go for the movie as you have promised
C. Apologise and make fresh promise
D. Tell him that you are sick, so you can't go with him

40. When you hear the news of a soldier getting killed on the borders, you feel:
A. He is paid by the Government to die for his country
B. It is a part of his duty to sacrifice his life
C. Such soldiers must be honoured by us
D. All of us should go to borders to help soldiers

41. You think that you have been given too much extra work by the School, due to which your studies are getting hampered. You will:
A. Complain to your father about it
B. Complain to your Principal about it
C. Tell everyone about it
D. Talk to your Class Teacher about it

42. A street light in your Society is not working, you will:
A. Ask for some donation and get it repaired
B. Inform the local Municipal Corporation to get it repaired
C. Do not worry as it is not your job
D. Put up a signage to highlight the condition of the light and ask people to be careful

43. In your opinion your Colleague is very stubborn. You will:
A. Inform other Colleagues
B. Inform your Boss
C. Keep talking to him and counsel
D. Speak loudly to make yourself heard

32. C	**33.** B	**34.** A	**35.** B	**36.** A	**37.** A	**38.** C	**39.** C	**40.** C	**41.** D
42. B	**43.** C								

44. According to you, for most jobs it is most important to hire persons with good attitudes and adequate intelligence rather than the ones with technical knowledge:
A. As per you, more qualities are required
B. You agree with the status
C. You disagree with the status
D. As per you, technical knowledge is not required

45. While making some changes in Company policy some of your staff think that changes create anxiety and not opportunity, then you:
A. Demonstrate your genuine concern
B. Do nothing about what your staff think
C. Ask him to speak to HR
D. Tell them the decision was not yours but of the management

46. You received a spam mail that you have won some cash prize, and to transfer the same, you are required to send your bank details. You will:
A. Immediately begin to send bank details
B. Will keep aside this mail and will not reply again
C. Just keep on thinking why you have received this mail
D. Will make a complaint to the local Police Station

47. If you read "women as Teachers and maids while men as Doctors and Pilots". This type of attitude/deception is likely to promote
A. Gender empowerment B. Gender stereotype
C. Gender role play D. Gender constancy

48. Sarthak is a day dreamer, having interest in reading books; not able to express his views before seniors; non friendly and idealistic employee, the type of attitude he has:
A. Extrovert B. Introvert
C. Ambient D. Athletic

49. How would you handle, a drunken Guest in the hotel?
A. Embarrass the Guest especially in front of other Guests
B. Deal with the intoxicated Guest, full of anger
C. Lock him until he behaves normally
D. Deal with the situation in a calm, friendly way

50. What are the attributes of an effective learner?
A. Self-directed
B. Curious and open minded
C. Self-aware
D. Self-directed, curious, open minded and self-aware

ENGLISH LANGUAGE

51. Following question consists of a word given in capital letters followed by four words. Choose the word that is most nearly the same in meaning to the word given in CAPITALS.

ABANDON
A. Leave B. Condone
C. Uphold D. Support

Directions (Qs. No. 52): *In the given sentence a word or phrase is written in capital letters. For each such word four words/phrases are listed below the sentence. Choose the word nearest in meaning to word in capitals.*

52. The inspector was a VIGILANT young man.
A. Smart B. Ambitious
C. Watchful D. Intelligent

53. Select the word which is most similar in meaning to AWKWARD.
A. Rough B. Clever
C. Dexterous D. Skillful

54. Select the word that is most similar in meaning to AMASS.
A. Spend B. Store
C. Dissipate D. Scatter

Directions (Qs. No. 55-59): *In the given Questions one part of the sentence has an error and the other parts of the sentence are correct. Find which part of the sentence has an error and choose that part as your answer out of (A), (B) and (C). If the sentence is free from error then choose your answer as choice (D).*

55. A. Vermin
B. Does much harm
C. to crops
D. No error

56. A. I am very anxious
B. to know how are you
C. and your mother doing well
D. No error

44. B	**45.** A	**46.** B	**47.** B	**48.** B	**49.** D	**50.** D	**51.** A	**52.** C	**53.** *
54. B	**55.** B	**56.** B, C							

57. A. Based on the newspaper reports
B. we can conclude that
C. many accidents caused by reckless driving
D. No error

58. A. He said it was the first time
B. that such a trick
C. is discovered
D. No error

59. A. He did not go
B. to the temple on foot
C. he went by the car
D. No error

Directions (Qs. No. 60-64): *In the following sentences, some of the words have been left out. Read the sentence carefully and choose the correct answer to each question out of four alternatives and fill in the blanks.*

60. The King was __________ while he was addressing his subjects.
A. Murdered B. Executed
C. Assassinated D. Exterminated

61. He would always be late with submissions because he would __________ whatever he was supposed to do.
A. Prevaricate B. Procrastinate
C. Interrogate D. Discriminate

62. He talked on and on __________.
A. Ad infinitum B. Voraciously
C. Hesitatingly D. Ad Interim

63. His __________ tastes and habits explain why he is always in debt.
A. Judicious B. Moderate
C. Thrifty D. Extravagant

64. We offer __________ to all who ask.
A. Council B. Councillor
C. Counsellor D. Counsel

Directions (Qs. No. 65): *In each of the following questions out of alternatives, choose the one which is most nearly opposite in meaning to underlined word.*

65. The ferocious ruler ruled.
A. Gentle B. Barbarous
C. Fierce D. Dangerous

Directions (Qs. No. 66 and 67): *In the given question containing main word followed by four words. Select the word that is most nearly the opposite in meaning.*

66. GRISLY
A. Attractive B. Monstrous
C. Disgusting D. Loathsome

67. GRACIOUS
A. Rude B. Beneficent
C. Magnificent D. Dignified

Directions (Qs. No. 68 and 69): *Out of the four alternatives, choose the one which can be substituted for the given words/sentences.*

68. One who is not sure about God's existence.
A. Agnostic B. Altruist
C. Amateur D. Ambidextrous

69. A lover of good food.
A. Connoisseur B. Gourmet
C. Honorary D. Insolvent

Directions (Qs. No. 70-72): *Four alternatives are given for the idiom/phrase underlined in the sentence. Choose the alternative which best expresses the meaning of the idiom/phrase.*

70. This medicine worked liked a charm and my health has greatly improved.
A. To be completely successful or effective
B. To be helpful
C. To be healthy
D. To be charming

71. The role of Priyanka Chopra in a popular series of Quantico was tailor - made for her.
A. To be completely suitable for someone.
B. To feel more comfortable or relaxed.
C. To make the situation worse.
D. To treat someone.

72. Rashi was really in seventh heaven when she got the promotion.
A. To be nervous and worried.
B. Extremely happy.
C. To prepare for trouble.
D. to feel more comfortable and relaxed.

73. The given sentence consists of a word or a phrase which is written in capital letters. Four options are given. Select the word or phrase which is closest to the opposite of the meaning of the word in capital letters.

The visit of the Vice - Chancellor has been DEFERRED indefinitely.
A. Expedited B. Dissolved
C. Postponed D. Put off

57. C	58. C	59. C	60. C	61. B	62. A	63. D	64. D	65. A	66. A
67. A	68. A	69. B	70. A	71. A	72. B	73. A			

74. Four alternatives are given for the idiom/phrase underlined in the sentence. Choose the alternative which best expresses the meaning of the idiom/ phrase.

Deepak tried to break the ice, but Hari was little cold.

A. To feel more comfortable or relaxed with a person whom you have not met earlier, to start a conversation.
B. To be impossible to understand.
C. To be completely suitable for someone.
D. To be happy.

75. In the given sentence a word is written in capital letters. Four options are given from which antonym is to be found out.

ACCOMPLISH

A. Compel B. Forgive
C. Disappoint D. Accuse

76. In the following question, out of the given alternatives, choose the one which is nearest in meaning to the underlined word in sentence.

For a lot of boys in India, becoming a successful cricket star has become an obsession. Earlier it was a hobby and sometimes passion.

A. Preoccupation B. Suspicion
C. Frustration D. Failure

Directions (Qs. No. 77-80): *Four words are given, out of which only one word is spelt correctly. Choose the correctly spelt word.*

77. A. Ocurencee B. Ocurrence
C. Occurence D. Occurrence

78. A. Nigardly B. Nuisence
C. Magnificient D. Eminent

79. A. Millionair B. Millionnaire
C. Millionaire D. Milionnaire

80. A. Bureocracy B. Burcucracy
C. Bureaucreacy D. Bureaucracy

Directions (Qs. No. 81-85): *In the given Question one part of the sentence has an error and the other parts of the sentence are correct. Find which part of the sentence has an error and choose that part as your answer out of (A), (B) and (C). If the sentence is free from errors then choose your answer as choice (D).*

81. A. Everyday new inventions
B. are make
C. for the good of humanity
D. No error

82. A. I finished my household chores
B. before he reached
C. to my place after so long
D. No Error

83. A. He is having an attack
B. of fever everyday
C. for the last few days
D. No error

84. A. If the farmer got the washing machine.
B. his wife can
C. do the laundry quickly
D. No Error

85. A. The Tata group owns
B. many industries that are spread
C. across the globe
D. No error

Directions (Qs. No. 86-90): *In the following sentences some of the words have been left out. Read the sentence carefully and choose the correct word out of the four alternatives and fill in the blanks.*

86. We should go ________ doing more good than harm.

A. On B. About
C. Above D. To

87. The two families have been engaged in a bitter ________ for the past two decades.

A. Anger B. Argument
C. Discussion D. Feud

88. The Traditional way of saying that you feel fine is to say that you are ________.

A. Alright B. All correct
C. All good D. All right

89. I haven't seen you ____________ a week.

A. Within B. Since
C. For D. From

90. Once he has signed the agreement, he won't be able to ________.

A. Back up B. Back in
C. Back it D. Back out

74. A	**75.** C	**76.** A	**77.** D	**78.** D	**79.** C	**80.** D	**81.** B	**82.** A, C	**83.** A
84. B	**85.** B	**86.** B	**87.** D	**88.** D	**89.** C	**90.** D			

GENERAL KNOWLEDGE AND CURRENT AFFAIRS

91. What device is used to measure the purity of milk?
A. Barometer B. Thermometer
C. Lactometer D. Hydrometer

92. What was the name of the first Indian Satellite launched in 1975?
A. Bhaskara B. Aryabhatta
C. Rohini D. Apple

93. Which is the longest epic in the world?
A. Bible B. Ramayana
C. Shakuntala D. Mahabharata

94. World's first test tube baby was born in which country?
A. India B. USA
C. England D. Australia

95. Which player of the Indian Women's Hockey team has been nominated for the "World Games Athlete of the Year" Award 2019, by the International Hockey Federation (FIH)?
A. Richa Rampal B. Bichu Devi Kharibam
C. Reena Khokhar D. Rajani Etimaspu

96. In which year were commonwealth games held in Delhi (India)?
A. 2006 B. 2010
C. 2014 D. 2018

97. Which part of the human body gets impaired due to Meningitis?
A. Joints
B. Lungs
C. Brain and spinal cord
D. Liver

98. The Prime minister of Britain stays in which of the following accommodation?
A. 10, Downing Street B. White House
C. Buckingham Palace D. Elysee Palace

99. The book "Long walk to freedom" was written by whom?
A. Nelson Mandela B. Jawahar Lal Nehru
C. M. K. Gandhi D. Bal Gangadhar Tilak

100. The only satellite of the earth is:
A. Moon B. Sun
C. Jupiter D. Saturn

101. Durand line is the boundary line between which two countries?
A. India and Pakistan
B. India and China
C. Pakistan and Afghanistan
D. India and Afghanistan

102. Reserve Bank of India was established in which year?
A. 1929 B. 1935
C. 1947 D. 1949

103. The college of Air warfare is located in which city of India?
A. Hyderabad B. Coimbatore
C. Secunderabad D. Chennai

104. Nicolaus Copernicus is known for:
A. He established that the planets orbited the Sun rather than the earth.
B. First person to reach south pole
C. First person to reach north pole
D. Discovery of Greenland and mountains of north pole

105. What is sea-farming *i.e.*, Cultivation of marine plants and animals for commercial purposes called?
A. Olericulture
B. Sericulture
C. Apiculture
D. Mariculture

106. Which is the longest National highway in the country?
A. NH-4 B. NH-8
C. NH-44 D. NH-49

107. The newspaper named "Guardian" is published in which country?
A. Britain B. USA
C. India D. China

108. The largest desert of the world is:
A. Arabian B. Australian
C. Thar D. Sahara

109. What is the ratio between land surface and water surface of earth?
A. 40 : 60 B. 71:21
C. 29 : 71 D. 49:51

91. C	**92.** B	**93.** D	**94.** C	**95.** *	**96.** B	**97.** C	**98.** A	**99.** A	**100.** A
101. C	**102.** B	**103.** C	**104.** A	**105.** D	**106.** C	**107.** A	**108.** D	**109.** C	

110. "Covid Katha" A multimedia guide for Mass Awareness on Covid-19 was launched by the union minister of science and technology health and family welfare and earth science. Who is the Science and Technology Minister of India?
A. Ravi Shankar Prasad
B. Raj Nath Singh
C. Harsh Vardhan
D. Amit Shah

111. Which town has been declared as cleanest Ganga town, by Swachh Survekshan Awards 2020, organized by Ministry of Housing and Urban Affairs?
A. Haridwar B. Varanasi
C. Allahabad D. Rishikesh

112. Who is the present president of USA?
A. Donald Trump B. Kamala Harris
C. Joe Biden D. Clinton

113. The largest salt water lagoon lake of India among the followings is:
A. Hussain Sagar, Telangana
B. Vembanad Lake, Kerala
C. Kolleru, Andhra Pradesh
D. Chilika Lake, Odisha

114. Which indian cricket player hit six sixes in one over in a T-20 international match?
A. M. S. Dhoni B. Virat Kohli
C. Kapil Dev D. Yuvraj

115. The well known Quote "Saare Jahan Se Achcha Hindustan Hamara" was penned by which scholar?
A. Jawahar Lal Nehru
B. Mohammed Iqbal
C. Bal Gangadhar Tilak
D. Bankim Chandra Chatterjee

116. Maharana Pratap was defeated by the Mughal Emperor Akbar in which famous battle?
A. Battle of Panipat B. Battle of Haldighati
C. Battle of Plassey D. Battle of Chausa

117. Who wrote the famous line: "A thing of beauty is a joy forever"?
A. John Keats B. Sir Richard Burton
C. V. S. Naipaul D. Larry Collins

118. Which country is known as the "Sugar Bowl" of the world?
A. Cuba B. Brazil
C. India D. USA

119. Which scale is used to measure the intensity of an earthquake?
A. Metric B. Centigrade
C. Richter D. Newton

120. When does solar eclipse take place?
A. When the sun is between Moon and Earth
B. When the Earth is between Moon and Sun
C. When the Moon is between Sun and Earth
D. When the Moon does not lie on the line joining the Sun and Earth

NUMERICAL ABILITY

121. Which of the following is divisible by 13?
A. 91 B. 94
C. 96 D. 99

122. Simplify: 7777 + 777 + 77 + 7
A. 8368 B. 8638
C. 8748 D. 8858

123. Find the average of the following set of scores:
105, 235, 326, 422
A. 222 B. 232
C. 252 D. 272

124. Ramesh brought 15 magazines for ₹ 30 from one shop and 25 magazines for ₹ 38 from another. What is the average price he paid per magazine?
A. ₹ 3 B. ₹ 33
C. ₹ 35 D. ₹ 37

125. Find a number such that when 7 is subtracted from 3 times the number, the result is 9 more than twice.
A. 10 B. 12
C. 14 D. 16

126. The sum of the squares of two positive integers is 130 and the difference of their squares is 32. The sum of the number is:
A. 13 B. 14
C. 15 D. 16

127. Evaluate: 80% of 480 + 25% of 640
A. 444 B. 544
C. 644 D. 744

110. C	**111.** B	**112.** C	**113.** D	**114.** D	**115.** B	**116.** B	**117.** A	**118.** A	**119.** C
120. C	**121.** A	**122.** B	**123.** D	**124.** *	**125.** D	**126.** D	**127.** B		

128. The present population of the villages is 6200. If the number of males increases by 12% and the number of female increases by 16%, then the population will become 7072. What is the present population of females in the village?

A. 3200 B. 3300
C. 3400 D. 3500

129. Sarla invests ₹ 97,200 which is 18% of her annual income, in fixed deposits. What is her monthly income?

A. ₹ 50,000 B. ₹ 45,000
C. ₹ 40,000 D. ₹ 35,000

130. 100 bananas are bought at rate of ₹ 400 and sold at the rate of ₹ 60 per dozen. The percentage of profit or loss is:

A. 10% gain B. 25% gain
C. 10% loss D. 25% loss

131. Aman buys an article for 20% less than its value and sells it for 20% more than its value. His gain or loss per cent is:

A. no profit, no loss B. less than 25% profit
C. more than 25% loss D. 50% profit

132. A man spends a part of his monthly income and saves a part of it. The ratio of his expenditure to his savings is 16 : 3. If his monthly income is ₹ 28500, what is the amount of his monthly savings?

A. ₹ 4,000 B. ₹ 4,500
C. ₹ 5,000 D. ₹ 5,500

133. Two numbers x and y are in the ratio 8 : 9 and their sum is 34. Then x is:

A. 10 B. 12
C. 14 D. 16

134. The ratio of ages of father to son is 13 : 2. Eighteen years later the ratio of their ages will be 2 : 1 respectively. What is son's present age?

A. 4 years B. 6 years
C. 8 years D. 10 years

135. Ram and Shyam can plough a field in 12 days. Shyam alone can plough the field in 18 days. In how many days will Ram alone plough the field?

A. 24 days B. 28 days
C. 32 days D. 36 days

136. A train running at the speed of 60 km/hr crosses a pole in 9 seconds. What is the length of the train?

A. 150 m B. 180 m
C. 210 m D. 240 m

137. A train of length 350 m takes 96 seconds to cross a tunnel of length 450 meters. What is the speed of train in km/hr?

A. 20 B. 25
C. 30 D. 35

138. The speed of the boat when travelling downstream is 38 km/hr, whereas when travelling upstream it is 32 km/hr, what is the speed (in km/hr) of boat in still water?

A. 33 B. 34
C. 35 D. 36

139. A boatman rows 2 km in 4 minutes, along the stream and 6 km in 30 minutes against the stream. The speed of the stream is:

A. 3 kmph B. 6 kmph
C. 9 kmph D. 12 kmph

140. In how many years will a sum of money double itself at $8\frac{1}{3}\%$ simple interest per annum?

A. 8 years B. 12 years
C. 16 years D. 20 years

141. At the rate of $8\frac{1}{2}\%$ p.a simple interest, a sum of ₹ 4800 will earn how much interest in 3 years?

A. ₹ 876 B. ₹ 1026
C. ₹ 1148 D. ₹ 1124

142. The value of $\sqrt{10+\sqrt{25+\sqrt{108+\sqrt{154+\sqrt{225}}}}}$ is:

A. 4 B. 6
C. 8 D. 10

143. $\sqrt{\frac{5}{4}}-\sqrt{\frac{4}{5}}=?$

A. $\frac{5\sqrt{3}}{2}$ B. $\frac{1}{5\sqrt{2}}$
C. $\frac{1}{2\sqrt{5}}$ D. 1

144. If the length of a rectangle is increased by 10% and it's breadth is decreased by 10%, the change in its area will be:

A. 1% increase
B. 1% decrease
C. 10% increase
D. No change

128. A	**129.** B	**130.** B	**131.** D	**132.** B	**133.** D	**134.** A	**135.** D	**136.** A	**137.** C
138. C	**139.** C	**140.** B	**141.** *	**142.** A	**143.** C	**144.** B			

145. The cost of copyright a room long with a carpet 75 cm wide at ₹ 4.50 per meter is ₹ 810. The breadth of the room is:

A. 7 m B. 7.5 m
C. 8 m D. 8.5 m

Directions (Qs. No. 146-150): *Study the bar diagram given below carefully and answer the following questions based on it.*

Birth Rate in Different Countries

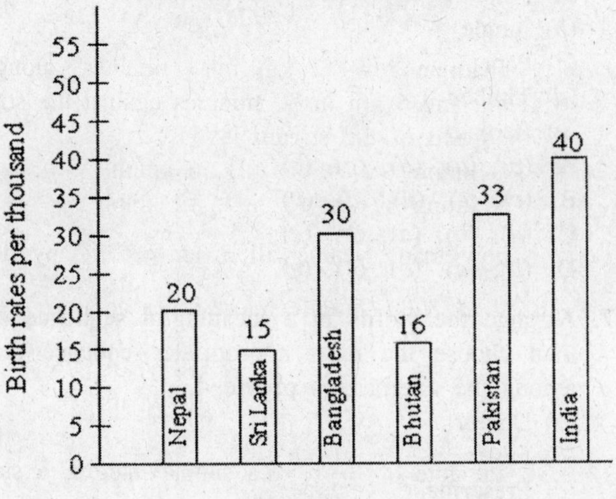

146. The birth rate of which country is 25% more than that of Bhutan?

A. Pakistan
B. India
C. Nepal
D. Bangladesh

147. The birth rate of Pakistan is what per cent of birth of Nepal?

A. 165% B. 155%
C. 140% D. 100%

148. The birth rate of India is how many times the birth rate of Bhutan?

A. 0.4 B. 5.2
C. 4 D. 2.5

149. What is the ratio of birth rate of Pakistan to Sri Lanka?

A. 5 : 11 B. 11 : 5
C. 2 : 1 D. 1 : 2

150. By how much per cent is the birth rate of Nepal less than the birth rates of Bangladesh?

A. 30% B. $33\frac{1}{3}$%
C. 45% D. 50%

REASONING AND LOGICAL DEDUCTION

151. Number series is with one term missing. Choose the correct alternative from given options.

1, 9, 25, ?, 81, 121

A. 64 B. 36
C. 91 D. 49

152. In the following question one item in the number series is wrong. Find out the wrong item.

3, 5, 15, 75, 1125, 20000

A. 3 B. 15
C. 1125 D. 20000

153. If BIBLIO is coded as BIBOIL and NEARER as AENRER, then ALIGATOR will be coded as:

A. ROTAALIG B. ALIGROTA
C. GILAROTA D. GILAATOR

154. In a certain language, BRIDE is coded as APEZZ, then which word would be coded as LKUMB:

A. MMXQG B. MLVNC
C. KIRIW D. KJTLA

155. Introducing a man, a woman said, "He is only son of my mother's mother." How is the woman related to the man?

A. Mother B. Aunt
C. Sister D. Niece

156. Pointing to a photograph, a person tells his friend, "She is grand daughter of elder brother of my father. "How is the girl in the photograph related to this man?

A. Sister B. Aunt
C. Sister-in-law D. Niece

157. A B C D E F G H I J K L M N O P Q R S T U V W X Y Z Which letter is exactly midway between F and R in the alphabet series?

A. K B. M
C. L D. N

145. * **146.** C **147.** A **148.** D **149.** B **150.** B **151.** D **152.** D **153.** C **154.** *
155. D **156.** D **157.** C

158. A B C D E F G H I J K L M N O P Q R S T U V W X Y Z Which letter is fifteenth to the right of the letter which is fourth to the left of I?

A. T　　B. U
C. S　　D. R

159. 4, 8, 16, 32, 64, ? , 256, 512

A. 128　　B. 127
C. 126　　D. 132

160. 6, 9, 12, 15, 18, ?

A. 20　　B. 21
C. 22　　D. 23

161. Introducing Usha to the guests, Piyush said, "Her father is the only son of my father." How is Usha related to Piyush?

A. Mother　　B. Sister
C. Daughter　　D. Niece

162. Introducing a man, Murali said, "His wife is the only daughter of my wife." How is Murali related to that man?

A. Father
B. Son
C. Grandfather
D. Father-in-law

163. 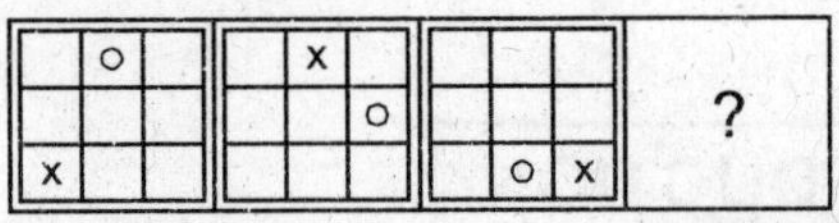

A. 　　B. 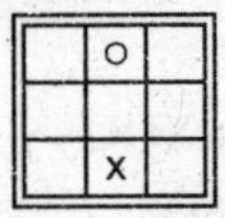

C. 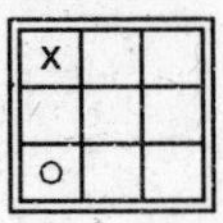　　D. 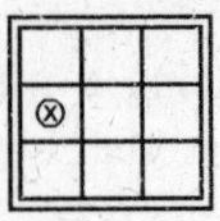

164. 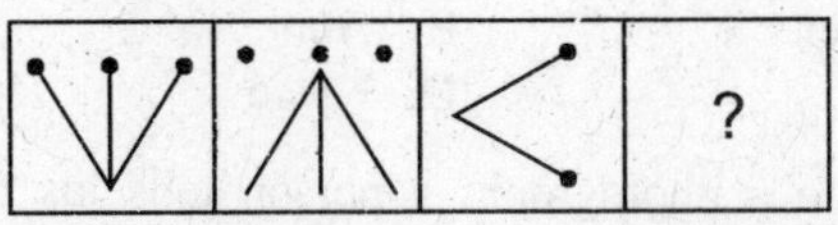

A. 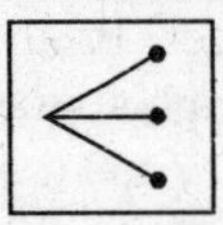　　B. 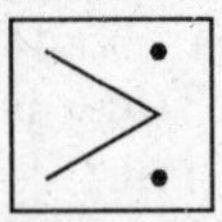

C. 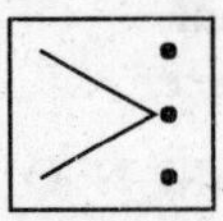　　D. 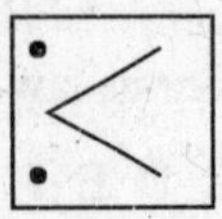

165. Arrange the words in a meaningful sequence and then choose the most appropriate seque-nce from among the alternatives provided.

(*a*) Wax
(*b*) Bee
(*c*) Honey
(*d*) Flower

A. (*b*), (*a*), (*c*), (*d*)　　B. (*d*), (*b*), (*c*), (*a*)
C. (*d*), (*c*), (*b*), (*a*)　　D. (*c*), (*d*), (*b*), (*a*)

166. Arrange the words in a meaningful sequence and then choose the most appropriate sequence from amongst the alternatives provided.

(*a*) Pulp
(*b*) Jungle
(*c*) Paper
(*d*) Timber
(*e*) Book

A. (*b*), (*a*), (*d*), (*c*), (*e*)
B. (*c*), (*e*), (*a*), (*d*), (*b*)
C. (*d*), (*b*), (*a*), (*c*), (*e*)
D. (*b*), (*d*), (*a*), (*c*), (*e*)

167. Arrange the words in a meaningful sequence and then choose the most appropriate sequence from among the alternatives provided.

(*a*) Doctor
(*b*) Fever
(*c*) Prescribe
(*d*) Diagnose
(*e*) Medicine

A. (*a*), (*d*), (*c*), (*b*), (*e*)
B. (*b*), (*a*), (*c*), (*d*), (*e*)
C. (*b*), (*a*), (*d*), (*c*), (*e*)
D. (*b*), (*d*), (*c*), (*e*), (*a*)

168. Choose the alternative which most closely resembles the mirror-image of the given word.

WHITE

A. ƎꓕIHW　　B. EꓕIHM
C. ƎTIHM　　D. ƎTIHW

169. Choose the alternative which most closely resembles the mirror-image of the given word.

START

A. SꓕAЯꓕ　　B. ƧTAЯT
C. ƧTVRT　　D. SꓕVRꓕ

170. Choose the alternative which most closely resembles the mirror-image of the given word.

SUN

A. ƧUИ　　B. SՈN
C. ƧՈИ　　D. SUИ

158. A　**159.** A　**160.** B　**161.** C　**162.** D　**163.** D　**164.** B　**165.** B　**166.** D　**167.** C
168. D　**169.** B　**170.** A

171. Find out the odd among the four:
A. Patna B. Mumbai
C. Ahmedabad D. Dehradun

172. Find out the odd among the four:
A. Arrow B. Spear
C. Bullet D. Sword

173. Find out the odd among the four:
A. Hands B. Legs
C. Ears D. Nose

174. What is the next term in the series?

FEVU, IHSR, LKPO, ONML
A. QPPH B. RQJI
C. POQK D. LROI

175. What is the next term in the series?

P, T, X, B, F
A. I B. J
C. K D. H

Directions (Qs. No. 176 and 177): *There is a certain relation between two given words on one side of : : and one word is given on another side of : : While another word is to be found from the given alternatives, having the same relation with this word as the given pair has. Select the best alternative.*

176. Himachal : Nati : : Kerala : ?
A. Bharatnatyam B. Kathak
C. Kuchipudi D. Kathakali

177. Moon : Satellite : : Earth : ?
A. Planet B. Sun
C. Round D. Solar system

178. Simran walks 12 km towards North. From there she walks 8 km towards South. Then she walks 3 km towards East. How far and in which direction is she with reference to her starting point?
A. 5 km East B. 7 km East
C. 5 km North-East D. 7 km North-East

179. In the following question, arrange the given words in the sequence in which they occur in the dictionary and then choose the correct sequence.
(*a*) Wound (*b*) Writer
(*c*) Whiter (*d*) Worst
(*e*) Worked
A. (*a*), (*d*), (*c*), (*e*), (*b*)
B. (*b*), (*a*), (*c*), (*d*), (*e*)
C. (*c*), (*e*), (*d*), (*a*), (*b*)
D. (*e*), (*c*), (*b*), (*a*), (*d*)

180. You are requested to construct a word from the letters given below. Each letters are numbered and the word is followed by four options. Choose the option which gives the correct order of the letters as indicated by the numbers to form a word.

T R F U I
1 2 3 4 5

A. 1, 2, 3, 4, 5 B. 2, 4, 3, 5, 1
C. 3, 4, 2, 5, 1 D. 3, 2, 4, 5, 1

COMPREHENSION

Directions (Qs. No. 181-184): *Read the following passages carefully and answer the questions that follow.*

Stammering is a habit disorder linked with lack of self confidence. Basically for a child to understand a language, there are four stages. The first is learning to understand the spoken language and the second is speaking. Both of these develop around age of two years.

The third stage is speaking complex sentences, which develops at around 3rd and 4th i.e. when the child recognizes the written alphabet. In 80% of children while the 3rd & 4th stage are at play, the first two get disturbed as something new is being incorporated in the mind.

This is absolutely normal. But what over cautious mothers do is fret a lot and the child develops fear which later manifests itself as stammering. In fact, most text books on stammering state in bold that "Had there not been any over cautious mothers, hardly anyone would have suffered from stammering." Fluency can be incorporated in the speech of such patients through hypnosis.

181. Stammering is caused because of:
A. physical disorder
B. hindered growth
C. lack of self-confidence
D. lack of understanding

182. The second stage of a child's understanding the language is:
A. speaking B. writing
C. listening D. reading

171. C **172.** D **173.** D **174.** B **175.** B **176.** D **177.** A **178.** C **179.** C **180.** D
181. C **182.** A

183. Fluency can be incorporated in the speech of such patients through:
A. hypnosis B. slap
C. punishment D. symbiosis

184. By the time the child becomes two years old he/she can:
A. speak complex sentences
B. only understand spoken language
C. understand and speak simple language
D. write the alphabets

Directions (Qs. No. 185-189): *Read the following passages carefully and answer the questions that follow.*

Street theatre in India is a well established ancient art form. Despite the proliferation of modern means of entertainment and communication, street theatre continues to flourish in India. Street theatre as a channel of communication has for centuries been propagating reforms by highlighting social, economic and political issues present in the society. Unlike in the olden days, its performance is no longer restricted to villages or small localities of the city. Today small group of performers including students would stage performances to mobilize public opinion or to help create or raise awareness over an issue of particular public importance.

Themes on substance abuse, AIDS awareness and domestic violence are some of the areas highlighted by contemporary street theatre. Unlike in regular drama, street dramas employ very little props and images. The human body become the main tool in which choreography, mime, dialogues, songs and slogans are extensively used.

Street theatre is one of the most intimate media. Its appeal is to the emotions leading to quick psychological impact on audiences. By being local and live they also are able to establish not only direct contact with audience, but being cost effective and flexible they are popular among all age groups.

185. Modern means of entertainment and communication ________ street theatre.
A. does affect
B. does not affect
C. helps popularize
D. help establish

186. In the olden days street theatre ________.
A. was restricted
B. was not restricted
C. was opened
D. was entertained

187. Street theatre usually ________ with issues of public importance.
A. is distanced
B. is performed
C. deals
D. does not deal

188. Street theatre is ________ as compared to stage.
A. Nothing B. Costly
C. Reasonable D. Affordable

189. Street theatre creates an/a ________ impact on audiences.
A. Intimate B. Emotional
C. Mystical D. Physical

Directions (Qs. No. 190-193): *Read the following passages carefully and answer the questions that follow.*

One simple physical contact lies behind the formation of a star, gravitational instability. The concept is not new. Newton first perceived it late in the 17th century.

Imagine a uniform, static cloud of gas in space. Imagine then that the gas is somehow disturbed so that one small spherical region becomes a little denser than the gas around it so that the small region's gravitational field becomes slightly stronger. It now attracts more matter to it and its gravity increases further, causing it to begin to contract. As it contracts its density increases which increases the gravity even more, so that it picks up even more matter and contracts even further. The process continues until the small region of gas finally forms a gravitationally bound object.

190. The primary purpose of the passage is to:
A. describe a static condition
B. support a theory considered out dated
C. depict the successive stages of a phenomenon
D. demonstrate the evolution of the meaning of term

191. It can be inferred from this passage that the author views the information contained within it as:
A. Lacking in elaboration
B. Original but obscure
C. Speculative and unprofitable
D. Uncomplicated and traditional

192. With which following words can you replace the word uniform as given in this passage?
A. Uniting
B. Varying
C. Gaseous
D. Unvarying

183. A	184. C	185. A	186. A	187. C	188. D	189. A	190. C	191. D	192. D

193. What does the underlined word 'it' stand for in the passage?
A. Gravitational instability
B. Cloud of gas
C. Small spherical denser region
D. Matter

Directions (Qs. No. 194 and 195): *Read the following passages carefully and answer the questions that follow.*

In our approach to life, be it pragmatic or otherwise, a basic fact that confronts us squarely and mistakenly is desire for peace, security and happiness. Different forms of life at different levels of existence make up the teeming denizens of this earth of ours. And no matter whether they belong to the higher groups such as animals, all beings primarily seek peace, comfort and security. Life is as dear to a mute creature as it is to Man. Even the lowliest insect strives for protection against dangers that threaten its life. Just as each one of us wants to live and not to die, so do all other creatures.

194. What is the main point of the author?
A. Different forms of life are found on earth
B. Different levels of existence are possible in nature
C. Peace and security are the chief goals of all living beings
D. Even the weakest creature struggles to protect its life.

195. Which one of the following assumptions is essential for developing the author's position?
A. All forms of life have a single overriding goal.
B. The will to survive of a creature is identified with a desire for peace.
C. All beings are divided into higher and lower groups.
D. A parallel is drawn between happiness and life and pain and death.

Directions (Qs. No. 196-199): *Read the following passages carefully and answer the questions that follow.*

The capitalist system of the society does not foster healthy relations among human beings. A few people own all the means of production and others though nominally few have to sell their labour under conditions imposed upon them, the emphasis of capitalism being on the supreme importance of material wealth. The intensity of its appeal is to the acquisitive intensity. It promotes worship of economic power with little regard to the means employed for its acquisition and the end that it serves. By its exploitation of human beings to the limits of endurance, its concentration is on the largest profit rather than maximum production.

Thus division of human family is done on the basis of economic circumstances. All this is injurious to division of human dignity. And when the harrowed Poor turn to the founders of religion for succor, they rather offer a subtle defence of the established order. They promise future happiness for their present suffering and conjure up vision of paradise to redress the balance to soothe the suffering and the revolt of the tortured man. The system imposes injustice, religion justifies it.

196. The passage indicates the capitalist system is:
A. Fair
B. Ambitious
C. Prosperous
D. Dehumanizing

197. The established order is supported by religion to:
A. alleviate the suffering of the poor in the capitalist system.
B. perpetuate the injustice imposed by the capitalist system.
C. balance the suffering of the poor with hope of future rewards.
D. help the tortured man to seek redress.

198. In a capitalist system:
A. the means justify the ends
B. the ends justify the means
C. the means endorsed by religion are strictly followed
D. means which lead to exploitation are strictly prohibited

199. Capitalism is injurious to human relations because it divides society into groups *i.e.*
A. working and non-working
B. exploiters and exploited
C. religious and irreligious
D. buyers and sellers

200. Four words are given, out of which only one word is spelt correctly.

Choose the correctly spelt word.
A. Sattelite
B. Satalite
C. Sattelit
D. Satellite

193. C	**194.** C	**195.** B	**196.** D	**197.** B	**198.** B	**199.** B	**200.** D

EXPLANATORY ANSWERS

121. A. $91 = 7 \times 13$

B. $74 = 2 \times 47$

C. $96 = 4 \times 24$

D. $99 = 9 \times 11$

Hence, (A) 91 is divisible by 13.

122. $7777 + 777 + 77 + 7 = 8638.$

123. $$\text{Average} = \frac{105+235+326+422}{4} = \frac{1088}{4} = 272.$$

125. Let number $= x$

Then, $3x - 7 = 2x + 9$

$\Rightarrow \quad 3x - 2x = 7 + 9$

$\Rightarrow \quad x = 16$

126. Let the two positive integers are x and y

Then, $x^2 + y^2 = 130 \quad ...(i)$

$x^2 - y^2 = 32 \quad ...(ii)$

From Adding (*i*) and (*ii*),

$2x^2 = 162$

$\Rightarrow \quad x^2 = 81$

$\Rightarrow \quad x = 9$

From (*i*),

$y^2 = 130 - x^2$

$= 130 - 81 = 49$

$\Rightarrow \quad y^2 = (7)^2$

$\Rightarrow \quad y = 7$

Hence, the sum of the number $= x + y$

$= 9 + 7 = 16.$

127. 80% of 480 + 25% of 640

$$= 480\times\frac{80}{100}+640\times\frac{25}{100}$$

$$= 48\times8+640\times\frac{1}{4}$$

$= 384 + 160$

$= 544.$

128. Let the present population of males and females are x and $(6200 - x)$ in the village.

Then, $$x\times\frac{112}{100}+(6200-x)\times\frac{116}{100} = 7072$$

$$\Rightarrow \frac{112}{100}x-\frac{116}{100}x+62\times116 = 7072$$

$$\Rightarrow -\frac{4x}{100} = 7072 - 7192$$

$$\Rightarrow -\frac{4x}{100} = -120$$

$\Rightarrow \quad 4x = 120 \times 100$

$\Rightarrow \quad x = 3000$

Hence, the present population of females in the village

$= (6200 - x) = 6200 - 3000 = 3200$

129. 18% of annual income = ₹ 97,200

$$\Rightarrow \text{annual income } \frac{18}{100} = 97200$$

$$\Rightarrow \text{annual income } = \frac{97200\times100}{18}$$

$= 5400 \times 100$

Hence, Sarita's monthly income

$$= \frac{5400\times100}{12}$$

$= 450 \times 100$

= ₹ 45000

130. The cost price of 1 banana = ₹ $\frac{400}{100}$ = ₹ 4

and the selling price of 1 dozen banana = ₹ 60

$\Rightarrow$ the selling price of 1 banana $= \frac{60}{12}$ = ₹ 5

Profit = S.P. – C.P. = 5 – 4 = ₹ 1

$$\therefore \text{Profit\%} = \frac{\text{Profit}\times100}{\text{C.P.}} = \frac{1\times100}{4} = 25\%$$

131. Let value of an article = ₹ 100

Then the cost price = ₹ 80

and the selling price = ₹ 120

$\therefore$ Profit = S.P. – C.P.

$= 120 - 80 = 40$

$$\therefore \text{Profit \%} = \frac{\text{Profit}\times100}{\text{C.P.}}$$

$$= \frac{40\times100}{80} = 50\%$$

132. Let expenditure and saving are $16x$ and $3x$

Then, income = expenditure + saving

$\Rightarrow \quad 28500 = 16x + 3x$

$\Rightarrow \quad 19x = 28500$

$\Rightarrow \quad x = \frac{28500}{19}$

$= 1500$

Hence, his monthly savings

$= 3x = 3 \times 1500$

$= ₹\ 4500$

133. Let two number x and y are $8k$ and $9k$.

Then, $8k + 9k = 34$

$\Rightarrow \quad 17k = 34$

$\Rightarrow \quad k = 2$

Hence, $\quad x = 8k$

$= 8 \times 2 = 16.$

134. Let the present age of father and son are $13x$ years and $2x$ years.

Then, after 18 years

$$\frac{13x+18}{2x+18} = \frac{2}{1}$$

$\Rightarrow \quad 13x + 18 = 4x + 36$

$\Rightarrow \quad 13x - 4x = 36 - 18$

$\Rightarrow \quad 9x = 18$

$\Rightarrow \quad x = 2$

Hence, Son's present age

$= 2x = 2 \times 2$

$= 4$ years.

135. (Ram + Shyam)'s 1 day's plough a field $= \frac{1}{12}$

and Shyam's 1 day's plough a field $= \frac{1}{18}$

$\therefore$ Ram's 1 day's plough a field $= \frac{1}{12} - \frac{1}{18}$

$= \frac{3-2}{36} = \frac{1}{36}$

Hence, Ram will alone plough the field in 36 days.

136. Given, speed of a train = 60 km/hr

$= 60 \times \frac{5}{18}$ m/sec.

Time = 9 seconds

$\because \quad \frac{\text{Length of the train}}{\text{Time}} = \text{Speed of a train}$

$\therefore$ Length of train = Time $\times$ speed of a train

$= 9 \times 60 \times \frac{5}{18}$ m

$= 30 \times 5 = 150$ m

137. The speed of train $= \frac{\text{Distance}}{\text{Time}}$

$= \frac{350+450}{96}$ m/s

$= \frac{800}{96} \times \frac{18}{5}$ km/hr

$= \frac{160 \times 3}{16} = 30$ km/hr

138. Let the speed of a boat in still water is u km/hr and the speed of the stream is v km/hr.

Then, $\quad u + v = 38 \quad \ldots(i)$

$u - v = 32 \quad \ldots(ii)$

From adding (i) and (ii)

$2u = 70, \Rightarrow u = 35$ km/hr.

Hence, the speed of boat in still water

$= 35$ km/hr.

139. Speed downstream $= (u + v)$ km/hr

$= \frac{2}{4} \times 60 = 30$ km/hr

$\Rightarrow u + v = 30 \quad \ldots(i)$

and speed upstream $= (u - v)$ km/hr.

$= \frac{6}{30} \times 60$

$= 12$ km/hr

$\Rightarrow \quad u - v = 12 \quad \ldots(ii)$

From adding (i) and (ii),

$2u = 42$

$\Rightarrow \quad u = 21$ km/hr.

Putting the value of u in (i)

$\therefore 21 + v = 30$

$\Rightarrow \quad v = 30 - 21$

$= 9$

$\Rightarrow \quad v = 9$ km/hr.

Therefore, the speed of boat in still water

$= u = 21$ km/hr.

and the speed of the stream

$= v = 9$ km/hr.

140. Let sum of money $= p$

Then, $\quad$ A = Amount $= 2p$

$\therefore$ Interest $= 2p - p = p$

Given, rate $= 8\frac{1}{3}\%$

$= \frac{25}{3}\%$

$\therefore$ Time $= \dfrac{I \times 100}{p \times r}$

$= \dfrac{p \times 100}{p \times \dfrac{25}{3}}$

$= 100 \times \dfrac{3}{25}$

$= 12$ years

Hence, time = 12 years.

142. $\sqrt{10+\sqrt{25+\sqrt{108+\sqrt{154+\sqrt{225}}}}}$

$= \sqrt{10+\sqrt{25+\sqrt{108+\sqrt{154+15}}}}$

$= \sqrt{10+\sqrt{25+\sqrt{108+\sqrt{169}}}}$

$= \sqrt{10+\sqrt{25+\sqrt{108+13}}}$

$= \sqrt{10+\sqrt{25+\sqrt{121}}}$

$= \sqrt{10+\sqrt{25+11}}$

$= \sqrt{10+\sqrt{36}}$

$= \sqrt{16}$

$= 4.$

143. $\sqrt{\dfrac{5}{4}}-\sqrt{\dfrac{4}{5}} = \dfrac{\sqrt{5}}{\sqrt{4}}-\dfrac{\sqrt{4}}{\sqrt{5}} = \dfrac{\sqrt{5}}{2}-\dfrac{2}{\sqrt{5}}$

$= \dfrac{5-4}{2\sqrt{5}}$

$= \dfrac{1}{2\sqrt{5}}.$

144. Let length $= x$ and breadth $= y$

Then, area of a rectangle $= xy$

and given,

length $= x+\dfrac{10}{100}x$

$= \dfrac{110x}{100} = \dfrac{11}{10}x$

and breadth $= y-\dfrac{10}{100}y$

$= \dfrac{90y}{100}$

$= \dfrac{9}{10}y$

$\therefore$ area of a rectangle $= \dfrac{11}{10}x \times \dfrac{9}{10}y$

$= \dfrac{99}{100}xy$

Hence, the change in its area

$= \dfrac{xy-\dfrac{99}{100}xy}{xy} \times 100\%$

$= \dfrac{\dfrac{1}{100}xy}{xy} \times 100\%$

$= 1\%$

Hence, its area will decrease by 1%.

146. From given bar diagram

Bhutan = 16

$\because$ 25% more than that of Bhutan

$= 16 \times \dfrac{125}{100}$

$= 16 \times \dfrac{5}{4}$

$= 4 \times 5$

$= 20$

Hence, Nepal (20) is 25% more than that of Bhutan.

147. From given bar diagram

Pakistan = 33,

Nepal = 20

$\because$ Pakistan $= x$ % of Nepal

$\therefore$ $33 = x\%$ of 20

$\Rightarrow$ $20 \times \dfrac{x}{100} = 33$

$\Rightarrow$ $\dfrac{1}{5}x = 33$

$\Rightarrow$ $x = 5 \times 33$

$= 165$

Hence, $x = 165\%$

148. From given bar diagram

Birth rate

India = 40,

and Bhutan = 16

$\because$ $40 = x \times 16$

$\therefore$ $x = \dfrac{40}{16} = \dfrac{5}{2} = 2.5$

Hence, the birth rate of India is 2.5 times the birth rate of Bhutan.

149. From given bar diagram

The ratio of birth rate of Pakistan to Sri Lanka

$= 33 : 15$

$= 11 : 5.$

150. From given bar diagram

Birth rate :

Nepal $= 20,$

Bangladesh $= 30$

Required per cent $= \dfrac{30-20}{30} \times 100$

$= \dfrac{10}{30} \times 100$

$= 33\dfrac{1}{3}\%.$

151. Given, number series

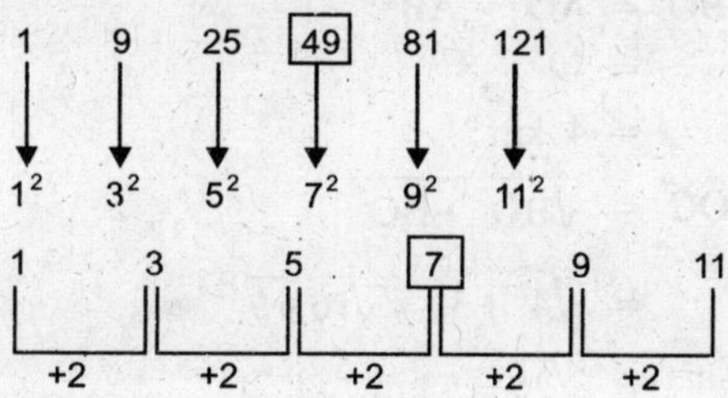

Here, ? = Missing term $= 7^2 = 49.$

152. Given, the number series.

3, 5, 15, 75, 1125, 20000

Here,

3rd term = 1st term × 2nd term

$= 3 \times 5$

$= 15$

4th term = 2nd term × 3rd term

$= 5 \times 15$

$= 75$

5th term = 3rd term × 4th term

$= 15 \times 75$

$= 1125$

6th term = 4th term × 5th term

$= 75 \times 1125$

$= 84375$

So, In place of 20000 it should be 84375

∴ Wrong item = 20000

153. Given, BIBLIO is coded as BIBOIL

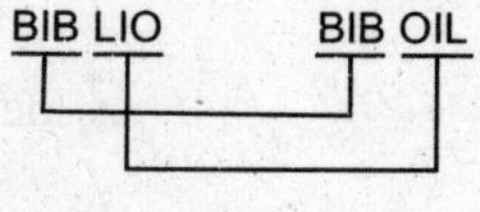

and NEARER as AENRER

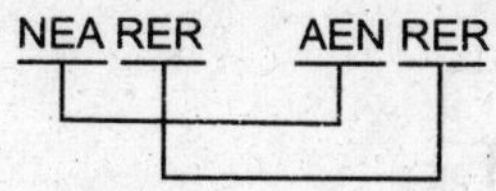

Similarly,

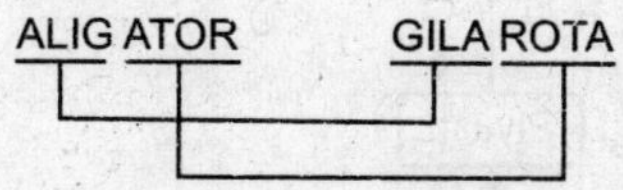

The word is divided into two section and the letters are written backwards.

Hence, ALIGATOR will be coded as GILAROTA.

155.

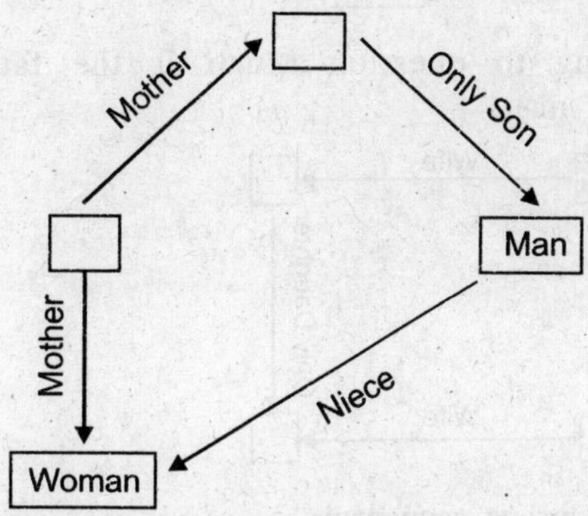

Here, woman is the niece of the man.

156.

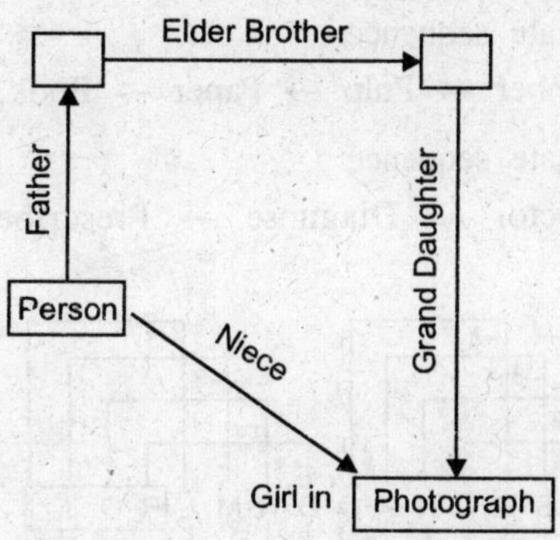

Here, The girl in the photograph is niece of person.

157. Midway between F and R in the alphabet series = L.

158. ∵ Fourth to the left of I = E.

∴ Fifteenth letter to the right of E = T.

159.

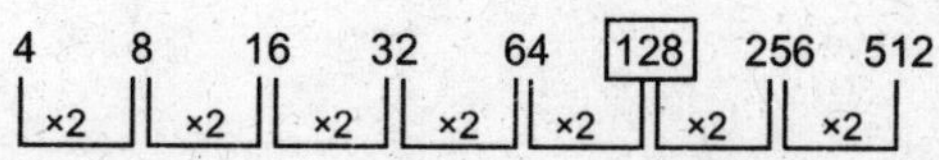

? = Missing number = 128.

160.

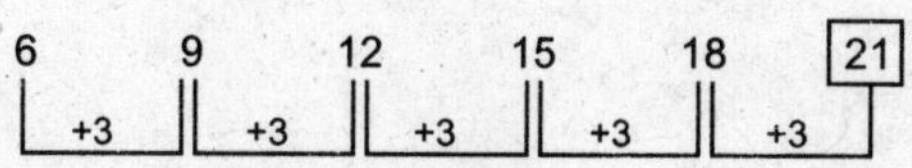

Here, the next number = ? = 21.

161. According to question Usha is the Daughter of Piyush.

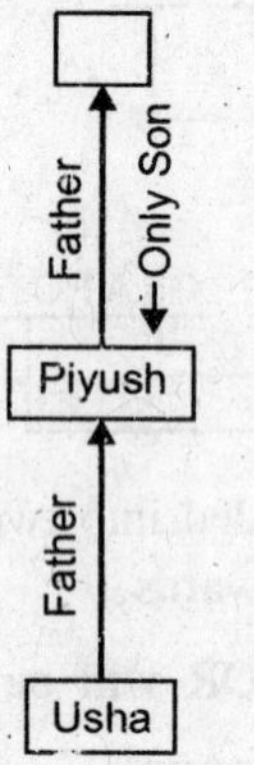

162. According to question Murli is the father-in-law of man.

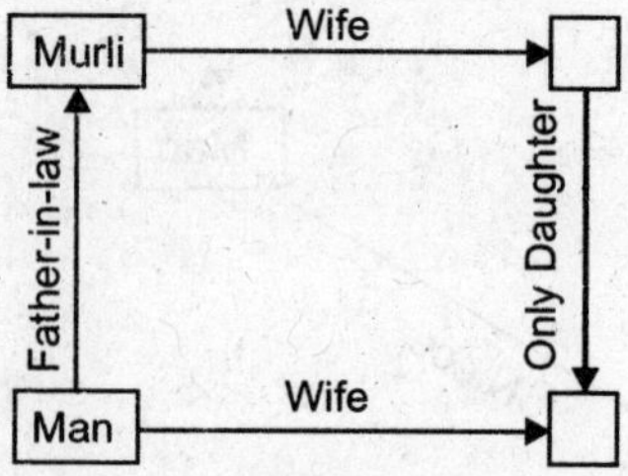

165. The appropriate sequence:
Flower → Bee → Honey → Wax

166. Most appropriate sequence
Jungle → Timber → Pulp → Paper → Book.

167. Most appropriate sequence
Fever → Doctor → Diagnose → Prescribe → Medicine.

174.

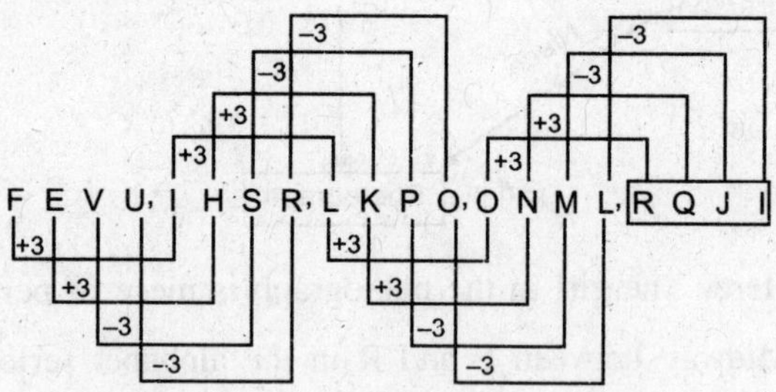

The next term in the series = RQJI.

175.

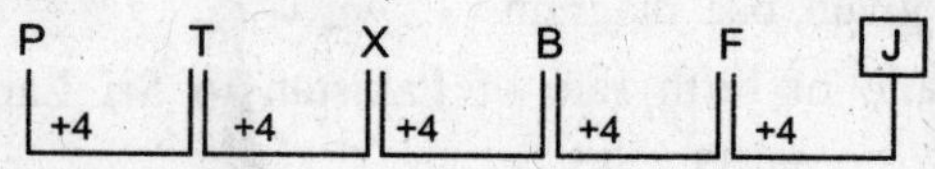

The next term in the series = J.

178. Here, starting point = O

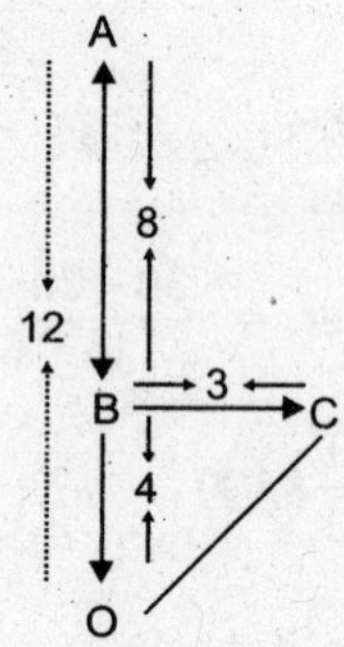

OA = 12 km, AB = 8 km

BC = 3 km

BO = AO − AB

= 12 − 8

= 4 km

$$OC = \sqrt{BO^2 + BC^2}$$

$$= \sqrt{4^2 + 3^2} = \sqrt{16+9}$$

$$= \sqrt{25} = 5 \text{ km}$$

Hence, C(Simran) is 5 km far North-East from her starting point.

179. According to dictionary,
words can be arranged in the following sequence.
Whites → Worked → Worst → Wound → Writer

180. Given, letter

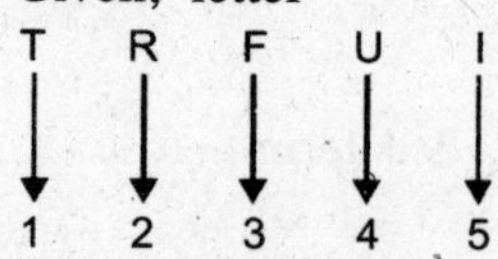

We construct a word from the given letters

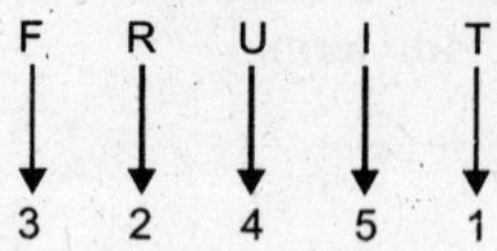

Aptitude For Service Sector

OBJECTIVE QUESTIONS

1. Your opinion about yourself is that
A. my work is not helping me
B. my luck is not supporting me
C. I am a burden on the earth
D. I should continue to do my work without worrying about its result

2. When you participate in a conference as a listener, you
A. do not agree with the ideas of the speaker
B. interrupt the speaker time and again while he speaks
C. listen to the speech with patience and then, express your reaction
D. do not say anything as you are too reluctant to express yourself

3. When you are invited to attend social gatherings, you
A. are reluctant to attend
B. are in a dilly-dally mood (*i.e.*, to attend or not to attend)
C. happily accept such invitations
D. openly criticise such gatherings and meetings

4. When you are short of money, you
A. work hard and earn money
B. borrow money from someone
C. get depressed
D. cry over your fate

5. When someone comes to you for help, you
A. tell him to come on some other day
B. immediately ponder over his problem
C. start telling him about your own problems and woes
D. listen to his problem and express sorrow

6. You have firm belief in
A. religion
B. language
C. caste
D. None of these

7. You always believe in
A. truth
B. falsehood
C. greed and hankering for things
D. good as well as evil

8. A person is unable to help you; even then, you
A. do not help him
B. help him according to your capacity
C. help him at an opportune moment
D. promise to help him but don't

9. If somebody criticises you, you
A. also criticise him
B. do not have any ill-will for him
C. follow the policy, "let any one speak ill about me but I do not speak ill about anybody."
D. do not like people who criticise others

10. You are away from your home and studying in another city. Due to an urgent piece of work, your father is not able to send you money in time. Then, you
A. fly into a rage
B. try to understand his handicaps
C. enquire from him by making phone calls
D. arrange money from another source and carry on your work

11. Sometimes, when you fail in your efforts, you
A. stop trying further
B. continue to try again and again till you succeed
C. blame your fate for failure
D. lose interest in your work

12. Your attitude towards yourself is
A. as a very harsh person
B. as a very soft-spoken person
C. as a person of few words
D. as a very humble person

13. Your valuable asset is
A. religion B. courage
C. self-confidence D. All of these

1. D	**2.** C	**3.** C	**4.** A	**5.** B	**6.** D	**7.** A	**8.** B	**9.** C
10. D	**11.** B	**12.** D	**13.** D					

14. Your ideal virtue is
A. telling lies for the least number of times
B. expecting truth from others
C. being less jealous towards others
D. believing in your toil

15. Your view about ideals and morality is the following
A. ideals and morality are confined to the walls of the college/educational institute
B. ideals and morality are confined only to books
C. ideals and morality are confined only to the speeches of teachers
D. ideals and morality are being followed even today

16. You always believe in
A. the adage of "eat, drink and be merry"
B. the adage of "laugh and remain cheerful"
C. the adage of "good mind, good find"
D. the adage of "without any malice towards anyone"

17. Your view about yourself is the following
A. I adore the friendship of my friends
B. I do not trust my friends
C. I believe in work as well as fate
D. I do not feel ashamed to do work

18. People like me because
A. I do not get swayed by the talks of other people
B. I concentrate only on my work
C. I have a lot of money
D. I believe in giving my knowledge to everybody

19. You are viewed by people as
A. secluded and self-centred
B. prudential and truthful
C. social and good-tempered
D. None of these

20. What kind of quality you possess?
A. Ability to work hard
B. Self-confidence
C. Good character
D. All of these

21. When you are in trouble, what do you think?
A. Troubles are a part of life
B. My confidence increases after I bear troubles
C. Troubles shake my self-confidence
D. Troubles poison my life

22. When you start your work, then on which topic, you concentrate the most?
A. The nature of and plan for the piece of work
B. The time period and expenses involved in the execution of the piece of work
C. The success of failure of the piece of work
D. All these aspects (A), (B) and (C)

23. If someone involves you in an argument, then what is your (expected) behaviour towards him?
A. You will not hesitate in arguing with him
B. You will try to get rid of him
C. You will try to learn a lesson or two from the person who is arguing
D. You will not take interest in the person who is arguing

24. If someone tries to obstruct your work time and again, you will
A. take these events seriously
B. take these events in your stride
C. try to stop him from obstructing/interfering in your affairs
D. ask him the reason for obstructing/interfering and give him a suitable reply

25. What is your attitude towards the daily chores of life?
A. Carrying them out in a scientific manner
B. Carrying them out in a normal manner
C. Carrying them out in a practical manner
D. Carrying them out according to your own convenience

26. At a place, the environment has been vitiated. Your reaction towards the people of that place would be
A. to isolate yourself from that environment
B. that vicious environment obstructs the growth of a nation
C. that improvement is feasible only if we live in that environment
D. to take everyone at the place into your confidence and then, initiate the process of rectification/ reform

27. You consider the first priority to be
A. reform of the self
B. reform of the society
C. reform of students
D. reform of the nation

28. If you are a poor man, you
A. concentrate on earning more money by any method
B. are not affected by penury
C. laugh at yourself
D. work hard to eliminate your poverty

14. D	**15.** D	**16.** C	**17.** D	**18.** D	**19.** C	**20.** D	**21.** B	**22.** D
23. C	**24.** D	**25.** C	**26.** D	**27.** A	**28.** B			

29. If someone rightly and logically criticises you, you will behave with him

A. as a friend B. as a critic
C. as an enemy D. as a fool

30. If someone criticises for a mistake you have committed, you will

A. rectify your mistakes
B. criticise that person in response to his criticism
C. have a fight with him
D. never talk to him

31. When you are not capable of taking a decision, then whose suggestion or advice you would like to take?

A. Of your nearest relatives
B. Of your parents
C. Of your friends
D. Of all those mentioned earlier

32. In order to move on the path of truth and righteousness, whom do you try to follow?

A. Leaders of the nation
B. Educationists of the nation
C. Orders/commands of great people
D. All the good persons

33. While at work, you lay special emphasis on

A. the quality of work
B. the external barriers
C. your failures
D. your abilities

34. You consider yourself to be an able candidate for the post of a General Manager because

A. your father is also a General Manager
B. your parents nurture the ambition that you should become a General Manager
C. you have completed a course in Hotel Management
D. your friends have forwarded this suggestion/ opinion

35. In the context of listening to the news, your opinion is that

A. this activity wastes time
B. it helps you know about all the happenings
C. there is no use of listening to the news
D. none of these

36. In your daily life, you give emphasis on

A. solving the problems of others
B. solving your own problems
C. protecting your nearest kith and kin and family members
D. protecting ideals and morality

37. In adverse circumstances, you

A. remain calm
B. get confused and perplexed
C. think carefully
D. continue to do your work

38. When other people misbehave with you,

A. you will also misbehave with them
B. you will try to find why they misbehave with you
C. you will avoid them too
D. you will not take notice of such people and do your work

39. Quite often, you like to get your job/work done by

A. inflicting pain on others
B. telling half-truths and half-lies
C. utilising your time properly
D. None of these

40. Your friend has received high academic degrees. But still, he has not been able to get a job. You will

A. try to locate a job for him
B. tell him that he himself has some limitation, which needs amendment
C. tell him that due to wrong policies of the government, most of the people are unemployed despite having good degrees
D. tell him not to lose heart and keep on appearing in competitive examinations. He is likely to succeed in the long run

41. The newspaper hawker comes late in the evening and therefore, you go to work without reading the newspaper. You will

A. give him a piece of your mind and tell him to deliver the newspaper early in the morning
B. stop taking newspapers from him from the very next day
C. not pay him in time
D. apprise him about your problem

42. You want respect and reputation in the society. Then, what would you consider the right action to be?

A. Develop friendly relationships with all the persons
B. Keep on interacting with all the respected persons
C. Develop strong relationships with antisocial people so that all the people give you respect and treat you as a reputed person
D. Forsake your personal selfish interests and work for the benefit of the masses

29. A	**30.** A	**31.** D	**32.** D	**33.** A	**34.** C	**35.** B	**36.** D	**37.** C	**38.** B
39. C	**40.** B	**41.** D	**42.** D						

43. In the society, you are
A. a withdrawn and self-centred person
B. a wise and truthful person
C. a gregarious and vivacious person
D. None of these

44. Your behaviour towards antisocial persons is that of a/an
A. gregarious individual reformer
B. reformer
C. critic
D. ordinary/normal person

45. In your opinion, during the times of joy and sorrow, people should live like the following
A. sorrowful during the times of sorrow
B. happy during the times of happiness
C. have the same disposition during joys or sorrows
D. they should always laugh

46. Girls should be imparted only that much of education, with which, they should be
A. able to shoulder the responsibilities of an efficient housewife
B. able to become a successful assistant teacher
C. able to give elementary education to children
D. able to become independent

47. According to your opinion, inherent abilities and qualities can be compared with earned abilities and qualities as follows
A. inherent abilities and qualities are less in number *vis-a-vis* earned abilities and qualities
B. inherent abilities and qualities are much more in number than earned abilities and qualities
C. there are many differences between both the types of abilities and qualities
D. there are many similarities in both the types of abilities and qualities

48. Only a hard working person can move ahead in life. What is your opinion?
A. hard working people are not successful quite often
B. the time to work hard has come now
C. this statement is in the context by one hundred per cent
D. only hardworking persons succeed

49. While making an action plan, many aspects or facets of the plan are overlooked on the pretext of the proverb, "shall be taken care of when the time comes." What is your opinion about this ignorance?
A. A pessimistic thought
B. An optimistic thought
C. The best thought
D. A foolish idea

50. What should be your opinion about the proverb "simple living and high thinking?"
A. The key to success is inherent in this proverb
B. It is an idealistic statement that is a must for all the enlightened persons
C. This principle is important only for teachers
D. None of these

51. Your opinion is that a man is respected because of his
A. abilities
B. idealistic principles
C. behaviour
D. riches

52. Before doing any piece of work, its plan is to be made. In this context, your opinion is that
A. planning is wastage of time
B. planning is good use of time
C. planning for work is only a personal opinion
D. planning is an indicator of success

53. Complicated problems
A. motivate you to do more work
B. persuade to generate more self-confidence
C. motivate you to do lesser volume of work
D. persuade you to be disappointed

54. According to you, the main reason for decay in the national character is
A. excessive use of television in the field of education
B. reduction in the efficiency of teachers
C. corruption in education
D. lack of moral values

55. You are a rich person. Therefore, your expected behaviour towards the poor is that you will
A. respect poor as well
B. help the poor to the maximum possible extent
C. let poor children sit in the front rows in your class
D. motivate the poor to make progress

56. The character of a person is affected to the maximum extent by
A. the boundaries of the family
B. the boundaries of the school
C. living with friends
D. the boundaries of the hostel

43. B	**44.** B	**45.** C	**46.** D	**47.** C	**48.** C	**49.** D	**50.** A	**51.** C	**52.** D
53. B	**54.** D	**55.** B	**56.** A						

57. The values of life are falling. You consider the reason to be that
A. people do not have commitments for one another
B. people do not have commitments towards hard work
C. there is no feeling of cooperation
D. all the people live for selfish motives

58. What do you think is necessary for getting respect in the society?
A. The standard of life should be high
B. The person(s) should be educated
C. One should respect the good and the evil persons alike
D. A school should be opened

59. You have been allocated such tasks as are strictly timebound. Then you think that
A. they create tension in your mind
B. there is a possibility of making mistakes while doing such types of tasks
C. there is no difficulty at all
D. the responsibility of doing piece(s) of work increases

60. You like to live in the company of those who
A. are peaceful and thoughtful
B. are beautiful and clever
C. are soft-spoken and frank
D. speak very high of you

61. Nowadays, the problem of unemployment is prevalent to a large extent among the educated people. In order to remove it, your opinion is that
A. education should be linked to employment
B. education should be increased in terms of level and spread
C. the age of retirement of employed individuals should be reduced
D. educated people should adopt the teaching profession

62. How do you want to keep your position secured in the society?
A. By joining a political party
B. By remaining away from all the political parties
C. By working and behaving according to the dignity of your position/status
D. By working in a social service organisation

63. In our country, the problem of pollution is assuming dangerous proportions. In order to check this menace, you will like that
A. all the polluting factories should be closed with immediate effect
B. all the factories should be closed, whether they are polluting or not
C. at least those factories should be closed that affect the lives of citizens and masses
D. it is the duty of the citizens to check the growth of pollution

64. You are a respected leader of a high class of the society. A leader of the lower class comes to meet you. How will you like to behave with him?
A. Just like one leader behaves with another
B. You will be reluctant to give him respect
C. You will talk to him for some time
D. You will offer him tea and then see him off

65. In order to do your work at an early date and efficiently, you will
A. do your work honestly and through inputs of toil
B. give bribe to the concerned person
C. approach the person concerned (for work) through an official of good status/power
D. get help of someone

66. If your favourite player is found to be guilty of match-fixing, you will
A. like a ban to be imposed on his play
B. meet highly placed officials in order to save his neck
C. like strict punitive measures to be incorporated with respect to such blunders in the rules of the game
D. like him to be banned from playing for a period of five years

67. You have two daughters. You long for a son. You will
A. like to fulfill this desire as soon as may be possible
B. remain committed to the principle that "two children make a perfect family."
C. make use of the family planning programme
D. think about the issue and remain perplexed

68. In your society, several evils are still well entrenched. That is why you always talk about social reforms. If some people belonging to scheduled castes (*harijans*) invite you to attend lunch/dinner, you will
A. accept the invitation but will not eat food
B. discuss before eating food
C. take only one glass of cold drink
D. accept food with warmth and love

57. A	**58.** B	**59.** D	**60.** A	**61.** A	**62.** C	**63.** C	**64.** A	**65.** A
66. C	**67.** B	**68.** D						

69. You are travelling in a bus or train. A child is opening and closing the window time and again, you will
A. scold the boy and make him sit
B. tell his mother to make him sit
C. advise him that he may get hurt if he continues to do so
D. make him sit near you

70. That is how you behave with other passengers in a train or bus.
A. You give seats to old women and men
B. You smile at those passengers (who are standing) from your heart but don't show this feeling
C. If someone does not give you a seat, you get engaged in a duel or fist fight
D. Talk with every person with humility and warmth

71. Your younger brothers and sisters do not utilise their time in the right manner and watch television during the time of studies. You will
A. forbid them from watching television
B. tell them that they should not watch television during the study hours
C. inform them about the diseases of eyes that can be invited by watching television
D. advise them to utilise their time in a useful manner

72. Some of your friends smoke. They tell you also to get on with the habit. You will
A. tell them about the diseases that can be invited due to this habit
B. love to smoke in their company
C. bluntly reject their advice
D. tell them that smoking is injurious to health

73. A friend of yours is always unhappy due to your behaviour. In order to develop warm relationship with him, you will
A. apologise to him for your wrong behaviour
B. talk to him according to the make-up of his mind and psyche
C. try to enquire about your misbehaviour and bring necessary reforms in the context of the same
D. always behave with him in a decent manner

74. Quite often, you take interest in watching movies. Due to this habit, sometimes you put off important pieces of work. Some of your friends advise you not to watch movies. You
A. ignore their advice
B. ponder over their advice
C. persuade them to watch cinema along with you
D. try to give priority to your work in the first instance

75. A friend of yours, who stays along with you, has the habit of remaining awake late in the night. Due to this habit of your friend, your sleep is disturbed. You will
A. motivate him to sleep early
B. tell him that he should take care of his health and sleep on time
C. apprise him of the diseases that can arise by being awake late in the night
D. give him information about the rules that lead to good health

76. A person is a liquor addict. How will you remove this bad habit of that person?
A. He should live in a good society
B. All the liquor shops should be closed
C. The person in question should practise *yoga* on a regular basil
D. Explain to him empathetically that liquor spoils the life of man

77. If a beggar asks for alms from you, you will
A. tell him to ask for the same from some other person
B. give him alms if you have the change
C. make an excuse that you do not have change
D. advise the beggar not to ask for alms as this activity is a crime according to the law

78. If your son steals some money from your pocket, you will
A. get him thrashed by the little children of your home
B. tell him about the ill-effects of stealing
C. throw him out of home
D. tell him that he should not steal in his own home

79. Some of your friends chew *paan* or *gutkha* and throw the refuse here and there. You will
A. tell them to spit the refuse in the spitoon only
B. try to tell them that they should take care of the cleanliness aspects
C. clean that place, which has been made awesome by them
D. write on walls that spitting should not be resorted to at those walls

69. C	**70.** A	**71.** B	**72.** D	**73.** C	**74.** D	**75.** B	**76.** C	**77.** D
78. B	**79.** B							

80. You get up late in the morning and your neighbour utilises this opportunity to read your newspaper. You will

A. try to get up early in the morning so that you yourself read the newspaper
B. tell him that he should foot half of the bill of newspapers
C. tell him to quickly read the newspaper and return it to you
D. tell him that he himself should buy the newspaper and read it

81. Your son throws stones and pebbles on passers-by. In order to eliminate this habit of your son, you will

A. beat him
B. give him a financial incentive if he does not throw stones and pebbles on others
C. always remain with him so that you may be able to stop him from throwing stones and pebbles on others
D. tell him that he should do away with this bad habit

82. If a boy has all the evil habits, then in order to effect changes in his behaviour, you will like to

A. punish him first of all
B. identify his bad habits and then rectify them
C. hand him over to the police
D. None of these

83. A fight is going on between two groups of villagers. Both are sticking to their decisions/opinions. You will

A. try to convince both the groups to the maximum possible extent that they should do away with arguments and take a necessary corrective step
B. convince them that bitter battles do not lead to the solution of the problem
C. convince both the groups that their respective decisions/opinions are correct/justified
D. ignore them and leave the scene

84. If a person thinks that crossing of the way by a cat or the act of sudden sneezing of someone is a sign of ill omen, you will

A. try to convince that person that this is only a blind faith
B. tell him not to go out
C. give a long lecture on the issue of blind faith
D. tell him about the losses that may be incurred due to blind faith

85. Your son wants to celebrate his birthday. But you do not have enough of money to buy cake and invite his friends to the birthday party. So, you will

A. celebrate his birthday by taking loan from someone
B. tell him that his next birthday will be celebrated with great pomp and show
C. persuade him tactfully and tell him not to celebrate his birthday
D. not allow him to celebrate his birthday

86. If your neighbourhood is on fire, then you will

A. join other people and watch the inferno
B. get perplexed
C. inform the fire brigade about the fire at the earliest possible time
D. remain at your home
D. old people stop learning

87. The following is your thought about Gandhiji

A. he earned freedom for the nation
B. he was a philosopher of a high order
C. he brought many reforms in the field of education
D. all of these

88. Your view about the success of a person is that

A. it is the result of his hard work and efforts
B. he must have earned this success through dishonest and evil deeds
C. he must be doing his work at the right time
D. he must be truthful

89. While doing any new piece of work, you

A. are reluctant
B. start it with great enthusiasm
C. commence it after careful planning
D. take opinions of elders

90. If two persons are having a fight, you will

A. support that person who is known to you
B. learn about the issue and try to end the conflict
C. let them fight with each other
D. inform the police

91. A football match is going on and you like one team but your group favours the other one. Then

A. you will become neutral
B. you will try to persuade other members to like your team better
C. you will cheer for the team the group favours
D. you will stick to your own favourite

80. C **81.** D **82.** B **83.** A **84.** A **85.** C **86.** C **87.** D **88.** A **89.** C
90. B **91.** D

92. Your colleague is having problem at work.
A. You avoid discussing her/his problem but do so if she/he asks
B. You advise her/him but let her/him decide on her/his own
C. You lend her/him support and help her/him in resolving the issue
D. You try to stay out of her/his affairs

93. If you see your nephew crying, you want to
A. call someone else to calm the baby, but avoid doing so yourself
B. immediately pick up the baby, even if the mother is present
C. only pick up the baby, if the mother is not there
D. let the mother calm the baby, but try to avoid as much as you can

94. When communicating information on an important company policy change, what sort of medium would you choose?
A. Oral communication followed by written communication
B. Oral communication alone
C. Written communication alone
D. Written communication followed by oral communication

95. If you want to start with something new and you have little savings and few employees, what will be your first priority?
A. Generate cash flow
B. Figure out what business to be in
C. Launch products
D. Develop customers

96. You are a team leader and two of your colleagues are having a strained relationship with each other. As a result they are not contributing well in group activities. How will you handle such a situation?
A. You will give them complementary tasks in which both have to work together
B. You will punish them for not contributing by keeping them out of the team
C. You will make an explicit effort to help them shake hands
D. How am I bothered with such petty issues? At least the task is being done by others' so it is fine!

97. If you are a manager and one of your employees is not working properly, as a manager you would
A. try to develop the man's abilities and interest in another job
B. give the man two weeks to improve
C. fire him
D. talk to him and try to find out his problem

98. You have a pharmaceutical company. You have received information that someone who is not an employee has tampered with a certain type of tablets in a specific area, which has caused some deaths in that area. In this type of crisis, what will you do?
A. Recall those tablets from the entire country despite the fact that the tampering of tablets has occurred in a certain area
B. Recall tablets from only the specific area and not the whole country
C. Launch a campaign to alert the public and recall tablets from the specific area
D. This incident can have a negative effect on your companys' earnings and can lead to loss. In order to avoid this you don't launch a campaign to alert the people

99. You are making a presentation on a new project that you have planned. But two of the other members are trying to snub you and emphasize their point.
A. You tend to understand their intentions so ignore them and keep concentrating on your presentation
B. You feel really hurt and indulge in an argument with them
C. You tell them politely as well as firmly to make their point later and let you continue
D. You insult them and say it on their face to shut them up

100. Suppose you are the leader of a group and the group members have a problem with your style of working. How would you manage the situation?
A. Continue with your style of working
B. Talk to your team members and come to a solution
C. Change your style of working
D. Leave the team

101. If you find yourself in a situation where you are required to make a Powerpoint presentation and you are already bogged down by too much work, as the manager what would you do?
A. Pass the buck to your subordinate, you are the boss, no one can question you
B. Prioritize your work and try to squeeze out time for it
C. Cancel the seminar and reschedule according to your convenience
D. Take an alternative mode of presentation

92. C	**93.** B	**94.** A	**95.** B	**96.** C	**97.** D	**98.** C	**99.** C	**100.** B	**101.** B

102. What is your attitude like when a subordinate approaches you to discuss a work-related problem?
A. I am the boss
B. I am the boss but let's talk
C. Forget I am the boss, let's talk
D. None of the above

103. The board appoints a hard-hearted CEO on your company who is extremely uncaring, makes fun of people and criticizes work for no reason. People feel scared and betrayed. No one is working and is barely able to function. As a senior HR what would you do?
A. You allow people to vent their frustrations behind closed doors
B. Take the role of the CEO's front and convince people that underneath all this, he wants the best for the company
C. Find it difficult for you to handle the situation so decide to change the job
D. Help people cool down by listening to them without interruption and try to come to a solution

104. You are the leader of a group and a new member joins it. How would you make the member comfortable?
A. By making the job interesting to him by praising him when he does well
B. Correcting him tactfully when he shows his weak points
C. Giving him a complete set of instructions to study
D. Explaining what the job requires, and then allowing him to develop his own methods

105. What would you normally do in a crisis situation, for instance in a situation where two of your colleagues are involved in a conflict—turned bitter—and one of them has resigned? This is a huge loss as he is quite a competent personnel. You would
A. not care as long as your pay scale is not affected
B. replace him with someone else
C. try to rationalize with both of them and reduce the animosity between them as it will affect the harmonious working environment
D. increase the work-load on the rest of the employees to overcome the loss

106. You have a pharmaceutical company. At the time of epidemic, several people are suffering from a painful disease that can be cured with the drug that your company produces. People don't have the resources to buy the drug and the government has refused to pay for the drug. What will you do?
A. Distribute the drug to people free of cost
B. Will reduce the price of your drug
C. Will not change the price of your drug
D. Launch a fund-raising campaign for the people

107. As an ideal leader, how would you interact with your group?
A. Give prompt, firm, clear instructions that other members will respect and follow
B. Respect the employees' opinions and attitudes
C. Avoid using authority
D. Work according to your own style and not respect the opinion of the other members

108. After having committed to your family that you would be taking them out on a vacation, you suddenly find yourself wanted in a board-meeting which unfortunately clashes with the vacation. What would you do?
A. Try and get out of that situation by asking your colleague to cover up for you
B. Proceed with your vacation plans without making any arrangement
C. Find out what the urgent meeting is all about and make necessary arrangements and postpone your vacation
D. Assuming it to be urgent, start making necessary arrangement to ensure that the reason for the meeting is fulfilled, thus cancelling the vacation

109. What would you as a manager do to improve employees' communication skills?
A. Training workshop by an outside consultant
B. Writing organizational documents at a reading level that matches the reading level of most employees
C. Engage in 2-way communication with stress on feedback
D. All the above

110. There has been a recent death in your family, and you are still grieving. However, your quarterly appraisal is round the corner, and for this you have to catch up with a lot of work. What would you do?
A. You will get back to the work immediately
B. You will just try your best to wriggle out of the situation by asking your superior to just postpone the appraisal for your this time
C. Ignore the appraisal and continue grieving since the appraisal happens every three months. You feel you can make up the next time.
D. Take the help of your organization counsellor to get overcome your emotions

102. B	**103.** D	**104.** D	**105.** C	**106.** B	**107.** A	**108.** C	**109.** A	**110.** A

111. You are a sincere and dedicated manager in a reputed 5-star hotel. You have been appointed as the chief manager of the Guwahati branch which needs to be developed. Your salary has been hiked but still

A. you crib for limited resources and try to convince the superior to send somebody else instead of you
B. you accept another offer and leave the job
C. you accept the challenge and go ahead with the project
D. you give it a shot for two months and see how it goes

112. Suppose you are the manager and one of your subordinates is not working satisfactorily. How would you approach him?

A. Send him an e-mail pointing out his performance
B. Call him to your room and explain the situation
C. Hold a meeting of all the group members and discuss what is to be done
D. Give him an ultimatum to improve his performance or else he will get the pink slip

113. You are in the middle of an important dinner party when the waiter spills hot soup all over the boss' lap. How would you cope?

A. You pour the entire contents of a jug of water over his lap, explaining that your prompt action will prevent burns, and then lay out a change of clothes in the guest bedroom and return to the party while the boss changes
B. You dab frantically at the ruined outfit with a napkin while screaming at the waiter
C. Arrange for the first aid and make arrangements to rush him or her off to the hospital
D. You panic and start shouting on the waiter

114. You are the manager of the department. You get to know that one of the subordinates is having a problem with his family, since his father is supposed to undergo bypass surgery. But at the same time the subordinate is very important for the current project which you have undertaken. The subordinate wants two-weeks leave. What would you do?

A. Not empathize with the employee's situation and ask him to stay
B. Transfer the work to some other employee of similar calibre
C. Get an extension for the project to be submitted as the employee is very efficient and you can't trust anyone else
D. Give him your support by assuring him that his work will be looked after

115. You are a team leader and you are supposed to hold a convention of HR issues. But your team members are unable to get adequate sponsorship.

A. You tell them things can work out like this and cancel the event
B. You postpone it for another day and give them some more time
C. You try and motivate them that they can do it
D. You put in your money and hold the event as scheduled

116. You are facing a problem working in the style your boss has asked you to do. You feel like modifying the plan and act according to your style.

A. You e-mail your boss and tell him that you want to work in your own style
B. You directly talk to him and explain the situation
C. You don't think that he will get convinced
D. You ignore it and move ahead as it is

117. You went on a leave for three days. After joining duties you are supposed to finish the pending jobs. Suddenly your boss assigns you a task that was supposed to be finished within ten days, but due to shortage of time it is to be done in seven days. You feel

A. like you are stuck in a complicated situation
B. like taking another long leave
C. enthusiastic and energetic
D. like taking the challenge in your stride

118. You have worked hard on an idea which you believe would be a breakthrough. But the presentation does not go as you had hoped it would. You

A. feel like a loser
B. take this as a learning experience and convince yourself that you would do better the next time
C. break down and get all the emotional
D. ignore all the suggestions and believes that you were correct

119. You have a Powerpoint presentation to make today and the hard disk of your computer has crashed and you don't have a power back-up and your presentation is after four hours.

A. You cancel the presentation
B. You utilize the four hours and make a fresh Powerpoint presentation
C. You change the mode of the presentation
D. You start panicking and don't know what to do

111. C	**112.** B	**113.** C	**114.** B	**115.** C	**116.** B	**117.** D	**118.** B	**119.** C

120. To understand how employees really feel about things, the supervisor should
A. arrange for informal private interviews with each employee
B. keep objective records of things that reflect their feelings like production, suggestions and complaints
C. notice their reactions to the orders and the works given to them
D. maintain a frank, informal, give and take relationship with them

121. A person managing the front office of an organisation should have
A. patience B. discipline
C. personality D. leadership

122. Providing service to people would imply
A. good insight B. planning
C. public dealing D. dutifulness

123. To be a team leader I must possess
A. trust B. supervision
C. support D. decision making ability

124. To be a good employer the management must stress on these qualities:
A. Employee satisfaction
B. Job content
C. Grievance management
D. Motivation

125. An angry customer wants to meet the senior manager for grievance reporting. What will you do?
A. Talk to him yourself
B. Tell him it is not easy to meet the senior manager
C. Be patient and try to cool him down
D. Try to remove his inconveniences by consulting seniors

126. Your colleague is not performing his duties upto the mark. You will
A. report to the seniors
B. try and handle his customers to maintain the company's status
C. take advantage of it to promote yourself
D. just do your part of the duties and enjoy your work

127. If on a tough day you are the only person available to handle the customers, you should
A. just do your part of the work
B. try and work to the maximum of your ability to satisfy customers
C. take leave and go back home
D. ask for additional help from the boss

128. A product launched by the company is having initial hiccups and complaints. You will
A. try and convince the customers it is temporary
B. warn the customers for initial hiccups
C. convey about the working and positive aspects of the product
D. tell your boss this product should be withdrawn to save the reputation

129. The front office in the organisation has a very uncomfortable physical set-up to work in. You will
A. manage somehow with reluctance
B. ignore everything and concentrate on your job
C. complain to seniors about it
D. launch a campaign to set the things right

130. Your boss has very piercing eyes and spies on your performance all the time. You will
A. just do you work
B. ignore the uncomfortable glances as it is his job
C. subtly convey it to the boss
D. tell your seniors clearly that such supervision affects your performance

131. A quick decision has to be taken against the norms. You will
A. wait and watch
B. take a justified view of the situation and arrive at a decision
C. consult and arrive at a decision
D. walk out of the room

132. All the hard work done by you is hijacked by your boss and the brickbats are left for you. You will
A. continue as hard work always pays
B. start praising yourself for all the achievements
C. learn to make right moves at right times
D. leave the job and look for greener pastures

133. You have a language handicap. Customer has many problems.
A. Words don't matter, feelings and services do
B. Look for better communicator
C. Ask for transfer
D. Manage to find problems and set them right

120. B **121.** A **122.** C **123.** D **124.** A **125.** D **126.** D **127.** B **128.** A **129.** D
130. A **131.** B **132.** C **133.** D

134. The present job is very satisfying but doesn't offer growth avenues. You
A. continue with it as it is giving enough
B. ask management for better job prospects
C. look for another job
D. Both (A) and (B)

135. My present job of dealing with public pays me well but is not socially respected.
A. I will leave
B. I will continue
C. I will continue but won't tell the nature of my job to others
D. I will convince my acquaintances that it is a good job

136. If someone approaches me with an offer of giving out the secrets of the organization I work in, in exchange for a higher position in another organization, I would
A. immediately say yes
B. immediately say no
C. ask for time to think
D. don't know

137. In an interview you are asked to describe yourself. You
A. use monosyllables to do so
B. go ahead full steam
C. fumble as it is embarrassing to talk about yourself
D. paint an unrealistic positive picture

138. Your subordinate accidentally spills soup on you in a party. You
A. laugh it off
B. say it's 'OK' but sulk nevertheless
C. snub him
D. spoil his dress too

139. You have a new boss. You
A. welcome him warmly
B. go flatter him as he will help you out in future
C. have problems adjusting as you are still loyal to your old boss
D. will be indifferent

140. To be a good manager, one must have
A. a pleasant personality
B. good communication skills
C. decision making ability
D. All of the above

141. In public dealing jobs, one must be
A. punctual
B. polite and humble
C. quick at taking decisions
D. a good listener

142. To be a good worker one must be
A. hardworking
B. sincere
C. honest
D. All of the above

143. To be an ideal manager, you should
A. organize seminars for your subordinates
B. present yourself as an example
C. be authoritarian in your approach
D. stick to your rules

144. To cater to the needs of clients you should
A. be "at your feet" all the time
B. instruct the workers to do the job
C. keep yourself informed of work progress
D. assign work according to their capabilities

145. If I had a choice, I would take up a task that has
A. very high chance of social mobility
B. low chance of social mobility
C. high chance of social mobility
D. very low chance of social mobility

146. You are a member of the sports-team of your college. One day due to misunderstanding, other members stop talking to you. You
A. wait till they come and start talking again
B. go forward, and start talking
C. keep to yourself and let things take their time for improving
D. ask someone to mediate

147. You got less marks than expected in the examination, which has jeopardized your chances for further studies. You
A. doubt the evaluation of the papers
B. forget about further studies and take up a job
C. try to take up a job and go for further studies through correspondence course
D. change your discipline and go for some easier courses

148. You are working on your computer and suddenly it gives trouble. You
A. call the technical staff on duty
B. switch off the computer and take a break
C. work on your colleague's computer
D. try to fix it yourself

134. B	**135.** A	**136.** B	**137.** A	**138.** B	**139.** A	**140.** D	**141.** D	**142.** D	**143.** B
144. D	**145.** A	**146.** B	**147.** C	**148.** A					

149. I would like to go up in life.
A. Personal contacts are more important
B. Quality work makes one go up in life
C. Work and relations makes one reach the high positions
D. Money power can achieve anything in life

150. Whenever you do some work you commit a lot of errors and mistakes which are always noticed by someone.
A. Makes you irritated about your own self
B. Curse your fate and get angry easily on the person who says
C. Try to keep quiet at that moment and wait for the opportunity to catch the other person
D. Consider error is human nature

151. After your graduation, you are offered a well-paid government job. However, your friend says that you have to bribe to get the appointment order. You
A. flatly refuse the offer
B. accept the job by paying the bribe, but firmly resolve that this is the last time you will pay bribe
C. accept the job by paying the bribe, consoling yourself that this is the present social set-up
D. go to some influential politician who can help

152. You have been given a new assignment. You
A. complete it with totally new ideas
B. consult your colleagues for new ideas
C. mix old ideas with your new ideas
D. will think being innovative involves risks

153. Your classmate comes and tells you that your friends were talking ill of you. You
A. go to them and talk it out
B. ask him not to tell this to you
C. don't bother about them
D. say you already know about it

154. The previous day of your interview, your friend comes and tells you that the expert for the interview is a very tough person. You
A. pray that only simple questions are asked
B. are not bothered, as you have prepared well
C. are consoled that you have applied for other posts also
D. stop preparation

155. While helping your younger sibling to solve maths problems you would like to
A. explain every aspect of the solution in detail
B. give general steps and expect him to finish the work properly
C. help him/her as and when he/she gets stuck
D. leave the problem totally on him/her to do

156. While going for a party wearing your best clothes, you were hit by a cyclist and your clothes became dirty. You
A. pick up a quarrel with the cyclist
B. do not take it seriously, but change your clothes and join the party later
C. remove the dirt from the clothes as far as possible and join the party in time
D. do not go for the party

157. You have to carry out an important assignment by visiting four different locations. You
A. chalk out the plan
B. consult your seniors
C. postpone the assignments
D. ask for help

158. A New Year's Party is to be arranged in your college. You
A. try to organize it on your own
B. take the help of your colleagues
C. volunteer but let someone else take the lead
D. let them organize it themselves

159. After talking to somebody for the first time, you
A. take steps to find out how your behaviour was perceived
B. don't take it all that seriously
C. think about how the other person improves you
D. pick up some hints and change the behaviour accordingly

160. When somebody criticizes you for a trivial issue you get easily irritated. You
A. try to keep your distance with the person
B. tell him he is not better than you
C. think over the criticism
D. express your views in a manner so that next time that person will never do it again.

161. A figure is a circle because :
A. it is divided into four equal parts
B. it has two right angles
C. it has a large area
D. it has no angles

149. B **150.** D **151.** A **152.** C **153.** C **154.** B **155.** B **156.** B **157.** A **158.** B
159. D **160.** C **161.** D

162. Electricians wear rubber gloves because :
A. they keep their hands soft
B. they are bad conductors of electricity
C. they are cheaper than other gloves
D. it is fashionable for them to do so

163. Those working in laboratories must wear aprons because:
A. they are a part of the uniform
B. aprons keep their dresses safe
C. only scholars wear aprons
D. aprons are made of colourful dress material

164. Platinum is costlier than silver because it is:
A. rarely found
B. whiter than silver
C. more in demand
D. lighter than silver

165. Traffic signals are necessary at all cross-roads because:
A. they add colour to the black roads
B. they are the indications of being on crossroads
C. they help in regulating the traffic
D. traffic policemen are not on duty during night time

166. Children must read more and more books because:
A. they are being collected in school library
B. teachers insist on reading them
C. they are helpful in increasing the knowledge
D. the reading habit will give less time for watching television

167. It is necessary to exercise in the morning because:
A. it keeps our body fit
B. it is easier to pass the time if one walks up very early
C. it is a good habit
D. many people are illiterate and they cannot read the morning newspaper

168. Women wear jewellery because :
A. they want to flaunt their riches
B. they cannot keep the ornaments at home where no one is there in their absence
C. men like women who wear jewellery
D. they want to look beautiful

169. Every nation must maintain a strong army because:
A. many people can be employed
B. it is essential for the nation's defence
C. it helps in maintaining law and order in the country
D. it will control the terrorist activities

170. Person sitting next to me is my best friend because:
A. he takes me out for a movie every week
B. he stood by me during my difficult times
C. he is praised by one and all
D. he helps me with my studies

171. Poking of the fire brightens it because:
A. unburnt parts catch fire
B. it scatters sparks in all direction
C. it allows in more air
D. the burnt particles move away

172. Rubber soles are used in shoes because:
A. they are porous than leather
B. they are cheaper
C. they are durable
D. they can be mended easily

173. Sea-water tastes saltish because:
A. salt is deposited in the sea by rivers
B. water bodies secrete salt
C. of the presence of salt rocks at the sea bed
D. sea weeds produce salt

174. Privatisation is advocated because:
A. Government requires funds to bridge deficits in the budget
B. Public sector undertaking's performance has been poor
C. of the shift in philosophy of the public sector's role
D. Government and public sector cannot merge their functionings

175. Breathing gets difficult at greater heights because:
A. of the lack of oxygen at higher places
B. the person is tired by the time he reaches his destination
C. the person is suffering from asthma
D. the air of places at greater heights is polluted

176. It is easier to walk on road than on hardened ice because:
A. people are accustomed to walking on road.
B. traffic on roads is regulated
C. the shoe companies are not efficient in making shoes fit for walking on ice
D. there is less friction on ice

162. B	**163.** B	**164.** A	**165.** C	**166.** C	**167.** A	**168.** D	**169.** B	**170.** B	**171.** C
172. A	**173.** A	**174.** B	**175.** A	**176.** D					

177. A clown always acts funny because:
A. he is paid only if he acts thus
B. he is not suitable for serious performances
C. it is his job to make others laugh
D. his mind is full of pranks

178. It is necessary for every company to advertise its products because
A. advertising is an effective way of boosting the sale of their products
B. every big company advertises its products
C. it provides employment to many models
D. it is officially recommended by the company's financial department

179. A person's blood pressure is normally lower in the morning because
A. he has had a good sound sleep
B. the person ate a light dinner and slept early
C. it is a natural biological rhythm.
D. all of the above

180. Parents give pocket-money to their children because
A. they have extra money in hand
B. they want their children to know the value of money
C. they want their children to be spend-thrift
D. they do not want their children to feel inferior to their friends belonging to richer families

181. Preservation of oil is necessary because
A. the government has passed such law
B. the gulf countries are gradually refusing to export oil
C. the oil preserved for longer period of time has more properties
D. improper use will exhaust the resources

182. All industrial units should be away from the residential units because
A. the workers will go home for lunch and work will suffer
B. industry's expansion projects can be easily carried out.
C. the smoke emitted from industries is harmful
D. the town-planners are more concerned about their rules of designing

183. The Selection Board call the candidates for the interview because
A. they want to see the candidate's physical appearance
B. it is then easier to decide which candidate is fit for the job
C. the members of the Selection Board have no other work during office hours
D. none of the above

184. Smoking near a leaking gas cylinder is dangerous because
A. the gas may catch fire and cylinder may burst
B. the warning sign on the cylinder says so
C. the person who is smoking may get burns in his mouth
D. all gas cylinders have oxygen in them

185. People send New Year cards to their friends and relatives because
A. it is customary
B. people don't have time to write letters
C. they want to wish their loved ones every happiness and prosperity
D. it is easier and cheaper to wish all the friends and relatives by sending cards

186. In the examination hall, you find that your question paper is too tough to be answered satisfactorily by you. The best thing you can do is
A. try cheating from your neighbouring candidate
B. leave the paper and walk out
C. try attempting those questions first of which you know something
D. complain to the examiner about the toughness of the question paper

187. Your best friend is annoyed with you for certain reasons. You will
A. try your best to reason out your friend annoyance
B. go out and make new friends
C. show indifference
D. remind the friend of your good friendship

188. You were invited to a party, but on the day of the party you are informed that the party has been cancelled. You will
A. try to find out the reason for its cancellation
B. decide that you will never go to that place ever again
C. not discuss the matter with anyone
D. hold the party at your place instead

189. You find that the cooking gas cylinder is leaking. The first thing you would do is
A. switch off the light
B. close the knob of the cylinder
C. call the fire brigade for help
D. alert all the members at home

177. C **178.** A **179.** C **180.** B **181.** D **182.** C **183.** B **184.** A **185.** C **186.** C
187. A **188.** A **189.** B

190. While returning home from a far away place you find that your pocket has been picked. You will:
A. try to hitch-hike till home
B. hire a taxi and pay on reaching home
C. go to the nearest police station and lodge a FIR
D. call home and ask someone to pick you from the place you make the phone call

191. A man is your good friend if:
A. He helps you with money
B. He helps you at the time of adversity
C. He remains always with you
D. He always admires you

192. Walking is a good exercise because:
A. It takes less time
B. It is done during the leisure period in the morning
C. It is the least exhaustive of all the other exercises
D. It provides opportunity to meet other persons who have come for a walk

193. What will a person do if he finds himself standing near someone whose clothes are on fire?
A. He will make a noise and call for help
B. He will go and call his family members quickly
C. He will put out the fire by pouring water
D. He will tear off his burning clothes and thus he will put out the fire

194. Kamal wants to help the poor, because:
A. He will earn fame by doing so
B. This is his holy duty
C. This will help him in getting more votes in his favour for election to the post of M.L.A
D. Such deed on his part will be admired by poor

195. A child collided against a bicycle which was coming from the wrong side. What should the child do?
A. He should let bicycle rider go away without creating any trouble for him
B. He should lodge in police a complaint against the bicycle rider
C. He should advise the bicycle rider to always keep his left while on road
D. He should advise the bicycle rider to always keep his right while on road

196. We should not sleep under a tree during night because
A. Trees exhale carbon dioxide gas during night
B. Evil spirits take shelter on trees during night
C. Trees might fall during night and persons sleeping under the tree could be crushed to death
D. Dew drops fall from the leaves during night

197. We can achieve success in our life only when:
A. We help others
B. We remain healthy
C. We work hard and have self-confidence
D. We get recommendation from others

198. Cables used for carrying electricity, are insulated with rubber. This is because:
A. Insulation makes the cable strong
B. By providing insulation we can easily hold the cable
C. Rubber is bad conductor of electricity
D. Insulation saves cable from the effect of water

199. If you happen to meet a handicapped person on the road, then:
A. You will not pay attention that side
B. You will drag him to one side of the road
C. You will be filled with anger to see him standing on the road and creating hindrance to traffic
D. You will help him in reaching to his destination

200. A few persons don't like eating sugar, because
A. They don't want to spend money on sugar
B. They are diabetic patients
C. They hate eating sugar
D. They don't get sugar easily

201. Ladies wear ornaments because:
A. They want to save their ornaments from thieves
B. They want to hide their ugliness
C. They want to look beautiful
D. Wearing ornaments is a symbol of their wifehood

202. During summer we wear light coloured clothes because:
A. Light coloured clothes are quite cheap
B. Light coloured clothes absorb heat falling on the body from outside
C. In light coloured clothes they appeared smart and good looking
D. Light coloured clothes protect from atmospheric heat

203. Persons having disease related to blood pressure, often go on hill stations because:
A. Cold climate is useful for them
B. Doctors suggest them for doing so
C. They go there with a view to change the climate
D. Atmospheric pressure is low at the places located on high altitude

190. B **191.** B **192.** C **193.** D **194.** B **195.** C **196.** A **197.** C **198.** C **199.** D
200. B **201.** C **202.** D **203.** B

204. Youths generally prefer to marry educated girls, because:
A. Educated wife is more trust worthy
B. An educated wife can handle the household situations in a better way
C. An educated wife can prove a earning hand if needed
D. Educated wives are generally beautiful

205. Policemen wear uniforms because:
A. Uniform keeps the criminal away
B. Uniform is approved by the Government
C. It keeps them smart
D. Policemen in uniform can be identified easily

206. These days youths prefer to wear high heel shoes because:
A. High heel shoes keep a better balance of their body
B. This is the fashion of these days
C. It increases height of the person who has worn it
D. This keeps them safe

207. If your friend borrows your scooter for some time and returns it back to you without giving thanks to you, what will you think about him?
A. No idea will come in mind
B. It was a mistake to handover scooter to such a person
C. The friend does not possess good manners
D. Exchange of thanks is not required among friends

208. Fire engines are generally painted in red colour because:
A. Red colour is durable
B. Red colour gives indication of danger
C. Red colour makes fire engines different from other vehicles
D. It is a colour prescribed by the Fire Service Department

209. A younger brother brings a beautiful saree for his wife. Seeing that the elder brother's wife resists for the same saree. If financial position of the elder brother does not permit for that then what will he do?
A. He will bring the saree on credit
B. He will create an understanding with his wife and express his inability
C. He will scold his wife for being obstinate
D. He will ask his younger brother's wife to give the saree to his wife on certain occasions.

210. Scientists and Research Associates wear apron because:
A. It keeps them Smart
B. It is a symbol of learnedness
C. It keeps their clothes safe
D. It indicates that they are the members of Research Department

211. A few persons wear spectacles because:
A. They want to protect their eyes
B. They want to look graceful
C. They want to hide their eyes
D. They suffer from error of vision

212. Deaf children generally become dumb also because:
A. They are deprived of this gift of God by birth
B. Ear and throat and interconnected
C. Others speak in front of children and hearing their voice, children learn to speak
D. Deaf children do not try to speak

213. A car running with high speed crushed a child and ran away from the place of accident with the same high speed. This all happened in front of a person who was passing by the place of accident. What should he do in such a case?
A. He should inform the police as soon as possible
B. He should note the number of the car
C. He should go accompanied with the child to a clinic and make arrangement for his treatment

214. It is the midnight when a person is passing by an utterly deserted place. Just at that place a few armed persons appear who ask him to cast off his wrist watch and gold chain. What should he do in such a moment?
A. He should tell them that they are strangers for him and so he will not do so
B. He should offer them his wrist watch and other valuables happily
C. He should try to run away from scene
D. He should instead scold them for such an immoral practice

215. Every nation must maintain a strong army because:
A. This makes the people of the nation strong
B. This helps in upliftment of the nation
C. This is essential for the nation's defence
D. This will contain the population of the country

204. C	**205.** D	**206.** B	**207.** C	**208.** B	**209.** B	**210.** C	**211.** D	**212.** C
213. C	**214.** B	**215.** C						

216. Mr. X and Mr. Y do not like each other because
A. Mr. X is a dark-complexioned man
B. Mr. X is a man of short status
C. Mr. X is not a gentleman
D. Mr. X is not a poor man

217. Ice floates on water because
A. Its weight is less than the weight of the water of equal volume
B. It is transparent
C. It is spongy
D. It melts quickly

218. In summer, wet clothes dry earlier than in rainy days because:
A. We can not see the sun during rainy days
B. In rainy days atmospheric air contains more humidity than in summer days
C. In rainy days wet clothes absorb humidity from air
D. During summer sharp wind blows

219. Five persons have been produced as eye-witnesses to an accident but the person who has been charged with committing the accident says that he can produce fifty persons against these five persons who will say that they have not seen him committing the accidents. The argument of the accused will not be accepted because:
A. We can not believe on an accused
B. A witness is needed who can prove the careless driving of the accused
C. Reality of the crime depends upon the authenticity of the witness not on the number of witnesses
D. Respondents always produce false witnesses

220. In a piece of land, there are snakes and vultures who eat rats. What will be instantaneous effect of coming wild dogs in this field?
A. Number of vultures will decrease
B. Number of rats will decrease
C. Number of snakes will decrease
D. Number of snakes will increase

221. In the game of cards, the game depends upon the cards shown by the opponent player and cards held by him. Which of the following is essential to win in this game?
A. Memory
B. Chance
C. Paying attention on the pace of game
D. Foresight

222. In a certain year a cooperative milk society earned the net profit of ₹ 41,000. Next year his amount of profit increased to ₹ 59000. It was declared that year that 50% had been earned as profit. This profit was earned by:
A. Decreasing expenditure
B. Maintaining the price of milk
C. Containing the establishment expenditure of the society
D. Maintaining the quality of milk

223. We generally affix Rubber sole on our shoes because:
A. It prevents noise
B. Rubber is more prefered than Leather
C. Rubber fitted shoes look beautiful
D. Affixing rubber is a fashion

224. Platinum is costly than Silver because:
A. It has more weight
B. It is rarer than silver
C. It is more white in colour
D. It is harder than silver

225. One should not Smoke because
A. Smoking is not a good habit
B. Cigarette consists of tobacco
C. money spent on smoking goes waste
D. Tobacco is injurious to health

226. I found a suit case full of money on the road. I
A. donated the amount among poors
B. gave it to the police
C. Both (A) and (B)
D. None of these

227. I am punctual regarding
A. going to bed B. time
C. meals D. None of these

228. You are travelling on a boat which capsized. Firstly, you
A. rescued others B. saved yourself
C. closed by eyes D. None of these

229. The game of chess involves
A. physical labour B. monetary loss
C. mental labour D. None of these

230. In case my writst watch is out of order, I
A. would try to repair it myself
B. would give it to watch maker
C. would buy a new watch
D. None of these

231. Often I change my opinion in the last moment.
A. Yes B. No
C. Some times D. None of these

216. C	**217.** A	**218.** B	**219.** C	**220.** B	**221.** A	**222.** C	**223.** B	**224.** B
225. D	**226.** B	**227.** B	**228.** B	**229.** C	**230.** B	**231.** B		

232. Generally I am extrovert and well behaved
A. Yes B. No
C. Some times D. None of these

233. I like to use new technique of work
A. Yes B. No
C. Some times D. None of these

234. I do like rules and regulations
A. Yes B. No
C. Some times D. None of these

235. Excellent ideas come to my mind
A. while working alone
B. while working in group
C. I do not know
D. None of these

236. Whenever my little baby cries loudly, then I
A. beat him/her B. feed milk to him/her
C. make him/her sleep D. None of these

237. When I see a mad person, I
A. approach towards him/her
B. maintain distance from him/her
C. throw stone at him/her
D. None of these

238. While driving my car I offer lift who ask for the lift
A. always B. some times
C. never D. None of these

239. Whenever some one knocks on my closed door then, firstly I
A. open the door
B. peep through the lens fitted in the door
C. do not open the door
D. None of these

240. I speak to others about my expectation and dreams
A. rarely B. often
C. some times D. None of these

241. When I do any foolish work then
A. I feel ashamed B. I feel proud of my self
C. Nothing happens D. None of these

242. If I were correspondent of any newspaper then I will write on the following subject
A. Cinema and theatre B. Political events
C. Neither (A) nor (B) D. None of these

243. If I were not human being then
A. I wish to be a bird B. I wish to be a horse
C. Can not say D. None of these

244. Suppose, you have worn a new shirt your friend passed a comment that it is not looking good on you. You
A. will change the shirt immediately
B. will take it lightly as it is your style
C. will not change the shirt but feel offended
D. None of these

245. I wish to live alone always.
A. Yes B. No
C. Some times D. None of these

246. I want to spend my spare (extra) time
A. in reading interesting books
B. in reading comics
C. Both (A) and (B)
D. None of these

247. Before doing any work I ask myself 'Is it appropriate'?
A. Yes B. No
C. Some times D. None of these

248. If I see the GOD. I will ask for
A. huge wealth B. honesty
C. love D. None of these

249. I, in cold days or during winter
A. wake up in the morning
B. wake up very late
C. wake up on scheduled time
D. None of these

250. While taking to friends I do not like to express my very personal matters.
A. Yes B. No
C. Sometimes D. None of these

251. Consultation with others helps me to take any decision.
A. Yes B. No
C. I get confused D. None of these

252. I want to be convinced by arguments
A. Yes B. No
C. Some times D. None of these

253. If an argument starts with someone, then I invariably
A. listen to the viewpoint of that person carefully and then, speak what is in my mind
B. state my view at the very outset
C. start saying whatever comes to my mind
D. become confused and perplexed

232. A	**233.** A	**234.** A	**235.** A	**236.** B	**237.** B	**238.** B	**239.** B	**240.** A	**241.** A	**242.** B
243. A	**244.** B	**245.** C	**246.** A	**247.** A	**248.** C	**249.** C	**250.** C	**251.** A	**252.** A	**253.** A

254. If you were a woman and if it were within your control, then what would you like to become?
A. Miss World
B. A player of international level
C. Politician
D. Actress

255. I like to fight the intricate problems
A. Only sometimes B. No
C. Yes D. Never

256. Whenever I join a new group, then
A. I am not able to understand them
B. I take some time to understand people
C. I feel pretty soon that I have known all of them
D. I take some time to identify and understand them

257. After having a meal to my heart's content, if someone requests me to eat a sweet, then I
A. refuse politely
B. eat some of the sweets
C. do not care about the proposition
D. Scold the person who makes a request

258. When I accomplish a task in a foolish manner, then
A. I feel proud
B. I like the action very much
C. I feel ashamed of it
D. nothing happens

259. When someone knocks at my closed door, then first of all, I
A. scold him from inside
B. do not open the door
C. open the door
D. see through the lens installed in the door

260. Best ideas come to my mind
A. when I work in a group
B. when I work alone
C. never
D. do not know when they come

261. You inform your close friend
A. all the important issues
B. all the bad issues
C. all the thoughts going on in your mind
D. nothing at all

262. Normally, I am an extrovert and gregarious
A. Sometimes B. No
C. Yes D. Never

263. When my bicycle goes out of order, then I
A. show it to the bicycle mechanic
B. try to repair it myself
C. tell my friends to repair it
D. buy a new bicycle

264. I search for the possibilities of the solution of every problem.
A. Sometimes B. Never
C. Yes D. No

265. I am punctual about
A. eating
B. going to the cinema
C. sleeping
D. time

266. If a person takes away my things without getting my permission, then I feel pain.
A. Yes B. Sometimes
C. No D. Never

267. Whenever I talk to somebody, then I
A. look at his face
B. look into his eyes
C. look at the things around him
D. look at his feet

268. Whenever someone interrupts my speech, then I
A. do not pay attention to him
B. start speaking at a faster pace than before
C. stop my speech and let him speak
D. nothing is certain

269. You have adorned a new shirt. Your companion passes a remark that your shirt is misfit for your personal. So, you will
A. start scolding him in the presence of all others
B. change the shirt immediately
C. not change the shirt but singe from the heart of your hearts
D. laugh away the remark, starting that it is your style

270. When you go to buy cloth for yourself, then what is the most important issue/factor looked after by you?
A. The cloth must be suitable for you
B. The cloth that is stated to be good by the shopkeeper
C. The costliest cloth
D. The design of the cloth should be different from those of all others

254. B	**255.** C	**256.** B	**257.** A	**258.** C	**259.** D	**260.** B	**261.** A	**262.** C
263. A	**264.** C	**265.** D	**266.** A	**267.** B	**268.** C	**269.** D	**270.** A	

271. If I were to acquire a lot of money, then I will
A. distribute it among neighbours
B. spend it and have whale of a time
C. save most of it for the future
D. cannot say anything about it

272. If I were a bat, then I would
A. fly during the day
B. fly during the night
C. fly during the day as well as the night
D. increase the number of ultrasonic waves

273. During the period of difficulty, I invariably take the help of another person.
A. Never B. Yes
C. No D. Sometimes

274. I like to eat ice-cream during winters.
A. No B. Yes
C. Sometimes D. Never

275. I will to spend my idle time by
A. chatting aimlessly with friends
B. reading a book containing interesting facts
C. reading comics
D. none of these

276. If you are a woman, then, while talking to others
A. you fly into a rage when the talk related to age is commenced
B. you tell your age by reducing a few years from the actual age
C. refrain from going any set of information related to age
D. you inform about your correct age, if asked about the same

277. I love to live alone.
A. Sometimes B. Yes
C. No D. Never

278. I tell people about my hopes and dreams
A. Quite often B. Very rarely
C. Never D. Sometimes

279. When my little child cries loudly, then I
A. give him food
B. thrash him with vigour
C. make him sleep
D. give him feed of milk

280. I like to use new procedures of work.
A. Never B. yes
C. Sometimes D. No

281. During winter days, I
A. get up at a fixed time
B. get up only in the morning
C. get up late
D. get up at an uncertain time

282. I like to be convinced by facts.
A. Sometimes B. No
C. Yes D. Never

283. When someone tells me to make a promise, then I
A. do never make a promise
B. think before finally making a promise
C. make a promise immediately
D. cannot say anything in the context

284. If I were the correspondent of a magazine, then I will write on the following subject
A. Health
B. Cinema and theatre
C. Current Politics
D. None of these three

285. The house of my hate-worthy neighbour is on fire. I
A. am very happy to learn about this
B. am going to put out the fire
C. am not going to put out the fire
D. am still thinking

286. I get help when I discuss things/issues with others
A. Sometimes B. No
C. Yes D. I get into a fix

287. I found a purse full of money in the college. I
A. gave it to the Principal
B. purchased books with that money
C. distributed the money amongst the poor
D. distributed the money amongst friends

288. Upon seeing a lunatic, you
A. start making hue and cry
B. throw stones on him
C. go near him
D. keep yourself away from him

289. I like pre-defined rules and regulations.
A. Sometimes
B. No
C. Yes
D. According to the occasion

290. I myself open the door of the car to enable my wife to sit inside the car.
A. If I am happy B. Sometimes
C. Never D. Always

271. C	**272.** B	**273.** D	**274.** A	**275.** B	**276.** D	**277.** A	**278.** B	**279.** D	**280.** B
281. A	**282.** C	**283.** B	**284.** C	**285.** B	**286.** C	**287.** A	**288.** D	**289.** C	**290.** D

291. Quite often, I change my mind at the last moment.
A. No
B. Yes
C. Sometimes
D. According to my benefit

292. Before starting my scooter, first of all, I
A. check its brakes
B. check the quantity of patrol in the fuel tank
C. check air in the tyres
D. check the headlight

293. When I decide something, then I
A. get into a fix
B. think about the decision
C. feel myself to be contented and satisfied
D. change my decision afterwards

294. When I am alone at my home, then, quite often, I
A. sing a song
B. sleep
C. watch television
D. read literature

295. I like to explore various possibilities/ opportunities, even though it may lead to delay in the piece of work.
A. Sometimes B. Yes
C. No D. Never

296. Before doing my piece of work, I ask myself, "Is it correct?"
A. Sometimes B. Yes
C. No D. Never

297. While talking to my friends, I do not like to express my personal feelings.
A. Sometimes
B. Yes
C. No
D. It depends of the gravity of feelings

298. When I go by the car, I always give lift to hitchhikers.
A. Only to ladies B. Always
C. Never D. Sometimes

299. If put under pressure, I give emphasis on giving myself more time so that I may be able to think more clearly.
A. I get into a fix B. Yes
C. No D. Sometimes

300. The boat I was travelling in, sank midway. First of all, I
A. started coaxing the boatman
B. saved others
C. saved myself
D. closed my eyes

301. While doing work, invariably, I
A. remain in the dilly-dally situation—"to do or not to do"
B. feel difficulty during the beginning
C. find the end to be tedious
D. start doing it immediately

302. I like to carry out the agricultural work according to the scientific method
A. For some time
B. Always
C. Sometimes
D. Never

303. If I find two persons fighting each other, on my way, I
A. try to help them arrive at a truce/settlement of the dispute
B. start fighting on behalf of the weaker person
C. let them fight and move on
D. watch the show

304. If I meet God sometime, then I would ask for Him.
A. Gold and Silver
B. Unlimited property/assets
C. Honestly
D. Love

305. What you would like to be if you were not a man
A. like to be a cow
B. become a horse in a big stable
C. like to be a bird
D. cannot say any thing in this context

306. Whenever some one demands any thing from me I
A. return him empty-handed
B. abuse him
C. give something
D. do not talk to him

307. Whenever I take a decision, then I
A. do not change it
B. change it
C. never change it
D. do not know

291. A	**292.** B	**293.** C	**294.** D	**295.** C	**296.** B	**297.** A	**298.** D	**299.** B	**300.** C
301. B	**302.** B	**303.** A	**304.** D	**305.** C	**306.** C	**307.** C			

308. Cricket is a game involving
A. physical labour B. mental labour
C. physical damage D. economic loss

309. I like to
A. wander B. study
C. watch television D. indulge in gossips

310. When I go to appear in an interview, then I wear a clean
A. shirt B. pantaloon
C. dress D. under wear

311. Your Boss is short tempered and always shouts at everybody, you will:
Your boss is angry and always yells at all look like you?
A. Take sportingly and look for some ways to control his temper.
Don't take it too seriously and find some ways to keep his anger under control.
B. Feel that Boss can have short temper, as he has a right to shout at everybody.
Bosses are angry, so it is normal for him to get angry with someone.
C. Tell him that he is wrong as he has no right to shout at everyone.
Tell him that he is making a mistake and he has no right to be angry with anyone.
D. Tell your boss how you feel and that this situation is not acceptable to you.
Tell your boss how we feel and we don't accept this situation.

312. While going to your Office, one day your neighbour asks for lift, for going to his office which is in opposite direction, you will:
Have a day at the office while your neighbour is opposite asks you lift towards you:
A. Tell him that it may not be possible.
Tell him it is not possible.
B. Tell him that you are not there for these kinds of jobs.
Tell him that you don't do such things.
C. Shout at him that you are getting late.
Shout at him that you are late.
D. Politely refuse him that his office is just in the opposite direction and that you have to reach office on time.
Refuse politely that his office is on the opposite side and that he has to reach office on time.

313. Your driver's daughter is getting married and he needs some money, you will:
A. Ask him to take a loan from Bank
B. Give him some money which is in your capacity & ask him to refund
C. Straight away refuse him as you have nothing to do with that matter
D. Raise a fund from your friends and help him.

314. In your Society, you have people throwing garbage here & there, you will:
A. Try to educate people and keep a dustbin in Society
B. Forget as it is not only your job
C. Penalise the person who is throwing the garbage
D. Nothing can be done

315. After studying hard for your exams, you did not score well, you will:
A. Stop studying hard
B. Start blaming the teacher, that he is unfair
C. Continue to work hard and perform your duty to show better results
D. Ask your friends not to study hard as they will also not get good marks

316. Due to your mistake your car has hit an old man who was riding a cycle. You will:
A. Run away from the place
B. Start shouting and blaming the old man
C. Ask your friend to get his cycle repaired
D. Feel sorry, pay some money to get his cycle repaired and arrange Medical Aid.

317. While you are about to cross a major crossing, you notice a blind man struggling to cross the road. You will:
A. Ask a young boy to help him cross the road
B. Go and catch his hand and help him cross the road
C. Curse the blind man and say why he should come to such busy roads
D. Continue to go your way and ignore him

318. At the Airport, Security asks you to remove your shoes, belt etc. You will:
A. Do it as per instructions
B. Refuse, as they are your personal property
C. You will call the Police for help
D. First you will fight with Security. After that you will remove it.

308. A **309.** B **310.** C **311.** A **312.** D **313.** B **314.** A **315.** C **316.** D
317. B **318.** A

319. Your Classmate is very rude with the Teacher. You have seen him talking rudely many times. You will:
A. Ignore as this issue is between him and the Teacher
B. Talk to his parents and try to find out why is he behaving like this
C. Ask your teacher to cut his name from the Class as it is disturbing to entire Class
D. Talk to your friend reminding him that Teacher is to be respected.

320. Your Boss has shared with you a new plan for the Company, You will:
A. Leak the plan to the Competitors
B. Share the plan with Colleagues immediately
C. Keep it confidential as it is a new plan
D. Share only with your best friend

321. After reaching the destination, you come to know that the Airline Company has forgotten to load your luggage. You will:
A. Start shouting at the airport as it is not your mistake
B. Complain to the Police Station about the incident
C. Give in the Print Media about the incident
D. Forgive them as this happens very rarely

322. Everyone in your Class has received new uniforms except you. What would you do?
A. Ask your Uniform In charge and question him why you have not got a new set of uniform
B. Complain to the Principal
C. Purchase from the market & submit bill to the School
D. Keep on coming to the School without uniform as you have not been provided the same

323. Your Office has gifted you a Diwali present, which you did not like much. You will:
A. Return it
B. Exchange with friends
C. Sell in the market and get money
D. Accept gracefully

324. Even after taking coaching from an Institute, you failed to get admission through competitive exam. You will:
A. Ask the Coaching Institute to return money
B. Ask your friends not to join that Institute
C. Try sincerely this time
D. Ask for 1 year free coaching

325. You are the Principal of a School. One of your teachers always comes late. You will:
A. Terminate him immediately
B. Initiate disciplinary action
C. Call him and counsel him
D. Ignore his mistakes

326. While staying in a Hotel you have given a shirt for laundry. Upon receiving, you found that shirt is damaged. You will:
A. Vacate the room immediately
B. Ask for the money against the damage
C. Call the laundry manager and lodge a complaint
D. Inform the person who is giving the shirt to you and advise him not to repeat it

327. In your opinion, how the poor should become rich:
A. The Poor should not dream to become rich
B. The Poor should be given good education, to help them find a job
C. Nothing can be done
D. Govt. should give money every month to the Poor

328. In a city, a large number of clubs organize Blood Donation Camps. You feel:
A. Some clubs are really doing a very good job to serve the society
B. Most clubs are making money, selling blood in market
C. The concept of club itself is useless concept
D. Clubs are doing just to get money from the Government

329. During your final examination D.J. party is going on next to your house. You will:
A. Try and ignore the issue
B. Politely request him to play music softly
C. Go and pick up a fight with him to stop the music
D. Go to friend's house and study there for exams

330. Near your Colony, some people are cutting trees, you will:
A. Ask your friends to do something about this matter
B. Think that this to be dealt by the Government only
C. Go and talk to the people who are cutting trees and make them understand the benefits of trees
D. Straight away file a complaint in Police Station

319. D	**320.** C	**321.** D	**322.** A	**323.** D	**324.** C	**325.** C	**326.** D	**327.** B
328. A	**329.** B	**330.** C						

331. In your Class one boy is differently abled and most of your friends avoid interactions with him. You will:
A. Try and ignore that boy, like many others
B. Request all the students to help him
C. Always be in touch with him, and provide assistance as needed
D. Give him money as and when he requires

332. Your boss criticizes you in front of your colleagues. He does it repeatedly and this makes you feel insulted. You will:
A. Complain to seniors
B. Ignore the situation
C. Talk to him openly about the way you feel and request him not to do it any more
D. Go to other staff members, discuss with them and talk to him jointly

333. A classmate of yours tells you in confidence that he plans to report sick, while he is actually going for a movie, what will you do?
A. Inform the class Teacher
B. Not do anything & let him go
C. Tell him to be cautious and ask if he needs some cash
D. Advise him to be honest with his class

334. The work of a subordinate or a Team Member of yours is not up to expectations. What will you do?
A. Report to higher Authority
B. Insult him for not doing his work properly
C. Ignore the issue as it is not improvable
D. Talk to him in person about the issue and provide all assistance required by him to improve.

335. What would be your course of action if management changes priorities of a Project suddenly?
A. Immediately leave that Project
B. Notify everyone working on the Project of the changes
C. Ask all the members to leave the Project
D. Register your grievance as you don't like it at all

336. You see some persons are trying to rob an old woman by snatching her purse. You will:
A. Start shouting & try to save her
B. Go away from the place
C. Call the Police and wait there
D. Ask the woman to leave her purse

337. In case your school switches over to new Technology for modernization, as a Principal you would:
A. Make arrangements to train staff as per the new Technology
B. Remove all the staff who are not familiar with the new Technology
C. Forget about the implementation of new Technology
D. Get rid of the employees whom you think are surplus

338. In your opinion, you consider a person as a good human being if:
A. He praises everyone all the time
B. He lends money to everyone all the time
C. He always helps everyone when they are in trouble
D. He remains with everyone all the time

339. If your elder brother does not look after your old parents well, you would:
A. Like to talk to your brother about this issue
B. Feel that the old parents have got to live like this only
C. Feel that it may not be possible for your brother to do the needful due to some problem
D. Tell your parents to adjust with the situation

340. While working in a Hotel if you came across a Guest who is unhappy with the services and starts misbehaving at the Reception with you, you would:
A. Keep yourself cool and tell him/her that you would do your best to help him/her
B. Tell him/her that he/she has no business to misbehave at the Reception
C. Inform your Manager & and wait for their instructions
D. Call the Police & handover the Guest

341. Describe how you would handle a situation where your Company is resisting a new idea or policy
A. Tell them you already know everything
B. Tell them that you are already qualified and trained
C. Understand the benefits and implement the new idea or policy
D. Understand the new policy but stick to old policy only

342. In a class, you find that the Teacher has a thick accent and you can't understand, what's being said, what would you do?
A. Point it out to the Teacher about it
B. Ask someone to translate everything that what the Teacher is saying
C. Try your best to understand what the Teacher is saying
D. Don't attend the class and ask your friend to teach you later

331. C	**332.** C	**333.** D	**334.** D	**335.** B	**336.** A	**337.** A	**338.** C	**339.** A
340. A	**341.** C	**342.** C						

343. As per you, which is the best quality one leader should have:
A. Function according to his/her own style & need not bother about others' opinion
B. Listen to others and then accordingly tackle the situation
C. Go always by what others say or suggest
D. Wait for others to take decision

344. A group of people were beating a thief on the roadside who has been caught red handed. Your reaction:
A. Will inform the Police and hand him over to them
B. Will allow people to keep on beating
C. Let him go after advising him not to repeat
D. Will myself start beating him until he bleeds

345. According to you, in Election you should vote:
A. Who happens to be rich
B. Who is well educated and also a man of good character
C. Who just happens to be known to your family
D. Who just simply belongs to a political family

346. You are working at the Reception of a Hotel. Presently there is no guest at the Reception. You will:
A. Be attentive & remain present at the Reception only
B. Start watching videos on mobile
C. Go to Cafeteria & relax
D. Start talking with your family and friends over mobile phone

347. A teacher of yours, always make fun of you in class. You will:
A. Ignore and focus on your studies
B. Complain to the chairman of the school
C. Never attend his/her class
D. Change the school

348. Due to security reasons, Security Services have locked down the Hotel. You are inside and in a hurry to get back home, what will you do?
A. Check for any sign of immediate danger and open to leave
B. You are sure that it is just a drill, so you will open the back door, which is locked from inside
C. Remain calm and wait for Security to give instructions
D. Put some music on mobile and enjoy your favourite songs

349. You have promised your friend to go with him for a movie on Saturday. Your sister falls sick on Saturday and would like to stay at home. What would you do?
A. Tell your friend that you have changed your mind
B. Go for the movie as you have promised
C. Apologise and make fresh promise
D. Tell him that you are sick, so you can't go with him

350. When you hear the news of a soldier getting killed on the borders, you feel:
A. He is paid by the Government to die for his country
B. It is a part of his duty to sacrifice his life
C. Such soldiers must be honoured by us
D. All of us should go to borders to help soldiers

351. You think that you have been given too much extra work by the School, due to which your studies are getting hampered. You will:
A. Complain to your father about it
B. Complain to your Principal about it
C. Tell everyone about it
D. Talk to your Class Teacher about it

352. A street light in your Society is not working, you will:
A. Ask for some donation and get it repaired
B. Inform the local Municipal Corporation to get it repaired
C. Do not worry as it is not your job
D. Put up a signage to highlight the condition of the light and ask people to be careful

353. In your opinion your Colleague is very stubborn. You will:
A. Inform other Colleagues
B. Inform your Boss
C. Keep talking to him and counsel
D. Speak loudly to make yourself heard

354. According to you, for most jobs it is most important to hire persons with good attitudes and adequate intelligence rather than the ones with technical knowledge:
A. As per you, more qualities are required
B. You agree with the status
C. You disagree with the status
D. As per you, technical knowledge is not required

343. B **344.** A **345.** B **346.** A **347.** A **348.** C **349.** C **350.** C **351.** D
352. B **353.** C **354.** B

355. While making some changes in Company policy some of your staff think that changes create anxiety and not opportunity, then you:
A. Demonstrate your genuine concern
B. Do nothing about what your staff think
C. Ask him to speak to HR
D. Tell them the decision was not yours but of the management

356. You received a spam mail that you have won some cash prize, and to transfer the same, you are required to send your bank details. You will:
A. Immediately begin to send bank details
B. Will keep aside this mail and will not reply again
C. Just keep on thinking why you have received this mail
D. Will make a complaint to the local Police Station

357. If you read "women as Teachers and maids while men as Doctors and Pilots". This type of attitude/ deception is likely to promote
A. Gender empowerment
B. Gender stereotype
C. Gender role play
D. Gender constancy

358. Sarthak is a day dreamer, having interest in reading books; not able to express his views before seniors; non friendly and idealistic employee, the type of attitude he has:
A. Extrovert B. Introvert
C. Ambient D. Athletic

359. How would you handle, a drunken Guest in the hotel?
A. Embarrass the Guest especially in front of other Guests
B. Deal with the intoxicated Guest, full of anger
C. Lock him until he behaves normally
D. Deal with the situation in a calm, friendly way

360. What are the attributes of an effective learner?
A. Self-directed
B. Curious and open minded
C. Self-aware
D. Self-directed, curious, open minded and self-aware

361. You are in an elevator with two other strangers and the electricity goes off in between. What would you do?
A. Panic and scream in the elevator.
B. Let the other people decide the course of action while you stand there and watch.
C. Try to break open the elevator.
D. Keep calm and try and ring the emergency alarm to seek help.

362. Annual day function is to be organised in your school, the responsibility of this has been assigned to you. You would :
A. Try to get rid of this responsibility.
B. Try to organize it with the help of your batchmates.
C. Avoid all your responsibilities.
D. Delegate it to someone else.

363. What do you do when you reach late for your class?
A. Quietly try to sneak into the class without being noticed by the teacher.
B. Do not attend the class only.
C. Admit your reason for being late in the class and whole heartedly accept the teacher's decision.
D. Make up excuses to convince the teacher.

364. In an examination hall, you find that your question paper is too tough. The best thing you can do is:
A. Try cheating from your neighbouring student.
B. Leave the paper and walk out.
C. Try attempting those questions first, of which you know the answers.
D. Write irrelevant matter to just fill in the pages.

365. While working in a group, you tend to:
A. Adjust with other members, but as per your convenience.
B. Be a bit hesitant.
C. Not involved with the group activity.
D. Extend full cooperation to the other group members.

366. You are transferred to a section in your school where you do not have any friends, you would:
A. Sit in one corner of the class and not take interest in anything.
B. Cry, for you do not like your surroundings.
C. Try and make new friends in the new section.
D. Ignore everything and just concentrate on your studies.

355. A **356.** B **357.** B **358.** B **359.** D **360.** D **361.** D **362.** B **363.** A
364. C **365.** D **366.** C

367. You find a lady entering your restaurant carrying a lot of bags in hand, you will:
A. Rush to open the door and help her with her bags.
B. Not bother about the same.
C. Be agitated due to shortage of space in the restaurant.
D. Ask her to leave her bags outside.

368. As a manager you notice there has been repeated customer complaints against a subordinate, you will:
A. Reprimand him and give him a deadline to improve.
B. Fire him from the job.
C. Ask other colleagues to warn him about the same.
D. Try to find out the problem and give him a remedial training.

369. Only a hard working person can move ahead in life. What is your opinion?
A. Hard working people are not always successful.
B. Hard working people are never successful.
C. A hardworking person will definitely succeed, sooner or later.
D. It all depends on your luck.

370. One of your roommate has the habit of speaking loudly over the phone which disturbs you while studying. Despite your repeated requests, his habit seems to be getting worse. You:
A. Start speaking loudly when your roommate is studying to teach him a lesson.
B. Fight with your roommate.
C. Complain about your roommate to the hostel warden.
D. Have an open discussion with your roommate about your problem and try to solve it amicably.

371. In the class you are delivering a speech when a classmate of yours is continuously interrupting you with several queries, you would:
A. Not pay attention to him.
B. Start speaking at a faster pace than before.
C. Stop the speech and let him speak.
D. Politely let him know that all his queries will be addressed at the end.

372. There has been a sudden death in the family recently and you are still grieving. However you have your annual examination round the corner and for that you have to catch up with a lot of studies. What would you do?
A. You will get back to studying after you get over your grief.
B. You will ignore your examination and continue grieving.
C. You will motivate yourself to get back to studying as only grieving will not do any good to you.
D. You will run away from everything.

373. If an argument starts with someone, then I invariably:
A. Listen to the viewpoint of that person carefully and then speak what is in my mind.
B. State my view at the very outset.
C. Start saying whatever comes to my mind.
D. Be confused and perplexed.

374. Your neighbour is continuously throwing garbage in your premise despite repeated warnings. You would:
A. Go to their house and engage into a fight with them.
B. Inform the police about this incident.
C. Take the garbage and throw it back in their premise.
D. Ask them the reason for their action and sternly yet politely ask them to stop this nuisance.

375. Your close relative has gifted you a birthday present, which you did not like much. You will:
A. Openly express your dislike.
B. Request him to exchange the item.
C. Respect the feelings of the person and use the gift appropriately.
D. Give a hint that the gift is not to your liking.

376. You observe that you are burdened with extra work in your workplace compared to your other colleagues. You would:
A. Continue doing the work in spite of increasing stress levels.
B. Revolt outright.
C. Politely reason out the situation with your supervisor.
D. Gain sympathy of others.

377. You are never in limelight or focus inspite of your efficiency at work. You would:
A. Lower your performance level.
B. Continue working and wait for the moment of recognition.
C. Keep silent regarding your grievances.
D. Openly publicise your efficiency and proclaim that you are the best.

367. A **368.** D **369.** C **370.** D **371.** D **372.** C **373.** A **374.** D **375.** C
376. C **377.** B

378. A typical airline flight might have about 150 passengers served by 4 flight attendants. Upon getting this information:

A. You start wondering about the work pressure.
B. Vouch never to work as a flight attendant.
C. You ignore as you are not interested in aviation industry.
D. You wonder how challenging and thrilling the job of a flight attendant must be.

379. Your supervisor repeatedly criticizes you in front of your subordinates. You feel insulted. You would:

A. Speak to other colleagues regarding this and consider leaving the job.
B. Ignore the situation but feel very angry and hurt by his words.
C. Hit back harshly and make him gulp his own words.
D. Approach him directly and explain your feelings to him.

380. You have observed lately that one of your colleague at work place has taken you for granted and often tries to pass off his responsibilities to you. You would:

A. Tolerate for some more time and then counter fiercely.
B. Shout at him in front of every one.
C. Discuss the matter with him in one to one mode.
D. Stay normal and ignore, although you don't like it.

381. You accidently over hear a colleague talking negatively about you to your boss. You would:

A. Storm-in straight away to deny the charges.
B. Calmly step in and establish logic for your behaviour and actions.
C. Start fighting with your colleague in front of the boss.
D. Ignore and walk away.

382. You have been instructed to do a job by your supervisor. You have not understood a part of the instructions. You would:

A. Seek clarification again before you commence the job.
B. Plunge into the job and clarify only when stuck.
C. Confidently go ahead without bothering about the consequences of mistake.
D. Keep your supervisor informed that some future clarification may be needed.

383. You as a class monitor have been asked to select a team for accomplishing a job. You would select students:

A. Only those who are close to you.
B. Only those who would do something when asked.
C. Only those who are ready to adapt to any situation they may come across.
D. Those who are close to you, those who would do something when asked and those who are ready to adapt to any situation they may come across.

384. Your friends have invited you for a gathering. You accept that and on returning home you are informed that there is a family get together on the same day. You would:

A. Flatly refuse to attend the family gathering.
B. Blame your friends for holding the gathering on the same day.
C. Decide to attend none of the functions.
D. Very politely refuse to go to one of the places.

385. Your neighbour's daughter is getting married and on the day of the wedding, a fire breaks out. You would:

A. Panic and run away.
B. Secure the children and the aged people first before you try to help others
C. Go to a safe distance and watch what is happening.
D. Come back home and relax.

386. You were going through your younger brother's maths exam copy which was checked and returned by the class teacher. You noticed a correct answer marked wrong. You would:

A. Straight away place a written complaint to the principal of the school.
B. Blame you brother rudely saying that he should have taken it to the concerned teacher.
C. Go and speak to the concerned teacher yourself without creating a fuss.
D. Put up a quarrel with the concerned teacher.

387. How would you ensure that you become the focal point in a group discussion?

A. By aggressive gestures and words.
B. Logical talking with appropriate humour.
C. Snubbing others while they want to speak.
D. Trying to stop aggressive outburst of others.

378. D **379.** D **380.** C **381.** B **382.** A **383.** C&D **384.** D **385.** B **386.** C **387.** B

388. The welfare society of your locality is organizing a Blood Donation Camp You would:
A. Express. only verbal desire to support such an initiative.
B. Refrain from going to the venue
C. Get irritated as you do not have time for such activities.
D. Show full enthusiasm and ensure that you are present on the day of the event.

389. Which of the following is not a part of a well groomed individual?
A. Streaked hair B. Well kept nails
C. Ironed shirt D. Formal shoes

390. Two of your close friends are having a strained relationship. You would:
A. Leave them to handle the situation on their own.
B. Allow time to naturally heal up the relationship.
C. Take initiative and try to find out the root cause of the strained relationship.
D. Sever your friendship with both of them.

391. If your batchmate confides his secrets, you would:
A. Use the information shared to your advantage.
B. Tell them to few of your other friends.
C. Discuss them with your parents.
D. Discuss the secrets only with the batchmate, if required.

392. A new member joins the cricket team of which you are the captain. A day after his joining, he gives a suggestion to you. You would:
A. Snap at him, saying that his suggestions are not required at such an early stage of joining.
B. Advice him to understand how the team works.
C. Think about the suggestions and judge their relevance.
D. Listen to it and forget about it.

393. You are attending a class and suddenly, your mobile phone rings loudly. You would:
A. Try to hide so that it would be difficult to locate the source
B. Own up and apologize to the teacher
C. Quickly switch off the mobile phone
D. Give excuses for keeping your phone in the 'ring' mode.

394. You are seated in an aircraft at the window seat. A little boy comes and requests you for the window seat and tells you to take the middle seat. You would:
A. Explain him politely that it is illegal.
B. Give up your seat on request.
C. Flatly refuse.
D. Offer a chocolate and deny the little boy the window seat.

395. As a team leader, you find one of your team members is not performing up to the mark. You would:
A. Shout at him in front of everybody.
B. Arrange for a counselling session.
C. Give a poor appraisal to him straight away.
D. Ignore thinking that he would develop with time.

396. Your manager calls you in his cabin and points out some deficiencies in your performance. You would:
A. Consider the manager as 'over analytical'.
B. Consider the manager as a person who wants you to improve.
C. Consider the manager as a 'dominating' person.
D. Listen and judge nothing.

397. Your team has failed to win a final match. As the captain of the team:
A. Take all blame on yourself for the defeat.
B. Blame your team members for the defeat.
C. Try to find out reasons of defeat by discussing with the team members.
D. Resign from the captaincy.

398. You are carrying two heavy bags and waiting at a railway station. The train arrives. You struggle with your bags and manage to board the train. Just then, you see an old lady trying hard to lift her bag. You will:
A, Advice her to call a porter.
B. Try to find your own seat thinking you can help her after wards.
C. Help her to lift her bag.
D. Tell a passer-by to help her.

399. You are in a crowded railway station. Suddenly you spot a little girl all alone and looking confused. You would:
A. Hand her over to the Railway Police for further help.
B. Ask her if she is lost and ask her to look for her parents or relatives.
C. Take no action.
D. Take her to your house for further assistance.

388. D **389.** A&D **390.** C **391.** D **392.** C **393.** B **394.** B **395.** B **396.** B
397. C **398.** C **399.** A

400. You have visited your uncle's place. At the middle of the night your uncle suffers a 'heart attack'. You will:
A. Ignore and go back to sleep.
B. Wake up immediately and call for an ambulance.
C. Google some medicines for him.
D. Wait till somebody instructs you for some action.

401. You have visited a place of tourist interest. You see a group of people littering on the road. You would:
A. Politely tell them that there is a dustbin nearby.
B. Shout at them for such a behaviour.
C. Express your displeasure with a stern look.
D. Ignore and walk away.

402. A customer has booked a room in your hotel but at the time of arrival, Room is not available. You will :
A. Take him to your Residence.
B. Regret and tell him that hotel is sold out.
C. Regret and arrange the room in another comparable category of hotels.
D. Provide him the list of other hotels in the city.

403. A technique that might be used by an active listener is to:
A. Describe a situation
B. Express anxiety
C. Paraphrase the speakers words
D. Offer a point of view when in conversation

404. An old lady, slipped and fell in the lobby of the hotel while walking and she starts shouting, you would:
A. Tell her its her fault
B. Look for a lady staff to help her
C. Help and make her comfortable
D. Nothing can be done as incident has already taken place.

405. A co-worker tells you in confidence that she plans to call in sick while she is actually taking a week's vacations, you will:
A. Inform the Authorities
B. Ignore the information
C. Advise her to be honest at the work place
D. Take all her responsibilities and encourage her to go for the vacation

406. While travelling in a train, you see a purse lying on the seat next to you, you will:
A. Pocket the cash and throw the purse.
B. Ignore as it you did not notice.
C. Change your seat to avoid touching that purse.
D. Take the purse and hand over to Police or Railway officer on duty.

407. While working as a school teacher, you find a child is unable to understand the lesson always. You will:
A. Take him to the Principal for strict action.
B. Discuss with the parents of the child and do the needful.
C. Ignore him in the class.
D. Ask him to take private tuitions from you.

408. What would you do if you realise at the last moment that the assignment you have done is not up to the mark?
A. Presume that the teacher may not notice it.
B. Ask the teacher for an extension and promise an up to the mark submission in future.
C. Ignore what teacher says after checking.
D. Give excuses for not doing the task up to the mark.

409. At your school, your friend asks your opinion about an issue, you will:
A. Present your honest opinion as you are an expert of that particular subject.
B. Give wrong answer purposely.
C. Rely on other's opinion.
D. Avoid the questions stating that you are busy.

410. Your boss doesn't pay attention to what you have just said, as he was busy at his computer, you will:
A. speak loudly to make yourself heard.
B. wait for sometime to talk.
C. leave his office and stop talking in future.
D. tell everyone about this incident.

411. Your class has been given a group task by your faculty and members of group assigned to you are not known to you.

You:
A. Don't participate with enthusiasm in the task.
B. Request your faculty to change your group.
C. You take this as an opportunity to learn things in the new group.
D. On your own decide to change the group and start working with a known group.

400. B	**401.** A	**402.** C	**403.** C	**404.** C	**405.** C	**406.** D	**407.** B	**408.** B
409. A	**410.** B	**411.** C						

412. You are preparing for your 10+2 final exams. Your neighbour's children make a lot of noise while playing and that disturbs you. You will:
A. Go and shout at the children.
B. Tell other neighbours about these children and the fact that they were such rowdy kids.
C. Ignore the whole situation.
D. Request to the parents of these children to stop them from creating such disturbances.

413. At times despite your best efforts, you still fail to impress your superiors with quality of your work, you:
A. Blame your fate for this.
B. Continue doing the same quality of work as it doesn't affect you.
C. Lose interest in your work.
D. Discuss with superiors and try again till you succeed.

414. You meet a motorist with a flat tyre. You will:
A. Help him by calling a mechanic.
B. Stop and try to change the tyre even though you don't have the expertise.
C. Help him park his car on one side of the road.
D. Ignore the situation and drive on.

415. You are staying in a hostel and sharing room with fellow mates. When you leave the room to go to college, you:
A. always put all things at their right places.
B. expect your room-mates to clean up the room.
C. be bossy and ask others to clean it up for you.
D. leave the room in complete mess.

416. You have to prepare for a vital examination as well as an important project at the same time. You will:
A. Prepare a time table allocating the required time to each and follow it.
B. You will start panicking and as a result will not be able to do anything satisfactorily.
C. You will prepare for any one of them.
D. Prepare for the examination and get your project done by your sibling.

417. While dining at a reputed restaurant you ordered vegetarian soup but you have been served with non-vegetarian soup. You will:
A. Call the server and shout at him/her.
B. Call the manager and complain to him/her.
C. Leave the restaurant immediately.
D. Forget the incident and do nothing about it.

418. You have planned a day trip with your friends and you are leading the group. One of your friend from other town who is in your town and staying in a hotel, calls up that he needs your help as he is not feeling well. You will:
A. Ask him to wait till you come back from the trip.
B. Ask him to call someone else.
C. Reschedule the whole day trip.
D. Call some other friend and ask him to help the sick friend of yours.

419. A farewell party is to be organized at your college by group of students. You:
A. Try to make another group and challenge the same.
B. Volunteer for the group.
C. Not be bothered about it.
D. Let others organize it themselves.

420. A new role for leaders is to take on responsibility as:
A. Overseer
B. Mentors only
C. Coaches only
D. Both Coaches and Mentors

421. You are a cashier at the cash counter of a hospital. There is no one waiting at the window to pay. You will:
A. Go and help a co-worker.
B. Quit your seat, go behind the office and relax.
C. Remain seated at your counter and be attentive to anybody requiring help.
D. Stay at the counter but listen to the mobile phone music through a pair of ear phones.

422. If someone criticises you for your mistakes, you will:
A. Fight with the person.
B. Start talking to others about his mistakes.
C. Not pay any attention to it.
D. Listen to him and take it as feedback for improvement.

423. You are the leader of a group and new member joins it. How would you make the member comfortable?
A. Giving him a complicated task.
B. Giving him a complete set of instructions to study and leave him alone.
C. Ignore him and do your business.
D. By making the job interesting to him and by praising him when he does well.

412. D **413.** D **414.** A **415.** A **416.** A **417.** D **418.** C **419.** B **420.** D
421. C **422.** D **423.** D

424. You have been sent to a Historical Monument for a cleanliness project and to educate the locals over the same. You know that there will not be any supervision there, you:
A. will ask your younger brother to go there and do it for you.
B. show no enthusiasm and just complete the project.
C. whole-heartedly participate in the project and try to put in your best efforts.
D. will not go there, at all.

425. Whenever any new assignment, which is out of your routine comfort, is given to you, you will:
A. Eagerly take up such assignments.
B. Try to stick to your comfort zone only.
C. Take up the assignment and make excuses for the delayed submission.
D. Never initiate the same.

426. You are working in a hotel and staying along with other staff in the official accommodation provided by the company. One day you fall sick. In your opinion:
A. You apply for leave as per company policy.
B. You expect your friends to apply for the leave on your behalf.
C. Expect your boss to grant your leave.
D. You don't need to apply for leave as everyone is aware.

427. A park in your locality has an open drain. You will:
A. Request your neighbours to pool money to convert that to a closed drain.
B. Inform the local Councillor.
C. Put up a signage to highlight the condition of the drain and ask people to be careful.
D. Expect your friends to cover it up.

428. While working as a manager in a hotel, you are informed that one guest in the hotel has suddenly fallen ill. You will:
A. Call a doctor and send him to the guest.
B. Let the guest handle things on his/her own.
C. Meet the guest and then urgently call the doctor and help the patient as required.
D. Ask your junior manager to deal with it.

429. You are in a crowded city bus when you see an old person and a lady with an infant get on to the bus. What would you do?
A. Ignore the situation and keep sitting in your seat.
B. Offer your seat to one and ask someone else to vacate their seat for the other.
C. Judge the situation and offer the seat to the appropriate person.
D. Offer your seat to the lady with the infant and direct the old person to the senior citizen seat.

430. You have secured a management job in an organization. Upon joining, you realised that the environment is overbearing. Your reaction would be:
A. To isolate yourself from the environment and keep blaming the staff.
B. Carry on and do nothing about it.
C. Leave the job.
D. To talk to staff, take them into your confidence and then initiate the process of rectification.

431. You are a sincere and dedicated manager of a well established hotel. Your company wants you to go and handle a property which is not doing well in business. You will:
A. Leave the job and take another job.
B. Crib about the new assignment.
C. Try to convince the superiors to send someone else, instead of you.
D. You accept the challenge and go ahead with the assignment.

432. One of your team member always tries to obstruct your work, repeatedly. You will:
A. Not do anything.
B. Start interfering in his tasks, too.
C. Take these exerts seriously.
D. Try to discuss with him about his obstructing behaviour.

433. To work efficiently and effectively in the service industry, which of the following you think is/are the essential ability(ies)/qualities?
A. Being introvert
B. Being responsible only
C. Being helpful and outgoing only
D. Both being responsible and being helpful and outgoing

434. In the examination hall you find that your Question Paper is too tough to be Answered. The best thing you can do is:
A. complain to the Examiner to change the Question Paper.
B. try to cheat.
C. leave the paper and walk out of the Examination hall.
D. try to attempt the questions you know first.

424. C **425.** A **426.** A **427.** C **428.** C **429.** D **430.** D **431.** D **432.** D
433. D **434.** D

435. One of your team-mates is repeatedly failing to score in cricket matches despite being talented and skilled. You will:
A. Collect money from other team mates and send him to a coaching school.
B. Ignore and drop him, making room for other extra player.
C. Do not give him a chance to play.
D. Organise a coaching and practice sessions with all your team mates and ensure he succeeds.

436. If all of a sudden your maid becomes seriously ill at night, you would:
A. Not care for the situation.
B. Ask someone else to help and leave from there.
C. Take her to the nearest hospital.
D. Wait for the morning to contact a doctor.

437. You Receive calls from Customer-Care continuously for the same matter. What will you do?
A. Don't Receive the call
B. Put your phone in silent mode and ignore the calls.
C. Put Customer-Care number on block list.
D. Receive the call but instruct them about not continuing with the calls.

438. You are going to cinema hall to watch a movie. You have some edible items in your bag. The cinema hall does not allow eatables inside. Watchman asks if you are carrying any food items in your bag.
A. You will hand over the food items.
B. You will argue with the watchman and insist on carrying the food items.
C. Gather a crowd and create a scene of the cinema hall.
D. You will not tell him anything.

439. You have got an assignment from your Boss. Before you execute it, the plan is to be made and discussed. In your opinion:
A. planning is half the task done.
B. planning is sheer waste of time.
C. planning is only a personal opinion.
D. planning is not required at all.

440. While working as restaurant supervisor in a hotel, one of your guests asks you to send food from the buffet to his room as he is hosting a party. This practice is totally against the hotel policy. You will:
A. Inform him about the policy and refuse politely.
B. Still send the food to his room.
C. Will ask for money in lieu of the food service.
D. Refuse him the food service, rudely.

441. If you happen to see someone getting hit by a car and getting badly injured, you would:
A. Run away from the place in fear of getting involved in a police case.
B. Immediately try and help the victim.
C. Try to chase the car to get hold of the driver.
D. Run and call the police.

442. You are preparing for the final examination scheduled on the next day, but your neighbour plays loud music and you are getting disturbed. What will you do?
A. You also start playing music louder than your neighbour.
B. Request your neighbour and inform him about your examination.
C. Inform the local Police and complain.
D. Ignore and try to concentrate on your preparation.

443. You are busy in a departmental store in the children's clothing section. You find an old lady looking for help in the packaged food section. You will:
A. Ignore the situation.
B. Excuse yourself from your own customers and quickly help the lady in the other section
C. Inform the appropriate sales staff to attend to her.
D. Pretend to be busy at your own counter.

444. The entrance path of your college is littered with paper and plastic on a daily basis. You will:
A. Criticize the sweeper of that area.
B. Leave it as it is and do not do anything.
C. Think that this is college responsibility.
D. Make a group of like-minded friends and create awareness in the college.

445. You are on your way to appear for a Job Interview and while walking down the road, your Dress is spoilt by a vehicle passing by on the road. You will:
A. Pick up a stone and throw at the vehicle and start an argument.
B. You decide to drop the interview and go back home.
C. You clean up your clothes as much as you can and keep your mind focused on the interview.
D. You will click a photograph of the car number and inform the traffic police about the incident.

435. D **436.** C **437.** D **438.** A **439.** A **440.** A **441.** B **442.** B **443.** C
444. D **445.** C

446. One of your classmates has lost his mobile and you know that one of your good friends has found the same mobile. You will:
A. Ignore the whole incident.
B. Ask your friend to return it to the owner.
C. Tell your classmate which of your friends has stolen it.
D. Suggest your friend not to return the mobile.

447. According to you, what should you do to control the ill effects of stress of modern day life:
A. Only sufficient relaxation and rest
B. Only diet control
C. Only physical exercise
D. Diet control, sufficient relaxation and rest and physical exercise

448. You have stomach ache and nausea and you have some very urgent work lined up at office. You feel that it is:
A. Necessary to attend work just to complete the urgent work.
B. Not necessary to attend office but you need to inform them about not being present.
C. Not required to visit office if you are unwell.
D. Not necessary to bother about work and no need to inform office as well.

449. One of your junior staff who has been working with you for a long time, now does not take his job seriously and even replies to you. You will:
A. Try to transfer him to some other department.
B. Shout at him and ask him to behave.
C. Talk to him and try to understand his problem and then act.
D. Shift his tasks to other staff members.

450. A classmate of yours has become addicted to some vile habits, you have been noticing changes in his behaviour, you will:
A. Start avoiding him.
B. Punish him.
C. Not do anything.
D. Counsel him and assist him to overcome the addiction.

451. A guest is not satisfied with the service of the department you are heading and you come to know about this from another colleague. You will:
A. Approach the guest and try to find out the situation and act accordingly.
B. Tell the other person to take care of this.
C. Do nothing about it.
D. Immediately inform your boss.

452. Your maid's son met with an accident and needs blood immediately. You will:
A. Collect money and give it to the maid to pay for the blood.
B. Gather some of your friends to donate the blood and refrain from donating yourself.
C. Volunteer to donate spontaneously.
D. Be indifferent and totally neglect the situation.

453. A fight takes place between two of your Best Friends. What will you do?
A. You also involve yourself in fighting.
B. Try to convince both to stop fighting and try to find a solution to the problem.
C. Ignore them and leave the scene.
D. Take side of one of the friends, who you think is right.

454. You are part of a group assignment in your school. You will:
A. agree with the ideas of others and not participate much.
B. dominate with your ideas over the others.
C. share your ideas with others.
D. shall be generating your own ideas after listening to the other people's ideas.

455. On the way back home from office after a very tiring day, you see an old lady standing in the bus next to where you are seated and requesting for the seat from you. You will:
A. Shout at the lady for riding in a crowded bus.
B. Offer your seat to the lady.
C. Tell her that you are also very tired and can't offer the seat.
D. Ignore the request.

456. You are driving a car without fastening the Seat Belt. You are stopped by the traffic police. You will:
A. Stop the car and start arguing with the traffic police.
B. Immediately stop the car and follow the instructions given by the traffic police.
C. Increase the speed of your car and try to escape.
D. Take away your hands off the car steering and try to put on your seat belt.

446. B	**447.** D	**448.** A	**449.** C	**450.** D	**451.** A	**452.** C	**453.** B	**454.** C
455. B	**456.** B							

457. Imagine a colleague of yours whom you don't get along with well, needs your help on an important assignment given to him. When he approaches you, you will:

A. Ignore him completely.
B. Welcome him and assist, to the best of your ability.
C. Misguide him and enjoy his failure.
D. Ask him to seek help from others.

458. Your friend has become angry with you without any apparent reason. You:

A. will try to please him.
B. will criticise him among your other friends.
C. will not talk to him at all.
D. will sort out the misunderstanding by talking to him.

459. One of your classmate with whom you don't get along very well slips and falls down in front of you in the college corridor and your friends started laughing. You will:

A. Just sit and watch.
B. Join your friends in laughter.
C. Help him and ask your friends not to laugh.
D. Walk away from the scene.

460. A new year Party is to be arranged in your office. You will:

A. sit back and wait for the invitation.
B. try to organize it on your own.
C. organize by taking help of your colleagues.
D. let someone else take the lead.

461. A park in front of your house has hardly any trees. Your neighbours have often expressed their desire to plant trees in the park. You will

A. not be interested in the matter since it is a community work.
B. expect some neighbour to take initiative and start the project.
C. ask some neighbour to start planting trees with others help.
D. take initiative yourself and start the work, while also asking others to help.

462. A family staying nearby your house has a kid who is a child with special needs. Most people in your locality avoid any interactions with the family. You will

A. request family staying next door to help the family, if possible.
B. try and ignore the family like many others.
C. visit them and render whatever help you could render.
D. keep contact with them regularly and ask others to visit them and provide assistance as needed.

463. Pollution levels in the metro town you stay have reached dangerous proportions. People discuss this subject all the time. You will

A. ask your friends to do something about the matter.
B. think that this is to be dealt by the government only.
C. criticize the government all the time for creating this situation.
D. reduce the usage of your own car to the minimum and utilize public transport to the maximum.

464. Your close friend expresses a desire to organize a 'Blood Donation Camp' to collect blood for a local hospital. You will

A. expect your friend to seek help from others and not disturb you.
B. take active part in the project and get fully involved.
C. tell him that it is not his job and you cannot help him in this venture.
D. take limited interest and request others to help in the task.

465. To work efficiently in a social sector, which of the following personality traits is considered most significant?

A. Perseverance and hard work
B. Helping attitude
C. Higher academic achievements.
D. Good looks.

466. According to you, efforts made by our government to facilitate movements of handicapped people to reach public places is considered

A. quite inadequate
B. much more than needed
C. needing considerable improvement
D. highly adequate

467. If you are earning adequately from your business

A. you need not give any money for charity, because you have earned it.
B. you should regularly give money for charity.
C. you may give some money for charity.
D. you should give money for charity, if others are also giving.

457. B **458.** D **459.** C **460.** C **461.** D **462.** D **463.** D **464.** B **465.** B
466. A **467.** B

488. Your close friend, who is also a social worker, plans to organize a free medical check up for the poor people of your area. He approaches you to help him in this task, you will
A. tell your friend bluntly that you are very busy with your work presently.
B. try and find some time to assist him.
C. be glad to help him and request other friends to also help him.
D. think it is a sheer waste of time for you and will try and ignore your friend for a few days.

489. In the recent past, treatment of patients by reputed private hospitals has been much in the news. According to you presently patient care by these hospitals
A. is highly satisfactory.
B. is much beyond expectations.
C. is just about satisfactory.
D. needs much improvement.

490. During the last few years law and order situation in your colony has been deteriorating substantially. You will
A. plan to shift to some other locality.
B. try and manage with the existing situation.
C. discuss with people of your colony and take up the issue with concerned agencies/authorities.
D. expect others to do the needful but apprise others of the prevailing condition.

491. During the past few years, tourism industry has progressed considerably. During this period, availability of hotel rooms with desirable facilities and reasonable charges has
A. decreased drastically B. remained the same
C. decreased marginally D. increased somewhat

492. In your opinion, medical facilities in rural India are considered
A. just about adequate
B. highly satisfactory
C. quite inadequate
D. excellent and commendable

493. Your maid servant has been working for you for more than 5 years now. Suddenly she informs you that owing to some family issues, she wants to quit the job. You will
A. get angry and tell her that she could not do so suddenly.
B. give her salary and ask her to get out.
C. ask her to complete the month and then leave by the month end.
D. give her a patient hearing and then decide accordingly.

494. The airlines with whom you have booked your ticket suddenly informs you one day prior, that the flight is cancelled due to some technical reason. You will
A. ask them to cancel your ticket and refund your money immediately.
B. get angry and pick-up a fight with the airlines staff.
C. lodge a complaint against the airlines with the concerned authority.
D. book your ticket as per options offered by the same airlines on the same date.

495. While working in hotel industry as an executive, which of the following personality traits you think is most significant to deal with an angry and unreasonable customer?
A. Good looks B. Higher intelligence
C. Patience and tact D. Hard working attitude

496. While going on your scooter, you happen to slightly hit a cyclist inadvertently and cause him a minor injury. You will
A. try to run away from the place of accident.
B. get angry and abuse the cyclist for not driving carefully.
C. hit the cyclist at the earliest and blame him fully for the accident.
D. talk to the cyclist nicely and help him to go to the nearest clinic for treatment of his injury.

497. Your good friend one day suddenly gets angry and tries to misbehave with you. You will
A. feel extremely bad and tell him that you did not expect this from him.
B. tell him that you want to break up with him immediately.
C. not feel bad but talk to him patiently and try to understand as to why did he behave in that fashion.
D. also shout at him and tell him to behave properly.

498. While you are making a project and working in a group, you tend to
A. dominate over other members of the team.
B. do your very best to look after the project and help yourself as well.
C. enjoy cooperating with other team members.
D. lose interest in the project.

488. C **489.** D **490.** C **491.** A **492.** C **493.** D **494.** D **495.** C **496.** D
497. C **498.** B

499. Your boss does not appreciate your work and continues to ignore you. You will
A. get angry and ask your boss to behave properly.
B. ask him politely as to why is he not happy and then try to adjust with what he tells you was the problem.
C. ignore your boss and continue doing your duty.
D. look for another job.

500. When your boss assigns you a big task, you tend to
A. jump into it without any preparation.
B. get annoyed and prefer to take long leave.
C. prepare yourself adequately and then accept it.
D. avoid it somehow by politely declining it.

501. You suddenly decide to visit your nephew and enjoy your holiday with him. On reaching his house, you realise that he is not keeping well and he did not extend the warmth you were expecting. You will
A. tell him that you were highly disappointed with his behaviour.
B. leave his house after a few hours, being badly hurt.
C. stay with him and since he is not well, try and help him in whatever way you can.
D. lose your cool and leave his house immediately after telling him that you will never see him again.

502. Your close relative has gifted you a birthday present, which you did not like much. You will
A. openly express your dislike.
B. request him to exchange the item.
C. respect the feelings of the person and use the gift appropriately.
D. give a hint that the gift is not of your liking.

503. While you went abroad on an official tour, on reaching your destination, you realise that your luggage has not arrived and it may take 3 to 4 days before you would receive it. You will
A. ignore the incident and forget about the luggage.
B. lodge an official complaint with airlines and demand compensation for causing such terrible inconvenience.
C. get extremely annoyed and go and pick up a fight with the airlines staff for such careless behaviour.
D. request the airlines to deliver the luggage at the earliest possible.

504. The shopping complex near your house is not handicap friendly. Due to which old and people with special needs find it difficult to shop for their daily needs. You will
A. take the subject with local authorities with the help of other people of your area.
B. expect people with special needs to shop elsewhere.
C. wait patiently for the concerned authorities to take some action to remedy the present situation.
D. try and ignore this situation as it exists now.

505. The medicine you purchased from the nearby medical store is not curing your disease. You suspect the medicine to be spurious and not genuine. You will
A. try and ignore the incident.
B. ask other neighbours, if they had similar experience and if yes, then take up the matter with consumer court/other agencies.
C. tell the medical store to change the medicine.
D. ask others to take up the matter, if they also suspect that medicines sold by that medical store are not considered genuine.

506. In a recent direction by the Supreme Court of India, the court has directed that police should not harass people who bring victims of road accidents to hospitals. You feel this direction will
A. not make any difference in the attitude of police personnel.
B. discourage people to help road accident victims.
C. encourage people to help road accident victims.
D. encourage police people to harass people who are helping others.

507. Since two schools are located near your house, everyday both in the morning and afternoon, when schools open and close, there is complete road blockage due to so many vehicles, which causes tremendous inconvenience to all residents of the area. You will
A. ask other residents of the area to do something about it.
B. consider shifting out of the colony where you are presently staying.
C. accept it as your fate and try to forget about it.
D. take up the issue with police/other authorities through your Resident's Welfare Association (RWA) after taking other residents into confidence.

499. B	**500.** C	**501.** C	**502.** C	**503.** D	**504.** A	**505.** B	**506.** C	**507.** D

508. While staying in a reputed hotel room, you ordered your vegetarian food, but to your surprise, you see that you have been served a non-vegetarian dish as well. You will
A. call the waiter who served the food and shout at him.
B. vacate room of the hotel and stay elsewhere immediately.
C. call the manager room-service and lodge a written complaint.
D. inform the waiter and try and forget about the incident.

509. While you are functioning as a manager in a hotel, one of your senior staff members has started coming late for work and also misbehaved with other employees frequently. You will
A. get angry and warn him verbally as well as in writing.
B. not take it seriously and try and ignore his changed behavioural pattern.
C. call him and counsel him to assess his problem and then try and help him as needed.
D. initiate disciplinary action against him at the earliest to correct him.

510. While travelling in a Metro train you observe that a number of seats are reserved for ladies, old people and handicapped. You feel
A. there is so much rush in Metro train, this reservation is highly inappropriate.
B. this facility be avoided in all compartments and may be provided in a few.
C. it is desirable since people in general do not care much for the old and the handicapped.
D. this can be a reason for fights and arguments among people who are travelling, therefore should be avoided.

511. Which of the following do you consider as the most important quality of social worker?
A. Helping attitude B. Hard working nature
C. Adequate motivation D. All of these

512. When you are going on your motorcycle, you happen to meet with a minor accident involving a scooter. You will
A. try to avoid the scene and get away.
B. park your motorcycle and shout at the scooterist blaming him.
C. park your motorcycle and hit the scooterist at the earliest.
D. help the scooterist to get up and tender an apology for the inadvertent accident.

513. A small park in front of your house usually remains dirty and you have been observing this situation for a long time now. You will
A. expect others to do something about it.
B. try and ignore it, as it does not directly concern you.
C. ask your neighbours to do something about it.
D. take initiative to clean the park and request others to helpout as well.

514. When some representative of a well known old age home approaches you for some monetary help, you will
A. ask him to got away and not waste your time.
B. feel that homes like this are quite dishonest and deserve no help.
C. try and ignore him by looking busy in something else.
D. spare whatever money you can and donate.

515. While working as a member of a team, due to a mistake by a team member, your task is not completed and your boss gets quite angry. You will
A. go to the boss and tell him what has happened.
B. blame your team member for the lapse and embarrass him.
C. take the blame on the entire team and say sorry.
D. fight and abuse the team member in front of all others.

516. While you are talking to your friend on the road, one man asks you an address in your colony. You will
A. bluntly tell him that you are not there to guide people.
B. tell him the general direction where he could find the address.
C. guide him adequately so that he understands.
D. ask him to take somebody else's help.

517. While travelling in a crowded metro, you are busy taking on your mobile when your co-passengers object as they are getting disturbed. You will
A. quickly finish your call and say sorry.
B. continue with your call as if nothing has happened.
C. raise your voice and pickup a fight.
D. tell them that you have nothing to do with them and they should mind their own business.

508. D	**509.** C	**510.** C	**511.** A	**512.** D	**513.** D	**514.** D	**515.** C
516. C	**517.** A						

518. One of your colleagues in the office is facing some financial problem and seeks your help. You will
A. tell him bluntly that he needs to manage his finance in a much better fashion.
B. spare some money and try to help him.
C. politely tell him that you do not believe in such financial transactions.
D. ask some other colleague to help him if he can.

519. While travelling in Shatabdi Express, you see the passenger in front of your seat has forgotten to take off the charger he was using. You will
A. quietly remove the charger and keep in your bag.
B. ignore the charger and mind your own business.
C. tell the passenger who is the owner of the charger to keep it with him.
D. pick up an argument to claim it is your charger.

520. Being the leader of a team to complete a project to take important decisions, you would
A. let others decide without seeking your opinion.
B. decide first and then let others know of it subsequently.
C. seek others opinion and then take a decision.
D. ask some other members of the team to decide on your behalf.

521. While you are out of your house, you realise that there has been a theft in your house and a number of costly items have been stolen. You will
A. talk to your neighbours and try to hold them responsible, since they were at home when the theft occurred.
B. feel extremely bad and curse your luck.
C. start searching for a new house to shift there.
D. try to forget the incident and be more careful in the future.

522. While working in an office which has public dealings on a day when a number of employees are absent, you will
A. also take leave and go home.
B. tell your superior to arrange more manpower.
C. just perform your share of work and refuse other work.
D. try to do extra work and help deal with other matters to help public.

523. While working in a corporate, suddenly you receive transfer orders to work in another office on a different location, you will
A. take long leave and avoid going there.
B. try and adjust with new environment of work as usual.
C. lose interest in your work and just carry on.
D. avoid working at the new place and try changing your transfer orders.

524. While dealing with an angry customer in a hotel, you will
A. ask to meet your senior and refuse to talk to him.
B. consult your senior and try to resolve the issue at the earliest.
C. shout back at him and tell him he has no business to show his temper.
D. ignore him totally and mind your business.

525. While functioning in your office if you commit a mistake, you will
A. try and blame others for the same.
B. try to cover up the issue somehow.
C. accept your fault and say sorry.
D. just try to rectify your mistake by putting extra work.

526. While driving your scooter, you inadvertently hit a woman and she gets injured. You will
A. outrightly blame her for the accident.
B. try to runaway from the accident scene.
C. accept your mistake and take her to the nearest hospital.
D. ask others on the road to help her.

527. In your office an employee working under you comes late for work often. You will
A. take steps to remove him from his job.
B. call him and severally warn him to become punctual.
C. speak to him personally and try to find reasons for such behaviour and counsel him.
D. ignore him and let him come late.

528. In your office, your boss finds fault with your work often and does not appreciate the good work done by you, you will
A. ignore him and mind your own business.
B. pick up a fight with him and argue on small issues.
C. ask your colleagues to speak to your boss on your behalf.
D. talk to your boss and try to find out the real issue and subsequently initiate corrective action.

518. B **519.** C **520.** C **521.** D **522.** B **523.** B **524.** B **525.** C
526. C **527.** C **528.** D

529. Your immediate neighbour often parks his car in the slot meant for you in front of your office. You will

A. tell your friends in your neighbourhood about the stupidity of your neighbour.
B. pickup a fight with him on the issue.
C. politely tell him to park his car in his slot and not yours.
D. park your car in such a fashion that he cannot take out his car.

530. A family in your neighbourhood often plays music loudly causing tremendous disturbance to all in the area. You will

A. try and forget about it.
B. go and request your neighbour not to disturb you.
C. tell your other neighbours about this repeated disturbance.
D. pick up a fight with the neighbour, who plays loud music.

531. While you leave your office in the evening, you will

A. personally see that all lights and fans are switched off.
B. feel that this is certainly not your job.
C. expect your lower staff to do it.
D. ask your subordinates to ensure this.

532. While travelling in a train, you purchase and drink a bottle of mineral water. After that, you will

A. leave the empty bottle in the train.
B. throw the bottle out of the running train.
C. keep the bottle with you and after twisting it throw it in a dustbin.
D. expect your co-passenger to throw the bottle in a dustbin.

533. While you ordered a shirt for yourself online, you realise that the shirt received does not fit the size you had ordered. You will

A. shout at the delivery boy and tell him that he did not know his job.
B. refuse to take the delivery of the shirt.
C. take the delivery and contact the company online to exchange the shirt.
D. never order any item online.

534. In the night you hear shouts of panic in your neighbourhood, perhaps there could be a theft. You will

A. ignore the incident and think others should help.
B. wake up your other neighbours and ask them to help.
C. feel it is none of your job to interfere.
D. go to the house concerned and offer help as required.

535. While travelling by air, you see the passenger sitting next to you is not feeling too well and needs help. You will

A. change your seat immediately and shift to a vacant seat near you.
B. ignore him completely and mind your own business.
C. call the air hostess and ask her to help the person.
D. help him physically and at the same time call the air hostess also.

536. A member of your team often behaves awkwardly and also does not complete the share of work assigned to him. You will

A. take steps to remove him from the team.
B. tell other members to speak to him to mend his ways.
C. pickup a fight with him and threaten him that he would be dropped from the team.
D. talk to him patiently and understand his problems and then motivate him to take part in the team effort more enthusiastically.

537. If you have just been denied promotion and your junior has been selected, what should you do?

A. Leave the organization.
B. Abuse the junior for manipulation and protest against the management.
C. Move to the court.
D. Talk to your boss, bring out your contribution and ask for reconsideration.

538. While selecting a candidate for a service industry job, you will go for a candidate who is

A. highly academic.
B. social and helpful.
C. quiet and an introvert.
D. responsible.

539. While working in a group, you tend to be

A. a bit assertive.
B. cooperating with others.
C. adjusting with other members, but as it suits you.
D. not getting much involved with group activities.

529. C	**530.** B	**531.** A	**532.** C	**533.** C	**534.** B	**535.** D	**536.** D
537. D	**538.** B	**539.** B					

540. When you meet a very angry customer, you
A. must tell him not to show his temper.
B. tell him to cool down and try to resolve his problem.
C. tell him you would refer the issue to your seniors.
D. tell him that there is not much you could do about the problem.

541. On coming across a very demanding and dominating customer, one should
A. tell him that he has no business to behave like that.
B. shout back at him and tell him that he is unreasonable.
C. politely tell him that he is unreasonable.
D. try and resolve his problem or inform your seniors.

542. If you mistakenly occupy a wrong berth in the train, on arrival of the rightful passenger, you would
A. quietly vacate the berth.
B. apologise and then vacate the berth.
C. tell the passenger that you would vacate after you get a berth.
D. vacate but tell the passenger that nothing much has happened and he should not make a fuss.

543. If you had a fight with one of your close friends due to a communication gap, what would you do?
A. Break up with the person for ever.
B. Make efforts to become friends again.
C. Purposely avoid meeting the person.
D. Make efforts to have a working relationship.

544. Your colleague on his own gives you negative feedback about your work, you will
A. tell him it is none of his business.
B. tell him that no one is perfect.
C. tell your boss about all this.
D. take it sportingly and thank him for the feedback.

545. In service industry, handling difficult people and tense situations with diplomacy and tact is considered as a
A. very important ability.
B. fairly significant quality.
C. not very important ability.
D. quality which can be ignored.

546. You don't like a few habits of one of your close friends, you would
A. tell him so and ask him to change his habits.
B. start ignoring him since you cannot change him.
C. accept him as he is.
D. tell him bluntly that you did not like those habits.

547. If you are a manager and one of your employees is not working properly, as a manager you would
A. try to develop his abilities and interest in another job.
B. give him two weeks to improve.
C. fire him.
D. talk to him and try to find out his problem.

548. You are a leader of a group and the group members have a problem with your style of working. How would you manage the situation?
A. Continue with your style of working.
B. Talk to your team members and come to a solution.
C. Change your style of working.
D. Leave the team.

549. The front office in the organization has a very uncomfortable physical set-up to work in, you would
A. launch a campaign to set things right.
B. complain to seniors regarding it.
C. manage somehow with reluctance.
D. ignore everything and concentrate on your job.

550. You find that some people in your office do not have much work, so you will endeavour
A. to get rid of them somehow.
B. to train them and make them fit for promotion to higher grade.
C. to shift them to other sections where there is shortage of people.
D. not to think much about it as the responsibility lies with others.

551. If you notice some of your colleagues cheating the organization, and making money by huge embezzlements, you would
A. never tell the owners because your relations with those colleagues will be strained.
B. tell the owners on the condition that your name should be kept secret.
C. blackmail the culprits by threatening to tell the owners.
D. ask for your share in the money they are making.

540. B	**541.** D	**542.** B	**543.** B	**544.** D	**545.** B	**546.** A	**547.** D
548. B	**549.** B	**550.** C	**551.** B				

552. Your colleague in the office is a heart patient and often does not feel well. He at times finds it difficult to finish his task and seeks help from others. You will

A. think that he must finish his assigned job, if he can.
B. try to avoid him.
C. ask other colleagues to help him.
D. go over to him and offer help.

553. While going to your office, you see an accident taking place on the road. You will

A. observe whether others are helping or not.
B. help if others are helping.
C. volunteer help along with others.
D. ignore the accident and proceed further.

554. Your immediate neighbour seeks your help for going to hospital as some one in their family has suffered a heart attack. You will

A. tell them that you are terribly busy and could not help.
B. drive them to the hospital and offer necessary assistance.
C. ask them to call an ambulance themselves.
D. ask other neighbour to help.

555. Which of the following human qualities you value most in your mind?

A. Being extremely rich and selfish.
B. Having tall and good looking personality.
C. Being kind hearted and helpful.
D. Being self-centered and having egos.

556. While you are getting ready to go to market with your family, your close friend drops in to spend sometime with you. You will

A. feel extremely angry by this development but feel you have no option.
B. feel happy to receive him and go to market some other time.
C. receive him but think to send him away at the earliest.
D. inform him that you would see him some other time as you were going out.

557. Welfare society of your colony is organizing a camp to plant trees in your neighbourhood. You will

A. feel angry as you have no spare time for such activities.
B. like participating, but could not go due to some sudden family commitment.
C. show your face by going there but come back at the earliest opportunity.
D. enthusiastically participate and plant as many trees as you could.

558. To work efficiently in service sector, you must be

A. highly confident
B. compassionate
C. caring
D. hard working

559. While boarding a bus, you notice that the person ahead of you has dropped his purse on the road. You will

A. keep the purse, since you have found it.
B. over look it.
C. collect the purse and hand over the owner.
D. expect somebody else to collect the purse and give it to the owner.

560. Your close friend requests you to join him in organising blood donation camp to collect a large quantity of blood to give to a major hospital of your city. You will

A. feel that this is certainly not your job.
B. tell him that you have no spare time.
C. request your other friends to take part, since you have no spare time.
D. rearrange your schedule and go and help your friend.

561. While driving your car in the market, you inadvertently met with a minor accident involving a cyclist. You will

A. angrily abuse the cyclist and tell him it was his fault.
B. try and run away from the scene of the accident.
C. help the cyclist get up and apologise for the mistake involving both of you.
D. get out of your car and hit the cyclist and create a scene.

562. When you observe a cluster of slums in the heart of a modern city, you feel

A. there is absolutely no place for such poor people in a modern city.
B. the government must give these poor people some alternative space and then shift them without force.
C. these slums must be immediately removed forcibly and area cleared.
D. these poor people should be given a notice of one month to shift to some other place.

552. D	**553.** C	**554.** B	**555.** C	**556.** C	**557.** D	**558.** C	**559.** C
560. D	**561.** C	**562.** B					

563. While you are studying for your examination, your neighbour's children make a lot of loud noise while playing and disturb you a great deal. You will
A. ignore the whole thing and try to focus on your studies.
B. tell other neighbours about these children and the fact they were such rowdy kids.
C. go and shout at the children and threaten them that you will beat them if they make loud noise.
D. go and request the parents of the children to stop them from making such disturbances.

564. While you are walking in the park in front of your house, you observe there are very few good trees in the park. You will
A. expect other residents to do something about it.
B. plant some trees yourself and request others also to do the same.
C. discuss the situation with other residents and plan some action.
D. try and forget about it.

565. While travelling in a bus, you drink a bottle of Coke and will then
A. push the empty bottle under the luggage of a co-passenger.
B. carry the bottle with you till you find a waste disposal place.
C. throw the empty bottle on the road.
D. look for some lonely place to throw the empty bottle.

566. While travelling on a long journey in a train, you notice a co-passenger not keeping too well and was looking for some help. You will
A. ask other passenger to assist him as required.
B. change your seat and avoid him.
C. ask other passengers if somebody was a doctor and yourself assist him in whatever way you could.
D. tell him that you were not a doctor so could not help him.

567. While working as a primary school teacher, you find a poor student is not able to pay his tuition fee. You will
A. take him to the Principal for strict action.
B. speak to his parents and ask them to pay fee.
C. find the reason for non-payment of fee and then personally help the boy, if needed.
D. punish him severely in front of the whole class.

568. When a new person joins your department in the office, you feel
A. your boss should call you and introduce him to you.
B. you should go and meet him and help him, if he needs any help.
C. you must ignore him totally.
D. he must come and introduce himself to you.

569. Your driver, who has worked for you for more than 10 years honestly, wants to quit his job, you will
A. pay him off immediately and ask him to leave.
B. talk to him nicely and try to find his problem and then act.
C. ask him to leave by the month end.
D. shout at him and call him a cheat.

570. In your office, one of your colleagues often takes credit for jobs that you have done, you will
A. tell him bluntly that he is a dishonest man
B. inform your boss as to what kind of a man he is
C. speak to him politely and tell him that such things do not help
D. tell other colleagues about it to bring his image down

571. While shopping in a busy market, one 10 year old child approaches you and says that he is lost You will
A. ask the child to approach somebody else, as you are busy.
B. request some shopkeeper to help him, if he can.
C. talk to the child and hand him over to the police.
D. ignore him and continue your shopping.

572. When you are having a walk along the sea-shore, you notice a man drowning and shouting for help. You will
A. draw the attention of others and keep on walking.
B. not like to get involved and continue your walk.
C. go into the water to help him, as you know swimming.
D. raise an alarm and request some other swimmer to help him.

573. While walking on the road, you find an envelope which contains an Aadhar Card. You will
A. leave the envelope there only and move on.
B. post the Aadhar card to the address of its owner.
C. give the envelope to your friend and ask him to deal with it.
D. curse the owner of the card and call him extremely careless.

563. D	**564.** B	**565.** B	**566.** C	**567.** C	**568.** B	**569.** B	**570.** C
571. C	**572.** C	**573.** B					

574. The office you own, has recently acquired a new software and some employees are not able to work with it efficiently. You will
A. sack these employees and recruit trained persons.
B. give them a short notice to get trained or leave the job.
C. organise a short training program for these employees.
D. accept some inefficiency and let them continue working.

575. While receiving your salary, you discover that your employer has paid extra money. You will
A. not give the money even after employer feels he has paid extra money to you.
B. think that you are lucky and keep the money.
C. return the money immediately to the employer.
D. keep the money, but plan to return the money at a later date.

576. While working as a manager in a hotel, you are informed that one of your guests has suddenly become very unwell. You would
A. ask the guest to go to some doctor.
B. call a doctor and send him to the guest.
C. meet the guest and then urgently call the doctor and help the patient as required.
D. ask your subordinate to deal with it and need not bother you.

577. Truly speaking, who among the following do you admire most?
A. Charles Shobhraj B. Kapil Dev
C. Sooraj Pancholi D. Mother Teresa

578. You are waiting at the bus-stop for your bus, when a passerby comes towards you and enquires about an address nearby. You will
A. inform him bluntly that you are not there to guide everybody around.
B. guide him generally in the direction only.
C. try and explain the route patiently so that he understands.
D. tell him to ask somebody else about it.

579. While you are working in your office, one colleague asks you to help him complete his urgent assignment. You will
A. tell him that you are busy with your work and it was not feasible to help him also.
B. quickly finish your work and help him as best as you can.
C. tell him that could not he see that you were engrossed with your work.
D. tell him that you would try and help him if possible.

580. When waiting to board a train, you notice an old man struggling with his luggage. You will
A. ask the old man to seek somebody's help.
B. wait for somebody else to come forward and help him.
C. willingly go to him and help him with his luggage.
D. look the other way and ignore him.

581. After having a cup of coffee in a plastic disposable cup at the railway platform, you are unable to see a dustbin around. You will
A. leave it on the platform and move away.
B. find a place where some muck is lying and throw the cup there.
C. keep it with you till you find a dustbin nearby.
D. throw it on the railway tracks.

582. While you are rushing to your office, your immediate neighbour requests you to drop his cheque in the bank, which is located about 500 yards from your office. You will
A. tell him that it may not be possible immediately, but you may do so in a day or two.
B. take his cheque and drop during the lunch break.
C. tell him that you are not there for these kind of jobs.
D. frankly tell him that it won't be possible for you to do so.

583. When travelling in a train, one of your co-passengers suddenly realises that he has lost his purse and mobile phone. You will
A. wait for other passengers to react.
B. console him and offer some minor help that you can.
C. ask him to take the help of other passengers.
D. change your seat to avoid him.

584. While you are having a walk on the road with your dog, suddenly your dog barks and injures a man on the road. You will
A. tell the man that you have no control over your dog.
B. tell the man that your are sorry.
C. console the man and offer him to take him to the nearby hospital.
D. try to run away from the scene.

574. C	**575.** C	**576.** C	**577.** D	**578.** C	**579.** B	**580.** C	**581.** C
582. B	**583.** B	**584.** C					

585. Your next door neighbour does not care for his old parents and constantly ignores them. You will
A. tell other neighbours to do something and help the old parents.
B. discuss this with other neighbours and try to find some way out.
C. politely discuss the topic with the neighbour and offer your help as needed.
D. not bother about it.

586. While you are working as a manager in the house-keeping department of a 5-star hotel, one day one of your guests gets extremely angry and shouts at the staff for a minor lapse. You will
A. inform him that mistakes can be made by anyone and there is no reason for him to behave like that.
B. tell him to contact your boss and sort the matter out.
C. apologise on behalf of the staff and make amends to satisfy him.
D. tell the guest that you could shout louder than him and he must behave properly.

587. While you are busy preparing yourself for a job interview after two days, your younger sister requests you to help her solve a maths question. You will
A. ask her to contact some friends and seek their help.
B. ask your mother to help her since you have no time to spare.
C. while having your dinner, you will find sometimes and help her.
D. bluntly tell her that it is just not possible for you to spare sometime for her.

588. You are going to meet your friend in the evening when your neighbour calls to help him as he is feeling unwell. You will
A. request him to call somebody else.
B. ask your another neighbour to help him.
C. change your program to meet your friend and instead help the neighbour.
D. ask him to wait till you return.

589. You are travelling in a reserved compartment on a journey from Delhi to Lucknow, when an old man approaches you to help him as he had no reservation, but had to travell due to an emergency. You will
A. ask him to request some other passenger to help him.
B. request the rail authorities in the train to help him out.
C. tell him that it is none of your business to accommodate him.
D. agree to share your berth with the man, if needed.

590. When your preparations for board exams of class 12 are in progress, one of your friends asks you to help him out solve a few questions. You will
A. tell him that since you have to revise so much, you have no time.
B. request him to check with some other friend and go to him.
C. adjust your timing in such a way that you can also help him.
D. avoid talking to him.

591. You and your brother are staying in a joint family. Your brother wishes to stay away from your parents. You will
A. request your brother not to separate, as you both have to look after your parents in their old age.
B. continue to stay with your parents even if your brother separates.
C. ask some other close relatives to convince your brother not to separate.
D. opt yourself to stay separately before your brother separates.

592. Which of the following is considered to be one of the most desirable quality for a person working in service sector?
A. Good health B. Team work
C. Helping attitude D. Patience

593. While working as a teacher, you find one student is not able to cope with the lessons. You will
A. take him to the Principal.
B. tell his parents to deal with him.
C. speak to him separately and find out his problem.
D. punish him severely in front of the whole class.

594. While travelling in a train, you observe a co-passenger drops a hundred rupee note. You will
A. ignore the incident and mind your business.
B. take the note and handover to the passenger who dropped it.
C. keep the note in your pocket as if you had found it.
D. make a noise and tell the passenger that he had dropped the note.

585. C	**586.** C	**587.** C	**588.** C	**589.** D	**590.** C	**591.** C	**592.** B
593. C	**594.** B						

595. While you are about to cross a major crossing, you notice a blind man struggling to cross the road. You will
A. ask a young boy to help him cross the road.
B. go and catch his hand and help him cross the road.
C. curse the blind man and say why should he come to such busy roads.
D. continue to go your way and ignore him.

596. When you reach your home after your office in the evening, you find your immediate neighbour has parked his car in the slot earmarked for you. You will
A. call him and shout at him to make him realise his mistake.
B. call him and politely tell him that perhaps by mistake he has parked his car in your slot.
C. park your car in such a way that he cannot take out his car.
D. tell your other neighbours that how stupid is your immediate neighbour and that he has no manners.

597. While you work sincerely in your office and deliver goods, your boss never appreciates your work. You will
A. confront your boss and tell him in front of others that he is very unfair.
B. stop working and look for another job.
C. continue to work hard and perform your duty to show better results.
D. meet him separately and tell him that you are doing your work to the best of your ability.

598. Everyday morning when you leave your room for your office, you
A. leave your room in a mess and go to office.
B. tell your younger brother to arrange your room.
C. always put all things at their right places.
D. expect other family members to organise your room.

599. You observe two of your neighbours are having a heated argument in front of your house. You will
A. go to your immediate neighbour and ask him to intervene.
B. tell your other neighbours how stupid are the people who are fighting.
C. remain indoors and close your main door.
D. go and ask them to cool down and resolve the matter in an amicable manner.

600. In the market, you observe a boy is driving his car rashly and hits a poor labourer, who is going on his cycle. Subsequently, the boy starts hitting the labourer blaming him. You will
A. start shouting and hitting the boy to save the labourer.
B. ignore the accident and mind your business.
C. stop the boy from hitting the labourer and ask him to pay some money to get his cycle repaired and arrange medical aid.
D. also join the boy to abuse and humiliate the labourer.

601. Your company ask you to work in another department of company, which you do not like. You will
A. perform most inefficiently to show your disgust.
B. try to go back to your old department.
C. start avoiding your work and ask for leave frequently.
D. try to get used to the new work environment and adjust.

602. In case, your colleagues tell you that you are often short tempered, you will
A. listen to it but tell them that almost everybody loses his temper, so there is nothing serious about it.
B. tell them to mind their own business and need not comment about others.
C. take sportingly and look for some ways to control temper.
D. argue with them and assert that they are wrong.

603. While dealing with a customer who is very upset about some services provided by your hotel, which of the following you need most?
A. Cleverness
B. Politeness
C. Logic
D. Patience

604. You observe one of your close friends is often unfare with you. You will
A. tell other friends about it.
B. tell your friend how you feel and that this situation is not acceptable to you.
C. continue to be friendly with him and let him realise his mistake.
D. start avoiding meeting him.

595. B	**596.** B	**597.** C	**598.** C	**599.** D	**600.** C	**601.** D	**602.** C
603. B	**604.** C						

605. Your maid servant, who has been working for you for the past two years, now does not take her job so seriously and even replies you back. You will

A. shout at her loudly and tell her that you would not tolerate all this.
B. ask her to mend her ways sternly.
C. talk to her and try to understand her problem and then act.
D. remove her from the job immediately.

606. One of your old friends wants to borrow ₹ 20,000 from you, you will

A. tell him that you do not like anybody borrowing any money from you.
B. make efforts not to interact with him any more.
C. tell others that he is so poor in managing his finances.
D. tell him to return the money before a stipulated time but give him money.

607. In case you are allotted substantial additional work in your office, you would

A. request your boss to provide you additional manpower.
B. try and do your best to cope with the additional load of work.
C. tell all others that your boss has been very unfair with you.
D. tell your boss that you just cannot handle this much of work.

608. While you are locking your flat to go somewhere, you will

A. expect some family member to switch off all lights and fans.
B. ask somebody younger to you to do it.
C. personally ensure that it is done.
D. think that this is none of your concern.

609. When you are paying him money, the old rickshaw pullar requests you for little extra money than what you normally give, you would

A. shout at him loudly and insult him for asking little extra money.
B. not give him any money and ask him to do whatever he felt like.
C. give him the extra bit of money without much fuss.
D. tell him that you would only give him what you normally give and nothing extra.

610. When some old and handicapped beggar approaches you begging for money, you think that

A. we should not encourage begging at all costs.
B. government should make provision for beggars so that they do not beg.
C. begging must be declared an offence and beggars should be put in jails.
D. you must help such people in whatever way you can and give some money or help.

611. While walking on the road, you find a man accidently dropping his wallet and walking away unaware, you will.

A. pick up the wallet and hand it over to him.
B. leave it as it is none of your business.
C. shout out and tell him he has dropped his wallet.
D. pick up the wallet and keep it with you as you found it.

612. You have to go shopping while your friend calls you for help as he is ill. You will

A. postpone your shopping and go to help your friend.
B. ask him to call someone else.
C. call another friend and ask him to help the ill friend.
D. ask him to hang on while you return from your shopping.

613. You finished your chocolate and now you can't find any dustbin around to dispose of the wrapper. You

A. will throw it anywhere.
B. keep it with you until you find a dustbin.
C. find a heap of trash where other people are throwing their garbage and you do the same.
D. try and stuff it in someone else's luggage.

614. A stranger comes to you asking about an address while you are waiting for someone. You will

A. ask him to ask someone else.
B. direct him casually without being too precise about the address.
C. explain him properly and repeatedly until he understands the directions properly.
D. tell him that you are not standing there to direct people.

615. One of your friends arrives to your house unannounced while you are preparing to go out with your family. You

A. would feel disappointed.
B. are happy to see him and postpone your outing and welcome him.
C. would welcome him but keep thinking how to get rid of him quickly.
D. would tell him that you will see him later because you are going out right now.

605. C	**606.** D	**607.** B	**608.** C	**609.** C	**610.** D	**611.** A	**612.** A
613. B	**614.** C	**615.** B					

616. A guy slipped and fell in front of you while walking through the college corridor and your friends started laughing. You will
A. join your friends in the laughter.
B. add some comment to increase the fun.
C. help him and ask your friends not to laugh.
D. just sit and watch.

617. One of your relatives invites you to visit them. Reaching there you find that he is not well and is unable to give a proper welcome. You would
A. get angry and return.
B. stay there but feel disappointed.
C. stay and help him.
D. not react at all.

618. You are getting late for a meeting and while driving, you witness an accident. You would
A. ignore the meeting and help the injured.
B. ignore it and rush for the meeting.
C. try and ask someone else to help him.
D. curse others for not helping and rush for the meeting.

619. You are travelling in a train and one of your co-passengers is left on a platform while the train starts moving. You would
A. not bother.
B. look around waiting for someone to react.
C. ask others to do something.
D. get up and pull the chain.

620. While travelling in an airline, you ordered something and there is some delay in your request for which air hostess apologizes to you. You
A. would not consider the apology.
B. get angry and start fighting.
C. would accept the apology and request them to process your request as quickly as possible.
D. would get disappointed and say nothing.

621. You are talking on your phone while travelling in a public transport while your co-passengers are getting disturbed. You
A. will start fighting.
B. would ask them to mind their own business.
C. would continue talking on your phone and ignore them.
D. would hang up and apologize.

622. While doing a transaction with a shopkeeper, he accidently returned you more amount than he was supposed to. You realize this when you get back home. You
A. won't tell him and keep the extra amount.
B. keep the money thinking you got lucky.
C. return the extra amount immediately telling that he made a mistake.
D. keep the money thinking that you will return it later.

623. A foreign tourist approaches you for some help but you don't share any common language. You
A. would waive him off telling that you don't understand his language.
B. would try and arrange a translator in order to help him.
C. try and help him as much as you could using sign language.
D. try making fun of him.

624. One of your friends is in distress and needs some financial help but is too shy to ask. You.
A. will go to him and help him saying he can return the money whenever he can.
B. will cash this chance to make fun of him.
C. would wait for him to ask for your help.
D. do not intend to help him.

625. There are some bad characters influencing the living conditions of people in your community. You
A. will gather people around you and oppose them.
B. will manage with the condition.
C. would wait for some help from others.
D. would leave the community.

626. There has been a death in a family in your community. At the same time some other family is planning a celebration. You, being the representative of your community
A. will ask the other family to delay the celebration.
B. won't interrupt in the matter.
C. will ask members of the community to come together for the first family and then congratulate the other family but ask them to postpone their celebration.
D. will join the celebration as well.

627. There is a function in your close relation and they need your assistance. You
A. would tell them that you are too busy to help.
B. would help them with great enthusiasm.
C. would tell about this to other relatives and ask them to help.
D. will take it like a burden.

616. C	**617.** C	**618.** A	**619.** D	**620.** C	**621.** D	**622.** C	**623.** B
624. A	**625.** A	**626.** C	**627.** B				

628. You have been sent on a visit to a rural area on a project to educate the local children. You
A. whole heartedly take part in the project and try to put in your maximum effort.
B. start complaining about the mismanagement.
C. show no enthusiasm but anyhow complete your project.
D. bailout of the project.

629. There is a function in your school/college and the management requests your participation but you are also busy with some other project. You
A. deny your participation saying you are too busy.
B. express your apologies and try to contribute as much as possible.
C. start feeling annoyed with such requests.
D. participate whole heartedly in the event and manage your project as well.

630. You see water running from a tap at any public place while no one is using it. You
A. walk away without bothering.
B. close the tap properly and ensure no water is wasted.
C. attract attention of other people toward it.
D. also leave the water funning after using taps.

631. After exiting your room in your house. You
A. switch off all the electrical appliances that are not required.
B. leave the lights and fans as they were.
C. expect someone else to do this for you.
D. forget to do these things but follow whenever you remember.

632. In your house you
A. keep littering here and there expecting others to clean it.
B. keep your things properly and don't care for others.
C. arrange everything and try to maintain hygiene everywhere.
D. make such a mess making life of others miserable too.

633. There is plenty of rain clogging in your society creating problems in communication. You would
A. face the difficulty every day without complaining.
B. report the matter in the local municipal office.
C. gather people and try to resolve the problem yourself.
D. motivate other people to resolve the problem.

634. During summers, on a very sunny day, you come across a poor person who is very thirsty and dehydrated. You
A. You buy him some water and juice from the market.
B. You tell him to stay at home when the weather is so hot.
C. You ask him to go to a dharmshala for help.
D. You buy him juice and ask him to pay.

635. While watching a movie in a theatre, a small child starts crying.
A. You yell at his/her parents for disturbing you in between the movie.
B. You try to ignore but instead pass comments on the child.
C. You ask their parents humbly to take their child out of the theatre.
D. You ask their parents if everything is ok with the child and if there is any help you can give to them.

636. While buying ticket in a bus, the conductor asks for change since you gave a large amount of note, you
A. shout at him, that he should have change and won't buy the ticket.
B. ask him to give you the ticket, keep the money and give change when he gets it.
C. get down from the bus and wait for the next one.
D. keep looking at other passengers until someone offers you change.

637. While standing in a queue at railway station, you see an illiterate person at the counter filling the form tor a ticket. You
A. tell him to move out of the line and fill the form as you are in hurry.
B. tell him to go back from where he came, since he does not know even how to fill a form.
C. go and offer him help in filling the form and buying the ticket.
D. ask the attendant at the counter to help him to fill the form.

638. In a park, you see two boys fighting and beating each other. You
A. go and start beating both of them.
B. ignore and walk away.
C. tell other people in the park that the fight should be stopped.
D. go to them and ask them politely to stop fighting and resolve the issue by talking and discussing.

628. A	**629.** D	**630.** B	**631.** A	**632.** C	**633.** B	**634.** A	**635.** D
636. B	**637.** C	**638.** D					

639. While eating at a restaurant, you are left with food. You
A. leave the food there as it is.
B. eat all of it even though you are not able to, which might result in bad health for you.
C. ask them to pack it so that you can have it with your next meal.
D. ask them to pack it so that you can give it to anyone who is in need of food.

640. In the hostel after taking a bath, you remember that you left the geyser ON. You
A. go back to the hostel to turn it OFF.
B. ask your friends in the hostel to switch it off.
C. ignore, thinking that it is not your concern.
D. do it again deliberately.

641. You are listening to loud music on your birthday night; your neighbour who has her exam tomorrow, comes to you to request you to slow down the volume. You
A. ask her to go to someone else's place to study.
B. tell her that you will slow down the volume but you don't do it.
C. turn off the music.
D. turn off the music and ask her if there is something that you can teach her for tomorrow's exam or may be clear any doubts that she has.

642. If you happen to be in a bus which meets with an accident you would
A. ask and motivate others to help out people who are hurt.
B. try and get away from the scene at the earliest.
C. extend physical help to people who need such help.
D. inform district authorities and police.

643. While you are away on a holiday, you have a theft in your house and you lose some jewellery and cash, you would
A. plan to shift to another house.
B. feel absolutely devastated and go into a depression.
C. be more security conscious and try and forget it.
D. blame your neighbours and have a fight with them.

644. Being a member of team while reaching a decision, you would
A. let others decide.
B. take a decision and inform others.
C. consult others and then decide.
D. let the matter be pending and later impose your decision.

645. To work efficiently and effectually in a service industry, which of the following you think is the most essential ability/quality?
A. being responsible.
B. being an introvert.
C. being helpful and outgoing.
D. being highly academically qualified.

646. One of your team members generally behaves in a selfish and clever manner quite often, you will
A. tell him about it in front of everyone.
B. tell him that this is not the way to behave.
C. counsel him separately after taking him into confidence.
D. ignore him as a member of the team.

647. A lot of the products of your company are defective but you come to know about it only after the products have been sold and customers start complaining of it. You would
A. issue a general information to all regarding defects in the product and advise them to get it exchanged for a defect-free product from the outlet.
B. ignore the complaints.
C. blame the customers for complaints.
D. do nothing.

648. If you want to computerize your office to make it more and more efficient and modern, you would
A. get rid of the old staff and arrange new staff who are well-versed in operating computers.
B. get the whole staff trained accordingly.
C. expel some of the employees due to surplus workers.
D. adjust the surplus workers at some other place for which they are fit.

649. What is the best quality in a person?
A. Ability to please others
B. Ability to work hard
C. Sincerity
D. Cordiality

639. D	**640.** B	**641.** D	**642.** C	**643.** C	**644.** C	**645.** A	**646.** C
647. A	**648.** D	**649.** C					

650. Whenever you do some work you commit a lot of errors and mistakes which are always noticed by someone. You then

A. get irritated about your own-self.

B. curse your fate and get angry easily on the other person.

C. try to keep quiet at that moment and wait for the opportunity to find fault in other person.

D. decide that to err is human.

651. What will be your response to an angry customer who wants to see the senior manager with a complaint?

A. You would be patient and try to cool him down.

B. Tell him it is very difficult to see the manager.

C. Talk to him yourself.

D. Try to solve his problem by consulting seniors.

652. If you are transferred to a place you do not like, you would

A. forget about your choice and work whole-heartedly.

B. try your best to get transferred to your favourite place.

C. not take interest in work.

D. take long leave.

653. The responsibility of hospitality of the guest or looking after their smooth and enjoyable stay in a hotel lies on the shoulders of

A. General Manager

B. Guest Relations Executive

C. Floor Supervisor

D. Front Office Manager

654. If on a tough day, you are the only person available to handle the customer, you should

A. just do your part of the work.

B. try and work to the maximum of your ability to satisfy customers.

C. take leave and go back home.

D. ask for additional help from the boss.

655. You see some smoke coming out of the building of your office and come to know that there is fire somewhere. First of all you would

A. go out of the building without considering the consequences thereof.

B. make a noise and inform all.

C. phone the fire brigade in no time.

D. first use the fire-fighting equipment or do something else to extinguish the fire.

656. Public dealings require

A. quick decisions

B. good listening

C. politeness

D. punctuality

657. Which of the following statements reflects your opinion about yourself?

A. I am not certain of my self-confidence.

B. I am even today as confident as before.

C. My self-confidence is declining day-by-day.

D. I have never been self-confident at all.

658. You are perplexed and find yourself in a fix when you are asked to

A. speak something from the stage.

B. do as others do.

C. listen and argue.

D. be among strangers.

659. What would you do if you get late in the morning due to bus timings?

A. Let it be as it is.

B. Take the consent of management.

C. Do not do anything.

D. Make some alternative arrangement.

660. If you are wrongly accused of something, you would

A. not even try to rebut the accusation, as it would be of no use.

B. be able to convince others of your innocence easily.

C. try to convince others, but without any hope of doing so.

D. try your best to convince others and hope that you succeed.

650. D	**651.** D	**652.** A	**653.** B	**654.** B	**655.** D	**656.** C	**657.** B
658. A	**659.** D	**660.** B					

MATHEMATICS

1

Numbers System

Whole Numbers

In our System of numeration, numbers are written by using the symbols 0, 1, 2, 3, 4, 5, 6, 7, 8 and 9 with each symbol getting a value depending on the place it occupies. These symbols are called digits. A number related to the objects in a collection gives an idea of how many objects are there in the collection.

The number 789345126 can be represented as:

Ten crores	Crores	Ten Lacs (Millions)	Lacs	Ten Thousands	Thousands	Hundreds	Tens	Units
10^8	10^7	10^6	10^5	10^4	10^3	10^2	10^1	10^0
7	8	9	3	4	5	1	2	6

This number can be read as: "Seventy-eight crores, ninety-three lacs, forty-five thousands, one hundred twenty six".

1. **Natural Numbers or Positive Integers (N = 1, 2, 3, 4, 5 .....):** These are also called counting numbers. When two natural numbers are added or multiplied together, the result is always a natural number. Therefore, all positive integers, used for counting objects, are always **natural numbers** whereas zero together with negative integers and fractional numbers are not natural numbers.
2. **Whole Numbers: (W = 0, 1, 2, 3, 4, 5, ...):** The number '0' together with the natural numbers gives us the numbers which are called **whole numbers,** e.g., 0, 1, 2, 3, 4 ..... etc. whereas –10, –15, –12 ..... or $\frac{1}{5}, \frac{2}{9}, \frac{4}{5}$..... etc. are not whole numbers.
3. **Integers: (I = ..., –5, –4, –3, –2, –1, 0, 1, 2, 3, 4, 5, ...):** The negative numbers together with the whole numbers are called integers. The numbers –1, –2, –3, –4, –5, ... are called negative integers and 1, 2, 3, 4, 5, ..., *i.e.,* natural numbers are called positive integers. The number 0 is simply an integer, *i.e.,* it is neither positive nor negative.
4. **Rational Numbers:** A rational number is a number that can be put in the form $\frac{p}{q}$ where p and q are both integers and $q \neq 0$, e.g., 8, $-\frac{7}{5}$, $-\frac{3}{4}$, $\frac{1}{7}$, 0 .... are all rational numbers i.e. a rational number may be positive, zero or negative.
5. **Irrational Numbers:** An irrational number is a number that can not be put in the form $\frac{p}{q}$ where p and q are both integers and $q \neq 0$, e.g., $\sqrt{5}, \sqrt{11}, \sqrt{15}$, $3 + \sqrt{5}$ .... etc. are all irrational numbers.
6. **Real Numbers:** All those numbers which are either rational or irrational, are called real numbers, e.g., $\frac{11}{17}$, $\frac{19}{21}$, $-\frac{7}{8}$, $\sqrt{7}$, $8 + \sqrt{3}$ etc. are real numbers.
7. **Even Numbers:** All those numbers which are exactly divisible by 2, are called 'even numbers', e.g., 2, 8, 14, 28, 52 etc. are even numbers.
8. **Odd Numbers:** All those numbers which are not exactly divisible by 2, are called 'odd numbers', e.g., 1, 3, 5, 7, 9, 19 etc. are odd numbers.

9. **Composite Numbers:** The numbers which are divisible not only by 1 or themselves, but by some other numbers also, are called the 'composite numbers'. In other words, the numbers which have more than two factors are called 'composite numbers.', e.g., 4, 9, 15, 18, 27, ... etc. are composite numbers.
10. **Prime Numbers:** The numbers which have only two factors, 1 and the number itself are called 'prime numbers', e.g., 2, 5, 11, 19, 23, 31, ... etc. are prime numbers.
11. **Co-primes:** Two numbers which have only 1 as the common factor are called 'co-primes'. 5 and 7 are co-primes. So are 15 and 16.
12. **Twin Primes:** Two prime numbers which differ by 2, are called 'twin primes', e.g., 3, 5; 5, 7; 11, 13; 71, 73 are some pairs of twin primes.
13. **Consecutive Numbers:** The numbers which are following or coming after other numbers in regular order, are called consecutive numbers. 4, 6, 8, 10 are consecutive even numbers and 9, 11, 13, 15 are consecutive odd numbers. 3, 4, 5, 6, 7 ..... etc. are consecutive numbers in the natural order of the number series.

TESTS FOR DIVISIBILITY OF NUMBERS

1. **Divisibility by 2:** A number is divisible by 2, if its units digit is 0, 2, 4, 6 or 8. For example, each of the numbers 130, 244, 566, 278, ... etc. is divisible by 2.
2. **Divisibility by 3:** A number is divisible by 3, if the sum of its digits is a multiple of 3. For example, each of the numbers 312, 213, 456 is divisible by 3 since sum of digits in each of these numbers is (3 + 1 + 2 = 6), (2 + 1 + 3 = 6) and (4 + 5 + 6 = 15) respectively, each of which is a multiple of 3.
3. **Divisibility by 4:** A number is divisible by 4, if the number formed by its digits in ten's and unit's places is divisible by 4. For example, numbers formed by ten's and unit's digits of 1132, 1312, 1400 and 1348 are 32, 12, 00 and 48 respectively which are divisible by 4. Hence, these numbers also are divisible by 4.
4. **Divisibility by 5:** A number is divisible by 5, if its unit's digit is either 0 or 5. For example, each of the numbers 100, 205, 315, 435 is divisible by 5 since unit's digit in each of these numbers is either 0 or 5.
5. **Divisibility by 6:** A number is divisible by 6, if it is divisible by both 2 and 3.
6. **Divisiblity by 8:** A number is divisible by 8, if the number formed by its digits in hundred's, ten's and unit's places is divisible by 8. For example, numbers formed by hundred's, ten's and unit's digits of 1864, 1024, 2008 and 5000 are 864, 024, 008 and 000 respectively which are divisible by 8. Hence, these numbers also are divisible by 8.
7. **Divisibility by 9:** A number is divisible by 9, if the sum of its digits is a multiple of 9. For example, each of the numbers 23409, 454554, 66636 is divisible by 9 since sum of digits in each of these numbers is (2 + 3 + 4 + 0 + 9 = 18), (4 + 5 + 4 + 5 + 5 + 4 = 27) and (6 + 6 + 6 + 3 + 6 = 27) respectively, each of which is a multiple of 9.
8. **Divisibility by 10:** A number is divisible by 10, if its unit's digit is zero. For example, each of the numbers 50, 80, 1310, 1400 is divisible by 10 since unit's digit in each of these numbers is 0.
9. **Divisibility by 11:** A number is divisible by 11, if the difference of the sum of its digits in even places and the sum of its digits in odd places (starting from unit's place) is either 0 or a multiple of 11. For example, each of the numbers 909183, 540045 and 184712 is divisible by 11 since in each of the numbers difference of the sum of digits in even places and sum of the digits in odd places is [(9 + 9 + 8) – (0 + 1 + 3) = 22], [(5 + 0 + 4) – (4 + 0 + 5) = 0] and [(8 + 7 + 2) – (1 + 4 + 1) = 11] respectively, each of which is either '0' or a multiple of '11'.
10. **Divisibility by 12:** A number is divisible by 12, if it is divisible by 3 and 4 both.

    For example, take a number 769824

    (*i*) Sum of digits = 7 + 6 + 9 + 8 + 2 + 4 = 36, it is divisible by 3.

    (*ii*) The number has 24 as its last two digits, which is divisible by 4.

    Hence, 769824 is divisible by 3 and 4 both, so it is divisible by 12.
11. **Divisibility by 14:** A number is divisible by 14, if it is divisible by 2 and 7 both.
12. **Divisibility by 15:** A number is divisible by 15, if it is divisible by 3 and 5 both.
13. **Divisibility by 16:** A number is divisible by 16, if the number formed by its last four digits is divisible by 16.

    For example, take a number 9877856, the number formed by its last four digits is 7856, which is divisible by 16. Hence, the number 9877856 is divisible by 16.
14. **Divisibility by 24:** A number is divisible by 24, if it is divisible by 3 and 8 both.
15. **Divisibility by 40:** A number is divisible by 40, if it is divisible by 5 and 8 both.
16. **Divisibility by 80:** A number is divisible by 80, if it is divisible by 5 and 16 both.

[**Note:** If a number is divisible by two co-primes separately, then the number will be also divisible by the product of co-primes.]

EXERCISE

1. The difference between the squares of two consecutive numbers is 25. The numbers are—
A. 11, 12 B. 12, 13
C. 15, 14 D. 14, 13

2. The sum of two digits of a number is 15. If 9 is added to the number, the digits are reversed. The number is—
A. 78 B. 87
C. 69 D. 96

3. A number which when multiplied by 11 is as much above 180 as it was originally below it. The number is—
A. 25 B. 30
C. 40 D. 45

4. Divide ₹ 53 among X, Y, Z so that X may receive ₹ 7 more than Y, and Y may receive ₹ 8 more than Z.
A. 10, 15, 18 B. 18, 10, 25
C. 20, 12, 27 D. 25, 18, 10

5. If a = 16 and b = 15, then what is the value of $\frac{a^2+b^2+ab}{a^3-b^3} = ?$
A. $\frac{1}{2}$ B. $\frac{1}{3}$
C. 1 D. 2

6. Find the number which when multiplied by 16 is increased by 225.
A. 13 B. 14
C. 15 D. 16

7. What is the largest number of four digits which is exactly divisible by 88?
A. 9999 B. 9988
C. 9944 D. 9998

8. If $\frac{a}{b} = \frac{4}{3}$, then $\frac{3a+2b}{3a-2b} = ?$
A. 2 B. 3
C. 4 D. 5

9. If $\frac{x}{y} = \frac{3}{4}$, then the value of $\frac{6}{7}+\frac{y-x}{y+x} = ?$
A. 1 B. 2
C. 3 D. 4

10. If the number $(10^n - 1)$ is divisible by 11, then n is—
A. odd number B. even number
C. any number D. multiple of 11

11. $\left(1-\frac{1}{3}\right)\left(1-\frac{1}{4}\right)\left(1-\frac{1}{5}\right)...\left(1-\frac{1}{n}\right) = ?$
A. $\frac{42}{29}$ B. $\frac{n-1}{n}$
C. $\frac{2}{n}$ D. 0

12. $\left(2-\frac{1}{3}\right)\left(2-\frac{3}{5}\right)\left(2-\frac{5}{7}\right)...\left(2-\frac{997}{999}\right) = ?$
A. $\frac{997}{999}$ B. ∞
C. $\frac{997}{3}$ D. $\frac{1001}{3}$

13. Divide 48 into two parts such that 7 times the first part added to 5 times the second part is 246. Find the first part.
A. 2 B. 3
C. 4 D. 5

14. The sum of a number and its reciprocal is thrice the difference of the number and its reciprocal. Find the number.
A. $\sqrt{2}$ B. $\sqrt{3}$
C. $\sqrt{5}$ D. $\sqrt{7}$

15. What should be added to the product of four consecutive odd numbers to make it a perfect square?
A. 13 B. 14
C. 15 D. 16

16. A boy was asked to find $\frac{7}{9}$ of a fraction. He made a mistake of dividing the fraction by $\frac{7}{9}$ and so got an answer which exceeded the correct answer by $\frac{8}{21}$. Find the correct answer.
A. 2/3 B. 5/7
C. 7/12 D. 7/15

17. If 40% of a number is 360, what will be 15% of 15% of that number?
A. 11.5 B. 20.25
C. 15.5 D. 21.75

18. The sum of two numbers is 25 and the difference of their square is 75. Find the difference between the numbers.
A. 2 B. 3
C. 4 D. 5

19. Ram eats 8 bananas in the morning, 5 in the afternoon and 2 in the evening. How many dozens of bananas does he eat in a day.
A. $1\frac{1}{4}$ B. $\frac{1}{4}$
C. $\frac{3}{13}$ D. $14\frac{17}{30}$

20. $47^{7.5} \div 47^{\frac{3}{2}} \times 47^{-3} = \left(\sqrt{47}\right)^{?}$ What should come in place of the question mark (?) in the following equation?
A. 5 B. 6
C. 7 D. 8

ANSWERS

1	2	3	4	5	6	7	8	9	10
B	A	B	B	C	C	C	B	A	B
11	**12**	**13**	**14**	**15**	**16**	**17**	**18**	**19**	**20**
C	D	B	A	D	C	B	B	A	B

EXPLANATORY ANSWERS

1. Let the numbers are x and $(x + 1)$

$\therefore \quad (x + 1)^2 - x^2 = 25$

$\Rightarrow \quad x^2 + 1 + 2x - x^2 = 25$

$\Rightarrow \quad 2x + 1 = 25$

$\Rightarrow \quad 2x = 25 - 1 = 24$

$\therefore \quad x = \dfrac{24}{2} = 12$

$\therefore \quad x + 1 = 12 + 1 = 13$

Hence, the numbers are 12, 13.

2. Let x be the digit in units place. Digit in ten's place is then $15 - x$.

$\therefore$ The number $= 10\,(15 - x) + x$

The new number with reverse digits

$= 10 \times x + (15 - x)$

$\therefore \quad 10(15 - x) + x + 9 = 10x + 15 - x$

$\Rightarrow \quad 150 - 10x + x + 9 = 9\,x + 15$

$\Rightarrow \quad 18x = 144$

$x = \dfrac{144}{18} = 8$

The digit of ten's place $= 15 - 8 = 7$

$\therefore$ The required number = 78.

3. Let the number is x

$\therefore \quad 180 - x = 11x - 180$

$\Rightarrow \quad 180 + 180 = 11x + x$

$\Rightarrow \quad 360 = 12x,$

$\Rightarrow \quad x = \dfrac{360}{12} = 30.$

4. Let Y receives ₹ a. Then X receives ₹ $(a + 7)$ and Z receives ₹ $(a - 8)$

But, $a + 7 + a + a - 8 =$ ₹ 53

$\Rightarrow \quad 3a - 1 = 53,$

$\Rightarrow \quad 3a = 53 + 1$

$\Rightarrow \quad 3a = 54,$

$\therefore \quad a = \dfrac{54}{3} =$ ₹ 18. = Y's share

X's share $= a + 7 = 18 + 7 =$ ₹ 25

Z's share $= a - 8 = 18 - 8 =$ ₹ 10.

5. Given $a = 16$ and $b = 15$, then $\dfrac{a^2 + b^2 + ab}{a^3 - b^3}$

$$= \frac{a^2 + b^2 + ab}{(a-b)(a^2 + b^2 + ab)} = \frac{1}{a-b} = \frac{1}{16-15} = 1$$

6. Let the required no. $= x$

then, $\quad 16x - x = 225$

$\Rightarrow \quad 15x = 225 \therefore x = 15$

7. The greatest no. of 4 digit = 9999

Now, after dividing 9999 by 88, we get Remainder = 55

Hence, the largest 4 digit no. = 9999 − 55 = 9944

8. $$\frac{3a+2b}{3a-2b} = \frac{3\frac{a}{b}+2}{3\frac{a}{b}-2} = \frac{3\times\frac{4}{3}+2}{3\times\frac{4}{3}-2} = \frac{6}{2} = 3$$

9. $$\frac{6}{7} + \frac{y-x}{y+x} = \frac{6}{7} + \frac{1-x/y}{1+x/y} = \frac{6}{7} + \frac{1-3/4}{1+3/4} = \frac{6}{7} + \frac{1}{7} = 1$$

10. n is even number.

11. $$\frac{2}{3}\times\frac{3}{4}\times\frac{4}{5}\times\ldots\times\frac{n-1}{n} = \frac{2}{n}$$

12. $$\frac{5}{3}\times\frac{7}{5}\times\frac{9}{7}\times\ldots\times\frac{1001}{999} = \frac{1001}{3}$$

13. Let the first part $= x$

then 2nd part $= (48 - x)$

By question, $\quad 7x + 5(48 - x) = 246$

$\Rightarrow \quad 2x = 246 - 240 \therefore x = 3$

14. Let the no. $= x$

then its reciprocal $= \dfrac{1}{x}$

By the question, $\left(x + \dfrac{1}{x}\right) = 3\left(x - \dfrac{1}{x}\right)$

$\Rightarrow \quad \dfrac{x^2 + 1}{x} = \dfrac{3(x^2 - 1)}{x}$

$\Rightarrow \quad x^2 + 1 = 3x^2 - 3$

$\Rightarrow \quad 3x^2 - x^2 = 3 + 1 \therefore x = \sqrt{2}.$

15. Let the four consecutive odd numbers be $(2x - 3)$, $(2x - 1)$, $(2x + 1)$ and $(2x + 3)$

$\therefore$ Their product $= (2x - 1)(2x + 1)(2x - 3)(2x + 3)$

$= (4x^2 - 1)(4x^2 - 9) = 16x^4 - 40x^2 + 9$

$= (4x^2 - 5)^2 - 16$

Hence, on adding 16, the result will be a perfect square.

16. Let the required fraction = x

then, by the question $x \div \frac{7}{9} - x \times \frac{7}{9} = \frac{8}{21}$

$$\Rightarrow \quad x \times \frac{9}{7} - \frac{7x}{9} = \frac{8}{21} \Rightarrow \frac{32x}{63} = \frac{8}{21}$$

$$\Rightarrow \quad x = \frac{8}{21} \times \frac{63}{32} = \frac{3}{4}$$

Hence, the correct answer = $\frac{3}{4} \times \frac{7}{9} = \frac{7}{12}$.

17. Let a number be x

then 40% of x = 360

$$\Rightarrow \quad \frac{40}{100} \times x = 360$$

$$\therefore \quad x = 360 \times \frac{100}{40} = 900$$

Now by the question,

$$15\% \text{ of } 15\% \text{ of } 900 = \frac{15}{100} \times \frac{15}{100} \times 900 = \frac{81}{4} = 20.25.$$

18. Let two numbers are a and b

Given, $a + b = 25$

and $a^2 - b^2 = 75$

$$\Rightarrow \quad (a + b)(a - b) = 75$$

$$\Rightarrow \quad (a - b) = \frac{75}{(a+b)} = \frac{75}{25} = 3.$$

19. Total dozen of bananas Ram eats in a day

$$= \frac{8}{12} + \frac{5}{12} + \frac{2}{12} = \frac{15}{12} = 1\frac{1}{4}$$

20. $47^{7.5} \div 47^{\frac{3}{2}} \times 47^{-3} = \left(\sqrt{47}\right)^{?}$

Let ? = x

then $(47)^{\frac{15}{2}} \div (47)^{\frac{3}{2}} \times (47)^{-3} = (47)^{\frac{x}{2}}$

$$\Rightarrow \quad (47)^{\frac{15}{2} - \frac{3}{2} - 3} = (47)^{\frac{x}{2}}$$

$$\Rightarrow \quad (47)^{\frac{6}{2}} = (47)^{\frac{x}{2}}$$

$$\therefore \quad x = 6.$$

Decimal Fraction

FRACTION

The relation to represent some part of the body to the whole body is known *Fraction*. For example $\frac{2}{5}$ is a fraction where 2 is the numerator and 5 is the denominator.

Important Facts :

(i) A fraction is also called a rational number.

(ii) A fraction is unity when its numerator and denominator are equal.

(iii) When a fraction is reduced in its lowest term, its numerator and denominator are prime to each other, *i.e.*, they have no common factor.

(iv) The value of fraction is not altered by multiplying or dividing the numerator and the denominator by the same number.

Vulgar or Common Fraction : The fraction such as $\frac{2}{9}, \frac{7}{11}, \frac{3}{10}, \frac{9}{100}$ are called vulgar fraction.

Decimal Fraction : Fractions in which denomi-nators are power of 10 are called decimal fractions.

For example : $\frac{1}{10}, \frac{1}{100}, \frac{7}{1000}$ etc.

Here, $\frac{1}{10}$ is 1 tenths, written as .1

$$\frac{1}{100} = .01$$

$$\frac{7}{1000} = .007$$

$$\frac{13}{100} = .13 \text{ and so on.}$$

Converting a Decimal into a Vulgar Fraction

First of all write down the given number as numerator without the decimal point, and for the denominator write 1 followed by as many zeros as many are there figures after the decimal point. Now reduce the fraction to its lowest terms.

Ex : *(i)* $0.63 = \frac{63}{100}$

(ii) $3.013 = 3\frac{013}{1000} = 3\frac{13}{1000}$

Addition and Subtraction of Decimal Fractions

First of all write down the numbers under one another. Other than the decimal point lies in one column. After arranging in this way, we add or subtract in usual fashion.

An example : Add 521 + 52.1 + 5.21 + 0.521

Sol : 521.000
52.100
5.210
0.521 After adding we get 578.831

Multiplication of decimal fraction

1. To multiply by 10, 100, 1000, etc

Example : *(i)* 63.02 × 10 = 630.2

(ii) $63.02 \times 100 = 6302$

(iii) $63.02 \times 1000 = 63020$

2. To multiply of two or more decimal fractions.

An example : *(i)* $5.91 \times 13 = 76.83$

(ii) $6.32 \times 0.59 = 3.7288$

(iii) $63.2 \times 0.01 = 0.632$

Conclusion: First of all multiply the given numbers assuming them without the decimal point. Now mark off the decimal point from extreme right in the product as many places of decimal as is the sum of the number of decimal places in the given numbers.

DIVISION OF DECIMALS

1. When the divisor is a counting number

Example : *(i)* $4.309 \div 10 = 0.4309$

(ii) $0.0182 \div 14 = 0.0013$

(iii) $9.586 \div 100 = 0.09586$

(iv) $0.05 \div 10^3 = 0.00005$

(v) $0.49 \div 7 = 0.07$

Conclusion : *(i)* When divisor is the power of 10, then shift the decimal point to the left by as many places of decimal as is the power of 10, prefixing zero if necessary.

(ii) When divisor is other than power of 10, then divide as in the case of integers, and in quotient, put the decimal point to give as many places of decimal as are there in the dividend.

2. When the divisor is a decimal

Example:

(i) $0.00066 \div 0.11 = \frac{0.00066}{0.11} = \frac{0.066}{11} = 0.006$

(ii) $42 \div 0.07 = \frac{42}{0.07} = \frac{4200}{7} = 600$

(iii) $32.5 \div 0.0064 = \frac{32.5}{0.0064} = \frac{325000}{64} = 5078.125$

Recurring Decimal : If in a decimal number a digit or a set of digits is repeated again and again, the decimal is known as recurring decimal.

For example:

(i) $2.666... = 2.\dot{6}$

(ii) $1.363636... = 1.\dot{3}\dot{6}$ or $1.\overline{36}$

(iii) $7.3424242... = 7.3\dot{4}\dot{2}$ or $7.3\overline{42}$

Recurring decimal numbers are of two types:

***(i)* Pure recurring decimals :** A decimal fraction in which all the figures after the decimal point are repeated is called a pure recurring decimal. For example, $0.\overline{3}$, $0.\overline{37}$, $3.\overline{4579}$ etc

***(ii)* Mixed recurring decimals :** A decimal fraction in which at least one figure after the decimal point is not repeated is called a mixed recurring decimal. For example, $0.3\overline{59}$, $0.29\overline{54}$, $0.2\dot{7}$ etc.

Conversion of Recurring into Vulgar Fraction

1. Pure recurring decimals

Rule : Put as many 9's in the denominator at the number of digits under recurring and delete the recurring sign.

For example, $0.\overline{5} = \frac{5}{9}$

$$0.\overline{35} = \frac{35}{99}$$

$$0.\overline{24} = \frac{24}{99} = \frac{8}{33}$$

2. Mixed Recurring Decimals

For example,

(i) $0.1\overline{8}$

Here, numerator $= 18 - 1 = 17$

and denominator $= 9 \times 10 = 90$

$$\therefore \quad 0.1\dot{8} = \frac{18-1}{90} = \frac{17}{90}$$

(ii) $0.2\dot{7}\dot{9}$

Here, numerator $= 279 - 2 = 277$

and denominator $= 99 \times 10 = 990$

$$\therefore \quad 0.2\overline{79} = \frac{279-2}{990} = \frac{277}{990}$$

(iii) $$0.3\overline{56} = \frac{356-3}{99 \times 10} = \frac{353}{990}$$

(iv) $$2.53\dot{6} = 2 + \frac{536-53}{9 \times 100} = 2 + \frac{483}{900}$$

$$= 2 + \frac{161}{300} = 2\frac{161}{300}$$

(v) $$0.43\overline{213} = \frac{43213-43}{999 \times 100}$$

$$= \frac{43170}{99900} = \frac{4317}{9990}$$

Addition and Subtraction of recurring decimals

Example : *(i)* Add $3.\overline{76}$ and $1.4\overline{576}$ and subtract also.

3.7	676767	67	
1.4	576576	57	
(+) 5.2	253344	24	$\Rightarrow 5.2\overline{253344}$
(–) 2.3	100191	10	$\Rightarrow 2.3100191$

(ii) Subtract $3.\overline{75}$ from $25.5\overline{473}$

25.5	473473	47
3.7	575757	57
21.7	897715	90

Hence, the required subtract $= 21.7\overline{897715}$

Multiplication and Division of Recurring Decimal

Example 1:

(*i*) $7.\overline{63} \times 11 = 7\frac{63}{99} \times 11$

$= 7\frac{7}{11} \times 11 = \frac{84}{11} \times 11 = 84$

(*ii*) $0.\overline{09} \times 7.\overline{3} = \frac{9}{99} \times 7\frac{3}{9}$

$= \frac{1}{11} \times \frac{66}{9} = \frac{6}{9} = 0.\overline{6}$

(*iii*) $0.\overline{6} \times 7.\overline{3} = \frac{6}{9} \times 7\frac{3}{9}$

$= \frac{6}{9} \times \frac{66}{9} = \frac{44}{9} = 4.\overline{8}$

(*iv*) $0.\overline{06} \div 100 = 0.060606... \div 100 = 0.00\overline{06}$

(*v*) $0.7\overline{32} \div 0.02\dot{7} = 0.73\dot{2}\dot{3} \div 0.02\dot{7}\dot{7}$

$= \frac{7323-73}{99 \times 100} \div \frac{277-2}{99 \times 100}$

$= \frac{7250}{9900} \div \frac{275}{9900} = \frac{7250}{275} = \frac{290}{11} = 26.\overline{36}$.

EXERCISE

1. Which of the following is equivalent to $\frac{15}{25}$?

A. $\frac{150}{25}$ B. $\frac{15}{250}$

C. $\frac{3}{5}$ D. $\frac{60}{75}$

2. If $\frac{9*3}{3*7}$ is equivalent to $\frac{9}{7}$, the sign * is replaced by

A. ÷ B. ×

C. + D. –

3. $\frac{5}{6}$ of an hour is equal to

A. half an hour B. 40 minutes

C. 50 minutes D. 55 minutes

4. An aircraft uses 2/5 of its fuel in flying 1,250 kilometres. The distance travelled on remaining fuel is

A. 1875 km B. 2125 km

C. 250 km D. 475 km

5. If $\frac{4}{3} * \frac{3}{4} = \frac{16}{9}$, then * means

A. + B. –

C. × D. ÷

6. Which of the following is the largest fraction?

$\frac{3}{15}, \frac{5}{20}, \frac{8}{64}, \frac{25}{1000}$

A. $\frac{3}{15}$ B. $\frac{5}{20}$

C. $\frac{8}{64}$ D. $\frac{25}{1000}$

7. Six times x increased by 12 is equal to

A. $\frac{x}{2}$ B. $2x$

C. $6x + 12$ D. $12x + 6$

8. Five times y diminished by 20 is equal to

A. $5y - 20$ B. $5y + 20$

C. $y/4$ D. $4y$

9. The number less than 15 by 7 is

A. $15x - 7$ B. 15/7

C. 15 D. 8

10. If 21 is add to four times a number, the result is 57. The number is

A. 7 B. 8

C. 9 D. 10

11. A number, the sum of whose fourth and fifth parts exceeds their third part by 28, is

A. 120 B. 240

C. 220 D. 160

12. Which fraction should be added to the sum of $5\frac{3}{4}$, $4\frac{4}{5}$ and $7\frac{3}{8}$ to make the result a whole number?

A. $\frac{1}{40}$ B. $\frac{2}{40}$

C. $\frac{3}{40}$ D. $\frac{4}{40}$

13. $\frac{1}{15}+\frac{3}{15}+\frac{5}{15}+\frac{6}{15} = ?$

A. $\frac{10}{15}$ B. $\frac{3}{5}$

C. $\frac{4}{5}$ D. 1

14. A number one-sixth of which exceeds its one-ninth by 100 is

A. 600 B. 900

C. 1500 D. 1800

15. The sum of 1/2, 1/4 and 1/8 of a number is 28. The number is

A. 28 B. 32

C. 36 D. 42

16. The sum of 1/9, 1/3, 1/6 and 7/18 of a number is 150. The number is

A. 120 B. 130

C. 140 D. 150

17. Which is the greatest?
.999, .1011, .1995, .9985
A. .999 B. .1011
C. .1995 D. .9985

18. In decimal system, $9\frac{1}{8}$ may be represented as
A. 9.18 B. 9.125
C. 9.025 D. 9.225

19. $2.205 \div 0.15 = ?$
A. 1.47 B. 14.7
C. 147 D. 0.147

20. G.C.M. of .24, 3.2 and 16.0 is
A. 80 B. 8
C. .8 D. .08

ANSWERS

1	2	3	4	5	6	7	8	9	10
C	B	C	A	D	B	C	A	D	C
11	**12**	**13**	**14**	**15**	**16**	**17**	**18**	**19**	**20**
B	C	D	D	B	D	A	B	B	D

EXPLANATORY ANSWERS

1. $\frac{15}{25} = \frac{3\times5}{5\times5} = \frac{3}{5}$

2. $\frac{9*3}{3*7} = \frac{9}{7}$, or, $\frac{9\times3}{7\times3} = \frac{9}{7}$, $\therefore$ The sign * is ×.

3. $\frac{5}{6}$ of 1 hr. $= \frac{5}{6}\times60$ minutes $= 50$ minutes.

4. Remaining fuel $= 1-\frac{2}{5} = \frac{5-2}{5} = \frac{3}{5}$

Distance flown by $\frac{2}{5}$ of fuel = 1250 km.

Distance flown by full fuel $= \frac{1250}{2/5} = \frac{1250\times5}{2}$ km.

Distance flown by $\frac{3}{5}$ of fuel

$= \frac{1250\times5\times3}{2\times5} = 1875$ km.

6. $\frac{3}{15} = \frac{1}{5}, \frac{8}{64} = \frac{1}{8}, \frac{5}{20} = \frac{1}{4}, \frac{25}{1000} = \frac{1}{40}$

Now, the fractions are $\frac{1}{5}, \frac{1}{4}, \frac{1}{8}, \frac{1}{40}$

$\therefore$ The largest fraction is $\frac{1}{4} = \frac{5}{20}$

7. $x \times 6 + 12 = 6x + 12$

8. $5 \times y - 20 = 5y - 20$

9. $15 - 7 = 8$

10. Let the number be x

$\therefore \quad 4x + 21 = 57$ or, $4x = 57 - 21 = 36$

Hence, $x = \frac{36}{4} = 9$

11. Let the number be x

$\therefore \quad \frac{x}{4}+\frac{x}{5} = \frac{x}{3}+28$

$\Rightarrow \quad \frac{9x}{20} = \frac{x}{3}+28 \Rightarrow \frac{9x}{20}-\frac{x}{3} = 28$

$\Rightarrow \quad \frac{27x-20x}{60} = 28 \therefore x = \frac{28\times60}{7} = 240.$

12. $5\frac{3}{4}+4\frac{4}{5}+7\frac{3}{8} = \frac{23}{4}+\frac{24}{5}+\frac{59}{8} = \frac{717}{40}$

717/40 becomes whole number when 3/40 is added to it, *i.e.,*

$\frac{717}{40}+\frac{3}{40} = \frac{720}{40} = 18$ which is a whole number.

13. $\frac{1}{15}+\frac{3}{15}+\frac{5}{15}+\frac{6}{15} = \frac{1+3+5+6}{15} = \frac{15}{15} = 1$

14. Let the number be x

$\frac{x}{6} = \frac{x}{9}+100$

$\Rightarrow \quad \frac{x}{6}-\frac{x}{9} = 100, \Rightarrow \frac{x}{18} = 100$

$\therefore \quad x = 100 \times 18 = 1800.$

15. Let the number be x

$\therefore \quad \frac{x}{2}+\frac{x}{4}+\frac{x}{8} = 28 \Rightarrow \frac{7x}{8} = 28$

$\therefore \quad x = \frac{28\times8}{7} = 32.$

16. Let the number be x

$\therefore \quad \frac{x}{9}+\frac{x}{3}+\frac{x}{6}+\frac{7x}{18} = 150$

$\Rightarrow \quad \frac{2x+6x+3x+7x}{18} = \frac{18x}{18} = 150 \therefore x = 150.$

17. .999 is the greatest.

18. $9\frac{1}{8} = 9+\frac{1}{8} = 9 + .125 = 9.125$

19. $2.205 \div 0.15 = \frac{2.205}{.15} = \frac{2205}{1000}\times\frac{100}{15} = \frac{2205}{150} = 14.7.$

20. G.C.M. of .24, 3.2 and 16.0

$=$ G.C.M. of $\frac{24, 320 \text{ and } 1600}{100} = \frac{8}{100} = 0.08$

Relation Between Numbers

Simplification is a mathematical operation by which a complex expression of numbers or fractions is converted into a simpler or less difficult form. It is erroneous to solve this type of questions on random basis and a very appropriate method is to apply BODMAS Rule for arriving at the solution of such problems. Each of the letters of the word 'BODMAS' when explained serially, has following implications:

1.	B	→	Bracket	[{ (‾) }]
2.	O	→	of	of
3.	D	→	Division	÷
4.	M	→	Multiplication	×
5.	A	→	Addition	+
6.	S	→	Subtraction	–

Therefore, for simplification, we should remove the brackets first. Thereafter operation for 'of', then for 'division', after that the operation for 'multiplication' and thereafter for 'addition' and at last operation for 'subtraction' should be carried out.

Important Notes

A. In mathematical operations the word 'of' indicates multiplication.

B. While removing brackets, first of all bar bracket '‾' and after that small bracket '( )' is removed. Thereafter the curly bracket '{ }' and at last square bracket [ ] is removed.

EXERCISE

1. The value of 51 ÷ 17 ÷ 3 is:
A. 9 B. 4
C. 3 D. 1

2. What will be the value of
40 × 2 ÷ 10 + 5 – 4?
A. 5 B. 8
C. 11 D. 9

3. The value of 28 × 104 ÷ (18 + 6) + 3 is:
A. $124\frac{1}{3}$ B. $104\frac{1}{3}$
C. $125\frac{1}{3}$ D. 128

4. If $75^2 - 65^2 = 2x$, then value of x is:
A. 715 B. 700
C. 688 D. 711

5. The value of 99 × 14 ÷ 11 ÷ 0.7 is:
A. 2.9 B. 1.6
C. 1.8 D. 2.8

6. If 45 – [28 – {37 – (15 – ?) }] = 58, then which of the following should replace the sign of interrogation (?)?
A. 18 B. 17
C. 13 D. 19

7. The value of $8\frac{1}{3}+5\frac{1}{4}\times13\frac{1}{5}\div6\frac{3}{5}$ is:
A. $19\frac{1}{3}$ B. $18\frac{5}{6}$
C. $21\frac{1}{3}$ D. $22\frac{1}{2}$

8. The value of $\frac{14}{3}$ of $\frac{5}{8}$ of 72 is:
A. 209 B. 217
C. 210 D. 199

9. What will be the value of
10 × 10 × 10 ÷ (20 ÷ 10 × 10 – 10) + 6?
A. 108 B. 111
C. 106 D. 114

10. What will be the value of $\dfrac{\frac{1}{3}\times20\div4}{\frac{1}{4}\times25\div5}$?
A. 7/3 B. 4/3
C. 5/3 D. 10/3

11. Which of the following is the standard form of $\dfrac{(24\times13)+(28\div7)}{(24+13)-\left(\frac{14}{3}\text{ of }\frac{5}{8}\right)}$?
A. $\frac{3792}{409}$ B. $\frac{4792}{309}$
C. $\frac{3792}{411}$ D. $\frac{3092}{409}$

12. If $\dfrac{144+32\div?-8}{35\div\frac{1}{2}\text{ of }\frac{1}{2}}=1$, then which of the following should replace the sign of interrogation?
A. 7 B. 6
C. 10 D. 8

13. What is the value of
$\dfrac{2.70\times2.70+4.30\times4.30+8.60\times2.70}{2.70+4.30}$?
A. 6.8 B. 7.0
C. 7.6 D. 8.5

14. What will be the value of $\dfrac{\left(\sqrt{6}+\frac{1}{\sqrt{6}}\right)^2}{\frac{1}{2}\text{ of }18+4}+\frac{2}{3}$?
A. 101/78 B. 104/71
C. 101/88 D. 99/57

15. 1150 ÷ 50 ÷ 23 + 15 = ?
A. 16 B. 20
C. 22 D. 18

ANSWERS

1	2	3	4	5	6	7	8	9	10
D	D	A	B	C	D	B	C	C	B
11	**12**	**13**	**14**	**15**					
A	D	B	A	A					

EXPLANATORY ANSWERS

1. $\because\ 51 \div 17 \div 3 = \frac{51}{17} \div 3 = 3 \div 3 = \frac{3}{3} = 1$

2. $\because\ 40 \times 2 \div 10 + 5 - 4$

$= 40 \times \frac{2}{10} + 5 - 4 = 8 + 5 - 4 = 9.$

3. $\because\ 28 \times 104 \div (18 + 6) + 3$

$= 28 \times 104 \div 24 + 3$

$= 28 \times \frac{104}{24} + 3 = 28 \times \frac{13}{3} + 3$

$= \frac{364}{3} + 3 = \frac{373}{3} = 124\frac{1}{3}$

4. $\because\ 75^2 - 65^2 = 2x$

$\Rightarrow (75 + 65)(75 - 65) = 2x$

$[\because\ a^2 - b^2 = (a + b)(a - b)]$

$\Rightarrow\ 140 \times 10 = 2x \Rightarrow x = 70 \times 10 = 700$

$\therefore$ Value of x is 700.

5. $\because\ .99 \times 14 \div 11 \div 0.7$

$= .99 \times \frac{14}{11} \div 0.7 = \frac{.99 \times 14}{11 \times 0.7} = 1.8$

6. $\because\ 45 - [28 - \{37 - (15 - ?)\}] = 58$

$\Rightarrow\ 45 - [28 - \{37 - 15 + ?\}] = 58$

$\Rightarrow\ 45 - [28 - \{22 + ?\}] = 58$

$\Rightarrow\ 45 - [28 - 22 - ?\} = 58$

$\Rightarrow\ 45 - 28 + 22 + ? = 58$

$\Rightarrow\ 39 + ? = 58$

$\Rightarrow\ ? = 58 - 39 = 19$

Therefore, the interrogation sign should be replaced by 19.

7. $\because\ 8\frac{1}{3} + 5\frac{1}{4} \times 13\frac{1}{5} \div 6\frac{3}{5}$

$= \frac{25}{3} + \frac{21}{4} \times \frac{66}{5} \div \frac{33}{5} = \frac{25}{3} + \frac{21}{4} \times \frac{66}{5} \times \frac{5}{33}$

$= \frac{25}{3} + \frac{21}{2} = \frac{50 + 63}{6} = \frac{113}{6} = 18\frac{5}{6}$

8. $\because\ \frac{14}{3}$ of $\frac{5}{8}$ of $72 = \frac{14 \times 5 \times 72}{3 \times 8} = 210$

9. $10 \times 10 \times 10 \div (20 \div 10 \times 10 - 10) + 6$

$= 10 \times 10 \times 10 \div \left(\frac{20}{10} \times 10 - 10\right) + 6$

$= 10 \times 10 \times 10 \div (20 - 10) + 6$

$= 10 \times 10 \times 10 \div 10 + 6$

$= 10 \times 10 \times \frac{10}{10} + 6$

$= 10 \times 10 \times 1 + 6 = 100 + 6 = 106$

10. $\because\ \dfrac{\frac{1}{3} \times 20 \div 4}{\frac{1}{4} \times 25 \div 5} = \dfrac{\frac{1}{3} \times 5}{\frac{1}{4} \times 5} = \dfrac{\frac{5}{3}}{\frac{5}{4}} = \frac{4}{3}$

11. $\because\ \dfrac{(24 \times 13) + (28 \div 7)}{(24 + 13) - \left(\frac{14}{3} \text{ of } \frac{5}{8}\right)} = \dfrac{312 + 4}{37 - \frac{35}{12}} = \dfrac{316}{\frac{409}{12}} = \dfrac{3792}{409}$

12. If $\dfrac{144 + 32 \div ? - 8}{35 \div \frac{1}{2} \text{ of } \frac{1}{2}} = 1 \Rightarrow \dfrac{144 + \frac{32}{?} - 8}{35 \div \frac{1}{4}} = 1 \Rightarrow \dfrac{136 + \frac{32}{?}}{\frac{35}{\frac{1}{4}}} = 1$

$\Rightarrow\ 136 + \frac{32}{?} = 35 \times 4 = 140$

$\Rightarrow\ \frac{32}{?} = 140 - 136 = 4 \Rightarrow ? = \frac{32}{4} = 8$

$\therefore$ Sign of interrogation (?) will be replaced by 8.

13. $\dfrac{2.70 \times 2.70 + 4.30 \times 4.30 + 8.60 \times 2.70}{2.70 + 4.30}$

$= \dfrac{(2.70)^2 + (4.30)^2 + 2 \times 4.30 \times 2.70}{2.70 + 4.30}$

$= \dfrac{(2.70 + 4.30)^2}{2.70 + 4.30}\ [\because a^2 + b^2 + 2ab = (a + b)^2]$

$= 2.70 + 4.30 = 7.00$

14. $\therefore\ \dfrac{\left(\sqrt{6} + \frac{1}{\sqrt{6}}\right)^2}{\frac{1}{2} \text{ of } 18 + 4} + \frac{2}{3} = \dfrac{(\sqrt{6})^2 + \left(\frac{1}{\sqrt{6}}\right)^2 + 2.\sqrt{6}\,\frac{1}{\sqrt{6}}}{9 + 4} + \frac{2}{3}$

$= \dfrac{6 + \frac{1}{6} + 2}{13} + \frac{2}{3} = \dfrac{\frac{49}{6}}{13} + \frac{2}{3} = \frac{49}{78} + \frac{2}{3} = \frac{101}{78}$

15. $1150 \div 50 \div 23 + 15$

$= \frac{1150}{50} \div 23 + 15 = 23 \div 23 + 15 = \frac{23}{23} + 15$

$= 1 + 15 = 16.$

2

Comparing Quantities

Percentage

The word 'per cent' or 'percentage' means 'for every one hundred'. In other words, it gives an indication of rate per hundred. It is denoted by the symbol %.

For example, 5% means 5 out of one hundred or $\frac{5}{100}$.

Remember:

(*i*) For converting a per cent into a fraction, divide it by 100.

(*ii*) For converting a fraction into a per cent, multiply it by 100.

(*iii*) For converting a per cent into a decimal, shift the decimal point two places to the left.

(*iv*) For converting one given quantity *(x)* as a percentage of another given quantity *(y)*, find $\frac{x}{y} \times 100$.

(*v*) There is no unit of percentage.

Important Facts—For quickly solving the problems related to percentage, remember following rules:

Rule 1:

(***a***) Of the given two numbers if the first is $x\%$ more than the second, then the second will be $\left(\frac{100 \times x}{100 + x}\right)\%$ less than the first.

(***b***) Of the given two numbers if the first is $x\%$ less than the second, then the second will be $\left(\frac{100 \times x}{100 - x}\right)\%$ more than the first.

(***c***) If two numbers are respectively $x\%$ and $y\%$ more than a third number, then the first number will be $\left(\frac{100 + x}{100 + y} \times 100\right)\%$ of the second.

(***d***) If two numbers are respectively $x\%$ and $y\%$ less than a third number, then the first number will be $\left(\frac{100 - x}{100 - y} \times 100\right)\%$ of the second.

Rule 2:

(***a***) If a number or quantity is increased by $x\%$ then in order to restore its original value it must be decreased by $\left[\frac{100 \times x}{100 + x}\right]\%$.

(***b***) If a number or quantity is decreased by $x\%$ then in order to restore its original value it must be increased by $\left[\frac{100 \times x}{100 - x}\right]\%$.

Rule 3:

(***a***) If a number is successively increased by $x\%$ and $y\%$ then a single equivalent increase in that number will be $\left(x + y + \frac{xy}{100}\right)\%$

(***b***) If two successive discounts of $x\%$ and $y\%$ are allowed on a particular amount, then a single discount that is equivalent to the two successive discounts will be $\left(x + y - \frac{xy}{100}\right)\%$

(***c***) If a number is successively increased by $x\%$, $y\%$ and $z\%$, then a single equivalent increase in that number will be $\left[(x + y + z) + \left(\frac{xy + yz + zx}{100}\right) + \frac{(xyz)}{10000}\right]\%$

(***d***) If three successive discounts of $x\%$, $y\%$ and $z\%$ are allowed on an amount, then a single discount that is equivalent to the three successive discounts will be $\left[x + y + z - \frac{(xy + yz + zx)}{100} + \frac{xyz}{10000}\right]\%$

Rule 4:

(***a***) If a number is increased by $x\%$ and thereafter reduced by $x\%$, then the number will be reduced by $\left(\frac{x^2}{100}\right)$ per cent.

(*b*) If a number is reduced by $x\%$ and thereafter increased by $x\%$ then the number will be reduced by $\left(\frac{x^2}{100}\right)$ per cent.

(*c*) If due to an increase of $x\%$ in the selling price of certain commodity the sell/consumption of the commodity decreases by $y\%$, then gross receipts on account of sale of that commodity will be increased or decreased by $\left(x-y-\frac{xy}{100}\right)\%$, where $x > y$ and will be decreased by $\left(y-x+\frac{xy}{100}\right)\%$, where $y > x$.

EXERCISE

1. In the expression xy^2, the values of both variables x and y are decreased by 20%. By this, the value of the expression is decreased by

A. 40% B. 48.8%
C. 51.2% D. 80%

2. 15 litres of mixture contains 20% alcohol and rest water. If 3 litres of water be mixed in it, the percentage of alcohol in the new mixture will be:

A. 15 B. $16\frac{2}{3}$
C. 17 D. $18\frac{1}{2}$

3. The difference between 70% and 55% of a number is 72. The number is:

A. 370 B. 460
C. 480 D. 520

4. 20% of a number is 10% of:

A. half the number
B. double the number
C. ten times the number
D. twenty times the number

5. 75% of what area is 15 sq. metres?

A. 10 sq. metres B. 15 sq. metres
C. 20 sq. metres D. 25 sq. metres

6. In an examination 80% of the students passed in Mathematics and 70% passed in English, while 10% students failed in both the subjects. If 360 students passed in both the subjects, find the total number of students who appeared in the examination.

A. 400 B. 600
C. 630 D. 640

7. In an election, there are two candidates. A candidate secured 57% of the total votes polled and elected by a margin of 2100 votes. Find the total number of votes polled.

A. 15000 B. 17500
C. 18000 D. 21000

8. Electric tax is increased by 20% and its consumption is decreased by 20%. The change in the expenditure is:

A. 4% decrease B. 4% increase
C. 5% decrease D. 5% increase

9. A man loses 10% of his money, after spending 20% of the remainder he is left with ₹ 2160. Initially the man had:

A. ₹ 1800 B. ₹ 2500
C. ₹ 3000 D. ₹ 3200

10. In a school 55% of the students are below 9 years of age and the remaining 153 above 9 years of age. The total number of students in the school is:

A. 296 B. 300
C. 340 D. 1000

11. The selling price of certain commodity was reduced by 25%. As a result of it, the sales increased by 30%. What was the effect of it on cash collected by daily sales?

A. 2.5% decrease B. 2.5% increase
C. 5% decrease D. 5% increase

12. A cooler marked at ₹ 1500 is offered at ₹ 1350 due to off-season discount. Find the rate of off-season discount offered.

A. 9.5% B. 10%
C. 10.5% D. 12%

13. The number of Gypsy-cars sold in 2008 was 16,500 and that sold in 2007 was 16580. How much was the percentage decrease in sales of the Gypsy-cars from 2007 to 2008?

A. less than 1 per cent
B. more than 1 per cent
C. zero per cent
D. cannot be determined

14. A company decided to sell ₹ 50,000 T.V. set for ₹ 48,000 as a world cup offer. What is the percentage discount offered by the company?

A. 6.5 B. 7
C. 7.5 D. 4

15. 9% of a number is $\frac{81}{200}$, what is $\frac{2}{7}$ of that number?

A. $1\frac{1}{5}$ B. $1\frac{2}{7}$
C. $2\frac{1}{7}$ D. $2\frac{1}{5}$

ANSWERS

1	2	3	4	5	6	7	8	9	10
B	B	C	B	C	B	A	A	C	C
11	12	13	14	15					
A	B	A	D	B					

EXPLANATORY ANSWERS

1. Decrease in expression

$$= xy^2 - \frac{80}{100} \times x\left(\frac{80}{100}y\right)^2 = xy^2 - \frac{64}{125}xy^2 = \frac{61xy^2}{125}$$

Hence, decrease per cent

$$= \frac{61xy^2}{125 \times xy^2} \times 100 = 48.8\%$$

2. Amount of alcohol $= \frac{20}{100} \times 15 = 3$ litre

Hence, required percentage $= \frac{3}{18} \times 100 = 16\frac{2}{3}\%$

3. Let the number be x; then

$$(70 - 55) \times \frac{1}{100} \times x = 72$$

$$\therefore \quad x = \frac{100 \times 72}{15} = 480$$

4. Let number be 100, then 20% and 10% of the number be 20 and 10 respectively.

Hence, 20% of a number is 10% of double the number.

5. Let required area be x sq. metre; then

$$\frac{75}{100} \times x = 15$$

$$\therefore \ x = \frac{15 \times 100}{75} = 20 \text{ sq metre}$$

6. Here, percentage of students failed in Mathematics and English be 30% and 20% respectively.

Percentage of students failed either one or both subjects $= 30 + 20 - 10 = 40\%$

Hence, percentage of pass students $= 100 - 40 = 60\%$

Now, $60\% = 360$

$$\therefore \quad 100\% = \frac{360}{60} \times 100 = 600$$

7. Let total number of votes be x; then

$$(57 - 43) \times \frac{1}{10}x = 2100$$

$$\therefore \quad x = \frac{100 \times 2100}{14} = 15000$$

8. Let initially electric tax is ₹ 100 and consumption = 100 units

Decrease in consumption

$= 100 \times 100 - 120 \times 80 =$ ₹ 400

Hence, decrease percentage $= \frac{400 \times 100}{100 \times 100} = 4\%$

9. Let initally the man had ₹ x, then

amount of money loses $= \frac{10}{100} \times x = ₹\frac{x}{10}$

Remaining amount of money $= x - \frac{x}{10} = ₹\frac{9x}{10}$

Money spent $= \frac{20}{100} \times \frac{9x}{10} = ₹\frac{9x}{50}$

Now, $\frac{9x}{10} - \frac{9x}{50} = 2160 \Rightarrow \frac{36x}{50} = 2160$

$$\therefore \ x = \frac{2160 \times 50}{36} = ₹\ 3000$$

10. Let total number of students be x, then

$$\frac{45}{100} \times x = 153 \ \therefore \ x = \frac{100 \times 153}{45} = 340$$

11. Let the selling price of a commodity be ₹ 100 and number of sales = 100 units

Decrease in daily cash

$= 100 \times 100 - 75 \times 130 =$ ₹ 250

Hence, decrease percentage $= \frac{250 \times 100}{100 \times 100} = 2.5\%$

12. Discount per cent

$$= \frac{1500 - 1350}{1500} \times 100 = \frac{150}{1500} \times 100 = 10\%$$

13. Required decrease percentage

$$= \frac{16580 - 16500}{16580} \times 100 = \frac{80}{16580} \times 100 = 0.48\%$$

14. Discount per cent $= \frac{2000}{50{,}000} \times 100 = 4\%$

15. Let the number be x; then

$$\frac{9}{100} \times x = \frac{81}{200} \ \therefore \ x = \frac{100 \times 81}{9 \times 200} = \frac{9}{2}$$

Hence, $\frac{2}{7}x = \frac{2}{7} \times \frac{9}{2} = \frac{9}{7} = 1\frac{2}{7}$.

Discount

Market Price (M.P.)—The attached price is called the market price (M.P.) or list price (L.P.) of the article and the reduction allowed in the price is called the **discount**.

(*i*) Discount = M.P. – S.P.

(*ii*) Discount % = $\dfrac{\text{Discount} \times 100}{\text{M.P.}}$

(*iii*) S.P. = M.P. – $\dfrac{\text{Discount\%} \times \text{M.P.}}{100}$

(*iv*) S.P. = M.P. × $\left(1 - \dfrac{\text{Discount\%}}{100}\right)$

(*v*) M.P. = $\dfrac{100 \times \text{S.P.}}{100 - \text{Discount\%}}$

S.P. = M.P. $\left(\dfrac{100 - \text{Discount\%}}{100}\right)$

M.P. – S.P. = $\dfrac{\text{M.P.} \times \text{Discount\%}}{100}$

Discount% = $\left(\dfrac{\text{M.P.} - \text{S.P.}}{\text{M.P.}}\right) \times 100$

EXERCISE

1. A cloth merchant offers 15% festival discount on every saree sold. If a certain saree is sold for ₹ 680, what is its marked price?
A. ₹ 800 B. ₹ 900
C. ₹ 1250 D. ₹ 1300

2. A shopkeeper offers 10% discount on an article and still makes a profit of 20%. What is the C.P. of the article if the marked price is ₹ 350?
A. ₹ 259.20 B. ₹ 262.50
C. ₹ 265.75 D. ₹ 272.5

3. A manufactures marks his goods in such a way that after allowing 20% discount, he makes a profit of 18%. What is the marked price of an item which costs him ₹ 200?
A. ₹ 295 B. ₹ 310
C. ₹ 315 D. ₹ 375

4. The marked price of a brand of coffee is ₹ 35 for 100g. But the shopkeeper gives a cup costing ₹ 7.50 free with it. Even then he gets a gain of 10%. What is the cost price of 100g of coffee?
A. ₹ 15 B. ₹ 25
C. ₹ 35 D. ₹ 65

5. A car is marked at ₹ 2,25,000. The manufacturer gives a discount of 10%. The dealer also gives a discount of 5%. What is the S.P. of the car?
A. ₹ 1,72,369 B. ₹ 1,64,370
C. ₹ 1,52,393 D. ₹ 1,92,375

6. A cycle merchant allows 25% commission on his advertised price and still makes a profit of 20%. If he gains ₹ 60 over the sale of one cycle. What is his advertised price?
A. ₹ 290 B. ₹ 310
C. ₹ 480 D. ₹ 520

7. The marked price of a shirt was ₹ 165 and it was at a discount of 12%. What the selling price of the shirt?
A. ₹ 145.20 B. ₹ 155.30
C. ₹ 165.20 D. ₹ 175.25

8. A trader marks his goods 40% above the cost price and gives a discount of 20% on the marked price. What is his gain per cent?
A. 8% B. 9%
C. 12% D. 15%

9. How much per cent more than the C.P. should a manufacturer mark his goods so that after allowing a discount of 20% on the marked price, he gains 10%.
A. 34.5% B. 27.5%
C. 37.5% D. 38.5%

10. A shopkeeper allows a discount of 10% to his customers and still gains 20%. What is the marked price of an article which costs ₹ 450 to the shopkeeper?
A. ₹ 600 B. ₹ 700
C. ₹ 800 D. ₹ 900

ANSWERS

1	2	3	4	5	6	7	8	9	10
A	B	A	B	D	C	A	C	C	A

EXPLANATORY ANSWERS

1. S.P. = ₹ 680, Discount = 15%

$$\text{M.P.} = \frac{100 \times \text{S.P.}}{100 - \text{Discount\%}}$$

$$= \frac{100 \times 680}{100 - 15} = \frac{100 \times 680}{85} = ₹\ 800$$

2. C.P. = ₹ x, 120% of x = 350 – 350 × 10%

$$\frac{120}{100} \times x = 350 - 35 = 315.$$

$$x = \frac{315 \times 5}{6} = \frac{525}{2}, \text{ C.P.} = ₹\ 262.50.$$

3. Let M.P. = ₹ x

$80\%\ x = 118\%$ of 200

$$\frac{80}{100}\times x = \frac{118}{100}\times 200 \Rightarrow x = \frac{236\times 5}{4} = ₹\ 295.$$

4. Let C.P. of 100 gm coffee = ₹ x

110% of $x = 35 - 7.50 = 27.50$

$$\frac{110}{100}\times x = 27.50$$

$$x = \frac{27.50\times 100}{110\times 100}$$

C.P. = ₹ 25.

5. M.P. = ₹ 225000

$$\text{1st S.P.} = 225000 - 225000 \times \frac{10}{100}$$

$$= 225000 - 22500 = 202500$$

$$\text{2nd S.P.} = 202500 - 202500 \times \frac{5}{100}$$

$$= 202500 - 10125 = ₹\ 192375$$

6. Let M.P. = 100

Commission = 25%

S.P. = 100 − 25 = 75

Profit = 20%

$$\text{C.P.} = \frac{100}{120}\times 75 = \frac{375}{6} = 62.50$$

Gain = 75 − 62.50 = ₹ 12.50

$$\text{M.P.} = \frac{100}{12.50}\times 60 = ₹\ 480$$

7. $$\text{S.P.} = \frac{\text{M.P.}(100-\text{Discount})}{100}$$

$$= \frac{165\times(100-12)}{100} = \frac{165\times 88}{100}$$

$= 33 \times 4.4 = ₹\ 145.20$

8. Let C.P. = 100, M.P. = 140, Discount = 20%

$$\text{S.P.} = 140 - 140\times\frac{20}{100} = 140 - 28 = 112$$

Profit = 112 − 100 = 12

$$\text{Profit } \% = \frac{12\times 100}{100} = 12\%$$

9. Let C.P. = ₹ x, S.P. = 110% of $x = \frac{110}{100}\times x = \frac{11}{10}x.$

Discount = 20%

$$\text{M.P.} = \frac{100\times\frac{11}{10}x}{100-20} = \frac{100\times\frac{11}{10}x}{80} = \frac{11}{8}x.$$

$$\text{Required } \% = \frac{\frac{11x}{8}-x}{x}\times 100 = \frac{3x\times 100}{8x} = 37.5\%$$

10. C.P. = 450, Gain = 20%

$$\text{S.P.} = 450 + 450\times\frac{20}{100} = 450 + 90 = 540$$

Discount = 10%

$$\text{M.P.} = \frac{100\times\text{S.P.}}{100-\text{Discount}} = \frac{100\times 540}{100-10}$$

$$= \frac{100\times 540}{90} = ₹\ 600$$

Profit & Loss

A consumer who goes to the market and buys certain goods. The buyer is called a customer and the shopkeeper who sells the goods to him is called a retailer. The retailer purchases goods in turn in bulk from a wholesaler who keeps a large stock of good and in this case, the retailer becomes the customer.

1. **Cost price (C.P.):** Cost price is that price at which a particular article is bought. Profit and loss both are marked at cost price.
2. **Selling Price (S.P.):** Selling price is that price at which a particular article is sold.
3. **Overheads:** The expenses incurred on transportation, maintenance, packaging, advertise-ments and the like are included as *Overhead.* These overheads and the profit when added to the cost price determine the selling price.
4. **Profit or Gain** : Whenever a person sells an article at price greater than the cost price he is said to have made a profit or gain.
   Profit or Gain = S.P. − C.P.
5. **Loss :** If S.P. is less than the C.P. there is loss.
   Loss = C.P − S.P

Some Basic Formulae:

(i) Gain = S.P. − C.P.

(ii) Loss = C.P. − S.P.

(iii) $\text{Gain } \% = \frac{\text{Gain}\times 100}{\text{C.P.}}$

(iv) $\text{Loss } \% = \frac{\text{Loss}\times 100}{\text{C.P.}}$

From these we can write direct expressions for S.P. and C.P.

(v) $\text{S.P.} = \left(\frac{100+\text{Gain}\%}{100}\right)\times\text{C.P.}$ in case of gain or profit

(vi) $\text{S.P.} = \left(\frac{100-\text{Loss}\%}{100}\right)\times\text{C.P.}$ in case of loss

These can be rewritten as

$\text{C.P.} = \frac{100}{100+\text{Gain}\%}\times\text{S.P.}$ in case of profit

$\text{C.P.} = \frac{100}{100-\text{Loss}\%}\times\text{S.P.}$ in case of loss *(vii)* If the C.P. of x goods = S.P. of y goods, then

(a) Gain % = $\frac{x-y}{y}\times 100$ [In case of $x > y$]

(b) Loss % = $\frac{y-x}{y}\times 100$ [In case of $y > x$]

(viii) When a man sells two things at the same price each and in this process his loss on first things is x% and gain on second things is x%, then in such a type question, there is always a loss.

$$\text{Loss \%} = x\% \text{ of } x = \frac{x^2}{100} = \left(\frac{x}{10}\right)^2.$$

$$\text{and Loss} = \frac{2\times \text{S.P.}}{\left(\frac{100}{x}\right)^2 - 1}$$

(ix) An article is sold at a profit of x%. Had it been sold for ₹ a some more, y% would have gained. Then, C.P. of an article =

$$\frac{\text{More gain}\times 100}{\text{Difference in percentage profit}}.$$

(x) A dishonest shopkeeper prefers to sell goods at his cost price but uses a false weight of x grams for each kilogram. Then his gain per cent,

$$\text{gain \%} = \frac{\text{Error}}{\text{True value} - \text{Error}}\times 100$$

$$= \frac{1000 - x}{x}\times 100$$

$$\text{or, gain \%} = \frac{\text{True weight} - \text{False weight}}{\text{False weight}}\times 100.$$

EXERCISE

1. Ashok bought 25 kg of rice at the rate of ₹ 6 per kg and 35 kg of rice at the rate of ₹ 7 per kg. He mixed the two and sold the mixture at the rate of ₹ 6.75 per kg. What was his gain or loss in the transaction?

A. ₹ 16 gain B. ₹ 16 loss
C. ₹ 10 gain D. None of these

2. A horse and a cow were sold for ₹ 12000 each. The horse was sold at a loss of 20% and the cow at a gain of 20%. The entire transaction resulted in

A. no loss no gain B. loss of ₹ 1000
C. gain of ₹ 1000 D. loss of ₹ 2000

3. Profit after selling a commodity for ₹ 425 is same as loss after selling it for ₹ 355. The cost of the commodity is :

A. ₹ 285 B. ₹ 390
C. ₹ 295 D. ₹ 400

4. Bhajan Singh purchased 120 reams of paper at ₹ 80 per ream. He spent ₹ 280 on transportation, paid octroi at the rate of 40 paise per ream and paid ₹ 72 to the coolie. If he wants to have a gain of 8%, what must be the selling price per ream?

A. ₹ 86 B. ₹ 86.48
C. ₹ 79 D. ₹ 90

5. Ram bought 4 dozen apples at ₹ 12 per dozen and 2 dozen at ₹ 16 per dozen. He sold all of them to earn 20%. At what price per dozen did he sell the apples?

A. ₹ 14.40 B. ₹ 16.00
C. ₹ 16.80 D. ₹ 16.20

6. Jimmy bought paper sheets for ₹ 7200 and spent ₹ 200 in transport. Paying ₹ 600 he had 330 boxes made, which he sold at ₹ 28 each. What is his profit percentage?

A. 15.5 B. 40
C. 50 D. None of these

7. A owns a house worth ₹ 10000. He sells it to B at a profit of 10% based on the worth of the house. B sells the house back to A at a loss of 10%. In this transaction A gets:

A. no profit no loss B. profit of ₹ 1000
C. profit of ₹ 1100 D. profit of ₹ 1200

8. At what price must Kantilal sell a mixture of 80 kg sugar at ₹ 6.75 per kg with 120 kg at ₹ 8 per kg to gain 20%?

A. ₹ 7.50 per kg B. ₹ 8.20 per kg
C. ₹ 8.35 per kg D. ₹ 9 per kg

9. Subhash purchased a taperecorder at $\frac{9}{10}$ of its selling price and sold it at 8% more than its S.P. His gain is:

A. 8% B. 10%
C. 18% D. 20%

10. A dealer marks his goods 20% above cost price. He then allows some discount on it and makes a profit of 8%. The rate of discount is :

A. 12% B. 10%
C. 6% D. 4%

11. A trader lists his articles 20% above C.P. and allows a discount of 10% on cash payment. His gain per cent is :

A. 10% B. 8%
C. 6% D. 4%

12. Tarun bought a T.V. with 20% discount on the labelled price. Had he bought it with 25% discount, he would have saved ₹ 500. At what price did he buy the T.V.?

A. ₹ 5000 B. ₹ 8000
C. ₹ 10000 D. ₹ 12000

13. While selling a watch, a shopkeeper gives a discount of 5%. If he gives a discount of 7%, he earns ₹ 15 less as profit. The marked price of the watch is :

A. ₹ 697.50 B. ₹ 712.50

C. ₹ 787.50 D. None of these

14. Kabir buys an article with 25% discount on its marked price. He makes a profit of 10% by selling it at ₹ 660. The marked price is :

A. ₹ 600 B. ₹ 700

C. ₹ 800 D. ₹ 885

15. A person bought an article and sold it at a loss of 10%. If he had bought it for 20% less and sold it for ₹ 55 more, he would have had a profit of 40%. The C.P. of the article is :

A. ₹ 200 B. ₹ 225

C. ₹ 250 D. None of these

ANSWERS

1	2	3	4	5	6	7	8	9	10
C	B	B	D	B	A	C	D	D	B
11	12	13	14	15					
B	B	D	C	C					

EXPLANATORY ANSWERS

1. C.P. of 60 kg mixture = ₹ (25 × 6 + 35 × 7) = ₹ 395

S.P. of 60 kg mixtire = ₹ (60 × 6.75) = ₹ 405

∴ Gain = ₹ (405 − 395) = ₹ 10

2. Loss % = $\left(\frac{20}{10}\right)^2 = (2)^2 = 4\%$

Total S.P. = ₹ 24000

and Total C.P. = ₹$\left(\frac{100}{96} \times 24000\right)$ = ₹ 25000

∴ Loss = ₹ (25000 − 24000) = ₹ 1000

3. Let C.P. = ₹ x, Then, $425 - x = x - 355$

⇒ $2x = 780$ ∴ x = ₹ 390

4. C.P. of 1 ream = $80 + \frac{280}{120} + \frac{72}{120} + 0.40$

$= 80 + \frac{7}{3} + \frac{3}{5} + \frac{2}{5}$ = ₹ $\frac{250}{3}$

∴ S.P. of 1 ream = ₹$\left(\frac{108}{100} \times \frac{250}{3}\right)$ = ₹ 90

5. C.P. of 6 dozen apples = ₹ (12 × 4 + 16 × 2) = ₹ 80

∴ S.P. = ₹$\left(\frac{120}{100} \times 80\right)$ = ₹ 96

∴ S.P. per dozen = ₹$\left(\frac{96}{6}\right)$ = ₹ 16

6. C.P. of 1 box = $\frac{7200 + 200 + 600}{330}$ = ₹ $\frac{800}{33}$

Hence, Gain% = $\frac{28 - \frac{800}{33}}{800/33} \times 100 = \frac{124}{800} \times 100 = 15.5\%$

7. Final C.P. for A = $\frac{110}{100} \times \frac{90}{100}$ × ₹ 10000 = ₹ 9900

Hence, profit for A

= $\frac{10}{100}$ × ₹ 10,000 + ₹ (10,000 − 9900) = ₹ 1100

8. C.P. of 1 kg sugar = $\frac{80 \times 6.75 + 120 \times 8}{200}$ = ₹ 7.50

∴ S.P. of 1 kg = ₹$\left(\frac{120}{100} \times 7.50\right)$ = ₹ 9 per kg

9. Let S.P. = ₹ 100;

C.P. for Subhash = $\frac{9}{10} \times 100$ = ₹ 90 and S.P. = ₹ 108

Hence, gain % for Subhash = $\frac{108 - 90}{90} \times 100 = 20\%$

10. Let C.P. be ₹ 100; then Marked price = ₹ 120 and S.P. = ₹ 108

∴ Discount = $\left(\frac{12}{120} \times 100\right)\% = 10\%$

11. Let C.P. be ₹ 100

Then, marked price = ₹ 120

S.P. = ₹$\left(\frac{90}{100} \times 120\right)$ = ₹ 108

∴ Gain % = $\left(\frac{8}{100} \times 100\right)\% = 8\%$

12. Here, 5% = 500

∴ 100% = $\frac{500}{5} \times 100$ = ₹ 10,000

Hence, labelled price = ₹ 10,000

∴ S.P. = $\frac{80}{100}$ × ₹ 10,000 = ₹ 8000

13. Let the marked price = ₹ x

Then, $\frac{7x}{100} - \frac{5x}{100} = 15 \Rightarrow \frac{x}{50} = 15$ ∴ x = ₹ 750

14. C.P. = $\frac{100}{110} \times 660$ = ₹ 600

Hence, M.P. = $\frac{100}{75} \times 600$ = ₹ 800.

Simple Interest

Interest is the money paid for the use of money borrowed, *i.e.*, extra money paid for using other's money is called *interest.*

The sum borrowed is called the principal. The sum of interest and principal is called the *Amount.*

If the interest on a certain sum borrowed for a certain period is reckoned uniformly, then it is called simple interest, denoted by S.I.

Thus, if A = Amount, P = Principal, I = Interest, T = Time (in year), R = Rate per cent per annum, then

(*a*) $I = \frac{P \times R \times T}{100}$ (*b*) $P = \frac{100 \times I}{R \times T}$

(*c*) $T = \frac{100 \times I}{P \times R}$ (*d*) $R = \frac{100 \times I}{P \times T}$

(*e*) $P = \frac{100\,A}{100 + RT}$ (*f*) A = P + I.

EXERCISE

1. If the simple interest on a certain sum of money at 6% per annum for 3 years is ₹ 90, the sum will be:
A. ₹ 500 B. ₹ 450
C. ₹ 525 D. ₹ 560

2. If the simple interest on ₹ 1 for 1 month is 1 paise, the rate per cent p.a. will be :
A. 10% B. 8%
C. 12% D. 6%

3. A sum of money doubles itself in 20 years. In how many years will it triple itself at the same rate of simple interest?
A. 30 years B. 50 years
C. 40 years D. 45 years

4. If the simple interest on ₹ 500 for 4 years is ₹ 40, find the rate per cent p.a.
A. 3½% B. 2%
C. 2½% D. 3%

5. After what time will the sum of ₹ 2000 become ₹ 2240 at 4% per annum simple interest?
A. 3 years B. 2 years
C. 5 years D. 4 years

6. The simple interest on a certain sum of money is $\frac{25}{64}$ of the sum and the number of years equals the rate per cent p.a. The rate per cent p.a. will be :
A. $7\frac{1}{2}\%$ B. $5\frac{1}{4}\%$
C. $6\frac{3}{4}\%$ D. $6\frac{1}{4}\%$

7. A sum of money amounts to ₹ 1150 in 3 years and to ₹ 1250 in 5 years at a certain rate per cent p.a. simple interest. The rate per cent p.a. will be :
A. 5% B. 8%
C. 7% D. 6%

8. The simple interest on a sum of ₹ 892 lent out at 6% p.a. for 8 months will be :
A. ₹ 36.68 B. ₹ 35.68
C. ₹ 48.58 D. ₹ 33.38

9. If the simple interest on a certain sum of money at 6% p.a. for 4½ years is ₹ 81, the sum will be:
A. ₹ 325 B. ₹ 225
C. ₹ 300 D. ₹ 340

10. A sum of ₹ 1850 lent out for 5 years at 3% p.a. simple interest will amount to:
A. ₹ 2227.75 B. ₹ 2127.50
C. ₹ 2137.50 D. ₹ 2086.50

11. A lent a sum of ₹ 1250 to B at a certain rate of interest for 3 years and a sum of ₹ 1500 to C at the same rate of interest for 2 years. If he was paid total ₹ 258.75 as interest in both cases, find the rate of interest at which money was lent by him.
A. $4\frac{1}{6}\%$ B. $6\frac{1}{4}\%$
C. $2\frac{1}{7}\%$ D. $3\frac{5}{6}\%$

12. A invested ₹ 5000 at a certain rate of simple interest and ₹ 4000 for the same period at 1% higher rate of interest. If the interest in both cases is same, the former rate of interest is :
A. 3% B. 4%
C. 6% D. 5%

13. A man lends ₹ 500 for 4 years and ₹ 600 for 3 years at a certain rate of simple interest. If he gets total ₹ 190 as interest in both cases, the rate per cent per annum is:
A. 8% B. 5%
C. 10% D. 4%

14. What annual instalment should be paid to clear the debt of ₹ 645 in 4 years at the rate of 5% p.a. simple interest?
A. ₹ 160 B. ₹ 185
C. ₹ 180 D. ₹ 190

15. If a certain sum of money at simple interest amounts to ₹ 1900 in 3 years and to ₹ 2050 in 5 years, the rate per cent per annum is:
A. 4½% B. 3½%
C. 2½% D. 5¼%

ANSWERS

1	2	3	4	5	6	7	8	9	10
A	C	C	B	A	D	A	B	C	B
11	**12**	**13**	**14**	**15**					
D	B	B	C	A					

EXPLANATORY ANSWERS

1. $P = \frac{90 \times 100}{6 \times 3} = ₹\ 500$

2. $\text{Rate} = \frac{1 \times 100}{100 \times \frac{1}{12}} = 12\%.$

3. Let principal = ₹ x; Amount = ₹ $2x$;
then $I = 2x - x = ₹\ x$

$\therefore\ R = \frac{x \times 100}{x \times 20} = 5\%$

Again, if principal = ₹ x;
Amount = ₹ $3x$; then $I = 3x - x = ₹\ 2x$

Hence, $T = \frac{2x \times 100}{x \times 5} = 40$ years

4. $\text{Rate} = \frac{40 \times 100}{500 \times 4} = 2\%$

5. Here, I = 2240 − 2000 = ₹ 240

$\therefore\ T = \frac{240 \times 100}{2000 \times 4} = 3$ years

6. Let, $R = T = x$; then

$\frac{25}{64}P = \frac{P \times x \times x}{100} \Rightarrow x^2 = \frac{25 \times 100}{64}$

$\therefore\ x = \frac{5 \times 10}{8} = \frac{25}{4};\ R = 6\frac{1}{4}\%$

7. Here, Simple interest for 2 years
= ₹ 1250 − ₹ 1150 = ₹ 100

$\therefore$ Simple interest for 3 years $= \frac{100 \times 3}{2} = ₹\ 150$

Hence, P = ₹ 1150 − ₹ 150 = ₹ 1000

$\therefore\ \text{Rate} = \frac{50 \times 100}{1000 \times 1} = 5\%$

8. Here, $I = \frac{892 \times 6 \times \frac{2}{3}}{100} = ₹\ 35.68$

9. $P = \frac{81 \times 100 \times 2}{6 \times 9} = ₹\ 300$

10. $I = \frac{1850 \times 3 \times 5}{100} = ₹\ 277.50$

$\therefore$ Amount = ₹ 1850 + ₹ 277.50
= ₹ 2127.50

11. $\frac{1250 \times R \times 3}{100} + \frac{1500 \times R \times 2}{100} = 258.75$

$\Rightarrow\ 6750\ R = 25875$

$\therefore\ R = \frac{25875}{6750} = \frac{23}{6} = 3\frac{5}{6}\%$

12. Here, $\frac{5000 \times R \times T}{100} = \frac{4000 \times (R+1) \times T}{100}$

$\Rightarrow\ 5R = 4R + 4\ \therefore\ R = 4\%$

13. Here, $\frac{500 \times R \times 4}{100} + \frac{600 \times R \times 3}{100} = 190$

$\Rightarrow\ 38R = 190$

$\therefore\ R = \frac{190}{38} = 5\%.$

14. Let annual instalment be ₹ x; then

$x + \frac{x \times 3 \times 5}{100} + x + \frac{x \times 2 \times 5}{100} + x + \frac{x \times 1 \times 5}{100} + x = 645 + \frac{645 \times 4 \times 5}{100}$

$\Rightarrow\ 4x + \frac{3x}{10} = 774 \Rightarrow \frac{43x}{10} = 774$

$\therefore\ x = \frac{774 \times 10}{43} = ₹\ 180$

15. Simple interest for 2 years
= ₹ 2050 − ₹ 1900 = ₹ 150
$\therefore$ Simple interest for 1 year

$= ₹\ \frac{150}{2} = ₹\ 75$

Since simple interest for 3 years
= ₹ 75 × 3 = ₹ 225

$\therefore$ Principal = ₹ 1900 − ₹ 225 = ₹ 1675

Hence, $\text{Rate} = \frac{75 \times 100}{1675 \times 1} = 4½\%$

Compound Interest

In business transaction if interest as it becomes due is not paid to the lender but is added on to the principal, the money is said to be lent at *compound interest* and the total sum owed after a given time is called the amount at compound interest for that time.

After a certain period, the difference between the amount and the original principal is called the compound Interest (C.I.).

Some Important Formulae :

Let Principal = P, Time = n years

Rate = r% p.a.

then, the amount,

(*a*) when interest is compounded annually:

then, $\text{Amount} = P\left(1+\frac{r}{100}\right)^n$

(*b*) when interest is compounded half yearly:

then, $\text{Amount} = P\left(1+\frac{r/2}{100}\right)^{2n}$

(*c*) when interest is compounded quarterly :

then, $\text{Amount} = P\left(1+\frac{r/4}{100}\right)^{4n}$

(*d*) when time is fraction of a year, say $4\frac{1}{3}$ years,

then, $\text{Amount} = P\left(1+\frac{r}{100}\right)^4 \times \left(1+\frac{\frac{1}{3}r}{100}\right)$

(*e*) when rates are r_1%, r_2% and r_3% for Ist, IInd and IIIrd year respectively; then,

$$\text{Amount} = P\left(1+\frac{r_1}{100}\right)\left(1+\frac{r_2}{100}\right)\left(1+\frac{r_3}{100}\right)$$

EXERCISE

1. What will be the compound interest on ₹ 8000 for 3 years at 5% p.a.?

A. ₹ 1361 B. ₹ 1261
C. ₹ 1260 D. ₹ 1250

2. What will be the amount if a sum of ₹ 2500 is invested for 1 year at 4% per annum compound interest, interest being compounded half-yearly?

A. ₹ 2625 B. ₹ 2601
C. ₹ 2830 D. ₹ 2901

3. Find the compound interest on ₹ 2560 for ½ year at 12½% per annum, interest payable quarterly.

A. ₹ 3720.50 B. ₹ 2722.50
C. ₹ 2752.50 D. ₹ 2250.50

4. After how many years will ₹ 3375 become ₹ 4096 at $6\frac{2}{3}$% per annum compound interest?

A. 4 years B. 2 years
C. 2½ years D. 3 years

5. A certain sum of money placed at compound interest amounts to ₹ 110 in 1 year and to ₹ 121 in 2 years. The rate of interest per annum is :

A. 5% B. 10%
C. 8% D. 4%

6. The present population of a city is 80,000. If the rate of growth is 5% per year, find its population after 3 years.

A. 88,100 B. 95,600
C. 92,610 D. 84,600

7. First year's interest on a sum of money placed at compound interest at the rate of 8% per annum is ₹ 72. What will be interest for the second year?

A. ₹ 77.76 B. ₹ 78.66
C. ₹ 85.66 D. ₹ 78.76

8. The difference between compound and simple interest on a certain sum of money for 2 years at 5% per annum is ₹ 21. Find the sum.

A. ₹ 7200 B. ₹ 8400
C. ₹ 9200 D. ₹ 8500

9. In how many years will a sum of ₹ 19200 placed at 10% per annum compound interest yield an interest of ₹ 4032?

A. 1½ years B. 2½ years
C. 2 years D. 3 years

10. The compound interest on a certain sum of money invested for 3 years at 5% per annum is ₹ 1891.50. What will be the simple interest on the same sum at the same rate for 2 years?

A. ₹ 1700 B. ₹ 1200
C. ₹ 1500 D. ₹ 2100

11. The simple interest on a sum of ₹ 4800 for 2 years is ₹ 768. What will be the compound interest on the same sum at the same rate and for the same period?

A. ₹ 798.72 B. ₹ 870.75
C. ₹ 920.69 D. ₹ 884.20

12. A sum of money lent out at a certain rate of simple interest amounts to ₹ 6600 in 2 years and to ₹ 6900 in 3 years. What will be the compound interest on the same sum of money if lent out at the same rate for 2 years?

A. ₹ 605 B. ₹ 715
C. ₹ 615 D. ₹ 595

13. If the first year's interest on a certain sum of money placed at 5% p.a. compound interest is ₹ 1200, what will be the interest for the third year?

A. ₹ 1220 B. ₹ 1323

C. ₹ 1423 D. ₹ 1330

14. If a certain sum of money placed at compound interest amounts to ₹ 960 in 3 years and to ₹ 1000 in 4 years, find the rate of compound interest.

A. $4\frac{1}{6}\%$ B. $5\frac{1}{6}\%$

C. $2\frac{1}{3}\%$ D. 3%

15. What would be the compound interest on ₹ 3200 at 25% per annum for 3 years?

A. ₹ 2050 B. ₹ 2775

C. ₹ 3050 D. ₹ 3180

ANSWERS

1	2	3	4	5	6	7	8	9	10
B	B	B	D	B	C	A	B	C	B
11	**12**	**13**	**14**	**15**					
A	C	B	A	C					

EXPLANATORY ANSWERS

1. ∴ $\text{C.I.} = 8000\left[\left(1+\frac{5}{100}\right)^3 - 1\right]$

$= 8000\left[\left(\frac{21}{20}\right)^3 - 1\right] = \frac{8000 \times 1261}{8000} = ₹\ 1261$

2. $A = 2500\left(1+\frac{2}{100}\right)^2 = 2500\left(\frac{51}{50}\right)^2 = \frac{2500 \times 51 \times 51}{50 \times 50}$

= ₹ 2601.

3. $\text{Amount} = 2560\left(1+\frac{25}{8 \times 100}\right)^2 = \frac{2560 \times 33 \times 33}{32 \times 32}$

= ₹ 2722.50

4. Here, $4096 = 3375\left(1+\frac{20}{3 \times 100}\right)^n$

$\Rightarrow \frac{4096}{3375} = \left(1+\frac{1}{15}\right)^n \Rightarrow \left(\frac{16}{15}\right)^3 = \left(\frac{16}{15}\right)^n$

∴ n = 3 years

5. Here, simple interest of ₹ 110 for 1 year

= 121 – 110 = ₹ 11

Hence, rate $= \frac{11 \times 100}{110 \times 1} = 10\%$

6. Population of the city after 3 years

$= 80{,}000\left(1+\frac{5}{100}\right)^3 = 80{,}000 \times \frac{21}{20} \times \frac{21}{20} \times \frac{21}{20} = 92610$

7. Second year's interest = 72 + 8% of 72

$= 72 + \frac{72 \times 8}{100} = 72 + 5.76 = ₹\ 77.76$

8. Here, $P\left[\left(1+\frac{5}{100}\right)^2 - 1\right] - \frac{P \times 5 \times 2}{100} = 21$

$\Rightarrow P\left[\frac{441}{400} - 1\right] - \frac{P}{10} = 21$

$\Rightarrow P\left[\frac{41}{400} - \frac{1}{10}\right] = 21 \Rightarrow P \times \frac{1}{400} = 21$

∴ $P = 21 \times 400 = ₹\ 8400$

9. Amount = ₹ 19200 + ₹ 4032 = ₹ 23232

Now, $23232 = 19200\left(1+\frac{10}{100}\right)^n$

$\Rightarrow \frac{23232}{19200} = \left(\frac{11}{10}\right)^n \Rightarrow \frac{121}{100} = \left(\frac{11}{10}\right)^n$

$\Rightarrow \left(\frac{11}{10}\right)^2 = \left(\frac{11}{10}\right)^n$

∴ $n = 2$ years

11. $\text{Rate} = \frac{768 \times 100}{4800 \times 2} = 8\%$

∴ $\text{C.I.} = 4800\left[\left(1+\frac{8}{100}\right)^2 - 1\right]$

$= 4800\left[\left(\frac{27}{25}\right)^2 - 1\right] = \frac{4800 \times 104}{625} = ₹\ 798.72$

13. Required interest

$= 1200\left(1+\frac{5}{100}\right)^2 = 1200 \times \frac{21}{20} \times \frac{21}{20} = ₹\ 1323$

14. Here, simple interest of ₹ 960 for 1 year

= 1000 – 960 = ₹ 40

Hence, Rate $= \frac{40 \times 100}{960 \times 1} = \frac{25}{6} = 4\frac{1}{6}\%$

15. Compound interest

$= 3200\left[\left(1+\frac{25}{100}\right)^3 - 1\right] = 3200\left[\left(\frac{5}{4}\right)^3 - 1\right]$

$= \frac{3200 \times 61}{64} = ₹\ 3050.$

●●●

3

Ratio and Proportion

RATIO

In ratio we compare two quantities of the same kind and consider what multiple, part or parts one is of the other. In comparing 8 with 4, observe that it is 2 times 4. This comparison can be represented as $8 \div 4$ or $\frac{8}{4}$.

Hence, *ratio is that relation between two numbers which is expressed by the fraction, the numerator is which is the measure of the first quantity and denominator is the measure of the second quantity.*

If the terms of a ratio be multiplied or divided by the same quantity the value of the ratio remains unaltered.

Thus, 3 : 4 is the same as 9 : 12 and 9 : 12 is the same as 3 : 4.

PROPORTION

The equality of two ratio is called proportion.

Consider the two ratios:

Ist ratio 2nd ratio

5 : 15 7 : 21

Since, 5 is one-third of 15 and 7 is one-third of 21, the two ratios are equal. The equality of two ratios is called proportion and the numbers 5, 15, and 7, 21 are said to be in **proportion.**

The proportion may be written as 5 : 15 : : 7 : 21 (5 is to 15 as 7 is to 21)

$\Rightarrow$ 5 : 15 = 7 : 21

$$\Rightarrow \quad \frac{5}{15} = \frac{7}{21}$$

The numbers 5, 15, 7 and 21 are called the terms. 5 is the first term, 15 the second, 7 the third, and 21 the fourth.

The first and fourth terms, *i.e.*, 5 and 21 are called extremes (end terms), and the second and the third terms, *i.e.*, 15 and 7 are called the **means** (middle terms), 21 is called the fourth proportional.

Some Important Facts:

1. If a and b are two quantities, then

(*a*) Duplicate ratio of $a : b = a^2 : b^2$

(*b*) Sub-duplicate ratio of $a : b = \sqrt{a} : \sqrt{b}$

(*c*) Triplicate ratio of $a : b = a^3 : b^3$

(*d*) Sub-triplicate ratio $a : b = \sqrt[3]{a} : \sqrt[3]{b}$

(*e*) Inverse or reciprocal ratio of $a : b = \frac{1}{a} : \frac{1}{b}$

(*f*) Third proportional to 'a' and 'b' $= \frac{b^2}{a}$

2. If A : B = $x : y$ and B : C = $p : q$, then

(*a*) $A : C = \frac{x \times p}{y \times q}$

(*b*) A : B : C = $px : py : qy$

3. In what *ratio* the two kinds of tea must be mixed together one at ₹ x per kg and another at ₹ y per kg, so that the mixture may cost ₹ z per kg?

$$\text{Ratio} = \frac{z - y}{x - z}$$

4. A grey hound persues a hare as takes J_1 leaps for every J_2 leaps of the hare. If K_1 leaps of the hound are equal to K_2 leaps of the hare, then the Ratio of speeds of the hound and hare is

$$\frac{J_2 \times K_1}{J_1 \times K_2}$$

5. The incomes of two persons are in the ratio of $a : b$ and their expenditure are in the ratio of $x : y$. If the saving of each person is ₹ s, then income of each is ₹ $\frac{as(y-x)}{ay-bx}$ and ₹ $\frac{bs(y-x)}{ay-bx}$ respectively.

6. In a mixture of z litre, the ratio of milk and water is $x : y$. If another p litres of water is added to the mixture, the ratio of milk and water in the resulting mixture $= \dfrac{xz}{yz + p(x+y)}$

7. There are four members a, b, c and d, then formula for

(a) What should be added to each of these numbers so that the remaining numbers may be proportional $= \dfrac{ad - bc}{(b+c) - (a+d)}$

(b) What should be subtracted from each of these numbers so that the remaining numbers may be proportional $= \dfrac{ad - bc}{(a+d) - (b+c)}$

8. In a mixture the ratio of milk and water is $a : b$. If in this mixture another K litre of water is added, then the ratio of milk and water in the resulting mixture becomes $a : m$. Then the quantity of milk in the original mixture $= \dfrac{ak}{m-b}$ and quantity of water $= \dfrac{bk}{m-b}$

EXERCISE

1. If A : B = 6 : 7 and B : C = 8 : 9, then A : B : C is:

A. 24 : 28 : 63 B. 48 : 28 : 63
C. 48 : 56 : 63 D. None of these

2. The sum of two numbers is 20 and their difference is $2\frac{1}{2}$. What is the ratio of the numbers?

A. 11 : 7 B. 9 : 11
C. 9 : 7 D. None of these

3. If 0.7 of one number is equal to 0.075 of another, what is the ratio of the two numbers?

A. 6 : 14 B. 3 : 28
C. 5 : 7 D. None of these

4. If 10% of x is the same as 20% of y, then $x : y$ is equal to :

A. 1 : 2 B. 2 : 1
C. 5 : 1 D. 10 : 1

5. Two numbers are in the ratio 3 : 5. If each number is increased by 10, the ratio becomes 5 : 7. The numbers are:

A. 3, 5 B. 7, 9
C. 13, 22 D. 15, 25

6. The mean proportional between 0.32 and 0.02 is:

A. 0.34 B. 0.3
C. 0.16 D. 0.08

7. The sum of three numbers is 98. If the ratio between the first and second be 2 : 3 and that between the second and third be 5 : 8, then what is the second number?

A. 20 B. 30
C. 10 D. 40

8. One man adds 3 litres of water to 12 litres of milk and another 4 litres of water to 10 litres of milk. What is the ratio of the strenghts of the milk in the two mixtures?

A. 15 : 25 B. 25 : 28
C. 28 : 25 D. None of these

9. ₹ 425 is divided among 4 men, 5 women and 6 boys such that the share of a man, a woman and a boy may be in the ratio of 9 : 8 : 4. What is the share of a woman?

A. ₹ 34 B. ₹ 24
C. ₹ 44 D. None of these

10. A vessel contains liquids P and Q in the ratio 5 : 3. If 6 litres of the mixture are removed and the same quantity of liquid q is added, the ratio becomes 3 : 5. What quantity does the vessel hold?

A. 40 litres B. 50 litres
C. 30 litres D. None of these

11. A bucket contains a mixture of two liquids P and Q in the proportion 7 : 5. If 9 litres of the mixture is replaced by 9 litres of liquid Q, then the ratio of the two liquid becomes 7 : 9. How much of the liquid P was there in the bucket?

A. 11 litres B. 21 litres
C. 31 litres D. None of these

12. Three glasses P, Q and R with their capacities in the ratio 2 : 3 : 4 are filled with a mixture of spirit and water. The ratio of spirit to water in P, Q and R is 1 : 5, 3 : 5 and 5 : 7 respectively. If the contents of these glasses are mixed together, what is the ratio of spirit to water in the mixture?

A. 14 : 27 B. 23 : 47
C. 25 : 47 D. None of these

13. A and B are two alloys of gold and copper prepared by mixing metals in proportions 7 : 2 and 7 : 11 respectively. If equal quantities of the alloys are melted to form a third alloy C, the proportion of gold and copper in C will be

A. 5 : 9 B. 5 : 7
C. 7 : 5 D. 9 : 5

14. Gold is 19 times as heavy as water and copper 9 times as heavy as water. The ratio in which these two metals be mixed so that the mixtures is 15 times as heavy as water is:

A. 1 : 2 B. 2 : 3
C. 3 : 2 D. 19 : 135

15. The contents of two vessels containing water and milk are in the ratio 1 : 2 and 2 : 5 are mixed in the ratio 1 : 4. The resulting mixture will have water and milk in the ratio:

A. 21 : 54
B. 31 : 74
C. 27 : 74
D. None of these

16. One year ago, the ratio between Mahesh and Suresh's salaries was 3 : 5. The ratio of their individual salaries of last year and present year are 2 : 3 and 4 : 5 respectively. If their total salaries for the present year are ₹ 4300, what is the present salary of Mahesh?
A. ₹ 1800
B. ₹ 1900
C. ₹ 1600
D. None of these

17. The ratio of P's and Q's income last year was 3 : 4. The ratio of their own incomes of last year and this year is 4 : 5 and 2 : 3 respectively. If the total sum of their present income is ₹ 4160. What is the present income of P?
A. ₹ 1500
B. ₹ 1400
C. ₹ 1600
D. None of these

18. The monthly salary of A, B, C is in the proportion of 2 : 3 ; 5. If C's monthly salary is ₹ 1200 more than that of A, then B's annual salary is:
A. ₹ 14400
B. ₹ 24000
C. ₹ 1200
D. ₹ 2000

19. ₹ 1050 is divided among P, Q and R. The share of P is $\frac{2}{5}$ of the combined share of Q and R. Thus P gets:
A. ₹ 200
B. ₹ 300
C. ₹ 400
D. ₹ 420

20. The ratio between Sumit's and Prakash's age at present is 2 : 3. Sumit is 6 years younger than Prakash. The ratio of Sumit's age to Prakash's age after 6 years will be:
A. 1 : 2
B. 2 : 3
C. 3 : 4
D. 3 : 8

ANSWERS

1	2	3	4	5	6	7	8	9	10
C	C	B	B	D	D	B	C	A	A
11	**12**	**13**	**14**	**15**	**16**	**17**	**18**	**19**	**20**
B	C	C	C	B	A	C	C	B	C

EXPLANATORY ANSWERS

1. A : B = 6 : 7
B : C = 8 : 9
∴ A : B : C = 6 × 8 : 7 × 8 : 7 × 9 = 48 : 56 : 63

2. Ratio $= \dfrac{20+\frac{5}{2}}{20-\frac{5}{2}} = \dfrac{22.5}{17.5} = \dfrac{225}{175} = \dfrac{9}{7} = 9:7$

3. We have, $0.7x = 0.075\,y$

$$\frac{x}{y} = \frac{0.075}{0.7} = \frac{75}{700} = \frac{3}{28} = 3:28$$

4. 10% of x = 20% of y

$$\Rightarrow \frac{10}{100}x = \frac{20}{100}y$$

$$\therefore \frac{x}{10} = \frac{y}{5} \Rightarrow \frac{x}{y} = \frac{10}{5} = \frac{2}{1} \Rightarrow x:y = 2:1$$

5. Let the number be $3x$ and $5x$.

Then, $\dfrac{3x+10}{5x+10} = \dfrac{5}{7} \Rightarrow 7(3x+10) = 5(5x+10)$

$\Rightarrow 21x + 70 = 25x + 50 \Rightarrow 4x = 20 \Rightarrow x = 5$

So, the numbers are 15, 25.

6. Mean proportional $= \sqrt{0.32 \times 0.02} = \sqrt{0.0064} = 0.08$

7. The ratio among the three numbers is
2 : 3
5 : 8
and 10 : 15 : 24

∴ The second number $= \dfrac{98}{10+15+24} \times 15 = 30$

8. Strength of milk in the first mixture $= \dfrac{12}{12+3} = \dfrac{12}{15}$

Strength of milk in the second mixture $= \dfrac{10}{10+4} = \dfrac{10}{14}$

∴ The ratio of their strengths $= \dfrac{12}{15} : \dfrac{10}{14}$

$= 12 \times 14 : 15 \times 10 = 28 : 25$

9. The ratio of shares of group of men, women and boys
$= 9 \times 4 : 8 \times 5 : 4 \times 6 = 9 : 10 : 6$

∴ Share of 5 women $= \dfrac{425}{9+10+6} \times 10 =$ ₹ 170

∴ Share of 1 woman $= \dfrac{170}{5} =$ ₹ 34

10. Let the vessel contains $5x$ litres and $3x$ litres of liquid P and Q respectively. The removed quantity contains

$\dfrac{16}{5+3} \times 5 = 10$ litres of P

and 16 – 10 = 6 litres of Q.

Now, $(5x - 10) : (3x - 6 + 16) = 3 : 5$

$\Rightarrow \dfrac{5x-10}{3x+10} = \dfrac{3}{5} \Rightarrow 25x - 50 = 9x + 30$

$\Rightarrow 16x = 80 \Rightarrow x = 5$

∴ Vessel contains $8x = 8 \times 5 = 40$ litres.

11. Let the two liquids P and Q are $7x$ litres and $5x$ litres repectively.

Now, when 9 litres of mixture are taken out, P remains

$$7x - 9\left(\frac{7}{7+5}\right) = 7x - \frac{9 \times 7}{12} = \left(7x - \frac{21}{4}\right) \text{ litres}$$

and Q remains

$$5x - 9\left(\frac{5}{7+5}\right) = 5x - \frac{9 \times 5}{12} = \left(5x - \frac{15}{4}\right) \text{ litres}$$

Now, when 9 litres of liquid Q are added,

$$\left(7x - \frac{21}{4}\right) : \left(5x - \frac{15}{4} + 9\right) = 7 : 9$$

$$\Rightarrow \frac{7x - \frac{21}{4}}{5x - \frac{15}{4} + 9} = \frac{7}{9}$$

$$\Rightarrow 63x - \frac{189}{4} = 35x + \frac{147}{4}$$

$$\Rightarrow 28x = \frac{189}{4} + \frac{147}{4} = \frac{336}{4} = 84$$

$$\Rightarrow x = \frac{84}{28} = 3 \Rightarrow 7x = 7 \times 3 = 21 \text{ litres.}$$

12. P : Q : R

2 : 3 : 4

Spirit : Water = 1 : 5, 3 : 5 and 5 : 7

When they are mixed, the ratio of spirit to water

$$= \left(2\times\frac{1}{1+5} + 3\times\frac{3}{3+5} + 4\times\frac{5}{5+7}\right) : \left(2\times\frac{5}{1+5} + 3\times\frac{5}{3+5} + 4\times\frac{7}{5+7}\right)$$

$$= \left(\frac{1}{3} + \frac{9}{8} + \frac{5}{3}\right) : \left(\frac{5}{3} + \frac{15}{8} + \frac{7}{3}\right) = \frac{25}{8} : \frac{47}{8} = 25 : 47$$

13. Gold in C $= \left(\frac{7}{9} + \frac{7}{18}\right) = \frac{21}{18} = \frac{7}{6}$

Copper in C $= \left(\frac{2}{9} + \frac{11}{18}\right) = \frac{15}{18} = \frac{5}{6}$

$\therefore$ Gold : Copper $= \frac{7}{6} : \frac{5}{6} = 7 : 5$

14. Let 1 gm of gold be mixed with x gm of copper to give $(1 + x)$ gm of mixture.

Now, $1G = 19w$

and $1C = 9w$

and mixture $= 15w$

Now, 1 gm gold + x gm copper = $(1 + x)$ gm mixture

$\therefore 19w + 9w \times x = (1 + x) \times 15w$

Thus, $4w = 6wx$

$$\Rightarrow x = \frac{4w}{6w} = \frac{4}{6} = \frac{2}{3}$$

So, the required ratio is $1 : \frac{2}{3}$, *i.e.*, 3 : 2.

15.

	Water	***Milk***
Vessel I	$\frac{1}{3}$	$\frac{2}{3}$
Vessel II	$\frac{2}{7}$	$\frac{5}{7}$

From vessel I, $\frac{1}{5}$ is taken and from vessel II, $\frac{4}{5}$ is taken. Therefore, the ratio of water to milk in the new vessel

$$= \left(\frac{1}{3}\times\frac{1}{5} + \frac{2}{7}\times\frac{4}{5}\right) : \left(\frac{2}{3}\times\frac{1}{5} + \frac{5}{7}\times\frac{4}{5}\right)$$

$$= \left(\frac{1}{15} + \frac{8}{35}\right) : \left(\frac{2}{15} + \frac{20}{35}\right) = \frac{31}{105} : \frac{74}{105} = 31 : 74$$

16. The ratio of Mahesh's salary for the two years = 2 : 3

The ratio of Suresh's salary for the two years = 4 : 5

We have also given that the ratio of their salary during the last year = 3 : 5

Now, we change the antecedents (2 and 4) of the first two ratios so that the antecedents in the first becomes 3 (antecedent of the third ratio) and the antecedent in the second becomes 5 (consequent of the third ratio).

Thus, $2 : 3 = 3 : \frac{9}{2}$ and $4 : 5 = 4\left(\frac{5}{4}\right) : 5\left(\frac{5}{4}\right) = 5 : \frac{25}{4}$

Now, it is clear that the ratio of their salaries for the present year is $\frac{9}{2} : \frac{25}{4} = 18 : 25$

$\therefore$ The present salary of Mahesh

$$= \frac{4300}{18+25} \times 18 = ₹\ 1800$$

17. The ratio of present incomes

$$= 3\times\frac{5}{4} : 4\times\frac{3}{2} = \frac{15}{4} : \frac{12}{2} = 30 : 48 = 5 : 8$$

$\therefore$ P's present income $= \frac{4160}{5+8} \times 5 = ₹\ 1600$

18. Let the monthly salary of A, B, C be $2x$, $3x$ and $5x$

Then, $5x - 2x = 1200$

or, $3x = 1200$

$\therefore$ $x = 400$

B's monthly salary = $3x = 3 \times 400 =$ ₹ 1200

19. P : (Q + R) = 2 : 5

$\therefore$ P's share = ₹ $\left(1050 \times \frac{2}{7}\right)$ = ₹ 300

20. Let their ages be $2x$ and $3x$ years.

$\Rightarrow$ $3x - 2x = 6 \Rightarrow x = 6$

Sumit's age = 12 years

Prakash's age = 18 years

After 6 years, Sumit's age = 18 years and Prakash's age = 24 years

$\therefore$ Ratio of their ages = 18 : 24 = 3 : 4

●●●

4

Algebra

Square Roots

☛ Points To Remember

- A number n is a perfect square number, if $n = m^2$
- A perfect square number is never negative.
- A square number never ends in 2, 3, 7 or 8.
- The number of zeros at the end of a perfect square is even.
- The square of an even number is even.
- The square of an odd number is odd.
- There are no natural number p and q such that $p^2 = 2q^2$.
- A number m is a square root of n, if $n = m \times m = m^2$. Positive square root of n is written as $\sqrt{n}$.
- If p and q are perfect squares ($q \neq 0$), then
  (*i*) $\sqrt{p \times q} = \sqrt{p} \times \sqrt{q}$

  (*ii*) $\sqrt{\dfrac{p}{q}} = \dfrac{\sqrt{p}}{\sqrt{q}}$
- A perfect squares leaves remainder 0 or 1 on division by 3.
  The following table gives the possible remainders for some other prime divisors.

Divisor	Possible Remainders
3	0, 1
5	0, 1, 4
7	0, 1, 2, 4
11	0, 1, 3, 4, 5, 9
13	0, 1, 3, 4, 9, 10, 12

- The unit's digit of the square of a natural number is the unit's digit of the square of the digit at unit's place of the given natural number.

Unit's digit of the number	Unit's digit of the square of the number
0	0
1 or 9	1
2 or 8	4
3 or 7	9
4 or 6	6
5	5

- For every natural number n,
  $(n + 1)^2 - n^2 = (n + 1) + n$
  e.g.; $9^2 - 8^2 = 9 + 8 = 17$
  $19^2 - 18^2 = 19 + 18 = 37$
- The square of a natural number n is equal to the sum of first n odd natural numbers.
  e.g.; $2^2 = 1 + 3$
  $4^2 = 1 + 3 + 5 + 7 = 16$
  n^2 = Sum of first n odd natural numbers.
- A triplet (m, n, p) of three natural numbers m, n and p is called a pythagorean triplet if $m^2 + n^2 = p^2$
- The square root of a perfect square number can be obtained by :
  (*i*) the prime factorization. (*ii*) the division method.
- If n is not a perfect square, then $\sqrt{n}$ is not a rational number.
- Squares of natural numbers having all digits 1 have a following pattern:
  $1^2 = 1$
  $11^2 = 1\,\mathbf{2}\,1$
  $111^2 = 1\,2\,\mathbf{3}\,2\,1$
  $1111^2 = 1\,2\,3\,\mathbf{4}\,3\,2\,1$

$11111^2 = 1\,2\,3\,4\,\mathbf{5}\,4\,3\,2\,1$

$111111^2 = 1\,2\,3\,4\,5\,\mathbf{6}\,5\,4\,3\,2\,1$

⋮

$111111111^2 = 1\,2\,3\,4\,5\,6\,7\,8\,\mathbf{9}\,8\,7\,6\,5\,4\,3\,2\,1$

In this pattern the sum of the digits of every number on the right hand side is a perfect square at given below:

$1 + 2 + 1 = 4 = 2^2$

$1 + 2 + 3 + 2 + 1 = 9 = 3^2$

$1 + 2 + 3 + 4 + 3 + 2 + 1 = 16 = 4^2$

. . . .

$1 + 2 + 3 + 4 + 5 + 6 + 7 + 8 + 9 + 8 + 7 + 6 + 5 + 4 + 3 + 2 + 1 = 81 = 9^2.$

- Observe the following pattern

$11^2 = 121$

$101^2 = 10201$

$1001^2 = 1002001$

$10001^2 = 100020001$

- Observe the following pattern

$11^2 = 121$

$101^2 = 10201$

$10101^2 = 102030201$

$1010101^2 = 1020304030201$

$101010101^2 = 10203040504030201$

- **Short Cut Method to find Squares Column Method**

Using $(a + b)^2 = a^2 + 2ab + b^2$.

Make three columns: What is square of 86

$a = 8, b = 6$

Step	Column I (a^2)	Column II $2ab$	Column III b^2
I	$(8)^2 = 64$	$2 \times 8 \times 6 = 96$	$(6)^2 = 36$
II	64	96 + 3 99	36
III	64 + 9 **73**	96 + 3 99	**36**

The bold digits give the required square $86^2 = 7396$.

Square Root

Square root of a given number is that number which is multiplied by itself is equal to the given number. For example, square root of 81 is 9 because 92 = 9 × 9 = 81.

Methods of Finding the square root

(*a*) **Prime Factorization Method**

(*i*) Prime Factorization Method

(*ii*) Group the Factors in Paris

(*iii*) Take one number from each pair of factors and then multiply them together.

Example: Find the square root of 4761?

Solution: $4761 = \underbrace{23 \times 23} \times \underbrace{3 \times 3}$

$\therefore \sqrt{4761} = 23 \times 3 = 69.$

(*b*) **Method of Division:** This method is used when the number is large and the factors cannot be easily determined.

Example: Find the square root of 226576?

Solution:

```
         476
  4    226516
        16
 87      665
  7      609
946      5676
  6      5676
           ×
```

$\sqrt[2]{226576} = 476.$

EXERCISE

1. $\sqrt{53824} = ?$

A. 202 B. 232

C. 242 D. 332

2. The value of $\sqrt{10+\sqrt{25+\sqrt{108+\sqrt{154+\sqrt{255}}}}}$ is:

A. 4 B. 6

C. 8 D. 10

3. Evaluate : $\sqrt{41-\sqrt{21+\sqrt{19-\sqrt{9}}}}$.

A. 3 B. 5

C. 6 D. 6.4

4. $\left(\frac{\sqrt{625}}{11} \times \frac{14}{\sqrt{25}} \times \frac{11}{\sqrt{196}}\right)$ is equal to:

A. 5

B. 6

C. 8

D. 11

5. If $x * y = x + y + \sqrt{xy}$, the value of 6*24 is:

A. 41 B. 42

C. 43 D. 44

6. $\sqrt{\frac{25}{81}-\frac{1}{9}} = ?$

A. $\frac{2}{3}$ B. $\frac{4}{9}$

C. $\frac{16}{81}$ D. $\frac{25}{81}$

7. The value of $\sqrt{0.01}+\sqrt{0.81}+\sqrt{1.21}+\sqrt{0.0009}$ is:

A. 2.03 B. 2.1

C. 2.11 D. 2.13

8. If $\sqrt{18225} = 135$, then the value of

$\left(\sqrt{182.25}+\sqrt{1.8225}+\sqrt{0.018225}+\sqrt{0.00018225}\right)$ is:

A. 1.49985 B. 14.9985

C. 149.985 D. 1499.85

9. If $\sqrt{3^n} = 729$, then the value of n is:

A. 6 B. 8

C. 10 D. 12

10. If $\sqrt{1+\frac{x}{169}}=\frac{14}{13}$, then x is equal to:

A. 1 B. 13

C. 27 D. None of these

11. If $\sqrt{1+\frac{55}{729}}=1+\frac{x}{27}$, then the value of x is:

A. 1 B. 3

C. 5 D. 7

12. The value of $\frac{\sqrt{80}-\sqrt{112}}{\sqrt{45}-\sqrt{63}}$ is:

A. $\frac{3}{4}$ B. $1\frac{1}{3}$

C. $1\frac{7}{9}$ D. $1\frac{3}{4}$

13. Given $\sqrt{2}=1.414$. The value of

$\sqrt{8}+2\sqrt{32}-3\sqrt{128}+4\sqrt{50}$ is:

A. 8.426 B. 8.484

C. 8.526 D. 8.876

14. $\sqrt{\frac{0.081\times0.324\times4.624}{1.5625\times0.0289\times72.9\times64}}$ is equal to:

A. 0.024 B. 0.24

C. 2.4 D. 24

15. The value of $\sqrt{\frac{(0.03)^2+(0.21)^2+(0.065)^2}{(0.003)^2+(0.021)^2+(0.0065)^2}}$ is:

A. 0.1 B. 10

C. 10^2 D. 10^3

16. The square root of $\left(7+3\sqrt{5}\right)\left(7-3\sqrt{5}\right)$ is:

A. $\sqrt{5}$ B. 2

C. 4 D. $3\sqrt{5}$

17. $\left(\sqrt{3}-\frac{1}{\sqrt{3}}\right)^2$ simplifies to:

A. $\frac{3}{4}$ B. $\frac{4}{\sqrt{3}}$

C. $\frac{4}{3}$ D. None of these

18. $\left(\sqrt{2}+\frac{1}{\sqrt{2}}\right)^2$ is equal to :

A. $2\frac{1}{2}$ B. $3\frac{1}{2}$

C. $4\frac{1}{2}$ D. $5\frac{1}{2}$

19. If $3a = 4b = 6c$ and $a+b+c = 27\sqrt{29}$, then $\sqrt{a^2+b^2+c^2}$ is:

A. $3\sqrt{29}$

B. 81

C. 87

D. None of these

20. The square root of $0.\overline{4}$ is:

A. $0.\overline{6}$ B. $0.\overline{7}$

C. $0.\overline{8}$ D. $0.\overline{9}$

ANSWERS

1	2	3	4	5	6	7	8	9	10
B	A	C	A	B	B	D	B	D	C
11	**12**	**13**	**14**	**15**	**16**	**17**	**18**	**19**	**20**
A	B	B	A	B	B	C	C	C	A

EXPLANATORY ANSWERS

1.

```
  2 | 53824 (232
    | 4
 43 | 138
    | 129
462 |  924
    |  924
    |   ×
```

$\therefore \sqrt{53824} = 232.$

2. Given exp. = $\sqrt{10+\sqrt{25+\sqrt{108+\sqrt{154+15}}}}$

$= \sqrt{10+\sqrt{25+\sqrt{108+\sqrt{169}}}}$

$= \sqrt{10+\sqrt{25+\sqrt{108+13}}} = \sqrt{10+\sqrt{25+\sqrt{121}}}$

$= \sqrt{10+\sqrt{25+11}} = \sqrt{10+\sqrt{36}}$

$= \sqrt{10+6} = \sqrt{16} = 4$

3. Given exp. = $\sqrt{41-\sqrt{21+\sqrt{19-3}}}$

$= \sqrt{41-\sqrt{21+\sqrt{16}}} = \sqrt{41-\sqrt{21+4}}$

$= \sqrt{41-\sqrt{25}} = \sqrt{41-5} = \sqrt{36} = 6$

4. Given exp. = $\frac{25}{11}\times\frac{14}{5}\times\frac{11}{14} = 5$

5. $6*24 = 6 + 24 + \sqrt{6\times24} = 30+\sqrt{144} = 30+12 = 42$

6. $\sqrt{\frac{25}{81}-\frac{1}{9}} = \sqrt{\frac{25-9}{81}} = \sqrt{\frac{16}{81}} = \frac{\sqrt{16}}{\sqrt{81}} = \frac{4}{9}$

7. Given exp.

$= \sqrt{\frac{1}{100}}+\sqrt{\frac{81}{100}}+\sqrt{\frac{121}{100}}+\sqrt{\frac{9}{10000}}$

$= \frac{1}{10}+\frac{9}{10}+\frac{11}{10}+\frac{3}{100}$

$= 0.1 + 0.9 + 1.1 + 0.03 = 2.13$

8. Given exp.

$= \sqrt{\frac{18225}{10^2}}+\sqrt{\frac{18225}{10^4}}+\sqrt{\frac{18225}{10^6}}+\sqrt{\frac{18225}{10^8}}$

$= \sqrt{\frac{18225}{10}}+\sqrt{\frac{18225}{10^2}}+\sqrt{\frac{18225}{10^3}}+\sqrt{\frac{18225}{10^4}}$

$= \frac{135}{10}+\frac{135}{100}+\frac{135}{1000}+\frac{135}{10000}$

$= 13.5 + 1.35 + 0.135 + 0.0135 = 14.9985$

9. $\sqrt{3^n} = 729 = 3^6$

$\Leftrightarrow \left(\sqrt{3^n}\right)^2 = (3^6)^2$

$\Leftrightarrow 3^n = 3^{12}$

$\Leftrightarrow n = 12$

10. $\sqrt{1+\frac{x}{169}} = \frac{14}{13} \Rightarrow 1+\frac{x}{169} = \frac{196}{169}$

$\Rightarrow \frac{x}{169} = \left(\frac{196}{169}-1\right) = \frac{27}{169}$

$\Rightarrow x = 27.$

11. $\sqrt{1+\frac{55}{729}} = 1+\frac{x}{27}$

$\Rightarrow \sqrt{\frac{784}{729}} = \frac{27+x}{27}$

$\Rightarrow \frac{28}{27} = \frac{27+x}{27}$

$\Rightarrow 27 + x = 28 \Rightarrow x = 1$

12. $\frac{\sqrt{80}-\sqrt{112}}{\sqrt{45}-\sqrt{63}} = \frac{\sqrt{16\times5}-\sqrt{16\times7}}{\sqrt{9\times5}-\sqrt{9\times7}}$

$= \frac{4\sqrt{5}-4\sqrt{7}}{3\sqrt{5}-3\sqrt{7}} = \frac{4\left(\sqrt{5}-\sqrt{7}\right)}{3\left(\sqrt{5}-\sqrt{7}\right)} = \frac{4}{3} = 1\frac{1}{3}$

13. Given exp.

$= \sqrt{4\times2}+2\sqrt{16\times2}-3\sqrt{64\times2}+4\sqrt{25\times2}$

$= 2\sqrt{2}+8\sqrt{2}-24\sqrt{2}+20\sqrt{2}$

$= 6\sqrt{2} = 6 \times 1.414 = 8.484$

14. Given exp. = $\sqrt{\frac{81\times324\times4624}{15625\times289\times729\times64}}$

$= \frac{9\times18\times68}{125\times17\times27\times8} = \frac{3}{125} = 0.024$

15. Given exp. = $\sqrt{\frac{(0.03)^2+(0.21)^2+(0.065)^2}{\left(\frac{0.03}{10}\right)^2+\left(\frac{0.21}{10}\right)^2+\left(\frac{0.065}{10}\right)^2}}$

$= \sqrt{\frac{100\ [(0.03)^2+(0.21)^2+(0.065)^2]}{(0.03)^2+(0.21)^2+(0.065)^2}}$

$= \sqrt{100} = 10$

16. $\sqrt{(7+3\sqrt{5})(7-3\sqrt{5})} = \sqrt{(7)^2-(3\sqrt{5})^2}$

$= \sqrt{49-45} = \sqrt{4} = 2$

17. $\left(\sqrt{3}-\frac{1}{\sqrt{3}}\right)^2 = \left(\sqrt{3}\right)^2 + \left(\frac{1}{\sqrt{3}}\right)^2 - 2\times\sqrt{3}\times\frac{1}{\sqrt{3}}$

$= 3+\frac{1}{3}-2 = 1+\frac{1}{3} = \frac{4}{3}$

18. $\left(\sqrt{2}+\frac{1}{\sqrt{2}}\right)^2 = \left(\sqrt{2}\right)^2 + \left(\frac{1}{\sqrt{2}}\right)^2 + 2\times\sqrt{2}\times\frac{1}{\sqrt{2}}$

$= 2+\frac{1}{2}+2 = 4+\frac{1}{2} = 4\frac{1}{2}$

19. $4b = 6c \Rightarrow b = \frac{3}{2}c$ and $3a = 4b$

$\Rightarrow \quad a = \frac{4}{3}b = \frac{4}{3}\left(\frac{3}{2}c\right) = 2c$

$a + b + c = 27\sqrt{29}$

$2c+\frac{3}{2}c+c = 27\sqrt{29}$

$\Rightarrow \quad \frac{9}{2}c = 27\sqrt{29}$

$\Rightarrow \quad c = 6\sqrt{29}$

$\therefore \sqrt{a^2+b^2+c^2}$

$= \sqrt{(a+b+c)-2(ab+bc+ca)}$

$= \sqrt{\left(27\sqrt{29}\right)^2 - 2\left(2c\times\frac{3}{2}c+\frac{3}{2}c\times c+c\times 2c\right)}$

$= \sqrt{(729\times 29)-2\left(3c^2+\frac{3}{2}c^2+2c^2\right)}$

$= \sqrt{(729\times 29)-2\times\frac{13}{2}c^2}$

$= \sqrt{(729\times 29)-13\times\left(6\sqrt{29}\right)^2}$

$= \sqrt{29(729-468)}$

$= \sqrt{29\times 261} = \sqrt{29\times 29\times 9}$

$= 29 \times 3 = 87$

20. $\sqrt{0.\overline{4}} = \sqrt{\frac{4}{9}} = \frac{2}{3} = 0.666.... = 0.\overline{6}$.

Basic Algebraic Identities of School Algebra & Elementary Surds

Algebric Identies

Some Important Formula

(*i*) $(a + b)^2 = a^2 + 2ab + b^2$

(*ii*) $(a - b)^2 = a^2 - 2ab + b^2$

(*iii*) $a^2 - b^2 = (a - b)(a + b)$

(*iv*) $(a + b + c)^2 = a^2 + b^2 + c^2 + 2ab + 2bc + 2ca$

(*v*) $(a + b - c)^2 = a^2 + b^2 + c^2 + 2ab - 2bc - 2ca$

(*vi*) $(a - b + c)^2 = a^2 + b^2 + c^2 - 2ab - 2bc + 2ca$

(*vii*) $(-a + b + c)^2 = a^2 + b^2 + c^2 - 2ab + 2bc - 2ca$

(*viii*) $(a + b)^3 = a^3 + b^3 + 3ab(a + b)$ or

$= a^3 + b^3 + 3a^2b + 3ab^2$

(*ix*) $(a - b)^3 = a^3 - b^3 - 3ab\,(a - b)$ or

$= a^3 - b^3 - 3a^2b + 3ab^2$

(*x*) $a^3 + b^3 = (a + b)\,(a^2 + b^2 - ab)$ or

$= (a + b)^3 - 3ab(a + b)$

(*xi*) $a^3 - b^3 = (a - b)\,(a^2 + b^2 + ab)$ or

$= (a - b)^3 + 3ab\,(a - b)$

(*xii*) $a^3 + b^3 + c^3 - 3abc$

$= (a + b + c)(a^2 + b^2 + c^2 - ab - bc - ca)$

If $a + b + c = 0$

$a^3 + b^3 + c^3 = 3abc$

(*xiii*) $(x + a)\,(x + b) = x^2 + (a + b)x + ab$

(*xiv*) $(a + b)^2 + (a - b)^2 = 2(a^2 + b^2)$

(*xv*) $(a + b)^2 - (a - b)^2 = 4ab$

(*xvi*) $(a + b)^3 + (a - b)^3 = 2(a^3 + 3ab^2)$

(*xvii*) $(a + b)^3 - (a - b)^3 = (2(b^3 + 3a^2b)$

(*xviii*) If $x+\frac{1}{x} = t$ Then, $x^2+\frac{1}{x^2} = t^2-2$

(*xix*) If $x-\frac{1}{x} = t$ Then, $x^2+\frac{1}{x^2} = t^2+2$

(*xx*) $x^3+\frac{1}{x^3} = \left(x+\frac{1}{x}\right)^3 - 3\left(x+\frac{1}{x}\right)$

(*xxi*) $x^2-\frac{1}{x^3} = \left(x-\frac{1}{x}\right)^3 + 3\left(x-\frac{1}{x}\right)$

(*xxii*) $x+\frac{1}{x} = \sqrt{x^2+\frac{1}{x^2}+2}$

(*xxiii*) $x-\frac{1}{x} = \sqrt{x^2+\frac{1}{x^2}-2}$

Factorization of Algebraic Expressions

Factorization : The process of writing an algebraic expression as the product of two or more algebraic expressions is called factorization.

Factors : The algebraic expressions that may be multiplied to obtain the given algebraic expressions are called factors of the given expression.

Factor Theorem : If $f(x)$ is completely divisible by $(x - a)$ then $f(a) = 0$, $(x - a)$ is called factor of $f(x)$, if and only if $f(a) = 0$

Remainder Theorem : If an expression $f(x)$ is divided by $(x - a)$ then the remainder is $f(a)$.

e.g., $f(x) = ax^3 + bx + cx + d$

$f(a) = a \cdot a^3 + b \cdot a + c \cdot a + d$ is known as remainder of the given polynomials.

Surds

Given a number, it is not always possible to find some whole number which when multiplied by itself will give the given number. In other words all given numbers are not perfect square numbers. For example, square root of 9, *i.e.,* $\sqrt{9}$ is 3, which is a whole number. But square root of 15, *i.e.,* $\sqrt{15}$ = 3.873, which is not a whole number.

Hence square roots of natural numbers which are not perfect squares are not rational numbers. These are irrational numbers and are called **Surds**.

For example, $\sqrt{3}$, $\sqrt{7}$, $2+\sqrt{11}$, $4+\sqrt{13}$ ..... etc. are Surds.

Given below are a few formulas which are quite helpful in solving the problems related to surds:

1. $\sqrt{a} \times \sqrt{a} = a$

2. $\sqrt{a} \times \sqrt{b} = \sqrt{ab}$

3. $\left(\sqrt{a}+\sqrt{b}\right)^2 = a + b + 2\sqrt{ab}$

4. $\left(\sqrt{a}-\sqrt{b}\right)^2 = a + b - 2\sqrt{ab}$

5. $x\sqrt{a} + x\sqrt{b} = x\left(\sqrt{a}+\sqrt{b}\right)$

6. $\dfrac{1}{\sqrt{a}+\sqrt{b}} = \dfrac{1}{\sqrt{a}+\sqrt{b}} \times \dfrac{\sqrt{a}-\sqrt{b}}{\sqrt{a}-\sqrt{b}} = \dfrac{\sqrt{a}-\sqrt{b}}{a-b}$

7. $\dfrac{1}{\sqrt{a}-\sqrt{b}} = \dfrac{1}{\sqrt{a}-\sqrt{b}} \times \dfrac{\sqrt{a}+\sqrt{b}}{\sqrt{a}+\sqrt{b}} = \dfrac{\sqrt{a}+\sqrt{b}}{a-b}$

8. $a + \sqrt{b} = c + \sqrt{d} \Rightarrow a = c$ and $b = d$

9. $\sqrt{2}$ = 1.41421, $\sqrt{3}$ = 1.73205, $\sqrt{5}$ = 2.23607, $\sqrt{6}$ = 2.4494 $\sqrt{7}$ = 2.64575, $\sqrt{8}$ = 2.82842, $\sqrt{10}$ = 3.16227, $\sqrt{11}$ = 3.31662

EXERCISE

1. $(28)^3 + (-15)^3 + (-13)^3 = ?$

A. 16380 B. 16250
C. 16420 D. 16280

2. If $x+\dfrac{1}{x} = 5$, What is the value of $x^3+\dfrac{1}{x^3}$:

A. 120 B. 210
C. 110 D. 105

3. If $x^2+\dfrac{1}{x^2} = 83$, what is the value of $x^3-\dfrac{1}{x^3} = ?$

A. 756 B. 754
C. 856 D. 932

4. $23^3 - 17^3 = ?$

A. 7254 B. 7153
C. 7271 D. 7154

5. If $x + \dfrac{1}{x} = 15$, then the value of $x^2 + \dfrac{1}{x^2}$ will be:

A. 228 B. 230
C. 323 D. 223

6. If $x = 12$ and $y = 4$, the value of $(x+y)^{x/y}$ will be:

A. 4096 B. 3896
C. 4196 D. 5086

7. If $x + y = 2z$, then the value of $\left(\dfrac{x}{x-z}+\dfrac{z}{y-z}\right)$ will be:

A. 1 B. 4
C. 3/2 D. 2

8. If $x + y + z = 0$, then the value of $\dfrac{(x+y)(y+z)(z+x)}{xyz}$ will be:

A. –3 B. –2
C. 0 D. –1

9. If $x + \dfrac{1}{x} = 3$, the value of $x^4 + \dfrac{1}{x^4}$ will be:

A. 49 B. 47
C. 37 D. 42

10. If $\left(x+\dfrac{1}{x}\right)^2 = 0$, then the value of $\left(x^2+\dfrac{1}{x^2}\right)$ will be:

A. 1 B. –1
C. 2 D. –2

11. If $\left(a+\dfrac{2}{a}\right) = 3$, then the value of $\left(a-\dfrac{2}{a}\right)$ will be:

A. ± 4 B. ± 5
C. ± 2 D. ± 1

12. If $\sqrt{a}+\frac{1}{\sqrt{a}} = 4$, then the value of $a^2 + \frac{1}{a^2}$ will be:

A. 194 B. 199
C. 178 D. 192

13. Factors of $x^2 - 25$ are:

A. $(x - 1)(x - 25)$
B. $(x + 25)(x - 1)$
C. $(x + 5)(x - 5)$
D. $(x - 5)(x - 5)$

14. Square of $\left(x-\frac{1}{x}\right)$ will be

A. $x^2 - 2 - \frac{1}{x^2}$ B. $x^2 - 2 + \frac{1}{x^2}$
C. $x^2 - 4 - \frac{1}{x^2}$ D. $x^2 - 2 + \frac{1}{x}$

15. Factors of $36 - 9x^2$ will be:

A. $(6 + 3x)(6 - 3x)$ B. $(3x - 6)(6 - 3x)$
C. $(3x + 6)(3x - 6)$ D. $(12x - 3x)(3 + 3x)$

ANSWERS

1	2	3	4	5	6	7	8	9	10
A	C	A	A	D	A	A	D	B	D
11	12	13	14	15					
D	A	C	B	A					

EXPLANATORY ANSWERS

1. Let $a = 28$, $b = -15$ and $c = -13$. Then

$$a + b + c = 28 - 15 - 13 = 0$$
$$a^3 + b^3 + c^3 = 3abc$$
$$(28)^3 + (-15)^3 + (-13)^3 = 3 \times 28 \times (-15) \times (-13) = 16380$$

2. $$x^3 + \frac{1}{x^3} = \left(x+\frac{1}{x}\right)^3 - 3\left(x+\frac{1}{x}\right)$$
$$= (5)^3 - 3 \times 5 = 125 - 15 = 110.$$

3. If $x^2 + \frac{1}{x^2} = 83$, what is the value of $x^3 - \frac{1}{x^3} = ?$

$$\left(x-\frac{1}{x}\right)^2 = x^2 + \frac{1}{x^2} - 2$$
$$x-\frac{1}{x} = \sqrt{83-2} = \sqrt{81}$$
$$x-\frac{1}{x} = 9$$
$$\therefore \left(x^3-\frac{1}{x^3}\right) = \left(x-\frac{1}{x}\right)^3 + 3\left(x-\frac{1}{x}\right)$$
$$= (9)^3 + 3 \times 9 = 729 + 27 = 756$$

4. $23^3 - 17^3 = (20 + 3)^3 - (20 - 3)^3 = 2(3^3 + 3 \times 20^2 \times 3)$

$[\because (a + b)^3 - (a - b)^3 = 2(b^3 + 3a^2b)]$

$= 2(27 + 3600) = 54 + 7200 = 7254$

5. $\because x + \frac{1}{x} = 15 \Rightarrow \left(x+\frac{1}{x}\right)^2 = (15)^2$

$$\Rightarrow x^2 + \frac{1}{x^2} + 2.x\frac{1}{x} = 225$$
$$\therefore x^2 + \frac{1}{x^2} = 225 - 2 = 223.$$

6. $(x+y)^{x/y} = (12+4)^{12/4} = (16)^3 = 4096.$

$[\because x = 12, y = 4]$

7. $\because x + y = 2z \Rightarrow x - z = z - y = -(y - z)$

$$\therefore \frac{x}{x-z} + \frac{z}{y-z} = \frac{x}{-(y-z)} + \frac{z}{y-z} = \frac{z-x}{y-z} = 1.$$

$[\because x - z = z - y]$

8. $\because$ $x + y + z = 0 \Rightarrow x + y = -z$

$x + y + z = 0 \Rightarrow y + z = -x$

and $x + y + z = 0 \Rightarrow z + x = -y$

$$\therefore \frac{(x+y)(y+z)(z+x)}{xyz} = \frac{(-z)(-x)(-y)}{xyz} = -1.$$

9. $\because x + \frac{1}{x} = 3 \Rightarrow \left(x+\frac{1}{x}\right)^2 = (3)^2$

$$\Rightarrow x^2 + \frac{1}{x^2} + 2.x.\frac{1}{x} = 9$$
$$\Rightarrow x^2 + \frac{1}{x^2} = 9 - 2 = 7$$
$$\because x^2 + \frac{1}{x^2} = 7 \Rightarrow \left(x^2+\frac{1}{x^2}\right)^2 = (7)^2$$
$$\Rightarrow x^4 + \frac{1}{x^4} + 2.x^2.\frac{1}{x^2} = 49$$
$$\therefore x^4 + \frac{1}{x^4} = 49 - 2 = 47.$$

10. $\left(x+\frac{1}{x}\right)^2 = 0 \Rightarrow x^2 + \frac{1}{x^2} + 2x.\frac{1}{x} = 0$

$$\Rightarrow x^2 + \frac{1}{x^2} = -2.$$

11. $\because \quad \left(a-\frac{2}{a}\right)^2 = \left(a+\frac{2}{a}\right)^2 - 4.a.\frac{2}{a} = (3)^2 - 8 = 9 - 8 = 1$

$\therefore \quad \left(a-\frac{2}{a}\right) = \pm\sqrt{1} = \pm 1.$

12. $\because \quad \sqrt{a}+\frac{1}{\sqrt{a}} = 4 \Rightarrow \left(\sqrt{a}+\frac{1}{\sqrt{a}}\right)^2 = (4)^2$

$\Rightarrow a + \frac{1}{a} + 2.\sqrt{a}.\frac{1}{\sqrt{a}} = 16 \because \left(a+\frac{1}{a}\right) = 14$

$\Rightarrow \left(a+\frac{1}{a}\right)^2 = (14)^2 \Rightarrow a^2 + \frac{1}{a^2} + 2.a.\frac{1}{a} = 196$

$\therefore \quad a^2 + \frac{1}{a^2} = 196 - 2 = 194.$

13. $x^2 - 25 = (x)^2 - (5)^2$,
[which is of the form $a^2 - b^2$]
$= (x + 5)(x - 5).$

14. According to question:

Square of $\left(x-\frac{1}{x}\right) = \left(x-\frac{1}{x}\right)^2$

$= x^2 - 2.x.\frac{1}{x} + \left(\frac{1}{x}\right)^2$

$= x^2 - 2 + \frac{1}{x^2}.$

15. $36 - 9x^2 = (6)^2 - (3x)^2$ [which is of the form $a^2 - b^2$]
$= (6 + 3x)(6 - 3x).$

Graphs of Linear Equations

Linear Equation in One Variable

Definition: A linear equation in one variable is an equation of the form $ax + b = 0$ or, $ax = c$ where, a, b, c are real numbers, $a \neq 0$ and x is a variable. Its graph is a straight line.

(*i*) If equation is on X-axis, then Y = 0

(*ii*) If equation is on Y-axis, then X = 0

Linear Equation in Two Variables

Definition: An equation of the form $ax + by + c = 0$ or, $ax + by = c$ where, a, b, c are real numbers, $a \neq 0$, $b \neq 0$ and x, y are variables, is called a linear equation in two variables.

For example: (*i*) $2x + 3y = 12$ (*ii*) $x + 2y = 8$

The System of Equations

$a_1x + b_1y + c_1 = 0$ and $a_2x + b_2y + c_2 = 0$ may be either unique solution or no solution or infinitely many solutions.

Unique solution is known as consistent or not parallel. No solution is known as inconsistent or parallel, while many solutions are known as coincident or dependent.

(*a*) **For unique solution:** $\frac{a_1}{a_2} \neq \frac{b_1}{b_2}$

(*b*) **For no solution:** $\frac{a_1}{a_2} = \frac{b_1}{b_2} \neq \frac{c_1}{c_2}$

(*c*) **For many solutions:** $\frac{a_1}{a_2} = \frac{b_1}{b_2} = \frac{c_1}{c_2}$

Graph of linear equations

Graph of a linear equation in two variables x and y *i.e.*, the graph of the equation of the form

$ax + by + c = 0, a \neq 0, b \neq 0$

we consider the equation,

$2x + y = 6$

then, $y = 6 - 2x$

We find different values of this equation

x	0	1	2	3
y	6	4	2	0

Now, we plot these points (x, y) on a graph paper and then join these points

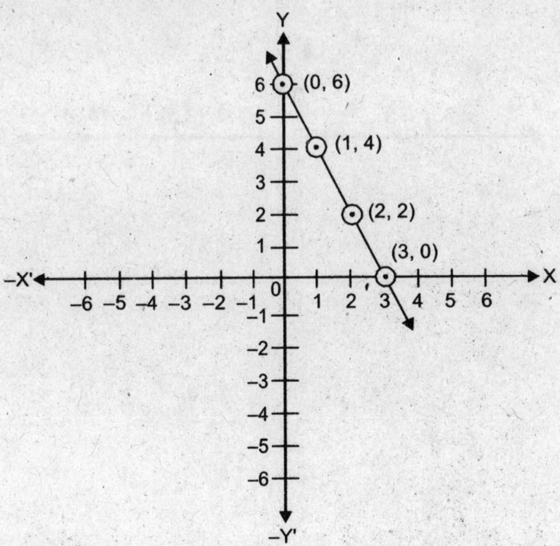

Hence, the line l is called the graph of the equation

$2x + y = 6$

Example 1: Draw the graph:

(*i*) $x = 2$, (*ii*) $y = 3$, (*iii*) $y = 0$

Solution: (*i*) The given equation, $x = 2$ does not contain y

Table of values

x	2	2	2	fixed
y	1	3	4	any value

ploting the points (2, 1), (2, 3) and (2, 4) and joining them

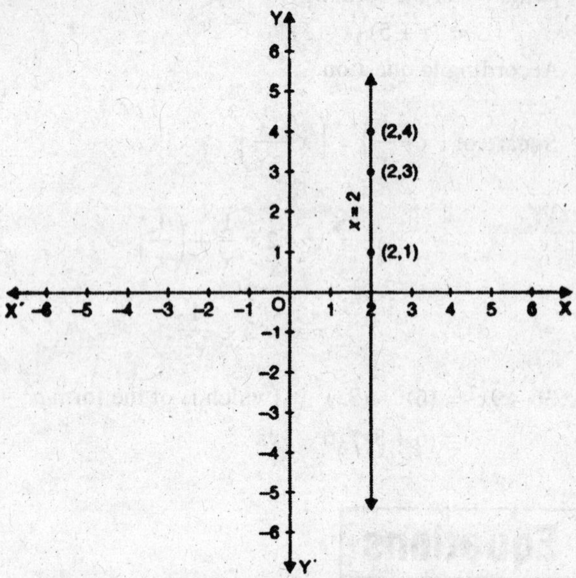

Hence, the graph of the given equation is a line parallel to y-axis

(*ii*) The given equation $y = 3$ does not contain x

Table of values

x	1	2	4	any value
y	3	3	3	fixed

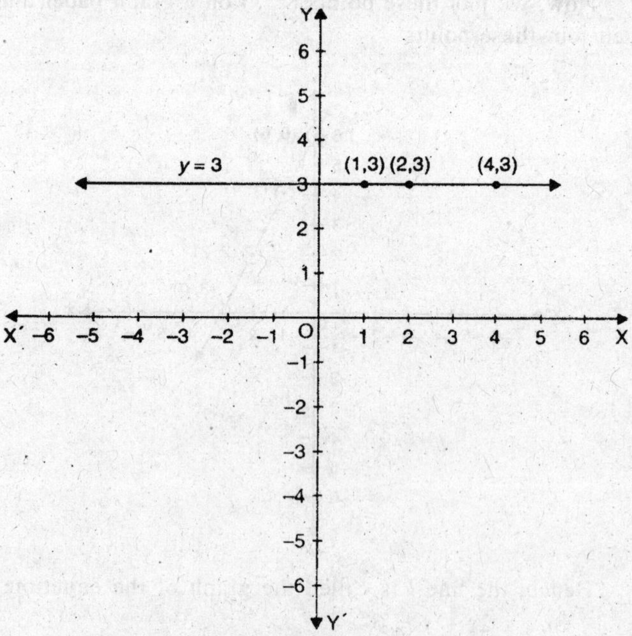

Hence, the graph of the given equation is a line parallel to x-axis.

(*iii*) The given equation is $y = 0$

Table of values

x	1	2	3	any value
y	0	0	0	fixed

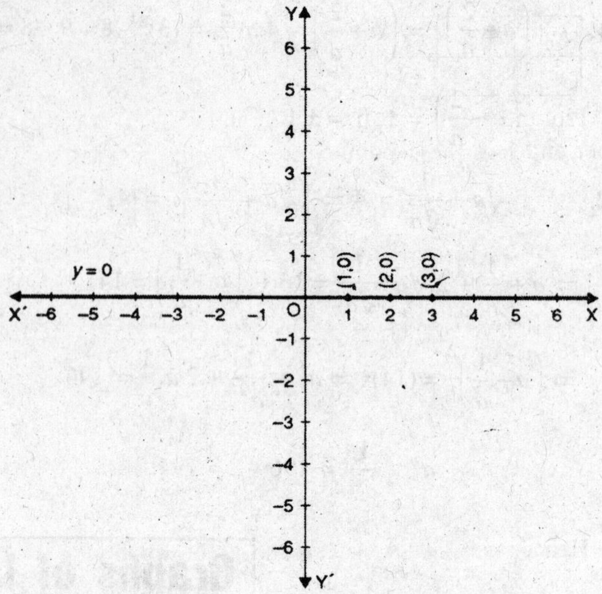

Hence, $y = 0$ is the equation of x-axis.

Example 2. Draw the graph of the line $x - 2y = 3$. From the graph find co-ordinates of the points when (*i*) $x = -5$, (*ii*) $y = 0$

Solution: The given equation is $x - 2y = 3$

Table of value

x	3	5	1
y	0	1	–1

$\because \quad 2y = x - 3$

$\therefore \quad y = \frac{x-3}{2}$

Plotting the points (3, 0), (5, 1) and (1, –1) on the graph paper and joining these points.

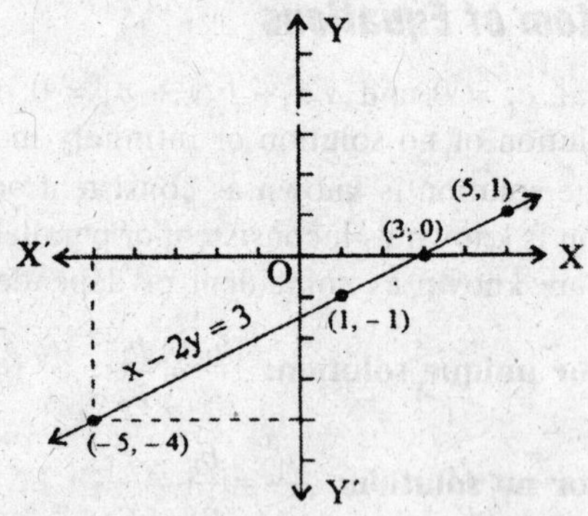

From the graph,

(*i*) when $x = -5$, then $y = -4$

(*ii*) when $y = 0$, then $x = 3$

Example 3. Draw the graph of the equations

$$5x + 3y = 4.$$

Solution: The given equation is $5x + 3y = 4$

$\Rightarrow \quad y = \frac{4-5x}{3}$

Table of values

x	–1	2	5
y	3	–2	–7

Plot the points (–1, 3), (2, –2) and (5, –7) on the graph paper and join these points.

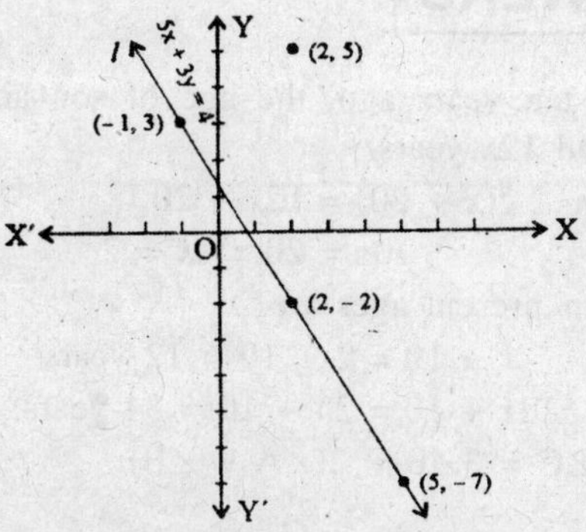

Hence, the line l is called the graph of the equation,

$$5x + 3y = 4$$

Example 4. Draw the graph of the equation

$$2x - 3y = -11.$$

Solution: The given equation is

$$2x - 3y = -11$$

$$\Rightarrow \quad 3y = 2x + 11$$

$$\Rightarrow \quad y = \frac{2x+11}{3}$$

Table of values

x	–1	2	–4
y	3	5	1

plot the points (–1, 3), (2, 5) and (–4, 1) on the graph paper and join these points

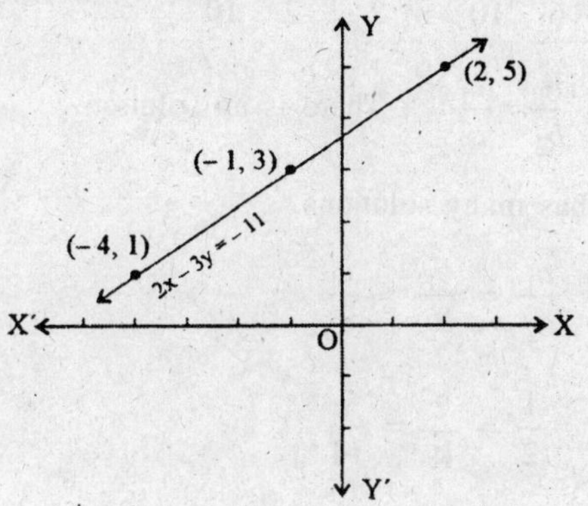

Hence, this line l is called the graph of the equation

$$2x - 3y = -11.$$

EXERCISE

1. The system of linear equations $2x + 3y = 7$ and $4x + 6y = 10$ has:
A. no solution
B. unique solution
C. infinite solution
D. no conclusion can be drawn

2. The value of k for which the system of equations $x + 2y + 7 = 0$ and $2x + ky + 14 = 0$ will have infinitely many solutions is:
A. 2 B. 4
C. 6 D. 8

3. For what value of α, the system of equations $\alpha x + 3y = \alpha - 3$ and $12x + \alpha y = \alpha$ will have a unique solution?
A. $\alpha \neq \pm 6$ B. $\alpha \neq \pm 3$
C. $\alpha \neq \mp 6$ D. None of these

4. For what value of k, the system of equations will represent the coincident lines $x+5y-7=0$ and $4x+20y+k=0$?
A. 28 B. –28
C. –26 D. None of these

5. A lady has 50 paise and ₹ 1 coins in her purse. If in all, she has 40 coins totally ₹ 25.50 how many of each type of coins does she have?
A. 26, 11 B. 11, 29
C. 29, 11 D. None of these

6. A father is three times as old as his son. After twelve years his age will be twice as the age of his son. Find their present ages in years.
A. 12, 26 B. 24, 36
C. 36, 12 D. None of these

7. Ten years ago, father was twelve times as old as his son. Ten years after, he will be twice as old as his son will be. Find their present ages in years.
A. 12, 36 B. 12, 24
C. 12, 34 D. None of these

8. The present age of a father is 3 years more than three times the age of son. Three years hence father's age will be 10 years more than twice the age of son. Determine their present ages in years.
A. 10, 33 B. 33, 10
C. 10, 30 D. None of these

9. In a triangle ABC, $\angle C = 3\angle B = 2(\angle A + \angle B)$. Find three angles in degrees.
A. 20°, 50°, 120° B. 30°, 40°, 120°
C. 20°, 40°, 120° D. None of these

10. The fraction becomes 2 when 1 is added to both the numerator and the denominator, and it becomes 3 when 1 is subtracted from both the numerator and denominator. The given fraction is :
A. 7/3 B. 4/7
C. 3/7 D. 7/4

ANSWERS

1	2	3	4	5	6	7	8	9	10
A	B	A	B	C	C	C	A	C	A

EXPLANATORY ANSWERS

1. $\frac{2}{4} = \frac{3}{6} \neq \frac{7}{10} \Rightarrow \frac{1}{2} = \frac{1}{2} \neq \frac{7}{10}$

$\frac{a_1}{a_2} = \frac{b_1}{b_2} \neq \frac{c_1}{c_2}$ ∴ There is no solution.

2. Since, it has many solutions.

∴ $\frac{a_1}{a_2} = \frac{b_1}{b_2} = \frac{c_1}{c_2}$

$\frac{1}{2} = \frac{2}{K} = \frac{7}{14}$

$\frac{1}{2} = \frac{2}{K} \Rightarrow K = 4.$

3. Since, the given equations have unique solution.

∴ $\frac{a_1}{a_2} \neq \frac{b_1}{b_2}$

$\frac{\alpha}{12} \neq \frac{3}{\alpha}$

$\Rightarrow \alpha^2 \neq 36 \Rightarrow \alpha \neq \pm 6$

4. Since, the given set of equations represent coincident lines.

then, $\frac{1}{4} = \frac{5}{20} = \frac{-7}{K} \Rightarrow K = -28$

5. Let, x be the number of 50 paise coins and y be the number of ₹ 1 coins.

According to the question,

$x + y = 40$ ...(*i*)

and $\frac{x}{2} + y = 25.50$

$\Rightarrow x + 2y = 51$ ...(*ii*)

Subtracting equation (*i*) from (*ii*) and solving we get, $x = 29, y = 11$

6. Let, age of son = x years.

∴ age of father = $3x$ years.

According to the question,

$2(x + 12) = 3x + 12 \Rightarrow x = 12$

∴ Son's age = 12 years; Father's age = 36 years.

7. Let ten years ago, the age of son and father were x and $12x$ years.

Then, $2(x + 20) = 12x + 20$

$\Rightarrow 10x = 20 \Rightarrow x = 2$

Their present ages are

$x + 10 = 2 + 10 = 12$ years

$12x + 10 = 24 + 10 = 34$ years.

9. ∴ $\angle C = 3\angle B = 2(\angle A + \angle B)$

$\angle A + \angle B = \frac{\angle C}{2}$

We have, $\angle A + \angle B + \angle C = 180°$

(Sum of angles of a triangle is 180°)

$\frac{\angle C}{2} + \angle C = 180°$

$3\angle C = 2 \times 180°$

$\angle C = \frac{2 \times 180°}{3} = 120°$

$3\angle B = \angle C$

$\angle B = \frac{\angle C}{3} = \frac{120°}{3} = 40°$

∴ $\angle A = 180° - (120° + 40°) = 180° - 160° = 20°.$

10. Let the fraction be $\frac{x}{y} \Rightarrow \frac{x+1}{y+1} = 2$

$\Rightarrow x + 1 = 2y + 2$

$\Rightarrow x - 2y = 1$ ...(*i*)

Again $\frac{x-1}{y-1} = 3$

$\Rightarrow x - 1 = 3y - 3$

$\Rightarrow x - 3y = -2$ ...(*ii*)

from (*i*) and (*ii*)

$x - 2y = 1$

$x - 3y = -2$

$- \quad + \quad +$

$y = 3$

Putting the value of y in (*i*) then we get, $x = 7$

∴ fraction $= \frac{x}{y} = \frac{7}{3}$

5

Average

The average of any number of quantities of the same kind can be found by dividing their sum by their number.

Thus,

$$\text{Average} = \frac{\text{Sum of quantities}}{\text{No. of quantities}}$$

Sum of quantities = Their average × Their number

$$\text{Number of quantities} = \frac{\text{Sum of quantities}}{\text{Their average}}$$

When a body coveres the same distance at two different speeds p km/hr and q km/hr, then its average speed for the whole journey is $\frac{2pq}{p+q}$ km/hr.

EXERCISE

1. The average of the fractions $1\frac{1}{2}$, $2\frac{1}{3}$, $3\frac{1}{3}$ and $4\frac{5}{6}$ is:

A. 2 B. $2\frac{1}{2}$

C. 3 D. 4

2. The average of first nine multiples of 3 is

A. 12.0 B. 12.5

C. 15.0 D. 18.5

3. The average of 13 numbers is 68, the average of first 7 numbers is 63 and the average of last 7 numbers is 70. What is the 7th number?

A. 43 B. 45

C. 47 D. 49

4. One-third of a certain journey was covered at the rate of 25 km per hour, one-fourth at the rate of 30 km per hour and the rest at the 50 km per hour. What is the average speed per hour for whole journey?

A. $33\frac{1}{3}$ kmph B. $44\frac{1}{4}$ kmph

C. $22\frac{1}{2}$ kmph D. 33 kmph

5. Nine men went to a hotel. Eight of them spent ₹ 3 for each over their meals and the ninth spent ₹ 2 more than the average expenditure of all the nine. What is the total money spent by them?

A. ₹ 29.25 B. ₹ 29.50

C. ₹ 29 D. ₹ 30

6. An establishment is permitted an average monthly contingency expenditure of ₹ 500 per month during the financial year. When a trial check was made at the end of the first nine months of the year it was found that the average monthly contingency expenditure worked out to be ₹ 511. What average monthly expenditure for the next three months should be aimed at in order to attain the permissible average of ₹ 500 per month for the whole year?

A. ₹ 567 B. ₹ 467

C. 367 D. ₹ 667

7. Average age of 8 persons increased by 2 years, when two men whose ages are 20 and 24 years are replaced by two women. What is the average age of women?

A. 30 years B. 31 years

C. 28 years D. 33 years

8. A man had seven children. When their average age was 12 years, the child who was 6 years of age died. What was the average of the surviving children 5 years after the death of the child?

A. 15 years B. 16 years

C. 17 years D. 18 years

9. The weight of a body, calculated as the average of seven different experiments is 53.735 grams. The average of the first three is 54.005 grams, the fourth was greater than the fifth by 0.004 gram, while the average of the sixth and seventh was 0.010 gram less than the average of the first three. What is the weight of the body as obtained by the fourth experiment?

A. 53.068 gm B. 53.078 gm
C. 53.086 gm D. 53.072 gm

10. A batsman has a certain average of runs for 16 innings. In the 17th innings, he makes a score of 85 runs thereby increasing his average by 3. What is the average after the 17th inning?

A. 33 runs B. 34 runs
C. 37 runs D. 36 runs

11. The average of 50 numbers is 38. If two numbers namely 45 and 55 are discarded, the average of the remaining numbers is

A. 36.5 B. 37
C. 37.5 D. 37.52

12. The average of 6 observations is 12. A new seventh observation is included and the new average is decreased by 1. The seventh observation is

A. 1 B. 3
C. 5 D. 6

13. A man whose bowling average is 12.4 takes 5 wickets for 26 runs and thereby decreases his average by 0.4. The number of wickets, taken by him, before his last match, is

A. 85 B. 78
C. 72 D. 64

14. The average of marks obtained by 120 candidates was 35. If the average of marks of passed candidates was 39 and that of failed candidates was 15, the number of candidates who passed the examination is

A. 100 B. 110
C. 120 D. 150

15. The average of three numbers is 42. The first is twice the second and the second is twice the third. The difference between the largest and the smallest number is

A. 18 B. 36
C. 54 D. 72

ANSWERS

1	2	3	4	5	6	7	8	9	10
C	C	C	A	A	B	A	D	D	C
11	**12**	**13**	**14**	**15**					
C	C	A	A	C					

EXPLANATORY ANSWERS

1. Average $= \frac{1}{4}\left(\frac{3}{2}+\frac{7}{3}+\frac{10}{3}+\frac{29}{6}\right)$

$= \left(\frac{9+14+20+29}{24}\right) = \frac{72}{24} = 3$

2. Average $= \frac{3(1+2+3+4+5+6+7+8+9)}{9} = \frac{135}{9}$

$= 15$

3. Average of 13 numbers = 68

$\therefore$ Total of 13 numbers = 13 × 68 = 884

Average of last 7 numbers = 70

$\therefore$ Total of last 7 numbers = 7 × 70 = 490

$\therefore$ Average of first 6 numbers

= 884 − 490 = 394

$\therefore$ Average of first 7 numbers = 63

$\therefore$ Total of first 7 numbers = 63 × 7 = 441

$\therefore$ 7th number = 441 − 394 = 47

4. Let the total distance covered during journey = 60 km

$\frac{1}{3}$ of the distance covered during journey

$= 60 \times \frac{1}{3} = 20$ km

$\frac{1}{4}$ of the distance covered during journey

$= \frac{1}{4} \times 60 = 15$ km

$\therefore$ The distance covered during the rest of journey = 60 − (20 + 15) = 25 km

Time taken to cover 20 km at 25 km/h

$= \frac{20}{25}$ hours $= \frac{4}{5}$ hour

Time taken to cover 15 km at 30 km/h

$= \frac{15}{30}$ hours $= \frac{1}{2}$ hour

Time taken to cover 25 km at 50 km/h

$= \frac{25}{50}$ hours $= \frac{1}{2}$ hour

Total time taken $= \frac{4}{5}+\frac{1}{2}+\frac{1}{2} = \frac{9}{5}$ hours

Hence average speed per hour

$= 60 \div \frac{9}{5} = \frac{60 \times 5}{9}$

$= \frac{100}{3}$ km/h $= 33\frac{1}{3}$ km/h

5. Let the average expenditure of all the nine
= ₹ x
Now amount spent by eight
= ₹ 3 × 8 = ₹ 24
and total spent by the ninth = ₹ $x + 2$

$$\Rightarrow \quad \frac{26+x}{9} = x$$

∴ Average amount spent by nine = $\frac{26+x}{9}$

Total amount spent by nine = 24 + x + 2 = 26 + x

$\Rightarrow \quad 9x = 26 + x$

or, $\quad 8x = 26$

$$\Rightarrow \quad x = \frac{26}{8} = ₹\ 3.25$$

Hence total money spent
= ₹ (3.25 × 9) = ₹ 29.25

6. Average monthly expenditure permitted = ₹ 500
Total expenditure permitted for 12 months
= ₹ 500 × 12 = ₹ 6000
Expenditure incurred during the first nine months
= ₹ 511 × 9 = ₹ 4,599
Expenditure for the last three month
= ₹ (6000 – 4599) = ₹ 1,401
∴ Average monthly expenditure for the three months

$$= ₹\ \frac{1401}{3} = ₹\ 467$$

7. Total increase in the age of 8 persons
= 2 × 8 = 16 years
Total age of two men being replaced
= 20 + 24 = 44 years
Total of the age of two women = 44 + 16 = 60 years
⇒ The average age of women

$$= \frac{60}{2} = 30 \text{ years.}$$

8. Average age of 7 children = 12 years
Total ages of 7 children = 12 × 7 = 84 years
Age of 1 child who died = 6 years
Total ages of remaining 6 children
= 84 – 6 = 78 years

∴ Average age of 6 children = $\frac{78}{6}$ = 13 years

∴ Average age of 6 children after 5 years
= 13 + 5 = 18 years

9. Total weight of 7 experiments
= 53.735 × 7 = 376.145 gm
Total weight of first three
= 54.005 × 3 = 162.015 gm
The average of the 6th and 7th was 0.010 gm less than that of the first three.
∴ Average of the 6th and 7th
= 54.005 – 0.010 = 53.995 gm
∴ Total of the 6th and 7th = 53.995 × 2 = 107.990 gm
Thus, total of 4th and 5th
= 376.145 – (162.015 + 107.990) = 106.140 gm
The fourth was greater than the fifth by 0.004 gm

$$\therefore \quad \text{The fifth} = (106.140 - 0.004) \times \frac{1}{2} = \frac{106.136}{2}$$

= 53.068 gm
Hence, the fourth = 53.068 + 0.004
= 53.072 gm

10. Average increase in the score of 17 innings
= 3 runs
Total increase in the score of 17 innings
= 3 × 17 = 51 runs
∴ His average of 16 innings
= 85 – 51 = 34 runs
Hence, average after the 17th innings
= 34 + 3 = 37 runs

11. Total of 50 numbers = 50 × 38 = 1900
Total of 48 numbers
= 1900 – (45 + 55) = 1800

$$\therefore \quad \text{Average} = \frac{1800}{48} = 37.5$$

12. Seventh observation
= (7 × 11 – 6 × 12) = 5

13. Suppose the number of wickets taken before the last match = x

$$\Rightarrow \quad \frac{12.4x + 26}{x+5} = 12$$

$\Rightarrow \quad 12.4x + 26 = 12x + 60$

$\Rightarrow \quad x = 85$

14. Let the number of candidates who passed = x

$\Rightarrow \quad 39 \times x + 15 \times (120 - x) = 120 \times 35$

$\Rightarrow \quad 24x = 4200 - 1800$

$$\therefore \quad x = \frac{2400}{24} = 100$$

15. Let the third number = x
Then, second number = $2x$ and first number = $4x$

$$\therefore \quad \frac{x + 2x + 4x}{3} = 42$$

$$\Rightarrow \quad \frac{7x}{3} = 42 \Rightarrow x = \frac{42 \times 3}{7}$$

$\Rightarrow \quad x = 18$

So, (largest) – (smallest) = $(4x - x) = 3x = 54$

●●●

6

Partnership Business

When two or more than two persons agree to invest money to run a business jointly, this association or deal is called *partnership* and those who invest money are called *pertners.* The total investment is called the *capital.*

Kind of partners : There are two kinds of partners.

1. **Working or active partner :** When a partner devotes his time for the business in addition to invest his money, he is called a working partner.

   With mutual agreement, the active partners get some fixed percentage of profit as *working allowance.*

2. **Sleeping or non-active partner :** A partner who simply invests money, but does not attend to the business is called a sleeping partner.

Kind of partnership :

(i) **Simple partnership :** If the capitals of several partners are invested for the same period, it is called a simple partnership.

(ii) **Compound or complex partnership :** If the capitals of the partners are invested for diffrent intervals of time, the partnership is called compound or complex.

EXERCISE

1. A and B started a business with the investment of ₹ 80000 and ₹ 60000 respectively. At the end of the year total profit in the business will be divided between them in the ratio of :

A. 2 : 3 B. 3 : 4
C. 2 : 1 D. 4 : 3

2. A and B started a business in partnership with the investment of ₹ 4000 and ₹ 6000 respectively. If at the end of the year total profit is ₹ 2250, what will each of them get?

A. ₹ 900, ₹ 1350
B. ₹ 800, ₹ 1450
C. ₹ 1000, ₹ 1250
D. ₹ 1200, ₹ 1050

3. Sonu, Monu and Mohit together start a business with the investment of ₹ 1800, ₹ 1500 and ₹ 1600 respectively. If at the end of the year, Monu gains a profit of ₹ 900 the total profit in the business is :

A. ₹ 2880 B. ₹ 2940
C. ₹ 3200 D. ₹ 3240

4. Omdutt started a business with a capital of ₹ 8000. After six months, Sanjay joined him with investment of some capital. If at the end of the year each of them gets equal amount as profit, how much did Sanjay invest in the business?

A. ₹ 18000 B. ₹ 17500
C. ₹ 16000 D. ₹ 16500

5. A, B and C buy a farm for ₹ 100000. A contributes ₹ 40000 in it. They sell it, and from the profit B gets ₹ 2750 and C gets ₹ 1750. What would be the profit of A?

A. ₹ 2780 B. ₹ 3000
C. ₹ 3280 D. ₹ 2785

6. A and B jointly invest ₹ 2100 and ₹ 3100 respectively in a firm. A is an active partner and hence he gets 25% of the profit separately. If their business yields them total ₹ 1040 as profit, what will be the gain of each of them?

A. ₹ 415, ₹ 625 B. ₹ 575, ₹ 465
C. ₹ 515, ₹ 525 D. ₹ 560, ₹ 480

7. Two partners invested ₹ 12500 and ₹ 8500 respectively in a business and decided that 60% of the profit incurred from the business will be equally divided between them while remaining profit will be assumed as interest on their capitals. If one of the partners gets ₹ 300 more profit than the other, what is the total profit in the business?

A. ₹ 3937.50 B. ₹ 4940.50
C. ₹ 3936.50 D. ₹ 4156

8. Neeraj and Birju are partners in a business. They divide between them the profit incurred in the business in such a proportion that $\frac{2}{5}$th portion of the profit gained by Neeraj is equal to $\frac{1}{3}$rd portion of the profit gained by Birju. If total profit in the business is ₹ 1210, find the profit earned by Birju.

A. ₹ 780 B. ₹ 660
C. ₹ 680 D. ₹ 590

9. A, B and C together took under lease a pasture ground for ₹ 888. If in this pasture ground A put his 20 sheep out to graze for 2½ months, B put his 30 sheep out to graze for 4 months and C put his 36 sheep out to graze for 3½ months, find the lease amount paid by each of them.

A. ₹ 205, ₹ 315, ₹ 378 B. ₹ 150, ₹ 360, ₹ 378
C. ₹ 170, ₹ 360, ₹ 358 D. ₹ 228, ₹ 360, ₹ 300

10. A, B and C started a business with the investment of ₹ 5000, ₹ 6000 and ₹ 4000 respectively. A is an active partner and therefore he gets 30% of the profit separately. Rest of the profit is divided in the ratio of their capitals. If at the end of year, A's profit is ₹ 200 more than the sum of the profits made by B and C, find the profit made by each of them.

A. ₹ 1620, ₹ 1242, ₹ 1178
B. ₹ 1720, ₹ 1252, ₹ 1228
C. ₹ 1510, ₹ 1187, ₹ 1133
D. ₹ 1600, ₹ 840, ₹ 560

11. Premchand, Nanak and Prabhat together rented a house for 2 years and settled to pay ₹ 1368 as rent. They lived together in this house for 5 months. Then Prabhat left the house and went away. 8 months after Nanak also went away and left the house for Premchand to live alone. How much did Premchand pay as rent of this house?

A. ₹ 1025 B. ₹ 950
C. ₹ 880 D. ₹ 780

12. A started a business with an investment of ₹ 4000. B joined him after 4 months and C joined him after 5 months. At the end of year they get profit in the ratio of 3 : 4 : 7. Find the ratio of capitals invested in the business by B and C.

A. 1 : 2 B. 2 : 1
C. 3 : 2 D. 1 : 3

13. Amit, Sumeet and Suresh started a business with capitals in the ratio of 2 : 3 : 4. Amit took back half of his investment after 3 months and Sumeet took back one-third portion of his investment after 4 months. If at the end of year, Suresh gets a profit of ₹ 3200, what is the total profit in the business?

A. ₹ $6076\frac{2}{3}$ B. ₹ $6066\frac{2}{3}$
C. ₹ 8000 D. ₹ $8333\frac{1}{3}$

14. A, B and C started a business in partnership. A invested ₹ 4000 for 8 months and ₹ 6000 for 4 months. B invested ₹ 3000 for 6 months and ₹ 5000 for next 6 months of the year while C invested ₹ 3000 for whole of the year. If at the end of year, total profit is ₹ 7000, what will be the shares of A, B and C in the profit?

A. ₹ 2800, ₹ 2400, ₹ 1800
B. ₹ 2500, ₹ 2600, ₹ 1900
C. ₹ 2600, ₹ 2500, ₹ 1900
D. ₹ 2000, ₹ 2700, ₹ 2300

15. A, B and C started a business in partnership with respective investment of ₹ 20000, ₹ 18000 and ₹ 12000. A and B are active partners and therefore they get an additional profit of 12% and 8% respectively for supervision and other related work they do for improvement of the trade. Rest of the profit is divided among them in the proportion of their capitals. If profit made by A is ₹ 648 more than B, find the profit earned by each of them.

A. ₹ 3960, ₹ 3312, ₹ 1728
B. ₹ 4960, ₹ 3312, ₹ 1728
C. ₹ 3690, ₹ 3132, ₹ 1820
D. ₹ 5960, ₹ 3600, ₹ 1750

16. Three labourers work for 5 hours, 6 hours and 7 hours respectively in a field and get wages in the proportion of time of working in the field. Three days after they increase their working hours by 1 hour. 4 days after they increase their working hours, work in the field gets finished. If their total wages is ₹ 276, find the share of wages earned by each of them.

A. ₹ 78, ₹ 92, ₹ 106 B. ₹ 88, ₹ 87, ₹ 101
C. ₹ 80, ₹ 90, ₹ 106 D. ₹ 81, ₹ 95, ₹ 100

17. A, B and C together took a pasture ground on rent at ₹ 16 per month with a view to graze their sheep in this ground. A, B and C owned 70, 50 and 40 sheep respectively. After 4 months A sold $\frac{2}{7}$th portion of his sheep to B and 3 month after that C sold $\frac{2}{5}$th portion of his sheep to A. How much will each of them pay as rent after the end of a year?

A. ₹ 70, ₹ 70, ₹ 52 B. ₹ 76, ₹ 76, ₹ 40
C. ₹ 80, ₹ 76, ₹ 36 D. ₹ 40, ₹ 76.30, ₹ 76

18. Samir and Saurabh started a joint firm. Samir's investment was thrice the investment of Saurabh and the period of his investment was two times the period of investment of Saurabh. If Saurabh got ₹ 4000 as profit, then their total profit is:

A. ₹ 16000 B. ₹ 20000
C. ₹ 24000 D. ₹ 28000

19. A, B and C together start a business. The amounts invested by A and B are in the ratio of 4 : 3 whereas the ratio of investments of B and C is 2 : 3. If the total profit earned is ₹ 46000, what is C's share in the profit?

A. ₹ 14000 B. ₹ 15000
C. ₹ 16000 D. ₹ 18000

20. Rani and Nisha started a business initially with ₹ 5100 and ₹ 6600 respectively. If the total profit is ₹ 2730, what is the Rani's share in the profit?

A. ₹ 1190 B. ₹ 1200
C. ₹ 1530 D. ₹ 1540

ANSWERS

1	2	3	4	5	6	7	8	9	10
D	A	B	C	B	B	A	B	B	D
11	**12**	**13**	**14**	**15**	**16**	**17**	**18**	**19**	**20**
B	A	B	A	A	A	B	D	D	A

EXPLANATORY ANSWERS

1. Ratio between their profits = 80000 : 60000 = 4 : 3.

2. Ratio of capitals of A and B = 4000 : 6000 = 2 : 3

A's share in the profit = $\frac{2}{5} \times 2250$ = ₹ 900

B's share in the profit = $\frac{3}{5} \times 2250$ = ₹ 1350

3. Ratio of their capitals
= 1800 : 1500 : 1600 = 18 : 15 : 16
Sum of proportionals = 18 +15 + 16 = 49
Monu's profit = ₹ 900

∴ Total profit in the business = $\frac{900}{15} \times 49$ = ₹ 2940

4. Investment by Omdutt for 1 month
= ₹ 8000 × 12 = ₹ 96000
Let Sanjay invested ₹ x for 6 months
∴ Capital of Sanjay for 1 month = ₹ x × 6 = ₹ $6x$
Now, $6x = 96000$
∴ x = ₹ 16000

5. Here, ratio of capitals of A and (B + C)
= 40000 : 60000 = 2 : 3
Profit of (B + C) = 2750 + 1750 = ₹ 4500

Hence, A's profit = $\frac{4500}{3} \times 2$ = ₹ 3000

6. Separate profit for A = $\frac{1040 \times 25}{100}$ = ₹ 260

Remaining profit = ₹ (1040 – 260) = ₹ 780
Ratio of capitals of A and B = 2100 : 3100 = 21 : 31

A's profit = $\frac{21}{52} \times 780$ = ₹ 315

B's profit = $\frac{31}{52} \times 780$ = ₹ 465

Total profit of A = ₹ (315 + 260) = ₹ 575
Therefore A and B will make profit of ₹ 575 and ₹ 465 respectively.

7. Ratio of their capitals = 12500 : 8500 = 25 : 17
Hence, sum of their ratios = 25 + 17 = 42 and difference of ratios = 25 – 17 = 8
Now total profit taken as interest

= $\frac{300}{8} \times 42$ = ₹ 1575

Hence, total profit in the business

= $\frac{100}{40} \times 1575$ = ₹ 3937.50

8. Let shares of Neeraj and Birju in profit are ₹ x and ₹ y respectively; then,

$\frac{2}{5}x = \frac{1}{3}y$ ∴ $x : y = 5 : 6$

Hence, share of Birju = $\frac{6}{11} \times 1210$ = ₹ 660

9. Ratio of their shares = (20 × 5/2) : (30 × 4) : (36 × 7/2) = 25 : 60 : 63
Sum of proportionals = 25 + 60 + 63 = 148
Total lease amount = ₹ 888

∴ Amount paid by A = $\frac{25}{148} \times 888$ = ₹ 150

Amount paid by B = $\frac{60}{148} \times 888$ = ₹ 360

Amount paid by C = $\frac{63}{148} \times 888$ = ₹ 378

10. Ratio of capitals of A, B and C = 5000 : 6000 : 4000 = 5 : 6 : 4
Let total profit in the business = ₹ x; then

$$\frac{30x}{100} + \frac{5}{15} \times \frac{70x}{100} - \frac{(6+4)}{15} \times \frac{70x}{100} = 200$$

$\Rightarrow \frac{8x}{15} - \frac{7x}{15} = 200$ ∴ x = ₹ 3000

Hence, A's profit = $\frac{8 \times 3000}{15}$ = ₹ 1600;

B's profit = $\frac{6}{15}\times\frac{7\times3000}{10}$ = ₹ 840;

C's profit = $\frac{4}{15}\times\frac{7\times3000}{10}$ = ₹ 560

11. Rent for 1 month = $\frac{1368}{24}$ = ₹ 57

Total rent paid by Premchand

$= 5 \times \frac{57}{3} + 8 \times \frac{57}{2} + 11\times57$

= 95 + 228 + 627 = ₹ 950.

12. Let, B and C invest ₹ x and ₹ y respectively

∴ Ratio of their capitals = 48000 : $8x$: $7y$

But given ratio of the profits = 3 : 4 : 7

$8x : 7y = 4 : 7 \Rightarrow \frac{x}{y}=\frac{1}{2}$

Hence, $x : y = 1 : 2$

13. Ratio of capitals of Amit, Sumeet and Suresh

= (2 × 3 + 1 × 9) : (3 × 4 + 2 × 8) : (4 × 12)

= 15 : 28 : 48

Sum of the ratios = 15 + 28 + 48 = 91

∴ Total profit in the business

$= \frac{91}{48}\times3200 =$ ₹ $6066\frac{2}{3}$

14. Ratio of their capitals

= (4000 × 8 + 6000 × 4) : (3000 × 6 + 5000 × 6) : (3000 × 12)

= 56000 : 48000 : 36000 = 14 : 12 : 9

Sum of proportionals = 14 + 12 + 9 = 35

Share of A in the profit = $\frac{14}{35}\times7000$ = ₹ 2800

Share of B in the profit = $\frac{12}{35}\times7000$ = ₹ 2400

Share of C in the profit = $\frac{9}{35}\times7000$ = ₹ 1800

15. Ratio of their capitals

= 20000 : 18000 : 12000 = 10 : 9 : 6

Let total profit in the business = ₹ x; then

$$\left(\frac{12x}{100}+\frac{10}{25}\times\frac{80x}{100}\right)-\left(\frac{8x}{100}+\frac{9}{25}\times\frac{80x}{100}\right) = 648$$

$$\Rightarrow \frac{11x}{25}-\frac{46x}{125}=648 \Rightarrow \frac{9x}{125}=648$$

$$\therefore \quad x = \frac{648\times125}{9} = ₹\ 9000$$

Hence, share of A = $\frac{11x}{25} = \frac{11\times9000}{25}$

= ₹ 3960;

Share of B = $\frac{46x}{125}=\frac{46\times9000}{125}$ = ₹ 3312

Share of C = $\frac{6}{25}\times\frac{80x}{100} = \frac{6}{25}\times\frac{4}{5}\times 9000$ = ₹ 1728

16. Ratio of their working hours

= (5 × 3 + 6 × 4) : (6 × 3 + 7 × 4) : (7 × 3 + 8 × 4)

= 39 : 46 : 53

Sum of proportionals = 39 + 46 + 53 = 138

∴ Wages for the 1st labourer = $\frac{39}{138}\times276$ = ₹ 78

Wages for the 2nd labourer = $\frac{46}{138}\times276$ = ₹ 92

Wages for the 3rd labourer = $\frac{53}{138}\times276$ = ₹ 106

17. Number of sheep of A for 1 month

$= [70 \times 4 + (70 - \frac{2}{7} \times 70) \times 3 + (70 - \frac{2}{7}\times 70 + \frac{2}{5} \times 40) \times 5]$

= 280 + 150 + 330 = 760

Number of sheep of B for 1 month

$= [50 \times 4 + (50 + \frac{2}{7}\times 70) \times 8] = 200 + 560 = 760$

Number of sheep of C for 1 month

$= [40 \times 7 + (40 - \frac{2}{5} \times 40) \times 5] = 280 + 120 = 400$

Hence, ratio of their sheep

= 760 : 760 : 400 = 19 : 19 : 10

Sum of proportionals = 19 + 19 + 10 = 48

1 year's rent of the pasture ground = 16 × 12 = ₹ 192

∴ Rent to be paid by A = $\frac{19}{48}\times192$ = ₹ 76

Rent to be paid by B = $\frac{19}{48}\times192$ = ₹ 76

Rent to be paid by C = $\frac{10}{48}\times192$ = ₹ 40

18. Ratio of Capitals of Samir and Saurabh

= (3 × 2) : (1 × 1) = 6 : 1

Saurabh's profit = ₹ 4000

Hence, total profit in the business

= 7 × ₹ 4000 = ₹ 28000

19. A : B = 4 : 3 and B : C = 2 : 3,

Therefore, A : B : C = 8 : 6 : 9

Hence, C's profit = $\frac{9}{23}\times46000$ = ₹ 18000

20. Ratio of their Capitals = 5100 : 6600 = 17 : 22

Hence, Rani's profit = $\frac{17}{39}\times2730$ = ₹ 1190

●●●

7

Mixture and Alligation

Alligation deals with calculation of values or properties of a mixture. Alligation is the rule that enables us—

(1) to find the proportion in which the two or more ingredients at the given prices must be mixed to yield a mixture at the given price. This is termed as "Alligation Alternate".

(2) to calculate the average or mean value of a mixture when the prices of two or more ingredients which are to be mixed together and proportion in which they are to be mixed are given. This is termed as "Alligation Medial".

1. Rule of Alligation:

$$\frac{\text{Amount of Cheaper ingredient}}{\text{Amount of Dearer ingredient}} = \frac{\text{Cost price of Dearer} - \text{Mean Price}}{\text{Mean Price} - \text{Cost Price of Cheaper}}$$

Here cost price of unit quantity of the mixture is called the *Mean Price.*

The above rule may be represented schematically as under:

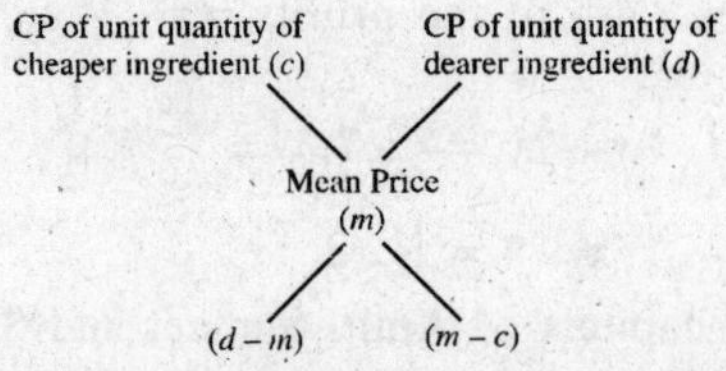

(Cheaper quantity) : (Dearer quantity) $= (d - m) : (m - c)$

This relationship is very helpful in solving problems on mixture involving percentage values, rates, prices, speeds etc.

2. *m* gm of sugar solution has *x* % sugar in it. To increase the sugar content in the solution to *y* %, quantity of sugar need to be added $= \dfrac{m(y-x)}{100-y}$

3. A vessel contains *x* litres of liquid A. *y* litres are withdrawn and replaced by liquid B. Next *y* litres of the mixture is withdrawn and again replaced by liquid B. This operation is repeated *n* times.

$$\frac{\text{Quantity of liquid A left after } n\text{th operation}}{\text{Whole quantity of liquid A initially present}} = \left(\frac{x-y}{x}\right)^n \text{ or } \left(1-\frac{y}{x}\right)^n$$

EXERCISE

1. In what proportion must tea at ₹ 62 per kg be mixed with tea at ₹ 72 per kg in order to obtain the mixture worth ₹ 65 per kg?

A. 4 : 6 B. 7 : 3
C. 2 : 3 D. 4 : 7

2. Find the quantity of rice @ ₹ 10 per kg. which should be mixed with 25 kgs of rice @ ₹ 8 per kg, so that on selling the mixture @ 15 per kg there is 80% profit.

A. 6 kgs B. 7 kgs
C. 3 kgs D. 5 kgs

3. A shopkeeper buys 26 kgs of milk @ ₹ 16 per kg. He also buys from another source an inferior quality of milk @ ₹ 10 per kg. How much quantity of the latter should he buy to mix it with the former so that he can sell the mixture @ ₹ 14 per kg without making any loss?

A. 13 kgs B. 12 kgs
C. 14 kgs D. 16 kgs

4. Two vessels A and B contain milk and water in the ratio 7 : 5 and 17 : 7 respectively. In what ratio mixtures from two vessels should be mixed to get a new mixture containing milk and water in the ratio 5 : 3?

A. 1 : 2 B. 2 : 1
C. 2 : 3 D. 3 : 2

5. Two vessels A and B contain mixture of milk and water in the ratio 4 : 1 and 9 : 11 respectively. They are mixed in the ratio of 3 : 2. Find the ratio of milk : water in the resulting mixture.

A. 34 : 16 B. 33 : 17
C. 16 : 34 D. 17 : 33

6. A person has two solutions of sugar with 30% and 50% concentration respectively. In what proportion should he mix two solutions to get 45% concentration in the resulting mixture?

A. 1 : 3 B. 3 : 1
C. 2 : 3 D. 3 : 2

7. 6 litres of milk and water mixture has 75% milk in it. How much milk should be added to the mixture to make it 90% pure?

A. 8 litres B. 9 litres
C. 10 litres D. 12 litres

8. In what ratio must water be added to spirit to gain 25% by selling it at cost price?

A. 1 : 4 B. 4 : 1
C. 3 : 4 D. 4 : 3

9. A shopkeeper has 50 kgs of rice. He sells a part of it at 20% profit and the rest at 40% profit. If he gains 25% on the whole, find the quantity of each part.

A. 12.5 kgs and 37.5 kgs B. 37.5 kgs and 12.5 kgs
C. 23.5 kgs and 21.5 kgs D. 21.5 kgs and 23.5 kgs

10. A shopkeeper has 100 kgs of tea. He sells a part of it at 20% profit and the rest at 5% loss. If his overall profit is 10%, find the quantity for each part.

A. 20 kgs B. 25 kgs
C. 30 kgs D. 40 kgs

11. A merchant has 160 kgs of wheat. He sells a part of it at 10% profit and the rest of 6% loss. If he incurs 4% loss on the whole, find the quantity for each part.

A. 120 kgs B. 140 kgs
C. 150 kgs D. 160 kgs

12. A man bought a certain quantity of sugar for ₹ 8000. He sells one-fourth of it at 20% loss. At what per cent profit should he sell the remainder stock so as to make an overall profit of 20%?

A. 20% B. 30%
C. 35% D. 40%

13. A person has ₹ 5000. He invests a part of it at 3% per annum and the remainder at 8% per annum simple interest. His total income in 3 years is ₹ 750. Find the sum invested at different rates of interest.

A. ₹ 2000 and ₹ 3000 B. ₹ 2500 and ₹ 2500
C. ₹ 3000 and ₹ 2000 D. ₹ 2750 and ₹ 2250

14. A person covers a dista2nce of 100 kms in 10 hours, partly by walking at 7 km/hr and rest by running at 12 km/hr. Find the distance covered in each part.

A. 48 kms B. 72 kms
C. 108 kms D. 124 kms

15. The average monthly salary of employees, consisting of officers and workers, of an organisation is ₹ 3000. The average salary of an officer is ₹ 10,000 while that of a worker is ₹ 2000 per month. If there are total 400 employees in the organisation, find the number of officers and workers separately.

A. 300, 100 B. 50, 350
C. 250, 150 D. 310, 90

16. The average daily wages of staff, consisting of supervisors and labourers, of a company is ₹ 50. The average wages of supervisors is ₹ 150 while that of labourers is ₹ 40 per day. If the number of supervisors is 15, find the number of labourers in the company.

A. 150 B. 175
C. 180 D. 200

17. ₹ 675 was divided among 75 boys and girls. Each boy gets ₹ 20 whereas a girl gets ₹ 5. Find the number of boys and girls.

A. 20, 55 B. 15, 60
C. 25, 50 D. 30, 45

18. A sum of ₹ 70 is divided among 10 children. Each boy gets ₹ 10 whereas a girl gets ₹ 5. If the number of boys is 4, find the number of girls.

A. 6 B. 7
C. 8 D. 9

19. From a cask of wine containing 25 litres, 5 litres are withdrawn and the cask is refilled with water. The process is repeated a second and then a third time. Find the quantity of wine left in the cask and also the ratio of wine to water in the resulting mixture.

A. 61 : 64 B. 16 : 46
C. 46 : 16 D. 64 : 61

20. A vessel contains 80 litres of milk. 16 litres of milk was taken out of the vessel and replaced by water. Then 16 litres of mixture was withdrawn and again replaced by water. The operation was repeated for third time. How much milk is now left in the vessel?

A. 96.40 litres B. 50.36 litres
C. 40.96 litres D. 32.76 litres

ANSWERS

1	2	3	4	5	6	7	8	9	10
B	D	A	B	B	A	B	A	B	D
11	**12**	**13**	**14**	**15**	**16**	**17**	**18**	**19**	**20**
B	B	C	B	B	A	A	A	D	C

EXPLANATORY ANSWERS

1. 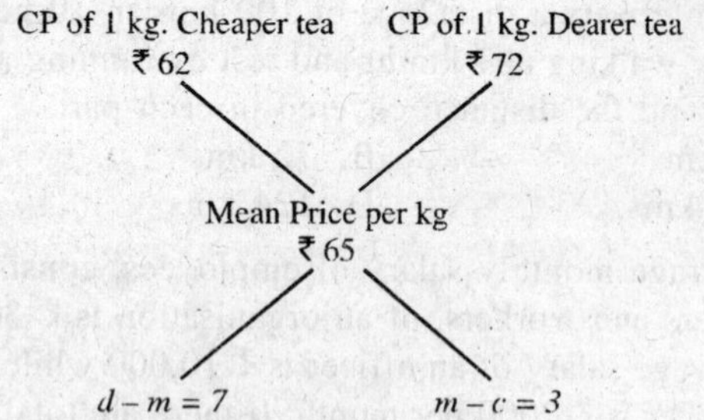

Using Alligation rule,

$$\frac{\text{Quantity of cheaper tea}}{\text{Quantity of dearer tea}} = \frac{d-m}{m-c} = \frac{7}{3}$$

Therefore, they must be mixed in the ratio of 7 : 3.

3. 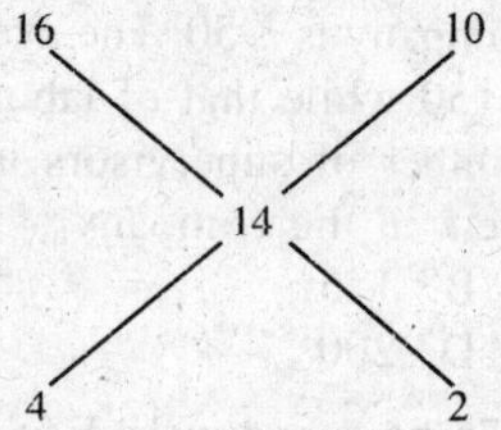

or 2 : 1 $\dfrac{\text{Quantity of milk @ ₹ 10 per kg}}{\text{Quantity of milk @ ₹ 16 per kg}} = \dfrac{1}{2}$

So, quantity of milk @ ₹ 10 per kg. $= \dfrac{26}{2} = 13$ kgs.

5. Fraction is *Milk* *Water*

A : $\dfrac{4}{5}$ $\dfrac{1}{5}$

B : $\dfrac{9}{20}$ $\dfrac{11}{20}$

(3A + 2B) = A and B : $\left(\dfrac{12}{5}+\dfrac{9}{10}\right)\left(\dfrac{3}{5}+\dfrac{11}{10}\right)$

$\dfrac{33}{10}$ $\dfrac{17}{10}$

So, Ratio of milk : water in the resulting mixture = 33 : 17.

6. 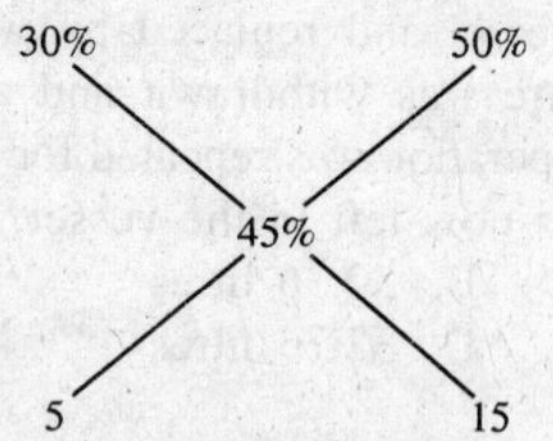

He should mix 30% and 50% in the ratio 5 : 15 or 1 : 3.

$\dfrac{\text{30\% Solution}}{\text{50\% Solution}} = \dfrac{1}{3}$ or 1 : 3

7. The given solution has 75% milk.

Milk to be added has 100% milk.

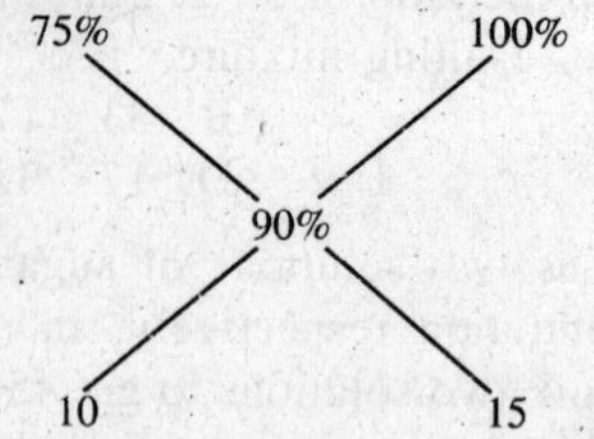

Milk should be added to the given mixture in the ratio 15 : 10 or 3 : 2.

$\therefore$ Quantity of milk to be added $= \dfrac{3}{2} \times 6 = 9$ litres.

8. Let cost price of spirit be ₹ 1 per litre.

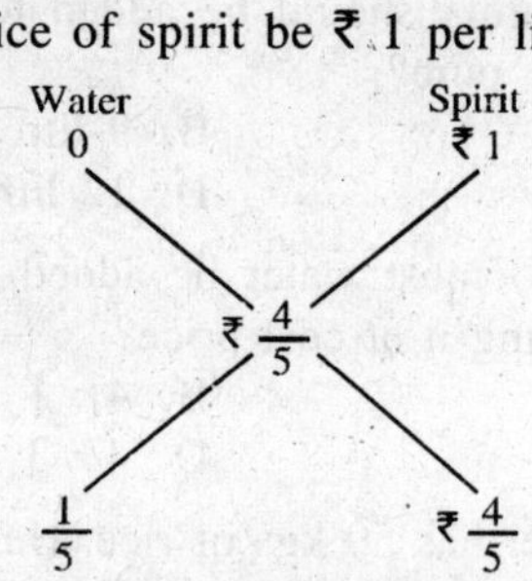

Then SP of mixture = ₹ 1 per litre

Gain = 25%

So, CP of mixture $= 1 \times \dfrac{100}{125} = ₹\ \dfrac{4}{5}$

We assume that CP of water is zero.

Using alligation rule on cost price,

Water should be mixed to spirit in the ratio $\dfrac{1}{5} : \dfrac{4}{5}$ or 1 : 4.

9. 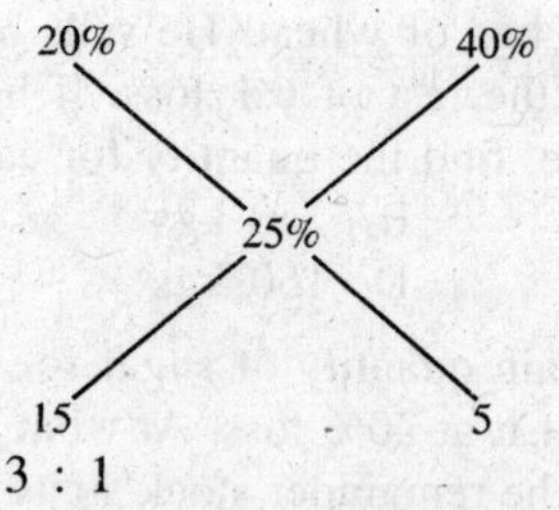

or 3 : 1

Quantity sold at 20% profit $= \dfrac{3}{3+1} \times 50 = 37.5$ kgs.

Quantity sold at 40% profit = (50 – 37.5) = 12.5 kgs.

10. 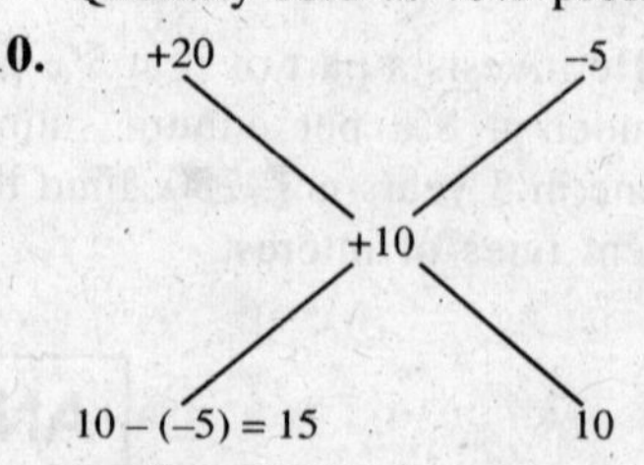

or 3 : 2

Quantity sold at 20% profit $= \dfrac{3}{3+2} \times 100 = 60$ kgs.

Quantity sold at 5% loss = (100 – 60) = 40 kgs.

11.

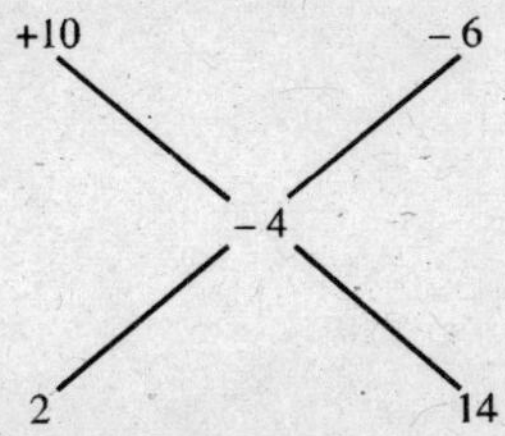

or 1 : 7

Quantity sold at 10% profit = $\frac{1}{1+7}$ × 160 = 20 kgs.

Quantity sold at 6% loss = 160 − 20 = 140 kgs.

12. Let the remainder stock be sold at x% profit.

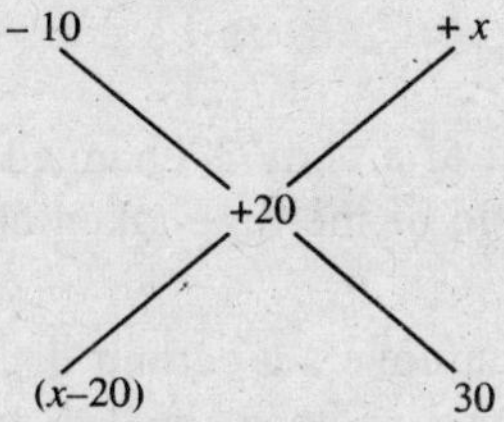

$$\frac{x-20}{30} = \frac{1/4}{3/4} \text{ or } x - 20 = 30 \times \frac{1}{3}$$

or $x = 20 + 10$, $x = 30\%$ profit.

13. Average rate of interest

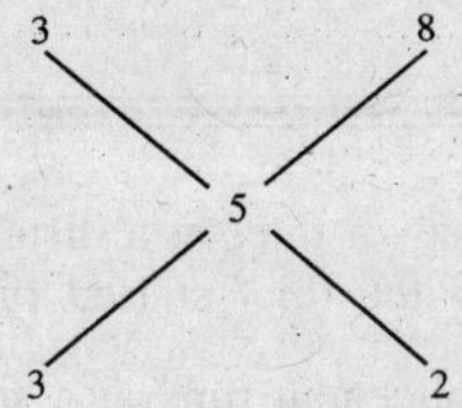

$= \frac{100 \times 750}{5000 \times 3}$ = 5% per annum

Investment at 3% per annum = $\frac{3}{3+2}$ × 5000 = ₹ 3000

Investment at 8% per annum = $\frac{2}{3+2}$ × 5000 = ₹ 2000.

14. Average speed = $\frac{100}{10}$ = 10 km/hr.

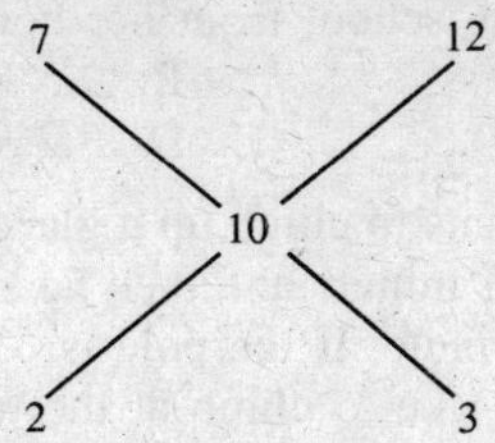

Ratio of time taken at 7 km/hr to 12 km/hr = 2 : 3

Time taken at 7 km/hr = $\frac{2}{2+3}$ × 10 = 4 hrs.

Distance covered at 7 km/hr = 7 × 4 = 28 km.

Distance covered at 12 km/hr = 100 − 28 = 72 km.

15.

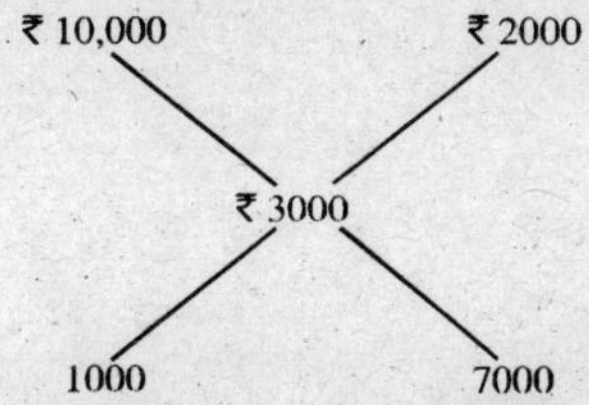

$$\frac{\text{Number of officers}}{\text{Number of workers}} = \frac{1000}{7000} = \frac{1}{7}$$

No. of officers = $\frac{1}{1+7}$ × 400 = 50

No. of workers = 400 − 50 = 350

16.

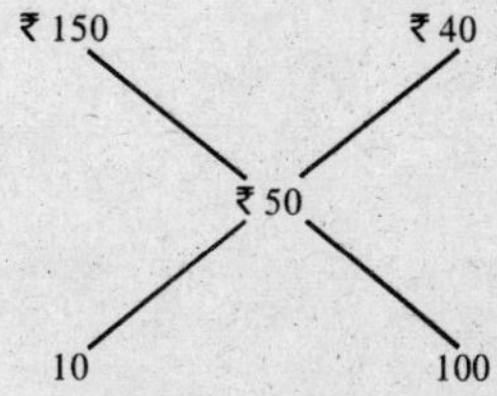

$$\frac{\text{Number of supervisors}}{\text{Number of labourers}} = \frac{10}{100} = \frac{1}{10}$$

Total number of labourers
= Total no. of supervisors × 10
= 15 × 10 = 150.

18.

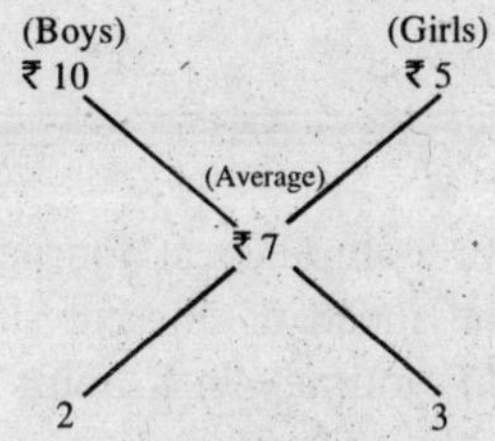

$$\frac{\text{Number of girls}}{\text{Number of boys}} = \frac{3}{2}$$

Number of girls = $\frac{3}{2}$ × 4 = 6

19. Here, quantity of wine left after third operation

$$= \left(1 - \frac{5}{25}\right)^3 \times 25$$

$$= \left(\frac{4}{5}\right)^3 \times 25 = \frac{64}{125} \times 25 = \frac{64}{5} = 12\frac{4}{5} \text{ litres.}$$

Final ratio of wine to water

$$= \frac{(64/125)}{(1-64/125)} = \frac{64/125}{61/125}$$

Wine : Water = $\frac{64}{61}$.

20. Amount of milk left

$$= 80\left(1 - \frac{16}{80}\right)^3 = 80\left(\frac{4}{5}\right)^3 = 80 \times \frac{64}{125}$$

= 40.96 litres.

8

Time and Distance

Important Formulae:

1. Speed = Distance ÷ Time
2. Distance = Time × Speed
3. Time = Distance ÷ Speed
4. x km/hr = $\left(x \times \frac{5}{18}\right)$ m/sec
5. x metres/sec = $\left(x \times \frac{18}{5}\right)$ km/hr.
6. If the speed of a body is changed in the ratio $m : n$, then the ratio of the time taken changes in the ratio $n : m$.
7. When a man covers a certain distance with a speed of x km/h and another equal distance at the rate of y km/h, then for the whole journey, the average speed is given by

   Average speed = $\frac{2xy}{x+y}$ km/h.

EXERCISE

1. A car moving at 48 km/hr completes a journey in 10 hours. By how much the speed of this car should be increased so as to do this journey in 8 hours?

A. 8 km/hr. B. 12 km/hr
C. 10 km/hr D. 15 km/hr

2. Starting from a point at a speed of 4 km/hr a man reaches at a cerain place and returns back to the point from where he had started journey on bicycle at the speed of 16 km/hr. His average speed during the entire journey will be:

A. 6.4 km/h B. 8.4 km/h
C. 5.4 km/h D. 10 km/h

3. A motorist covers a certain distance at a average speed of 48 km/h in 45 minutes. What speed in km/h he must maintain to cover the same distance in 30 minutes?

A. 66 km/h B. 79 km/h
C. 80 km/h D. 72 km/h

4. Two points A and B are 150 km apart. A man completes his onward journey from A to B in 3 hours 20 minutes and return journey from B to A in 4 hours 10 minutes. His average speed during the entire journey will be less than his average speed during the journey from A to B by:

A. 5 km/h B. 7.5 km/h
C. 9 km/h D. 3 km/h

5. A policeman saw a thief at a distance of 200 m. The policeman and the thief started running at the same time. If the policeman runs at a speed of $4\frac{1}{6}$ m per second and the thief at a speed of $3\frac{1}{3}$m per second, after what time the policeman will catch the thief?

A. 12 min B. 10 min
C. 9 min D. 4 min

6. Kanchan walks from her home at 4 kms per hour and reaches her school 5 minutes late. If she walks at 5 kms per hour, she reaches the school 2½ minutes earlier. How far is the school from her home?

A. 3.5 kms B. 2.5 kms
C. 2.75 kms D. 3.2 kms

7. A monkey wants to climb up a glazed pole. He climbs 12 metres in 1 minute and then he slips back 3 metres in the next minute. If the pole is 63 metre high, how long does he take to climb at the top of the pole?

A. $11\frac{1}{4}$ min B. $12\frac{1}{2}$ min
C. $12\frac{3}{4}$ min D. $14\frac{3}{4}$ min

8. A and B start walking at the same time on a circular path with circumference 35 metre. If they walk in the same direction at 4 km/hr and 5 km/hr respectively, after what time will they meet together?

A. 35 hours B. 27 hours
C. 24 hours D. 40 hours

9. While walking at $\frac{3}{5}$ of his usual speed Kamalkant reaches at his destination late by 30 minutes. His usual time consumed in reaching to his destination is:
A. 32 min B. 40 min
C. 45 min D. 42 min

10. The distance between two stations A and B is 300 km. A train leaves the station A with a speed of 40 km/hr. At the same time another train departs from the station B with a speed of 50 km/hr. How much time will these two trains take to cross each other?
A. 3 hrs 40 min B. 3 hrs 20 min
C. 2 hrs 20 min D. 3 hrs 45 min

11. Gulshan starts from a place P at 2 p.m. and walks to Q at 5 km per hour. Tarun starts from P at 3 p.m. and follows Gulshan on bicycle at 10 km per hour. By when Tarun will catch Gulshan?
A. At 5.30 p.m. B. At 4.00 p.m.
C. At 4.30 p.m. D. At 6.00 p.m.

12. Nilesh goes to school from his village at the speed of 4 km/hr and returns from school to village at the speed of 2 km/hr. If he takes 6 hours in all, then what is the distance between the village and the school?
A. 8 km B. 6 km
C. 5 km D. 4 km

13. A school bus covers a distance from a village to school at the speed of 12 km/hr and reaches the school 8 minute late. The next day the bus covers the same distance at the speed of 20 km/hr and reaches the school 10 minutes early. What is the distance between village and the school?
A. 6 km B. 9 km
C. 12 km D. 15 km

14. By increasing the speed of the bus by 10 km/hr the time of journey for 72 km is reduced by 36 minutes. What was the original speed of the bus?
A. 30 km/hr B. 35 km/hr
C. 40 km/hr D. 45 km/hr

15. A car completes a fixed journey in 8 hours. It covers half distance at the speed of 40 km/hr and rest at the 60 km/hr, the distance of the journey is:
A. 400 km B. 420 km
C. 384 km D. 350 km

16. A car covers four consecutive extensions of 3 km each at the speeds of 10 km/hr, 20 km/hr, 30 km/hr and 60 km/hr. Its average speed of journey is:
A. 30 km/hr B. 25 km/hr
C. 20 km/hr D. 10 km/hr

17. A girl rides her bicycle 10 km at an average speed of 12 km/hr and another 12 km at an average speed of 10 km/hr. Her average speed for the entire journey is approximately:
A. 12.2 km/hr B. 11.2 km/hr
C. 10.8 km/hr D. 10.4 km/hr

18. Raman drove from home to a neighbouring town at the speed of 50 km/hr and on his returning journey, he drove at the speed of 45 km/hr and also took an hour longer to reach home. What distance did he cover each way?
A. 900 km B. 500 km
C. 450 km D. 225 km

19. A man takes 6 hours 35 minutes in walking to a certain place and riding back. He would have taken 2 hours less by riding both ways. What would be the time he would take to walk both ways?
A. 10 hours B. 8 hours 35 minutes
C. 8 hours 25 minutes D. 8 hrs

20. A man covers a distance of 6 km at the rate of 4 km/hr and other 4 km at 3 km/hr this average speed is
A. $3\frac{5}{9}$ km/hr B. $3\frac{9}{17}$ km/hr
C. $5\frac{9}{17}$ km/hr D. $9\frac{3}{17}$ km/hr

ANSWERS

1	2	3	4	5	6	7	8	9	10
B	A	D	A	D	B	C	A	C	B
11	**12**	**13**	**14**	**15**	**16**	**17**	**18**	**19**	**20**
B	A	B	A	C	C	C	C	B	B

EXPLANATORY ANSWERS

1. Let he has to increase his speed by x km/hr for given condition; then,

$$(48 + x) \times 8 = 48 \times 10$$

$$\Rightarrow \quad 48 + x = 60 \therefore x = 12 \text{ km/hr}$$

2. Average speed during the entire journey

$$= \frac{2xy}{x+y} = \frac{2 \times 4 \times 16}{4+16} = \frac{8 \times 16}{20} = 6.4 \text{ km/hr.}$$

3. Let required speed be x km/hr; then

$$x \times \frac{1}{2} = 48 \times \frac{3}{4} \therefore x = 48 \times \frac{3}{4} \times 2 = 72 \text{ km/hr}$$

4. During onward journey from A to B:

$$\text{Average speed} = \frac{150}{10/3} = \frac{150 \times 3}{10} = 45 \text{ km/hr.}$$

During entire jouney:

$$\text{Average speed} = \frac{300}{\frac{10}{3}+\frac{25}{6}} = \frac{300\times 6}{45} = 40 \text{ km/hr.}$$

Hence, difference of average speed

$= 45 - 40 = 5$ km/hr.

5. Suppose the policeman will catch the thief after t sec

then, $\left(\frac{25}{6}-\frac{10}{3}\right)t = 200 \Rightarrow \frac{5}{6}t = 200$

$\therefore\ t = \frac{200\times 6}{5} = 240$ sec $= 4$ min.

6. Suppose the distance between her house to the school $= x$ km

Difference of time $= \frac{5}{2} - (-5) = \frac{15}{2}$ min $= \frac{1}{8}$ hr.

$\frac{x}{4}-\frac{x}{5}=\frac{1}{8} \Rightarrow \frac{x}{20}=\frac{1}{8}\ \therefore\ x = \frac{20}{8} = 2.5$ km

7. The monkey climbs 12 metres in 1 minute and then he slips back 3 metres in the next minute

$\therefore$ The monkey climbs in the first 2 minutes $= 12 - 3 = 9$ metres

$\therefore$ In the first 12 minutes the monkey climbs $= 9 \times 6 = 54$ metres

Remaining height of the pole to be covered by the monkey $= 63 - 54 = 9$ metre

$\therefore$ The monkey will climb the height of 9 metres in the 13th minute

$\because$ The monkey climbs 12 metres in 1 minute

$\therefore$ The monkey will climb 9 metres in

$\frac{1}{12}\times 9 = \frac{3}{4}$ minute

$\therefore$ Time spent in climbing at the top of the pole

$= \left(12+\frac{3}{4}\right)$ minutes $= 12\frac{3}{4}$ minutes

8. The two persons walk in the same direction

$\therefore$ Their relative speed $= 5 - 4 = 1$ km/hr

Distance covered in 1 round on the circular path $= 35$ km

$\therefore$ They will meet after $\frac{35}{1} = 35$ hours.

9. Suppose usual speed of Kamalkant is v km/hr and his destination is at a distance of x kms; then usual time taken $= \frac{x}{v}$ hours.

$\frac{x}{3v/5}-\frac{x}{v}=\frac{1}{2} \Rightarrow \frac{2x}{3v}=\frac{1}{2}\ \therefore\ \frac{x}{v}=\frac{3}{4}$ hour $= 45$ min.

10. The two trains are moving in the opposite directions

$\therefore$ Relative speed $= 40 + 50 = 90$ km/hr.

$\therefore$ Time taken to cross each other

$= \frac{300}{90} = 3\frac{1}{3}$ hours or, 3 hours 20 minutes.

11. Let Tarun will catch Gulshan after t hours the starting of Tarun; then, $10t = 5(t + 1)$

$\Rightarrow 5t = 5\ \therefore\ t = 1$ hr

Hence, required time $=$ 3 p.m. $+$ 1 hr. $=$ 4 p.m.

12. Let x km be the distance between village and the school; then

$\frac{x}{4}+\frac{x}{2}=6 \Rightarrow \frac{3x}{4}=6\ \therefore\ x = \frac{6\times 4}{3} = 8$ km

13. Let x km be the distance from village to school, then

$\frac{x}{12}-\frac{x}{20} = [8 - (-10)] \times \frac{1}{60}$

$\Rightarrow \frac{x}{30}=\frac{18}{60}\ \therefore\ x = \frac{18}{60}\times 30 = 9$ km

14. Let original speed of the bus be x km/hr; then

$\frac{72}{x}-\frac{72}{x+10}=\frac{36}{60} \Rightarrow \frac{72(x+10-x)}{x^2+10x}=\frac{3}{5}$

$\Rightarrow\ 1200 = x^2 + 10x$

$\Rightarrow x^2 + 10x - 1200 = 0$

$\Rightarrow (x + 40)(x - 30) = 0$

$\therefore\ x = 30$ or $x = -40$

Taking positive value only, so speed of the bus $= 30$ km/hr.

15. Let the distance of the journey be x km, then,

$\frac{x}{2\times 40}+\frac{x}{2\times 60} = 8 \Rightarrow \frac{5x}{240}=8$

$\therefore\ x = 8 \times 48 = 384$ km

16. Total distance of the journey $= 4 \times 3$ km $= 12$ km

Total time taken $= \frac{3}{10}+\frac{3}{20}+\frac{3}{30}+\frac{3}{60}=\frac{36}{60}=\frac{3}{5}$ hr.

Hence, average speed $= \frac{12}{3/5}=\frac{12\times 5}{3} = 20$ km/hr.

17. Average speed

$= \frac{10+12}{\frac{10}{12}+\frac{12}{10}}=\frac{22}{61/30}=\frac{22\times 30}{61}=\frac{660}{61} = 10.8$ km/hr

18. Let his distance of journey of each way be x km; then

$\frac{x}{45}-\frac{x}{50}=1 \Rightarrow \frac{x}{450} = 1$

$\therefore\ x = 450$ km

19. Here, Walking to a certain place + riding back = 6 hrs 35 min. ...*(i)*

$2 \times$ riding the same distance = 4 hrs 35 min. ...*(ii)*

Multiplying equation *(i)* $\times$ 2 and subtracting *(ii)* we get

Time taken in walking both ways = 13 hrs 70 min – 4 hrs. 35 min = 8 hrs. 35 min.

20. His average speed $= \frac{6+4}{\frac{6}{4}+\frac{4}{3}}=\frac{10}{17/6}=\frac{60}{17}=3\frac{9}{17}$ km/hr

●●●

9

Time and Work

IMPORTANT FACTS:

1. If A can do a piece of work in n days, then work done by A in 1 day = $\frac{1}{n}$.

2. If work done by A in 1 day = $\frac{1}{n}$; then A can finish the whole work in n days.

3. If A is twice as good a workman as B then; Ratio of work done by A and B = 2 : 1
Ratio of times taken by A and B to finish a work = 1 : 2.

EXERCISE

1. 12 boys can do a piece of work in 16 days. In how many days can 6 boys do the same work?
A. 16 days B. 32 days
C. 23 days D. 24 days

2. A can do a piece of work in 8 days while B can do the same work in 16 days. If they start working together, how long would they take to complete half portion of this work?
A. $2\frac{2}{3}$ days B. $3\frac{5}{7}$ days
C. $4\frac{1}{2}$ days D. $3\frac{1}{2}$ days

3. A can do a piece of work in 4 days. B is 50% more efficient than A. How long would B alone take to finish this work?
A. $3\frac{1}{3}$ days B. $5\frac{1}{4}$ days
C. $2\frac{2}{3}$ days D. $1\frac{2}{3}$ days

4. A and B working together complete a work in 35 days. If A takes 60 days to complete it, how long would B alone take to complete it?
A. 64 days B. 72 days
C. 81 days D. 84 days

5. A few children working together can do a piece of work in 18 days. If the number of children employed on the work is made double, how long would they take to complete half of the work?
A. $4\frac{1}{2}$ days B. $2\frac{1}{3}$ days
C. $8\frac{3}{4}$ days D. $6\frac{1}{2}$ days

6. 10 men or 18 boys can do a piece of work in 15 days. In how many days would 25 men and 15 boys complete the same work working together?
A. $5\frac{1}{2}$ days B. $4\frac{1}{2}$ days
C. $6\frac{2}{3}$ days D. $2\frac{1}{3}$ days

7. A can do a piece of work in 40 days. He starts working, but having some other engagements he drops out after 5 days. Thereafter B completes this work in 21 days. How many days would A and B take to complete this work working together?
A. 15 days B. 16 days
C. 17 days D. 11 days

8. Two persons A and B can complete a piece of work in 8 hours and 16 hours respectively. If they work at it alternately for an hour, A starting first, in how many hours will the work be finished?
A. $9\frac{1}{3}$ hours B. $10\frac{1}{2}$ hours
C. $11\frac{1}{2}$ hours D. $8\frac{1}{2}$ hours

ANSWERS

1	2	3	4	5	6	7	8
B	A	C	D	A	B	A	B

EXPLANATORY ANSWERS

1. $\because$ 12 boys can do a piece of work in 16 days.

$\therefore$ 1 boy will do the same piece of work in 16×12 days.

$\therefore$ 6 boys will do the same piece of work in

$\frac{16 \times 12}{6}$ days = 32 days.

2. (A + B)'s 1 day's work = $\frac{1}{8}+\frac{1}{16}=\frac{3}{16}$

Hence, (A + B) will do the whole work in $\frac{16}{3}$ days

So, they will do the half portion of the work in $\frac{16}{3 \times 2}$ days = $\frac{8}{3}=2\frac{2}{3}$ days.

3. A's 1 day's work = $\frac{1}{4}$;

Hence, B's 1 day's work = $\frac{150}{100} \times \frac{1}{4}=\frac{3}{8}$

So, B will do the whole work in $\frac{8}{3}=2\frac{2}{3}$ days.

4. (A + B)'s 1 day's work = $\frac{1}{35}$

and also, A's 1 day's work = $\frac{1}{60}$

Hence, B's 1 day's work

$=\frac{1}{35}-\frac{1}{60}=\frac{5}{420}=\frac{1}{84}$

So, B will do the whole work in 84 days.

5. Let number of children be x;

Now x children can do the work in 18 days.

Hence, $2x$ children will do $\frac{1}{2}$ of the work in

$\frac{18 \times x}{2x \times 2}=\frac{9}{2}$ days = $4\frac{1}{2}$ days.

6. 10 men $\equiv$ 18 boys; 25 men $\equiv \frac{18}{10} \times 25 = 45$ boys

Hence, 25 men + 15 boys = 45 + 15 = 60 boys

Now, 18 boys can do a piece of work in 15 days.

Hence, 60 boys will do a piece of work in

$\frac{15 \times 18}{60}=\frac{9}{2}$ days = $4\frac{1}{2}$ days.

7. A's 5 days' work = $5 \times \frac{1}{40}=\frac{1}{8}$

Remaining work = $1-\frac{1}{8}=\frac{7}{8}$, which is done by B in 21 days.

Hence, B's 1 day's work = $\frac{7}{8 \times 21}=\frac{1}{24}$

Now, (A + B)'s 1 day's work = $\frac{1}{40}+\frac{1}{24}=\frac{8}{120}=\frac{1}{15}$

Hence, (A + B) will complete the work in 15 days.

8. In 2 hours the part of work = $\frac{1}{8}+\frac{1}{16}=\frac{3}{16}$ will be completed.

Hence, in 5 pairs of hours the part of work

$= 5 \times \frac{3}{16}=\frac{15}{16}$ will be completed

Remaining work = $1-\frac{15}{16}=\frac{1}{16}$ which will be done by A.

Time taken by A to complete the $\frac{1}{16}$ work

$=\frac{1/16}{1/8}=\frac{1}{2}$ hour.

Hence, required number of hours

$= 10 + \frac{1}{2}=10\frac{1}{2}$ hours.

●●●

10

L.C.M. & H.C.F.

LCM

Multiple : A number is said to be multiple of other when it is exactly divisible by the other.

Common multiple : A common multiple of two or more numbers is a number which is exactly divisible by each of them. For example, for 2 and 3, common multiples are 6, 12, 18, 24 and so on.

Explanation:

Consider the two numbers 2 and 3

Multiple of 2 are 2, 4, 6, 8, 10, 12, ...

Multiple of 3 are 3, 6, 9, 12, 15, ...

∴ Common multiples are 6, 12, 18, ...

Least Common Multiple (L.C.M.) : L.C.M. of two or more given numbers is the least number which is exactly divisible by each of them. For example,

6 is a common multiple of 2 and 3

12 is also common multiple of 2 and 3

18 is also common multiple of 2 and 3

But 6 is the least common multiple (L.C.M.) of 2 and 3.

Methods to find out L.C.M.

L.C.M. of two or more given numbers is determined by following two methods:

1. By prime factorization method

2. By division method

HCF

Factor : One number is said to be a factor of other when it divides the other exactly. Hence, 5 and 7 are factors of 35.

Common factor : A common factor of two or more numbers is a number that divides each of them exactly. Hence, 5 is a common factor of 15, 25, 35 and 55.

Highest Common Factor (H.C.F.) : H.C.F. of two or more numbers is the largest number by which each given number is divisible without leaving any remainder.

An example : It is required to find the H.C.F. of 6 and 8.

Factors of 6 are 1, 2, 3, 6 and

Factors of 8 are 1, 2, 4, 8.

The common factors are 1, 2, but highest of these is 2. Hence, 2 is the H.C.F.

Relationship Between Two Numbers and Their L.C.M. and H.C.F.

Product of the H.C.F. and the L.C.M. of two numbers is equal to the product of the given numbers.

i.e., 1st number × 2nd number = H.C.F. × L.C.M.

EXERCISE

1. The largest three-digit number, when divided by 6, 9 and 12 leaves 1 as remainder in each case, will be

A. 887 B. 987
C. 973 D. 730

2. Two numbers are in the ratio of 8 : 15. If their H.C.F. is 4, the numbers are

A. 32 and 60 B. 16 and 30
C. 80 and 150 D. 64 and 120

3. The largest number that will divide 226 and 272 leaving 1 and 2 as remainders respectively, is

A. 36 B. 45
C. 55 D. 59

4. Which of the following is the greatest common divisor of 1170 and 102?

A. 8 B. 4
C. 6 D. 3

5. A number, when 3 is added to it, becomes divisible by 36, 45 and 50. The smallest such number is

A. 987 B. 798
C. 986 D. 897

6. The least perfect square number which is completely divisible by 10, 20, 30 and 40 is

A. 4800 B. 3600
C. 4400 D. 2500

7. The product of two numbers is 2160 and their H.C.F. is 12. How many such pairs of numbers can be possibly formed?

A. 3 B. 1
C. 2 D. None

8. The greatest number that will divide 366, 513 and 324 leaving the same remainder in each case is

A. 21 B. 18
C. 27 D. 42

ANSWERS

1	2	3	4	5	6	7	8
C	A	B	C	D	B	C	A

EXPLANATORY ANSWERS

1. L.C.M. of 6, 9 and 12

$$\begin{array}{c|ccc} 3 & 6, & 9, & 12 \\ \hline 2 & 2, & 3, & 4 \\ \hline & 1, & 3, & 2 \end{array}$$

$\therefore$ LCM = 3 × 2 × 3 × 2 = 36.

$\because$ Largest 3-digit number = 999

36) 999 (27
72
279
252
× 27

$\therefore$ Largest 3-digit number which is exactly divisible by 6, 9 and 12

= 999 − 27 = 972

$\therefore$ The required number = 972 + 1 = 973

2. Let the numbers be $8x$ and $15x$

$8x = 2 \times 2 \times 2 \times x$

$15x = 3 \times 5 \times x$

$\therefore$ LCM of $8x$ and $15x = 2 \times 2 \times 2 \times x \times 3 \times 5 = 120x$

Now, 1st number × 2nd number = HCF × LCM

$\Rightarrow 8x \times 15x = 4 \times 120x$

$\Rightarrow 120x^2 = 4 \times 120x$

$\Rightarrow x = 4$

$\therefore$ Numbers are 8 × 4 = 32 and 15 × 4 = 60

3. 226 − 1 = 225 and 272 − 2 = 270

Now, HCF of 225 and 270

225) 270 (1
225
45) 225 (5
225
×

$\therefore$ The required number is 45.

4. 1170 = 2 × 5 × 3 × 3 × 13

102 = 2 × 3 × 17

$\therefore$ Greatest common divisor = 2 × 3 = 6

5. It is clear from the given conditions of the problem that the smallest number will be 3 less than the LCM of 36, 45 and 50.

$\therefore$ LCM of 36, 45 and 50

$$\begin{array}{c|ccc} 3 & 36, & 45, & 50 \\ \hline 2 & 12, & 15, & 50 \\ \hline 3 & 6, & 15, & 25 \\ \hline 5 & 2, & 5, & 25 \\ \hline & 2, & 1, & 5 \end{array}$$

$\therefore$ LCM = 3 × 2 × 3 × 5 × 2 × 5 = 900

$\therefore$ Required number = 900 − 3 = 897.

6. LCM of 10, 20, 30 and 40

$$\begin{array}{c|cccc} 2 & 10, & 20, & 30, & 40 \\ \hline 5 & 5, & 10, & 15, & 20 \\ \hline 2 & 1, & 2, & 3, & 4 \\ \hline & 1, & 1, & 3, & 2 \end{array}$$

$\therefore$ LCM = 2 × 2 × 5 × 3 × 2

But the number is a perfect square number

$\therefore$ Required number = 2 × 2 × 5 × 5 × 3 × 3 × 2 × 2 = 3600.

7. Product of two numbers = their HCF × their LCM

2160 = 12 × LCM

$$\therefore \quad \text{LCM} = \frac{2160}{12} = 180$$

Therefore such pairs of numbers in which product of numbers is 2160 and HCF is 12 will be only 2. *i.e.,* 12 × 180 and 36 × 60.

8. Difference between 366 and 513

= 513 − 366 = 147

and difference between 513 and 324

= 513 − 324 = 189

$\therefore$ HCF of 147 and 189

147) 189 (1
147
× 42) 147 (3
126
× 21) 42 (2
42
×

$\therefore$ The required largest number is 21.

●●●

ENGLISH LANGUAGE & COMPREHENSION

1 Spelling Errors

The most common errors in English are of spellings of words. Even the most learned men are sometimes confused about the correct spellings of some words. One must keep and use a dictionary religiously. Never ignore and let pass a new word casually.

A number of question to test your knowledge of spellings are compiled here. Try to solve as many as you can.

Multiple Choice Questions

Directions: *Find the correctly spelt word out of the four options in each question.*

1. A. Accompalish B. Ackmplesh C. Acomplush D. Accomplish

2. A. Acommodation B. Acomodation C. Accomodation D. Accommodation

3. A. Astonished B. Astronished C. Astoneshed D. Asstonished

4. A. Benefeted B. Benefitted C. Benifited D. Benefited

5. A. Belligerent B. Beligirent C. Belligarant D. Belligerrent

6. A. Chancelery B. Chancellery C. Chancellary D. Chancelary

7. A. Discriminate B. Discremineta C. Discrimenate D. Discriminat

8. A. Damage B. Dammage C. Damaige D. Dammege

9. A. Efficiant B. Effecient C. Efficient D. Eficient

10. A. Extravagant B. Extreragent C. Extreregant D. Extravegent

11. A. Efflorascence B. Eflorescene C. Effllorescence D. Efflorescence

12. A. Equinimity B. Equanimmity C. Equannimity D. Equanimity

13. A. Farmament B. Farmement C. Fermament D. Fremament

14. A. Grieff B. Grief C. Grieef D. Grrief

15. A. Guarantee B. Garuntee C. Guaruntee D. Gaurantee

16. A. Hypocritical B. Hypocretical C. Hypocriticel D. Hypocirticel

17. A. Humurous B. Humorous C. Humoreus D. Humorrous

18. A. Itenerary B. Itinarery C. Itinarary D. Itinerary

19. A. Indipenseble B. Indispansible C. Indispensable D. Indipensable

20. A. Imprecticability B. Impracticebility C. Impracticibility D. Impracticability

21. A. Incradulous B. Incredulous C. Incridulous D. Incredalous

22. A. Juddicious B. Judiceous C. Judicious D. Judiceus

23. A. Kleptomonia B. Kleptemonia C. Kleptomania D. Klaptomania

24. A. Lackdaisical B. Lackadaisical C. Lckadaisicle D. Lackadisical

25. A. Licentious B. Licontious C. Licenttious D. Licientious

26. A. Meddicine B. Medicine C. Medicene D. Medicinne

27. A. Meritricious B. Merefrecious C. Meretricious D. Merritricious

28. A. Missunderstood B. Miesunderstood C. Misunderstood D. Misunderstod

29. A. Occurad B. Occurred C. Ocurred D. Occured

30. A. Osttentatious B. Ostentetious C. Ostentatious D. Ostenttatious

31. A. Obnosious B. Obnoxeous C. Obnoxious D. Obnoseous

32. A. Omenous B. Ominous C. Ommineous D. Omineous

33. A. Pecification B. Pacification C. Pecifacation D. Pecefication

34. A. Prograssive B. Progressive C. Progresive D. Prograsive

35. A. Pasiveness B. Passiveness C. Passeveniss D. Passivines

36. A. Polyendry B. Poliendry C. Pollyendry D. Polyandry

37. A. Puerille B. Puerrile C. Puerile D. Purrile

38. A. Pesanger B. Passenger C. Pessenger D. Pasanger

39. A. Querrelsome B. Quarrelsame C. Quarrelsome D. Querralsome

40. A. Rigourous B. Rigerous C. Rigorous D. Regerous

41. A. Survellance B. Surveilance C. Surveillance D. Survaillance

42. A. Schedule B. Schdule C. Schedale D. Schedeule

43. A. Sepalchrle B. Sepalchral C. Sepulchrle D. Sepulchral

44. A. Sympathetic B. Smypathetic C. Sympothetic D. Sympethetic

45. A. Sincerely B. Sencerely C. Sincerelly D. Sincerrely

46. A. Satellite B. Sattellite C. Satelite D. Sattelite

47. A. Teracherous B. Treacherous C. Treacheraus D. Treachereans

48. A. Uncivilized B. Uncevilized C. Uncivillized D. Uncevelized

49. A. Vainglorious B. Vaniglorious C. Vaniglerious D. Vaingloreus

50. A. Vulnarable B. Valnerable C. Velnerable D. Vulnerable

ANSWERS

1	2	3	4	5	6	7	8	9	10
D	D	A	B	A	C	A	A	C	A
11	12	13	14	15	16	17	18	19	20
D	D	C	B	A	A	B	D	C	D
21	22	23	24	25	26	27	28	29	30
B	C	C	B	A	B	C	C	B	C
31	32	33	34	35	36	37	38	39	40
C	B	B	B	B	D	C	B	C	C
41	42	43	44	45	46	47	48	49	50
C	A	D	A	A	A	B	A	A	D

❑❑❑

2 Spotting Errors

The most common errors in English are of spellings, grammar and usage of words. By regular practice, the errors can be easily spotted and minimised.

Common Errors with Nouns and Noun-Phrases

	Incorrect	Correct
1.	I have bought new *furnitures.*	I have bought new *furniture.*
2.	The wages of sin *are* death.	The wages of sin *is* death.
3.	She told these *news* to her mother.	She told her mother this *news.*
4.	He took *troubles* to do his work.	He took *trouble* (or pains) over his work.
5.	The *cattles* were grazing.	The *cattle* were grazing.
6.	He showered *many abuses* on me.	He showered *much abuse* on me.
7.	I spent the holidays with my *family members.*	I spent the holidays with my *family.*
8.	There is no *place* in this compartment.	There is no *room* in this compartment.
9.	Write this new *poetry* in your *copy.*	Write this new *poem* in your *note-book.*
10.	He took *insult* at this.	He took *offence* at this.
11.	Put your *sign* here.	Put your *signatures* here.
12.	She is my *cousin sister.*	She is my *cousin.*
13.	*Sunil's* my *neighbour's* house was burgled.	*Sunil* my *neighbour's* house was burgled.
14.	I lost a *ten-rupees* note.	I lost *a ten-rupee* note.
15.	Road closed for *repair.*	Road closed for *repairs.*
16.	His house is out of *repairs.*	His house is out of *repair.*
17.	What is the *reason* of an earthquake?	What is the *cause* of an earthquake?
18.	This building is made of *stones.*	This building is made of *stone.*
19.	I disapprove of *these kinds* of games.	I disapprove of *this kind* of games.
20.	Veena's and Sheela's father is ill.	Veena and Sheela's father is ill.
21.	His *son-in-laws* are doctors.	His *sons-in-law* are doctors.
22.	*Alms* is given to the *poor.*	*Alms* are given to the poor.
23.	He always keeps his words.	He always keeps his *word.*
24.	I carried the *luggages.*	I carried the *luggage.*
25.	*Two-third* of the work is left.	*Two-thirds* of the work is left.

Common Errors with Pronouns

	Incorrect	Correct
1.	Both did not go.	Neither went.
2.	We all did not go.	None of us went.
3.	Each of these boys play.	Each of these boys plays.
4.	Whoever does best he will get a prize.	Whoever does best will get a prize.
5.	One should not waste his time.	A man should not waste his time.
6.	I and she are sisters.	She and I are sisters.
7.	He is wiser than me.	He is wiser than I.
8.	Between you and I, Anil is not to be trusted.	Between you and me, Anil is not to be trusted.
9.	Nobody was there but I.	Nobody was there but me.
10.	Who is there ? It is me.	Who is there ? It is I.
11.	Only he and me can use this card.	Only he and I can use this card.
12.	Let you and I go now.	Let you and me go now.
13.	Everyone got one's pay.	Everyone got his pay.
14.	Everyone is frightened when they see a tiger.	Everyone is frightened when he sees a tiger.
15.	These two friends are fond of one another.	These two friends are fond of each other.
16.	I did not like him coming at that hour.	I did not like his coming at that hour.
17.	Who do you think I met?	Whom do you think I met?
18.	You should avail this opportunity.	You should avail yourself this opportunity.
19.	When you have read these books, please return the same to me.	When you have read the books, please return them to me.
20.	They that are humble need fear no fall.	Those that are humble need fear no fall.

Common Errors with Adjectives

	Incorrect	Correct
1.	These all oranges are good.	All these oranges are good.
2.	He held the book in the both hands.	He held the book in both hands.
3.	Both men have not come.	Neither man has come.
4.	That man should do some or other work.	That man should do some work or other.
5.	He is elder than I.	He is older than I.
6.	Shakespeare is greater than any other poets.	Shakespeare is greater than any other poet.
7.	He is a coward man.	He is a cowardly man.
8.	Many villagers cannot write his own name.	Many villagers cannot write their own name.
9.	Each of us loves our home.	Each of us loves his home.
10.	Much efforts bring their reward.	Much effort brings its reward.
11.	He found hundred rupees.	He found a hundred rupees.
12.	He had leave of four days.	He had four days leave.
13.	This is a worth seeing sight.	This is a sight worth seeing.
14.	He will spend his future life here.	He will spend the rest of his life here.
15.	There is a best teacher in that class.	There is a very good teacher in that class.
16.	Of the two plans this is the best.	Of the two plans this is the better.
17.	He is becoming strong every day.	He is becoming stronger every day.
18.	He is worst than I.	He is worse than I.
19.	Jaipur is hot than Delhi.	Jaipur is hotter than Delhi.
20.	In our library the number of books is less.	In our library the number of books is small.

Common Errors with Verbs

	Incorrect	Correct
1.	He asked had we taken our luggage.	He asked if we had taken our luggage.
2.	She asked what are you doing.	She asked what we were doing.
3.	Rama asked to Anil why he is angry.	Rama asked Anil why he was angry.
4.	He does not care for his money.	He does not take care of his money.
5.	He does not care for his work.	He takes no care over his work.
6.	No one cared for him after his mother died.	No one took care of him after his mother died.
7.	He got angry before I said a word.	He got angry before I had said a word.
8.	I met a man who was my tutor 20 years ago.	I met a man who had been my tutor twenty years ago.
9.	I had been for walking yesterday.	I went for a walk yesterday.
10.	If I shall do this I shall be wrong.	If I do this I shall be wrong.
11.	I have left trekking.	I have given up trekking.
12.	I came to know as to how he did this.	I learnt how he did this.
13.	I came to know why he was sad.	I found out why he was sad.
14.	He knows to swim.	He knows how to swim.
15.	The criminal's head was cut.	The criminal's head was cut off.
16.	I said to him to go.	I told him to go.
17.	I told the teacher to excuse me.	I asked the teacher to excuse me.
18.	He is troubling me.	He is giving me trouble.
19.	I have got a hurt on my leg.	I have hurt my leg.
20.	She gave a speech.	She made a speech.

Common Errors in Subject-Verb Agreement

	Incorrect	Correct
1.	The owners of this factory *is* very rich.	The owners of this factory *are* very rich.
2.	The pleasures of nature that one can experience at Shimla *is* beyond description.	The pleasures of nature that one can experience at Shimla *are* beyond description.
3.	There *is* no street lights in our colony.	There *are* no street lights in our colony.
4.	He and I *am* entrusted with the job.	He and I *are* entrusted with the job.
5.	Rice and curry *are* his favourite dish.	Rice and curry *is* his favourite dish.
6.	The honour and glory of our country *are* at stake.	The honour and glory of our country *is* at stake.
7.	Time and tide *waits* for none.	Time and tide *wait* for none.
8.	All the passengers with the driver *was* killed.	All the passengers, with the driver, *were* killed.
9.	The teacher, with her students, *were* going out.	The teacher, with her students, *was* going out.
10.	I as well as they *am* tired.	I as well as they *are* tired.
11.	Not only the soldiers but their captain also *were* captured.	Not only the soldiers but their captain also *was* captured.
12.	Neither you nor I *were* selected.	Neither you nor I *was* selected.
13.	Either of these two applicants *are* fit for the job but neither want to accept it.	Either of these two applicants *is* fit for the job but neither wants to accept it.
14.	One of these students are sure to stand first.	One of these students *is* sure to stand first.
15.	Everyone of these workers want a raise.	Everyone of these workers wants a raise.
16.	None of these letters has been answered so far.	None of these letters *have* been answered so far.
17.	None of the girls were present at the party.	None of the girls *was* present at the party.
18.	Many a battle were fought on Indian soil.	Many a battle *was* fought on Indian soil.
19.	A lot of work remain to be done.	A lot of work *remains* to be done.
20.	The majority of these girls likes music.	The majority of these girls *like* music.

Common Errors in the Use of Modals/Auxiliary Verbs

	Incorrect	Correct
1.	When I shall see him I shall tell him this.	When I *see* him, I shall tell him this.
2.	If I should do wrong, he would punish me.	If I *did* wrong, he would punish me.
3.	Until he will have confessed his fault, he will be kept in prison.	Until he *has* confessed his fault, he will be kept in prison.
4.	She will obey me.	She *shall* obey me.
5.	You would work hard.	You *should* work hard.
6.	You shall find him in the garden.	You *will* find him in the garden.
7.	He must have died of exposure, but we cannot be certain.	He *might* have died of exposure, but we cannot be certain.
8.	You might not show disrespect to your elders.	You *must* not show disrespect to your elders.
9.	You may take exercise in order to maintain good health.	You *must* take exercise in order to maintain good health.
10.	He must be a crook for all we know.	He *may* be a crook for all we know.

Common Errors in the Use of Adverbs

	Incorrect	Correct
1.	He is very much angry.	He is *very* angry.
2.	She was very good enough to help me.	She was *good enough* to help me.
3.	She runs much fast.	She runs *very* fast.
4.	She runs very faster than Seema.	She runs *much* faster than Seema.
5.	It is bitter cold today.	It is *bitterly* cold today.
6.	He is a much learned man.	He is a very learned man.
7.	She is thinking very hardly.	She is thinking very hard.
8.	To tell in brief the film was boring.	*In short* the film was boring.
9.	He told the story in details.	He told the story *in detail.*
10.	I did it anyhow.	I *managed to do* it somehow.
11.	Aeroplanes reach Europe soon.	Aeroplanes reach Europe quickly.
12.	Before long there were dinosaurs on the earth.	*Long ago,* there were dinosaurs on the earth.
13.	This book is too interesting.	This book is *very* interesting.
14.	He lives miserly.	He lives in *a miserly* way.
15.	Just I had gone when she came.	I had just gone when she came.
16.	He sings good.	He sings *well.*
17.	He sings good than I.	He sings *better* than I.
18.	Really speaking it is cold.	*As a matter of fact* it is cold.
19.	He is enough tall to reach the ceiling.	He is *tall enough* to reach the ceiling.
20.	He went directly to his college.	He went *direct* to his college.

Common Errors in the Use of Conjunctions

	Incorrect	Correct
1.	As he is fat so he runs slowly.	As he is fat *he* runs slowly.
2.	If he is fat then he will run slowly.	If he is fat, he will run slowly.
3.	Though he is fat still he runs fast.	Though he is fat, *he runs* fast.
4.	*As* I pulled the trigger at the sametime he shook my arm.	As I pulled the trigger, he shook my arm.
5.	No sooner I had spoken than he left.	No sooner *had* I spoken than he left.

	Incorrect	Correct
6.	Not only he will go, but also he will stay there.	Not only *will he* go, but he *will also* stay there.
7.	Neither he comes nor he writes.	Neither *does he* come nor *does he* write.
8.	Scarcely he entered the room than the telephone rang.	Scarcely *had* he entered the room *when the* telephone rang.
9.	Hardly she had left the house than it began to rain.	Hardly *had she* left the house *when* it began to rain.
10.	He is the fastest runner and he comes last.	He is the fastest runner *but* he comes last.
11.	She is as innocent as if she looks.	She is as innocent as she looks.
12.	Until he does not try he must be punished.	He must be punished unless he tries.
13.	I want to know as to why you are late.	I want to know why you are late.
14.	I am fond of Chinese food as for example sweet and sour prawns.	I am fond of Chinese food, for example, sweet and sour prawns.
15.	He was angry therefore I ran away.	He was angry so I ran away.
16.	I was trying to work, at that time he was disturbing me.	While I was trying to work, he was disturbing me.
17.	Supposing if he is late, what will happen?	Supposing he is late (or if he is late) what will happen?
18.	He asked me that why I was late.	He asked me why I was late.
19.	Let us catch a taxi lest we should not get late.	Let us catch a taxi lest we should get late.
20.	She dresses herself like the teacher does.	She dresses herself as the teacher does.
21.	Wait while I come.	Wait *until* (or *till)* I come.
22.	Until, there is corruption in India, there can be little progress.	*As long* as there is corruption in India there can be little progress.
23.	I have never told a lie nor cheated anybody.	I have never told a lie *nor have I* cheated anybody.
24.	Both Mohan as well as Arun are responsible for this action.	Both Mohan *and* Arun are responsible for this action.
25.	Hindus and Muslims both are to blame for the riots.	*Both Hindus* and Muslims are to blame for the riots.

Common Errors in the Use of Prepositions

	Incorrect	*Correct*
1.	I will not listen him.	I will not listen *to* him.
2.	Copy this word by word.	Copy this word *for* word.
3.	He enquired from her where she lived.	He enquired *of* her where she lived.
4.	Sign here with ink.	Sign here *in* ink.
5.	Has she come in train or by foot?	Has she come *by* train or *on* foot?
6.	She said this at his face.	She said this *to* his face.
7.	Open the book on page one.	Open the book *at* page one.
8.	I was invited for lunch.	I was *invited to* lunch.
9.	I am ill since three months.	I have been *ill for* three months.
10.	This paper is inferior than that.	This paper is inferior *to* that.
11.	This resembles to that.	This *resembles* that.
12.	My brother is superior than you in strength.	My brother is superior *to* you in strength.
13.	He wrote me.	He wrote *to* me.
14.	I shall explain them this.	I shall explain this *to* them.
15.	Send this letter on my address.	Send this letter *to* my address.
16.	He suggested me this.	He suggested this *to* me.
17.	He goes *on his* work.	He goes *to his* work.
18.	He *reached to* Nagpur.	He *reached* Nagpur.
19.	He told *to me* to go.	He told *me* to go.
20.	The term begins *from* July 1st.	The term begins *on* July 1st.

Miscellaneous Errors

	Incorrect	*Correct*
1.	Many *homes* are lying vacant.	Many *houses* are lying vacant.
2.	It is cool in the *shadow* of the tree.	It is cool in the *shade* of the tree.
3.	She *keeps* good health.	She *enjoys* good health.
4.	My leg is *paining*.	*I am feeling pain* in my leg.
5.	*See* this word in the dictionary.	*Look up* this word in the dictionary.
6.	The train will arrive *just now*.	The train will arrive *shortly*.
7.	They are *pulling* on well.	They are *getting* on well.
8.	The river has *over flown* its bank.	The river has *over flown* its banks.
9.	He was appointed *on* the post.	He was appointed *to* the post.
10.	Last but not *the least,* we have to discuss the problem of over population.	Last but not *least,* we have to discuss the problem of over population.
11.	*Cities* after *cities* fell.	*City* after *city* fell.
12.	What is the use Munir going there?	What is the use of Munir going there?
13.	He *did many mischief.*	He *made much mischief.*
14.	It is exact five *in* my watch.	It is exact five *by* my watch.
15.	I will dine with them on *next Sunday.*	I will dine with them *Sunday next.*
16.	Misfortunes when faced bravely and *manly* become less troublesome.	Misfortunes when faced bravely and *manfully* become less troublesome.
17.	I am *laid down* with fever.	I am *laid up* with fever.
18.	He is habituated to smoking.	He is *addicted* to smoking.
19.	*According to my opinion* he is right.	*In my opinion* (or according *to me)* he is right.
20.	Could you please *open* this knot?	Could you please *untie* this knot?

Multiple Choice Questions

Directions: *In this section, each sentence has three parts, indicated by (A), (B) and (C). Read each sentence to find out whether there is an error. If you find an error in any one of the parts (A, B, C), indicate your response by marking the letter related to that part. If a sentence has no error, indicate this by marking '(D)' which stands for "No error". Errors may belong to grammar, usage or idiom. Ignore errors of punctuation, if any.*

1. (A) Beware of/(B) a fair-weather friend/(C) who is neither a friend in need nor a friend indeed/(D) No error.

2. (A) Copernicus proved/(B) that Earth/(C) moves round the Sun./(D) No error.

3. (A) Seldom we have been treated/(B) in such a rude manner/(C) by the police personnel./(D) No error.

4. (A) Some men are born great,/(B) some achieve greatness/(C) and some had greatness thrust on them./(D) No error.

5. (A) The property/(B) was divided/(C) among the two brothers./(D) No error.

6. (A) I am quite certain/(B) that the lady is not only greedy/(C) but miserly./(D) No error.

7. (A) The aircraft overloaded/(B) there was something wrong of the battery/(C) and the engine was making a queer noise/(D) No error.

8. (A) A thorough inquiry of the misappropriation of funds/(B) is now imperative/(C) to bring the guilty to book/(D) No error.

9. (A) The brilliant success in the examination/(B) as well as his record in sports/(C) deserves high praise/(D) No error.

10. (A) While travelling by a train/(B) on a cold winter night/(C) an argument rose between two passengers in our compartment/(D) No error.

11. (A) I cannot find/(B) where has he gone/(C) though I have tried may best/(D) No error.

12. (A) If I was/(B) the Prime Minister of India/(C) I would work wonders/(D) No error.

13. (A) Amit's severe bout of flu/(B) debilitated him so much/(C) that he was too tired to do for work for a week./(D) No error.

14. (A) This is the crux of the entire problem;/(B) everything centres on/(C) it being resolved./(D) No error.

15. (A) One of the major aims of the Air Force/(B) was the complete demolition of all means of transportation/(C) by the bombing of rail lines and terminals./(D) No error.

16. (A) His strong voice cut over/(B) the hum of conversation/(C) like a knife through butter./(D) No error.

17. (A) Even though they weren't expecting us/(B) they managed to knock up/(C) a marvellous meal./(D) No error.

18. (A) The celebrated singer was/(B) surrounded by the usual crowd/(C) of lackeys and hanger-ons./(D) No error.

19. (A) If it weren't/(B) for you,/(C) I wouldn't be alive today./(D) No error.

20. (A) He looked like a lion/(B) baulked from/(C) its prey./(D) No error.

21. (A) Widespread flooding/(B) is effecting/(C) large areas of the villages./(D) No error.

22. (A) She regards/(B) negotiating prices with customers/(C) as her special preserve./(D) No error.

23. (A) Often in political campaigns, a point is reached at which/(B) the candidates take out their gloves./(C) and start slugging with bare fists./(D) No error.

24. (A) If we really set to/(B) we can get the whole house/(C) cleaned in an afternoon./(D) No error.

25. (A) Pieces of rock plummeted/(B) down the mountainside/(C) in the ground below./(D) No error.

26. (A) Since the two parties each won/(B) the same number of seats,/(C) the minority party holds the balance of power./(D) No error.

27. (A) It's arrogant for you/(B) to assume you'll/(C)win every time./(D) No error.

28. (A) We've paid for our travel and accommod-ation,/(B) so we need only to take/(C) some pocket-money with us./(D) No error.

29. (A) There's no evidence to show/(B) that information technology secrets are more/(C) vulnerable in India than Britain or the US./(D) No error.

30. (A) It is shameful that hunting/(B) is still considered sport/(C) by some unscrupulous people in the civilized world./(D) No error.

31. (A) The Prime Minister's good looks won him/(B)the election but he has still to prove/(C) that he's not a just pretty face./(D) No error.

32. (A) The two books are the same/(B) except for the fact that this/(C) has an answer in the back./(D) No error.

33. (A) He estimated his income tax bill/(B) by extrapolation over figures/(C) submitted in previous years./(D) No error.

34. (A) The modern office block/(B) sticks out like a sore thumb/(C) among the old buildings in the area./(D) No error.

35. (A) I will try to put over/(B) some feelers to gauge/(C) people's reactions to our proposal./(D) No error.

36. (A) A major contribution of Mathura sculptors/(B)of that period were the creation and popularization/(C) of the Buddha's image in human form./(D) No error.

37. (A) Amit has been deceiving Mona/(B) for many years but she/(C) has not still tumbled to it./(D) No error.

38. (A) Mahavira was an advocate of nonviolence and vegetarianism,/(B) who revived and reorganized the Jain doctrine/(C) and established rules for their monastic order. (D) No error.

39. (A) Microwaves are the principle carriers/(B) of television, telephone and data transmissions/(C)between stations on earth and between the earth and satellites./(D) No error.

40. (A) An unit is an abstract idea,/(B) defined either by reference to/(C) a randomly chosen material standard or to a natural phenomenon./(D) No error.

41. (A) With the crisis deepening,/(B) the critics sense an opportunity/(C) about putting in place a more radical strategy./(D) No error.

42. (A) The salesman gave us/(B) a big spiel about why/(C) we should buy his product./(D) No error.

43. (A) I will need several weeks/(B) to invent the lie of the land before/(C) I can make any decision about the future of the business./(D) No error.

44. (A) You should be cautious/(B) and make a few discrete enquiries about/(C) the firm before you sign anything./(D) No error.

45. (A) Your husband doesn't/(B) believe that you are older/(C) than I./(D) No error.

46. (A) We are meeting today afternoon/(B) to discuss the matter/(C) and reach a compromise./(D) No error.

47. (A) Either Ram or/(B) you is responsible/(C) for this action./(D) No error.

48. (A) The student flatly denied/(B) that he had copied/(C) in the examination hall./(D) No error.

49. (A) By the time you arrive tomorrow/(B) I have finished/(C) my work./(D) No error.

50. (A) The speaker stressed repeatedly on/(B) the importance of improving/(C) the condition of the slums./(D) No error.

51. (A) The captain with the members of his team/(B) are returning/(C) after a fortnight./(D) No error.

52. (A) After returning from/(B) an all-India tour/(C) I had to describe about it/(D) No error.

53. (A) The teacher asked his students/(B) if they had gone through/(C) either of the three chapters included in the prescribed text./(D) No error.

54. (A) Although they are living in the country/(B) since they were married/(C) they are now moving to the town./(D) No error.

55. (A) Do you know/(B) how old were you/(C) when you came here?/(D) No error.

ANSWERS

1	2	3	4	5	6	7	8	9	10
D	B	A	C	C	C	B	A	D	C
11	**12**	**13**	**14**	**15**	**16**	**17**	**18**	**19**	**20**
B	A	C	C	B	A	A	C	C	C
21	**22**	**23**	**24**	**25**	**26**	**27**	**28**	**29**	**30**
C	A	A	A	C	A	A	B	D	B
31	**32**	**33**	**34**	**35**	**36**	**37**	**38**	**39**	**40**
C	C	C	D	A	B	C	C	A	A
41	**42**	**43**	**44**	**45**	**46**	**47**	**48**	**49**	**50**
C	D	D	D	C	A	B	D	B	A
51	**52**	**53**	**54**	**55**					
B	C	C	B	D					

❑❑❑

3 Articles

Definite and Indefinite Articles

(*i*) 'A' and 'an' are Indefinite Articles.

(*ii*) 'The' is Definite Article.

(*iii*) 'A' and 'an' modify a noun in a general way.

(*iv*) 'The' particularises it. *e.g.*,

Mohan has **a pen.**

The pen which you gave me was expensive.

Vowel and Consonant Sounds

(*i*) 'A' is used before words starting with the sound of a consonant.

(*ii*) 'An' is used before a vowel sound (vowels a, e, i, o, u) *e.g.*, a book, a cat, a useful thing, a European girl, a university, but an FDR, an MA, an honest boy, an hour, an owl, an egg, an umbrella, etc.

Use of Articles 'A' and 'An'

A cat mews. (*i.e.,* every cat)

The cat of my neighbour mews day and night. (*i.e.,* a particular cat)

He gave me **an** egg. (Here 'an' means 'one')

Use of Article 'The'

1. 'The' is used before names of rivers, mountains, seas, oceans:

   The Himalayas, the Ganga, the Yamuna, the Bay of Bengal, the Indian Ocean, the Nile, the English Channel, *etc.*

2. Names of newspapers and magazines:

   The Times of India, the Tribune, The Sun, *etc.*

3. Names of the famous and holy books:

   The Guru Granth Sahib, The Gita, The Ramayana, *etc.*

4. Names of creations of nature:

   the sun, the earth, the moon, the sky, *etc.*

5. While using Adjectives as Nouns:

   The poor should be helped by **the rich.**

6. Sometimes with the Comparative Degree:

   The more you think, **the more** you worry.

7. With the Superlative Degree:

   She is **the most intelligent** girl in our school.

8. Before the imaginary lines and directions:

   The Latitude, The Equator, the east, the west, etc.

9. Before the names of musical instruments:

   The violin, the piano, the flute, etc.

10. While using a Proper Noun as a Common Noun:

    Mohan is **the Sachin** of our team.

Omission of Article 'The'

1. Before some Nouns used to convey general sense, articles are not used but are used to particularise them:

   Man is mortal.

2. Before Proper Nouns:

   Rakesh is an intelligent boy.

3. With Abstract Noun:

   Childhood is the prime time of one's life.

   The childhood of Sohan was full of sorrow.

4. With Material Nouns:

   Milk is an essential food.

   The milk of the cow is sweet.

5. Usually no article is used before names of diseases:

   Cancer is a fatal disease.

   However, when we talk about a disease figuratively, we use an article before its name, *e.g.*

   Corruption is a cancer.

6. Names of games and language:

   I like football.

   I can speak Punjabi, Hindi and English.

7. Gold is a precious metal.

   NOTE: As you must have noted above, the definite article 'the' has been used where a noun is particularised.

Double Use of Article 'The'

Read the following sentences carefully to understand this :

1. The poet and novelist has been honoured.
   (The same person is the poet as well as novelist)
2. The poet and the novelist have been honoured.
   (The poet and the novelist are two different persons).
3. I have a black and white dog.
   (that is, one dog)
4. I have a black and a white dog.
   (that is, two dogs)

Multiple Choice Questions

Directions : *Fill in the blanks with suitable articles. Mark 'D' if no article required.*

1. Do you know .... boy in white?
A. a B. an
C. the D. No article

2. She is .... girl I am looking for.
A. a B. an
C. the D. No article

3. Have you read .... Mahabharat?
A. a B. an
C. the D. No article

4. ....rich are not always happy.
A. A B. An
C. The D. No article

5. Oranges are sold by .... dozen.
A. a B. an
C. the D. No article

6. Milk is sold by .... litre.
A. a B. an
C. the D. No article

7. .... Amazon is the longest river in the world.
A. A B. An
C. The D. No article

8. .... higher you climb, the colder it gets.
A. A B. An
C. The D. No article

9. She is .... untidy girl.
A. a B. an
C. the D. No article

10. I am .... M.A. is English.
A. a B. an
C. the D. No article

11. I have already spent .... few rupees I had.
A. a B. an
C. the D. No article

12. .... English are very hard-working.
A. A B. An
C. The D. No article

13. April is the fourth month of .... year.
A. a B. an
C. the D. No article

14. Rice is sold by .... kilogram
A. a B. an
C. the D. No article

15. She is .... best of the three girls.
A. a B. an
C. the D. No article

16. .... man in the car is a friend of mine.
A. A B. An
C. The D. No article

17. Brevity is .... soul of wit.
A. a B. an
C. the D. No article

18. .... thing of beauty is a joy for ever.
A. A B. An
C. The D. No article

19. .... little learning is a dangerous thing.
A. A B. An
C. The D. No article

20. .... best sauce for food is hunger.
A. A B. An
C. The D. No article

21. Birds of .... feather flock together.
A. a B. an
C. the D. No article

22. He makes .... living by begging.
A. a B. an
C. the D. No article

23. It is .... pity that he died so young.
A. a B. an
C. the D. No article

24. What .... nuisance it is?
A. a B. an
C. the D. No article

25. Delhi is .... London of India.
A. a B. an
C. the D. No article

26. Where is .... will, there is a way.
A. a B. an
C. the D. No article

27. Her father is .... physician and surgeon.
A. a B. an
C. the D. No article

28. This will benefit .... poor.
A. a B. an
C. the D. No article

29. ....bird in hand is better than two in a bush.
A. A B. An
C. The D. No article

30. As he is hard-working, he will win .... prize.
A. a B. an
C. the D. No article

31. .... water of this well is dirty.
A. A B. An
C. The D. No article

32. Only .... wearer knows where the shoe pinches.
A. a B. an
C. the D. No article

33. .... action will be taken against you.
A. A B. An
C. The D. No article

34. .... sun rises in the east.
A. A B. An
C. The D. No article

35. She was promoted to .... highest post.
A. a B. an
C. the D. No article

36. Did you see .... Táj Mahal?
A. a B. an
C. the D. No article

37. He is .... one-eyed man.
A. a B. an
C. the D. No article

38. This is .... useful book.
A. a B. an
C. the D. No article

39. Cloth is sold by .... metre.
A. a B. an
C. the D. No article

40. The sun sets in .... west.
A. a B. an
C. the D. No article

41. Amar bought......umbrella yesterday.
A. a B. an
C. the D. No article

42. Surinder is ...... honest boy.
A. a B. an
C. the D. No article

43. She wrote ...... book in French.
A. a B. an
C. the D. No article

44. ...... lion roars.
A. A B. An
C. The D. No article

45. ..... apple a day keeps the doctor away.
A. A B. An
C. The D. No article

46. John bought ...... car yesterday.
A. a B. an
C. the D. No article

47. His father is ..... engineer in the U.S.A.
A. a B. an
C. the D. No article

48. It is hard for ..... owl to fly during the day times.
A. a B. an
C. the D. No article

49. She had ..... rimmed hat.
A. a B. an
C. the D. No article

50. My uncle is ..... heart specialist.
A. a B. an
C. the D. No article

51. He looks as foolish as .... ass.
A. a B. an
C. the D. No article

52. Did you go to .... prison to visit him?
A. a B. an
C. the D. No article

53. I found .... one-rupee note in the market.
A. a B. an
C. the D. No article

54. It is a pleasure to meet such .... efficient man.
A. a B. an
C. the D. No article

55. The Sanyasi lived in a cave in .... Himalayas.
A. a B. an
C. the D. No article

56. There is .... union in our factory.
A. a B. an
C. the D. No article

57. He hit his wife on the head with .... umbrella.
A. a B. an
C. the D. No article

58. I caught him by .... collar.

A. a B. an

C. the D. No article

59. Child is .... father of man.

A. a B. an

C. the D. No article

60. He gazed at .... moon for two hours.

A. a B. an

C. the D. No article

ANSWERS

1	2	3	4	5	6	7	8	9	10
C	C	C	C	C	C	C	C	B	B
11	**12**	**13**	**14**	**15**	**16**	**17**	**18**	**19**	**20**
C	C	C	C	C	C	C	A	A	C
21	**22**	**23**	**24**	**25**	**26**	**27**	**28**	**29**	**30**
A	A	A	A	C	A	A	C	A	A
31	**32**	**33**	**34**	**35**	**36**	**37**	**38**	**39**	**40**
C	C	B	C	C	C	A	A	C	C
41	**42**	**43**	**44**	**45**	**46**	**47**	**48**	**49**	**50**
B	B	A	A	B	A	B	B	A	A
51	**52**	**53**	**54**	**55**	**56**	**57**	**58**	**59**	**60**
B	C	A	B	C	A	B	C	C	C

❑❑❑

4 Prepositions

A Preposition is a word that comes before a Pronoun or a Noun and expresses the relationship between Noun or Pronoun and some part of the remaining sentence.

(*a*) He is busy **with** his work.
(*b*) The boy jumped **into** the river.
(*c*) The birds are chirping **in** the trees.

In these sentences the words **with**, **into** and **in** show the relationship between the verbs **busy, jumped** and **chirping** with the nouns **work, river** and **trees** respectively.

Position of the Preposition

A. A Preposition usually precedes its object.
(*i*) He laughs **at** the poor.
(*ii*) He is angry **with** you.
(*iii*) She agrees **with** me.

B. In the case of Relative Pronouns it comes after the subject.
(*i*) This is the boy whom I was looking **for**.
(*ii*) That is the pen whose mention I was making **of**.

C. In the following cases, the Preposition comes after its object.
(*i*) Where is the boy you were complaining **against**?
(*ii*) What things are there you are looking **for**?
(*iii*) Who is there, you are waiting **for**?

Omission of the Prepositon

In many cases when the sentences contain Nouns of Time or Place, the Prepositions **from**, **in** and **for** are often omitted.

(*i*) He walked many kilometres.
(*ii*) He came to see me last year.
(*iii*) As I could not find my puppy anywhere, I looked here and there.

Prepositions are small words that show the relationship between one word and another. Prepositions in the following sentences show the position of the paper in relation to the desk, the book, hand and the door.

The paper is **on** the desk.
The paper is **under** the book.
The paper is **in** his hand.
The paper is **by** the door.

Common Prepositions

about	at	by
in	onto	toward
above	before	concerning
inside	out	under
across	behind	despite
into	over	until
after	below	down
like	since	up
against	beneath	during
near	through	upon
along	beside	except
of	throughout	with
amid	between	for
off	till	within
among	beyond	from
on	to	without

Multiple Choice Questions

Directions: *Select the most appropriate preposition from the given alternatives to fill in the blanks and make the sentence meaningfully complete.*

1. Don't try to be an advocate ..... these criminals.
A. for B. with
C. across D. in

2. The audience admired him ..... his sweet voice.
A. to B. on
C. for D. at

3. I want to check your bag ..... fake currency notes.
A. to B. for
C. upon D. on

4. The dew drops clung .... the blades of grass.
A. for B. on
C. to D. in

5. The thief was chased ..... by the police.
A. on B. after
C. into D. at

6. Please carry this bag ..... my room.
A. on B. for
C. to D. in

7. A lorry bumped ..... a car.
A. on B. over
C. into D. to

8. They were begging ..... food.
A. for B. on
C. to D. after

9. She always boasts ..... her wealth.
A. of B. for
C. on D. after

10. She banged ..... the door violently.
A. for B. to
C. on D. down

11. I applied ..... the post of a clerk.
A. for B. on
C. in D. to

12. I applied ..... the Principal for the post of a teacher.
A. to B. on
C. with D. for

13. I begged ..... him not to divulge the secret.
A. for B. of
C. with D. to

14. You had better borrow a pen ..... Rakesh.
A. over B. into
C. from D. by

15. I baked a cake ..... the guests.
A. to B. for
C. on D. of

16. She is confident ..... (her) success.
A. with B. on
C. of D. for

17. The doctor will cure you ..... malaria.
A. of B. with
C. for D. from

18. This law is common ..... all.
A. to B. upon
C. over D. at

19. She was condemned ..... her bad hand writing.
A. on B. for
C. into D. of

20. In summer there will be a great demand ..... desert cooler.
A. on B. with
C. for D. of

21. We shall wait ..... you.
A. on B. for
C. towards D. after

22. Tom displayed his injury ..... all his friends.
A. for B. upon
C. to D. at

23. She distributed the sweets ..... the two brothers.
A. among B. between
C. for D. in

24. Please distribute these apples ..... all.
A. among B. to
C. for D. at

25. It rarely happened that he defended ..... an innocent person.
A. against B. for
C. upon D. at

26. The parents were disappointed ..... the performance of their son.
A. on B. with
C. at D. of

27. Common salt dissolves ..... water.
A. for B. in
C. with D. by

28. This medicare is free ..... sugar.
A. on B. to
C. from D. of

29. The manager granted leave ..... the clerk.
A. to B. on
C. into D. for

30. The air was heavy ..... aroma of perfumes.
A. on B. with
C. into D. from

31. She had a quick glance ..... the magazine.
A. at B. from
C. into D. to

32. The climate of Kashmir is favourable ..... me.
A. with B. in
C. to D. for

33. They hate you ..... your poverty.
A. for B. on
C. in D. of

34. He is eligible ..... this post.
A. for B. to
C. with D. at

35. The smoke was emerging ..... down the foot of the hill.
A. on B. to
C. from D. at

36. The criminal managed to escape ..... the prison.
A. upon B. from
C. with D. of

37. You should educate your friends ..... the benefits of living in villages.
A. on B. towards
C. upon D. in

38. She made a lot of efforts ..... win the match.
A. for B. to
C. upon D. at

39. The new inspector will enquire ..... the murder case.
A. on B. for
C. into D. at

40. The retired soldiers were exempted ..... all taxes.
A. from B. to
C. on D. of

41. She was adept ..... journalism.
A. at B. on
C. with D. in

42. She is afraid ..... snakes.
A. on B. to
C. of D. with

43. I agree ..... your proposal.
A. for B. on
C. to D. with

44. The children were amazed ..... so big a python.
A. at B. on
C. in D. with

45. She was anxious ..... the final match.
A. about B. on
C. with D. for

46. He apologized ..... his being late.
A. towards B. for
C. on D. as

47. The children were amused ..... his jokes.
A. for B. to
C. at D. on

48. She is angry ..... you.
A. to B. with
C. on D. for

49. She is angry ..... your teasing remark.
A. at B. in
C. for D. with

50. A big patch of land was allocated ..... the refugees.
A. to B. for
C. in D. upon

ANSWERS

1	2	3	4	5	6	7	8	9	10
A	C	B	C	B	C	C	A	A	C
11	12	13	14	15	16	17	18	19	20
A	A	B	C	B	C	A	A	B	C
21	22	23	24	25	26	27	28	29	30
B	C	B	A	A	C	B	C	A	B
31	32	33	34	35	36	37	38	39	40
A	C	A	A	C	B	A	B	C	A
41	42	43	44	45	46	47	48	49	50
A	C	C	A	A	B	C	B	A	A

❑❑❑

5 Synonyms & Antonyms

There are thousands of words in English language. No one can remember their meanings easily but with regular practice one can memorise most of them. A number of words with their Synonyms and Antonyms are compiled here. Try to learn as many as you can and answer the questions thereafter.

Words	Synonyms	Antonyms
Abandon	Cease, Forsake	Continue
Abhor	Hate, Loathe, Detest	Like, Love
Abiding	Enduring, Durable	Fleeting
Able	Proficient, Competent	Incompetent, Unfit
Ability	Skill, Power	Disability, Inability
Abortive	Fruitless, Futile	Fruitful, Successful
Abolish	Destroy, Undo	Restore, Revive
Abridge	Shorten, Curtail	Lengthen, Expand
Absolve	Forgive, Pardon, Excuse	Condemn
Accelerate	Hasten	Retard
Accord	Agreement, Harmony	Discord, Disagreement
Accumulate	Collect, Store, Amass	Distribute, Scatter
Adamant	Hard, Inflexible	Flexible
Adversity	Misfortune, Distress	Prosperity
Adept	Expert, Skilful	Inexpert, Unskillful
Aggravate	Heighten, Intensify	Quell, Suppress
Agile	Nimble	Clumsy, Undeft
Alert	Vigilant	Heedless
Allay	Calm, Soothe, Assuage	Arouse
Ameliorate	Improve, Advance, Amend	Worsen, Deteriorate
Ambiguous	Vague, Unclear	Clear
Amiable	Lovable, Agreeable	Disagreeable
Annihilate	Destroy	Create
Arduous	Hard, Strenuous	Easy
Attacks	Assault	Defend
Audacity	Boldness	Cowardice
Auspicious	Favourable, Propitious, Lucky	Ominous, Inauspicious, Unlucky
Austere	Harsh, Severe, Rigorous	Easy-going

Words	Synonyms	Antonyms
Authentic	True, Genuine	Spurious, False
Avarice	Greed	Generosity
Averse	Unwilling, Loath, Disinclined	Willing, Inclined
Aversion	Hostility, Hatred	Affinity, Liking
Base	Low, Mean, Ignoble	Noble, Exalted
Boisterous	Noisy, Stormy	Calm, Quiet
Brave	Courageous, Daring, Bold, Plucky	Cowardly, Dastardly, Timid
Brief	Short, Concise, Laconic	Lengthy, Diffuse
Bright	Vivid, Radiant	Dull, Dark
Brutal	Savage, Cruel	Humane, Kindly
Callous	Hard, Cruel, Indifferent	Soft, Tender, Concerned
Cautious	Careful, Wary	Rash, Reckless, Foolhardy
Censure (*n*)	Blame, Condemnation	Praise
Censure (*vb*)	Blame, Condemn	Praise, Commend
Circumscribed	Restricted, Confined, Limited	Unconfined, Unrestricted
Civil	Polite, Courteous, Gracious, Urbane	Rude, Uncivil, Impolite, Ungracious
Coerce	Compel, Force	Volunteer
Compassionate	Pitiful, Sympathetic, Merciful	Unsympathetic, Merciless, Cruel
Compress	Condense, Abbreviate	Expand, Lengthen
Conspicuous	Noticeable, Manifest	Inconspicuous
Constant	Steady, Steadfast, Uniform	Inconstant, Variable
Cordial	Friendly, Warm, Hearty	Cold, Unfriendly
Covert	Hidden, Secret	Overt, Open
Cruel	Savage, Ruthless, Vicious	Kind, Gentle, Benevolent
Cursory	Rapid, Superficial	Thorough, Exhaustive, Intensive
Credible	Believable, Probable, Plausible	Incredible, Unbelievable, Fantastic
Crafty	Cunning, Sly	Artless, Simple, Ingenuous
Costly	Expensive, Dear	Cheap, Inexpensive
Confidence	Trust, Reliance	Distrust, Doubt
Death	Decease, Demise	Existence, Life
Dearth	Scarcity, Lack, Want, Paucity, Shortage	Plenty, Abundance
Decay	Dissolution, Decline, Decomposition, Disintegration	Regeneration
Deference	Respect, Reverence	Disrespect, Irreverence
Deficient	Lacking, Inadequate	Complete, Sufficient
Desolate	Lonely, Deserted	Crowded, Occupied
Destitute	Wanting, Needy	Rich, Affluent
Diligence	Industry, Perseverance	Idleness
Disgrace	Dishonour, Discredit	Honour, Credit
Dwindle	Decrease, Shrink	Grow, Increase
Earthly	Terrestrial, Mundane	Celestial, Heavenly, Unearthly
Eligible	Qualified, Suitable	Ineligible, Unsuitable
Emancipate	Liberate, Free	Enslave
Excited	Impassioned, Stimulated	Composed, Cool, Impassive
Extraordinary	Uncommon, Remarkable, Marvellous	Commonplace, Ordinary
Extravagant	Lavish, Prodigal, Wastrel, Spendthrift	Thrifty, Economical, Frugal

Words	Synonyms	Antonyms
Fabricate	Construct, Make	Destroy
Fabulous	Fictitious, Mythical	Actual, Real
False	Untrue, Mendacious	True, Genuine
Famous	Well-known, Renowned	Obscure, Unknown
Fantastic	Fanciful, Imaginative, Visionary	Practical, Down to earth
Fearful	Nervous, Anxious, Afraid, Scared	Fearless, Dauntless
Felicity	Happiness	Sorrow
Gaiety	Joyousness, Hilarity	Mourning, Dullness
Garrulous	Talkative, Loquacious	Taciturn, Silent, Reserved
Generous	Liberal, Magnanimous	Stingy, Miserly
Gigantic	Huge, Colossal	Minute, Small
Graphic	Vivid, Pictorial, Meaningful	Vague
Guest	Visitor	Host
Guile	Fraud, Trickery	Artlessness, Ingenuousness
Gratitude	Gratefulness	Ingratitude, Ungratefulness
Gratuitous	Voluntary, Spontaneous, Unwarranted	Involuntary, Forced
Hamper	Hinder, Obstruct	Facilitate, Ease
Haughty	Arrogant, Proud	Humble, Modest
Hazardous	Dangerous, Perilous	Safe, Secure Protected
Headstrong	Obstinate, Stubborn	Weak-willed, Flexible
Hope	Belief, Conviction, Expectation	Despair, Hopelessness
Improvident	Prodigal, Carelessness	Provident, Economical
Incessant	Unceasing, Continuous	Discontinuous
Indolent	Slothful, Lethargic	Active, Energetic
Joy	Delight, Pleasure	Sadness, Gloom
Jolly	Jovial, Merry	Gloomy, Sad
Judicious	Discreet, Prudent	Indiscreet, Injudicious
Knowledge	Enlightenment, Learning	Ignorance, Stupidity
Laborious	Industrious, Assiduous	Slothful, Lazy
Laxity	Slackness, Looseness	Firmness
Lenient	Mild, Forbearing	Strict, Stern
Lethal	Deadly, Fatal, Mortal	Life-giving, Vital, Vivifying
Liberal	Generous, Tolerant	Intolerant, Illiberal
Liberty	Freedom, Independence	Slavery, Bondage
Lively	Animated, Active	Dull, Listless
Loyal	Faithful, Devoted	Treacherous, Disloyal, Unfaithful
Lucky	Fortunate	Unlucky, Unfortunate
Lucrative	Profitable	Unprofitable
Magnanimous	Generous, Largehearted	Ungenerous, Stingy
Malady	Illness, Ailment	Health
Manifest	Noticeable, Obvious	Obscure, Puzzling
Meagre	Small	Plentiful, Large
Mean	Low, Abject	Noble, Exalted
Mendacious	False, Untruthful	Truthful
Misery	Sorrow, Distress	Happiness, Joy

Words	Synonyms	Antonyms
Morbid	Sick, Diseased	Healthy
Mournful	Sorrowful, Sad	Joyful, Happy
Negligent	Careless, Heedless	Careful
Notorious	Infamous, Disreputable	Reputable
Obedient	Submissive, Compliant, Docile	Disobedient, Recalcitrant, Wayward
Obsolete	Antiquated, Out-of-Date	Current, Modern
Opportune	Timely, Seasonable	Inopportune
Opulence	Wealth, Riches	Penury, Poverty
Onerous	Heavy, Burdensome	Light, Easy
Palatable	Tasty, Delicious	Unpalatable
Pathetic	Touching	Joyous, Cheery
Persuade	Urge, Induce	Dissuade
Praise *(vb)*	Applaud, Eulogise	Condemn
Praise *(n)*	Applause, Eulogy	Condemnation
Precarious	Risky, Uncertain	Safe, Certain
Pretence	Pretext, Excuse	Candour, Frankness
Propagate	Breed, Circulate	Terminate, Restrict
Quaint	Odd, Singular	Usual, Ordinary
Quell	Suppress, Subdue	Agitate, Arouse
Rare	Uncommon, Scarce	Common, Ordinary
Refined	Polished, Elegant	Crude, Coarse
Remote	Distant	Near, Close
Renown	Fame, Reputation	Infamy, Notoriety
Rigid	Stiff, Unyielding	Flexible, Yielding
Remorseful	Regretful, Repentant	Unrepentant
Rebellion	Revolt, Mutiny, Insurgency	Loyalty
Scared	Holy, Consecrated	Profane, Unholy
Sane	Sensible, Sound	Insane
Scold	Chide, Rebuke	Praise
Serious	Grave, Earnest	Frivolous
Shy	Bashful	Bold, Impudent
Simple	Plain, Artless	Complex, Cunning, Shrewd
Solitary	Single, Lonely, Secluded	Numerous, Multitude
Shallow	Superficial	Deep
Solace	Comfort, Relief	Discomfort, Grief
Spurious	Sham, False	Genuine, Authentic
Stagnant	Still, Motionless	Moving
Surplus	Excess	Deficit, Shortage
Tame	Gentle, Mild, Domesticated	Savage, Wild
Teacher	Instructor, Educator	Student, Pupil
Tedious	Wearisome, Monotonous	Agreeable, Lively
Temporal	Worldly, Secular	Spiritual
Temperate	Moderate	Immoderate, Intemperate
Tortuous	Winding, Circuitous	Straight, Direct
Tough	Hard, Strong	Tender, Soft, Flexible

Words	Synonyms	Antonyms
Transient	Temporary, Fleeting	Lasting, Durable, Permanent
Trusworthy	Reliable	Unreliable, Untrustworthy
Tranquil	Calm	Agitated
Ugly	Unsightly, Repulsive	Beautiful, Attractive
Useful	Advantageous, Serviceable	Useless
Vehemence	Passion, Force	Apathy, Indifference
Vindictive	Revengeful	Forgiving
Wholesome	Healthy	Unwholesome, Morbid, Unhealthy, Diseased
Wicked	Evil, Impious	Pious, Good
Wise	Sagacious, Erudite	Foolish, Stupid
Wrath	Anger, Fury, Rage	Love, Peace, Calm
Wreck	Ruin, Destroy	Create, Construct
Yield	Surrender, Submit	Resist, Revolt
Yielding	Submissive, Supple	Inflexible, Intractable
Yoke	Oppression, Bondage	Freedom
Zeal	Passion, Fervour	Apathy, Indifference
Zest	Relish, Enthusiasm	Distaste, Disrelish

Multiple Choice Questions

Directions (Qs. 1 to 50): *In the following questions choose the word which best expresses the MEANING of the given word.*

1. TEPID
   A. Hot B. Warm
   C. Cold D. Boiling
2. MAYHEM
   A. Jubilation B. Havoc
   C. Excitement D. Defeat
3. TIMID
   A. Fast B. Slow
   C. Medium D. Shy
4. CANTANKEROUS
   A. Quarrelsome B. Rash
   C. Disrespectful D. Noisy
5. PRECARIOUS
   A. Cautious B. Critical
   C. Perilous D. Brittle
6. TACITURNITY
   A. Dumbness B. Changeableness
   C. Hesitation D. Reserve
7. INEBRIATE
   A. Dreamy B. Stupefied
   C. Unsteady D. Drunken
8. HARBINGER
   A. Massenger B. Steward
   C. Forerunner D. Pilot
9. INTIMIDATE
   A. To hint B. Frighten
   C. Bluff D. Harass
10. IRONIC
    A. Inflexible B. Bitter
    C. Good-natured D. Disguisedly sarcastic
11. STRINGENT
    A. Tense B. Stringy
    C. Strict D. Causing to shrink
12. ECSTATIC
    A. Animated B. Bewildered
    C. Enraptured D. Willful
13. COMMENSURATE
    A. Measurable B. Proportionate
    C. Beginning D. Appropriate
14. DESTITUTION
    A. Humility B. Moderation
    C. Poverty D. Beggary
15. ASCEND
    A. Leap B. Grow
    C. Deviate D. Mount
16. UNCOUTH
    A. Ungraceful B. Rough
    C. Slovenly D. Dirty

17. LYNCH
A. Hang B. Madden
C. Killed D. Shoot

18. LAUD
A. Lord B. Eulogy
C. Praise D. Extolled

19. CORRESPONDENCE
A. Agreements B. Contracts
C. Documents D. Letters

20. VENUE
A. Place B. Agenda
C. Time D. Duration

21. STERILE
A. Barren B. Arid
C. Childless D. Dry

22. SYNOPSIS
A. Index B. Mixture
C. Summary D. Puzzle

23. GERMANE
A. Responsible B. Logical
C. Possible D. Relevant

24. PONDER
A. Think B. Evaluate
C. Anticipate D. Increase

25. CANNY
A. Obstinate B. Handsome
C. Clever D. Stout

26. ABUNDANT
A. Ripe B. Cheap
C. Plenty D. Absent

27. CONSEQUENCES
A. Results B. Conclusions
C. Difficulties D. Applications

28. SHIVER
A. Shake B. Rock
C. Tremble D. Move

29. DILIGENT
A. Progressive B. Brilliant
C. Inventive D. Hard-working

30. DISTANT
A. Far B. Removed
C. Reserved D. Separate

31. FORAY
A. Excursion B. Contest
C. Ranger D. Intuition

32. FRUGALITY
A. Foolishness B. Extremity
C. Enthusiasm D. Economy

33. GARNISH
A. Paint B. Garner
C. Adorn D. Abuse

34. VIGOUR
A. Strength B. Boldness
C. Warmth D. Enthusiasm

35. CANDID
A. Apparent B. Explicit
C. Frank D. Bright

36. BRIEF
A. Limited B. Small
C. Little D. Short

37. GARRULITY
A. Credulity B. Senility
C. Loquaciousness D. Speciousness

38. FURORE
A. Excitement B. Worry
C. Flux D. Anteroom

39. NEUTRAL
A. Unbiased B. Non-aligned
C. Undecided D. Indifferent

40. LAMENT
A. Complain B. Comment
C. Condone D. Console

41. ADVERSITY
A. Failure B. Helplessness
C. Misfortune D. Crisis

42. TURN UP
A. Land up B. Show up
C. Crop up D. Come up

43. DEIFY
A. Flatter B. Challenge
C. Worship D. Face

44. ERROR
A. Misadventure B. Misgiving
C. Ambiguity D. Blunder

45. SHALLOW
A. Artificial B. Superficial
C. Foolish D. Worthless

46. MASSACRE
A. Murder B. Stab
C. Assassinate D. Slaughter

47. COMBAT
A. Conflict B. Quarrel
C. Feud D. Fight

48. VORACIOUS
A. Wild B. Hungry
C. Angry D. Quick

49. IMPROMPTU
A. Offhand B. Unimportant
C. Unreal D. Effective

50. RABBLE
A. Mob B. Noise
C. Roar D. Rubbish

Directions (Qs. 51 to 100): *In the following questions choose the word which is the exact OPPOSITE of the given words.*

51. STRINGENT
A. General B. Vehement
C. Lenient D. Magnanimous

52. FLIMSY
A. Frail B. Filthy
C. Firm D. Flippant

53. BUSY
A. Occupied B. Engrossed
C. Relaxed D. Engaged

54. ADAPTABLE
A. Adoptable B. Flexible
C. Yielding D. Rigid

55. LOVE
A. Villainy B. Hatred
C. Compulsion D. Force

56. BALANCE
A. Disbalance B. Misbalance
C. Debalance D. Imbalance

57. RELINQUISH
A. Abdicate B. Renounce
C. Possess D. Deny

58. MOUNTAIN
A. Plain B. Plateau
C. Precipice D. Valley

59. FICKLE
A. Courageous B. Sincere
C. Steadfast D. Humble

60. PERENNIAL
A. Frequent B. Regular
C. Lasting D. Rare

61. RARELY
A. Hardly B. Definitely
C. Frequently D. Periodically

62. STARTLED
A. Amused B. Relaxed
C. Endless D. Astonished

63. ADHERENT
A. Detractor B. Enemy
C. Alien D. Rival

64. QUIESCENT
A. Indifferent B. Troublesome
C. Weak D. Unconcerned

65. CONDENSE
A. Expand B. Distribute
C. Interpret D. Lengthen

66. BENIGN
A. Malevolent B. Soft
C. Friendly D. Unwise

67. OBSCURE
A. Implicit B. Obnoxious
C. Explicit D. Pedantic

68. HYPOCRITICAL
A. Gentle B. Sincere
C. Amiable D. Dependable

69. EVASIVE
A. Free B. Honest
C. Liberal D. Frank

70. INDUSTRIOUS
A. Indifferent B. Indolent
C. Casual D. Passive

71. EXTRICATE
A. Manifest B. Palpable
C. Release D. Entangle

72. LUCID
A. Glory B. Noisy
C. Obscure D. Distinct

73. INSIPID
A. Tasty B. Stupid
C. Discreet D. Feast

74. OBEYING
A. Ordering B. Following
C. Refusing D. Contradicting

75. VICTORIOUS
A. Defeated B. Annexed
C. Destroyed D. Vanquished

76. COMMISSIONED
A. Started B. Closed
C. Finished D. Terminated

77. VANITY
A. Pride B. Humility
C. Conceit D. Ostentious

78. ZENITH
A. Acme B. Top
C. Nadir D. Pinnacle

79. TANGIBLE
A. Ethereal B. Concrete
C. Actual D. Solid

80. REPRESS
A. Inhibit B. Liberate
C. Curb D. Quell

81. EPILOGUE
A. Dialogue B. Prelude
C. Post script D. Epigram

82. FRAUDULENT
A. Candid B. Direct
C. Forthright D. Genuine

83. LOQUACIOUS
A. Reticent B. Talkative
C. Garrulous D. Verbose

84. NIGGARDLY
A. Frugal B. Thrifty
C. Stingy D. Generous

85. PERTINENT
A. Irrational B. Irregular
C. Insistent D. Irrelevant

86. FAINT-HEARTED
A. Warm-hearted B. Full-blooded
C. Hot-blooded D. Stout-hearted

87. VIOLENT
A. Humble B. Harmless
C. Gentle D. Tame

88. STATIONARY
A. Active B. Mobile
C. Rapid D. Busy

89. HONORARY
A. Dishonourable B. Reputed
C. Paid D. Official

90. COMMON
A. Rare B. Small
C. Petty D. Poor

91. REPEL
A. Attend B. Concentrate
C. Continue D. Attract

92. ARTIFICIAL
A. Red B. Natural
C. Truthful D. Solid

93. CAPACIOUS
A. Limited B. Caring
C. Foolish D. Changeable

94. PROVOCATION
A. Vocation B. Pacification
C. Peace D. Destruction

95. METICULOUS
A. Mutual B. Shaggy
C. Meretricious D. Slovenly

96. ABLE
A. Disable B. Inable
C. Unable D. Enable

97. COMFORT
A. Uncomfort B. Miscomfort
C. Discomfort D. None of these

98. GAIN
A. Loose B. Fall
C. Lost D. Lose

99. SYNTHETIC
A. Affable B. Natural
C. Plastic D. Cosmetic

100. ACQUITTED
A. Freed B. Burdened
C. Convicted D. Entrusted

ANSWERS

1	2	3	4	5	6	7	8	9	10
B	B	D	A	B	D	D	C	B	D
11	**12**	**13**	**14**	**15**	**16**	**17**	**18**	**19**	**20**
C	C	B	C	D	A	C	C	D	A
21	**22**	**23**	**24**	**25**	**26**	**27**	**28**	**29**	**30**
A	C	D	A	C	C	A	C	D	A
31	**32**	**33**	**34**	**35**	**36**	**37**	**38**	**39**	**40**
A	D	C	A	C	D	C	A	A	A
41	**42**	**43**	**44**	**45**	**46**	**47**	**48**	**49**	**50**
C	B	C	D	B	D	D	B	A	A
51	**52**	**53**	**54**	**55**	**56**	**57**	**58**	**59**	**60**
C	C	C	D	B	D	C	D	C	D
61	**62**	**63**	**64**	**65**	**66**	**67**	**68**	**69**	**70**
D	B	B	A	C	A	C	B	B	B
71	**72**	**73**	**74**	**75**	**76**	**77**	**78**	**79**	**80**
D	C	A	A	A	D	B	C	A	B
81	**82**	**83**	**84**	**85**	**86**	**87**	**88**	**89**	**90**
B	D	B	D	D	D	C	B	C	A
91	**92**	**93**	**94**	**95**	**96**	**97**	**98**	**99**	**100**
D	B	A	B	D	C	C	D	B	C

❑❑❑

6 One Word Substitutions

There are many words in English language which can be perfectly used for a number of words. These words help in expressing ideas in a short and correct manner for the right occasion. Such words not only enhance the vocabulary but also enable you to economise in the use of words to a great extent. Try to learn as many as you can.

Denoting Numbers

- A collection of poems — *anthology*
- A number of merchant ships protected by warships (in war-time) — *convoy*
- A number of stars grouped together — *constellation*
- A number of hired applauders, *i.e.* persons paid to clap — *claque*
- A number of people at church — *congregation*
- A number of people gathered together for some common purpose — *gathering, assembly, society*
- A group of people who get together to work for some cause of common interest — *coterie*
- A number of workmen, prisoners, thieves — *gang*
- A number of sheep — *flock*
- A number of geese — *gaggle*
- A number of leopards — *leap*
- A number of lions, monkeys — *pride, troop*
- A number of herrings, mackerel — *shoal*
- A number of fish taken in a net — *catch, haul*
- A number of whales, porpoises — *school, gam*
- A number of oxen or horses (two or more) harnessed together — *team*
- A number of ships, cars, buses — *fleet*

Denoting Places

- A place where bees are kept — *apiary*
- A place where birds are kept — *aviary*
- A place where fishes are kept — *aquarium*
- A dwelling-place of an animal underground — *burrow*
- A squirrel's home — *drey*
- A nest of a bird of prey — *eyrie, aerie*
- A place where spirituous liquors are produced — *distillery*
- A place where clothes are washed and ironed — *laundry*
- A place where Government records are kept — *archives*
- A place where treasures of art, curiosities, etc. are preserved or exhibited — *museum*
- A place where fruit trees are grown — *orchard*

Pertaining to the Literary Sphere

- A work whose writer is unknown — *anonymous*
- A record of one's life written by oneself — *autobiography*
- The history of the life of a person — *biography*
- The heading or short description of a newspaper article, chapter of a book etc. — *caption*
- A humorous play, having a happy ending — *comedy*
- A list of books in a library — *catalogue, bibliography*
- A book in which the events of each day are recorded — *diary*
- A books containing the words of a language with their definitions, in alphabetical order — *dictionary*
- A book of names and addresses — *directory*
- A short speech by a player at the end of a play — *epilogue*
- A brief summary of a book — *epitome*
- A book containing information on all branches of knowledge — *encyclopedia*
- To remove the offensive portions of a book — *expurgate*
- A speech delivered without earlier preparation — *extempore*
- A noisy or vehement speech intended to excite passions — *harangue*
- A written account, usually in book form of the interesting and memorable experiences of one's life — *memoirs*
- A note to help the memory — *memorandum*
- A declaration of plans and promises put forward by a candidate for election, political party or a sovereign — *manifesto*
- A short speech by a player at the beginning of a play — *prologue*
- Literary theft, or passing off an author's original work as one's own — *plagiarism*
- Speaking aloud to oneself — *soliloquy*
- A play with a sad or tragic end — *tragedy*

Pertaining to Religion

- One who believes that man can have no knowledge of God but only of natural phenomena — *agnostic*
- One who renounces his religious vows or forsakes his religious principles — *apostate*
- One who does not believe in existence of God — *atheist*
- One intolerantly devoted to a particular creed — *bigot*
- To utter profane language against God or anything holy — *blaspheme*
- A breaker of church images — *iconoclast*
- Worship of images or idols — *idiolatory*
- One who believes in God — *theist*
- One who believes in only one God — *monotheist*
- One who believes in many Gods — *polytheist*

Pertaining to Government

- To give up a throne or other office of dignity — *abdicate*
- Absence of government — *anarchy*
- Government by Sovereign of uncontrolled authority — *autocracy, despotism*
- Government by departments of states — *bureaucracy*
- Government of the people, for the people and by the people — *democracy*
- Government by the nobility — *aristocracy*
- The right of self-government — *autonomy*
- Government by a few — *oligarchy*
- Government by the wealthy — *plutocracy*

- Government by divine guidance *theocracy*
- To decide a political question by the direct vote of the whole electorate *referendum*
- Sweeping governmental change *revolution*
- The science of government *politics*

Pertaining to Professions

- One who attends to the diseases of the eye *oculist*
- One who tests eyesight and sells spectacles *optician*
- One who attends to the teeth *dentist*
- One skilled in the care of hands and feet *chiropodist*
- A physician who assists women at child-birth *obstetrician*
- One who drives a motorcar *chauffeur*
- One who makes or sells candles *chandler*
- One who preserves the skins of animals and mounts them so as to resemble the living animals *taxidermist*
- One who compiles a dictionary *lexicographer*
- One who writes books *author*
- One skilled in the treatment of diseases of animals *veterinarian*
- A tradesman who manages funerals *undertaker*
- One who draws up contracts and lends money on interest *scrivener*
- One who lends money and keeps goods as security *pawnbroker*
- A teacher who travels from place to place to give instruction. *peripatetic*
- One who travels from place to place selling miscellaneous articles *hawker, pedlar*
- One who collects postage stamps *philatelist*
- One who lends money at exorbitant interest *usurer*
- One who takes care of a building *janitor*
- One who sells sweets and pastries *confectioner*
- One who works in a coalmine *collier*
- One who flies an aeroplane *pilot, aviator*
- One who studies rocks and soils *geologist*
- One who shoes horses *farrier*
- A professional rider in horses races *jockey*
- One who deals in silks, cotton, woollen, and linen goods *mercer*
- One who deals in wines *vintner*
- One who deals in fish *fishmonger*
- One who deals in iron and hardware *ironmonger*
- One who sells fruits, vegetables, etc. from a barrow *costermonger*
- One who sets type in a printing office *compositor*

Pertaining to Medicine

- A substance which destroys or weakens germs *antiseptic*
- Any medicine which produces insensibility *anaesthetic*
- A medicine to counteract poison *antidote*
- Want or poorness of blood *anaemia*
- A medicine which alleviates pain *anodyne*
- To cut off a person's body a part which is infected *amputate*
- One who is recovering from illness *convalescent*
- To be able to tell the nature of disease by its symptoms *diagnose*
- A disease affecting many persons at the same place and time *epidemic*
- A disease confined to a particular district or place *endemic*
- To disinfect by smoke *fumigate*

- Free or exempt from infection — *immune*
- A person who is sick — *invalid*
- A cure for all diseases — *panacea*
- A disease widely epidemic — *pandemic*
- Confinement to one place to avoid spread of infection — *quarantine*

Pertaining to Characteristics and Actions

- One who devotes his life to the welfare and interests of other people — *altruist*
- One who can use both hands with equal ease — *ambidexterous*
- One who fishes with a rod — *angler*
- One who kills secretly or by surprise — *assassin*
- A person who collects things belonging to ancient times — *antiquary*
- One who is always finding faults — *censorious*
- One living at the same time as another — *contemporary*
- One who sneers at the aims and beliefs of his fellowmen — *cynic*
- One who delights in speaking about oneself — *egotist*
- One who exalts his own opinion — *egoist*
- One who dies for a noble cause — *martyr*
- One who retires from society to live a solitary life — *recluse, hermit*
- One who maliciously sets fire to buildings — *incendiary*
- One who is banished from his home or his country — *exile*
- One who takes refuge in a foreign country — *refugee, alien*
- One who runs away from justice or the law — *fugitive*
- One who walks in his sleep — *somnambulist*
- One who looks on the bright side of things — *optimist*
- One who looks on the dark side of things — *pessimist*
- A hater of mankind — *misanthropist*
- One who knows everything — *omniscient*
- One who is all powerful — *omnipotent*
- One who is present everywhere — *omnipresent*
- One who devotes his service or wealth for the love of mankind — *philanthropist*
- One new to anything — *novice, tyro, neophyte*
- One who engages in any pursuit for the love of it, and not for gain — *amateur*
- One who journeys to a holy place — *pilgrim*
- A leader of the people who can sway his followers by his oratory — *demagogue*
- One who has special skill in judging art, music, tastes, etc. — *connoisseur*
- One whose reasoning is clever yet false — *sophist*
- One who makes a display of his learning — *pedant*
- One who is indifferent to pain or pleasure — *stoic*
- One who loves his country and serves it devotedly — *patriot*
- One devoted to the pleasures of eating and drinking — *epicure*
- One who poses to be what he is not — *hypocrite, impostor*
- One who foretells events — *prophet*
- One who pretends to know a great deal about everything — *mountebank, charlatan, quack*
- One versed in many languages — *linguist*
- One who cannot pay one's debts — *insolvent*
- One who takes over after another in office or employment — *successor*
- One who has been before another in office or employment — *predecessor*
- One who is opposed to intellectual progress — *obscurant*
- One who abstains from alcoholic drinks — *teetotaller*

- One who hides away on a ship to obtain a free passage — *stowaway*
- One who spends very little — *miser*
- One who spends too much — *spendthrift*

Pertaining to War

- An unprovoked attack by an enemy — *aggression*
- Shells, bombs, military stores — *ammunition*
- A place where naval or military weapons are made or stored — *ordnance*
- An agreement between belligerents to stop fighting — *armistice*
- A general pardon of offenders — *amnesty*
- To reduce to nothing — *annihilate*
- Nations carrying on warfare — *belligerents*
- To surround a place with the intention of capturing — *besiege*
- To camp in the open air without tents or covering — *bivouac*
- To seize for military use — *commandeer*
- A person who is forced by law to become a soldier — *conscript*
- An order prohibiting ships to leave the ports — *embargo*
- A number of firearms being discharged continuously — *fusillade*
- To make an examination or preliminary survey of enemy territory for military objectives — *reconnoitre*

Pertaining to Marriage and Children

- One who marries a second wife or husband while the legal spouse is alive — *bigamist*
- One vowed to a single or unmarried life — *celibate*
- One engaged to be married — *fiancé, fiancee*
- A child whose parents are dead — *orphan*
- A hater of marriage — *misogamist*
- One who has more than two wives at a time — *polygamist*

Pertaining to Death

- Dead and decaying flesh (esp. of animals) — *carrion*
- A monument set up for persons who are buried elsewhere — *cenotaph*
- To preserve a dead body from putrefaction — *embalm*
- Words inscribed on a tomb — *epitaph*
- An examination of dead body — *postmortem, autopsy*
- An account in the newspaper of the funeral of one deceased — *obituary*
- The property left to someone by a will — *legacy*
- Occurring after death — *posthumous*
- The act of killing a human being — *homicide*
- Murder of a new born child — *infanticide*
- Murder of a brother — *fratricide*
- Murder of a sister — *sororicide*
- Murder of a mother — *matricide*
- Murder of a father — *patricide*
- Murder of a parent — *parricide*
- Murder of a king — *regicide*

Pertaining to Sciences and Arts

- The study of all heavenly bodies and the earth in relation to them — *astronomy*
- The science of land management — *agronomics*

- The study of mankind — *anthropology*
- The study of physical life or living matter — *biology*
- The study of plants — *botany*
- The art of beautiful handwriting — *calligraphy*
- The science which deals with the varieties of human race — *ethnology*
- The study of the origin and history of words — *etymology*
- The study of coins — *numismatics*
- The study of human face — *physiognomy*
- The art of making fireworks — *pyrotechnics*
- The study of birds — *ornithology*
- The study of languages — *philology*
- At home equally on land or in water — *amphibious*
- The inside of a nut — *kernel*
- The central or innermost part of fruit — *core*
- The animals of a certain region — *fauna*
- The plants and vegetation of a certain region — *flora*
- Absence of rain for a long time — *drought*
- To supply land with water by artificial means — *irrigate*
- One who studies plant and animal life — *naturalist*
- A cud-chewing animal, *e.g.* the cow — *ruminant*
- A gnawing animal, *e.g.* the rat — *rodent*
- A four-footed animal — *quadruped*
- Animals which carry their young in a pouch, *e.g.* kangaroo — *marsupials*
- Soil composed largely of decayed vegetable matter — *humus*
- A preparation for killing insects — *insecticide*
- A plant or animal growing on another — *parasite*
- Living for many years — *perennial*

Miscellaneous

- Loud enough to be heard — *audible*
- Not distinct enough to be heard — *inaudible*
- Fit for food — *edible*
- Unfit for human consumption — *inedible*
- Fit to be chosen or selected — *eligible*
- Not having the qualities for being chosen — *ineligible*
- Writing that is easy to read — *legible*
- Writing that is difficult to decipher — *illegible*
- Able to read — *literate*
- Unable to read — *illiterate*
- Born of married parents — *legitimate*
- Born of unmarried parents — *illegitimate*
- To send back a person to his own country — *repatriate*
- To banish from one's country — *expatriate*
- To move from one country to another — *migrate*
- One who leaves his country to settle in another — *emigrant*
- One who comes into a foreign country to settle there — *immigrant*
- Incapable of being redeemed from evil, *i.e.* beyond correction — *incorrigible*
- That which cannot be rubbed out or blotted out — *ineffaceable, indelible*
- That which cannot be conquered — *invincible*
- Incapable of making errors — *infallible*

❑ That which cannot be avoided or prevented	*inevitable*
❑ Incapable of being burnt	*incombustible*
❑ That which easily catches fire	*inflammable, flammable*
❑ That which cannot be seen	*invisible*
❑ Living for ever	*immortal*
❑ Increase the gravity of an offence	*aggravate*
❑ Ordinary or commonplace remark	*platitude*
❑ That which cannot be satisfied	*insatiable*
❑ That which cannot be repaired	*irreparable*
❑ That which cannot be imitated	*inimitable*
❑ Persons (or efforts) that cannot be wearied	*indefatigable*
❑ One who eats too much	*glutton*
❑ To destroy completely	*annihilate*
❑ A statement open to more than one interpretation	*ambiguous*
❑ A round about way of speaking	*circumlocution*
❑ Cautious observation of events, etc.	*circumspection*
❑ That which cannot be hurt	*invulnerable*

Multiple Choice Questions

Directions: *Below are given some statements each of which is capable of being expressed by one word only. Each statement is followed by four such words of which only one is correct. Out of the given alternatives A, B, C and D choose the correct word which very closely fits each definition.*

1. A set of papers giving information about a person or event:
A. editorial B. agenda
C. dossier D. clippings

2. List and explanations of technical, difficult, etc. terms:
A. preface B. glossary
C. bibliography D. appendix

3. One who pays too much care to his clothes and personal appearance:
A. conscious B. dandy
C. cynosure D. leer

4. A child born after death of father:
A. effeminate B. immature
C. fatherless D. posthumous

5. A person who is hard to please:
A. insensible B. hypocrite
C. egoist D. fastidious

6. Complete failure in something attempted:
A. fiasco B. vain
C. falsies D. flop

7. A word which can be interpreted in any way:
A. confusing B. misnomer
C. ambiguous D. precise

8. A group of persons united by common interests:
A. society B. class
C. clique D. coterie

9. A person who is inexperienced and easily deceived:
A. fool B. immature
C. blackhorn D. greenhorn

10. Instruction by question and answer:
A. interrogatory B. catechism
C. bulletin D. alibi

11. Record of events by someone with first hand knowledge:
A. novice B. report
C. memoir D. itinerary

12. A mode of talk familiar to a particular group or profession:
A. jargon B. colloquial
C. slang D. abuses

13. Person who is crazy:
A. lackadaisical B. tarter
C. scrupulous D. loony

14. A person who readily believes others:
A. hasty B. immature
C. credulous D. credible

15. One who eats human flesh:
A. beast B. cannibal
C. maneater D. carnivorous

16. Intentional destruction of racial groups:
A. genocide B. homicide
C. fratricide D. communal riot

17. One with weakness of mind caused by old age:
A. dastard B. dotard
C. fop D. philanderer

18. Study of insects:
A. zoology B. philology
C. entomology D. etymology

19. A critical judge of any art particularly fine arts:
A. connoisseur B. veteran
C. philistine D. dilettante

20. One who introduces items of an entertainment:
A. consort B. compere
C. director D. introducer

21. A combination of business firms:
A. enterprise B. franchise
C. cartel D. autonomous

22. Freeing of suppressed emotions:
A. catastrophe B. catharsis
C. epilogue D. chagrin

23. One who believes in the power of fate:
A. optimist B. pessimist
C. fearful D. fatalist

24. The murder of brother:
A. genocide B. homicide
C. salvage D. fratricide

25. Additional to proper payment:
A. premium B. overtime
C. ex-gratia D. fringe

26. A person or thing used to tempt somebody into a position of danger:
A. decoy B. provocateur
C. jinx D. scapegoat

27. Custom of having more than one husband at the same time:
A. polygamy B. polyandry
C. bigamy D. sexagenary

28. A person of refined taste in food and drink:
A. emeritus B. epicure
C. glutton D. gourmand

29. A tombstone inscription:
A. epithet B. encomium
C. epistle D. epitaph

30. An office which has no work but high salary:
A. fortuitous B. gratuitous
C. sinecure D. ceremonial

31. One who is indifferent to pains and pleasure of life:
A. stoic B. metaphysical
C. pessimist D. sceptic

32. List of names of persons showing duties to be performed by each in turn:
A. notice B. bulletin
C. roster D. agenda

33. Long angry speech of criticism or accusation:
A. track record B. tirade
C. taut D. outburst

34. One who is in favour of never drinking alcoholic drinks:
A. idealist B. uxorious
C. teetotaller D. unalcoholic

35. Trying to win favour by flattery and charm:
A. smarmy B. shrewish
C. toady D. loquacious

36. A decision on which one cannot go back:
A. incorrigible B. irrevocable
C. rigid D. invulnerable

37. The science that studies the varieties of human race:
A. phrenology B. physiology
C. sociology D. ethnology

38. A person who hates women:
A. philogynist B. philatelist
C. misogamist D. misogynist

39. A group of people in a particular grade in an organisation:
A. colleague B. staff
C. echelon D. commission

40. Honourably discharged from service:
A. emeritus B. latitudinarian
C. infallible D. meritorious

41. One who does not believe in the existence of God:
A. atheist B. altruist
C. agnostic D. flippant

42. The large money paid for an early retirement:
A. goldmine B. golden handshake
C. gratuity D. lion's share

43. A hater of learning and knowledge:
A. misologist B. misogynist
C. philologist D. philanthropist

44. One who lives and acts for the welfare of others:
A. misanthrope B. credulous
C. altruist D. gregarious

45. Mental weariness for want of occupation:
A. desperate B. depression
C. fatigue D. ennui

46. That which makes it difficult to recognise the presence in real of somebody or something:
A. cover B. mask
C. make-up D. camouflage

47. To bear a hand in one's new business:
A. partnership B. interfere
C. assist D. join

48. One who renounces the world and practices self-discipline in order to attain salvation:
A. devotee
B. ascetic
C. theist
D. parsimonious

49. A place where gambling is practiced:
A. hotel
B. motel
C. casino
D. stadium

50. A sad song is a:
A. dirge
B. elegy
C. ditty
D. knell

ANSWERS

1	2	3	4	5	6	7	8	9	10
C	B	B	D	D	A	C	C	D	B
11	**12**	**13**	**14**	**15**	**16**	**17**	**18**	**19**	**20**
C	A	D	C	B	A	B	C	A	B
21	**22**	**23**	**24**	**25**	**26**	**27**	**28**	**29**	**30**
C	B	D	D	D	A	B	B	D	C
31	**32**	**33**	**34**	**35**	**36**	**37**	**38**	**39**	**40**
A	C	B	C	A	B	D	D	C	A
41	**42**	**43**	**44**	**45**	**46**	**47**	**48**	**49**	**50**
A	B	A	C	D	D	C	B	C	A

❑❑❑

7 Idioms and Phrases

- An idiom is a group of words established by usage as having a meaning different from the individual words.
- A phrase is a small group of words standing together as an idiomatic expression.

Learn and practise as may as you can.

Idioms and Idiomatic Phrases

✦ **ABC** (basic principles)
She does not know the ABC of photography.

✦ **At one's beck and call** (ready to obey)
He had a dozen men at his beck and call.

✦ **At sixes and sevens** (in disorder)
The drawing room articles were lying at sixes and sevens on the floor.

✦ **A wet blanket** (a discouraging person)
Don't allow Rakesh to accompany you to the hunting trip because he is a wet blanket.

✦ **A big gun** (an important person)
Mr Smith is a big gun in our city.

✦ **At a stone's throw** (at a short distance from)
My school is at a stone's throw from my house.

✦ **A man of word** (a person who keeps his promise)
Mr Sharma is a man of word.

✦ **A man of a few words** (a remarkable person)
Gandhiji was a man of a few words.

✦ **At arm's length** (to keep away)
We should always keep bad boys at arm's length

✦ **A bolt from the blue** (a sudden and unexpected event)
The news of my friend's death came to me like a bolt from the blue.

✦ **A man of letters** (a scholar)
Radha Krishnan was a man of letters.

✦ **A hard nut to crack.** (a puzzling problem)
To get a win over American basket ball team is a hard nut to crack for India.

✦ **A yeoman's service** (service which is beneficial to the human beings)
He did yeoman's service through his life.

✦ **A snake in the grass** (a hidden foe)
Beware of him because he seems to be a snake in the grass.

✦ **Acid test** (hard test)
The election will be an acid test for the ruling party.

✦ **A wolf in sheep's clothing** (a hypocrite)
You should not keep company with him because he is a wolf in sheep's clothing.

✦ **At the eleventh hour** (at the last moment)
The war was about to start but fortunately at the eleventh hour a messenger came to the PM with a message of peace.

✦ **A great card** (an important person)
Mr Sood is a great card in the ministry of finance.

✦ **A fool of the first water** (one completely foolish)
Being a fool of the first water he could not solve even the simplest sum.

✦ **A bone of contention** (to be the cause of quarrel)
Kashmir is the bone of contention between India and Pakistan.

✦ **A green hand** (not very much experienced)
We shall pay a little to a green hand.

✦ **All in all** (completely)
Rajesh is all in all in this office.

✦ **A bed of roses** (a comfort)
Life is not a bed of roses.

✦ **An apple of discord** (to be the cause of)
Kashmir is an apple of discord between India and Pakistan.

✦ **A white elephant** (of no use)
This sort of glib talker always proves a white elephant in the end.

✦ **A red letter day** (An important day)
15th August is a red letter day for the Indians.

✦ **By hook or by crook** (by any means fair or foul)

✦ **Black sheep** (a traitor)
Later on Mr XYZ proved a black sheep.

✦ **By dint of** (by means of)
By dint of hard work, she earned a lot of money.

✦ **Break ones back** (to work hard to get something)
He broke his back to earn his livelihood.

✦ **Break the back of** (accomplish the hardest part of a certain job)

There is nothing to be worried about as we've already broken the back of the problem.

✦ **Beat about the bush** (to go on talking on some worthless topic)
Stop this beating about the bush, come to the main task.

✦ **Beyond one's means** (beyond one's budget)
He is living beyond his means, therefore, he is sure to get ruined.

✦ **Cut loose** (Keep away)
India should cut loose from bad politics.

✦ **Chips of the same block** (having the same taste)
They are the chips of the same block.

✦ **Cut-throat competition** (a stiff competition)
There is a cut-throat competition among the publishers in the market.

✦ **Come what may** (no matter what happens)
I'll do it come what may.

✦ **Drop someone a line** (send a letter, etc.)
Please drop me a line of your well-being.

✦ **Dull the edge of** (reduce the intensity of)
Take this pill and it will dull the edge of pain.

✦ **From hand to mouth** (without any saving)
The poor factory worker is living from hand to mouth.

✦ **Fair and square** (clean)
One must be fair and square in one's dealing.

✦ **Hard of hearing** (somewhat deaf)
She is a bit hard of hearing.

✦ **In the good books of** (be good in one's mind)
Jack is in the good books of his teachers.

✦ **In black and white** (in written)
Don't give him anything in black and white.

✦ **In cold blood** (mercilessly)
The old woman was murdered in cold blood.

✦ **In a crack** (all of a sudden or rapidly)
The thief left the place in a crack.

✦ **In full swing** (in full force)
The studies of the students are going on in full swing.

✦ **In the twinkling of an eye** (quickly)
The monkey ate up grams in the twinkling of an eye.

✦ **Keep the ball rolling** (to maintain the progress of some activity)
After the death of his father he had to take the charge of his office to keep the ball rolling.

✦ **Neck and neck** (even)
There is a neck and neck fight between the two boxers.

✦ **Once in a blue moon** (seldom)
She visits her brother once in a blue moon.

✦ **Slow and steady** (slowly but continually)
Slow and steady wins the race.

✦ **To cut a sorry figure** (present oneself in a bad way)
She cut a sorry figure on the stage.

✦ **To give a red carpet reception** (to give a warm welcome)
The PM was given a red carpet reception in America.

✦ **To dance one's tune** (to follow someone submissively)
He always dances to his brother's tune.

✦ **To turn a deaf ear to** (to disregard)
She turned a deaf ear to her parents' advice.

✦ **To call a spade a spade** (to speak the truth)
Gandhiji always called a spade a spade.

✦ **To bring to book** (to scold)
The naughty boy was brought to book by the teacher.

✦ **To cut short** (to reduce)
Smoking will cut short your life.
He wants to get money by hook or by crook.

✦ **To grease the palm of** (to bribe)
Rohit greased the palm of the clerk and got the file moved.

✦ **Through thick and thin.** (under all circumstances)
We'll stand by you through thick and thin.

✦ **To die by inches** (to die a painful death)
The old man died by inches.

✦ **To eat one's words** (to retract one's statement)
You'll have to eat your words because you have spoken without thinking.

✦ **To burn the midnight oil** (to work hard)
You'll have to burn the midnight oil if you want to get good marks.

✦ **To poke one's nose into** (to meddle with)
It is bad to poke your nose into others' affair.

✦ **To fall flat** (to have no effect)
His father's advice fell flat on him.

✦ **To make a clean breast of** (to confess)
He made a clean breast of his involvement in the bomb blast.

✦ **To get the better of** (overcome)
Anger got the better of him.

✦ **To break somebody's back** (to give too much work to him to do)
She broke his back by giving him so much hard work to do.

✦ **Throw cold water on** (to discourage)
She tried to throw cold water on his plan but he was well-determined.

✦ **The long and short of** (in brief)
The long and short of his lecture is that we should live like brothers.

✦ **To burn one's fingers** (to get oneself in trouble)
You have burnt your fingers by speaking against him.

- **To turn over a new leaf** (to change the course of life)
  He has turned over a new leaf in his life.
- **To have one's own axe to grind** (to have vested interest)
  He has his own axe to grind in this matter.
- **To take to one's heels** (to run away)
  The thief took to his heels as soon as he saw the policeman.
- **To move heaven and earth** (to make too much effort)
  The young man moved heaven and earth to find a job.
- **To be caught red handed** (to be caught at the time of committing a crime)
  The clerk was caught red handed when he was accepting bribe from Mr ABC.
- **To receive with open arms** (to give a warm welcome)
  The new president of the club was received with open arms by the members.
- **To be born with a silver spoon in one's mouth** (to be born in a rich family)
  Mr. J. L. Nehru was born with a silver spoon in his mouth.
- **To come to light** (to be known)
  A new disease has recently come to light.
- **To be the apple of one's eye** (be very dear)
  He is the apple of his parent's eye.
- **To make fun of** (laugh at)
  The children made fun of the waiter in the hotel.
- **To let the cat out of the bag** (to divulge secret)
  It was Sohan who let the cat out of the bag by telling the real matter.
- **To open a new chapter** (to start some habit, etc.
  By drinking, you've opened a new chapter in your life.
- **To make the flesh creep** (to terrify)
  The story made my flesh creep.
- **To lose ground** (to retreat)
  After fighting for some time the Pakistani army began to lose ground.
- **To bring to book** (to punish)
  The student was brought to book by the teacher.
- **To show a clean pair of heels** (to run away)
  The thief showed a clean pair of heels as soon as he saw the policeman approaching.
- **To gain ground** (to be established)
  He gained ground in India in a few years.
- **To get wind of** (to get information)
  I got wind of his secret plans.
- **Under a cloud** (be in trouble or in a state of disgrace or suspicion)
  His company seemed to be under a cioud as it had no funds to pay the wages to the workers.

Verbal Phrases

- **Act upon** (to follow)
  I acted upon my father's advice.
- **Act upto** (to perform within limits)
  He acted upto his conscience.
- **Act beyond** (to perform crossing limits)
  We should not act beyond our capacity.
- **Act for** (to perform in place of someone else)
  The vice principal acted for the principal.
- **Back up** (to make a queue)
  The vehicles began to back up.
- **Back down** (withdraw claim in the presence of opposition)
  The leader backed down from his previous statement.
- **Back off** (draw back some plan or action)
  They backed off from building a flyover.
- **Back out** (withdraw from a promise, etc.)
  The government backed out of its promise.
- **Break down** (stop working) My car broke down on the highway.
- **Break into** (enter in certain premises by breaking the door, etc.)
  Last night a thief broke into my neighbour's.
- **Break off** (stop all of a sudden)
  She broke off and began to think over about her/his hand.
- **Break out** (spread)
  Cholera has broken out in the town.
- **Break out of** (escape from)
  A prisoner broke out of the prison last night.
- **Break up** (disperse)
  The cloud of fog began to break up as the sun rose.
- **Break something up** (Cause something to break into small pieces)
  She broke up the chocolate to distribute it among the girls.
- **Break with** (Cut off connection after quarrelling with someone)
  He has broken with his brother.
- **Call on** (pay a visit to somebody)
  I'll call on Mohan's today.
- **Call out** (to start)
  The workers have called out a strike.
- **Call off** (to stop the strike etc.)
  The workers have called off the strike.
- **Call at** (to visit someone's house)
  I called at his house yesterday.
- **Call in** (send for)
  Please call in the doctor.

✦ **Carry on** (continue)
Please carry on your work.

✦ **Carry something out** (perform a task)
Our company is carrying out a big deal with a foreign company.

✦ **Carry something over** (postpone)
The fancy dress competition had to be carried over till Monday)

✦ **Carry someone off** (kill somebody)
Cancer carried her off on the day of her 20th birthday.

✦ **Come of age** (get established)
As our company has come of age, so, there is no problem in selling our goods.

✦ **Come of** (belong to)
She comes of a royal family.

✦ **Come over** (surmount)
We at last came over all our problems.

✦ **Come off** (to take place)
The marriage of my brother comes off in the next month.

✦ **Come round** (agree)
At last he came round to my views.

✦ **Come under** (fall in the category of)
All these animals come under the same species.

✦ **Come down with** (suffer from)
She came down with whopping cough.

✦ **Come from** (be the nature of)
She came from London.

✦ **Come about** (happen)
The explosion came about when the worker struck the match to light a cigarette.

✦ **Cut off** (die)
The princess was cut off in the prime of her life.

✦ **Cut down** (reduce)
The prices of consumer goods should be cut down.

✦ **Cut someone out** (exclude someone)
His father cut him out of his will.

✦ **Fall in**
She fell in love with the prince.

✦ **Fall down** (fail)
The deal fell down for lack of transparency.

✦ **Fall out** (quarrel)
She fell out with his elder brother.

✦ **Fall through** (fail)
The project fell through for lack of funds.

✦ **Get away** (escape)
She got away with her life.

✦ **Get by** (to accomplish something with great difficulty)
She is not rich. She has just enough to get by.

✦ **Get on** (perform)
How are you getting on with your studies?

✦ **Get out** (become known)
The news got out that the PM was paying a visit to Russia.

✦ **Get over** (overcome)
At last I got over all obstacles.

✦ **Get up** (rise)
When do you get up in the morning?

✦ **Give up** (stop)
He gave up smoking.

✦ **Give out** (emit)
Garlic gives out a pungent smell.

✦ **Give in** (collapse)
The bridge gave in under the heavy load.

✦ **Give away** (distribute)
The Principal gave away the prizes.

✦ **Give out** (announce)
It was given out that the President of India would visit the place soon.

✦ **Go off** (explode)
The gun went off suddenly.

✦ **Go on** (continue)
She went on about how she flew the aeroplane.

✦ **Go through** (examine)
I'll go through this book later on.

✦ **Go up** (be built)
The construction of the house is going up.

✦ **Grind on** (continue for a long time in a tedious way)
The discussion over political issues ground on.

✦ **Grind something out** (produce something a tedious way)
She will grind some more short stories.

✦ **Look out** (be careful)
Look out! there is a snake.

✦ **Look down upon** (hate)
We should not look down upon the poor.

✦ **Look at** (watch)
Look at the blackboard.

✦ **Look after** (take care of)
We ought to look after our old parents.

✦ **Look into** (investigate)
The new police inspector will look into the matter.

✦ **Look up** (rise)
The prices of consumer goods are looking up.

✦ **Look back** (think of the past)
It made her feel disolate when she looked back on things of the past.

✦ **Make up** (to fulfil)
I'll make up my deficiency in Mathematics.

- ✦ **Make out** (understand)
  I could not make out what she said.
- ✦ **Make up one' mind** (to resolve)
  I have made up my mind to settle in the USA.
- ✦ **Make off** (leave hurriedly)
  She made off without informing anybody.
- ✦ **Make something over** (transfer)
  She should make her property over to her sons.
- ✦ **Make over** (hand over)
  He made over the charge of the file to Mr Robert.
- ✦ **Pull back** (retreat)
  The government has pulled back from its previous policy.
- ✦ **Pull something down** (demolish)
  The authorities concerned pulled down a few building which were illegally built on government land.
- ✦ **Pull out** (pluck)
  The child pulled out a few petals of the flower.
- ✦ **Pull through** (recover)
  The patient will pull through.
- ✦ **Push on** (continue a journey)
  It was getting darker but we pushed on.
- ✦ **Push at** (exert force)
  He pushed at the bell, but it did not ring.
- ✦ **Push for** (demand persistently)
  The workers have been pushing for the installation of new machines for five years.
- ✦ **Put out** (extinguish)
  She put out the light.
- ✦ **Put on** (wear)
  He put on an overcoat.
- ✦ **Put off** (postpone)
  The plan had to be put off.
- ✦ **Put by** (spare something for future)
  We must put by some money for future.
- ✦ **Put up with** (stay)
  Your aunt is out of town for a couple of days, you may put up with us till she comes.
- ✦ **Put something down** (record something)
  She put a new idea down on the paper.
- ✦ **Take after** (resemble)
  He takes after his father.
- ✦ **Take off** (remove)
  He took off his shoes.
- ✦ **Take something out** (obtain)
  You may take out some money from Rohit if you want to purchase this car.
- ✦ **Take to** (fall into the habit of)
  He took to gambling.
- ✦ **Turn something down** (reject something)
  The judge turned down his appeal.
- ✦ **Turn on** (attack)
  The thief turned on him with a knife.

Multiple Choice Questions

Directions: *Some idioms/phrases are given below with their probable meanings. Select the options with their correct meanings.*

1. Carry out
A. To take from one place to another
B. To continue
C. To obey
D. To make efforts

2. In the same boat
A. A worn out choice
B. Indifferent
C. In identical circumstances
D. Carry off

3. In one's good book
A. A costly book
B. A priceless treasure
C. In one's favour
D. An enchanting beauty

4. Keep a straight face
A. To do make up
B. To change clothes
C. Assume responsibility
D. To remain serious

5. To be above board
A. To have a good height
B. To be honest in any business deal
C. To have no debts
D. To try to be beautiful

6. On the face of it
A. To agree B. From an action
C. More than enough D. Apparently

7. Let the bygones be bygones
A. In one's favour B. To pretend
C. To forget the past D. Other choice

8. To split hairs
A. Major distinctions
B. Hair with two ends
C. To make minute distinction
D. Without distinction

9. Bread and butter
A. Both bread and butter
B. Something essential
C. Livelihood
D. Relevant things

10. To bell the cat
A. To catch a cat and tie a bell round its neck
B. To make an effort
C. To be quick
D. To face a risk

11. Hard and fast
A. Strict B. Solid
C. Fast moving D. Some hard surface

12. Part and parcel
A. The part of a parcel
B. An essential part
C. A missing parcel
D. Some part of a machine sent by parcel

13. Null and void
A. Something invalid
B. Something that can be avoided
C. Something that can be nullified
D. Something evil

14. To make clean breast of
A. To gain prominence
B. To praise oneself
C. To confess without reserve
D. To destroy before it blooms

15. Trump card
A. A powerful means of achieving an object
B. Resourcefulness
C. The best gamble to attain success
D. None of these

16. Tall talk
A. A discussion continued for a long time
B. A high sounding talk
C. A meaningful talk
D. A useless talk

17. Small talk
A. Gossip
B. A discussion carried on for a long time
C. A brief discussion
D. None of these

18. Throw out of gear
A. To replace B. Hinder, disturb
C. To decide D. Take up tune

19. To and fro
A. Back and forth B. Puzzled
C. Amazed D. Reprove

20. To bell the cat
A. To do an easy job
B. To be indifferent to
C. To undertake a difficult job
D. To clarify

21. To be under cloud
A. Puzzle
B. Enjoy the favour
C. Talk thoughtlessly
D. To be under suspicion

22. A labour of love
A. A tragic end
B. A funny thing
C. Not fruitful
D. Work done without payment

23. Follow suit
A. Follow an example B. Wear a new dress
C. Irrelevant D. A gay person

24. Foul play
A. Bad intentions
B. A play not well acted
C. A play not liked by the audience
D. None of these

25. To pick holes
A. To find some reason to quarrel
B. To destroy something
C. To criticise someone
D. To cut some part of an item

26. To smell a rat
A. To see signs of plague epidemic
B. To get bad smell of a dead rat
C. To suspect foul dealings
D. To be in a bad mood

27. To put a spoke in one's wheel
A. To encourage
B. Act without restraint
C. Risk something
D. To obstruct one's progress

28. To pull one's leg
A. To give up B. Take care of
C. To befool D. To know

29. To play with fire
A. Grasp the truth
B. To handle something dangerous
C. To ridicule
D. To flee away

30. To reckon with
A. Take up time
B. Make an inventory
C. To deal with
D. Submit to punishment

31. To run short
A. Talk until one is tired at
B. Apply to oneself
C. To get rid of
D. To have or be too little

32. A man of letters
A. A postman B. A learned man
C. A hypocrite D. An ignorant man

33. A maiden speech
A. A speech made in the parliament
B. A speech made before unmarried girls
C. A speech made by a political leader
D. A speech made for the first time

34. Order of the day
A. An order passed on a particular day
B. A current law
C. Something common or general
D. None of these

35. To end in smoke
A. To make completely understand
B. To ruin oneself
C. To excite great applause
D. None of these

36. To give vent to
A. To allow to flow forth
B. To prove a failure
C. To amass wealth
D. To evade

37. To eat humble pie
A. To apologise or confess
B. To order
C. To flatter
D. To get rid of

38. A black sheep
A. An unlucky person B. A negro
C. An ugly person D. None of these

39. To catch a tartar
A. To trap wanted criminal with great difficulty
B. To catch a dangerous person
C. To meet with disaster
D. To deal with a person who is more than one's watch

40. Sit on fence
A. To remain neutral
B. To show contempt
C. To enjoy the surroundings
D. To become fond of

41. Pay off old scores
A. To repay the debt B. To have revenge
C. To invite D. Secretly

42. Turn turtle
A. To cheat B. To be lopsided
C. To frustrate D. To dance to the tune

43. Wash one's hands of
A. To refuse B. To assist
C. To abuse D. To refuse to be

44. Under duress
A. Under compulsion B. Willing
C. To elicit information D. To demand

45. To turn the tables
A. To ruin someone
B. To turn the situation to one's own side
C. To reverse the situation
D. To move from one point to another

46. On the cards
A. Possibly B. Probably
C. Openly D. Likely

47. To leave someone in the lurch
A. To come to compromise with someone
B. Constant source of annoyance to someone
C. To put someone at ease
D. To desert someone in his difficulties

48. To play second fiddle
A. To be happy, cheerful and healthy
B. To reduce importance of one's senior
C. To support the role and view of another person
D. To do back seat driving

49. To yearn for
A. To weep for B. To remember
C. To admire D. To long for intensely

50. Call off
A. To finish B. To withdraw
C. To postpone D. To cry

ANSWERS

1	2	3	4	5	6	7	8	9	10
C	C	C	D	B	D	C	C	C	D
11	12	13	14	15	16	17	18	19	20
A	B	A	C	C	B	A	B	A	C
21	22	23	24	25	26	27	28	29	30
D	D	A	A	C	C	D	C	B	C
31	32	33	34	35	36	37	38	39	40
D	B	D	C	D	A	A	D	B	A
41	42	43	44	45	46	47	48	49	50
B	B	D	A	C	D	D	C	D	B

❑❑❑

8 Narration

Direct and Indirect Narration/Speech

The exact words spoken by the speaker are known as Direct Speech.

The words spoken by somebody and expressed by someone else with some modification are known as Indirect Speech.

(*a*) Ram says to me, "You do not help me."

(*b*) Ram tells me that I do not help him.

The sentence (*a*) shows the words spoken by Ram. So, it is a sentence of Direct Speech.

The sentence (*b*) shows the words spoken by Ram and expressed by someone else with certain modification. So, it is a sentence of Indirect Speech.

The following points should be noted while changing Direct Speech into Indirect speech:

1. The verb outside the inverted commas is called the Reporting Verb.
2. The verb or sentence inside the inverted commas is called the Reported Speech.
3. If the Reporting verb is in the Present or Future Tense, there is no change in the tense in the Reported Speech.
4. If the Reporting Verb is in the Past Tense, the Tense in the Reported Speech is changed.
5. The Reporting verb may be in any Tense, in it the Pronouns are changed as under:
   (*i*) First Person according to Subject
   (*ii*) Second Person according to Object
   (*iii*) Third Person, No change.
6. If the Reporting verb is in the Past Tense the Adverb will change as under in the Indirect Speech.

Direct	***Indirect***
now	then
here	there
after	before
today	that day
yesterday	the previous day
these	those
tomorrow	the next day
last week	the previous week
this	that

7. Adjectives/Determiners are changed as under:

Direct	***Indirect***
this	that
these	those

Rules for Change of Tense

Reporting Verb	Reporting Speech	Change of Tense
Present Tense	Any Tense	No change
Future Tense	Any Tense	No change
Past Tense	Present/Future Tense	Change into corresponding Past Tense
Past Tense	Past Indefinite Tense	Change into Past Perfect Tense
Past Tense	Past Continuous Tense	Change into Past Perfect Continuous Tense
Past Tense	Past Perfect/Perfect Continuous Tense	No change
Past Tense	Universal Truth	No change
Past Tense	Proverb	No change

Transformation of Speech Based on Special Rules

1. Rule Related to Interrogative Sentence

- If the answer of an interrogative sentence is possible in yes-no manner.

Illustration.

Dhoni said to Sachin, "Will you help me?"

Dhoni asked Sachin whether he would help him.

(**Note :** The answer of R.S. is possible in yes-no manner)

Rule of Transformation from Direct to Indirect speech

Step I : Change R.V. into ask.

Step II : In place of comma use 'if/whether'.

Step III : Change interrogative sentence into assertive sentence.

- If the answer of an interrogative sentence is not possible in yes-no manner.

Illustration:

Sachin said to Dhoni, "What do you want?"

Sachin asked Dhoni what he wanted.

(**Note :** Only in Step II, you have to avoid comma and inverted comma and rest will be same as mentioned above).

2. Rule related to Imperative Sentence

- Imperative sentence is a sentence which shows Order/ Advice/Request

Illustration:

My teacher said to me, "Go there".

My teacher ordered me to go there.

Rule of Transformation from Direct to Indirect Speech

Step I : Change R.V. as per meaning/sense of R.S. into order/request/advise.

Step II : In place of comma, use 'to'.

Step III : Rest portion will be same.

3. Rule related to Optative Sentence

- Optative sentence is a sentence which expresses the feeling of bless/curse/pray/wish.

Illustration:

Mother said to me, "May you live long!"

Mother blessed me that I might live long.

Rule of Transformation from Direct to Indirect Speech

Step I : Change R.V. as per meaning/sense of R.S. into bless/curse/pray/wish.

Step II : In place of comma, use 'that'.

Step III : Change optative sentence into assertive sentence.

4. Rule related to Exclamatory Sentence

- Exclamatory sentence is a sentence which takes note of exclamatory (!) mark in that sentence showing inner feeling.

Illustration:

She said, "Alas! I am ruined".

She exclaimed with sorrow that she was ruined.

Rule of Transformation from Direct to Indirect Speech

Step I : Change R.V. as per meaning/sense of R.S. into exclaim/exclaims/exclaimed/will or shall exclaim + joy/sorrow/anger/surprise/applause/ contempt.

Step II : Change comma into that.

Step III : Change note of exclamation (!) into full stop (.)

Step IV : Change exclamatory sentence into assertive sentence.

Universal, Historical truth, etc.

If the Reported Speech expresses a Universal or Historical or Habitual truth, its Tense will not change.

1. The teacher said to the students, "The sun rises in the east."
   The teacher told the students that the sun rises in the east.
2. My father said to me, "The First Battle of Panipat was fought in 1526."
   My father told me that the First Battle of Panipat was fought in 1526.

Multiple Choice Questions

Directions (Qs. 1 to 13): *Select the correct Indirect Speech for the following sentences:*

1. I said to him, "I shall help you."
   A. I told him that I can help him.
   B. I told him that I would help him.
   C. I told him that I will help him.
   D. I told him that I shall be helping him.

2. My Teacher said to me, "The earth revolves round the sun."
   A. My teacher told me that the earth revolves round the sun.
   B. My teacher told me that the earth revolve round the sun.
   C. My teacher told me that the earth had been revolving round the sun.
   D. My teacher told me that the earth has been revolving round the sun.

3. I said to my friend, "My father daily goes for a walk."
   A. I told my friend that my father daily goes for a walk.
   B. I told my friend that my father daily went for a walk.
   C. I told my friend that my father has to go for a walk.
   D. I told my friend that my father had gone for a walk.

4. He said to me, "May God bless you!"
   A. He requested that God can bless me.
   B. He prayed that God can bless me.
   C. He prayed that God might bless me.
   D. He prayed that God will bless me.

5. The patient said, "Thank you, doctor."
   A. The patient thanked the doctor.
   B. The patient requested the doctor with thanks.
   C. The patient told the doctor thanks.
   D. The patient suggested the doctor thanks.

6. Satish said, "No, I shall not talk to him."
   A. Satish told that he should not talk to him.
   B. Satish suggested that he would not have talked to him.
   C. Satish exclaimed with sorrow that he would not talk with him.
   D. Satish refused to talk to him.

7. The child said, "What a lovely place!"
   A. The child exclaimed with sorrow that it was a lovely place.
   B. The child thought that the place was lovely.
   C. The child exclaimed with joy that the place was very lovely.
   D. The child suggested that the place was lovely.

8. He said, "What a fool I have been!"
   A. He told himself with sorrow that he was a fool.
   B. He confessed with regret that he had been a great fool.
   C. He said himself a fool.
   D. He suggested that he could be a fool.

9. He said, "Alas! I am ruined."
   A. He told me that he had been ruined.
   B. He exclaimed with joy that he had been ruined.
   C. He exclaimed with sorrow that he was ruined.
   D. He told me that he should not be ruined.

10. The accused said, "I am not guilty."
    A. The accused exclaimed with sorrow that I am not guilty.
    B. The accused exclaimed with joy that he was not guilty.
    C. The accused stated that he was not guilty.
    D. The accused told me that he has not been guilty.

11. My teacher said, "The earth is round".
    A. My teacher said that the earth was round.
    B. My teacher says that the earth is round.
    C. My teacher said that the earth is round.
    D. My teacher ordered that the earth is round.

12. He said, "What a place it is!"
    A. He said that it was a very fine place.
    B. He said that is a very fine place.
    C. He said that the place is fine.
    D. He exclaimed with joy/surprise that it was a very fine place.

13. Ria said, "Shall I thread the needle?"
    A. Ria asked if she should thread the needle.
    B. Ria asked if she shall thread the needle.
    C. Ria ordered if she should thread the needle.
    D. Ria says that if she would thread the needle.

Directions (Qs. 14 to 33): *Pick out the correct alternative that completes the incomplete sentence which is changed into Indirect Narration.*

14. She said to me, "I shall see you as soon as I get time."
    She told me:
    A. that she will see me as soon as she will get time.
    B. that she would see me as soon as she would get time.
    C. she would see me whenever she got time.
    D. that she would see me whenever she gets time.

15. My secretary said to me, "Your plane will leave if you do not go at once."
    My secretary told me that:
    A. her plane would leave if she did not go at that time.
    B. her plane would leave if I do not go at once.
    C. my plane would leave if I did not go at that very time.
    D. my plane will leave if I did not go at that time.

16. My mother said to me, "Don't quarrel among yourselves".
    My mother:
    A. forbade me to quarrel among ourselves.
    B. asked me not to quarrel among ourselves.
    C. asked me that not to quarrel among ourselves.
    D. asked me to quarrel not among ourselves.

17. Her father said to her mother, "Excuse the daughter."
    Her father:
    A. requested her mother to excuse the daughter.
    B. asked her mother to excuse the daughter.
    C. asked her mother to have excused the daughter.
    D. asked her mother to have been excused.

18. He said to his friend, "Wait here till father comes."
    He requested his friend:
    A. to wait here till father had come.
    B. that to wait there till his friend came.
    C. to wait there till father came.
    D. to wait here until his friend came.

19. She said to her maid, "Run and catch the thief."
    She ordered her maid:
    A. ran and catch the thief.
    B. that to run and to catch the thief.
    C. ran and caught the thief.
    D. to run and catch the thief.

20. Anita said to Sunita, "What are you doing?"
    Anita asked Sunita:
    A. what she will be doing.
    B. that what she is doing.
    C. that what she was doing.
    D. what she was doing.

21. She said to me, "Are you meeting me today?"
    She enquired of me:
    A. whether I am meeting her that day.
    B. whether I was meeting her today.
    C. whether I was meeting her that day.
    D. I was meeting her that day.

22. Nitish said to me, "When did you buy this pen?"
    Nitish asked me:
    A. when I was to buy that pen.
    B. when I would buy that pen.
    C. when I had bought that pen.
    D. when I was buying that pen.

23. She said to me, "Are you going to market?"
She enquired of me:
A. I am going to market.
B. I was going to market.
C. if I was going to market.
D. if I had been going to the market.

24. Damini said, "Why did not you change your clothes?"
Damini asked me:
A. why I had not changed my clothes.
B. why I did not change my clothes.
C. why I would not change my clothes.
D. why I have not been changing my clothes.

25. Umesh said to me, "Have you read that novel?"
Umesh asked me:
A. if he was reading that novel.
B. if he had read that novel.
C. if I had read that novel.
D. if I was reading that novel.

26. She said to me, "I shall forgive you."
She told me:
A. that she will forgive me.
B. that she was going to forgive me.
C. that she will not forgive me.
D. that she would forgive me.

27. I said to her, "It was very hot last night."
I told her:
A. that it had been very hot the previous night.
B. that it was very hot the previous night.
C. that it has been very hot the last night.
D. that it had been very hot this night.

28. She said to me, "I thank you for the help you have given."
She:
A. told me that she thanked me for the help I had given.
B. thanked me for the help I have given.
C. thanked to me for the help I have given.
D. thanked me for the help I had given.

29. Mohini said to me, "Trust in God."
Mohini advised me:
A. that I should trust in God.
B. should trust in God.
C. trusted in God.
D. to trust in God.

30. I said to him, "Let us go to school."
I told him:
A. we would go to school.
B. we shall go to school.
C. that we would go to school.
D. that we should go to school.

31. Rajni said, "May God bless you?"
Rajni:
A. exclaimed with wish that God might bless me.
B. expressed a wish that God might bless me.
C. asked God to bless me.
D. shouted with joy to bless me.

32. My mother said me, "Do not have so many friends."
My mother forbade me:
A. to have so many friends.
B. not to have so many friends.
C. to have been so many friends.
D. to possess so many friends.

33. Ram said, "Pay attention to me."
Ram asked:
A. pay attention to him.
B. paid attention to him.
C. having paid attention to him.
D. to pay attention to him.

Directions (Qs. 34 to 50): *In questions below, the sentences have been given in Direct/Indirect Speech. Out of the four alternatives suggested select the one which best expresses the given sentence in Indirect/Direct Speech.*

34. She said that her brother was getting married
A. She said, "Her brother is getting married."
B. She told, "My brother is getting married"
C. She said, "My brother is getting married".
D. She said, "My brother was married".

35. "Please don't go away", she said.
A. She said to please her and not go away.
B. She told me to go away.
C. She begged me not to go away.
D. She begged that I not go away.

36. "If you don't keep quiet I shall shoot you", he said to her in a calm voice.
A. He warned her to shoot if she didn't keep quiet calmly.
B. He said calmly that I shall shoot you if you don't be quiet.
C. He warned her calmly that he would shoot her if she didn't keep quiet.
D. Calmly he warned her that be quiet or else he will have to shoot her.

37. I told him that he was not working hard.
A. I said to him, "You are not working hard."
B. I told him, "You are not working hard."
C. I said, "You are not working hard."
D. I said to him, "He is not working hard."

38. She said that she would finish the work the next day.
A. She said, "I will finish the work the next day."
B. She said, "I will finish the work tomorrow."
C. She said, "You will finish the work tomorrow."
D. She said, "I finished the work."

39. She said to him, "Why don't you go today?"
A. She asked him why he did not go that day.
B. She said to him that why he don't go today.
C. She asked him not to go today.
D. She asked him why he did not go today.

40. "Are you alone, my son?" asked a soft voice close behind me.
A. A soft voice asked that what I was doing there alone.
B. A soft voice said to me are you alone son.
C. A soft voice from my back asked if I was alone.
D. A soft voice behind me asked if I was alone.

41. My cousin said, "My room-mate had snored throughout the night."
A. My cousin said that her room-mate snored throughout the night.
B. My cousin told me that her room-mate snored throughout the night.
C. My cousin complained to me that her room-mate is snoring throughout the night.
D. My cousin felt that her room-mate may be snoring throughout the night.

42. He asked Rama if he needed his help then.
A. He said to Rama, "Do you need my help?"
B. He told Rama, "Tell me if you need help."
C. He asked Rama, "Do I need your help?"
D. He said to Rama, "Do you need my help now?"

43. Nita ordered her servant to bring her a cup of tea.
A. Nita told her servant, "Bring a cup of tea."
B. Nita said, "Bring me a cup of tea."
C. Nita said to her servant, "Bring me a cup of tea."
D. Nita said to her servant, "Bring her that cup of tea."

44. He exclaimed with joy that India had won the Sahara Cup.
A. He said, "India has won the Sahara Cup."
B. He said, "India won the Sahara Cup."
C. He said, "How! India will win the Sahara Cup."
D. He said, "Hurrah! India has won the Sahara Cup."

45. The boy said, "Who dare call you a thief?"
A. The boy enquired who dared call him a thief.
B. The boy asked who called him a thief.
C. The boy told that who dared call him a thief.
D. The boy wondered who dared call a thief.

46. The little girl said to her mother, "Did the sun rise in the East?
A. The little girl said to her mother that the sun rose in the East.
B. The little girl asked her mother if the sun rose in the East.
C. The little girl said to her mother if the sun rises in the East.
D. The little girl asked her mother if the sun is in the East.

47. Dhruv said that he was sick and tired of working for that Company.
A. Dhruv said, "I am sick and tired of working for this Company."
B. Dhruv said, "He was tired of that Company."
C. Dhruv said to me, "I am sick and tired of working for this Company."
D. Dhruv said, "I will be tired of working for that Company."

48. He said to his father, "Please increase my pocket-money."
A. He told his father, please increase the pocket-money.
B. He pleaded his father to please increase my pocket-money.
C. He requested his father to increase his pocket-money.
D. He asked his father increase his pocket-money.

49. She said to her friend, "I know where is everyone."
A. She told that she knew where was everyone.
B. She told her friend that she knew where was everyone.
C. She told her friend she knew where is everyone
D. She told her friend that she knows where was everyone.

50. His father ordered him to go to his room and study.
A. His father said, "Go to your room and study."
B. His father said to him, "Go and study in your room."
C. His father shouted, "Go right now to your study room."
D. His father said firmly, "Go and study in your room."

ANSWERS

1	2	3	4	5	6	7	8	9	10
B	A	A	C	A	D	C	B	C	C
11	**12**	**13**	**14**	**15**	**16**	**17**	**18**	**19**	**20**
C	D	A	B	C	A	B	C	D	D
21	**22**	**23**	**24**	**25**	**26**	**27**	**28**	**29**	**30**
C	C	C	A	C	D	A	A	A	D
31	**32**	**33**	**34**	**35**	**36**	**37**	**38**	**39**	**40**
B	A	D	C	C	C	A	B	A	D
41	**42**	**43**	**44**	**45**	**46**	**47**	**48**	**49**	**50**
A	D	C	B	A	B	A	C	B	A

9 Voice

A sentence in active voice focuses on the person or thing doing the action. A sentence in passive voice focuses on the person or thing affected by the action. *e.g.*,

The idol was built. (Active voice)
Someone built the idol. (Passive voice)

Transformation of Voice

- Voice and Tense are closely associated with each other.
- Tense plays an important role while transforming the voice.

On the basis of following points, voice can be transformed from active to passive voice.

The Present Indefinite Tense

Active voice: Subject + V_1 + Object
Passive voice: Subject + is, am, are + V_3 + by + Object

1. **Active voice:** He sings sweet songs.
   Passive voice: Sweet songs are sung by him.
2. **Active voice:** She does not cause any hindrance in my work.
   Passive voice: No hindrance in my work is caused by her.
3. **Active voice:** Do they love their country?
   Passive voice: Is their country loved by them?

The Present Continuous Tense

Active voice: Subject + is/am/are + V_1 + ing + Object.
Passive voice: Subject + is/am/are + being + V_3 + by + Object.

1. **Active voice:** She is cooking food.
   Passive voice: Food is being cooked by her.
2. **Active voice:** Rita is not knitting a sweater.
   Passive voice: A sweater is not being knitted by Rita.
3. **Active voice:** Is Meena baking a cake?
   Passive voice: Is a cake being baked by Meena?

The Present Perfect Tense

Active voice: Subject + has/have + V_3 + Object.
Passive voice: Subject + has/have + been + V_3 + by + Object.

1. **Active voice:** I have written an essay.
   Passive voice: An essay has been written by me.
2. **Active voice:** They have not whitewashed the fence.
   Passive voice: The fence has not been whitewashed by them.
3. **Active voice:** Have you cut the cake?
   Passive voice: Has the cake been cut by you?

The Past Indefinite Tense

Active voice: Subject + V_2 + Object
Passive voice: Subject + was/were + V_3 + by + Object

1. **Active voice:** He composed a new song.
   Passive voice: A new song was composed by him.
2. **Active voice:** He did not operate the computer.
   Passive voice: The computer was not operated by him.
3. **Active voice:** Did she catch a fish?
   Passive voice: Was a fish caught by her?

The Past Continuous Tense

Active voice: Subject + was/were + V_1 + ing + Object
Passive voice: Subject + was/were + being + V_3 + by + Object

1. **Active voice:** The farmers were ploughing the fields.
   Passive voice: The fields were being ploughed by the farmers.
2. **Active voice:** He was not administering the new drug to the patient.
   Passive voice: The new drug was not being administered to the patient by him.
3. **Active voice:** Was she sewing a dress?
   Passive voice: Was a dress being sewn by her?

The Past Perfect Tense

Active voice: Subject + had + V_3 + Object.
Passive voice: Subject + had + been + V_3 + by + Object

1. **Active voice:** He had issued me an import licence.
   Passive voice: I had been issued an import licence.
2. **Active voice:** We had not visited the Taj.
   Passive voice: The Taj had not been visited by us.
3. **Active voice:** Who had taught you English?
   Passive voice: By whom had you been taught English?

The Future Indefinite Tense

Active voice: Subject + will/shall + V_1 + Object.
Passive voice: Subject + will/shall + be + V_3 + by + Object.

1. **Active voice:** He will remove the dust from the shelf.
   Passive voice: The dust from the shelf will be removed by him.
2. **Active voice:** He will not open the main gate.
   Passive voice: The main gate will not be opened by him.
3. **Active voice:** Will you help us?
   Passive voice: Shall we be helped by you?

The Future Perfect Tense

Active voice: Subject + will/shall + have + V_3 + Object.
Passive voice: Subject + will/shall + have + been + V_3 + by + Object.

1. **Active voice:** They will have sold their house by then.
   Passive voice: Their house will have been sold by them by then.
2. **Active voice:** He will not have informed the police about it.
   Passive voice: The police will not have been informed about it by him.
3. **Active voice:** Will they have accepted the deal?
   Passive voice: Will the deal have been accepted by them?

Imperative Sentences

1. **Active voice:** Open the window.
   Passive voice: You are ordered to open the window.
   Or
   Let the window be opened.
2. **Active voice:** Please/kindly open the window.
   Passive voice: You are requested to open the window.
3. **Active voice:** Never make a noise.
   Passive voice: A noise should never be made.

Infinitives

1. **Active voice:** It is time to open the shop.
   Passive voice: It is time for the shop to be opened.
2. **Active voice:** He begged the officer to forgive him.
   Passive voice: He begged the officer to be forgiven.
3. **Active voice:** He has to break the door.
   Passive voice: The door has to be broken by him.

Prepositional Verb

1. **Active voice:** She laughed at the beggar.
   Passive voice: The beggar was laughed at by her.
2. **Active voice:** He listened to the news.
   Passive voice: The news was listened to by him.
3. **Active voice:** They called in the doctor.
   Passive voice: The doctor was called in by them.

Double Object

1. **Active voice:** He gave me a pen.
   Passive voice: A pen was given to me by him.
   Or
   I was given a pen by him.
2. **Active voice:** She told us a story.
   Passive voice: A story was told (to) us by her.
   Or
   We were told a story by her.

Use of Preposition other than 'by'

1. **Active voice:** The jug contains juice.
   Passive voice: Juice is contained in the jug.
2. **Active voice:** The audience thronged the hall.
   Passive voice: The hall was thronged with the audience.
3. **Active voice:** I know her.
   Passive voice: She is known to me.

Quasi Passive Verbs

1. **Active voice:** Quinine tastes bitter.
   Passive voice: Quinine is bitter when tasted.
   Or
   Quinine is bitter when it is tasted.
2. **Active voice:** Sugar is sweet (to taste).
   Passive voice: Sugar is sweet when tasted.
   Or
   Sugar is sweet when it is tasted.

Implied Sentences

1. **Active voice:** The driver drove the bus.
   Passive voice: The bus was driven.
2. **Active voice:** Someone read the news.
   Passive voice: The news was read.
3. **Active voice:** They say work is worship.
   Passive voice: It is said that work is worship.

Multiple Choice Questions

Directions (Qs. 1 to 20): *In the following questions, a sentence has been given in Active/Passive Voice. Out of the four alternatives suggested, select the one that Best Expresses the same sentence in Passive/Active Voice.*

1. Circumstances will oblige me to go.
   A. I will oblige the circumstances and go.
   B. I shall be obliged to go by the circumstances.

C. Under the circumstances, I should go.
D. I shall be obliged by the circumstances to go.

2. We waste much time on trifles.
A. Much time was wasted on trifles.
B. Much time will be wasted on trifles.
C. Much time is wasted by us on trifles.
D. Much time is wasted on trifles.

3. Mohan gave the beggar an old shirt.
A. An old shirt was given to Mohan by the beggar.
B. An old shirt was given to the beggar by Mohan
C. The begger was gave an old shirt by Mohan.
D. An old shirt was gave to the beggar by Mohan.

4. They have made him a king.
A. A king has been made by him.
B. He was made a king by them.
C. They have been made kings by him.
D. He has been made a king by them.

5. Who taught you English?
A. By whom English was taught to you?
B. By whom you were taught English?
C. By whom was English taught to you?
D. By whom are you taught English?

6. Was he knocking at the door?
A. Was the door being knocked at by him?
B. Was the door being knocked by him?
C. Was the door knocked by him?
D. Was the door knocking at him?

7. What was Rani doing?
A. What was done by Rani?
B. What was Rani being done?
C. What was being done by Rani?
D. What was being doing Rani?

8. Why were you wasting your time?
A. Why was your time being wasted?
B. Why was your time being wasted by you?
C. Why was your time wasted by you?
D. Why was your time wasted?

9. She has laid out a small garden.
A. A small garden has been laid by her.
B. A small garden has laid her.
C. A small garden being laid by her.
D. A small garden has been laid out by her.

10. She had already solved all the sums.
A. All the sums had already been solved by her.
B. All the sums have already been solved by her.
C. All the sums have been solved by her.
D. All the sums are solved by her.

11. He will have posted the letter.
A. The letter has been posted by him.
B. The letter will be posted by him.
C. The letter will have been posted by him.
D. The letter is posted by him.

12. They will have sold all the books by 4 P.M.
A. All the books will be sold by 4 P.M.
B. All the books will have been sold by 4 P.M.
C. All the books were being sold by 4 P.M.
D. All the books must be sold by 4 P.M.

13. Do you speak English?
A. Is English spoken by you?
B. Does English spoken by you?
C. Is English being spoken by you?
D. Does English being spoken by you?

14. Had they seen me before?
A. Had myself been seen by them before?
B. Had me being seen by them before?
C. Had I been seen by them before?
D. Had I being seen by them before?

15. May I take this pen?
A. May this pen will be taken by me?
B. May this pen shall be taken by me?
C. May this pen should be taken by me?
D. May this pen be taken by me?

16. Can we send it by air?
A. Can this be sent by air?
B. Can it be sent by air?
C. Can it go by air?
D. Can it be send by air?

17. Who wrote this book?
A. By whom was this book written?
B. By whom is this book written?
C. By whom was this book being written?
D. By whom is this book being written?

18. What did you buy?
A. What is bought by you?
B. What is being bought by you?
C. What was bought by you?
D. What was being bought by you?

19. Whom do you want?
A. Who is wanted by you?
B. Who is being wanted by you?
C. You are wanted by whom?
D. You are being wanted by whom?

20. When will you raise this question?
A. When this question will be raised by you?
B. When will this question be raised by you?
C. When this question is being raised by you?
D. When is this question being raised by you?

Directions (Qs. 21 to 35): *In each of the following questions, a sentence is given in Active Voice. Below it are given four alternatives suggesting the Passive Voice form of the above sentence. Choose the correct alternative.*

21. Who did this?
A. This was done by whom?
B. By whom was this done?
C. Who has done this?
D. By whom this was done?

22. One should keep ones promises.
A. Promises should be kept.
B. Ones promises should be kept by one.
C. Promises must be kept.
D. Ones promises one should keep.

23. Give the order.
A. Order given.
B. Order be given.
C. Let the order be given.
D. Order may be given by you.

24. You will have to do it.
A. It will be done by you.
B. It will have to be done by you.
C. It has to be done by you.
D. It would have to be done by you.

25. Keep to the left.
A. You are ordered to keep to the left.
B. You ought to keep to the left.
C. You are advised to keep to the left.
D. You must keep to the left.

26. They will arrange a party.
A. A party will have to be arranged by them.
B. A party they will have to arrange.
C. A party will be arranged by them.
D. A party by them will be arranged.

27. Someone has picked my pocket.
A. My pocket is picked.
B. My pocket has picked.
C. My pocket has been picked.
D. My pocket was picked.

28. He kept me waiting.
A. I kept waiting for him.
B. I kept waiting by him.
C. I was waiting for him.
D. I was kept waiting by him.

29. Why do you tell a lie?
A. Why is a lie told by you?
B. Why is told a lie by you?
C. Why is told by you a lie?
D. Why has a lie been told by you?

30. I have written a letter.
A. A letter is written by me.
B. A letter has been written by me.
C. A letter was written by me.
D. A letter had been written by me.

31. They will have helped you.
A. You will have helped by them.
B. You will have been helped by them.
C. You will be helped by them.
D. You will be helped by them.

32. Open the door.
A. Door may be opened.
B. Let the door be open.
C. Let the door be opened.
D. Door be opened.

33. I am reading a book.
A. A book is read by me.
B. A book is being read by me.
C. A book has been read by me.
D. A book in been read by me.

34. Why did your brother write such a letter?
A. Why your brother wrote such a letter?
B. Why was by brother written such a letter?
C. Why was such a letter written by your brother?
D. Why was written such a letter by your brother?

35. Did you run a great risk?
A. Was a great risk run by you?
B. Was run a great risk by you?
C. Was by you run a great risk?
D. Had you run a great risk?

Directions (Qs. 36 to 45): *In each of the following questions, a sentence is given in Passive Voice. Below it are given four alternatives suggesting the Active Voice form of the above sentence. Choose the correct alternative.*

36. He was made king.
A. He became king.
B. They made him king.
C. They had made him king.
D. He has been made king.

37. Good news is expected by us.
A. We are expecting good news.
B. We have been expecting good news.
C. We had expected good news.
D. We expect good news.

38. The child must be looked after.
A. The child you must look after.
B. You must look after the child.
C. You must look the child after.
D. You may look after the child.

39. What is wanted by you?
A. What you want?
B. What did you want?
C. What do you want?
D. What you do want?

40. Your father is known to me.
A. I am known to your father.
B. I know your father.
C. I have known your father.
D. I knew your father.

41. She may be told the story by you.
A. The story may be told by you to her.
B. You may tell the story to her.
C. You may tell her the story.
D. You may tell to her the story.

42. Duty ought to be done.
A. Let duty be done.
B. One ought to do one's duty.
C. One should do his duty.
D. Do you duty.

43. Is English spoken by you?
A. Did you speak English?
B. Do you speak English?
C. Have you spoken English?
D. Do you know how to speak English?

44. Gold coins are contained in this box.
A. This box contains gold coins.
B. This box has contained gold coins.
C. This box is containing gold coins.
D. This box has gold coins.

45. Character is revealed by manners.
A. Manners revealed character.
B. Manners reveal character.
C. Manners have revealed character.
D. Manners do reveal character.

ANSWERS

1	2	3	4	5	6	7	8	9	10
D	C	B	D	C	A	C	B	D	A
11	**12**	**13**	**14**	**15**	**16**	**17**	**18**	**19**	**20**
C	B	A	C	D	B	A	C	A	B
21	**22**	**23**	**24**	**25**	**26**	**27**	**28**	**29**	**30**
B	A	C	B	C	C	C	D	A	B
31	**32**	**33**	**34**	**35**	**36**	**37**	**38**	**39**	**40**
B	C	B	C	A	B	D	B	C	B
41	**42**	**43**	**44**	**45**					
C	B	B	A	B					

❑❑❑

10 Sentence Completion

> Filling the blanks is such an exercise that starts with the primary schools and continues at the highest level of competitive examinations. One must practise it regularly to score well.

Multiple Choice Questions

Directions: *Pick out the most effective word(s) from the given words to fill in the blanks and make the sentence meaningfully complete.*

1. One requires great .... to teach and handle little children who are restless.
A. patience B. attitude
C. determination D. knowledge

2. The researchers will .... some of the causes of increasing poverty in the state.
A. fund B. investigate
C. promote D. circulate

3. I usually perform .... when nobody is watching me.
A. alone B. good
C. better D. hard

4. It was .... to everyone that the minister had been drinking.
A. observed B. known
C. discovered D. realised

5. I would rather stay indoors .... the rain stops.
A. so B. waiting
C. until D. usually

6. The process should be completed as far as possible within a week, ... which the matter should be brought to notice of the officer concerned.
A. following B. failing
C. realizing D. referring

7. The officers are ..... to regular transfers.
A. free B. open
C. subject D. available

8. All letters received from Government should ..... be acknowledged.
A. suddenly B. obviously
C. immediately D. occasionally

9. Mumbai office ..... a meeting of senior officials to discuss the high incidence of frauds.
A. attended B. convened
C. reported D. registered

10. The note should be ..... to all the concerned departments for their consideration.
A. regulated B. requested
C. carried D. forwarded

11. Your present statement does not .... what you said last week.
A. accord to B. accord in
C. accord with D. accord for

12. I had a vague .... that the lady originally belonged to Scotland.
A. notion B. expression
C. imagination D. theory

13. The prisoner showed no .... for his crimes.
A. hatred B. obstinacy
C. remorse D. anger

14. It is inconceivable that in many schools children are subjected to physical .... in the name of discipline.
A. violation B. exercise
C. violence D. security

15. We have not yet fully realised the .... consequences of the war.
A. happy B. pleasing
C. grim D. exciting

16. Happiness consists in being .... what we have.
A. contented to B. contented with
C. contented for D. contented in

17. His rude behaviour is a .... his organization.
A. disgrace for B. disgrace on
C. disgrace upon D. disgrace to

18. No child is .... understanding. One has to wait and provide proper guidance.
A. dull to B. dull in
C. dull of D. dull for

19. I am fully .... the problems facing the industry.
A. alive with B. alive to
C. alive for D. alive on

20. The Romans were .... science.
A. bad in B. bad to
C. bad for D. bad at

21. Although I was .... of his plans, I encouraged him, because there was no one else who was willing to help.
A. sceptical B. remorseful
C. fearful D. excited

22. You have no business to .... pain on a weak and poor person.
A. inflict B. put
C. direct D. force

23. Her uncle died in a car accident. He was quite rich. She suddenly .... all her uncle's money.
A. succeeded B. caught
C. gave D. inherited

24. There was a major accident. The plane crashed. The pilot .... did not see the tower.
A. likely B. probably
C. scarcely D. hurriedly

25. The car we were travelling in .... a mile from home.
A. broke off B. broke down
C. broke into D. broke up

26. What are you .... in the kitchen cupboard?
A. looking in B. looking on
C. looking to D. looking for

27. I did not see the point of .... waiting for them, so I went home.
A. hanging around B. hang on
C. hang together D. hanging up

28. He lost confidence and .... of the deal at the last minute.
A. backed out B. backed on
C. backed down D. backed onto

29. To the dismay of all the students, the class monitor was ..... berated by the principal at a school assembly.
A. critically B. ignominiously
C. prudently D. fortuitously

30. All attempts to revive the fishing industry were ..... failure.
A. foredoomed to B. heading at
C. predicted for D. estimated to

31. There are ..... parked outside than yesterday.
A. fewer cars B. few cars
C. less cars D. a small number of cars

32. The minister had to ..... some awkward questions from reporters.
A. fend B. fend at
C. fend out D. fend off

33. The ..... of evidence was on the side of the plaintiff since all but one of the witnesses testified that his story was correct.
A. propensity B. force
C. preponderance D. brunt

34. Attention to detail is ..... of a fine craftsman.
A. hallmark B. stamp
C. seal of authority D. authenticity

35. Behaving in a .... and serious way, even in a .... situation, makes people respect you.
A. calm, difficult B. steady, angry
C. flamboyant, tricky D. cool astounding

36. Along with a sharp rise in ………, a recession would eventually result in more men, women, and children living in ………..
A. crime, apathy
B. fatalities, poor
C. deaths, slums
D. unemployment, poverty

37. The government has …………… to provide financial aid to the ones ……….. by severe floods in the city.
A. desired, troubled B. promised, havoc
C. failed, affected D. wanted, struck

38. An airplane with ………… passengers on board made an unscheduled .... as the airport to which it was heading was covered with thick fog.
A. imitable, slip B. faulty, stop
C. variety, halt D. numerous, landing

39. Deemed universities .... huge fees, but have not been successful in providing .... education to our students.
A. collect, maintaining
B. pay, better
C. ask, good
D. charge, quality

40. If the banks desire to .... profit, they should get rid of .... measures.
A. lose, concentrate B. increase, populist
C. earn, unhealthy D. maximise, traditional

41. Leadership defines what the future should look like and ...... people with that vision.
A. aligns B. develops
C. trains D. encourages

42. We upset ourselves by responding in an ...... manner to someone else's actions.
A. unabashed B. irrational
C. arduous D. arguable

43. All the people involved in that issue feel a great ...... to his suggestion.
A. contradiction B. adherence
C. indifference D. repugnance

44. These elections will be remembered as much for its anti-incumbency mood as for its ...... mandate.
A. invincible B. rational
C. unprecedented D. deliberate

45. How do you expect us to stay in such a ...... building even if it can be hired on a nominal rent?
A. scruffy B. disperate
C. fragmented D. robust

46. ...... efforts from all concerned are required to raise the social and economic conditions of our countrymen.
A. Perpetual B. Dynamic
C. Massive D. Exploring

47. Many companies see technology as a ...... for a whole host of business problems.
A. consideration B. preference
C. linking D. panacea

48. Known as devout and serious person, she also has ...... sense of humour.
A. better B. plentiful
C. quick D. good

49. The matter would have become serious if ...... action had not been taken.
A. hasty B. fast
C. timely D. unusual

50. The ...... with which he is able to yield the paint brush is really remarkable.
A. ease B. practice
C. majesty D. sweep

51. You must ensure the correctness of the information before ....
A. drawing B. enabling
C. learning D. jumping

52. The rocket .... the target and did not cause any casualty.
A. sensed B. reached
C. missed D. exploded

53. It is desirable to take .... in any business if you want to make profit.
A. advice B. risk
C. loan D. recourse

54. They wasted all the money on purchase of some .... items.
A. excellent B. important
C. significant D. trivial

55. When he found the wallet his face glowed but soon it faded as the wallet was ....
A. empty B. vacant
C. recovered D. stolen

56. He has served the country by .... many significant positions.
A. appointing B. creating
C. developing D. holding

57. The frequent errors are a result of the student's ....
A. talent B. smartness
C. carelessness D. perception

58. The robbers eventually .... in breaking into the house.
A. succeeded B. decided
C. caught D. trained

59. I finally .... her to stay another day.
A. advised B. persuaded
C. suggested D. called

60. Most of the people who .... the book exhibition were teachers.
A. witnessed B. presented
C. conducted D. attended

ANSWERS

1	2	3	4	5	6	7	8	9	10
A	B	C	A	C	B	C	C	B	D
11	12	13	14	15	16	17	18	19	20
C	A	C	C	C	B	D	B	B	D
21	22	23	24	25	26	27	28	29	30
B	C	C	B	C	C	D	A	B	A
31	32	33	34	35	36	37	38	39	40
A	D	D	A	A	D	C	D	C	B
41	42	43	44	45	46	47	48	49	50
A	A	D	C	A	A	D	D	C	A
51	52	53	54	55	56	57	58	59	60
A	C	B	D	A	D	C	A	B	D

❑❑❑

11 Sentence Improvement

One may use the same words in many ways but the best way is only one that makes the perfect usage of the words and conveys the proper meaning of the expression. Try it yourself in the following questions.

Multiple Choice Questions

Directions: *In these questions, a part of the sentence is bold. Below are given alternatives to the bold part at A, B and C which may improve the sentence. Choose the correct alternative. In case no improvement is needed, your answer is 'D'.*

1. Discreet salience **is extremely important** to create that 'irresistible-yet-unattainable' image for brands that want to take India seriously
A. was extremely important
B. is mainly important
C. was important extremely
D. No Improvement

2. This, over a designer outfit that he wanted for a friend's party and **that his sensitive** parents refused him.
A. which his sensitive
B. which his insensitive
C. that his insensitive
D. No Improvement

3. Goa was full of non-Goa property hunters **rushing about buying up the place** like tomorrow was an expired lease.
A. rushing in buying up the place
B. rushed about buying up the place
C. rushing about to buy up the place
D. No Improvement

4. Property hunting is a **tired and hungry** making business.
A. is a tiresome and hungry
B. is a tiring and hungry
C. is a tiring and waste
D. No Improvement

5. Cultural differences aside, **till luxury need speaks** in a manner that befits.
A. luxury still needs to speak
B. luxury still need to speak
C. luxury till need to speak
D. No Improvement

6. Indian food—the culinary avatar of the subcontinent's social history presented on a platter—**is without doubt the best food** in the world.
A. is undoubtedly the greatest food
B. is without doubt greatest food
C. is best food without doubt
D. No Improvement

7. It must retain the language of poetry. **It needed to create** stories, and not statements.
A. It needed creating
B. It needs creating
C. It needs to create
D. No Improvement

8. This year, Asia-Pacific has become the first region **to reach aggregate profiting** in biotech.
A. to reach aggregated profitability
B. to reach aggregate profitability
C. to reach aggregate of profit
D. No Improvement

9. India is deviating to embrace the West. If Western luxury brands deviate a little, **albeit selectively**, they will find rich Indian arms open far and wide.
A. though selectively

B. however selectively
C. albeit selectedly
D. No Improvement

10. China and India continued to attract attention and deals, motivated by the desire to increase access to these **largest and growing** drug markets and by the need to lower the costs of drug development.
A. larger and growing B. large and growing
C. larger and grown D. No Improvement

11. Luxury brands are **still above of the** clover curve here, with their elite (small) audiences.
A. still ahead of the B. still in the
C. still far of the D. No Improvement

12. Agencies **hence needed to be** sure of returns before investing, say admen.
A. hence needs to be B. so needs to be
C. hence need to be D. No Improvement

13. India is still a nascent market and that's the spirit everyone's **looking at it**.
A. looking for it B. looking in it
C. looking with it D. No Improvement

14. Questioning the state's move to allow women to serve liquor but not dance in bars **of the ground that** dancing aroused physical lust.
A. on the grounds that
B. of the grounds that
C. over the grounds that
D. No Improvement

15. For England the positives from their crushing series lose come in the shape of James Anderson and Kevin Pietersen, **both of which** have made significant strides up the rankings.
A. both of which B. both of whom
C. both of who D. No Improvement

16. International campaigns can work well for luxury here, **but context cannot be** ignored.
A. so context cannot be
B. but context cannot
C. but context couldn't
D. No Improvement

17. For one, the Indian luxury context, **while evolved rapidly**, still has its own meaning, and its own implications.
A. while evolved rapid
B. which evolving rapidly
C. while evolving rapidly
D. No Improvement

18. But too much of availability can compromise a luxury brand or **made it lose** its lustre.
A. make her lose B. make him lose
C. make it lose D. No Improvement

19. Still, it's under-the-upper **layers themselves who** are aspiring for slivers of luxury.
A. layers themselves which
B. layer itself who
C. layers themself which
D. No Improvement

20. It is like saying Hindi movies, with skimpily dressed dancers, would **effect public** order.
A. effect your B. affect public
C. affected public D. No Improvement

21. The court held that a few women being involved in prostitution was no **justice to deny other** bar girls the right to livelihood.
A. justification to declare other
B. justification to deny other
C. justice to let other
D. No Improvement

22. All-rounder cricketer has also made some progress **over the** player rankings.
A. above the B. at the
C. up the D. No Improvement

23. Former minister on Sunday **joined hands** with a suspended Lok Sabha member to float a new political outfit.
A. folded hands B. walked hand in hand
C. shaked hands D. No Improvement

24. Pakistan's former ministers will meet in London on Monday **to ask** a strategy to return home from exile.
A. to chalk out B. to negotiate
C. to create D. No Improvement

25. It's a family potboiler, medical thriller and political drama **all in one**–except that it's all too real and all too grim.
A. all 3 in one
B. all coupled into one
C. all rolled into one
D. No Improvement

26. India's efforts to get international support for its civil nuclear energy programme got **a go ahead on** Sunday as Germany indicated it would not come in the way of the India-US nuclear deal.
A. a life in B. a boost on
C. a boost at D. No Improvement

27. Is it time for old bungalows to **bite the dust**?
A. go down B. get down
C. come down D. No Improvement

28. The bungalows was an outward manifestation of a certain **way in life**, and with that era gone.
A. way for life B. way of life
C. way at life D. No Improvement

29. The builder Mittals will reportedly **raise their money**-raking high-rise behind it.
A. highten their money
B. rise their money
C. raise there money
D. No Improvement

30. The impatient present has usually demolished **more of the** past before we wake up to the irretrievable loss.
A. much of
B. much of their
C. much of the
D. No Improvement

31. Preservation is a romantic notion; demolition **quiet** more practical reasons.
A. has many,
B. had many,
C. have many,
D. No Improvement

32. You must get back to your **charming self** and impress the audience with your social skills.
A. own self
B. main self
C. own uniqueness
D. No Improvement

33. Stay focused on your goals and don't **get disturbed by** non-materialistic possessions.
A. get involved by
B. get betrayed by
C. get distracted by
D. No Improvement

34. You may appear more optimistic than your detractors **may want it to be**.
A. want you to be
B. wish yourself to be
C. seek you be
D. No Improvement

35. There are a number of mineral springs in the Czech territory, which **has been used** for medicinal purposes since the early 15th century.
A. have been used
B. had been used
C. has being used
D. No Improvement

36. The picturesque mountains **offer**s excellent bungee jumping spots.
A. shows
B. provides
C. offer
D. No Improvement

37. Begin your **meal with** traditional faves like potato soup, beef soup with liver dumplings or dill soup made from sour milk.
A. meals with
B. meal in
C. meals of
D. No Improvement

38. You can also **go to the** National Museum building and the famous Prague State Opera.
A. went to
B. visit the
C. saw
D. No Improvement

39. If they close the Gulf for a **length of time** to shipping, then certainly we could look at $150, probably higher.
A. larger amount of time
B. larger duration of time
C. larger amount of hours
D. No Improvement

40. **More of them** are owned by the state and even the privately-owned ones are open to the public.
A. Most of which
B. Most of them
C. Most of all
D. No Improvement

41. Constructed in the ninth century by the Prince Booivoj, the castle has transformed **oneself** from a wooden fortress surrounded by earthen bulwarks to the imposing form it has today.
A. himself
B. herself
C. itself
D. No Improvement

42. Apart from frequent art exhibitions, **their are also** permanent collections devoted to archaeology, anthropology, mineralogy, natural history and numismatics.
A. there is also
B. there are also
C. their are also
D. No Improvement

43. You can visit the Czech Museum of Fine Arts, **at a** permanent exhibition on Czech Kubism.
A. with a
B. for a
C. in a
D. No Improvement

44. Tensions **above** Iran come at a time of strong demand for energy.
A. under
B. inside
C. over
D. No Improvement

45. Because its shores line the narrow Straits of Hormuz, Iran **could quickly hit** both military and commercial shipping.
A. will quickly hit
B. shall quickly hit
C. will be quick hitting
D. No Improvement

46. For most people who exercise **at the** morning, there is no getting around the question: Eat and run? Or run and eat later?
A. in the
B. in
C. at the time of
D. No Improvement

47. Are ad agencies even attempting to peer into the keyhole of this indulgence sanctum to garner consumer insights **ahead of** the curve?
A. above
B. over
C. within
D. No Improvement

48. Too many people rush into the world of credit and don't stop to think about how **their actions could affect their** credit score and ability to qualify for credit in the future.
A. their actions may affect their
B. their actions might affect their
C. their actions will affect their
D. No Improvement

49. According to the report, **number of deal with** vaccines were energized by concerns around avian flu, SARS, and biodefence products, while looming patent expirations led to more deals in generics.

A. number of deals in
B. number of deal in
C. number of deals with
D. No Improvement

50. This is how the Bombay High Court responded to the state government's purported **moral stand which** dance bars were causing grave harm to society.
A. moral stand in B. moral stand at
C. moral stand that D. No Improvement

51. If you have a high credit limit, use **at least a** third of it.
A. atleast a B. at last a
C. utmost a D. No Improvement

52. Fitness experts will say that **first eating provides** fuel for a proper workout.
A. eating in the beginning provides
B. first eat provides
C. eating first provides
D. No Improvement

53. One study that examined the claim directly in 1995 found that a group of people did **burned much calories from fat on days** when they exercised on an empty stomach than on days when they had a small breakfast first.
A. burn more calories from fat on days
B. burn more calorie from fat on days
C. burnt more calories from fat on days
D. No Improvement

54. Carefree children spent their afternoons **to run about barefoot**, their clothes dusty, and telltale twigs of the neighbour's mango tree in their hair.
A. running barefoot in the sun
B. run about barefoot in the sun
C. running about barefoot in the sun
D. No Improvement

55. A year ago, a 13-year-old girl attempted suicide because her mother **refuses to pay his** mobile bills.
A. refuses to pay her B. refused to pay her
C. refused to pay his D. No Improvement

ANSWERS

1	2	3	4	5	6	7	8	9	10
D	C	D	B	A	D	C	C	D	B
11	**12**	**13**	**14**	**15**	**16**	**17**	**18**	**19**	**20**
C	C	D	A	C	D	C	C	C	C
21	**22**	**23**	**24**	**25**	**26**	**27**	**28**	**29**	**30**
B	C	C	A	C	B	D	B	D	C
31	**32**	**33**	**34**	**35**	**36**	**37**	**38**	**39**	**40**
A	D	C	A	D	C	A	B	D	B
41	**42**	**43**	**44**	**45**	**46**	**47**	**48**	**49**	**50**
C	B	A	C	D	A	D	C	A	C
51	**52**	**53**	**54**	**55**					
C	C	A	C	B					

❑❑❑

12 Reordering Words & Sentences

Different words form a sentence and convey their meaning only when arranged in a proper order. A Paragraph is formed from sentences, it will convey its true meaning and purpose only when the sentences are arranged in a proper manner. Try and practise it in this exercise.

Multiple Choice Questions

Directions (Qs. 1 to 20): *In the following questions, some parts of the sentence have been jumbled up. You are required to rearrange these parts which are labelled P, Q, R and S to produce the correct sentence. Choose the option with proper sequence.*

1. We are doing
P : to the people
Q : to give relief
R : all we can
S : but more funds are needed
The correct sequence should be
A. P Q R S B. R Q P S
C. Q P R S D. S P Q R

2. The man
P : when he was
Q : in the office last evening
R : could not finish
S : all his work
The correct sequence should be
A. P Q R S B. Q R S P
C. R Q P S D. R S P Q

3. The people decided
P : they were going
Q : how much
R : to spend
S : on the construction of the school building
The correct sequence should be
A. Q P R S B. P Q R S
C. P R Q S D. S Q P R

4. The man said that
P : those workers
Q : would be given a raise
R : who did not go on
S : strike last month
The correct sequence should be
A. P Q R S B. P R S Q
C. Q P R S D. R S P Q

5. I think
P : the members
Q : are basically in agreement
R : of the group
S : on the following points
The correct sequence should be
A. R Q P S B. S Q R P
C. P R Q S D. P Q S R

6. While it was true that
P : I had
Q : to invest in industry
R : some lands and houses
S : I did not have ready cash
The correct sequence should be
A. P Q R S B. P R S Q
C. S Q P R D. Q P R S

7. P : But for your help
Q : to finish this work
R : it would not have been possible
S : in time
The correct sequence should be
A. P R Q S B. S P Q R
C. R P Q S D. P Q R S

8. The boy
P : in the competition
Q : who was wearing spectacles
R : won many prizes
S : held in our college
The correct sequence should be
A. P Q R S B. R P S Q
C. Q R P S D. Q P S R

9. About 200 years ago,
P : in the south of India
Q : an old king
R : ruled over a kingdom
S : called Rajavarman
The correct sequence should be
A. Q S R P B. P Q R S
C. Q P S R D. Q S P R

10. P : his land
Q : a wooden plough
R : the Indian peasant still uses
S : to cultivate
The correct sequence should be
A. R Q P S B. Q P S R
C. S R Q P D. R Q S P

11. He was a man,
P : even if he had to starve
Q : who would not beg
R : borrow or steal
S : from anyone
The correct sequence should be
A. P Q R S B. P R Q S
C. Q R S P D. Q P R S

12. P : in the progress of
Q : universities play a crucial role
R : our civilization
S : in the present age
The correct sequence should be
A. S Q P R B. Q R S P
C. Q R P S D. S Q R P

13. P : far out into the sea
Q : for the next two weeks there were further explosions
R : which hurled
S : ashes and debris
The correct sequence should be
A. Q R P S B. R S P Q
C. Q R S P D. S R P Q

14. William Shakespeare,
P : in his lifetime
Q : the great English dramatist
R : wrote thirty-five plays
S : and several poems
The correct sequence should be
A. P Q R S B. R S P Q
C. Q S R P D. Q R S P

15. Whenever I am,
P : with an old friend of mine
Q : in New Delhi
R : to have dinner
S : I always try
The correct sequence should be
A. S Q P R B. Q S R P
C. R P S Q D. P R Q S

16. P : I don't know
Q : must have thought
R : what people sitting next to me
S : but I came away
The correct sequence should be
A. R S Q P B. R Q S P
C. P Q R S D. P R Q S

17. P : in estimating the size of the earth
Q : but they were hampered by the lack of instruments of precision
R : ancient astronomers
S : used methods which were theoretically valid
The correct sequence should be
A. R P Q S B. P R Q S
C. R S Q P D. R P S Q

18. P : It is a pity that
Q : by offering a handsome dowry
R : a number of parents think that
S : they will be able to ensure the happiness of their daughters
The correct sequence should be
A. S Q R P B. P R S Q
C. P S R Q D. P R Q S

19. The common man
P : in nurturing
Q : a more active role
R : communal harmony
S : should play
The correct sequence should be
A. P R S Q B. S Q P R
C. S Q R P D. P R Q S

20. The doctor
P : able to find out
Q : what has caused
R : the food poisoning
S : has not been
The correct sequence should be
A. S P R Q B. P R Q S
C. P R S Q D. S P Q R

Directions (Qs. 21 to 40): *A number of sentences are given below which when properly sequenced form a coherent paragraph. Each sentence is labelled as abcdef...... Choose the most logical order of sentences from among the given choices to construct a coherent paragraph:*

21. (a) Parts of northern region were pounded by heavy rains today,

(b) Vehicular traffic came to a near halt.
(c) As mid and high altitude areas of Himachal Pradesh were in grip of severe cold wave with snow lashing the tribal areas and mid ranges receiving showers.
(d) As the sky remained heavily overcast with dark clouds reducing the visibility considerably.
(e) A large number of tourists were forced to buy heavy woollens and stay indoors due to inclement weather.

A. ecabd B. adecb
C. edabc D. acbde

22. (a) The idea is that students should be able to find employment for themselves after the course.
(b) The Central Board of Secondary Education is planning a revamp of its vocational courses.
(c) For this it is necessary to tie up with the industry as well as mobilise schools for their support.
(d) While others will be made less academic and more in tune with the needs of the industry.
(e) A number of courses have been identified as 'deadwood' and will be done away with.

A. bedac B. abcde
C. acebd D. baced

23. (a) Clearly, age is not a deterrent in one's choice of learning.
(b) Perhaps, it was because of her childhood desire.
(c) When Rachna came to Delhi eight years back, she had not anticipated a career in the field of art.
(d) She has been successful in the various exhibitions that she has been part of in terms of business.
(e) She had got into expressing her thoughts with the help of a brush and colours only because her daughter refused to get initiated into it.
(f) She feels that her use of colour appeals to people.

A. aedcbf B. cdefba
C. cebadf D. acdebf

24. (a) The rehabilitation record has been dismal.
(b) It has been two years years since the earthquake rudely rattled the people of Gujarat.
(c) And since then, life has been a constant struggle.
(d) The quake set Gujarat's clock back by 10 years.
(e) Things changed forever.

A. bedca B. bcade
C. dbace D. edcba

25. (a) In fact, success in exams depended on rote learning from old notes.
(b) when he was studying civil engineering in a college in Gujarat.
(c) He was detained for lack of attendance.
(d) Lectures were soporific, classes rarely worth attending and 80 per cent attendance compulsory.
(e) The college became a trap he hated.
(f) His is a plight many engineers across India would identify with.
(g) He found the going tough.

A. abcdgef B. bgdacef
C. fabcdge D. abcdefg

26. (a) In a country that has close to 600 recognised engineering colleges, there are only seven IITs.
(b) Barring a few exeptions, the academic atmosphere in these is moribund.
(c) The very best students usually get there.
(d) many waste themselves in frustration.
(e) Most of those who get into engineering are good students.
(f) but about 1.25 lakh others and up in the remaining colleges.

A. aecfbd B. abecdf
C. abcdef D. acfbed

27. (a) Whatever the job market, common wisdom says that IIT graduates will find jobs where others have failed.
(b) The IIT brand name is a ticket to success.
(c) When recruiters go headhunting, the IITs are still top of their list.
(d) Its possessor is understood to have an excellent academic record and the will to succeed.
(e) In the job market, that counts.

A. bdeac B. abcde
C. abdce D. dbace

28. (a) It will pave the way ....
(b) signalling a new beginning in strategic ties......
(c) for a tangible Indian economic presence in Iran and Central Asia.
(d) Iran has offered India valuable road linkages to central Asia ......
(e) aimed at promoting peace and economic cooperation in the region.

A. dbeac B. debca
C. acebd D. abced

29. (a) A good college is essential for a successful career and admissions are based on marks.
(b) The marks-based system followed by all the boards in the country recognises only a small percentage of students as successful.
(c) The marks one scores in the crucial board exams dictate the path his life takes.
(d) Anyone scoring below a certain percentage is automatically branded a 'failure'.
(d) So if you cannot make it into the best college, your career is over even before it has started.

A. abcde B. bcdea
C. bdcae D. abdec

30. (a) The project has already started on an experimental basis in the west district.
(b) A website is soon going to be launched where application forms can be downloaded and submitted.

(c) Standing in a queue at a government office to submit application form will be a thing of the past.
(d) A unique code will be alloted while submitting the form which will help in finding the status of the application.

A. abcd B. dabc
C. cbda D. badc

31. (a) To curb bio-terrorism is a difficult task.
(b) To check these attacks and lessen their impact, we need an impartial team of sincere, strong and dedicated men.
(c) The media can play a strong role in stopping this unnecessary spread of panic.
(d) Since bio-terrorism is not visible or easily detectable, it can be used often.
(e) Men who honour the lives of their fellow countrymen before their own.

A. abcde B. dabce
C. adbec D. acbed

32. (a) He was dying.
(b) No one was ready to touch him as even shifting him from one place to another would lead to profuse bleeding.
(c) He was a five-day old infant, premature and bleeding profusely.
(d) Even if injected one small needle, blood would ooze out and continue to flow for an hour at a stretch.
(e) This small being had haematoma, a thick blood clot in his brain.

A. edbca B. cabde
C. eacdb D. cedba

33. (a) The day I don't treat a patient, I feel ......
(b) I have enough to eat, I crave for blessings now.
(c) But if a financially weak patient gives me only ₹ 50, I don't mind.
(d) Each month I do three to four operations free of cost.
(e) I have lost something in life.
(f) My consultation fee is ₹ 300.

A. fcdeab B. dfcbae
C. fcabde D. bdfcea

34. (a) When he was rushed to the nearby Primary Health Centre after his fall, the doctor referred him to a hospital.
(b) This worsened his injury.
(c) Had a little precaution been exercised after the accident, Tarun would have continued with his gymnastic classes.
(d) He was paralysed from waist downwards when he fell from the vaulting horse while doing gymnastics.
(e) However, the doctor forgot to tell Tarun's parents to take him on a stretcher as he had suffered spinal injuries.
(f) Tarun is wheelchair bound for two years.

A. fdeabc B. abcdef
C. fdcaeb D. fdbcae

35. (a) As the temperature rises, staying hydrated can become a greater challenge for people exercising both indoors and out.
(b) Several things can influence this process, including age, gender, physical conditioning. humidity and a lack of sufficient fluids.
(c) In hot weather, individuals can lose as much as two quarts of sweat per hour.
(d) As we age, we have a lower perceived level of thirst in response to fluid loss and early stages of dehydration.
(e) If not replenished, this can lead to dehydration, heat exhaustion and even heatstroke.

A. abcde B. dbcae
C. cbdea D. acebd

36. (a) The leopard was discovered in the servant quarters of a farmhouse.
(b) The injuries appeared to have been caused by the paws of the leopard, and were not teeth wounds.
(c) It took the wild life officials, Delhi Police and Delhi zoo vets eight hours to capture the leopard that had wandered into a factory in south Delhi.
(d) The leopard then jumped into the factory where the workers managed to lock it in a small generator room before calling in the police.
(e) Before its capture, the leopard attacked two women and a man in the farmhouse.

A. aebdc B. bdaec
C. eadbc D. adbec

37. (a) Police suspect a carpenter working at John's house as he has not reported for work since the day the boy went missing.
(b) John did not return home in the afternoon.
(c) John's mother had herself put the boy on the vehicle in the morning.
(d) John smiled at him and was last seen walking up to him.
(e) His parents called the school and were told John had not been to school at all and had been marked absent.
(f) He was about to enter the school when someone called out his name.

A. cfdbea B. debfca
C. bfdaec D. abcdef

38. (a) However, the mayhem over the last few months is deeply shocking.
(b) Yet I do not agree with the prophets of doom who see nothing but disaster ahead.
(c) When I came back to my motherland India after a stay in Switzerland, I felt I was trading a hotbed of

intense religious and political violence for peace and quiet.

(d) I think our nation is searching for an identity.

(e) And a new vision of the future will emerge from this.

A. abcde B. cabde
C. cebad D. bedca

39. (a) An integrated and combined approach was required to reveal the mystery of the brain —its structure, composition and function.

(b) Since the early 80's, scientists were clear that the brain would be the final frontier to conquer.

(c) The initiative was flagged off and came to be known as the Human Brain Project.

(d) But that wasn't easy because understanding the brain involved completely integrating information from the level of the gene to the level of behaviour.

(e) To fulfill this requirement a group of American scientists from various disciplines decided to work together.

A. acbed B. bdaec
C. abdec D. badec

40. (a) A product is something that is made in a factory, a brand is something that is bought by a consumer.

(b) The trick therefore, lies in the brand positioning.

(c) For a consumer, the satisfaction of becoming associated with a name that is the 'best' and the 'leader' is far more important and at times makes him ignore the price factor.

(d) Brands come and go.

(e) Still there are those who manage to stay and develop an affinity with consumers.

A. aebcd B. debac
C. decab D. aecdb

ANSWERS

1	2	3	4	5	6	7	8	9	10
B	D	A	B	C	C	A	C	A	D
11	**12**	**13**	**14**	**15**	**16**	**17**	**18**	**19**	**20**
C	A	C	D	B	D	C	B	B	D
21	**22**	**23**	**24**	**25**	**26**	**27**	**28**	**29**	**30**
D	A	C	A	B	D	A	A	C	C
31	**32**	**33**	**34**	**35**	**36**	**37**	**38**	**39**	**40**
C	D	B	C	D	A	A	B	B	B

❑❑❑

13 Comprehension Passages

PASSAGES

Directions: *Read the following passages and answer the questions given below each.*

PASSAGE-1

In the Roman times, defected enemies were generally put to death as criminals for having offended the emperor of Rome. In the middle ages, however, the practice of ransoming of returning prisoners in exchange for money became common. Though some saw this custom as a step towards a most humane society, the primary reasons behind it were economic rather than humanitarian.

In those times, rulers had only a limited ability to raise taxes. They could neither force their subject to fight nor pay them to do so. The promise of material compensation in the form of goods and ransom was therefore the only way of inducing combatants to participate in a war. In the middle ages, the predominant incentive for the individual soldiers was the expectation of spoils. Although collecting ransom clearly brought financial gain, keeping a prisoner and arranging for his exchange had its cost. Consequently, procedures were devised to reduce transaction costs.

One such device was a rule asserting that the prisoner had to assess his own value. This compelled the prisoner to establish a value *without too much distortion;* indicating too low a value would increase, the captive's chances of being killed, while indicating too high a value would either ruin him financially or create a prohibitively expensive ransom that would also result in death.

1. It can be inferred from the passage that a medieval soldier
- A. was less likely to kill captured members of opposing armies than was a soldier of the Roman Empire
- B. was similar to a 20th century terrorist in that he operated on a basically independent level and was motivated solely by economic incentives
- C. had few economic options and chose to fight because it was the only way to earn an adequate living
- D. was motivated to spare prisoners' lives by humanitarian rather than economic ideals

2. Which of the following best describes the change in policy from executing prisoners in Roman times to ransoming prisoners in the middle ages?
- A. The emperors of Rome demanded more respect than did medieval rulers and thus Roman subjects went to greater lengths to defend their nation
- B. It was a reflection of the lesser degree of direct control medieval ruler had over subjects
- C. It became a show of strength and honour warrior of the middles ages to be able to capture and return their enemies
- D. Medieval soldiers were not as hum-anitarian as their ransoming practices might have indicated

3. The primary purpose of the passage is to
- A. discuss the economic basis of the medieval practice of exchanging prisoners for ransom
- B. examine the history of the treatment of prisoner of war
- C. emphasize the importance of a warrior's code of honour during the middle ages
- D. explore a way of reducing the cost of ransom

4. The author uses the phrase *"without too much distortion"* in order to
- A. indicate that prisoners would fairly assess their worth
- B. emphasize the important role medieval prisoners played in determining whether they should be ransomed
- C. explain how prisoners often paid more than an appropriate ransom in order to increase their chances for survival
- D. suggest that captors and captives often had understanding relationships

PASSAGE-2

The world dismisses curiosity by calling it idle or mere idle curiosity—even though curious persons are seldom idle. Parents do their best to extinguish curiosity in their children because it makes life difficult to be faced everyday with a string of unanswerable questions about what makes fire hot or why grass grows. Children whose curiosity survives parental discipline are invited to join our university. With the university, they go on asking their questions and trying to find the answers. In the eyes of a scholar, that is what a university is for. Some of the questions which the scholars ask, seem to the world to be scarcely worth asking, let alone answering. They asked questions too minute specialised for you and me to understand without years of explanation. If the world inquires of one of them why he wants to know the answer to a particular question he may say especially if he is a scientist, that the answer will in some obscure way make possible a new machine or weapon or gadget. He talks that way because he knows that the world understands and respects utility.

But to you who are now part of the university, he will say that he wants to know the answer simply because he does not know it, the way the mountain climber wants to climb a mountain, simply because it is there. Similarly a historian asked by an outsider why he studies history may come out with the argument that he has learnt to repeat on such occasions, something about knowledge of the past making it possible to understand the present and mould the future. But if you really want to know why a historian studies the past, the answer is much simpler, something happened and he would like to know what. All this does not mean that the answers which scholars find to their questions have no consequences. They may have enormous consequences but these seldom form the reason for asking the questions or pursuing the answers. It is true that scholars can be put to work answering questions for the sake of the consequences as thousands are working, now, for example, in search of a cure for cancer. But this is not the primary function of the scholars. For the consequences are usually subordinate to the satisfaction of curiosity.

1. According to the passage, the children make life difficult for their parents
   A. by their ceaseless curiosity
   B. by unceasing bombardment of questions
   C. by asking irrelevant questions
   D. by posing profound questions
2. The common people consider some of the questions that the scholars ask unimportant
   A. as they are too lazy and idle
   B. as they are too modest
   C. as it's beyond their comprehension
   D. as it is considered a waste of time
3. A historian really studies the past
   A. to comprehend the present and to reconstruct the future
   B. to explain the present and plan the future
   C. to understand the present and make fortune
   D. to understand the present and mould the future
4. Children whose curiosity survives parental discipline means
   A. children retaining their curiosity in spite of being discouraged by their parents
   B. children pursuing their mental curiosity
   C. children's curiosity subdued due to parents' intervention
   D. children being disciplined by their parents
5. According to the passage, parents do their best to discourage curiosity in their children
   A. because they have no time
   B. because they have no patience to answer them
   C. because they feel that their children ask stupid questions continuously
   D. because they are unable to answer all their questions

PASSAGE-3

The factor of geographical distribution is equally, possibly even more, significant that English is spoken as first or native language in at least four continents of the world, Russian in two, Chinese and the Indian languages in one. English is without question the closest approach to a world language today. It goes without saying that no two persons ever have an identical command of their common language. Certainly, they have not precisely the same vocabulary. There are at least minor differences in pronunciation, indeed the same individual will not pronounce his vowels and consonants in absolutely identical fashion everytime he utters them. Everyone possesses, in addition, certain individual traits of grammatical form and syntactical order, constituting that peculiar and personal quality of language which we term as style. All of this is implicit in the well-known phrase, 'Style is the man.' No men are identical, no two styles are the same. If this be true of but two persons, the potential of differences resident in a language spoken by more than 200 million truly staggers imagination.

1. The author argues that English is the closest approach to a world language because
   A. there are more native speakers of English than of any other language
   B. English has less number of mutually unintelligible dialects
   C. the geographical distribution of English covers a much greater area
   D. other languages are much too complex to be world languages

2. The fact that the same individual will not pronounce his vowels and consonants identically everytime shows that
   A. literary style varies from person to person
   B. mutual intelligibility is a myth
   C. vocabulary varies from individual to individual
   D. no two persons speak the same language exactly the same way
3. It is evident from the passage that style is
   A. a strange type of language
   B. a language where one does not have to be particular about correctness and grammar
   C. language used in a particular way by an individual
   D. a question of grammatical and syntactic correctness
4. According to some authorities
   A. more people speak Chinese dialect than English
   B. more people speak English as an auxiliary language than as a first language
   C. more people speak English in the UK than in England
   D. about one-fourth of the world's population speaks English
5. The overall implication of the passage is that
   A. to suppose that 230 million people speak English as a native language would certainly be an underestimate
   B. the 55 million inhabitants of the British Isles speak like the 30 million inhabitants of the dominions and colonies
   C. a little less than half the native English speakers in the world live in the US
   D. about one-tenth of the total English-speaking world population lives in British dominions and colonies

PASSAGE-4

What is the future which awaits our children? The underlying assumption of the question, that Indian children have a common future, is itself dubious. It can legitimately be asked whether a student who is well-fed, attending a boarding school in the salubrious climate of the hills and learning to use computers has any future in common with a malnourished child who goes to a school with no blackboards, if indeed he does go to school. The latter may have no worthwhile future at all. And it might be worthwhile to analyse the significance of this marginalisation of more than 75 per cent of the children of this country.

The failure to provide an infrastructure for primary education in the villages of India more than 40 years after independence is in sharp contrast with the sophisticated institutions, for technical institutes of higher education are funded by the government, which essentially means that the money to support them comes from taxes. And, since indirect taxation forms a substantial part of the taxes collected by the government, the financial burden is borne by all the people. L.K. Jha put it graphically when he observed that 25 paise of every rupee spent on educating an IIT student comes from the pockets of men and women whose children may never enter a proper classroom.

1. The author is trying to highlight which of the following?
   A. Faulty system of direct taxes
   B. The greatness of L.K. Jha
   C. Need of sophisticated education for rural poor
   D. Need to have common future for Indian children
2. Which of the following pairs have been termed as 'sharp contrast' by the author?
   (*i*) Infrastructure for technical education
   (*ii*) Lack of infrastructure for rural primary schools
   (*iii*) 25 paise of every rupee earned by Government is spent on education
   (*iv*) The financial burden of higher technical education is borne by all people
   (*v*) 75% of children have limited opportunities
   A. (*ii*) and (*iv*) B. (*ii*) and (*iii*)
   C. (*iii*) and (*iv*) D. (*i*) and (*ii*)
3. Which of the following statements is not true?
   (*i*) The author welcomes Govt.'s initiative on primary education
   (*ii*) 75% of the children have a bright future
   (*iii*) 25% cost of educating a technocrat comes from poor people
   A. Only (*i*) B. Only (*ii*)
   C. Only (*iii*) D. Only (*i*) and (*ii*)
4. According to the author, who among the following does not have a hopeful and prosperous future?
   (*i*) All students from technical institutes
   (*ii*) All students financially supported by the Government
   A. Only (*i*) B. Only (*ii*)
   C. Both (*i*) and (*ii*) D. Neither (*i*) nor (*ii*)
5. What seems to be the likely answer of the author to the question posed by him in the first sentence of the passage?
   (*i*) There is no common future for the Indian children
   (*ii*) The future is worthwhile for majority of Indian children
   (*iii*) The majority may never enter a proper classroom
   A. Only (*i*) B. Only (*ii*)
   C. Only (*iii*) D. Both (*i*) and (*ii*)
6. What seems to be the purpose of the author in writing this passage?
   A. Setting goals for children of upper middle class
   B. Questioning the legitimacy of public schools
   C. Highlighting lack of infrastructural facilities for primary education
   D. Focusing on inequality in educational opportunities

PASSAGE-5

Cyber crime is the branded stigma defacing the culture and magnanimity of computer technology. It is upkeeping the flag with indomitable triumph against developing computer technology worldwide.

Modern age is striding with marching steps of technology revolution beating the past decade of ancestral belief with ultimate care. Computer invention has unfolded the mystery of quick access with the objective of minimum manpower and cutting the time consumption parameters.

As each coin has dual face of its portrait, likewise computer technology is sick of creeping virus. Synthetic man-made dilemma of site hackers activation is causing setback to the expanding anchor of revolutionary device with great loss of time, economy and data profile as suffered by consumers. A recent report from Internet security firm Websense estimates that 85.6 per cent of all the unwanted e-mails contained links to spam sites. The company's data suggests that the number of malicious sites grew 233 per cent in the last six months and saw 671 per cent growth in the number of malicious sites during the last year. In June alone, the total number of e-mails detected as containing viruses increased by 600 per cent compared to May.

Chat rooms, blogs and message-boards where the users post comments have been identified as the top targets of hackers and spammers due to the high traffic these attract. According to Websense, 95 per cent of user-generated comments to blogs, chat rooms and message-boards during the first half of the year were malicious.

It is advisable not to click on spurious links and stay away from keying in passwords at unknown sites as they are most likely to be spammed. Hackers can steal your passwords and log in to your account and access critical information like account numbers and contact details among other things.

1. The above passage is:
A. an advisory for the computer users.
B. an advisory for the Internet users.
C. a warning against possible threat to the Internet users.
D. related to chat rooms, blogs and message boards.

2. People who use chat rooms and blogs,
A. are safe and have no threats from spam.
B. are more prone to malicious e-mails.
C. create virus and hack the accounts of others.
D. are unsafe.

3. According to the writer, it is not safe to:
A. log on to spurious links.
B. access one's own account frequently.
C. have essential information stored in a computer.
D. include data-stealing code.

4. Hackers and spammers, according to the writer, are:
A. a new threat to the Internet users and the economy.
B. only pranksters and not serious threat to the system.
C. trained, professional technocrats who are an asset.
D. not expert professionals.

5. Which word in the passage is synonym of *weblog*?
A. blog B. password
C. site D. e-mail

6. Which agency has assessed the data record with spam sites?
A. Microsoft
B. Internet security from Google
C. Websense
D. Spammers

7. Which month dominates the e-mails detection data record?
A. May B. June
C. Last six months D. Last year

PASSAGE-6

Progress in life depends a good deal on crossing one threshold after another. Some time ago, a man watched his little nephew try to write his name. It was hard work, very hard work. The little boy had arrived at an effort threshold. Today he writes his name with comparative ease. No new threshold confronts him. This is the way with all of us. As soon as we cross one threshold, as soon as we conquer one difficulty, a new difficulty appears, or should appear. Some people make the mistake of steering clear of thresholds. Anything that requires genuine thinking and use of energy, they avoid. They prefer to stay in a rut where thresholds are not met. Probably, they have been at their job a number of years. Things are easy for them. They make no effort to seek out new obstacles to overcome. Real progress stops under such circumstances.

Some middle-aged and elderly people greatly enrich their lives by continuing to cross thresholds. One man went into an entirely new business when he was past middle life and made success of it, De Morgan didn't start to write novels until he was past sixty. Psychologists have discovered that man can continue to learn throughout his life. And it is undoubtedly better to try and fail than not to try at all. There one can be placed in the category of the Swiss mountaineer of whom it was said, *"He died climbing"*. When a new difficulty arises to obstruct your path, do not complain. Accept the challenge. Determine to cross this threshold as you have crossed numerous other thresholds in your past. In the words of a poet, do not rest but strive *to pass from dream to grander dream.*

1. What obstructs real progress in life?
A. Remaining at one and the same post
B. Avoiding the thinking and energy
C. Shunning every work
D. Stopping education

2. What does progress in life depend upon?
   A. Good habits
   B. Hardwork
   C. Overcoming one difficulty after another
   D. Spirit of service and cooperation
3. What does *'He died climbing'* signify?
   A. He died when he was climbing the hill
   B. He died before getting at the top
   C. He strove hard till the last moment of life
   D. He climbed the hill and then died
4. What does *'to pass from dream to grander dream'* mean?
   A. Always having greater and greater aspiration in life
   B. Seeing one good dream and then greater aspiration in life
   C. Making plan after plan
   D. Seeing one dream after the other
5. What did the man entering a new business past middle life do of his business?
   A. He miserably failed in it
   B. He achieved partial success
   C. He dropped the business after some time
   D. He achieved good success in it
6. How can you accomplish the most difficult tasks?
   A. By mobilizing all possible resources
   B. By avoiding all obstacles
   C. By sticking to hardwork
   D. By doing it bit by bit and persisting in the effort
7. What does De Morgan's life teach?
   A. That it is futile to learn many things
   B. That one is never old in case he has vigour
   C. That it is never too late to learn
   D. That creative writing can be made even late in life
8. How do middle-aged and elderly people add brilliance to their lives?
   A. By overcoming difficulty one after another
   B. By getting sycophants to surround them
   C. By making fine speeches
   D. By acquiring resourcefulness
9. What should we do when a new difficulty obstructs our path?
   A. Run away from it
   B. Be bold and face it
   C. Manoeuvre to get it removed
   D. Enlist other people's help to get it over
10. When did De Morgan start to write novels?
    A. When he was sixty years old
    B. When he was below sixty
    C. When he studied psychology
    D. None of these

PASSAGE-7

It is *heartening* to know that if one had not had any heart attack earlier and he stops smoking, his chances of having a heart attack *drop* to that of a non-smoker in about six months' time. Stopping of smoking is also the single most effective means of secondary prevention (recurrence of a heart attack) in heart patients.

Smoking leads to pain and stiffness in the legs while walking. No amount of drugs can help. The only remedy is to give up smoking. If women smoke during pregnancy, there is an increased risk of death of the baby in the womb or soon after birth. Even where the baby survives, there is likelihood of delayed physical and intellectual development of the baby till it reaches 11 years of age.

Still worse the fact about smoking is that passive smoking is equally dangerous. Passive smokers are those who do not smoke but being in the company of smokers have to inhale smoke exhaled by the smokers They are equally prone to heart diseases, lung cancer and bronchitis, for no fault of theirs. It is seen that the incidence of these diseases is greater among women whose husbands are *heavy* smokers As such, every non-smoker has a fundamental right to safeguard himself against the danger of passive smoking. "Your smoking is injurious to my health and I have a right to stop you from smoking" could be the slogan against passive smoking. It is a great threat to the health of the individual, the family and the society. In fact one has to choose between health and smoking including passive smoking. *One cannot have both.*

Another matter of *grave concern* about smoking is the long time interval between the start of smoking habit and the manifestation of deadly diseases like cancer, chronic bronchitis and heart attack. People are generally not aware of the link between smoking and the misery they have to undergo years later and younger people often fall victim to this menacing habit under the wrong impression that they are *immune* to its disastrous effects, not realising that they are *heading* towards catastrophe. The prolonged incubation period of many tobacco-related diseases has prevented recognition of the size of the threat and the *grim* picture of chronic and life-threatening diseases.

1. What is "passive smoking"?
   A. Giving up the habit of smoking abruptly
   B. Exhaling smoke by a non-smoker
   C. Unintended intake of smoke exhaled by smokers
   D. Smoking cigarettes which are harmless in nature
2. The effects of passive smoking are more and more prominently observed among
   A. the children
   B. the smokers
   C. the wives of smokers
   D. the non-smokers
3. Which of the following is a heartening thing, according to the author?

A. People who have had a heart attack stop smoking
B. It takes only six months for any person to quit smoking
C. The smoker carries the risk of heart attack for six months
D. None of these

4. Which of the following statements is/are false in the context of the passage?

(*i*) Passive smokers are not free from risk of heart diseases
(*ii*) Intake of certain medicines helps recover pain and stiffness in legs caused by smoking
(*iii*) Younger people are immune to the disastrous effects if their regular smoking is under control

A. (*i*) and (*ii*) only B. (*ii*) and (*iii*) only
C. (*ii*) only D. (*iii*) only

5. Which of the following is not mentioned in the passage as a likely result of smoking by women during pregnancy?

A. Death of baby before birth
B. Death of baby after birth
C. Survival of baby with some abnormality
D. Abnormal delay in the childbirth

6. Which of the following is considered by the author as a matter of "grave concern"?

A. Inordinate delay in appearance of symptoms of hazards of smoking
B. Long time required for giving up the habit of smoking
C. Manifestation of deadly. diseases like cancer, bronchitis, etc.
D. Lack of awareness of people regarding the hazards of smoking

7. The youth feel that they are immune to the hazardous effects of smoking because

A. these effects of smoking are not visible within a short time span
B. they do not realise that they are heading towards disaster
C. they feel a great thrill in acquiring the habit of smoking
D. the link between smoking and its disastrous effects cannot be established

8. Which factor prevents people from realising the extent of threat of smoking hazards?

A. Their lack of awareness of civic responsibilities
B. Their firm belief that they are not immune to these hazards
C. The less disastrous effects of tobacco- related diseases
D. None of these

9. The last sentence of the third para *"One cannot have both"* means

A. active smoking and passive smoking
B. smoking and risk of heart diseases
C. threat to the individual and also to the family
D. None of these

Directions (Qs. 10 to 12): *Choose the word which is most nearly the **SAME** in meaning as the word given in bold capitals as used in the passage.*

10. HEADING

A. crowning B. marching
C. adorning D. title

11. HEAVY

A. excessive B. bulky
C. large D. thick

12. DROP

A. roll B. escape
C. remove D. reduce

Directions (Qs. 13 to 15): *Choose the word which is most nearly the **OPPOSITE** in meaning of the word given in bold capitals as used in the passage.*

13. GRIM

A. dim B. dark
C. presentable D. pleasant

14. IMMUNE

A. free B. vulnerable
C. powerful D. weak

15. HEARTENING

A. cheerful B. miserable
C. frightening D. dangerous

PASSAGE-8

The happy man is the man who lives objectively, who has free affections and wide interests, who secures his happiness through these interests and affections and through the fact that they, in turn, make him an object of interest and affection to many others. To be the recipient of affection is a potent cause of happiness, but the man who demands affection is not the man upon whom it is *bestowed.* The man who receives affection is, speaking broadly, the man who gives it. But it is useless to attempt to give it as a calculation, in the way in which one might lend money at interest, for a calculated affection is not genuine and is not felt to be so by the recipient.

What then can a man do who is unhappy because he is encased in self? So long as he continues to think about the causes of his unhappiness, he continues to be self-centred and therefore does not get outside the vicious circle, if he is to get outside it, it must be genuine interests, not by simulated interests adopted merely as a medicine. Although this difficulty is real, there is nevertheless much that he can do if he has rightly diagnosed his trouble. If, for example, his trouble is due to a sense of sin, conscious or unconscious, he can first persuade his conscious mind that he has no reason to feel sinful and then proceed, to plant his rational conviction in his unconscious mind, concerning himself meanwhile with some more or less neutral activity. If he succeeds in *dispelling* the sense of sin, it is possible that genuine objective interests will arise spontaneously. If his trouble is self-pity, he can deal with it in the same manner after first persuading himself that there is nothing extraordinarily unfortunate in his circumstances.

If fear is his trouble, let him practise exercises designed to give courage. Courage has been recognised from time immemorial as an important virtue, and a great part of training of boys and young men has been devoted to producing a type of character capable of fearlessness in battle. But moral courage and intellectual courage have been much less studied, they also, however, have their technique. Admit to yourself everyday at least one painful truth, you will find this quite useful. Teach yourself to feel that life still be worth living even if you were not, as of course you are, immeasurably superior to all your friends in virtue and in intelligence. Exercises of this sort prolonged through several years will at last enable you to admit facts *without flinching* and will, in so doing, free you from the empire of fear over a very large field.

1. Who according to the passage is the happy man?
A. who is encased in self
B. who has free affection and wide interests
C. who is free from worldly passions
D. who has externally centre passions

2. According to the passage, calculated affection
A. appears to be false and fabricated
B. makes other pen-on to love you
C. turns into permanent affection over a period of time
D. leads to self-pity

3. Which of the following virtues, according to the passage, has been recognised for long as an important virtue?
A. Patriotism B. Sacrifice
C. Courage D. Self-consciousness

4. Which of the following, according to the passage, has not been studied much?
A. Feeling of guilt and self-pity
B. The state of mind of an unhappy man
C. How to get absorbed in other interests
D. Moral and intellectual courage

5. If a man is suffering from a sense of sin
A. he should invite opinion of others
B. he should admit his sin at once
C. he should consciously realize that he has no reason to feel sinful
D. he should develop a fearless character

6. What happens to a man who demands affection?
A. His feelings are reciprocated by others
B. He tends to take a calculated risk
C. He becomes a victim of a viscious circle
D. None of these

7. What should a man do who is suffering from the feeling of self-pity?
A. He should control his passions and emotions
B. He should persuade himself that everything is alright in his circumstances
C. He should seek affection from others
D. He should develop a feeling of fearlessness

8. How to get out of the viscious circle mentioned in the passage?
A. By practicing skills of concentration
B. By inculcating the habits of self-absorption
C. Being true to others and one's internal circumstances
D. None of these

9. Which of the following statements is not *true* in the context of the passage?
A. Happy man has wide interests
B. Courage has been recognized as an important virtue
C. Unhappy man is encased in self
D. Issue of intellectual courage has been extensively studied

10. Which of the following words is ***SIMILAR*** in meaning of the word **'bestowed'** as used in the passage?
A. Conferred B. Accommodated
C. Trusted D. Withdrawn

11. Which of the following statements is *true* in the context of the passage?
A. All passions stem from unhappiness
B. The happy man lives in subjectively
C. Any virtue has a dark side also
D. One feels happy if one receives affection

12. Which of the following words is ***SIMILAR*** in meaning to the word **'flinching'** as used in the passage?
A. Wincing B. Convincing
C. Explaining D. Debating

13. What happens when you think about cause of your unhappiness?
A. You try to introspect and look critically at yourself
B. You realize that the life can be lived in different ways
C. You try to practice exercise designed to give courage
D. You remain a self-centred person

14. What according to the passage is the real cause of happiness?
   A. Material rewards and incentives received
   B. Critical analysis of the happy state of mind
   C. Affection received from others
   D. Calculated risks taken

15. Which of the following words is ***OPPOSITE*** in meaning of the word **'dispelling'** as used in the passage?
   A. Giving   B. Accumulating
   C. Projecting   D. Scattering

PASSAGE-9

Education, particularly higher education, is the obvious but crucially important instrument for nation building. As Confucious has said:

"If you are thinking of one year, plant rice. If you are thinking of a decade, plant trees. If you are thinking of a century, educate the people."

When we set about the task of higher education, we should be absolutely clear in our perception of the goals of education in the specific context of our nation's development. No *doubt,* one of the important aims of education would be to create the required range and nature of trained manpower assessed to be needed by different sectors of national growth. The entire educational apparatus must be geared progressively to fulfill the requirements of different phases of our growth in every sector—primary, secondary and *tertiary.* The aim must be to ensure that our country does not experience either *paucity,* or a *surfeit* of trained manpower in any specific segment of our economy. The requirements of our country, as a free, democratic, secular, socialist, nation, *aspiring* for rapid development, *entail* a specific recipe for our educational institutions. Today's educational institutions must therefore be developed accordingly and must regulate themselves to give the country the precise nature and quantum of trained manpower as projected by the requirements of our planned economy.

1. The author has quoted thoughts of Confucious to stress
   A. importance of planting trees for human beings
   B. the worthless efforts in planting rice
   C. the benefits of investing in education
   D. the need for assessing manpower requirement

2. Which statement cannot be made on the basis of the passage?
   A. Higher education should keep in view the requirements of national economy
   B. Higher education has not been employed for nation building
   C. All levels of education have a role to play in nation's growth
   D. In our country we need to have a specially planned educational system

3. The writer believes that
   A. there are no problems related to higher education
   B. investment in education is of long-range
   C. higher education should be used to assess manpower needs
   D. aims of higher education in India are absolutely clear

4. The author's expectations from higher education, are essentially
   A. unrealistic   B. confusing
   C. critical   D. vague

5. The writer indicates that
   A. higher education did not play any role in national growth
   B. primary education did not play any role in national growth
   C. our nation experiences paucity of trained manpower in many sectors
   D. today's higher education has no precise goals to achieve

6. Author has used the word 'apparatus' to indicate the
   A. scientific nature of education
   B. complicated organization demanded by education
   C. readily visible benefits of education
   D. entire equipment of education to perform particular function

7. Which of the following has not been conveyed by the passage?
   A. Education at any level can contribute in nation building
   B. Manpower needs in many areas can be fulfilled through higher education
   C. Rapid development of our nation is possible through higher education
   D. Present higher education does not ensure surfeit of trained manpower

8. This passage is likely to be addressed to
   A. politicians only
   B. scientists only
   C. students only
   D. cannot be said

9. Choose a suitable title to the passage:
   A. Manpower Planning in India
   B. Importance of Higher Education
   C. Demands of Higher Education
   D. Role of Higher Education in India

Directions (Qs.10 to 12): *Choose the word which is most nearly the **SAME** in meaning as the word given in bold capitals as used in the passage.*

10. DOUBT
   A. suspicion   B. certain
   C. definite   D. sure

11. TERTIARY
A. last B. important
C. third D. terminal

12. ASPIRING
A. inquiring B. awaiting
C. involving D. striving

Directions (Qs.13 to 15): *Choose the word which is most* ***OPPOSITE*** *in meaning as the word given in bold capitals as used in the passage.*

13. PAUCITY
A. moderate B. enormity
C. mediocrity D. littleness

14. SURFEIT
A. abundance B. redundancy
C. repletion D. lack

15. ENTAIL
A. entitled B. ensure
C. dismiss D. retain

PASSAGE-10

Books are a great treasurehouse of knowledge. They are the living examples of man's *march* on the path to higher and higher civilisation. The great men who died long ago, live in their books. We feel their very personality and existence when we read their books. We feel as if they were conversing with us.

Books not only store civilization but also carry it forward. All coming generations get the light of knowledge from the books written by their ancestors and try to improve upon that knowledge. Civilization cannot make much *headway* in a country where there are not many *great* books. We get through books the latest knowledge in the fields of arts, science, commerce, etc. This knowledge is helpful to us and *enables* us to achieve success in the field of our choice.

Books are never failing friends. They never *desert* us, not even when all fair-weather friends have deserted us. They dispel the dark clouds of gloom from our minds and increase our happiness if we are already happy. Through the ages, the scriptures and other great books have provided immeasurable *solace* to the wounded and strife-torn humanity.

There may be books prescribed for some course or profession, but then there are books for general study. The books of literature—poetry, drama, novel, short stories, etc., are generally highly thrilling and inspiring if they are written by a good author. There may be tragic, comical or humorous books. The question is that of an individual's choice.

To be a lover of books, though not to be bookworm, is a sign of good luck. A voracious reader gets much *more pleasure* from reading bool·s than a miser gets in hoarding money. The knowledge embedded in books is valueless; so is pleasure obtained from reading them. A good book absorbs the whole spirit of man; the reader's pleasure is indescribable.

1. Which of the following, according to the passage, is not true about books?
A. They are source of inspiration
B. They are source of knowledge
C. They are source of happiness
D. They are means of livelihood

2. How do the books help in progress of civilization?
A. Based on the earlier books new knowledge is obtained
B. The books provide solution to many problems
C. The books inspire the scientists
D. Not mentioned in the passage

3. How do the books make people more happy?
A. They help the reader to overcome the shadows of uncertainty
B. They help bring in joy by amusing the reader through their content
C. They help the reader to understand the darker side of life
D. Not mentioned in the passage

4. Which of the following is the author's view about the knowledge and pleasure derived from books?
(*i*) We get more of knowledge and less of pleasure
(*ii*) We get more of pleasure and less of knowledge
(*iii*) We get knowledge and pleasure in equal measure
A. only (*i*) B. only (*ii*)
C. either (*i*) or (*ii*) D. only (*iii*)

5. The high quality of books produced by a country indicates:
A. it has a high rate of literacy
B. it has a progressive civilization
C. it is not an industrialised nation
D. it has learned ancestors

6. Why are the books, according to the passage, called never-failing friends?
A. Books do not betray individuals
B. Books are inanimate
C. Books always give companionship to the reader
D. Books are available in the market anytime unlike others

7. How do the books help in bringing peace in the minds of people?
A. Books provide information about the past civilization
B. Books help people learn to take correct steps with the help of the recorded information
C. Books act as a window to the minds of the great men
D. Not mentioned in the passage

8. Which of the following has been described as a sign of good luck?
   A. Being a miser
   B. Having lot of money
   C. Advancing the culture
   D. A passion for books

Directions (Qs. 9 to 12): *Choose the word which is most nearly the **SAME** in meaning as the word given in bold capitals as used in the passage.*

9. **SOLACE**
   A. peace B. tranquillity
   C. calmness D. console

10. **ENABLES**
    A. helps B. succeeds
    C. promotes D. stops

11. **HEADWAY**
    A. higher B. forge
    C. movement D. improve

12. **MARCH**
    A. move B. progress
    C. pass D. register

Directions (Qs. 13 to 15): *Choose the word which is most **OPPOSITE** in meaning of the word given in bold capitals as used in the passage.*

13. **GREAT**
    A. small B. thin
    C. short D. ordinary

14. **PLEASURE**
    A. displeasure B. pain
    C. happiness D. hardship

15. **DESERT**
    A. waterhole B. bitter
    C. accompany D. propel

ANSWERS

PASSAGE-1

1	2	3	4
A	B	A	A

PASSAGE-2

1	2	3	4	5
A	C	D	A	D

PASSAGE-3

1	2	3	4	5
A	D	C	D	A

PASSAGE-4

1	2	3	4	5	6
D	A	D	A	A	D

PASSAGE-5

1	2	3	4	5	6	7
A	D	A	A	A	C	B

PASSAGE-6

1	2	3	4	5
A	C	C	A	D
6	7	8	9	10
D	B	A	B	D

PASSAGE-7

1	2	3	4	5
C	C	D	B	D
6	7	8	9	10
A	A	D	D	B
11	12	13	14	15
A	D	D	B	C

PASSAGE-8

1	2	3	4	5
B	A	C	D	C
6	7	8	9	10
D	B	D	D	A
11	12	13	14	15
D	D	D	C	B

PASSAGE-9

1	2	3	4	5
D	D	C	D	D
6	7	8	9	10
D	A	D	B	A
11	12	13	14	15
C	D	B	D	C

PASSAGE-10

1	2	3	4	5
D	A	D	D	B
6	7	8	9	10
A	D	D	D	A
11	12	13	14	15
D	B	D	B	C

❑❑❑

14 Cloze Test

A cloze test is a procedure in which a person is asked to supply words that have been removed from a passage as a test of his ability to comprehend text. Practise it regularly to score well.

PASSAGES

Directions: *In each of the following passages some numbered blank spaces are given. For each numbered blank space four answer choices are given. Pick out the one which is the most appropriate for that blank space, keeping the trend of the passage in mind.*

Passage-1

Mankind's most ....(1).... treasure of thoughts is carefully preserved in the golden casket of books. The ....(2).... of books is as vast as the universe, for there is no comer of it which they have left ....(3).... . There is no ....(4).... of books on any topic, be it as simple as the composition of sodium nitrate or as ....(5).... as the mechanism of a spacecraft rocketing towards Mars. The ....(6).... of books is not only most easily available but is enlightened, dependable and lifelong. In times of distress they make us stoically ....(7).... of the object that causes uneasiness and we learn to ....(8).... with the sting of adversity.

Questions

1. A. costly B. important C. valuable D. vast
2. A. area B. scope C. storage D. kingdom
3. A. unexplored B. unseen C. untouched D. unapproached
4. A. lack B. dearth C. shortage D. insufficiency
5. A. extricate B. intricate C. intrinsic D. internecine
6. A. company B. assistance C. friendship D. companionship
7. A. defiant B. defendant C. defensible D. delusive
8. A. adapt B. adopt C. exist D. co-exist

Passage-2

Though the government has tried to ....(1).... Naxalism with all its might, much more needs to be done to totally root out the ....(2).... of Naxalism. The roots of Naxalism ....(3).... economic backward- ness and social exploitation of the peasants and the weaker classes. Thus, the best way to ....(4).... Naxalism is to bring the naxals ....(5).... the mainstream. ....(6).... policies and schemes should be implemented effectively ....(7).... the Naxals economically stable. They should be ....(8).... to participate in democratic processes. The government has to ....(9).... the social upliftment of the Naxals. Use of force in ....(10).... Naxalism will yield little success.

Questions

1. A. crush B. handle C. tackle D. suppress
2. A. menace B. whole C. gamut D. stems
3. A. lies in B. are in C. abound in D. exist in
4. A. crash B. crush C. break D. defy

5. A. in B. on
C. into D. within

6. A. Current B. Latest
C. Occurring D. Existing

7. A. so that B. so as to make
C. such that D. to make

8. A. insisted B. brought
C. encouraged D. forced

9. A. assure B. insure
C. guarantee D. ensure

10. A. countering B. defying
C. banishing D. desecrating

Passage-3

We are living in very exciting ....(1).... . The ....(2).... change is dizzying and the impact this progress is having on our present and — more importantly — on our future is difficult to ....(3).... in its ...(4).... . This is the age of ....(5).... micro-processors, sophisticated software, new hardware technology and high bandwidth, high-speed networks. The PC gave us a new way to work, play and ....(6).... . In fact, it brought ....(7).... our desktops computing power, which until a few years ....(8).... had only been available to corporates. With the ....(9).... of the internet, the PC ....(10).... us the most convenient and flexible way to head on to the Net.

Questions

1. A. periods B. days
C. phase D. times

2. A. phase B. pace
C. sphere D. drastic

3. A. guess B. forecast
C. comprehend D. approximate

4. A. whole B. entirety
C. fruition D. fullness

5. A. strong B. changing
C. powerful D. sonorous

6. A. convey B. communicate
C. entertain D. enjoy

7. A. onto B. to
C. on D. at

8. A. back B. earlier
C. behind D. before

9. A. addendum B. adherence
C. afoot D. advent

10. A. allowed B. privileged
C. brought D. offered

Passage-4

What is required today in our country is ....(1).... of a new political culture based on full respect for human liberty, on pluralism and on a better social deal for all. The major ....(2).... facing us today is to carry out democratic transformation in all the ....(3)...., social, cultural, economic and political. The events of the 20th century ....(4).... one thing absolutely clear that human ....(5)...., everywhere, specially in countries whose political structures were ....(6).... to reflect the revolutionary aspirations of the people ....(7).... not only under stress and strain but are ....(8).... vast upheavals because of the ....(9).... of democracy. At the same time it has also to be understood that democracy cannot be ....(10).... into a static mould.

Questions

1. A. growing B. developing
C. creating D. creation

2. A. development B. crisis
C. challenge D. drawback

3. A. corners B. context
C. realm D. spheres

4. A. have made B. has made
C. had made D. made

5. A. travails B. traverse
C. traps D. transverse

6. A. supposed B. meant
C. caused D. forced

7. A. were B. was
C. are D. have been

8. A. developing B. evolving
C. experiencing D. faced with

9. A. denial B. rebuff
C. rebuttal D. absence

10. A. shaped B. flex
C. frozen D. caused

Passage-5

For centuries, women not only in India but all over the world ....(1).... treated as ....(2).... secondary position to men. ....(3).... human history men ....(4).... far greater power then women to name, classify, and order the worlds in which they both live. ....(5).... studies in various parts of the world point out to a wide ....(6).... in male and female roles ....(7).... cultures and demonstrate the possibility of change in these sex-determined roles. The 20th century in particular ....(8).... the cause of gender justice by internationalizing struggles for equality ....(9).... women and other oppressed people. Women's struggles against their ....(10).... were intertwined in ....(11).... degrees with ideologies and movements based on the values of freedom, self-determination, equality, democracy and justice.

Questions

1. A. has been B. have been
C. had been D. were
2. A. occupying B. taking
C. possessing D. serving
3. A. All through B. Throughout
C. Since D. From
4. A. have B. had
C. have had D. enjoy
5. A. Sociological B. Anthropological
C. General D. Practical
6. A. concord B. repulsion
C. disagreement D. variation
7. A. among B. across
C. between D. of
8. A. developed B. evolved
C. promoted D. entertained
9. A. for B. to
C. among D. by
10. A. subsidiary B. subsequent
C. subservience D. subordination
11. A. various B. varying
C changing D. differing

Passage-6

Visualisation is a strong ....(1).... to memory. Those persons who ......(2)..... a powerful memory cannot do so without taking the help of visualisation. Such persons have developed the skills to ....(3).... visualisation even in such ....(4).... tasks as remembering names and numbers. These persons have the names and numbers ....(5).... in their brain even after hearing those names and figures only once. On the other hand those who take the help of revising to memorise ....(6).... to forget it once they have ....(7).... the practice of revising ....(8).... the ones who have applied visualisation to memorise. Psychologists ....(9).... in visualisation a powerful tool for personality development. The more you visualise, the more you are ....(10).... your attitude and behaviour to the blue prints of your vision and ....(11).... more you are inching towards success.

Questions

1. A. way B. path
C. aid D. symptom
2. A. command B. master
C. rule D. enjoy
3. A. use B. apply
C. put D. place
4. A. trivial B. difficult
C. mundane D. unscrupulous
5. A. impress B. imprinted
C. impinge D. store
6. A. bent B. incline
C. prone d. tend
7. A. dropped B. left
C. gave up D. given up
8. A. unlike B. opposite
C. contrary D. not like
9. A. found B. have found
C. sees D. finds
10. A. shaping B. moulding
C. making D. attuning
11. A. actually B. factually
C. subsequently D. consequently

Passage-7

The development of an area depends on the resources ....(1).... in the area, the needs and ....(2).... of the people living there and the technological skill ....(3).... by them. Humans play an important and decisive role in the ....(4).... of development of an area. We choose the ....(5).... of resources which could be developed to our ....(6).... . The natural ....(7).... available in an area ....(8).... value as a resource only when people find a use for them. There are ....(9).... where large potential resources are available, but they ....(10).... developed for economic reasons. Lack of capital for investments, roads and railway lines, and other ....(11).... facilities may stand in the way of resource development.

Questions

1. A. present B. prevalent
C. available D. exist
2. A. inspirations B. aspirations
C. ambitions D. curiosity
3. A. handled B. practised
C. availed D. possessed
4. A. system B. design
C. pattern D. style
5. A. class B. group
C. variety D. types
6. A. good B. advantage
C. approach D. favour
7. A. secrets B. phenomenon
C. products D. endowments
8. A. get B. acquire
C. possess D. takes
9. A. instances B. events
C. circumstances D. happenings
10. A. have not yet been B. haven't been
C. are not yet D. yet have not been

11. A. common B. general
C. infrastructural D. structural

Passage-8

The Naxal problem in India is basically socio-economic in ....(1).... . The main reasons ....(2).... the Naxal movement in India are the ....(3).... of peasants and their weak social and economic position. ....(4).... of the peasants are landless labourers whose lands have been ....(5).... occupied by the landlords. Moreover, the landlords give ....(6).... wages to the peasants. Their ....(7).... suffering at the hands of the landlords thus encourage many peasants to take law ....(8).... their own hands. Due to their poor economic condition the peasants easily ....(9).... the trap of the naxal leaders who have their ....(10).... interests. Illiteracy, unemployment, police excesses, corruption and ....(11).... administration further ....(12).... this complex problem.

Questions

1. A. form B. shape
C. behaviour D. nature
2. A. for B. of
C. in D. behind
3. A. complaisance B. exploitation
C. domination D. exculpation
4. A. Many B. Much
C. Most D. All
5. A. imperiously B. imperatively
C. forcefully D. forcibly
6. A. improper B. small
C. inadequate D. insufficient
7. A. long B. brutal
C. pathetic D. great
8. A. in B. into
C. on D. by
9. A. fall into B. fall in
C. fell in D. fell into
10. A. selfish B. vested
C. vicious D. vindictive
11. A. failed B. improper
C. inefficient D. bureaucratic
12. A. heighten B. deepen
C. add D. worsen

Passage-9

No doubt various ....(1).... and Acts are there to eliminate the ....(2).... practice of child labour. But the ....(3).... is that, these are not being implemented in both letter and spirit, for which the ....(4).... of the problem remains as it was. Therefore a judicious, pragmatic, integrated and time-bound ....(5).... supplemented by ....(6).... follow-up action is essential to ....(7).... the problem that ....(8).... deep root in our Society. It is true that child labour can't be ....(9)... with a magic wand. If we ....(10).... time-bound goals and follow, of course, with the ....(11).... assistance of ILO and UNICEF, it is possible to eliminate the problem of child labour. With strong political will power and people's backing nothing is ....(12).... . Rather ....(13).... the bud we should let it blossom and spread its fragrance all around. ....(14).... lies the progress and prosperity of the society.

Questions

1. A. means B. methods
C. source D. provisions
2. A. unjust B. inhuman
C. mal D. illegal
3. A. anxiety B. abrasion
C. tragedy D. conclusion
4. A. magnitude B. depth
C. gravity D. soaring
5. A. approach B. analysis
C. survey D. scheme
6. A. continuous B. thorough
C. throughout D. regular
7. A. outroot B. uproot
C. downroot D. grassroot
8. A. have B. has
C. had D. has taken
9. A. wipe out B. wipe off
C. wipe up D. wiped
10. A. keep B. put
C. put up D. set
11. A. ongoing B. continuing
C. unending D. frequent
12. A. insurmountable B. intangible
C. inscrutable D. incorrigible
13. A. killing B. hurting
C. destroying D. nipping
14. A. Here B. There
C. Therein D. Herein

Passage-10

Every action we perform ....(1).... a result. And, naturally, we lay claim ....(2).... the results or fruits ....(3).... from that action in the ....(4).... that it is we who perform the action. This is .....(5).... ignorance because ....(6).... is it the Lord who ....(7).... the result of any action, it is by His will ....(8).... that even the action is accomplished. The will of the Lord ....(9).... whether we cooperate with His will or strive ....(10).... . If God wills that an action takes place, he arranges for the ....(11).... for it to happen. It is ....(12).... experience that sometimes despite our best efforts we ....(13).... achieve the results we desire, and at other times the seemingly most ....(14).... situations mysteriously get ....(15).... . ....(16).... way man chooses to act, both the act and the outcome of the cost are dependent ....(17).... on the will of the Lord.

Questions

1. A. produce B. produces C. causes D. undergoes
2. A. on B. at C. to D. for
3. A. occurring B. obtaining C. deriving D. falling
4. A. belief B. hope C. fantasy D. folly
5. A. sheen B. keen C. sheer D. sheathe
6. A. alone B. only that C. not only D. for only
7. A. declares B. decides C. ordains D. ornate
8. A. completely B. entirely C. only D. alone
9. A. prevails always B. prevails everywhere C. is prevalent D. always prevails
10. A. alone B. always C. constantly D. independently
11. A. wherewithal B. whereabouts C. whatsoever D. wherefore
12. A. usual B. general C. universal D. common
13. A. does not B. may not C. do not D. might not
14. A. intractable B. intangible C. internecine D. intricate
15. A. subsided B. resolved C. solved D. converted
16. A. Whatever B. All the C. All those D. Whichever
17. A. mainly B. actually C. entirely D. generally

ANSWERS

PASSAGE-1

1	2	3	4	5	6	7	8
C	D	A	B	B	D	A	D

PASSAGE-2

1	2	3	4	5	6	7	8	9	10
C	A	A	B	C	D	B	C	D	A

PASSAGE-3

1	2	3	4	5	6	7	8	9	10
D	B	C	B	C	B	A	D	D	D

PASSAGE-4

1	2	3	4	5	6	7	8	9	10
D	C	D	A	A	B	C	C	A	C

PASSAGE-5

1	2	3	4	5	6	7	8	9	10	11
B	A	B	C	B	D	B	C	D	D	B

PASSAGE-6

1	2	3	4	5	6	7	8	9	10	11
C	A	B	C	B	D	A	A	B	D	D

PASSAGE-7

1	2	3	4	5	6	7	8	9	10	11
C	B	D	C	D	B	D	B	A	A	C

PASSAGE-8

1	2	3	4	5	6	7	8	9	10	11	12
D	A	B	C	D	C	A	B	A	B	C	D

PASSAGE-9

1	2	3	4	5	6	7	8	9	10	11	12	13	14
D	B	C	A	A	D	B	D	B	D	B	A	D	C

PASSAGE-10

1	2	3	4	5	6	7	8	9	10	11	12	13	14	15	16	17
B	C	B	A	C	C	C	D	D	D	A	D	C	A	B	D	C

GENERAL INTELLIGENCE

VERBAL

CHAPTER 1

Analogies

NUMBER ANALOGY

In number analogy also, the relationship between the given numbers is detected and then applied to the second part to find the missing numbers. This relationship between the numbers can be based on any of the following patterns : *(i)* numbers can be odd/even/prime numbers; *(ii)* numbers can be multiples of one number; *(iii)* numbers can be squares/cubes of different numbers; *(iv)* some numbers can be added to/subtracted from/multiplied to/divided into the first number to get the second number; *(v)* the second number can be the sum/product/difference of the digits of first number; and *(vi)* combinations of any mathematical calculations given above can apply to the relationship between the two given numbers.

MULTIPLE CHOICE QUESTIONS

Directions : *In the following questions, select the number from the given options which follows the same relationship as shared between the first two numbers.*

1. 1 : 11 : : 2 : ?
(*a*) 20 (*b*) 22
(*c*) 24 (*d*) 44

2. 18 : 27 : : 22 : ?
(*a*) 42 (*b*) 39
(*c*) 33 (*d*) 54

3. 14 : 20 : : 16 : ?
(*a*) 23 (*b*) 10
(*c*) 48 (*d*) 32

4. 8 : 27 : : 64 : ?
(*a*) 277 (*b*) 125
(*c*) 250 (*d*) 99

5. 0.16 : 0.0016 : : 1.02 : ?
(*a*) 10.20 (*b*) 0.102
(*c*) 0.0102 (*d*) 1.020

EXPLANATORY ANSWERS

1. (*b*) : The first number is repeated to obtain the second number.

2. (*c*) : In the given set, the numbers are multiples of 9 and in the second set, multiples of 11.

$$\begin{array}{ccccccc} 18 & : & 27 & :: & 22 & : & 33 \\ \downarrow & & \downarrow & & \downarrow & & \downarrow \\ 9 \times 2 & & 9 \times 3 & & 11 \times 2 & & 11 \times 3 \end{array}$$

3. (*a*) : The relationship between the numbers is :

$$\begin{array}{ccccccc} 14 & : & 20 & :: & 16 & : & 23 \\ \downarrow & & \downarrow & & \downarrow & & \downarrow \\ 7 \times 2 & & (7 \times 3) - 1 & & 8 \times 2 & & (8 \times 3) - 1 \end{array}$$

4. (*b*) : The numbers are cubes of different numbers.

$$\begin{array}{ccccccc} 8 & : & 27 & :: & 64 & : & 125 \\ \downarrow & & \downarrow & & \downarrow & & \downarrow \\ 2^3 & & 3^3 & & 4^3 & & 5^3 \end{array}$$

5. (*c*) : The decimals are divided by 100.

LETTER ANALOGY

In this type of analogy the relationship between two given set of letters is established and then applied to the other set to obtain the required set of letters as the answer. These letters can be moved some steps backward or forward; reversed in whole or in sections or have some common identity between each other.

MULTIPLE CHOICE QUESTIONS

Directions : *In the questions given below one term is missing. Based on the relationship of the two given terms find the missing term from the given options.*

1. GFC : CFG : : RPJ : ?
   (*a*) JRP (*b*) JPR
   (*c*) PJR (*d*) RJP
2. BCF : DEG : : MNQ : ?
   (*a*) OPR (*b*) PQS
   (*c*) OPP (*d*) QRT
3. NATION : ANITNO : : HUNGRY : ?
   (*a*) HNUGRY (*b*) UNHGYR
   (*c*) YRNGUH (*d*) UHGNYR
4. SSTU : MMNO : : AABC : ?
   (*a*) GGHH (*b*) IJKK
   (*c*) XXYZ (*d*) NOOP
5. ACE : FGH : : LNP : ?
   (*a*) QRS (*b*) PQR
   (*c*) QST (*d*) MOQ
6. UVW : SXU : : LMN : ?
   (*a*) JOL (*b*) KNM
   (*c*) JKL (*d*) MLO
7. EIGHTY : GIEYTH : : OUTPUT : ?
   (*a*) UTOPTU (*b*) UOTUPT
   (*c*) TUOUTP (*d*) TUOTUP
8. TSR : FED : : WVU : ?
   (*a*) CAB (*b*) MLK
   (*c*) PQS (*d*) GFH
9. CJDL : FMGR : : IKJR : ?
   (*a*) OQPT (*b*) RSTU
   (*c*) OQRT (*d*) KRMO

EXPLANATORY ANSWERS

1. (*b*) : The letters of the first group are reversed.

GFC : CFG : : RPJ : JPR

2. (*a*) : The three letters are moved 2, 2 and 1 steps forward respectively.

BCF : DEG : : MNQ : OPR
(+2, +2, +1) (+2, +2, +1)

3. (*d*) : The word is divided in sections of two letters and the letters are reversed.

NATION : ANITNO : : HUNGRY : UHGNYR

4. (*c*) : The first letter in each group is repeated and followed by two consecutive letters.

5. (*a*) : The three letters are moved 5, 4, and 3 steps forward respectively.

ACE : FGH : : LNP : QRS
(+5, +4, +3) (+5, +4, +3)

6. (*a*) : The three letters are moved –2, +2 and –2 steps respectively.

UVW : SXU : : LMN : JOL
(–2, +2, –2) (–2, +2, –2)

7. (*d*) : The word is divided into two sections and the letters are written backwards.

EIGHTY : GIEYTH : : OUTPUT : TUOTUP

8. (*b*) : The letters are consecutive and written in reverse order.

9. (*a*) : In each set of letters, the 1st and 3rd letters are consecutive.

CJDL : FMGR : : IKJR : OQPT

SEMANTIC ANALOGY

In Analogy Tests the relationship between two given words is established and then applied to the other words. The type of relationship may vary, so while attempting such questions the first step is to identify the type of relationship, which can be any one of the following.

MULTIPLE CHOICE QUESTIONS

Directions : *In the questions given below establish the relationship between the two words. Then from the given options select one which has the same relationship as of the given two words.*

1. HUNGER : FOOD : : THIRST : ?
(*a*) Water (*b*) Drink
(*c*) Tea (*d*) Coffee

2. HUNTER : GUN : : WRITER : ?
(*a*) Book (*b*) Pen
(*c*) Poem (*d*) Page

3. WOOL : SHEEP : : SILK : ?
(*a*) Saree
(*b*) String
(*c*) Silkworm
(*d*) Moth

4. FOOD : STOMACH : : FUEL : ?
(*a*) Engine (*b*) Automobile
(*c*) Rail (*d*) Aeroplane

5. WATER : SAND : : OCEAN : ?
(*a*) Island (*b*) River
(*c*) Desert (*d*) Waves

6. ADULT : BABY : : FLOWER : ?
(*a*) Seed (*b*) Bud
(*c*) Fruit (*d*) Butterfly

7. WRITER : READER : : PRODUCER : ?
(*a*) Creator (*b*) Contractor
(*c*) Creature (*d*) Consumer

8. ENTRANCE : EXIT : : LOYALTY : ?
(*a*) Treachery (*b*) Patriotism
(*c*) Fidelity (*d*) Reward

9. MOTHER : MATERNAL : : FATHER : ?
(*a*) Eternal (*b*) Detrimental
(*c*) Paternal (*d*) Formidable

10. PEARL : NECKLACE : : FLOWER : ?
(*a*) Plant (*b*) Garden
(*c*) Petal (*d*) Bouquet

11. ALPHABET : WORD : : WORD : ?
(*a*) Sound (*b*) Music
(*c*) Sentence (*d*) Dictionary

12. LIFE : DEATH : : HOPE : ?
(*a*) Cry (*b*) Pain
(*c*) Despair (*d*) Sad

13. GOOD : BAD : : VIRTUE : ?
(*a*) Blame (*b*) Sin
(*c*) Despair (*d*) Vice

14. BIRD : FLY : : SNAKE : ?
(*a*) Timid (*b*) Clatter
(*c*) Crawl (*d*) Hole

EXPLANATORY ANSWERS

1. (*a*) : Hunger is satiated by food, thirst by water.
2. (*b*) : Weapon of a hunter is a gun, weapon of a writer is a pen.
3. (*c*) : Wool is obtained from sheep, silk is obtained from silkworm.
4. (*a*) : Food is consumed in stomach, fuel is consumed in engine.
5. (*c*) : The related words are near opposites.
6. (*b*) : The youngone of an adult is a baby and that of a flower is a bud.
7. (*d*) : A writer aims to please the readers by his writings, a producer aims to please the consumers by his products.
8. (*a*) : The related words are opposites.
9. (*c*) : Relations on the mother's side are maternal and on the father's side paternal.
10. (*d*) : Many pearls make a necklace, many flowers make a bouquet.
11. (*c*) : More than one alphabet make a word, more than one word make a sentence.
12. (*c*) : The related words are opposites.
13. (*d*) : The related words are opposites.
14. (*c*) : Birds fly, snakes crawl.

CHAPTER 2

Number Classification

ODD ONE OUT—NUMBERS

In this type of classification, different numbers are given as options. These numbers have some commonness; except one which is the odd one. One has to identify the similarity and then strike the odd one out as answer option. The number can be odd/even/consecutive, prime numbers, multiple of some number, single, square or cubes of different numbers, plus/minus of some other number or combinations of any mathematical calculation.

MULTIPLE CHOICE QUESTIONS

Directions : *In each of the following questions, there are four options. Three numbers, in these options, are alike in certain manner. Only one number does not fit in. Choose the one which is different from the rest.*

1. (*a*) 1948 (*b*) 2401 (*c*) 966 (*d*) 1449

2. (*a*) 182 (*b*) 169 (*c*) 130 (*d*) 158

3. (*a*) 129 (*b*) 130 (*c*) 131 (*d*) 132

4. (*a*) 3215 (*b*) 9309 (*c*) 4721 (*d*) 2850

5. (*a*) 1776 (*b*) 2364 (*c*) 1976 (*d*) 3776

6. (*a*) 64 (*b*) 84 (*c*) 16 (*d*) 36

EXPLANATORY ANSWERS

1. (*a*) : Other numbers are divisible by 7.

2. (*d*) : Other numbers are multiples of 13.

3. (*c*) : 131 is a prime number.

4. (*b*) : In other numbers, no digit is repeated.

5. (*b*) : In other numbers the last two digits are same.

6. (*b*) : All other numbers are perfect squares.

ODD ONE OUT—LETTERS

In this classification of letters, four groups of letters or a series of letters is given as options. One has to select the option as answer which does not share the commonness of the others.

MULTIPLE CHOICE QUESTIONS

Directions : *In each of the following questions, four out of five alternatives contain alphabet placed in a particular form. Find the one that does not belong to the group.*

1. (*a*) BXCW (*b*) OTPS (*c*) GQHR (*d*) JNKM

2. (*a*) BVPS (*b*) OLMZ (*c*) RPSR (*d*) XTCD

3. (*a*) RNJH (*b*) SOKG (*c*) QMIE (*d*) MIEA

4. (*a*) QLJS (*b*) GVTI (*c*) KRPM (*d*) ONMP

5. (*a*) PEAR (*b*) TORE (*c*) REAP (*d*) TEAR

6. (*a*) ECA (*b*) JHF (*c*) OMK (*d*) UWY

7. (*a*) ACE (*b*) PRT (*c*) UWY (*d*) MNO

EXPLANATORY ANSWERS

1. (*c*) : In all other groups, first and third letters are consecutive and second and fourth letters are in reverse alphabetical order.

2. (*c*) : No letter is repeated in any other group.

3. (*a*) : In all other groups, there is a gap of three letters between two consecutive letters.

4. (*d*) : In all other groups, first and third letters are moved two steps forward to obtain fourth and second letters respectively.

5. (*b*) : All other groups contain E, A and R.

6. (*d*) : All other groups contain alternate letters from right to left.

7. (*d*) : All other groups contain alternate letters from left to right.

ODD ONE OUT—WORDS

In this type of classification, five words are given out of which four are almost same in matter or meaning and only one word is different from the common four. One has to find out the word which is different from the rest.

MULTIPLE CHOICE QUESTIONS

Directions : *In each of the following questions, four words are alike in some manner. Spot the odd one out.*

1. (*a*) Green (*b*) Red (*c*) Colour (*d*) Orange

2. (*a*) Stable (*b*) Hole (*c*) Canoe (*d*) Sty

3. (*a*) Nose (*b*) Eyes (*c*) Skin (*d*) Teeth

4. (*a*) Venus (*b*) Moon (*c*) Pluto (*d*) Mars

5. (*a*) Happy (*b*) Gloomy (*c*) Lively (*d*) Cheerful

6. (*a*) Cone (*b*) Circle (*c*) Triangle (*d*) Rectangle

7. (*a*) Lead (*b*) Mercury (*c*) Copper (*d*) Iron

8. (*a*) Kite (*b*) Bird (*c*) Radar (*d*) Jet

9. (*a*) Knee (*b*) Shoulder (*c*) Ankle (*d*) Palm

10. (*a*) Deluge (*b*) Calamity (*c*) Catastrophe (*d*) War

EXPLANATORY ANSWERS

1. (*c*) : All others are types of colour.

2. (*c*) : Canoe is a boat. Others are resting places of birds/ animals.

3. (*d*) : All others are sense organs.

4. (*b*) : All others are planets.

5. (*b*) : All others are expressions of joy

6. (*a*) : All others are geometrical figures.

7. (*b*) : All others are solid metals.

8. (*c*) : All others are flying objects. Radar traces the objects in sky.

9. (*d*) : All others are joints in human body.

10. (*d*) : All others are nature-bound. Only war is man-made.

CHAPTER 3

Small & Capital Letters/ Numbers Coding-Decoding and Classification

TYPE - I

Coding is a secretive language which is used to change the representation of the actual term/word/value. This coded language can be framed by *(i)* moving the letters one or more steps forward or backward; *(ii)* substituting numbers for letters and vice–versa; *(iii)* writing the letters of the given word in reverse order in part or in whole; and *(iv)* replacing the letters in their natural series by the same positioned letters in their reverse series.

Alphabet in natural series are :

A B C D E F G H I J K L M N O P Q R S T U V W X Y Z

A ↓ 1st, E ↓ 5th, J ↓ 10th, O ↓ 15th, T ↓ 20th, Y ↓ 25th

Alphabet in reverse series are :

Z Y X W V U T S R Q P O N M L K J I H G F E D C B A

Z ↓ 1st, V ↓ 5th, Q ↓ 10th, L ↓ 15th, G ↓ 20th, B ↓ 25th

Note : On reaching Z, the series restarts from A and on reaching A, it restarts from Z.

MULTIPLE CHOICE QUESTIONS

Directions : *In the following questions select the right option which indicates the correct code for the word or letter given in the question.*

1. If CHAIR is coded as FKDLU, then RAID is coded as :
(*a*) ULGD (*b*) ULKG
(*c*) ULDG (*d*) UDLG

2. If CONDEMN is coded as CNODMEN, then TEACHER is coded as :
(*a*) TEACHER (*b*) TAEECHR
(*c*) TCAEEHR (*d*) TAECEHR

3. In a code language COME is written as XLNV and ABLE as ZYOV. How will MOLLY be written in that code?
(*a*) NLOBO (*b*) NLBOO
(*c*) LNOOB (*d*) NLOOB

4. In a certain code PROFESSION is written as EFORPNOISS. In the same code DICTIONARY will be written as :
(*a*) YRANOITCID (*b*) ITCIDYRANO
(*c*) ITCIDYRNAO (*d*) ITCDIYARNO

5. JUNE is coded as NXPF, how will STAY be coded in the same manner?
(*a*) WWCZ (*b*) WVCZ
(*c*) WWDB (*d*) VWZC

6. If in a certain code GENIUS is coded as IGPKWU, then IDIOT will be written in the same code as :
(*a*) JEJPU (*b*) KFKQV
(*c*) LGLRW (*d*) HCHNS

7. If ACTION is coded as ZXGRLM, then HEALTH will be coded in the same way as :
(*a*) SVZOGS (*b*) TVZOGT
(*c*) RUZPGR (*d*) QVGOZQ

8. If THOUSAND is coded as SGNTRZMC, then FUMING will be coded as :
(*a*) GVNJOH (*b*) ETHLMF
(*c*) EVLJMH (*d*) ETLHMF

9. If EARTHQUAKE is coded as MOGPENJOSM, then EQUATE will be coded as :
(*a*) MENOPM (*b*) MENOMP
(*c*) MJOGPM (*d*) MNJOPM

10. In a certain code language HJIZT code is deciphered as MONEY, in the same way NOVGZ will be deciphered as :
(*a*) STUMP (*b*) STALE
(*c*) STICK (*d*) SPIRE

EXPLANATORY ANSWERS

1. (*d*) : The word is coded by moving the letters three steps forward.

CHAIR → FKDLU

+3, +3, +3, +3, +3

Similarly,

RAID → UDLG

+3, +3, +3, +3

2. (*d*) : In this word, the second and third letters interchange their places and the fifth and sixth letters do the same. Other letters retain their position.

CONDEMN → CNODMEN

Similarly,

TEACHER → TAECEHR

3. (*d*) : The letters of the word are coded by their represented letters in the reverse series.

C	O	M	E	→ letters in natural series
X	L	N	V	→ letters in reverse series
↓	↓	↓	↓	
3rd	15th	13th	5th	→ position of letters
A	B	L	E	→ letters in natural series
Z	Y	O	V	→ letters in reverse series
↓	↓	↓	↓	
1st	2nd	12th	5th	→ position of letters

Similarly,

M	O	L	L	Y	→ letters in natural series
N	L	O	O	B	→ letters in reverse series
↓	↓	↓	↓	↓	
13th	15th	12th	12th	25th	→ position of letters

4. (*b*) : The word is divided into two equal parts and the letters of each part are written backwards.

PROFE SSION → EFORP NOISS

Similarly,

DICTI ONARY → ITCID YRANO

5. (*a*) : The word is coded by moving the letters +4, +3, +2, and +1 steps respectively.

JUNE → NXPF

+4, +3, +2, +1

Similarly,

STAY → WWCZ

+4, +3, +2, +1

6. (*b*) : The word is coded by moving the letters two steps forward, *i.e.*,

GENIUS → IGPKWU

+2, +2, +2, +2, +2, +2

Similarly,

IDIOT KFKQV

+2
+2
+2
+2
+2

7. *(a)* **:** The letters of the word are coded by their represented letters in the reverse series.

A	C	T	I	O	N → letters in natural series
Z	X	G	R	L	M → letters in reverse series
↓ 1st	↓ 3rd	↓ 20th	↓ 9th	↓ 15th	↓ 14th position of letters

Similarly,

H	E	A	L	T	H → letters in natural series
S	V	Z	O	G	S → letters in reverse series
↓ 8th	↓ 5th	↓ 1st	↓ 12th	↓ 20th	↓ 8th → position of letters

8. *(d)* **:** The word is coded by moving the alphabet one step backwards, *i.e.*,

THOUSAND SGNTRZMC

–1
–1
–1
–1
–1
–1
–1
–1

Similarly,

FUMING ETLHMF

–1
–1
–1
–1
–1
–1

9. *(d)* **:** The alphabet in word EQUATE are taken from the given word EARTHQUAKE. Tally the letters from the coded word to get the answer code.

E A R T H Q U A K E → letters
M O G P E N J O S M → codes
E Q U A T E → letters to be coded
M N J O P M → answer codes

10. *(b)* **:** The coded alphabet are deciphered by moving five steps forward, *i.e.*,

HJIZT MONEY

+5
+5
+5
+5
+5

Similarly,

NOVGZ STALE

+5
+5
+5
+5
+5

TYPE - II

Column coding is a very complex form of coding. It needs a lot of attention and swift eye movement to decode the code for each letter of the given words. Proper words in capital letters are given in one column and the codes in small letters are given in another column. Based on the information given in both columns the candidate has to arrive at the correct answer option.

MULTIPLE CHOICE QUESTIONS

Directions: *The following questions are based on the column pattern. Understand the coding pattern and answer the questions.*

	Column I		Column II
(1)	FAMOUS	(a)	jcqhxp
(2)	SATIRE	(b)	hqdbyn
(3)	FRIGHT	(c)	ybcnke
(4)	TANGLE	(d)	zewhnd
(5)	ROVING	(e)	epbmyw
(6)	HUNTER	(f)	wdnbxk

1. What is the code used for the letter U?

(*a*) d (*b*) n
(*c*) b (*d*) x

2. What is the code used for the letter N?

(*a*) e (*b*) p
(*c*) m (*d*) w

3. What is the code used for the letter A?

(*a*) h (*b*) q
(*c*) b (*d*) n

4. What is the code used for the letter F?
(*a*) w (*b*) p
(*c*) d (*d*) c

5. What is the code used for the letter E?
(*a*) d (*b*) n
(*c*) b (*d*) k

Column I	Column II
(1) WRONG	(a) cklxd
(2) GRANT	(b) pdqkc
(3) STEAM	(c) qpuns
(4) CROWS	(d) lxnvk
(5) CEMET	(e) usqvs
(6) TERMS	(f) nukqs

EXPLANATORY ANSWERS

1. (*d*) : From statements (1) and (6), U = X.
2. (*d*) : From statements (5) and (6), RN = bw. From statement (4), N = w.
3. (*a*) : From statements (2) and (4), ATE = hdn. From statement (6), TE = dn. Therefore, A = h.
4. (*d*) : From statements (1) and (3), F = c.
5. (*a*) : From statements (2) and (4), ATE = hdn. From statement (6), TE = dn. From statement (3), T = n. Hence E = d.

TYPE - III

There is variety in ways of coding. Coding language is not only for words and numbers but also for hiding a group of words, statements or even sentences. This form of coding pattern may appear to be confusing but after solving only a few questions it is very easy to understand. Questions based on this coding pattern require no moving of steps or straining efforts of calculations, but only quick tallying or comparing ability. The codes can be letters or numbers.

MULTIPLE CHOICE QUESTIONS

Directions : *In the following questions study the coded patterns and then select the right option from the given alternatives.*

1. In a certain language, (a) 'go ju mi' stands for 'plenty of money'; (b) pao ju go nei vu' for 'money creates lots of problems'; (c) 'kol vu nei' for 'problems create tension'; and (d) 'sol tun ju haw' for 'still money is needed'. Which of the following words stand for 'money'?
(*a*) nei (*b*) ju
(*c*) haw (*d*) go

2. In a certain language, (a) 'FOR' stands for 'old is gold'; (b) 'ROT' stands for 'gold is pure'; (c) 'ROM' stands for 'gold is costly'. How will 'pure old gold is costly' be written?
(*a*) TFROM (*b*) FOTRM
(*c*) FTORM (*d*) TOMRF

3. In a certain code '415' means 'milk is hot'; '18' means 'hot soup'; and '895' means 'soup is tasty'. What number will indicate the word 'tasty'?
(*a*) 9 (*b*) 8
(*c*) 5 (*d*) 4

4. In a certain code '643' means 'she is beautiful', '593' means 'he is handsome', and '567' means 'handsome meets beautiful'. What number will indicate the word 'meets'?
(*a*) 5 (*b*) 3
(*c*) 7 (*d*) 6

5. In a certain code language, (a) 'dugo hui mul zo' stands for 'work is very hard'; (b) 'hui dugo ba ki' for 'Bingo is very smart'; (c) 'nano mul dugo' for 'cake is hard', and (d) 'mul ki qu' for 'smart and hard'. Which of the following words stand for 'Bingo'?
(*a*) jalu (*b*) dugo
(*c*) ki (*d*) ba

6. In a certain code language, (a) 'pic vic nic' stands for 'winter is cold'; (b) 'to nic re' for 'summer is hot'; (c) 're pic boo' for 'winter and summer' and (d) 'vic tho pa' for 'nights are cold'. Which of the following word is the code for 'summer'?
(*a*) nic (*b*) boo
(*c*) to (*d*) re

7. In a certain language, (a) 'mx das sci' means 'good little frock'; (b) 'jm coz sci' means 'girl behaves good'; (c) 'ngv drs coz' means 'girl makes mischief'; and (d) 'das gp coz' means 'little girl fell'. What is the code for 'frock' in this language?
(*a*) mx (*b*) das
(*c*) sci (*d*) gp

8. In a certain language 'mu mit es' means 'who is she' and 'elb mu es' means 'where is she'. What is the code for 'where' in this language?
(*a*) es (*b*) elb
(*c*) mu (*d*) mit

9. In a certain code language '069' means 'grapes are sweet', '476' means 'very sweet fruit' and '509' means 'grapes are ripe'. Which of the following digits means 'ripe' in that language?

(*a*) 0 (*b*) 5
(*c*) 9 (*d*) 7

10. In a certain code language 'roi ja kyo twa' means 'Moody is writing letters', 'pok ju ja twa' means 'Woody is writing cards', 'trn kyo pos un' means 'they are writing letters', and 'koi rus pok' means 'gifts and cards'. What is the code word for 'Moody'?

(*a*) ja (*b*) twa
(*c*) roi (*d*) kyo

EXPLANATORY ANSWERS

1. (*b*) :

Code	*Sentence*
1. go *ju* mi	plenty of *money*
2. pao *ju* go nei vu	*money* creates lots of problems
3. kol vu nei	problems create tension
4. sol tun *ju* haw	still *money* is needed

In 1st, 2nd and 4th codes and their sentences the word 'ju' is repeated and so is 'money'.

2. (*a*) :

Code	*Sentence*
1. FOR	old is gold
2. ROT	gold is pure
3. ROM	gold is costly

Therefore,

F stands for old
O stands for is
R stands for gold
T stands for pure
M stands for costly

So, 'pure old gold is costly' will be written as 'TFROM'.

3. (*a*) :

Code	*Sentence*
1. 415	milk is hot
2. 18	hot soup
3. 895	soup is *tasty*

From 3rd code and its sentence neither number '9' is repeated nor the word 'tasty'.

4. (*c*) :

Code	*Sentence*
1. 643	she is beautiful
2. 593	he is handsome
3. 56*7*	handsome *meets* beautiful

From 3rd code and its sentence, neither number '7' nor the word 'meets' is repeated.

5. (*d*) :

Code	*Sentence*
1. *dugo hui* mul zo	work *is very* hard
2. *hui dugo* **ba** *ki*	**Bingo** *is very smart*
3. nano mul *dugo*	cake is *hard*
4. mul *ki* qu	*smart* and hard

From 2nd code and its sentence, neither 'ba' nor 'Bingo' is repeated.

(Words repeated are in italics)

6. (*d*) :

Code	*Sentence*
1. pic vic nic	winter is cold
2. to nic *re*	*summer* is hot
3. *re* pic boo	winter and *summer*
4. vic tho pa	nights are cold

The word 'summer' is common in 2nd and 3rd sentences and so is the code 're'.

7. (*a*) :

Code	*Sentence*
1. **mx** *das sci*	*good little* **frock**
2. jm coz *sci*	girl behaves *good*
3. ngv drs coz	girl makes mischief
4. *das* gp coz	*little* girl fell

Word 'frock' is only in the 1st sentence. The code word 'das' is repeated in 4th sentence and 'sci' in 2nd sentence. So, 'mx' is the code for 'frock'.

8. (*b*) :

Code	*Sentence*
1. *mu* mit *es*	who *is she*
2. **elb** *mu* es	**where** *is she*

The code words 'mu' and 'es' are repeated in Ist sentence. The only code left is 'elb' which means 'where'.

9. (*b*) :

Code	*Sentence*
1. *069*	*grapes are* sweet
2. 476	very sweet fruit
3. **509**	*grapes are* **ripe**

The code numbers '0' and '9' are repeated in 1st and 3rd sentences. The only code remaining is '5' which stands for 'ripe'.

10. (*c*) :

Code	*Sentence*
1. **roi** *ja kyo twa*	**Moody** *is writing letters*
2. pok ju *ja twa*	Woody *is writing* cards
3. trn *kyo* pos un	they are writing *letters*
4. koi rus pok	gifts and cards

'Moody' is in 1st sentence only. The code words 'ja' and 'twa' are repeated in 2nd sentence and 'kyo' in 3rd sentence. Only code word 'roi' remains which stands for 'Moody'.

CHAPTER 4

Semantic Series

MULTIPLE CHOICE QUESTIONS

1. ADG, XVT, BEH, WUS, ?
(*a*) VTR (*b*) CFI
(*c*) DFJ (*d*) STU

2. GMSY, IOUA, KQWC, ?
(*a*) MSYE (*b*) NSYE
(*c*) MTYE (*d*) MSYF

3. ADG, GJM, ?, SVY
(*a*) MPS (*b*) MQR
(*c*) MQS (*d*) SPM

4. KNQ, TWZ, CFI, ?
(*a*) KOR (*b*) LOR
(*c*) MNQ (*d*) JLM

5. AEI, BFJ, CGK, ?
(*a*) DLH (*b*) EGF
(*c*) EFL (*d*) DHL

6. CFI, IKM, OPQ, ?
(*a*) UUU (*b*) UST
(*c*) VUS (*d*) TUV

7. LAZ, NEX, PIV, ?
(*a*) SLS (*b*) QNS
(*c*) RMT (*d*) RMS

8. DED, EFE, FGF, ?
(*a*) HGH (*b*) GHG
(*c*) EFE (*d*) FHF

9. XYZ, UVW, ?, OPQ
(*a*) RST (*b*) STU
(*c*) QRS (*d*) TUV

10. VCL, UEI, TGF, ?
(*a*) SJC (*b*) THI
(*c*) SIC (*d*) RHD

11. ABC, EFG, HIJ, ?
(*a*) IJK (*b*) KLM
(*c*) LMN (*d*) JKL

12. PQR, HIJ, DEF, ?
(*a*) DEF (*b*) CDE
(*c*) ABC (*d*) BCD

EXPLANATORY ANSWERS

1. (*b*) : There are two alternate series.

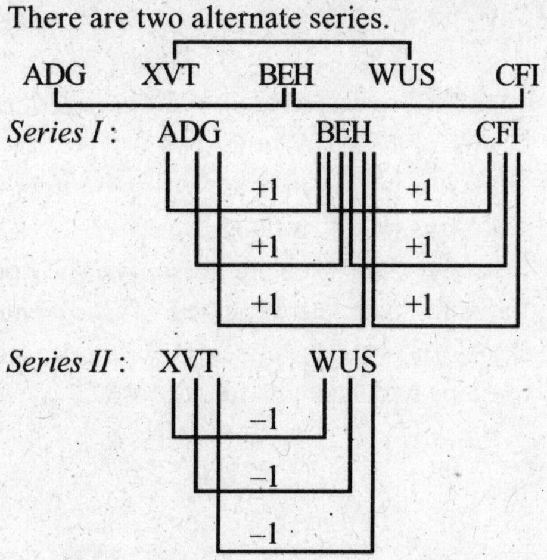

2. (*a*) : The series is formed by moving each letter two steps forward from one group to the next.

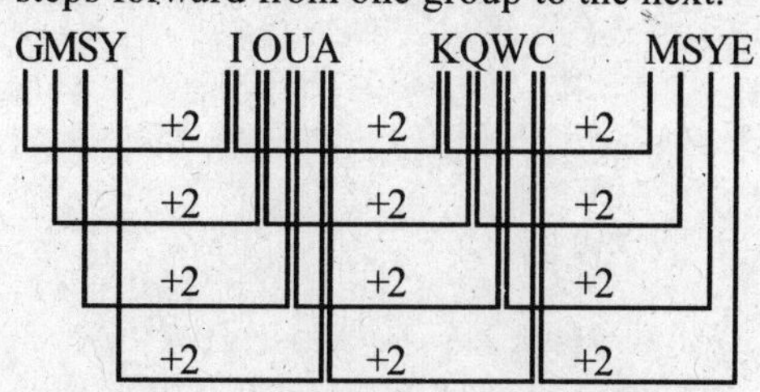

(The series restarts from A on reaching Z)

3. (*a*) : In each group of three letters the alphabet is in the succession of +3. The next group begins with the last alphabet of the previous group.

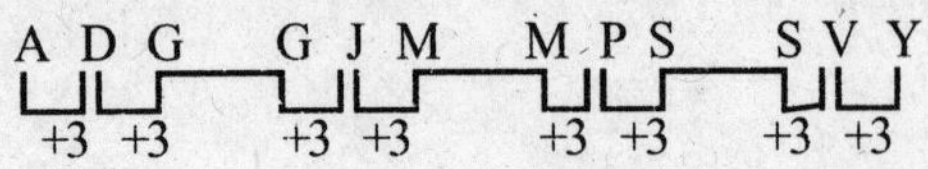

4. (*b*) : All the alphabet in this group series is in succession of +3. The alphabetical series repeat from 'A' on reaching 'Z'.

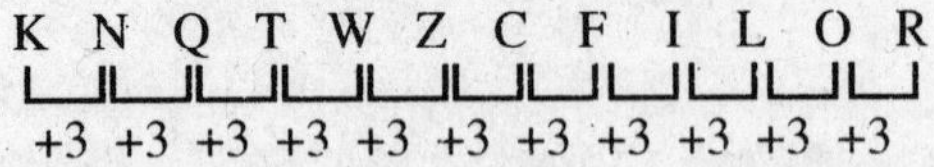

5. (*d*) : Each of the three alphabet in one group corresponds to the alphabet in the next group in the succession of +1, *i.e.,*

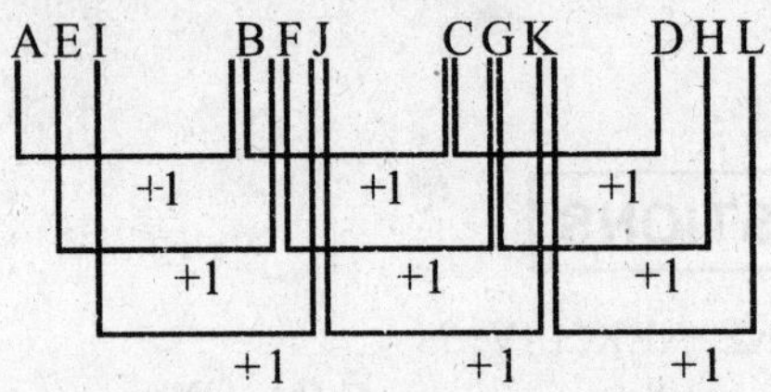

6. (*a*) : The three alphabet in one group correspond to the alphabet in the next group in the manner +6, +5, +4 respectively, *i.e.,*

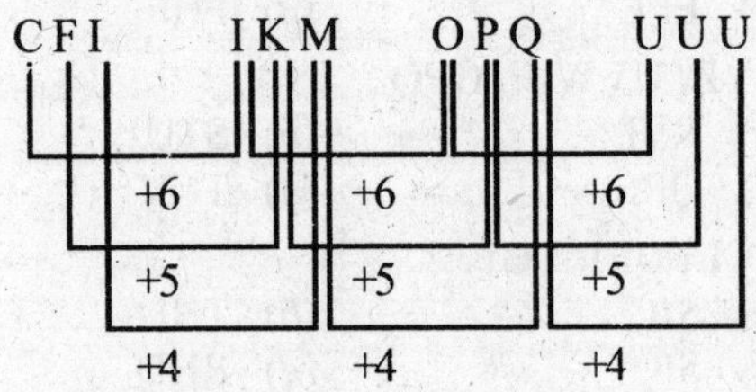

7. (*c*) : The three alphabet in one group correspond to the alphabet in the next group in the manner +2, +4, –2 respectively, *i.e.,*

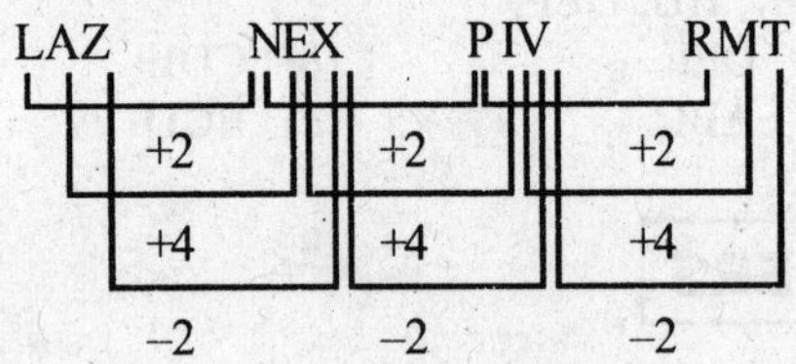

8. (*b*) : The alphabet from one group to the next are in succession of +1, *i.e.,*

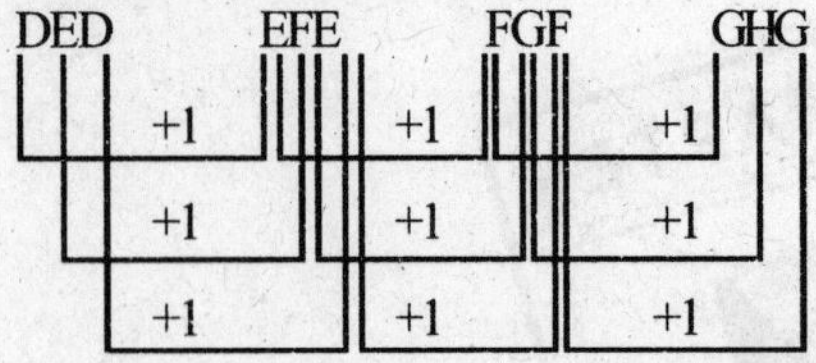

9. (*a*) : The alphabet from one group to the next are in recession of –3, *i.e.,*

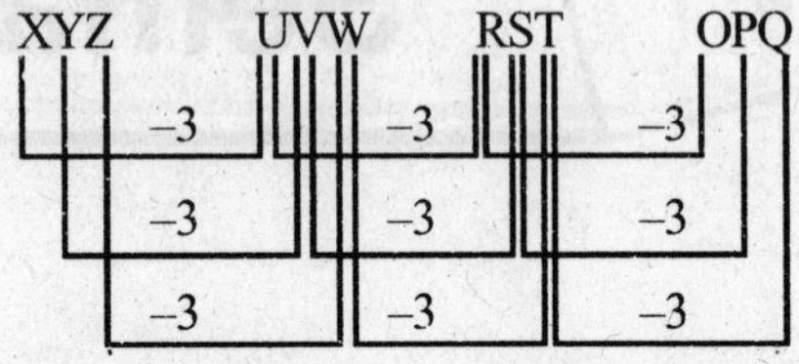

10. (*c*) : The alphabet in one group correspond to the alphabet in the next group in the manner –1, +2, –3 respectively, *i.e.,*

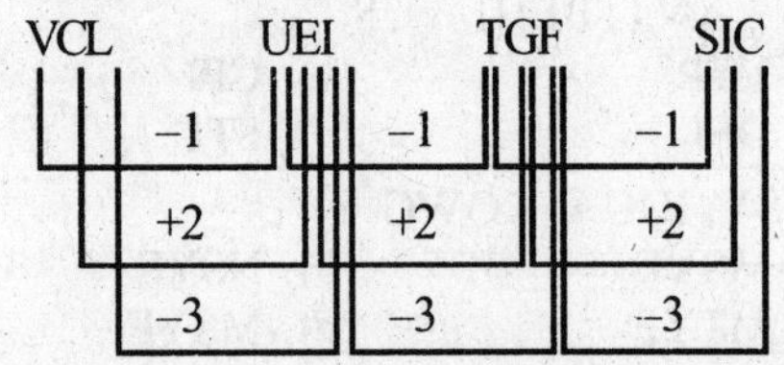

11. (*d*) : The difference between the last letter of the preceding group of alphabet and the first letter of the next group is decreasing by 1, *i.e.,*

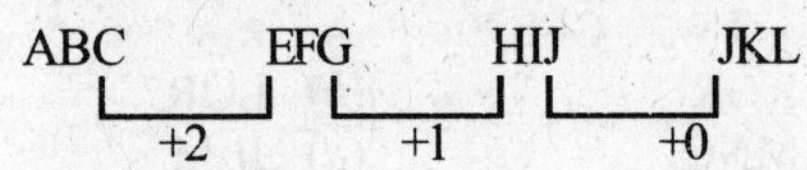

Otherwise the three letters in each group are in their natural order.

12. (*d*) : The letters in each group of alphabet are in the recession of –8, –4, –2 respectively.

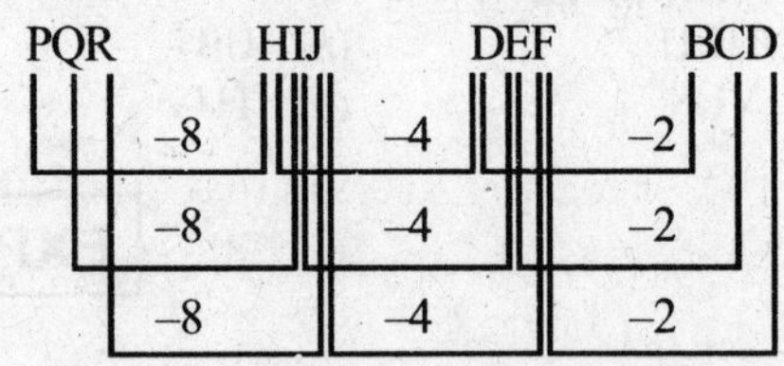

CHAPTER 5

Number Series

In this type of series, the set of given numbers in a series are related to one another in a particular pattern or manner. The relationship between the numbers may be (i) consecutive odd/even numbers; (ii) consecutive prime numbers; (iii) squares/cubes of some numbers with/without variation of addition or subtraction of some number; (iv) sum/product/difference of preceding numbers; (v) addition/subtraction/multiplication/division by some number; and (vi) many more combinations of the relationships given above.

MULTIPLE CHOICE QUESTIONS

Directions: *In the following questions, select the number(s) from the given options for completing the given series.*

1. 3, 9, 27, 81, 243, ?
(*a*) 486 (*b*) 729
(*c*) 972 (*d*) 359

2. 1, 6, 12, 19, 27, ?
(*a*) 38 (*b*) 35
(*c*) 36 (*d*) 54

3. 2, 6, 14, 30, 62, ?
(*a*) 126 (*b*) 128
(*c*) 120 (*d*) 130

4. 8, 48, 16, 96, 32, ?
(*a*) 192 (*b*) 150
(*c*) 64 (*d*) 288

5. 2, 8, 14, 24, 34, 48, ?
(*a*) 66 (*b*) 62
(*c*) 58 (*d*) 64

6. 4, 9, 19, 34, 54, ?, 109
(*a*) 89 (*b*) 84
(*c*) 74 (*d*) 79

7. 3, 15, 35, 63, 99, ?
(*a*) 144 (*b*) 143
(*c*) 121 (*d*) 169

8. 2, 3, 6, 18, 108, ?
(*a*) 1944 (*b*) 1658
(*c*) 648 (*d*) 1008

9. 1, 2, 3, 2, 3, 5, 4, 5, ?
(*a*) 9 (*b*) 6
(*c*) 10 (*d*) 7

10. 7776, 1296, 216, 36, 6, ?
(*a*) 6 (*b*) 0
(*c*) 3 (*d*) 1

11. 1, 8, 27, 64, 125, ?
(*a*) 172 (*b*) 176
(*c*) 216 (*d*) 189

12. 2, 3, 5, 7, 11, 13, ?
(*a*) 19 (*b*) 57
(*c*) 31 (*d*) 17

13. 80, 64, 48, 32, 16, ?
(*a*) 4 (*b*) 0
(*c*) 8 (*d*) 1

14. 3, 8, 13, 24, 41, ?
(*a*) 65 (*b*) 75
(*c*) 70 (*d*) 80

15. 9, 81, 90, 810, 819, ?
(*a*) 7371 (*b*) 900
(*c*) 8100 (*d*) 1638

16. 0, 8, 24, 48, 80, ?
(*a*) 110 (*b*) 96
(*c*) 120 (*d*) 140

17. 2, 4, 8, 3, 9, 27, 4, 16, ?
(*a*) 64 (*b*) 32
(*c*) 48 (*d*) 24

EXPLANATORY ANSWERS

1. (b) : The numbers in the series are multiplied by 3 to get the next numbers.

2. (c) : The difference between the numbers in the series increases by 1, after beginning from 5, *i.e.,*

1 6 12 19 27 36

+5 +6 +7 +8 +9

3. (a) : The difference between the numbers in the series doubles each time, after beginning from 4, *i.e.,*

2 6 14 30 62 126

+4 +8 +16 +32 +64

4. (a) : *Explanation I* : The sequence in the series is × 6, ÷ 3 which is repeated.

8 48 16 96 32 192

×6 ÷3 ×6 ÷3 ×6

Explanation II : There are two alternate series and the numbers are multiplied by 2.

8 48 16 96 32 192

(8 ×2 16 ×2 32; 48 ×2 96 ×2 192)

Series I : 8, 16, 32

Series II : 48, 96, 192

5. (b) : The sequence in the series is :

2 8 14 24 34 48 62

+6 +6 +10 +10 +14 +14

The difference increases by 4 at alternate step.

6. (d) : The difference between the numbers increases by 5, after beginning from 5, *i.e.,*

4 9 19 34 54 79 109

+5 +10 +15 +20 +25 +30

7. (b) : The series follows the sequence of the squares of even numbers beginning from 2, minus 1.

8. (a) : Every third number in the series is the product of previous two numbers.

2 3 6 18 108 1944

2 × 3, 3 × 6, 6 × 18, 18 × 108

9. (a) : In this series three numbers form a set. The first two numbers of each set are in natural order and the third number is the sum of first and second numbers. The first number of the next set begins with double the first number of the previous set.

× 2 × 2

1 2 3 2 3 5 4 5 9

1 + 2 2 + 3 4 + 5

10. (d) : The numbers in this sequence are divided by 6 each time.

11. (c) : The sequence in the series is cube of numbers in their natural order.

12. (d) : The series consists of prime numbers in increasing order.

13. (b) : The numbers in the series are decreasing with the difference of 16 at each step.

14. (c) : The sequence in the series is (number + next number) + addition of natural number increasing by 1 at each step, after beginning from 2.

3 8 13 24 41 70

(3+8) + 2

(8 + 13) + 3

(13 + 24) + 4

(24 + 41) + 5

15. (a) : The sequence in the series is × 9, + 9 which is repeated.

16. (c) : The sequence of the series consists of the product of 2 even numbers in natural order, *i.e.,*

0	8	24	48	80	120
↓	↓	↓	↓	↓	↓
(0 × 2)	(2 × 4)	(4 × 6)	(6 × 8)	(8 × 10)	(10 × 12)

17. (a) : In this series 3 numbers form a set. The first number is in natural order. The second number is the square of above number. The third number is the cube of first number.

CHAPTER

6 Arithmatical Reasoning

MULTIPLE CHOICE QUESTIONS

Directions (1–5) : *The following questions are based on the information given below :*

Data of 450 candidates, who took part in an examination in Social Science, Mathematics and Science is given below:

Passed in all the subject	167
Failed in all the subject	60
Failed in Mathematics	199
Failed in Social Science	175
Failed in Science	191
Passed in Science only	52
Passed in Mathematics only	48
Passed in Social Science only	62

1. How many passed in at least one subject?
(*a*) 450 (*b*) 390
(*c*) 304 (*d*) 167

2. How many failed in two subjects only?
(*a*) 56 (*b*) 61
(*c*) 152 (*d*) 162

3. How many passed in Mathematics and at least in one more subject?
(*a*) 210 (*b*) 203
(*c*) 170 (*d*) 94

4. How many failed in Social Science only?
(*a*) 15 (*b*) 21
(*c*) 30 (*d*) 42

5. How many failed in one subject only?
(*a*) 152 (*b*) 144
(*c*) 61 (*d*) 56

6. A, B, C, D and E play a game of cards. A says to B, "If you give me three cards, you will have as many as E has and if I give you three cards, you will have as many as D has." A and B together have 10 cards more than what D and E together have. If B has two cards more than what C has and the total number of cards be 133, how many cards does B have?
(*a*) 22 (*b*) 35
(*c*) 25 (*d*) 23

7. A bus starts from city X. The number of women in the bus is half of the number of men. In the city Y, 10 men left the bus and five women entered. Now, number of men and women is equal. In the beginning, how many passenger entered the bus?
(*a*) 15 (*b*) 30
(*c*) 36 (*d*) 45

8. I have a few sweets to be distributed. If I keep 2, 3 or 4 in a pack, I am left with one sweet. If I keep 5 in a pack, I am left with none. What is the minimum number of sweets I can have to pack and distributed?
(*a*) 25 (*b*) 37
(*c*) 54 (*d*) 65

9. A, B, C, D and E play a game of cards. A says to B, "If you give me 3 cards, you will have as many as I have at this moment while if D takes 5 cards from you, he will have as many as E has", A and C together have twice as many cards as E has B and D together also have the same number of cards as A and C taken together. I all together they have 150 cards, how many cards has C got.
(*a*) 28 (*b*) 29
(*c*) 31 (*d*) 35

10. At the end of a business conference, ten people present shake hands with each other once. How many handshakes will be there all together?
(*a*) 20 (*b*) 45
(*c*) 90 (*d*) 55

EXPLANATORY ANSWERS

1. (*b*) : Candidates passed at least in one subject = (Candidates passed in only one subjects) + (Candidates passed in only two subjects) + (Candidates passed in only all subjects). (Candidates failed in only two subjects) + (Candidates failed in only one subject) + (Candidates passed in all the subject)
= 162 + 61 + 167
= 390.

2. (*d*) : Candidates failed in two subjects only = Candidates passed in one subjects only
= 62 + 48 + 52
= 162.

3. (*b*) : Candidates failed in science only
=191 – (62 + 60 + 48)
= 21
Candidates failed in one social science only = 15
Therefore, candidates passed in maths and at least one more subject
= (21 + 15 + 167)
= 203

4. (*a*) : Candidates failed in social science only = (candidates failed in social science) – (candidates failed in all subjects + candidates passed in science only + candidates passed in maths only)
= 175 – (60 + 52 + 48)
= 175 – 160
= 15.

5. (*c*) : Candidates failed in one subject only
= (total number of candidates) – (candidates passed in all subjects + candidates failed in all the subjects + candidates passed in one subject only)
= 450 – (167 + 60 + 62 + 48 + 52)
= 450 – 389
= 61.

6. (*c*) : From the questions, we have
B – 3 = E ...... (i)
B + 3 = D ...... (ii)
A + B = D + E + 10 ...... (iii)
B = C + 2 ...... (iv)
A + B + C + D + E = 133 ...... (v)
From (i) and (ii)
B – E = D – B ⇒ E + D = 2 B ...... (vi)
From (iii) and (vi)
A + B = 2B + 10 ⇒ B = A – 10
or, A = B + 10 ...... (vii)
From (v), (vi), (iv) and (vii) we have
(B + 10) + (B) + (B – 2) + 2B = 133
5B = 133 – 8 = 125
= 25.

7. (*d*) : In the city X let the number of men be x

Then the number of women be $\frac{x}{2}$.

In the city y, $x - 10 = \frac{x}{2} + 5$

or, $\frac{x}{2} = 15$ or, $x = 30$ and $y = 15$.

Therefore, total number of passenger at the beginning were 30 + 15 = 45.

8. (*a*) : The required number will be obtained by taking LCM of 2, 3 and 4 and adding 1 into it. The number so obtained is 25.

9. (*a*) : From the questions it is clear that
B – 3 = A ...... (1)
D + 5 = E ...... (2)
A + C = 2 E ...... (3)
A + C = B + D ...... (4)
A + B + C + D + E = 150 ...... (5)
From (3), (4) and (5) we get
5E = 150 ∴ E = 30
Now from (2) D = 30 – 5 = 25
and from (4) A = 32
Now from (3) 32 + C = 2 × 30
C = 60 – 32 = 28.

10. (*b*) : Total number of handshakes = (9 + 8 + 7 + 6 + 5 + 4 + 3 + 2 + 1) = 45

CHAPTER 7

Problem Solving

Number problems consists of number sequences, problems with algebraic expressions, mathematical calculations and other compatiable problems.

MULTIPLE CHOICE QUESTIONS

1. How many 6's are there in the following series of numbers which are preceded by 7 but not immediately followed by 9?

6 7 9 5 6 9 7 6 8 7 6 7 8 6 9 4 6 7 7 6 9 5 7 6 3

(*a*) One (*b*) Two
(*c*) Three (*d*) Four

2. In a chess tournament each of six players will play every other player exactly once. How many matches will be played during the tournament?

(*a*) 12 (*b*) 15
(*c*) 30 (*d*) 36

3. How many 4's are there in the following series which are preceded by 7, but are not preceded by 8?

3 4 5 7 4 3 7 4 8 5 4 3 7 4 9 8 4 7 2 7 4 1 3 6

(*a*) 1 (*b*) 2
(*c*) 3 (*d*) 4

4. How many even numbers are there in the following series of numbers, each of which is immediately preceded by an odd number, but not immediately followed by an even number?

5 3 4 8 9 7 1 6 5 3 2 9 8 4 3 5

(*a*) Nil (*b*) 1
(*c*) 2 (*d*) 3

5. If all the numbers from 1 to 51 which are exactly divisible by 3 are arranged in descending order, which of the following numbers will come at the seventh and tenth places from the top?

(*a*) 33 & 27 (*b*) 33 & 21
(*c*) 21 & 30 (*d*) 33 & 24

6. Nitin was counting down from 32. Shasank was counting upwards, the numbers starting from 1 and he was calling out only the odd numbers. Which common number will they call out at the same time if they were calling out at the same speed?

(*a*) 21
(*b*) 22
(*c*) 19
(*d*) They will not call out the same number

7. In the following list of numerals, how many 3s are followed by 3, but NOT preceded by 3?

2 4 6 3 3 1 5 7 8 3 3 3 4 6 2 3 3 3 3 9 7 2 3

(*a*) 1 (*b*) 2
(*c*) 3 (*d*) 4

8. If in a given number 5 8 9 4 3 2 7 6 1 4, we interchange the first and the second digits, the third and the fourth, the fifth and the sixth and so on, then counting from the right end, which digit will be sixth?

(*a*) 3 (*b*) 2
(*c*) 4 (*d*) 5

9. Aparna cuts a cake into two halves and cuts one-half into smaller pieces of equal size. Each of the small pieces is twenty grams in weight. If she has seven pieces of the cake in all with her, how heavy was the original cake?

(*a*) 140 grams (*b*) 280 grams
(*c*) 240 grams (*d*) 120 grams

10. In the following number sequence how many such even numbers are there which are exactly divisible by its immediate preceding number but not exactly divisible by its immediate following number?

3 8 4 1 5 7 2 8 3 4 8 9 3 9 4 2 1 5 8 2

(*a*) Two (*b*) Three
(*c*) Four (*d*) More than four

11. How many 7s are there in the following series which are not immediately followed by 3 but immediately preceded by 8?

8 9 8 7 6 2 2 6 3 2 6 9 7 3 2 8 7 2 7 7 8 7 3 7 7 9 4

(*a*) Nil (*b*) One
(*c*) Two (*d*) Three

12. How many 9's are there in the following sequence which are neither preceded by 6 nor immediately followed by 3?

9 3 8 6 9 9 5 9 3 7 8 9 9 9 3 9 6 3 9

(*a*) One (*b*) Two
(*c*) Three (*d*) Four

13. If a number is five times as great as another number which is four less than forty, then the number is :

(*a*) 220 (*b*) 180
(*c*) 144 (*d*) 200

14. If 2/3rd of a number is 96, what will be the 3/4th of that number?

(*a*) 108 (*b*) 198
(*c*) 128 (*d*) 48

15. If such numbers which are divisible by 5, and also those which have 5 as one of the digits are eliminated from the numbers 1 to 60, how many numbers would remain?

(*a*) 53 (*b*) 47
(*c*) 40 (*d*) 45

EXPLANATORY ANSWERS

1. (*c*) : 679569768767869467769576 3
1 2 3

2. (*b*) : When all the players have to play with each other then the method of calculating the number of matches to be played is $\frac{n(n-1)}{2}$ where '*n*' is the number of players playing the match. So, the number of matches played will be :
$(6 \times 5) \div 2 = 30 \div 2 = 15$

3. (*d*) : 3457437485437498472741 36
1 2 3 4

4. (*c*) : 5 3 4 8 9 7 1 6 5 3 2 9 8 4 3 5
1 2

5. (*d*) : The numbers divisible by 3 in descending order are:
51, 48, 45, 42, 39, 36, 33, 30, 27, 24, 21, 18, 15, 12, 9, 6, 3.
(33 — 7th; 24 — 10th)

6. (*d*) : When Nitin is on count 22, Shasank is on 21 and when Nitin is on count 21, Shasank is on 23.

7. (*c*) : 2 4 6 3 3 1 5 7 8 3 3 3 4 6 2 3 3 3 3 9 7 2 3
1 2 3

8. (*b*) : The new number after interchanging the digits is :
8 5 4 9 2 3 6 7 4 1
6th

9. (*c*) : There is one bigger piece and six smaller pieces. One small piece weighs 20 gm. Total weight of six smaller speices is 120 gm.
∴ Weight of the bigger piece = 120 gm
∴ Weight of the original cake = 240 gm

10. (*a*) : 3 8 4 1 5 7 2 8 3 4 8 9 3 9 4 2 1 5 8 2
1 2

11. (*c*) : 898762263269732872778737794
1 2

12. (*d*) : 9 3 8 6 9 9 5 9 3 7 8 9 9 9 3 9 6 3 9
1 2 3 4

13. (*b*) : Number four less than forty is $40 - 4 = 36$
Five times the number is $= 36 \times 5 = 180$

14. (*a*) : If the number is x, then

$$\frac{2}{3}x = 96$$

$$x = \frac{96 \times 3}{2} = 144$$

$\frac{3}{4}$ th of the number is $144 \times \frac{3}{4} = 108$

15. (*c*) : The eliminated twenty numbers are : 5, 10, 15, 20, 25, 30, 35, 40, 45 and 50 to 60. The remaining numbers are $60 - 20 = 40$.

CHAPTER 8

Numerical Operations/ Symbol Substitution

Questions in this category are easy to attempt. Candidates must be quick in substituting symbols and calculations. The common pattern of questions asked are given below.

SOLVED EXAMPLES

1. If '+' stands for '×'; '×' stands for '÷'; '÷' stands for '–' and '–' stands for '+' then
2 – 8 × 2 + 6 ÷ 7 = ?

(*a*) 32 (*b*) 19 (*c*) 23 (*d*) 9

Ans. (*b*) : After substituting the symbols in the given expression the new expression will be :

2 + 8 ÷ 2 × 6 – 7

The solving steps will be :

2 + 4 × 6 – 7

2 + 24 – 7

26 – 7 = 19

2. If ▲ stands for '+'

■ stands for '–'

● stands for '÷'

✱ stands for '×' then

13 ▲ 5 ✱ 20 ● 10 ■ 9 = ?

(*a*) 26 (*b*) 37 (*c*) 14 (*d*) 55

Ans. (*c*) : After substituting the symbols the new expression will be :

13 + 5 × 20 ÷ 10 – 9

The solving steps will be :

13 + 5 × 2 – 9

13 + 10 – 9

23 – 9 = 14

MULTIPLE CHOICE QUESTIONS

Directions : *Each of the following questions is followed by four alternatives. Select the most appropriate answer.*

1. If "+" means "–"; "–" means "×"; "×"means "÷" and "÷" means "+", then
15 × 5 ÷ 10 + 5 – 3 = ?

(*a*) 9.5 (*b*) 0

(*c*) – 2 (*d*) 24

2. If "+" means "–"; "–" means "×"; "×"means "÷" and "÷" means "+", then
15 × 3 ÷ 15 + 5 – 2 = ?

(*a*) 0 (*b*) 10

(*c*) 20 (*d*) 6

3. If "+" means "÷"; "×" means "–"; "÷"means "+" and "–" means "×", then
16 ÷ 8 × 6 – 2 + 12 = ?

(*a*) 22 (*b*) 24

(*c*) 23 (*d*) 20

4. If "+" means "×"; "–" means "÷"; "÷"means "+" and "×" means "–", then what will be the value of $20 \div 40 - 4 \times 5 + 6 = ?$

(*a*) 60 (*b*) 1.67
(*c*) 150 (*d*) 0

5. If "+" means "×"; "–" means "÷"; "×"means "–" and "÷" means "+", then $5 + 8 - 4 \times 2 \div 9 = ?$

(*a*) 15 (*b*) 13
(*c*) 17 (*d*) 11

6. If × stands for addition, ÷ stands for subtraction, + stands for multiplication and – stands for division, then $(20 \times 6 \div 6 \times 4)$ is equal to

(*a*) 5 (*b*) 24
(*c*) 25 (*d*) 80

7. If "+" means "×"; "÷" means "–"; "×"means "÷" and "–" means "+", what will be the value of the following expression? $4 + 11 \div 5 - 50 = ?$

(*a*) 79 (*b*) –11
(*c*) 91 (*d*) 89

8. If "+" means "÷"; "÷" means "–"; "–"means "×" and "×" means "+", then $10 \div 2 - 15 + 3 \times 5 = ?$

(*a*) 10 (*b*) 15
(*c*) 25 (*d*) 5

9. If A stands for add, B for subtract, C for multiply and D for divide, then for what does 4A 3B 3A 2 stand?

(*a*) 2 (*b*) 4
(*c*) 6 (*d*) 8

10. If × stands for add, *y* stands for subract, *z* stands for divide and *p* stands for multiply, then what is the the value of (7 p 3) y 6 × 5?

(*a*) 5 (*b*) 10
(*c*) 15 (*d*) 20

11. If "+" means "÷"; "÷" means "–"; "–"means "×" and "×" means "+", what will be the value of $8 + 2 \div 3 - 4 \times 6 = ?$

(*a*) –2 (*b*) $-15\frac{1}{3}$
(*c*) 12 (*d*) 15

12. If "+" means "÷"; "×" means "–"; "÷"means "×" and "–" means "+", what will be the value of the following expression? $9 + 3 \div 4 - 8 \times 2 = ?$

(*a*) $6\frac{3}{4}$ (*b*) $-1\frac{3}{4}$
(*c*) $-6\frac{1}{4}$ (*d*) 18

13. If "–" means "÷"; "+" means "×"; "÷"means "–" and "×" means "+", then which of the following must be true?

(*a*) $1 \div 2 + 3 \times 6 - 8 = 12$
(*b*) $2 + 3 - 5 \times 8 \div 4 = 7$
(*c*) $5 + 6 \times 8 - 2 \div 3 = 31$
(*d*) $6 \div 1 + 2 - 8 \times 4 = 31$

14. If "÷" means "+"; "+" means "×"; "–"means "÷" and "×" means "–", then $5 + 8 - 4 \times 2 \div 9 = ?$

(*a*) 13 (*b*) 15
(*c*) 11 (*d*) 17

EXPLANATORY ANSWERS

1. (*c*) : $15 \div 5 + 10 - 5 \times 3$
$3 + 10 - 15 = -2$

2. (*b*) : $15 \div 3 + 15 - 5 \times 2$
$5 + 15 - 10 = 10$

3. (*c*) : $16 + 8 - 6 \times 2 \div 12$
$16 + 8 - 1 = 23$

4. (*d*) : $20 + 40 \div 4 - 5 \times 6$
$20 + 10 - 30 = 0$

5. (*c*) : $5 \times 8 \div 4 - 2 + 9$
$10 - 2 + 9 = 17$

6. (*b*) : $20 + 6 - 6 + 4 = 24$

7. (*d*) : $4 \times 11 - 5 + 50$
$44 - 5 + 50 = 89$

8. (*d*) : $10 - 2 \times 15 \div 3 + 5$
$10 - 10 + 5 = 5$

9. (*c*) : $4 + 3 - 3 + 2 = 6$

10. (*d*) : $(7 \times 3) - 6 + 5$
$21 - 6 + 5 = 20$

11. (*a*) : $8 \div 2 \;\; 3 \times 4 + 6$
$4 - 12 + 6 = -2$

12. (*d*) : $9 \div 3 \times 4 + 8 - 2$
$12 + 8 - 2 = 18$

13. (*c*) : (*a*) $1 - 2 \times 3 + 6 \div 8 = 12 \Rightarrow \frac{-17}{4} = 12$

(*b*) $2 \times 3 \div 5 + 8 - 4 = 7 \Rightarrow \frac{26}{5} = 7$

(*c*) $5 \times 6 + 8 \div 2 - 3 = 31 \Rightarrow 31 = 31$

(*d*) $6 - 1 \times 2 \div 8 + 4 = 31 \Rightarrow \frac{-39}{4} = 31$

14. (*d*) : $5 \times 8 \div 4 - 2 + 9$
$10 - 2 + 9 = 17$

CHAPTER 9

Word Building

These are spellings, word order and dictionary related questions. The candidate is given a word and asked to select the word that can/cannot be formed from its spellings. He/she may be asked to decide the meaningful order of the given words. He/she may also be asked to arrange the given words in the sequence in which they occur in the dictionary.

MULTIPLE CHOICE QUESTIONS

Directions (Qs. No. 1 to 12): *From the given alternatives select the word which* ***cannot*** *be formed using the letters of the given word.*

1. REPUBLICAN
(*a*) CLIP (*b*) PURE
(*c*) ANKLE (*d*) BANE

2. ESTRANGE
(*a*) GENERATE (*b*) SERGEANT
(*c*) REAGENTS (*d*) GREAT

3. DETERMINATION
(*a*) DETENTION (*b*) DESTINATION
(*c*) TERMINATE (*d*) DOMINATE

4. CHRISTMAS
(*a*) CHRIST (*b*) SMART
(*c*) CRUST (*d*) HARM

5. LEGALIZATION
(*a*) ALERT (*b*) ALEGATION
(*c*) GALLANT (*d*) NATAL

6. CHARACTER
(*a*) CRATE (*b*) CHARTER
(*c*) HEARTY (*d*) TRACER

7. ADMINISTRATION
(*a*) Station (*b*) Minister
(*c*) Ration (*d*) Mind

8. ORGANISATION
(*a*) ORGAN (*b*) ORGANISE
(*c*) NATION (*d*) ORATION

9. PERAMBULATOR
(*a*) RAMPANT
(*b*) LABOUR
(*c*) MARBLE
(*d*) RAMBLE

10. POSSESSION
(*a*) SESSION
(*b*) POSE
(*c*) POISE
(*d*) OBSESS

11. PRINTINGS
(*a*) SAINT (*b*) PRINT
(*c*) STING (*d*) RINGS

12. QUALIFICATION
(*a*) LIAR (*b*) FIAT
(*c*) LION (*d*) FICTION

13. From the given alternatives select the word which can be formed using the letters given in the word.
ULTRANATIONALISM
(*a*) ULTRAMONTANE
(*b*) ULTRAMODERN
(*c*) ULTRAIST
(*d*) ULULATE

14. A meaningful word starting with R is made from the first, second, fourth, fifth and eighth letters of the word CREATIVE. Which of the following is the middle letter of the word?
(*a*) E (*b*) T
(*c*) C (*d*) A

Directions (Qs. No. 15 to 18): *Which one of the given responses would be a meaningful order of the following words?*

15. 1. Amoeba 2. Oyster
3. Worm 4. Cow
(*a*) 1, 3, 2, 4 (*b*) 1, 2, 3, 4
(*c*) 4, 3, 2, 1 (*d*) 3, 2, 4, 1

16. 1. Birth 2. Death
3. Childhood 4. Infancy
5. Adolescence 6. Adulthood
7. Old age
(*a*) 2, 6, 7, 5, 4, 3, 1 (*b*) 1, 4, 3, 5, 6, 7, 2
(*c*) 1, 4, 3, 6, 5, 7, 2 (*d*) 2, 7, 6, 4, 5, 3, 1

17. 1. Police 2. Punishment
3. Crime 4. Judge
4. Judgement
(*a*) 3, 1, 2, 4, 5
(*b*) 1, 2, 4, 3, 5
(*c*) 5, 4, 3, 2, 1
(*d*) 3, 1, 4, 5, 2

18. 1. Orange 2. Indigo
3. Red 4. Blue
5. Green 6. Yellow
7. Violet
(*a*) 7, 2, 4, 5, 6, 1, 3 (*b*) 7, 2, 4, 6, 5, 1, 3
(*c*) 7, 2, 6, 4, 5, 1, 3 (*d*) 7, 2, 6, 4, 1, 5, 3

Directions (Qs. Nos. 19 and 24): *Arrange the given words in the sequence in which they occur in the dictionary.*

19. 1. Clone 2. Climate
3. Clutter 4. Create
5. Clapped
(*a*) 52143 (*b*) 51234
(*c*) 52134 (*d*) 53124

20. 1. Lasted 2. Loop
3. Lake 4. Litter
5. Listed
(*a*) 31542 B. 31254
(*c*) 31245 (*d*) 31452

21. 1. Intricate 2. Interview
3. Intransigent 4. Interrogation
5. Intravenous
(*a*) 2, 4, 5, 3, 1 (*b*) 5, 3, 1, 2, 4
(*c*) 4, 2, 3, 5, 1 (*d*) 3, 5, 2, 1, 4

22. 1. Forge 2. Forget
3. Forgo 4. Forgive
5. Format
(*a*) 1, 2, 4, 3, 5
(*b*) 5, 2, 4, 3, 1
(*c*) 1, 4, 3, 2, 5
(*d*) 3, 4, 5, 2, 1

23. 1. Forecast 2. Forget
3. Foreign 4. Forsook
5. Force
(*a*) 3, 5, 1, 2, 4 (*b*) 5, 1, 3, 2, 4
(*c*) 5, 1, 3, 4, 2 (*d*) 5, 1, 2, 3, 4

24. 1. Fenestration 2. Feather
3. Feed head 4. Feature
5. Feminine
(*a*) 2, 4, 3, 5, 1 (*b*) 4, 2, 3, 1, 5
(*c*) 2, 4, 1, 5, 3 (*d*) 4, 2, 3, 5, 1

25. Arrange the given words in the sequence in which they occur in the Dictionary and locate the last word.
(*a*) Frankenstein (*b*) Frankincense
(*c*) Frankalmoign (*d*) Frauendienst

26. Grouping of words are given. Choose the next word in the series from the given options.
AFGHAN, INDEFINITELY, SYNOPSIS, STUPENDOUS, BURST
(*a*) GLACIAL (*b*) COMPANION
(*c*) RESCRIPT (*d*) HIJACKER

ANSWERS

1	2	3	4	5	6	7	8	9	10
(*c*)	(*a*)	(*b*)	(*c*)	(*a*)	(*c*)	(*b*)	(*b*)	(*a*)	(*d*)
11	**12**	**13**	**14**	**15**	**16**	**17**	**18**	**19**	**20**
(*a*)	(*a*)	(*c*)	(*d*)	(*a*)	(*b*)	(*d*)	(*a*)	(*c*)	(*d*)
21	**22**	**23**	**24**	**25**	**26**				
(*c*)	(*a*)	(*b*)	(*a*)	(*d*)	(*d*)				

CHAPTER 10

Relationship Concept

While attempting questions on blood relations, one should be clear of all the relation patterns that can exist between any two individuals. These type of questions are given mainly to test one's relationship ability.

Very well known relations are :

Mother	Grandmother
Father	Grandfather
Son	Grandson
Daughter	Granddaughter
Brother	Brother-in-law
Sister	Sister-in-law
Niece	Father-in-law
Nephew	Mother-in-law
Uncle	Son-in-law
Aunt	Daughter-in-law
Husband	Cousin
Wife	

The patterns of some relationships which help in solving questions in these tests are :

Father's *or* Mother's Father	—	Grandfather (Paternal *or* Maternal)
Father's *or* Mother's Mother	—	Grandmother (Paternal *or* Maternal
Father's *or* Mother's Son	—	Brother
Father's *or* Mother's Daughter	—	Sister
Father's Brother	—	Paternal Uncle
Father's Sister	—	Paternal Aunt
Mother's Brother	—	Maternal Uncle
Mother's Sister	—	Maternal Aunt
Uncle *or* Aunt's Son *or* Daughter	—	Cousin
Son's Wife	—	Daughter-in-law
Daughter's Husband	—	Son-in-law
Husband's *or* Wife's Brother	—	Brother-in-law
Husband's *or* Wife's Sister	—	Sister-in-law
Brother's Wife	—	Sister-in-law
Sister's Husband	—	Brother-in-law
Brother's Son	—	Nephew
Brother's Daughter	—	Niece

MULTIPLE CHOICE QUESTIONS

Directions : *In each of the following questions keenly study the relationship mentioned between the persons, and then from the given options select the right relationship as the answer.*

1. 'A' is the father of 'B' and 'C'. 'B' is the son of 'A' but 'C' is not the son of 'A'. What is 'C's' relation with 'A'?
(*a*) Daughter (*b*) Son
(*c*) Niece (*d*) Nephew

2. A lady said, "The person standing there is my grandfather's only son's daughter". How is the lady related to the standing person?
(*a*) Sister (*b*) Mother
(*c*) Aunt (*d*) Cousin

3. Ravi is the brother of Amit's son's son. What is Amit's relation to Ravi?
(*a*) Cousin (*b*) Father
(*c*) Grandfather (*d*) Son

4. Mayank said, "My mother is the sister of Rajat's brother." What is Rajat's relation with Mayank?
(*a*) Cousin
(*b*) Maternal uncle
(*c*) Uncle
(*d*) Brother-in-law

5. Introducing Lily, Raghav said, "Her father is my mother's only son". How is Lily related to Raghav?
(*a*) Aunt (*b*) Daughter
(*c*) Mother (*d*) Sister

6. Ajay is the brother of Vijay. Mili is the Sister of Ajay. Sanjay is the brother of Rahul and Mehul is the daughter of Vijay. Who is Sanjay's Uncle?
(*a*) Rahul
(*b*) Ajay
(*c*) Mehul
(*d*) Data inadequate

7. Adity is Bhavi's brother, Bharat is Jayant's father. Ella is Bhavi's mother. Aditya and Jayant are brothers. What is Ella's relationship with Bharat?
(*a*) Sister
(*b*) Mother
(*c*) Daughter
(*d*) Wife

8. A man introduced the boy coming with him as "He is son of the father of my wife's daughter". What relation did the boy bear to the man?
(*a*) Son-in-law
(*b*) Son
(*c*) Brother
(*d*) Father

9. A and B are two brothers. C is sister of B. D is sister of E. E is son of A. Who is D's uncle?
(*a*) D (*b*) E
(*c*) B (*d*) C

10. Varun said pointing towards Arun, "He is my sister's only brother's son". How is Arun related to Varun?
(*a*) Son (*b*) Brother
(*c*) Nephew (*d*) Data insufficient

11. Pointing to a man, a lady said, "His brother's father is my grandfather's only son." How is the lady related to the man?
(*a*) Mother
(*b*) Sister
(*c*) Daughter
(*d*) Aunt

12. Vidya is the wife of Gopi and Gopi is the brother of Akhil. Akhil is the uncle of Vijay. What is Vijay's relation with Vidya?
(*a*) Son
(*b*) Nephew
(*c*) Brother-in-law
(*d*) Brother

EXPLANATORY ANSWERS

1. (*a*) :

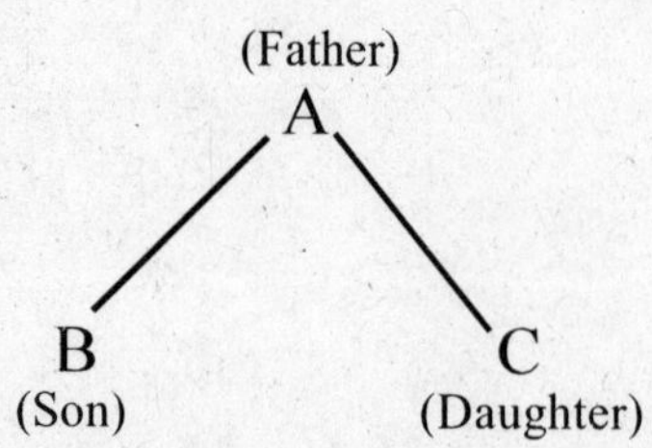

'C' is not the son of 'A', but 'A' is the father of 'C'. So, 'C' is the daughter of 'A'.

2. (*a*) :

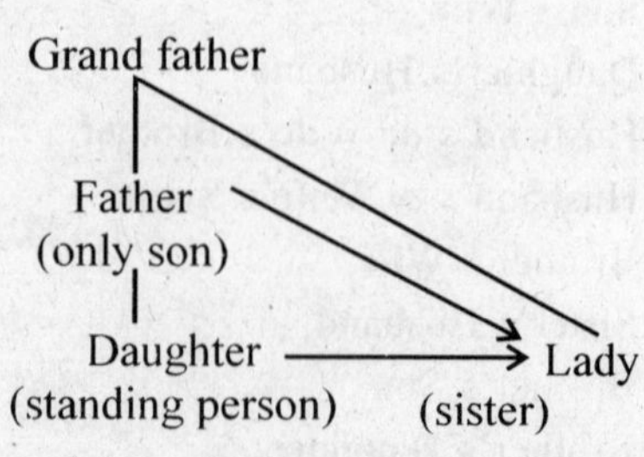

Lady's grandfather's son is lady's father and father's daughter will only be lady's sister.

3. (c) :

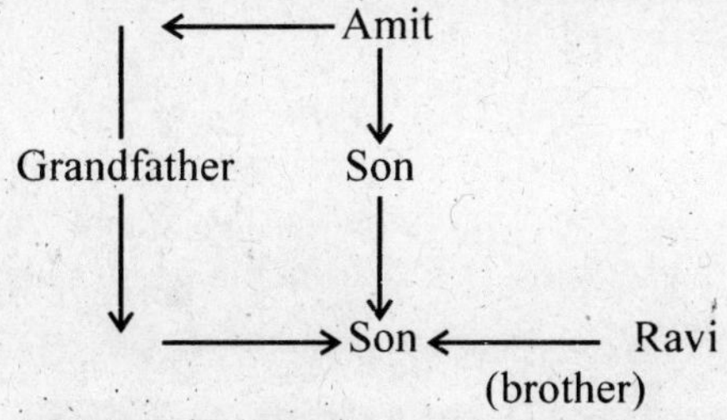

Amit's son's son is Amit's grandson. Ravi is the brother of Amit's son's son. So, Amit is also the grandfather of Ravi.

4. (b) :

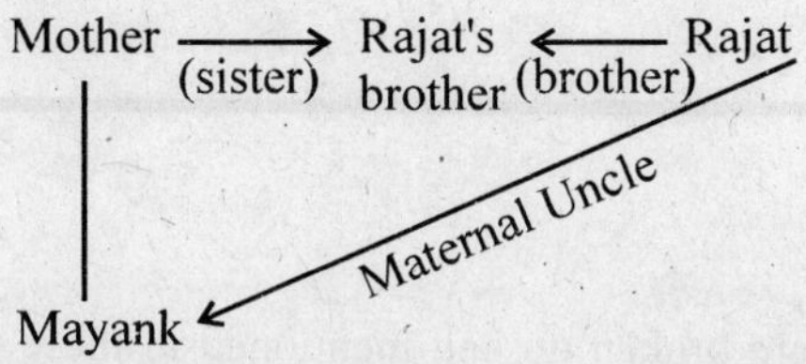

Mayank's mother is the sister of Rajat's brother. So Rajat is also the brother of Mayank's mother. Relation of the brother with his sister's child is maternal. So Rajat is Mayank's maternal uncle.

5. (b) : The relation is :

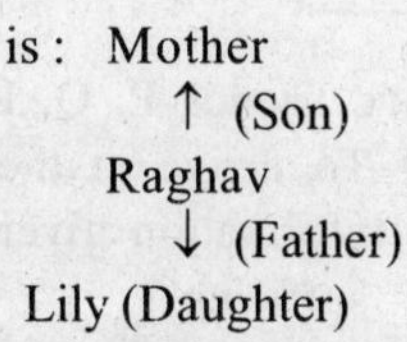

'My mother's only son' means Raghav himself. 'Her father' means Lily's father; *i.e.* Raghav and so, Lily is Raghav's daughter.

6. (d) :

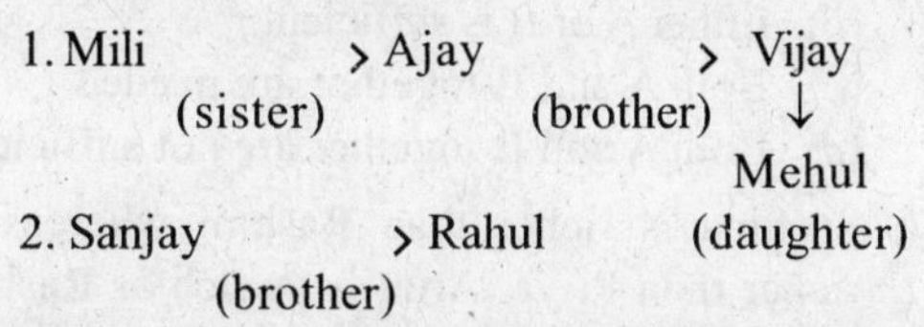

There are two sets of relationship. Information given is incomplete and no relation can be established between the two sets.

7. (d) : The relationship chart based on problem is :

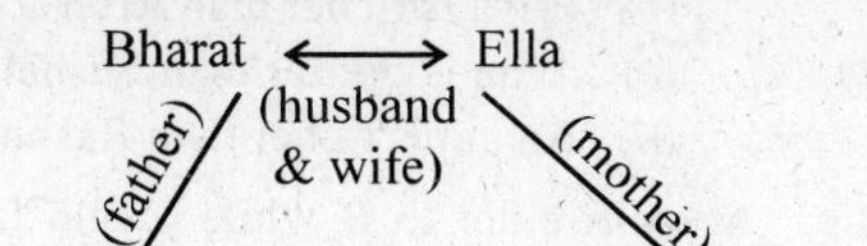

Jayant and Aditya are brothers. If Aditya is Bhavi's brother, then Jayant is also Bhavi's brother. If Bharat is Jayant's father, then he is also the father of Aditya and Bhavi. If Ella is Bhavi's mother, then she is also the mother of Aditya and Jayant. This means Bharat and Ella are husband and wife and the parents of three.

8. (b) : The relationship chart based on problem is :

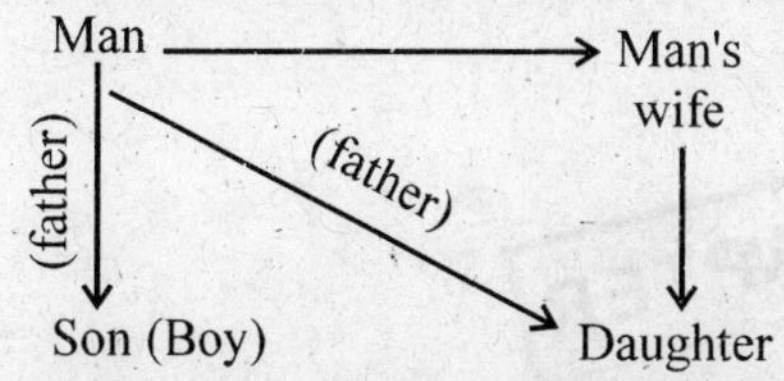

'Father of the man's wife's daughter' is the man himself and the boy in question is the man's son.

9. (c) : The relationship chart based on the problem is :

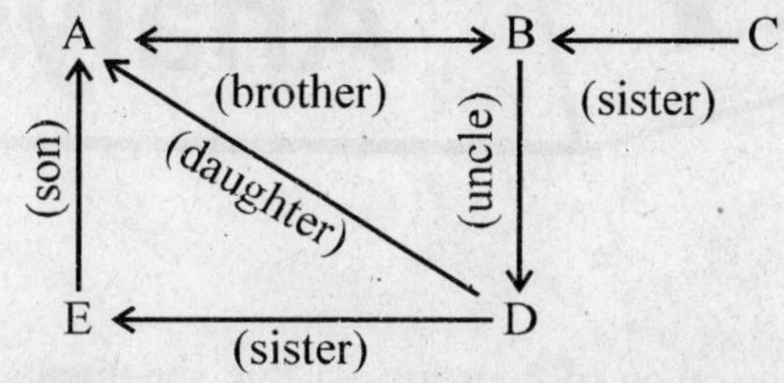

When D is sister of E, who is son of A then D is daughter of A. Brother of A is B and so, B is D's uncle.

10. (a) :

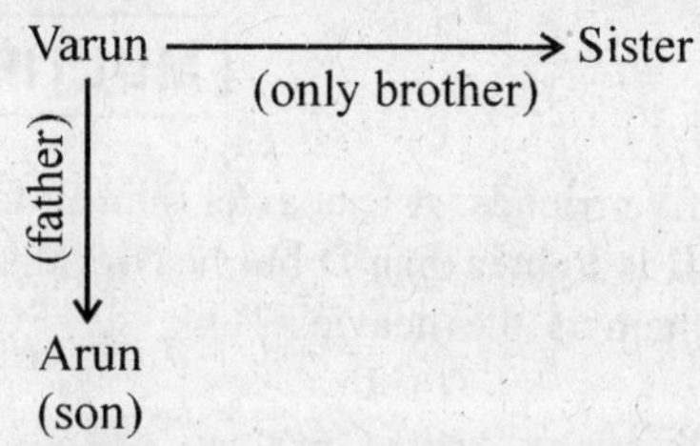

Varun's sister's only brother is Varun himself and Arun is his son.

11. (b) :

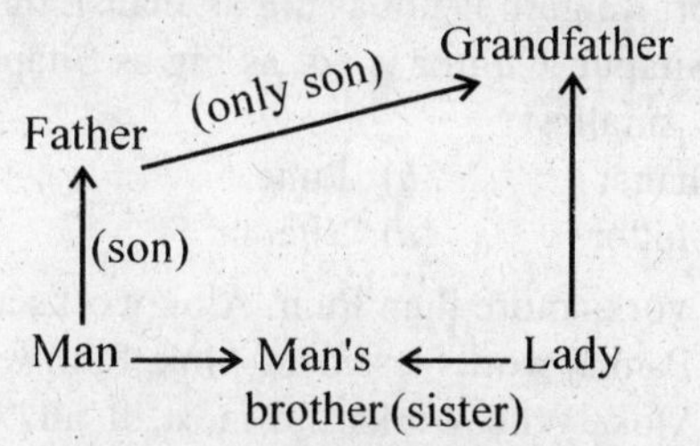

Man's brother's father is also the lady's father as he is the only son of lady's grandfather. So, the lady is man's sister.

12. (b) : The relationship chart based on problem is :

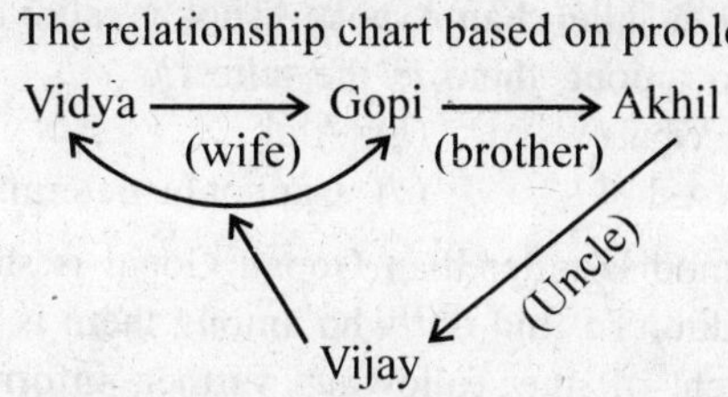

Vidya is wife of Gopi who is brother of Akhil. So, Vidya is sister-in-law of Akhil. If Akhil is uncle of Vijay then Gopi will naturally be the uncle of Vijay as it is not specified that any of the mentioned persons are Vijay's parents. Now, when Vijay is Gopi's nephew then he will also be Vidya's nephew.

CHAPTER

11 Analysis

In these type of questions, a few statements are given. Certain facts are broken up and mentioned in these statements. What is required is to analyse the statements, arrange and sort out the given facts and then answer the questions related to the given statements.

MULTIPLE CHOICE QUESTIONS

1. Among five friends, A is heavier than B; C is lighter than D; B is lighter than D but heavier than E. Who among them is the heaviest?
(*a*) B (*b*) C
(*c*) A (*d*) Can't say

2. Pune is bigger than Jhansi, Sitapur is bigger than Chittor. Raigarh is not as big as Jhansi, but is bigger than Sitapur. Chittor is not as big as Sitapur. Which is the smallest?
(*a*) Jhansi (*b*) Pune
(*c*) Chittor (*d*) Sitapur

3. Ajay works more than Ram. Alok works as much as Raju. Pankaj works less than Alok. Ram works more than Alok. Who works the most of all?
(*a*) Ajay (*b*) Ram
(*c*) Alok (*d*) Raju

4. Vipul is taller than Hans. Hans is taller than Anand. Alok is taller than Ashok. Ashok is taller than Hans. Who among them is the tallest?
(*a*) Vipul (*b*) Alok
(*c*) Ashok (*d*) Cannot be determined

5. Pramod is taller than Gopal. Gopal is shorter than Madhu. To find out who among them is the tallest, which of the following further informations is necessary?
(*a*) Madhu is taller than Gopal.
(*b*) Madhu is shorter than Pramod's brother
(*c*) Pramod is taller than Madhu.
(*d*) Pramod is taller than Madhu's brother.

6. Among five friends P, Q, R, S and T, who is the youngest? To arrive at the answer which of the following information given in the statements (A) and (B) is sufficient?
(A) R is younger than P and T.
(B) S is younger than Q.
(*a*) Only A alone is sufficient
(*b*) Either A or B is sufficient
(*c*) Both A and B together are needed
(*d*) Both A and B together are not sufficient

7. Sushma is richer than Rashmi whereas Anand is richer than Priya. Arun is as rich as Rashmi. Shoba is richer than Sushma.
Which of the following statements is correct according to the above propositions?
(*a*) Rashmi is poorer than Priya.
(*b*) Priya is richer than Arun
(*c*) Arun is poorer than Sushma.
(*d*) Anand is richer than Rashmi

8. A is elder to B while C and D are elder to E who lies between A and B. If C be elder to B, which one of the following statements is necessarily true?
(*a*) E is elder to B (*b*) A is elder to C
(*c*) C is elder to D (*d*) D is elder to C

9. Vikram is taller than Rajan but shorter than Annie. Jamal is taller than Annie. Sita is taller than Vikram. Rajan is shorter than Sita. Who is the shortest of all in the group?
(*a*) Sita (*b*) Rajan
(*c*) Vikram (*d*) Cannot be determined

10. Suresh is as much older than Kamal as he is younger than Prabodh. Navin is as old as Kamal. Which of the following statements is wrong?
(*a*) Suresh is older than Navin
(*b*) Kamal is younger than Suresh
(*c*) Prabodh is not the oldest
(*d*) Navin is younger than Prabodh

11. Ashok is heavier than Gopal. Mahesh is lighter than Jayesh. Prashant is heavier than Jayesh but lighter than Gopal. Who among them is the heaviest?
(*a*) Gopal (*b*) Jayesh
(*c*) Prashant (*d*) Ashok

12. Subodh's marks in English are as much more than Gopal's marks in History as less than Pramod's marks in English. To find out Subodh's marks in English, which of the following informations given in the statements (A) and (B) is/ are sufficient?
(A) Gopal's marks in History.
(B) Pramod's marks in History.
(*a*) Both A and B together are needed
(*b*) Only B is sufficient
(*c*) Either A or B is sufficient
(*d*) Both A and B together are not sufficient

Directions (Qs. 13-14) : *(A) Gopal is shorter than Ashok but taller than Kuhav; (B) Navin is shorter than Kuhav; (C) Jayesh is taller than Navin; (D) Ashok is taller than Jayesh.*

13. Who among them is the tallest?
(*a*) Gopal (*b*) Ashok
(*c*) Jayesh (*d*) Navin

14. Which of the following informations is not necessary to answer the above question?
(*a*) A (*b*) B
(*c*) C (*d*) D

Directions (Qs. 15-16) : *Five men A, B, C, D and E read a newspaper. The one who reads first gives it to C. The one who reads last had taken from A. E was not the first or last to read. There were two readers between B and A.*

15. B passed the newspaper to whom?
(*a*) E (*b*) B
(*c*) A (*d*) None of these

16. Who read the newspaper last?
(*a*) E (*b*) B
(*c*) D (*d*) Cannot be determined

EXPLANATORY ANSWERS

1. (*d*) : The five friends in descending order of weight are : A/D, B/C, E or A/D, B, C/E. Either A or D is the heaviest.

2. (*c*) : The order of cities in descending order of size is : Pune, Jhansi, Raigarh, Sitapur, Chittor.

3. (*a*) : On the basis of doing work, the descending order will be : Ajay, Ram, Alok/Raju, Pankaj.

4. (*d*) : On the basis of height, the descending order will be Vipul/Alok, Ashok, Hans, Anand. Either Vipul or Alok is the tallest.

5. (*c*) : According to the information both Pramod and Madhu are taller than Gopal. Option (c) decides who is the tallest.

6. (*d*) : Statements are not inter-related.

7. (*c*) : On the basis of wealth, the descending order will be :
1. Shobha, Sushma, Rashmi/Arun
2. Anand, *and* Priya
(The two statements are not inter-related.)

8. (*a*) : The order in descending seniority will be : A/C/D, E, B.

9. (*b*) : On the basis of height the descending order will be :
Jamal/Sita, Annie, Vikram, Rajan.
or
Jamal, Sita/Annie, Vikram, Rajan.

10. (*c*) : On the basis of age the descending order will be : Prabodh, Suresh, Kamal/Navin.

11. (*d*) : On the basis of weight, the descending order will be : Ashok, Gopal, Prashant, Jayesh, Mahesh.

12. (*d*) : Comparison in marks do no clarify Subodh's marks in a subject.

13. (*b*) : On the basis of height the descending order will be :
Ashok, Gopal/Jayesh, Kuhav, Navin
or
Ashok, Gopal, Kuhav/Jayesh, Navin.

14. (*c*)

15. (*d*) : The men read the newspaper in this order : B, C, E, A, D, and B passed the newspaper to C.

16. (*c*) : The men read the newspaper in this order : B, C, E, A, D, and B passed the newspaper to C.

CHAPTER 12

Judgement

MULTIPLE CHOICE QUESTIONS

1. Eileen is planning a special birthday dinner for her husband's 35th birthday. She wants the evening to be memorable, but her husband is a simple man who would rather be in jeans at a baseball game than in a suit at a fancy restaurant. Which restaurant below should Eileen choose?

(*a*) Alfredo's offers fine Italian cuisine and an elegant Tuscan decor. Patrons will feel as though they've spent the evening in a luxurious Italian villa.

(*b*) Pancho's Mexican Buffet is an all-you-can-eat family style smorgasbord with the best tacos in town.

(*c*) The Parisian Bistro is a four-star French restaurant where guests are treated like royalty. Chef Dilbert Olay is famous for his beef bourguignon.

(*d*) Marty's serves delicious, hearty meals in a charming setting reminiscent of a baseball clubhouse in honor of the owner,Marty Lester, a former major league baseball all-star. Answer & Explanation

2. The film director wants an actress for the lead role of Lucy who perfectly fits the description that appears in the original screenplay. He is not willing to consider actresses who do not resemble the character as she is described in the screenplay, no matter how talented they are. The screenplay describes Lucy as an average-sized, forty something redhead, with deep brown eyes, very fair skin, and a brilliant smile. The casting agent has four actresses in mind.

1. Actress #1 is a stunning red-haired beauty who is 5'9" and in her mid-twenties. Her eyes are brown and she has an olive complexion.
2. has red hair, big brown eyes, and a fair complexion. She is in her mid-forties and is 5'5".
3. is 5'4" and of medium build. She has red hair, brown eyes, and is in her early forties.
4. is a blue-eyed redhead in her early thirties. She's of very slight build and stands at 5'.

(*a*) 1, 2 (*b*) 2, 3
(*c*) 1, 4 (*d*) 2, 4

3. The school principal has received complaints from parents about bullying in the school yard during recess. He wants to investigate and end this situation as soon as possible, so he has asked the recess aides to watch closely. Which situation should the recess aides report to the principal?

(*a*) A girl is sitting glumly on a bench reading a book and not interacting with her peers.

(*b*) Four girls are surrounding another girl and seem to have possession of her backpack.

(*c*) Two boys are playing a one-on-one game of basketball and are arguing over the last basket scored.

(*d*) Three boys are huddled over a handheld video game, which isn't supposed to be on school grounds. Answer & Explanation

4. Mrs. Carson took a taxi to meet her three friends for lunch. They were waiting for her outside the restaurant when she pulled up in the car. She was so excited to see her friends that she left her tote bag in the taxi. As the taxi pulled away, she and her friends took notice of the license plate number so they would be able to identify the car when they called the taxi company.

1. The four women seem to agree that the plate starts out with the letter J.
2. Three of them agree that the plate ends with 12L.
3. Three of them think that the second letter is X, and a different three think that the third letter is K.

The four license plate numbers below represent what each of the four women thinks she saw. Which one is most likely the license plate number of the taxi?

(*a*) JXK 12L (*b*) JYK 12L
(*c*) JXK 12I (*d*) JXX 12L

5. Zachary has invited his three buddies over to watch the basketball game on his wide-screen television. They are all hungry, but no one wants to leave to get food. Just as they are arguing about who should make the food run, a commercial comes on for a local pizze-ria that delivers. The phone number flashes on the screen briefly and they all try to remember it. By the time Zachary grabs a pen and paper, each of them recollects a different number.

1. All of the men agree that the first three numbers are 995.
2. Three of them agree that the fourth number is 9.
3. Three agree that the fifth number is 2.
4. Three agree that the sixth number is 6; three others agree that the seventh number is also 6.

Which of the numbers is most likely the telephone number of the pizzeria?

(*a*) 995-9266 (*b*) 995-9336
(*c*) 995-9268 (*d*) 995-8266

EXPLANATORY ANSWERS

1.(*d*) : Since Eileen's husband does not enjoy fancy restaurants, choices (*a*) and (*c*) can be ruled out. Choice (*b*), although casual, doesn't sound as though it would be the kind of special and memorable evening that Eileen is looking for. Choice (*d*), which is owned by a former baseball star and is described as "charming" and "reminiscent of a baseball clubhouse", sounds perfect for Eileen's husband, who is described as a baseball fan and a man with simple tastes.

2.(*b*) : 2 and 3 possess most of the required traits. They both have red hair and brown eyes, are average-sized, and are in their forties. 1 is very tall and is only in her mid-twenties. She also has an olive complexion. 4 is of very slight build and is in her early thirties. She also has blue eyes.

3.(*b*) : Seeing four girls surrounding another girl, while in possession of her backpack, is the most suspicious of the incidents described.

4.(*a*) : The four women seem to agree that the plate starts out with the letter J. Three of them agree that the plate ends with 12L. Three of them think that the second letter is X, and a different three think that the third letter is K. The plate description that has all of these common elements is "Option A".

5.(*a*) : All of the men agree that the first three numbers are 995. Three of them agree that the fourth number is 9. Three agree that the fifth number is 2. Three agree that the sixth number is 6; three others agree that the seventh number is also 6. "Option A" is the best choice because it is made up of the numbers that most of the men agree they saw.

DECISION MAKING

MULTIPLE CHOICE QUESTIONS

Directions (Qs. 1 to 2) : *Read the following information carefully and answer the questions given below it.*

Following are the criteria for admitting a student in the first year engineering course in a college.

The student must—

(*i*) have passed XII standard examination in science with at least 80% marks.

(*ii*) not be more than 20 years old as on 1. 8. 1998.

(*iii*) have secured at least 90 marks in the entrance test out of a total of 150 marks.

(*iv*) be able to pay ₹ 15,000 as tuition fees for the first semester and ₹ 5,000 admission charges at the time of taking admission.

In the case of a candidate, who satisfies all other criteria except at—

(a) (iv) above but can pay at least 60% of the stipulated fees, the case may be referred to the Admission Committee.

(b) (iii) above but has secured more than 95% marks in the XIIth standard examination, the case may be referred to Chairman–Admissions.

You are given the following cases as on 1. 8. 1998. Depending upon the information provided in each case and based on the criteria mentioned above, recommend your decision. You are not to assume anything. If the information provided is not adequate to take a decision, mark 'Data inadequate' as the answer.

1. Subodh Mohaptara was 19 years old as on 20th December, 1997. He has secured 98% marks in XIIth standard examination with science and 80 marks in the entrance test. He can pay the requisite tuition fees and admission charges.

(a) Admit
(b) Refer to Admission Committee
(c) Data inadequate
(d) Do not admit
(e) Refer to Chairman–Admissions

2. Reema Jaiswal was born on 20th July, 1978. She has secured 85% and 75% marks in XIIth standard with science and entrance test respectively. She can pay the requisite tuition fees and admission charges.

(a) Refer to Chairman--Admission
(b) Refer to Admission Committee
(c) Data inadequate
(d) Do not admit
(e) Admit

Directions (Qs. 3 to 4) : *Read the following information to answer the given questions :*

Following are the criteria for selecting candidates for Research Fellowship :
The candidate must—

(i) be a post–graduate with minimum of 65% marks.
(ii) not be more than 30 years as on 15. 10. 1993.
(iii) have at least 3 years research experience.
(iv) have diploma in Statistics.
(v) have secured at least 50% marks in the entrance test.
(vi) have finalised the topic for research.

However, in case a candidate who fulfills all other criteria except

(a) (iii) above, but has M. Phil degree, should be referred to Dean.
(b) (iv) above, should be referred to Chairman.
(c) (i) above, but has at least 55% marks in post–graduation and 65% in the entrance test, should be given fellowship.
(d) (v) above, but has at lest 45% marks, should be wait–listed.

Based on these criteria and information provided below, decide the course of action in each case. You are not to assume anything. If the data provided is not adequate to decide the given course of action, your answer will be "data inadequate". These cases are given to you as on 15. 10. 1993.

3. 26 years old, Mamta Deo is a post graduate with 58%. She has got four years' research experience and has finalised topic for research. She got 70% marks in diploma in Statistics and 54% marks in the entrance examination.

(a) Fellowship not to be granted
(b) Refer to Dean
(c) Refer to Chairman
(d) Grant Fellowship
(e) Data inadequate

4. Shushila Nair has 65% marks in her post–graduation and is M. Phil. She has 5 years research experience. She has secured 65% in the entrance test and has finalised the research topic. Her date of birth is 11. 8. 65.

(a) Grant fellowship (b) Wait–list
(c) Refer to Dean (d) Refer to Chairman
(e) Data inadequate

Directions (Qs. 5 to 6) : *Read the following information to answer the given questions :*

Following are the conditions for selecting candidates for Research Fellowship :

The candidate must—

(i) be a post-graduate with minimum of 60% marks.
(ii) not be more than 30 years as on 1. 9. 1993.
(iii) have at least 3 years' research experience.
(iv) have diploma in statistics.
(v) have secured at least 55% marks in the entrance test.
(iv) have finalised the topic for research.

However, in the case of a candidate who fulfills all other criteria except—

(a) (iii) above but has M. Phil degree, should be given fellowship.
(b) (iv) above should be referred to Dean.
(c) (i) above but has atleast 55% marks in post–graduation, should be wait-listed.
(d) (v) above but has atleast 50% marks, should be referred to Chairman.

Based on these criteria and information provided below, decide the course of action in each case. You are not to assume anything. If the data provided is not adequate to decide the given course of action, your answer will be "data inadequate". These cases are given to you as on 1. 9. 1993.

5. Vijay Gupta is 24 years old and has got 58% marks in the entrance examination. He has secured 63% marks in his post-graduation and 55% marks in M.

Phil. He has got diploma in Statistics and has also finalised the topic for research.

(*a*) Grant Fellowship (*b*) Refer to Dean
(*c*) Refer to Chairman (*d*) Wait-list
(*e*) Data inadequate

6. Ajoy Dwivedi has secured 65% marks in the post-graduation and has secured 5 years research experience. He has secured 65% marks in the entrance test and has finalised the research topic. His date of birth is 11. 8. 1965.

(*a*) Grant Fellowship (*b*) Wait-list
(*c*) Refer to Dean (*d*) Data inadequate
(*e*) None of these

Directions (Qs. 7 to 8) : *Read the following information carefully and answer the questions given below :*

Following are the criteria of promotion from Junior Officer's Cadre to Senior Officer's Cadre in an organisation: The candidate must—

(*a*) have completed atleast 5 years in the organisation.
(*b*) have secured 65% marks in the written test for promotion.
(*c*) have secured 60% marks in the Group Discussion.
(*d*) have secured 70% marks in the interview.
(*e*) have good record of his work performance.
(*f*) have good communication skill and get along well with his colleagues.
(*g*) not be more than 40 years and less than 30 years as on 1. 9. 93.
(*h*) have good academic record with an average of at least 65% marks.

However, in the case of a candidate who—

(*i*) satisfies all other conditions except (*d*) above but has secured 75% marks in the written test and 65% marks in he Group Discussion, the case is to be referred to the General Manager (Personnel)–GM(P) for the decision.
(*j*) satisfies all other criteria except (*h*) above but has secured an average of more than 60% marks, the case is to be referred to the Managing Director (MD) of the organisation.

Now read the information provided in the case of each candidate in each of the questions given below and decide on the basis of the information provided and based on the above conditions, which of the courses of action you would suggest. These cases are given as on 5. 9. 1993. (Remember you are not to assume anything which is not provided in the question). If complete information is not provided, the answer would be Data inadequate.

7. 38 years old Rajesh has secured 65% marks in the written test for promotion, 73% marks in interview and 62% marks in Group Discussion. He has good record of his work performance, good communication skills and gets along well with his colleagues. He has good academic record with an average of 61% marks and has completed 7 years in the organisation.

(*a*) Refer to GM(P) (*b*) Refer to MD
(*c*) Promote (*d*) Do not promote
(*e*) Data inadequate

8. 34 years old Sudha has secured 60% marks in the written test for promotion, 72% marks in interview and 69% marks in Group discussion. She has good communication skill and gets along well with her colleagues. Her record of work performance is good and she has completed 6½ years in the organisation.

(*a*) Refer to MD (*b*) Do not promote
(*c*) Refer to GM(P) (*d*) Promote
(*e*) Data inadequate

EXPLANATORY ANSWERS

1. (*e*) : Criterion (*iii*) is not satisfied but Criterion (*b*) gives the decision.

2. (*d*) : Both Criterion (*iii*) and Criterion (*b*) are not satisfied.

3. (*a*) : Both Criterion (*i*) and Criterion (*c*) are not satisfied.

4. (*d*) : Criterion (*iv*) is not given but Criterion (*b*) gives the decision.

5. (*a*) : Criterion (*iii*) is not satisfied but Criterion (*a*) gives the decision.

6. (*c*) : Criterion (*iv*) is not satisfied but Criterion (*b*) gives the decision.

7. (*b*) : Criterion (*h*) is not satisfied but Criterion (*j*) gives the decision.

8. (*b*) : Criterion (*b*) is not satisfied.

CHAPTER 13

Statement Conclusion

In this reasoning pattern, a statement is given followed by two conclusions. The statement is to be taken as the fact. Then based on it one has to decide which of the conclusion(s) definitely follows or does not follow from the given statement.

MULTIPLE CHOICE QUESTIONS

Directions (Qs. 1 to 20): *In the following questions, each question has a statement followed by two conclusions. Taking the statement to be true, decide which of the given conclusions definitely follows from the given statement. Indicate your answer as (a) if only I follows; (b) if only II follows; (c) either I or II follows; (d) if neither I nor II follows; and (e) if both I and II follow.*

1. *Statement* : The Principal humiliated the teacher in the presence of students.

Conclusions I: The Principal did not like the teacher.

II: The teacher was not popular amongst his students.

2. *Statement* : Good health is dependent on right eating habits. Most of the people do not follow any rule regarding eating.

Conclusions I: Most of the people have poor health.

II: People are ignorant of proper eating habits.

3. *Statement* : Until our country achieves economic equality and political freedom, democracy would be meaningless.

Conclusions I: Political freedom and democracy go hand in hand.

II: Economic equality leads to real political freedom and democracy.

4. *Statement* : Black cloud follows thunder. Rains follow thunder.

Conclusions I: Thunder is the cause of rain.

II: Black cloud is the cause of thunder.

5. *Statement* : Practice is better than precept. Most doctors are heavy smokers.

Conclusions I: Most doctors cannot advise people not to smoke.

II: Doctors do not regard smoking as injurious.

6. *Statement* : Workers feel highly motivated when they get sense of involvement by participating in the management of companies.

Conclusions I: Workers should be motivated to produce more.

II: Workers should be allowed to participate in the management of companies.

7. *Statement* : Industrial revolution which first of all started in Europe has brought about modern age.

Conclusions I: Disparity between rich and poor results in revolution.

II: Revolution overhauls society.

8. *Statement* : America's defence secretary reiterated that they would continue to supply arms to Pakistan.

Conclusions I: Pakistan is incapable of manufacturing arms.

II: It would ensure peace in the region.

9. *Statement* : Poor people are more trust-worthy as compared to the rich. They can do wonders if they are taken into confidence.

Conclusions I: Poor people are wonderful people.

II: By and large rich people are not trustworthy.

10. *Statement* : Government has spoiled many top ranking financial institutions by appointing bureaucrats as Directors of these institutions.

Conclusions I : Government should appoint Directors of the financial institutes taking into consi-deration the expertise of the person in the area of finance.

II : The Director of the financial institute should have exper-tise commensurate with the financial work carried out by the institute.

Directions (Qs. 11 to 15): *In the following questions, the symbols* $*$, $\overset{*}{=}$, $=$, $@$ *and* $\underset{=}{@}$ *are used with the following meanings :*

(*a*) $*$ (*b*) means (*a*) is greater than (*b*),

(*a*) $\overset{*}{=}$ (*b*) means (*a*) is either greater than or equal to (*b*).

(*a*) = (*b*) means (*a*) is equal to (*b*).

(*a*) @ (*b*) means (*a*) is smaller than (*b*) and

(*a*) $\underset{=}{@}$ (*b*) means (*a*) is either smaller than or equal to (*b*).

Answer is given as:

(*a*) If only conclusion I is true;

(*b*) If only conclusion II is true;

(*c*) If either I or II is true;

(*d*) If neither I nor II is true;

(*e*) If both I and II are true.

11. *Statements* : $T \overset{*}{=} P, P @ S, P = M$

Conclusions : *I.* $S * M$ *II.* $T @ S$

12. *Statements* : $R \underset{=}{@} M, M * P, R \overset{*}{=} L$

Conclusions : *I.* $M = L$ *II.* $P = L$

13. *Statements* : $M = T, T \underset{=}{@} Z, S * M$

Conclusions : *I.* $Z * M$ *II.* $Z = M$

14. *Statements* : $L @ C, C * Z, Z \underset{=}{@} F$

Conclusions : *I.* $C * F$ *II.* $F = C$

15. *Statements* : $Z @ B, N \overset{*}{=} S, B @ N$

Conclusions : *I.* $B = Z$ *II.* $S \underset{=}{@} B$

EXPLANATORY ANSWERS

1. (*a*) : Only conclusion I follows. Conclusion II is not confirmed by the given statement.

2. (*a*) : Conclusion I definitely follows. Conclusion II is not confirmed by the given statement.

3. (*b*) : Only conclusion II follows. Conclusion I cannot be drawn from the given statement.

4. (*b*) : Only conclusion II follows. Conclusion I is wrong as rains are the cause of thunder.

5. (*e*) : Both conclusion I and conclusion II follow from the statements as the doctors who are heavy smokers indicate that they do not regard smoking as injurious and thus, cannot advise people not to smoke.

6. (*e*) : Both conclusions I and II follow from the statement as involvement of workers boosts production and benefits the companies.

7. (*b*) : Only conclusion II follows. Conclusion I is not related the statement.

8. (*d*) : Neither conclusion I nor conclusion II follows. Both the conclusions are unrelated to the statement.

9. (*b*) : Only conclusion II follows. Conclusion I is not related to the statement.

10. (*e*) : Both conclusion I and conclusion II follow.

11. (*a*) : $T \geq P, P < S, P = M$

$\therefore S > M$

12. (*d*) : $R \leq M, M > P, R \geq L$

$\therefore L \leq R \leq M$

13. (*c*) : $M = T, T \leq Z, Z = M$

If $T = Z$, then $Z = M$

If $T < Z$, then $Z > M$

14. (*d*) : $L < C, C > Z, Z \leq F$

No relation can be established between C and F.

15. (*d*) : $Z < B, N \geq S, B < N$

No relation can be established between B, S and Z.

CHAPTER 14

Syllogistic Reasoning

In this reasoning pattern two statements are followed by few conclusions drawn. Four options (*a*), (*b*), (*c*) & (*d*) are given as answers. Based on the statement the candidate has to select the right answer in each question.

MULTIPLE CHOICE QUESTIONS

Directions (Q. 1–4) : *In each question given below two statements are followed by four conclusions numbered I, II, III and IV. You have to take the two given statements to be true even if they seem to be at variance from commonly known facts. Read the statements and conclusions and decide which of the conclusions logically follows from the two given statements, disregarding commonly known facts.*

1. Statements: All the phones are scales. All the scales are calculators.

Conclusions:
I. All the calculators are scales.
II. All the phones are calculators.
III. All the scales are phones.
IV. Some calculators are phones.

(*a*) Only I and IV (*b*) Only III and IV
(*c*) Only II and IV (*d*) Only I and II

2. Statements: No door is dog. All the dogs are cats.

Conclusions:
I. No door is cat.
II. No cat is door.
III. Some cats are dogs.
IV. All the cats are dogs.

(*a*) Only II and IV (*b*) Only I and III
(*c*) Only III and IV (*d*) Only III

3. Statements: Some tables are T.V. Some T.V. are radios.

Conclusions:
I. Some tables are radios.
II. Some radios are tables.
III. All the radios are T.V.
IV. All the T.V. are tables.

(*a*) Only II and IV (*b*) Only I and III
(*c*) Only IV (*d*) None of the four

4. Statements: All men are vertebrates. Some mammals are vertebrates.

Conclusions:
I. All men are mammals.
II. All mammals are men.
III. Some vertebrates are mammals.
IV. All vertebrates are men.

(*a*) Only IV (*b*) Only II
(*c*) Only III (*d*) Only I

Directions (Q. 5–9) : *Every question below has a few statements, followed by four conclusions numbered I, II, III and IV. You have to consider every given statement as true, even if it does not conform to the well known facts. Read the conclusions and then decide which of the conclusions can be logically derived.*

5. Statements: Some keys are staplers. Some staplers are stickers. All the stickers are pens.

Conclusions:
I. Some pens are staplers.
II. Some stickers are keys.
III. No sticker is key.
IV. Some staplers are keys.

(*a*) Only I and II
(*b*) Only II and IV
(*c*) Only II and III
(*d*) Only I and IV and either II or III

6. Statements: All the locks are keys. All the keys are bats. Some watches are bats.

Conclusions:
I. Some bats are locks.
II. Some watches are keys.
III. All the keys are locks.
IV. Some keys are locks.

(*a*) Only I and II (*b*) Only I and IV
(*c*) Only II and III (*d*) Only I and III

7. **Statements:** All the papers are books. All the bags are books. Some purses are bags.
Conclusions:
I. Some papers are bags.
II. Some books are papers.
III. Some books are purses.
IV. Some papers are purses.
(*a*) Only I and IV (*b*) Only II and III
(*c*) Only I and II (*d*) Only I and III

8. **Statements:** All the bottles are boxes. All the boxes are bags. Some bags are trays.
Conclusions:
I. Some bottles are trays.
II. Some trays are boxes.
III. All the bottles are bags.
IV. Some trays are bags.
(*a*) Only III and IV (*b*) Only I and II
(*c*) Only II and III (*d*) Only I and IV

9. **Statements:** Some rats are cats. Some cats are dogs. No dog is cow.
Conclusions:
I. No cow is cat. II. No dog is rat.
III. Some cats are rats. IV. Some dogs are cats.
(*a*) Only I and IV (*b*) Only I and II
(*c*) Only I and III (*d*) Only III and IV

EXPLANATORY ANSWERS

1. (*c*)

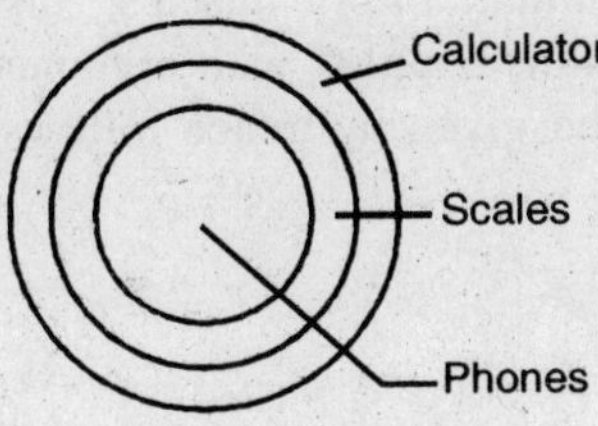

2. (*d*)

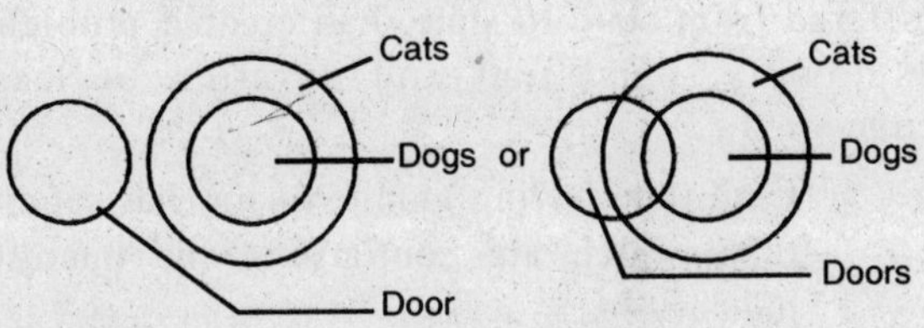

3. (*d*)

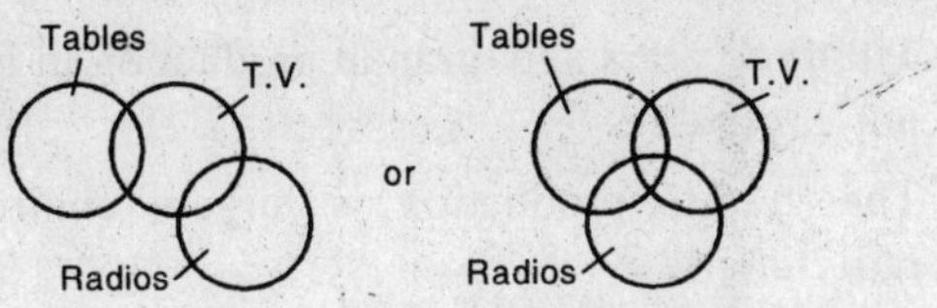

4. (*c*)

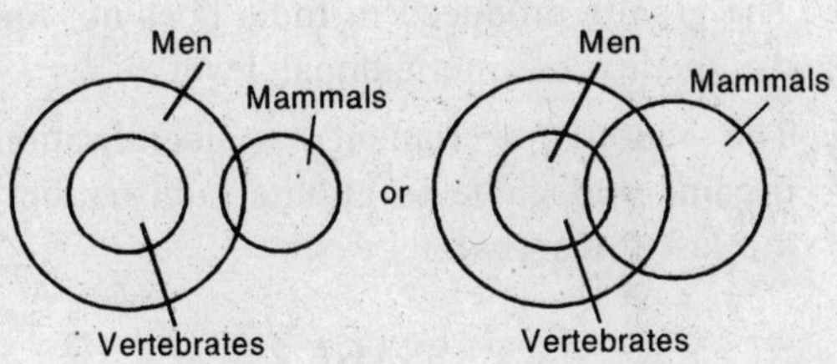

5. (*d*)

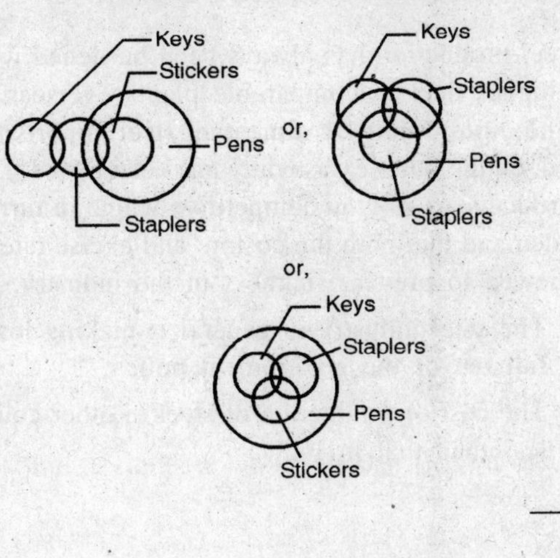

6. (*b*)

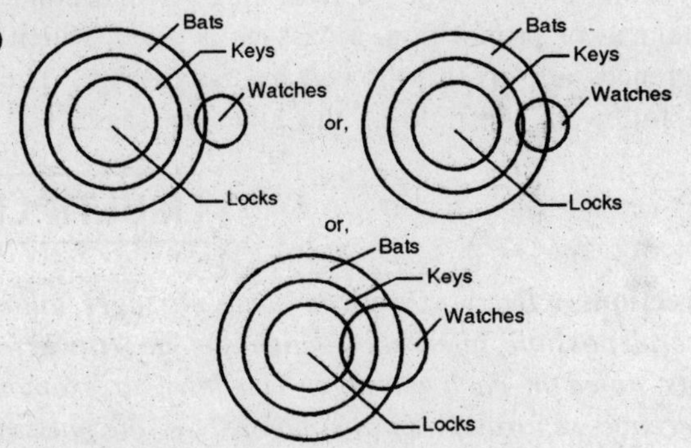

7. (*b*)

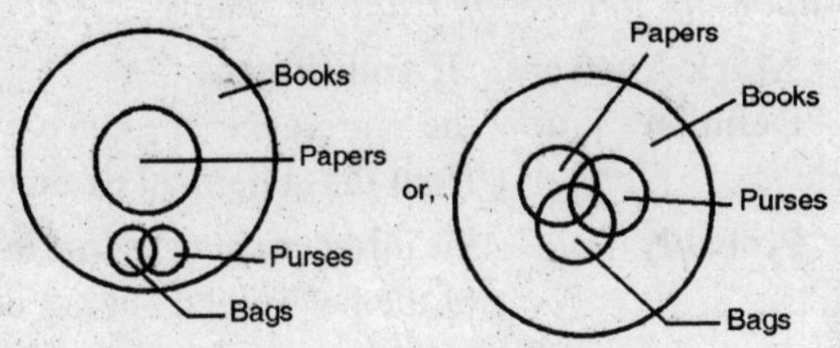

8. (*a*)

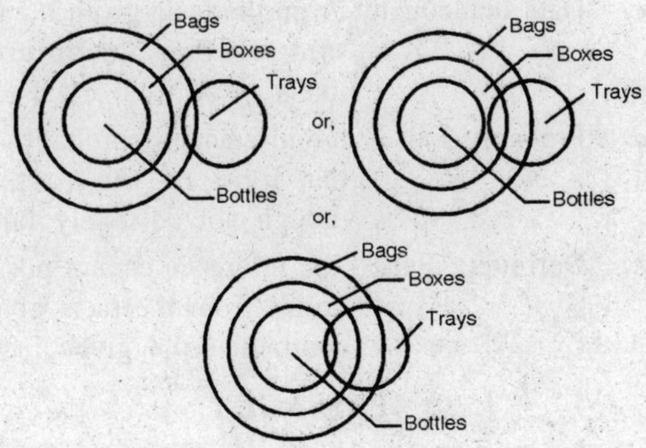

9. (*d*)

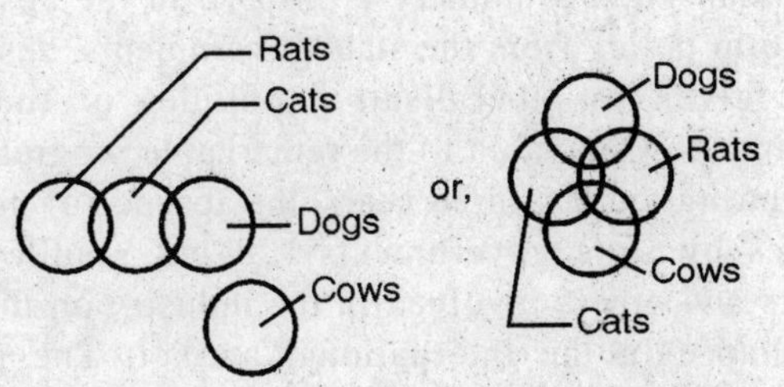

CHAPTER 15

Drawing Inferences

Questions on this type of reasoning have become quite common in competitive examinations. In this test, instead of a statement or proposition, a passage is given which is a congregation of many propositions coupled with arguments. Some inferences are given followed by the passage. The candidate has to decide whether the given inference follows, or does not follow in the light of the given passage.

MULTIPLE CHOICE QUESTIONS

Directions : *Below are given some passages followed by several possible inferences which can be drawn from the facts stated in each passage. You have to examine each inference separately in the context of the passage and decide upon its degree of truth or falsity.*

	Mark Answers	**If you think...**
(a)	"Definitely True"	the inference properly follows from the statement of facts given.
(b)	"Probably True"	the inference may be true in the light of the facts given but not definitely true.
(c)	"Data Inadequate"	from the facts given it cannot be said whether the inference is likely to be true or false.
(d)	"Probably False"	the inference is probably false in the light of the facts given though not definitely false.
(e)	"Definitely False"	the inference cannot possibly be drawn from the facts given or it contradicts the given facts.

PASSAGE 1

Indian granite industry is in peril in the absence of a uniform policy from the state governments, despite the thrust given by liberalisation policies of the union government. Compared to the remarkable progress in the field during the last three years, the absence of matching policies by state governments had put granite quarry owners and others involved in the industry on the verge of collapse in the international market. The policies differed from state to state, had created problems as far as loyalty, dead rent and duration of lease were concerned.

1. Each state having granite quarry has set up its own rules which are contrary to the interest of the industry.

2. Till three years ago, granite production in India was not profitable.

3. The granite production is largely controlled by individuals.

4. The granite produced in India does not match with the quality of international level.

5. The union government's liberalisation policy became applicable to granite industry only during the last three years.

PASSAGE 2

Steel production has always been burdened with costs much higher than in comparable plants overseas. On the one hand custom duty on almost all steel imports has been reduced, on the other excise duty has been raised. Domestic steel products are now uncompetitive which in turn has led to the demand that both the custom and excise rates should be reviewed to prevent sickness in the industry.

6. The steel industry in general is making losses as a fall out of the government policy.

7. The cost of production of steel in other countries is less than that in India.

8. India can compete with the foreign countries in re gard to the price of steel with a favourable government policy.

9. Foreign steel has become cheaper comparative to domestic steel.

10. The government is considering lowering of excise duty on steel products.

PASSAGE 3

The annual domestic consumption of plastics in India is expected to grow between 2.5 and 3 million tonnes by the end of the Ist balls of the century from the current level of about one million tonnes. The global consumption of plastics now stands at 100 million tonnes. To sustain the present growth pattern, India would need two additional polymer plants of 1,000 tonnes every year till the turn of the Ist half of this century. Entrepreneurs should now think in lines of globalisation and promote projects of international capacity and they would have to look at technology transfer as well as upgradation and strategic and creative alliances.

11. The total domestic consumption of plastics in India is about one per cent of the global consumption.

12. At present India does not import plastics.

13. India lacks in technological capabilities in producing plastics.

14. There is an expected growth of about .2 per cent in the plastic consumption every year.

15. Potentially India can be one of the major players in the production of plastics in the international market.

EXPLANATORY ANSWERS

1. *(a)* : The policies differed from state to state.

2. *(c)* : Remarkable progress during the last three years is mentioned in the paragraph but nothing suggests that the production was not profitable.

3. *(a)* : There is absence of a uniform policy from the state Governments.

4. *(c)* : According to the paragraph, absence of matching policies had put the quarry owners and others involved in the industry on the verge of collapse in the international market. Nothing is mentioned about the granite quality produced in India or of the international level.

5. *(e)* : The inference does not relate to the facts given in the statement.

6. *(d)* : Government policy alone may not be responsible for the losses. Cost or quality factor may also be responsible.

7. *(c)* : The paragraph mentions that steel production in India has always been burdened with costs much higher than in comparable plants overseas. But nowhere in the paragraph it is mentioned that the cost of production of steel is less in other countries.

8. *(a)* : If the government reviews its policy, India can definitely compete with the foreign countries in regard to the steel price.

9. *(a)* : Customs duty on almost all steel products has been reduced.

10. *(b)* : There is a demand that both the customs and excise rates should be reviewed.

11. *(a)* : The global consumption of plastics is 100 million tonnes and current level of consumption in India is 1 million tonnes.

12. *(c)* : The paragraph does not mention about the import or export of plastics.

13. *(a)* : Entrepreneurs would have to look at technology transfer as well as upgradation and strategic and creative alliances.

14. *(a)* : The expected growth by end of the Ist half of this century is between 2.5 and 3 million tonnes. India needs 2 additional polymer plants of 1,000 tonnes per year.

15. *(a)* : By thinking in lines of globalisation and promoting projects of international capacity India can be one of the major players in the production of plastics in the international market.

CHAPTER 16

Trends

This type of questions are asked to assess the thinking pattern or mental trends of the candidate. These are simple questions but should be answered honestly and carefully.

MULTIPLE CHOICE QUESTIONS

Directions : *In the questions given below four alternatives have been given below each one of them. You have to select the right alternative according to your mind and mark it in your answer sheet.*

1. I like pre-defined rules and regulations.
(*a*) Sometimes (*b*) No
(*c*) Yes (*d*) No idea

2. I found a purse full of money in college premise. I:
(*a*) donated the amount among poor
(*b*) gave it to the principal
(*c*) offered it at temple
(*d*) None of these

3. I am punctual regarding
(*a*) going to bed (*b*) time
(*c*) meals (*d*) dating

4. I was travelling on a boat which capsized. Firstly, I:
(*a*) rescued others (*b*) saved myself
(*c*) closed my eyes (*d*) cursed my luck

5. When someone asks you for help in odd situations then:
(*a*) you give him/her all possible help
(*b*) you promise him/her help
(*c*) you do not help him/her
(*d*) you turn a deaf ear

6. In case my wristwatch is out of order, I:
(*a*) would try to repair it myself
(*b*) would give it to watchmaker
(*c*) would buy a new watch
(*d*) would throw it away

7. Often I change my opinion in the last moment.
(*a*) Yes (*b*) No
(*c*) Sometimes (*d*) No idea

8. Generally I am extrovert and well behaved.
(*a*) Yes (*b*) No
(*c*) Sometimes (*d*) No idea

9. I like to use new technique of work.
(*a*) Yes (*b*) No
(*c*) Sometimes (*d*) No idea

10. When someone considers you wrong then:
(*a*) you do not react
(*b*) you consider him/her wrong
(*c*) you try to ward off the misunderstanding on proper occasion.
(*d*) you pick a fight

11. The secret of my success is:
(*a*) hard labour (*b*) awakening in night
(*c*) gossiping (*d*) luck

12. If you are a female and you are talking with a male:
(*a*) You hide your age
(*b*) You are afraid
(*c*) You talk without hesitation
(*d*) You avoid talks

13. I do like rules and regulations.
(*a*) Yes (*b*) No
(*c*) Sometimes (*d*) No idea

14. Excellent ideas come to my mind:
(*a*) while working alone
(*b*) while working in a group
(*c*) while in sleep
(*d*) while in bathroom

15. Whenever my little baby cries loudly, then I
(*a*) beat him/her
(*b*) feed milk to him/her
(*c*) make him/her sleep
(*d*) ask my husband to handle him/her

16. When I see a mad person, I :
(*a*) approach towards him/her
(*b*) maintain distance from him/her
(*c*) throw stone at him/her
(*d*) start laughing at him/her

17. While driving my car I offer lift to people who ask for lift.
(*a*) Always (*b*) Sometimes
(*c*) Never (*d*) If she is a girl

18. When someone tries to convince you then:
(*a*) You get convinced
(*b*) You do not get convinced
(*c*) You hear him/her passionately
(*d*) You turn a deaf ear

19. Whenever someone knocks on my closed door then firstly I
(*a*) open the door
(*b*) peep through the lens fitted in the door
(*c*) do not open the door
(*d*) yell at him/her

20. I speak to others about my expectation and dreams.
(*a*) Rarely (*b*) Often
(*c*) Sometimes (*d*) Never

21. Any dispute can be solved by :
(*a*) quarrelling (*b*) court
(*c*) dialogue (*d*) money

22. When I do any foolish work then :
(*a*) I feel ashamed (*b*) I feel proud of myself
(*c*) Nothing happens (*d*) I weep

23. If I were correspondent of any newspaper then I would write on the following subject :
(*a*) Cinema and theatre
(*b*) Political events
(*c*) Sports
(*d*) Stock market

24. If I were not human being then :
(*a*) I wish to be a bird (*b*) I wish to be a horse
(*c*) I wish to be God (*d*) Can't say

25. Suppose, you have worn a new shirt and your friend passed a comment that it is not looking good on you. You :
(*a*) will change the shirt immediately
(*b*) will take it lightly as it is your style
(*c*) will not change the shirt but feel offended
(*d*) will start quarrelling

26. I wish to live alone always.
(*a*) Yes (*b*) No
(*c*) Sometimes (*d*) Never

27. I want to spend my spare (extra) time :
(*a*) in reading interesting books
(*b*) in reading comics
(*c*) in viewing films
(*d*) in gossiping

28. Before doing any work I ask myself 'Is it appropriate'?
(*a*) Yes (*b*) No
(*c*) Sometimes (*d*) Never

29. If I see the GOD, I will ask for
(*a*) huge wealth (*b*) honesty
(*c*) love (*d*) heaven

30. People call you selfish.
(*a*) Always (*b*) Sometimes
(*c*) Never (*d*) No idea

31. While talking to friends I do not like to express my very personal matters.
(*a*) Yes (*b*) No
(*c*) Sometimes (*d*) Never

32. Consultation with others helps me to take a decision.
(*a*) Yes (*b*) No
(*c*) Sometimes (*d*) Never

33. After failure:
(*a*) One repents
(*b*) One tries again to succeed
(*c*) Nothing special is happened
(*d*) Nothing in life remains

34. I want to be convinced by arguments.
(*a*) Yes (*b*) No
(*c*) Sometimes (*d*) Never

ANSWERS

1	2	3	4	5	6	7	8	9	10
(*c*)	(*b*)	(*b*)	(*b*)	(*a*)	(*b*)	(*b*)	(*a*)	(*a*)	(*c*)
11	**12**	**13**	**14**	**15**	**16**	**17**	**18**	**19**	**20**
(*a*)	(*c*)	(*a*)	(*a*)	(*b*)	(*b*)	(*b*)	(*a*)	(*b*)	(*a*)
21	**22**	**23**	**24**	**25**	**26**	**27**	**28**	**29**	**30**
(*c*)	(*a*)	(*c*)	(*a*)	(*b*)	(*c*)	(*a*)	(*a*)	(*c*)	(*c*)
31	**32**	**33**	**34**						
(*c*)	(*a*)	(*b*)	(*a*)						

CHAPTER 17

Critical Thinking

In this type of reasoning, a statement is given and assumptions are drawn from it. An assumption is something assumed, supposed and taken for granted. The implicity of the two assumptions is in question. The implication means the hidden meaning, something which is derived from and as such based upon the statement.

MULTIPLE CHOICE QUESTIONS

Directions (Qs. 1 to 6): *In each question below are given two statements followed by two conclusions numbered I and II. You have to take the two given statements to be true even if they seem to be at variance from commonly known facts and then decide which of the given conclusions logically follows from the two given statements, disregarding commonly known facts. Read both the statements and—*

Give answer (a) if only conclusion I follows; give answer (b) if only conclusion II follows; give answer (c) if either I or II follows; give answer (d) if neither I nor II follows and give answer (e) if both I and II follows.

1. *Statements* *I:* All tomatoes are red.
II: All grapes are tomatoes.
Conclusions *I:* All grapes are red.
II: Some tomatoes are grapes.

2. *Statements* *I:* All painters are smilling.
II: Some authors are painters.
Conclusions *I:* All smiling authors are painters.
II: Some authors are smiling.

3. *Statements* *I:* All peons in this office are efficient.
II: Ramu is not efficient.
Conclusions *I:* Ramu is not peon in this office.
II: Ramu should be more efficient.

4. *Statements* *I:* All weavers are hard working.
II: No hard working men are foolish.
Conclusions *I:* No weavers are foolish.
II: Some foolish are weavers.

5. *Statements* *I:* All fishes are cars.
II: All cars are vegetables.
Conclusions *I:* Some vegetables are cars.
II: Some vegetables are fishes.

6. *Statements* *I:* Some dogs are pups.
II: All horses are pups.

Directions (Qs. 7 to 10): *In each question below is given a statement followed by three assumptions number I, II and III. An assumption is something supposed or taken for granted. You have to consider the statement along with the assumptions and decide which of the assumptions is implicit in the statement. Then decide which of the alternatives is the correct answer.*

7. *Statement :*
"Use Riya Cold Cream for fair complexion"—an advertisement.
Assumptions :
I. People like to use cream for fair complexion.
II. People are easily fooled.
III. People respond to advertisements.
(*a*) Only I is implicit.
(*b*) Only II is implicit.
(*c*) Only I and III are implicit.
(*d*) Only I and II are implicit.
(*e*) All are implicit.

8. *Statement :*
"Slogans against smoking in office should be put on the notice board"—an employee in an office suggests.
Assumptions :
I. The employee felt that his suggestion will be considered.
II. People smoke in the office.
III. Some people will stop smoking after reading the slogans.
(*a*) Only I is implicit.
(*b*) Only I and II are implicit.
(*c*) Only II and III are implicit.

(*d*) None is implicit.
(*e*) All are implicit.

9. *Statement :*
"I want to present him a book on techniques of yoga on his birthday"—A tells B.
Assumptions :
I. A and B will be invited for the birthday celebrations.
II. The person to whom the book is to be presented, is not keeping good health.
III. Book is the best gift for birthdays.
(*a*) Only I and II are implicit.
(*b*) Only II and III are implicit.
(*c*) Only I and III are implicit.
(*d*) None is implicit.
(*e*) All are implicit

10. *Statement :*
Keeping in view the financial constraint, the management institution has decided to charge at the time of providing employment in various organisations, a placement fee of ₹ 25000 from the organisation in which the student will be provided the employment.
Assumptions :
I. It will help in increasing the demand of the students belonging to the management institution.
II. The amount collected in this way will be purposeful.
III. It may be possible that the organisation providing employment may select less number of students in future.
(*a*) None follows.
(*b*) Only II and III follow.
(*c*) Only I follows.
(*d*) Only I and II follow.
(*e*) None of these

EXPLANATORY ANSWERS

1. (*e*) : When all tomatoes are red and all grapes are tomatoes, then all grapes are also red. When all grapes are tomatoes, then some tomatoes must be grapes. Therefore, both conclusions I and II are correct.

2. (*b*) : When all painters are smiling and some authors are painters, then some authors are smiling. Therefore. only conclusion II is correct.

3. (*a*) : When all the peons of the office are efficient, then Ramu cannot be a peon in this office. Therefore, only conclusion I is correct.

4. (*a*) : When all weavers are hardworking and no hardworking men are foolish, then no weavers are foolish. Therefore, only conclusion I is correct.

5. (*e*) : When all fishes are cars and all cars are vegetables, then all fishes will naturally be vegetables. This means that some vegetables are fishes. And when all cars are vegetables, then some vegetables will be cars naturally. Therefore, both the conclusions I and II are correct.

6. (*d*) : No relationship can be established between the two statements. Therefore, neither conclusion I nor conclusion II is correct.

7. (*c*) : The advertisement itself denotes that people like to use cream for fair complexion and they do respond to advertisements. Advertisements are for awareness of the product not for fooling people.

8. (*e*) : Suggestion for putting up the notice is made because some people must be smoking in office. Notice board is read by people in office and some may stop smoking after reading the slogans.

9. (*c*) : According to A presents are best gifts for birthdays and when A has bought the book he expects to be invited for the birthday celebration. Nothing is mentioned about health of the birthday person.

10. (*b*) : The amount collected will lessen the financial constraint and there is every possibility for selecting less number of students because of the fee charged.

CHAPTER 18

Emotional Intelligence

Emotional intelligence (EI) refers to the ability to perceive, control, and evaluate emotions. Emotional intelligence (EI) is the area of cognitive ability involving traits and social skills that facilitate interpersonal behaviour. Intelligence can be broadly defined as the capacity for goal-oriented adaptive behaviour; emotional intelligence focuses on the aspects of intelligence that govern self-knowledge and social adaptation.

Emotional Intelligence that is also called Emotional Intelligence Quotient or (EQ) narrates the capability, capacity, or deftness to understand. It evaluates and manages one's emotions.

MULTIPLE CHOICE QUESTIONS

Directions: *Answer the following questions by selecting the appropriate option.*

1. In my group of friends, I am generally aware of how each person feels about the other people in our social circle.
(*a*) Strongly Agree (*b*) Agree
(*c*) Disagree (*d*) Strongly Disagree

2. When I am upset, I can usually pinpoint exactly why I am distressed.
(*a*) Strongly Agree (*b*) Agree
(*c*) Disagree (*d*) Strongly Disagree

3. While there are some things that I would like to change, I generally like who I am.
(*a*) Strongly Agree (*b*) Agree
(*c*) Disagree (*d*) Strongly Disagree

4. When I make mistakes, I often berate and criticize myself and my abilities.
(*a*) Often (*b*) Sometimes
(*c*) Rarely (*d*) Almost Never

5. I feel uncomfortable in emotionally charged situations.
(*a*) Strongly Agree (*b*) Agree
(*c*) Disagree (*d*) Strongly Disagree

6. I tend to avoid confrontations. When I am involved in a confrontation, I become extremely anxious.
(*a*) Strongly Agree (*b*) Agree
(*c*) Disagree (*d*) Strongly Disagree

7. I am generally aloof and detached until I really get to know a person.
(*a*) Strongly Agree (*b*) Agree
(*c*) Disagree (*d*) Strongly Disagree

8. I tend to overreact to minor problems.
(*a*) Often (*b*) Sometimes
(*c*) Rarely (*d*) Almost Never

9. I feel confident about my own skills, talents, and abilities.
(*a*) Strongly Agree (*b*) Agree
(*c*) Disagree (*d*) Strongly Disagree

10. I would describe myself as a good judge of character.
(*a*) Strongly Agree (*b*) Agree
(*c*) Disagree (*d*) Strongly Disagree

11. When I am facing an unpleasant task, I tend to:
(*a*) Make a plan and work on it a little each day
(*b*) Get it over with as soon as possible
(*c*) Put it off until the last minute
(*d*) Don't do it at all

12. During a heated argument, I am more likely to:
(*a*) Stop the fight and agree to a short break before resuming the discussion.
(*b*) Shut down and stop responding to the other person.
(*c*) Give in and apologize in order to quickly end the argument.
(*d*) Start insulting the other person.

13. When making an important decision, I tend to:
(*a*) Follow my instincts
(*b*) Rely on direction from other people
(*c*) Go with the easiest option
(*d*) Guess randomly

14. Which of the following statements best describes you?
(*a*) I have an easy time making friends and getting to know new people.
(*b*) I get along well with others, but I have to really get to know someone before they become a true friend.
(*c*) I find it difficult to meet people and make friends.
(*d*) I cannot make friends.

15. You have invested a lot of time and energy into a project for one of your classes. While you feel confident about your work, your instructor gives you a C+ on the project. How do you deal with this situation?
(*a*) Decide the class is stupid and stop putting forth your best efforts.
(*b*) Berate and criticize your own work.
(*c*) Confront the instructor and ask for a better grade.
(*d*) Think about ways you could improve the project and apply these ideas to future schoolwork.

16. One of your best friends has suffered a miscarriage. How do you respond?
(*a*) Allow your friend to express her feelings and offer your support.
(*b*) Spend time with her, but avoid talking about her loss.
(*c*) Convince her to go out with some friends to get her mind off it.
(*d*) Give her some time to herself.

17. One of your co-workers has a habit that annoys you. The problem seems to be getting worse each day. How do you respond?
(*a*) Tell your co-worker what is bothering you.
(*b*) Make a complaint about the behaviour to your supervisor.
(*c*) Talk about your co-worker behind his back.
(*d*) Suffer in silence.

18. You've been feeling stressed out at work and haven't finished projects as quickly as you should. When your boss suddenly assigns you another large project, how do you feel?
(*a*) Anxious about getting all the work done.
(*b*) Overwhelmed by the task before you.
(*c*) Angry that your boss hasn't noticed how overworked you are.
(*d*) Depressed and sure that you can never finish it all.

19. If I am scheduled to meet a loved one at a certain time and that person is late, I get worried and eventually start to panic:
(*a*) Frequently (*b*) Sometimes
(*c*) Rarely (*d*) Never

20. Others do not want to spend time with me in public because my behaviour embarrasses them.
(*a*) Frequently (*b*) Sometimes
(*c*) Rarely (*d*) Never

21. I prevent being in situations where I need to show compassion and affection because I feel uncomfortable comforting others.
(*a*) Frequently (*b*) Sometimes
(*c*) Rarely (*d*) Never

22. When I am angry, I do not care about what I say or do and end up saying and doing things I regret later and need to apologize for.
(*a*) Frequently (*b*) Sometimes
(*c*) Rarely (*d*) Never

23. I feel frequently depressed and unhappy without really knowing why.
(*a*) Frequently (*b*) Sometimes
(*c*) Rarely (*d*) Never

24. If others point out my mistakes or give me negative feedback about myself, I feel ashamed, embarrassed and then become offensive and angry.
(*a*) Frequently (*b*) Sometimes
(*c*) Rarely (*d*) Never

25. Crying makes me feel better so I frequently cry when I am angry, ashamed, or embarrassed.
(*a*) Frequently (*b*) Sometimes
(*c*) Rarely (*d*) Never

ANSWERS

1	2	3	4	5	6	7	8	9	10
(*b*)	(*b*)	(*a*)	(*b*)	(*d*)	(*d*)	(*c*)	(*d*)	(*a*)	(*b*)
11	**12**	**13**	**14**	**15**	**16**	**17**	**18**	**19**	**20**
(*a*)	(*a*)	(*a*)	(*a*)	(*d*)	(*a*)	(*a*)	(*a*)	(*c*)	(*d*)
21	**22**	**23**	**24**	**25**					
(*d*)	(*d*)	(*d*)	(*d*)	(*d*)					

CHAPTER 19

Social Intelligence

Questions on social intelligence are asked to assess the common sense of the candidate in various social situations.

MULTIPLE CHOICE QUESTIONS

Directions : *Each of the following questions is followed by four alternatives. Select the most appropriate answer.*

1. In the examination hall, you find that your question paper is too tough to be answered satisfactorily by you. The best thing you can do is:
(*a*) try cheating from your neighbouring candidate.
(*b*) leave the paper and walk out.
(*c*) try attempting those questions first of which you know something.
(*d*) complain to the examiner about the toughness of the question paper.

2. Your best friend is annoyed with you for certain reasons. You will :
(*a*) try your best to reason out your friend's annoyance.
(*b*) go out and make new friends.
(*c*) show indifference.
(*d*) remind the friend of your good friendship.

3. You were invited to a party, but on the day of the party you are informed that the party has been cancelled. You will :
(*a*) try to find out the reason for its cancellation.
(*b*) decide that you will never go to that place ever again.
(*c*) not discuss the matter with anyone.
(*d*) hold the party at your place instead.

4. You find that the cooking gas cylinder is leaking. The first thing you would do is :
(*a*) switch off the light.
(*b*) close the knob of the cylinder.
(*c*) call the fire brigade for help.
(*d*) alert all the members at home.

5. While returning home from a far away place you find that your pocket has been picked. You will :
(*a*) try to hitch-hike to home.
(*b*) hire a taxi and pay on reaching home.
(*c*) go to the nearest police station and lodge an FIR.
(*d*) call home and ask someone to pick you from the place you made the phone call.

6. Your friend has not invited you to his marriage party, you will :
(*a*) ignore the whole affair.
(*b*) send him your best wishes.
(*c*) attend the ceremony.
(*d*) hold it against him.

7. You are interviewed for a new job. Which of the following questions is most important to you?
(*a*) Remuneration you will be paid.
(*b*) Opportunities for promotion.
(*c*) Scope to develop your ideas and use them to improve the working of the organisation.
(*d*) All the above are equally important.

8. You are walking down the street and suddenly you see two hundred-rupee notes on the pavement. What action will you take?
(*a*) Give the money to beggar.
(*b*) Pocket it yourself.
(*c*) Deposit it in the nearest police station.
(*d*) Leave it as it is.

ANSWERS

1	2	3	4	5	6	7	8
(*c*)	(*a*)	(*a*)	(*b*)	(*b*)	(*b*)	(*d*)	(*c*)

INDEXING ADDRESS MATCHING

Directions : *In each question below a combination of name and address is given in the first column at the left, followed by four such combinations, one each under the columns (a), (b), (c) and (d). You have to find out the combination which is exactly the same as the combination in the first column. The number of that column which contains that combination is the answer. If all the combinations are different, the answer is '(e)'.*

1. Triveni Atma
Opp Lal Banglow
Varanasi -221002

(*a*) Triveni Atma
Opp Lal Bangalow
Varanasi -221002

(*b*) Triveni Atma
Opp Lal Banglow
Varanasi -220012

(*c*) Triveni Atma
Opp Lal Banglow
Varanasi -221002

(*d*) Triveni Athma
Opp Lal Banglow
Varanasi -221002

2. Tara Lal Appa
Javagal street
Calicat 673005

(*a*) Tara Lal Appa
Javagal Street
Calicat 673005

(*b*) Tara Lal Appa
Javagal street
Calicut 673005

(*c*) Tara Lal Appa
Javagal street
Calicat 670035

(*d*) Tara Lal Appa
Javagal streat
Calicat 673005

3. Iqbal Rehman
Bhandri Gali
Post Box No -3097

(*a*) Iqbal Rehman
Bhandri Ghali
Post Box No -3097

(*b*) Iqbal Rehman
Bhandri Gali
Post Box No -3097

(*c*) Iqbal Rehman
Bhandri Gali
Post Box no -3097

(*d*) Iqbal Rahman
Bhandri Gali
Post Box No -3097

4. Jaganpa Shinde
Christ phot co.
Tel no -27363

(*a*) Jaganpa Shinde
Christ photo co.
Tel no -27363

(*b*) Jaganpa Shinde
Christ phot co.
Tel no -27363

(*c*) Jaganpa Shinde
Christ phot co.
Tel no -273633

(*d*) Jaganna Shinde
Christ phot co.
Tel no -27363

5. N.R. Savitri
Giri Girls hostal
Anapuram-167951

(*a*) N.R. Savitri
Giri Girls hostal
Anapuram-167951

(*b*) N.R. Savitri
Giri Girls hostel
Anapuram-167951

(*c*) N.R. Savitri
Giri Girls hostal
Anapuram-167851

(*d*) N.R. Savithri
Giri Girls hostal
Anapuram-167951

6. Madam Brulopher
Jung villa
Banjaram Hills

(*a*) Madam Bruloper
Jung villa
Banjaram Hills

(*b*) Madam Brulopher
Jung villa
Banjaram Hill

(*c*) Madam Brulopher
Jung Villa
Banjaram Hills

(*d*) Madam Brulopher
Jung villa
Banjaram Hills

7. Samartha sen
C 20/05 Guftga Bldg
B. No. - 1631

(*a*) Samartha sen
C 20/05 Guftga Blg
B. No. - 1631

(*b*) Samartha sen
C 200 Guftga Bldg
B. No. - 1631

(*c*) Samartha sen
C 20/05 Guftga Bldg
B. No. - 1631

(*d*) Samartha sen
C 20/05 Guflga Bldg
B. No. - 1631

8. Phiroz Gherabl
Harmit palace
Samaita nagar

(*a*) Phiroz Gerabi
Harmit palace
Samaita nagar

(*b*) Phiroz Gerabl
Harmit place
Samaita nagar

(*c*) Phiroz Gerabl
Harmit palace
Samaita nager

(*d*) Phiroz Gherabl
Harmit palace
Samaita nagar

9. Nitu gajadhar
Shersing Haveli
Jaipur -302006

(*a*) Nitu gajadhar
Shersing Haveli
Jaipur -302006

(*b*) Nitu gajadar
Shersing Haveli
Jaipur -302006

(*c*) Nitu gajadhar
Shersing Haveli
Jaipur -303006

(*d*) Nitu Gajadhar
Shersing Haveli
Jaipur -302006

ANSWERS

1	2	3	4	5	6	7	8	9
(*c*)	(*a*)	(*b*)	(*b*)	(*a*)	(*d*)	(*c*)	(*d*)	(*a*)

CHAPTER 20

Venn Diagrams

In these type of questions diagrammatic representation presents a logical illustration of particular class or statements based on which the questions are asked. A clear view of the diagram makes the concept clear for attempting such questions.

SOLVED EXAMPLE

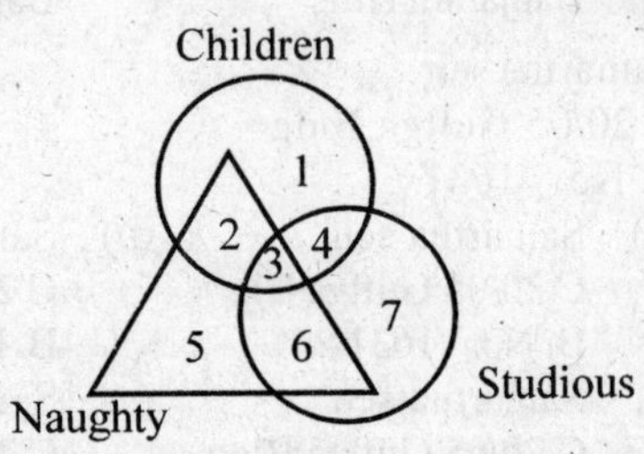

Study the above diagram and specify the region representing children who are naughty as well as studious.

(*a*) 3 and 6 (*b*) 2 and 4
(*c*) only 3 (*d*) only 4

Ans. (*c*) : The explanation depicting children who are naughty as well as studious will be :

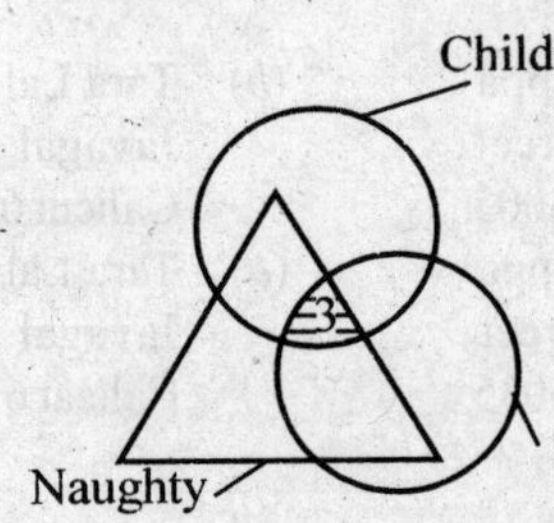

It is now clear that only region 3 represents all the three classes.

MULTIPLE CHOICE QUESTIONS

Directions (Qs. 1–3) : *In the following diagram, there are three figures interlocking each other – a rectangle, a square and a triangle. Each figure represents the class mentioned against it.*

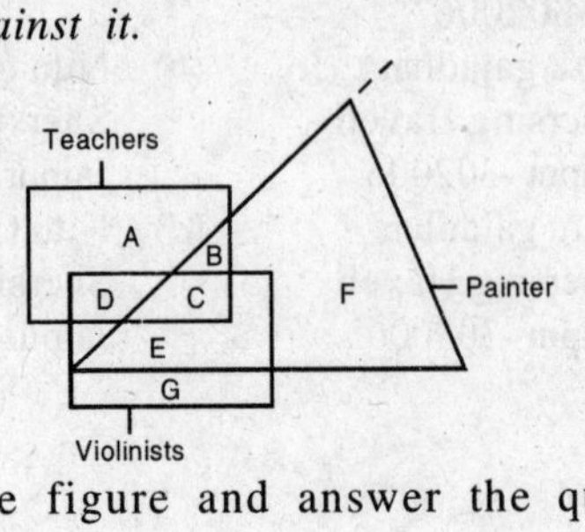

Study the figure and answer the questions that follows.

1. Teachers who are painters but not violinists are represented by

(*a*) B (*b*) C
(*c*) D (*d*) F

2. The region which represents painters and violinists but not teachers, is denoted by

(*a*) B (*b*) D
(*c*) E (*d*) F

3. Which letter represents teachers who are painters as well as violinists?

(*a*) B (*b*) C
(*c*) D (*d*) E

Directions (Qs. 4–6) : *In the figure given below, there are three interesting circles each representing certain section of people. Different regions are marked a-g. Read the statements in each of the following questions and choose the letter of the region which correctly represents the statements?*

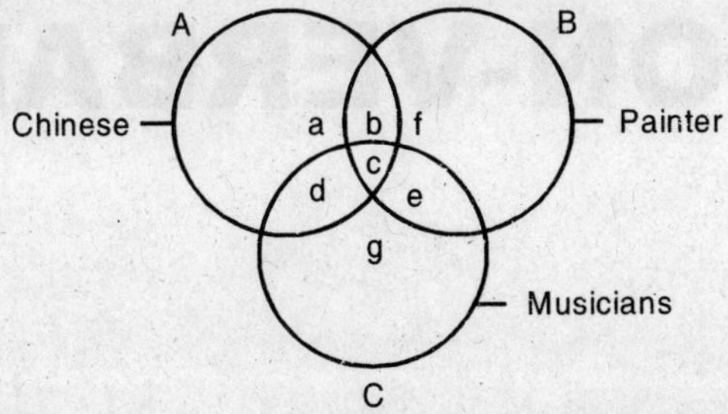

4. Chinese who are painters but not musicians?
(*a*) b (*b*) c
(*c*) d (*d*) g

5. Chinese who are musicians but not painters.
(*a*) d (*b*) c
(*c*) b (*d*) a

6. Painters who are neither Chinese nor musicians.
(*a*) b (*b*) c
(*c*) f (*d*) g

Directions (Qs. 7–10) : *In the following figure, the circle stands for employed, the square stands for hard-working, the triangle stands for rural and the rectangle stands for intelligent. Study the figure carefully and answer the questions that follow.*

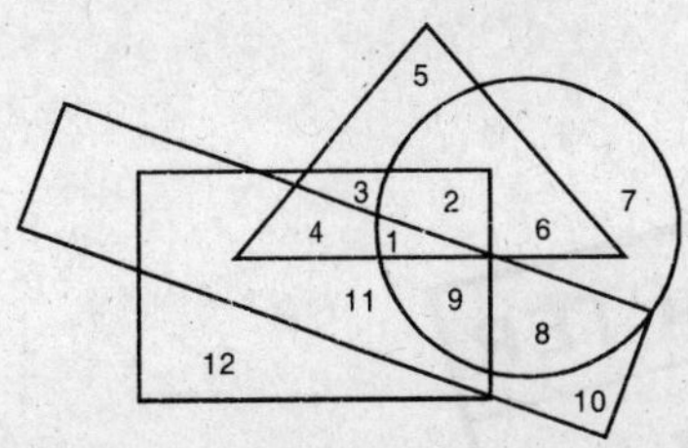

7. Rural employed people who are neither intelligent nor hard-working are indicated by region.
(*a*) 10 (*b*) 9
(*c*) 6 (*d*) 4

8. Unemployed rural hard-working and intelligent people are indicated by region.
(*a*) 1 (*b*) 2
(*c*) 3 (*d*) 4

9. Rural people who are hard-working and employed but not intelligent are indicated by region.
(*a*) 1 (*b*) 2
(*c*) 3 (*d*) 4

10. Rural employed people who are neither intelligent nor hard-working are indicated by region.
(*a*) 2 (*b*) 4
(*c*) 6 (*d*) 9

EXPLANATORY ANSWERS

1. (*a*) : The persons satisfying the given conditions are represented by the region which is common to the rectangle and the triangle but not the square *i.e.*, B.

2. (*c*) : The persons satisfying the given conditions are represented by the region which is common to the triangle and the square but is not a part of the rectangle *i.e.*, E.

3. (*b*) : The required set of persons is represented by the letter denoting the region common to the rectangle, triangle and the square *i.e.*, C.

4. (*a*) : The required region is the one which is common to the circles A and B and lies outside circle C *i.e.*, b.

5. (*a*) : The required region is the one which is common to the circles A and C but is not a part of circle B *i.e.*, d.

6. (*c*) : The required region is the one which lies inside the circle B but is not a part of either circle A or circle C *i.e.*, f.

7. (*c*) : The required set of people is represented by the region which is common to the triangle and circle but is not a part of either the rectangle or the square *i.e.*, 6.

8. (*d*) : The required set of people is represented by the region which lies outside the circle and is common to the triangle, square and rectangle *i.e.*, 4.

9. (*b*) : The required set of people is represented by the region which is common to the triangle, square and circle but is not a part of the rectangle *i.e.*, 2.

10. (*c*) : The required set of people is denoted by the region which is common to the triangle and the circle but is not a part of the rectangle *i.e.*, 2.

NON-VERBAL

CHAPTER 1

Series/Figural Series

MISSING SERIES

This form of series is almost identical to the one mentioned earlier. Here too are given two sets of figures, the Problem Figures and the Answer Figures. The problem figures follow a particular pattern of movement which constitute the series. The only difference from the earlier mentioned set of series is that instead of depicting the last figure that continues the pattern here one of the middle figures needs to be depicted from-the answer figures. This type needs a little more concentration and brain work as the continuity is broken and has to be set right. Understand the set up of elements, pattern and figures in each set and try different styles and rules to find the answer.

MULTIPLE CHOICE QUESTIONS

Directions : *In each of these questions, there are two sets of figures. The figures placed first are Problem Figures, and those follows are Answer Figures indicated by the letters (a), (b), (c), (d) and (e). A series is established if one of the five Answer Figures is placed at the question-marked space. Figures form a series if they change from left to right according to some specific rule. The letter of the Answer Figure which should be placed in the question-marked space is the answer. All the figures, i.e. three Problem Figures and one Answer Figure placed in the question-marked space should be considered as forming the series.*

1. Problem Figures

Answer Figures

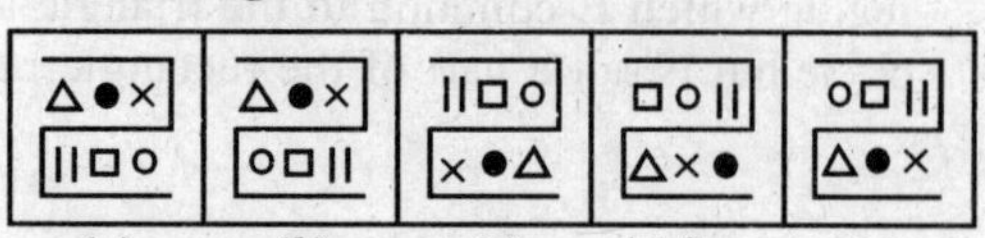

(a) (b) (c) (d) (e)

2. Problem Figures

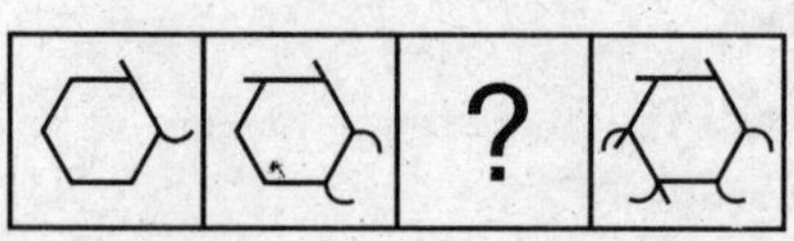

Answer Figures

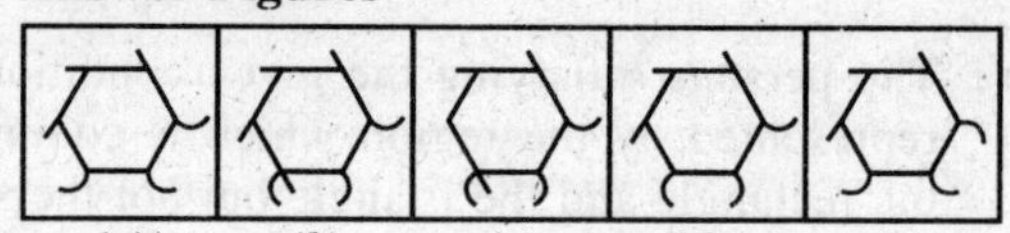

(a) (b) (c) (d) (e)

3. Problem Figures

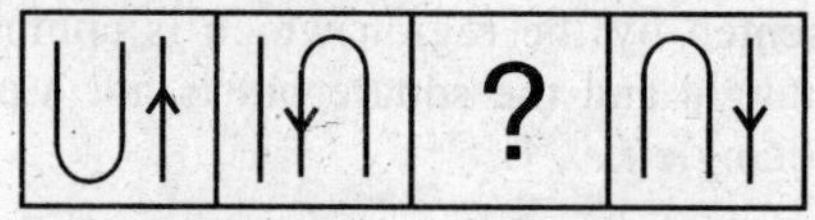

Answer Figures

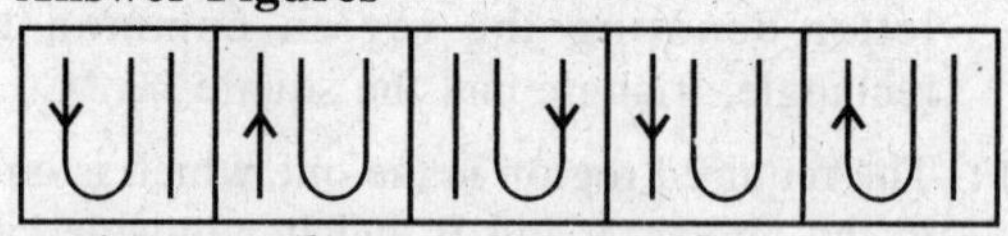

(a) (b) (c) (d) (e)

4. Problem Figures

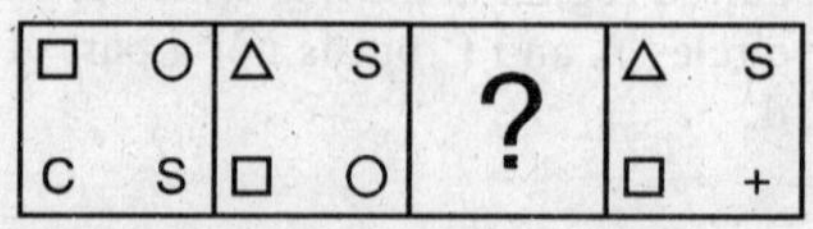

Answer Figures

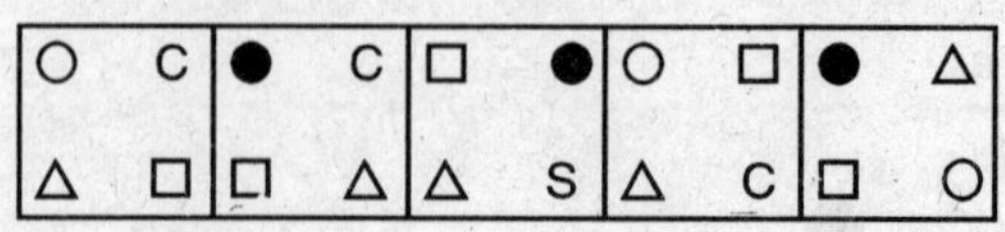

(a) (b) (c) (d) (e)

5. Problem Figures

Answer Figures

(*a*) (*b*) (*c*) (*d*) (*e*)

6. Problem Figures

Answer Figures

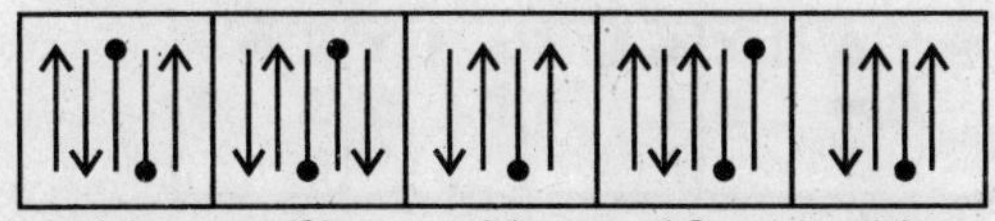

(*a*) (*b*) (*c*) (*d*) (*e*)

EXPLANATORY ANSWERS

1. (*c*) : From first problem figure to the second the elements on the top are shifted down and vice versa. In fourth problem figure there are three elements which, as per rule, are also shifted. So, in question marked space only option '(*c*)' can be considered as forming the series.

2. (*d*) : Anticlockwise one of the sides of the hexagon is extended and clockwise one arc is added. The direction of the arc is changed at each step. Answer figure 'D' is the right answer.

3. (*e*) : Both the elements are turned upside down, their places interchanged and the arrow head moved left from one element to the other. In the question marked space the 'U' shape and the arrowhead should be facing upwards, the line segment should be on the right and the arrowhead should be on the extreme left. To continue the series the next figure has the 'U' shape and the arrowhead facing downwards, the line segment on the right and the arrowhead on the extreme right. Option '(*e*)' fits into the question marked space.

4. (*c*) : At each step the places of two elements on the horizontal are interchanged and clockwise one element is made new. Option '(*c*)' fits in the pattern to complete the series.

5. (*b*) : At each step the enclosed figure is enlarged in the next and a new figure is placed inside the enlarged figure. Option '(*b*)' fits into the question marked space.

6. (*a*) : The arrow and the line with the dot are increased in a set pattern in opposite directions. The series they form is two arrows and two lines with the dot which is repeated. Answer figure '(*a*)' is the right choice.

FIGURAL SERIES

In this form of non-verbal series, which are the most common, four or five consecutive problem figures form a definite sequence and one is required to select the one figure from the given set of Answer Figures that will continue the same sequence.

One has to try different set of moves, changes, replacements, rotations, repetitions and a lot more variations to arrive at the logical pattern making the series. Practising alone will sharpen one's skill of solving such sequences.

MULTIPLE CHOICE QUESTIONS

Directions : *In each of the following questions which one of the five answer figures given below should come after the problem figures if the sequence are continued?*

1. Problem Figures

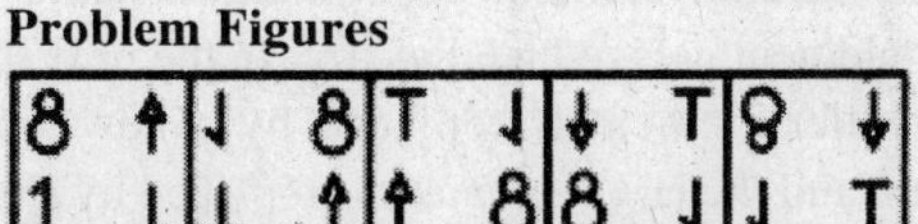

Answer Figures

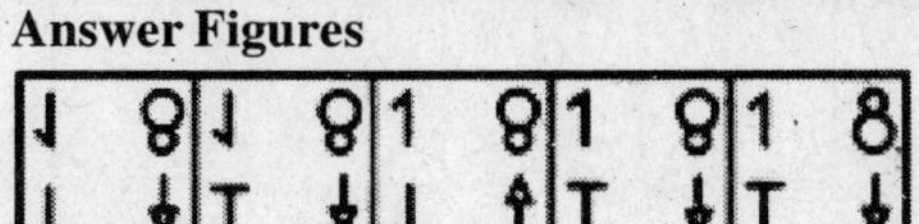

(*a*) (*b*) (*c*) (*d*) (*e*)

2. Problem Figures

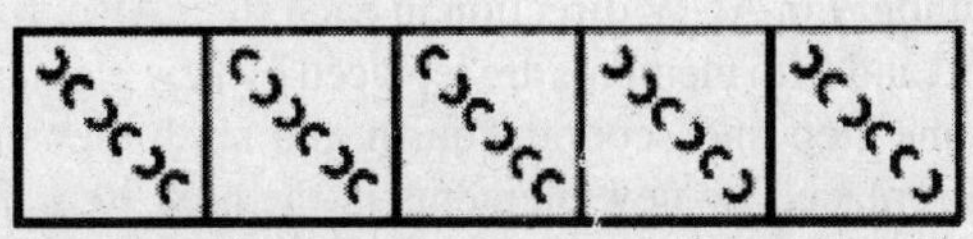

Answer Figures

(*a*) (*b*) (*c*) (*d*) (*e*)

3. Problem Figures

Answer Figures

(a) (b) (c) (d) (e)

4. Problem Figures

Answer Figures

(a) (b) (c) (d) (e)

5. Problem Figures

Answer Figures

(a) (b) (c) (d) (e)

6. Problem Figures

Answer Figures

(a) (b) (c) (d) (e)

7. Problem Figures

Answer Figures

(a) (b) (c) (d) (e)

8. Problem Figures

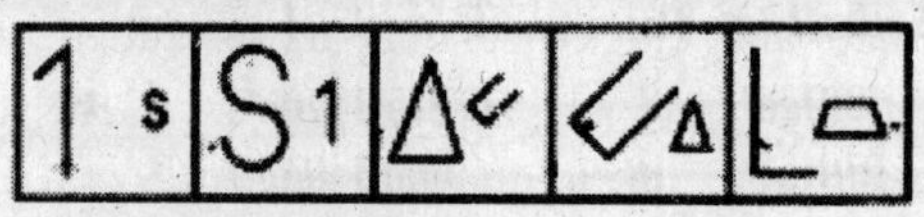

Answer Figures

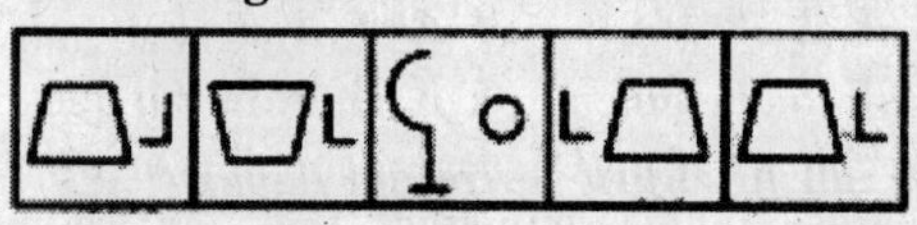

(a) (b) (c) (d) (e)

EXPLANATORY ANSWERS

1. (*d*) : In each step, all the elements move to the adjacent corner (of the square boundary) in a CW direction and the element that reaches the upper-left corner gets vertically inverted.

2. (*c*) : We can label the arcs as shown . The arcs get inverted in the sequence (1 & 2), (3, 4 & 5), (6 & 1), (2, 3 & 4), (5 & 6), ...

3. (*d*) : All the elements move half-a-side of the square boundary in ACW direction in each step. Also, first, third and fifth elements are replaced by new elements in one step and second, fourth and sixth elements are replaced by new elements in the next step. The two steps are repeated alternately.

4. (*a*) : In each step, the dot moves one space CW and the arrow moves two spaces CW.

5. (*c*) : One arc and four arcs get inverted alternately.

6. (*e*) : The number of parts increases by one along with the number of sides in the figure.

7. (*c*) : The pin rotates 45°CW and 90°CW alternately and moves one space (each space is equal to half-a-side of the square) and two spaces CW alternately. The arrow rotates 90°ACW and 45°ACW alternately and moves two spaces and one space.

8. (*e*) : In one step, the two elements interchange positions and the smaller element gets enlarged while the larger element gets reduced in size. In the next step, the smaller element is replaced by a new small element and the larger element is replaced by a new large element.

CHAPTER 2

Semantic Classification

Classification means arranging the given content in groups or classes having qualities of same kind. In classification type questions, the figures or items are sorted out in groups on the basis of their similarities in qualities in shapes, size, pattern, structure, genus, order, species, grade, style, constituents and other specifications, and thus the answer is found out.

TYPE-I

Classification of this type does not have two sets of figures known as Problem Figures and Answer Figures; instead they have only one set of four or five figures known as Problem Figures. One of these Problem Figures is not like the other four figures. In other words, three or four of the Answer Figures belong to a class while one which is the odd figures, does not belong to it.

MULTIPLE CHOICE QUESTIONS

Directions : *In each of the following questions one of the figures is different from the rest. Spot the figure.*

1. 

(a) (b) (c) (d) (e)

2. 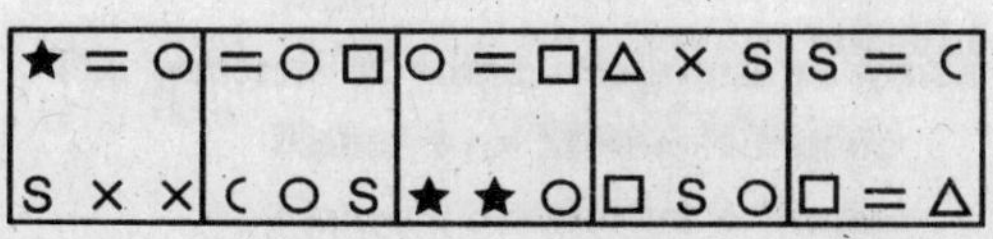

(a) (b) (c) (d) (e)

3. 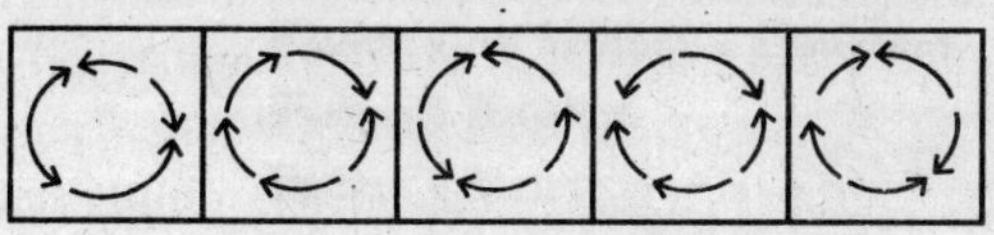

(a) (b) (c) (d) (e)

4. 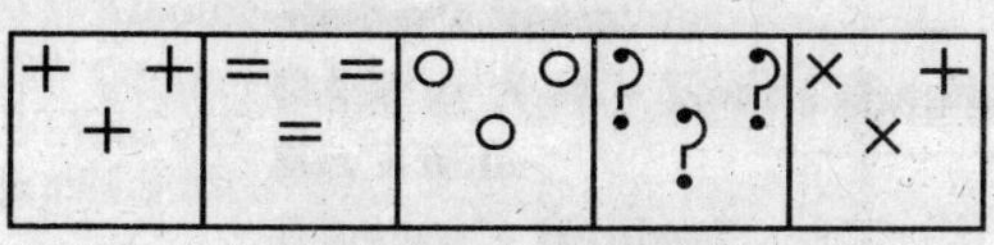

(a) (b) (c) (d) (e)

5. 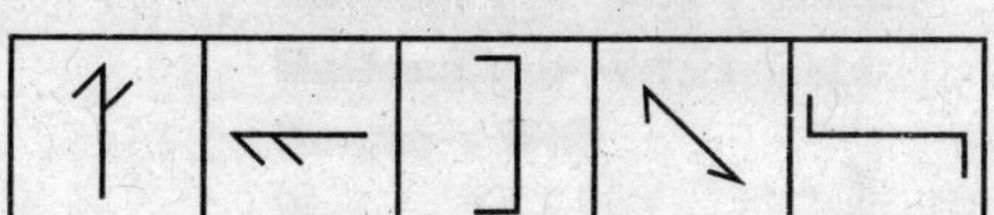

(a) (b) (c) (d) (e)

6. 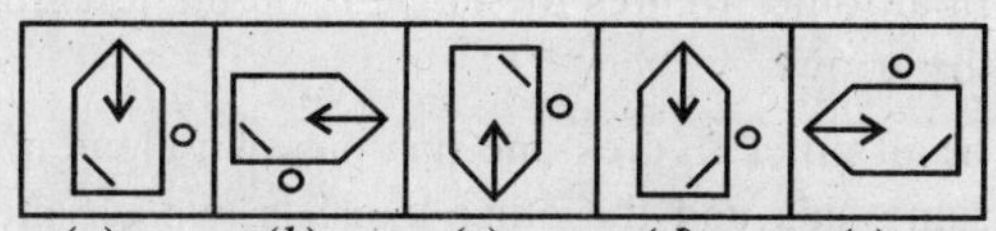

(a) (b) (c) (d) (e)

7. 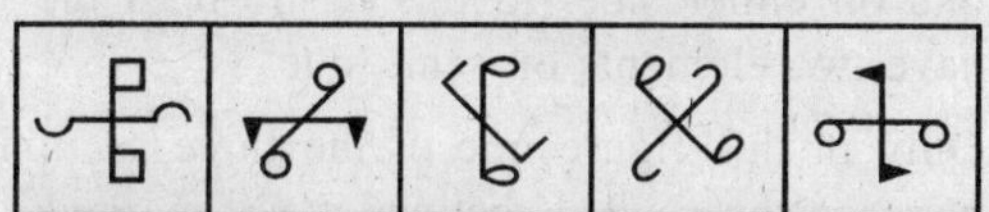

(a) (b) (c) (d) (e)

8. 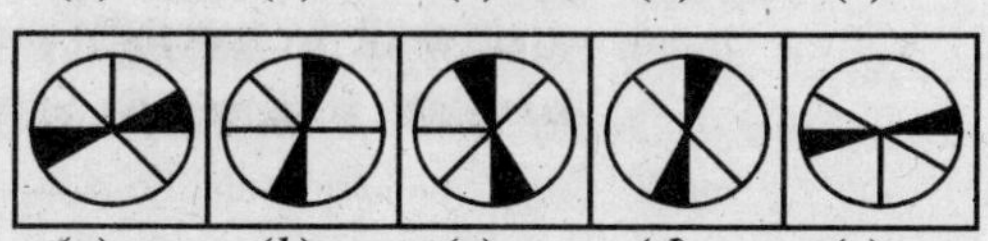

(a) (b) (c) (d) (e)

9. 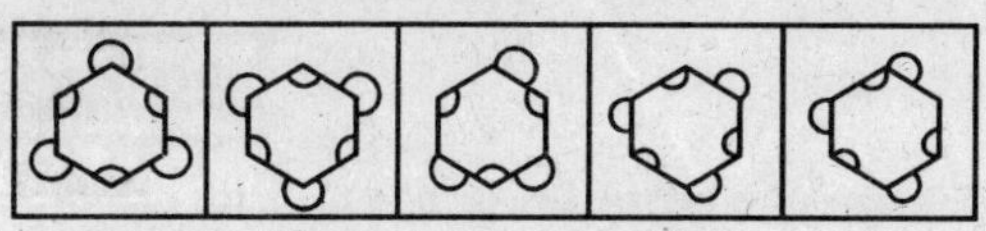

(a) (b) (c) (d) (e)

10. 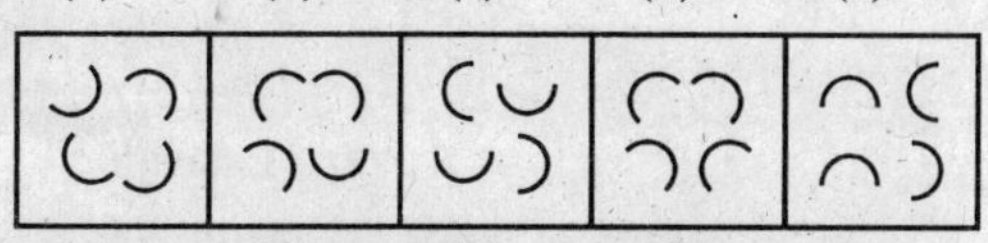

(a) (b) (c) (d) (e)

11. 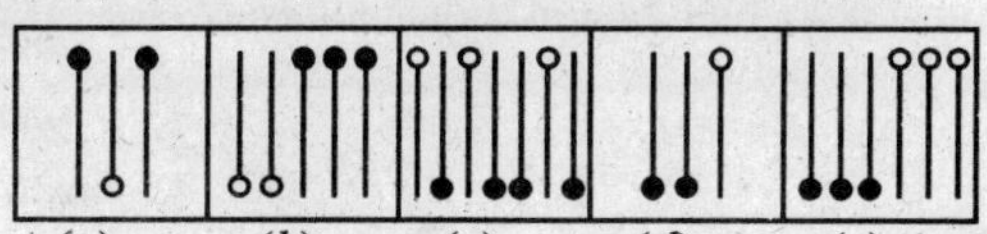

(a) (b) (c) (d) (e)

12. 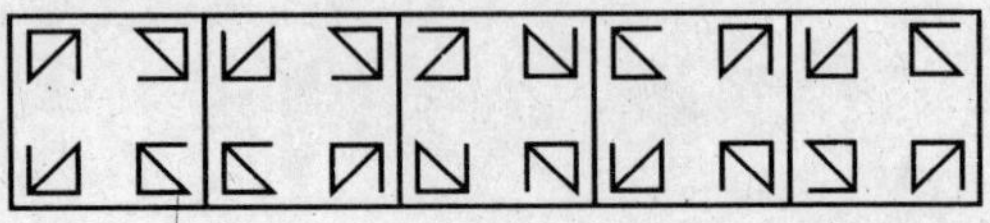

(a) (b) (c) (d) (e)

13. 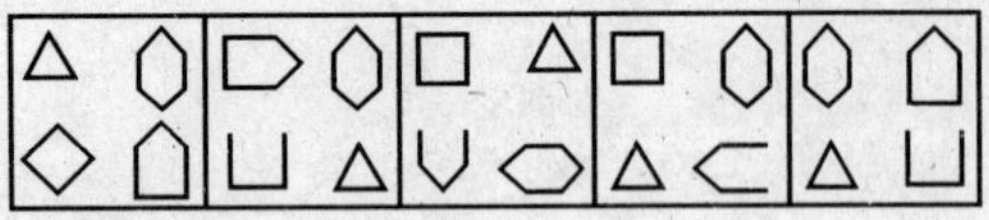

(a) (b) (c) (d) (e)

14. 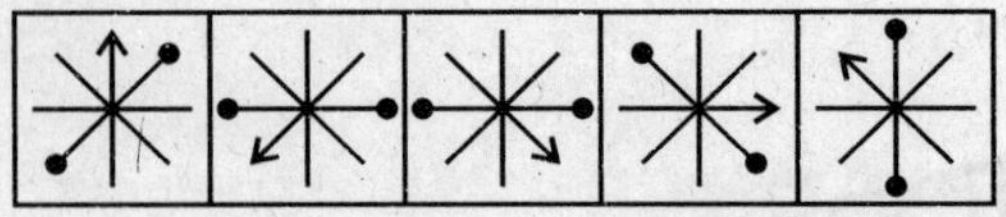

(a) (b) (c) (d) (e)

15. 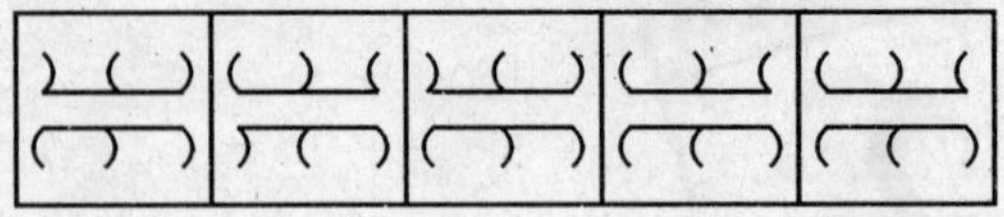

(a) (b) (c) (d) (e)

EXPLANATORY ANSWERS

1. (*d*) : Only in this figure all the lines making the hands and legs of the human shape are drawn downwards.

2. (*c*) : In all other figures only one set of elements is identical.

3. (*b*) : Only in this figure four arrows are pointing in same direction, and one arrow in its opposite direction. In other figures three arrows are in same direction and two in the opposite direction.

4. (*e*) : All other figures have three identical elements.

5. (*d*) : In all other figures two lines are parallelly drawn.

6. (*c*) : In all other figures the circle is on the left side of the arrow.

7. (*c*) : In all other figures one line has two elements on same side and the other line has two ele-ments, one on either side. In this figure both the lines have two elements on same side.

8. (*d*) : Only in this figure one of the three sections in between the shaded sections is not marked.

9. (*e*) : In all other figures the elements inside as well as outside the hexagon are placed at equal distance. In this figure the outside element at the top is wrongly placed (It should be near the other corner of the same line).

10. (*d*) : In all other figures two elements are in same direction and the other two elements are opposite to each other.

11. (*e*) : Only in this figure the two types of elements are equal in number.

12. (*c*) : In all other figures the diagonal line in all other elements is drawn from the right end.

13. (*a*) : In all other figures one of the four elements has one open side.

14. (*c*) : In all other figures the arrow is to the left of the dot.

15. (*b*) : In all other figures two of the three curves on one of the lines are in the same direction and are adjacent.

CHAPTER 3

Figural Analogy

Figural Analogy is a process of reasoning between two parallel cases. It relates to agreement or correspondence in certain respects between two things. It is a process whereby the underlying relationship that exists between two figures, designs or patterns is determined. Under the process, one has to discover the features common to the two figures or designs. This common feature is a model or base. The question seeks solution on the basis of this model or base.

In non-verbal analogy questions, there are two sets of figures which are known as *(i)* Problem Figures, and *(ii)* Answer Figures. The Problem Figures are divided into two parts. The Answer Figures are given below the Problem Figures.

MULTIPLE CHOICE QUESTIONS

Directions ; *The second figure in the first unit of the Problem Figures bears a certain relationship to the first figure. Similarly, one of the figures in the Answer Figures bears the same relationship to the first figure in the second unit of the Problem Figures. Locate the figure which would fit the question mark.*

1. Problem Figures

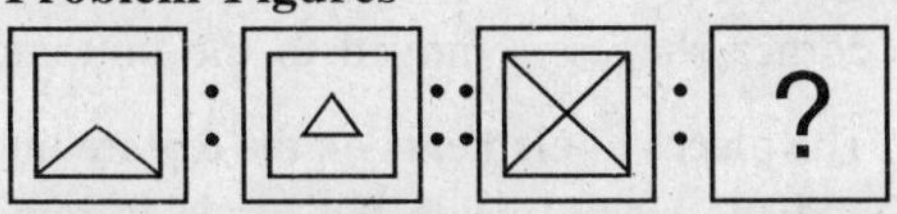

Answers Figures

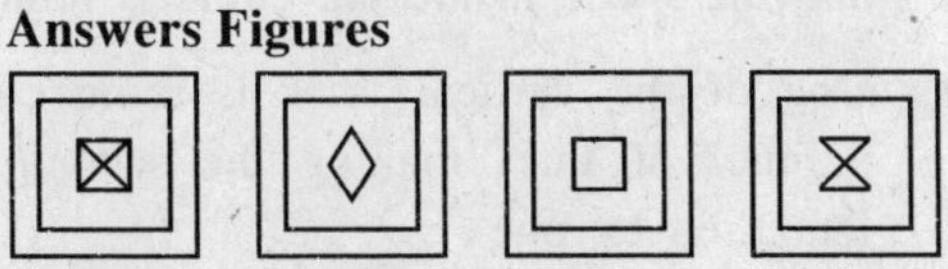

(*a*) (*b*) (*c*) (*d*)

2. Problem Figures

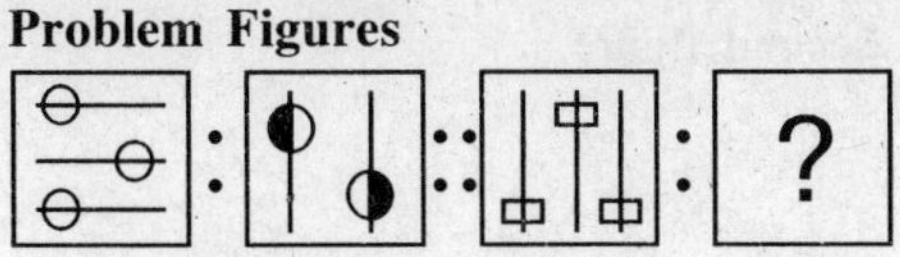

Answer Figures

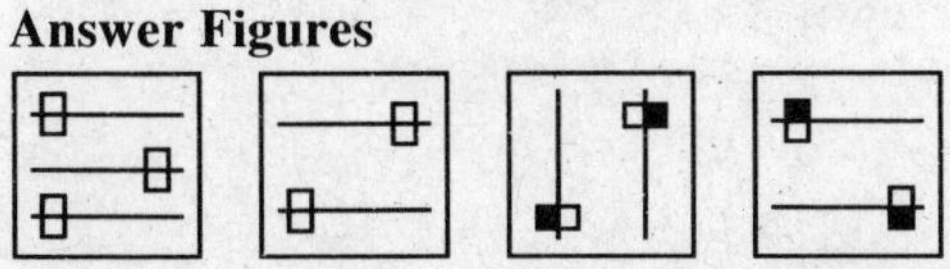

(*a*) (*b*) (*c*) (*d*)

3. Problem Figures

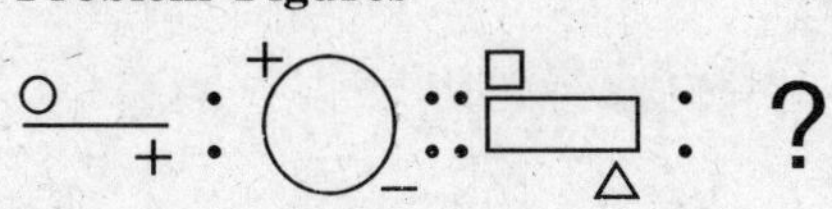

Answer Figures

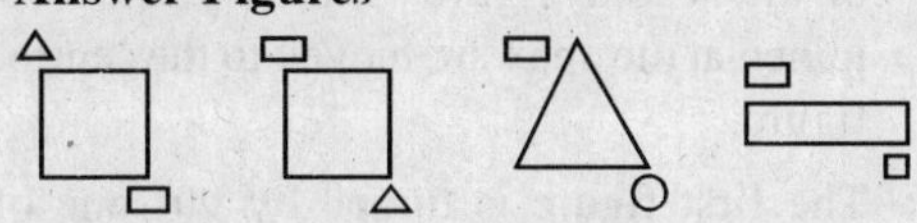

(*a*) (*b*) (*c*) (*d*)

4. Problem Figures

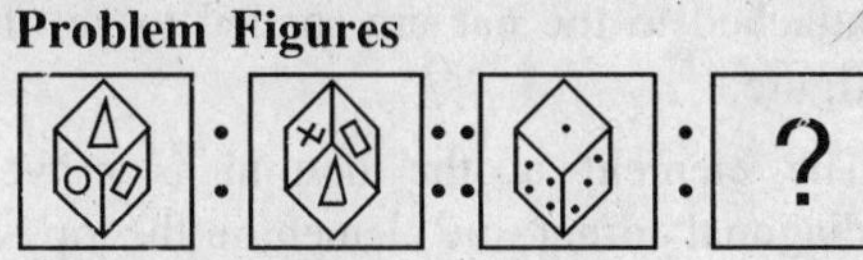

Answer Figures

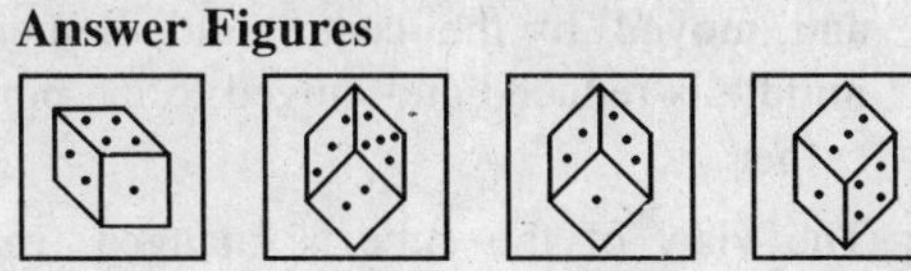

(*a*) (*b*) (*c*) (*d*)

5. Problem Figures

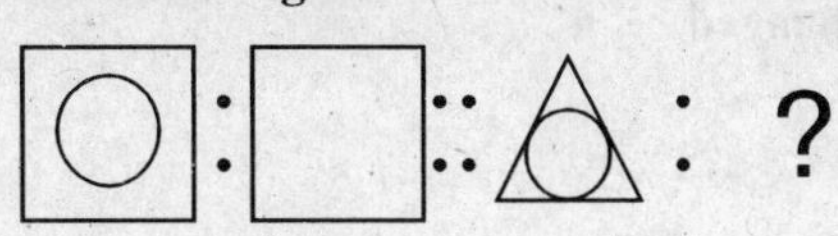

Answer Figures

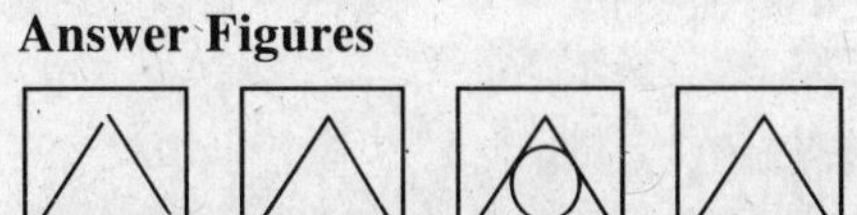

(*a*) (*b*) (*c*) (*d*)

6. Problem Figures

Answer Figures

(*a*) (*b*) (*c*) (*d*)

7. Problem Figures

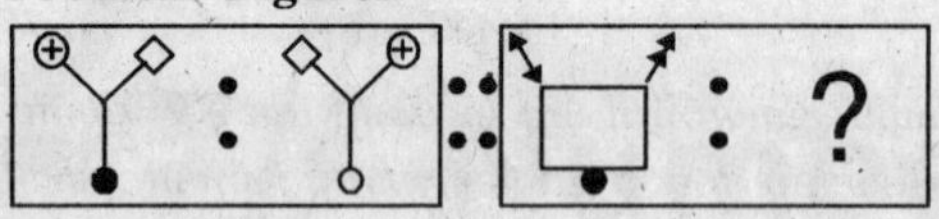

Answer Figures

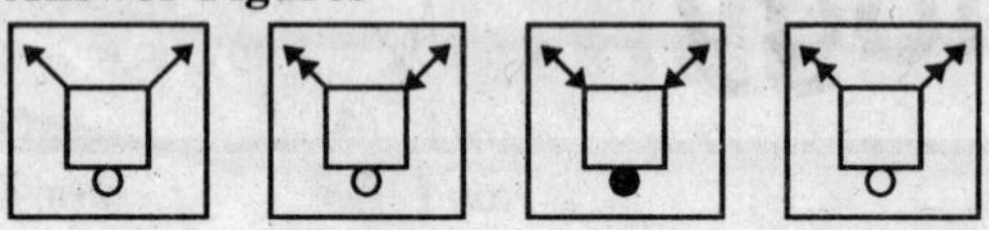

(*a*) (*b*) (*c*) (*d*)

8. Problem Figures

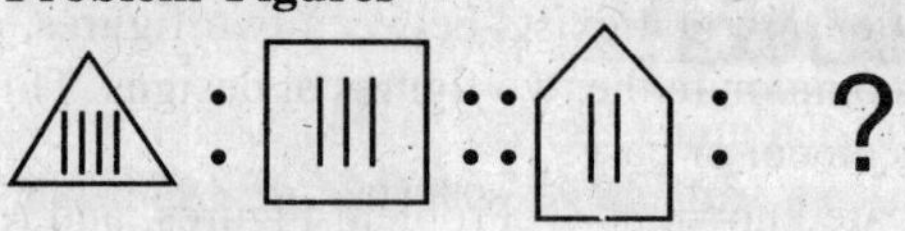

Answer Figures

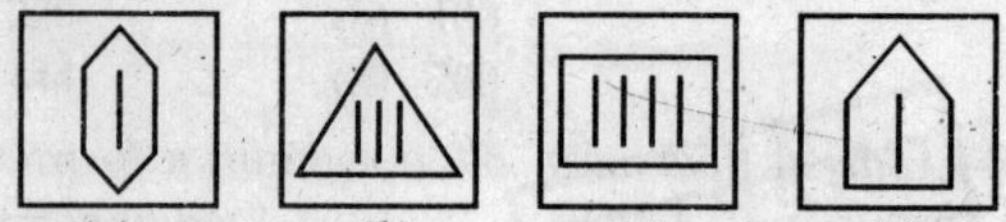

(*a*) (*b*) (*c*) (*d*)

9. Problem Figures

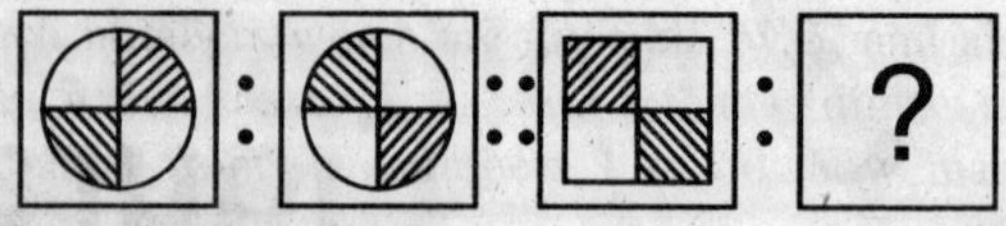

Answer Figures

(*a*) (*b*) (*c*) (*d*)

EXPLANATORY ANSWERS

1. (*d*) : The triangle in the first figure is moved to the centre of the second figure. Similarly, the two triangles joined at the apex are moved to the centre in answer figure.

2. (*d*) : The first figure is turned by 90° one of the bars is removed and opposite sides of the element attached to the bar are shaded to get the second figure.

3. (*a*) : The element at the bottom is moved to the diagonal corner, the element in the top is enlarged and moved to the centre and element in the middle is reduced and moved to the bottom right corner.

4. (*c*) : The view of the cube is changed from top to bottom. The design on the right side remains unchanged while the design on the left side is changed.

5. (*d*) : The inner shape in the first figure is removed to get the second figure.

6. (*b*) : The two half shapes placed vertically are turned upside down and joined, and this new shape is moved to the top. The two curved shapes placed horizontally are joined and this new shape is moved to the centre. One of the two remaining corner shapes is moved to the bottom.

7. (*b*) : The places of elements on the top are interchanged and the shade inside the circle is removed.

8. (*a*) : One of the vertical lines is removed and the number of lines making the second figure is increased by one.

9. (*a*) : First figure is rotated 90° anticlockwise to get the second figure.

CHAPTER 4

Spatial Visualization

In such questions, cut-out pieces are given alongwith the whole figure, that is the figure out of which the figures have been cut. By looking at the cut-out figures one has to find out the figure which may be constituted by putting the pieces together, i.e., one has to find out the figure of which the pieces have been cut. One has to be very imaginative and has to use space perception in finding out the solution. The whole process is mental and requires special skill in visualising different spatial patterns. It is not easy to develop this skill overnight but it can certainly be cultivated by practice and the method of trial and error.

MULTIPLE CHOICE QUESTIONS

Directions (Qs. 1-5) : *Which one figure can be made out of given paper cut-outs?*

1.

(a) (b) (c) (d)

2.

(a) (b) (c) (d)

3.

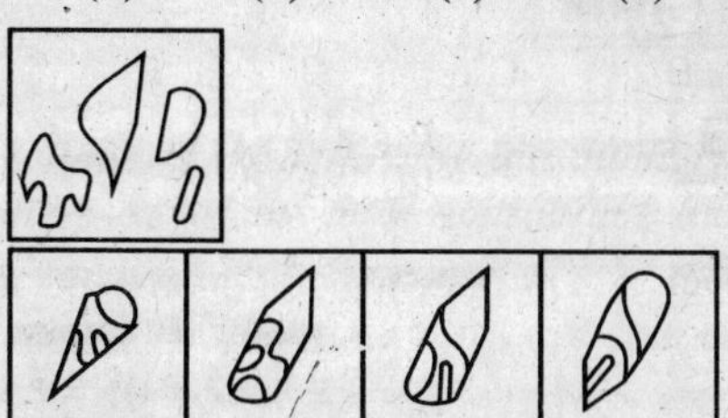

(a) (b) (c) (d)

4.

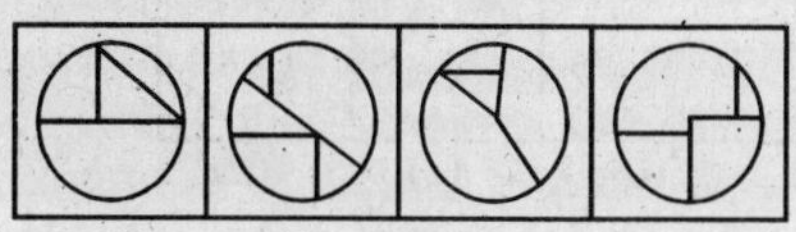

(a) (b) (c) (d)

5.

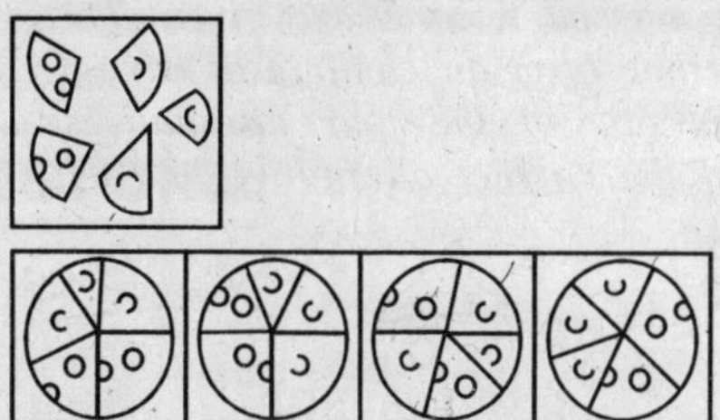

(a) (b) (c) (d)

Direction (Qs. 6-10) : *In each of the following questions an irregular piece of paper has been cut into two pieces. One piece has been shown on the left while the other piece has been given as one of the four alternatives against it. Find the correct alternative:*

6.

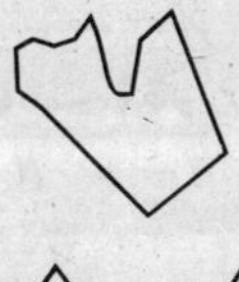

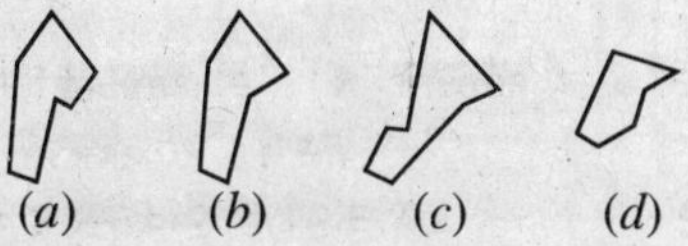

(a) (b) (c) (d)

7.

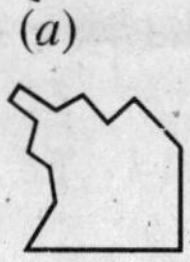

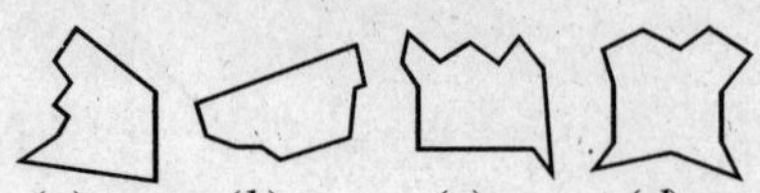

(a) (b) (c) (d)

8.

(a) (b) (c) (d)

9.

(a) (b) (c) (d)

10.

(a) (b) (c) (d)

Directions (Qs. 11-15) : *In each of the following questions five diagrams marked A to E are given. Three of these when put together form an equilateral triangle and have been given as one of the four alternatives under the question. Find the correct alternative in each case.*

11.

A B C D E

(a) ABE (b) BCE
(c) ADE (d) BDE

12.

A B C D E

(a) ABC (b) BCD
(c) CDE (d) BDE

13.

A B C D E

(a) BCD (b) CDE
(c) ABD (d) ABE

14.

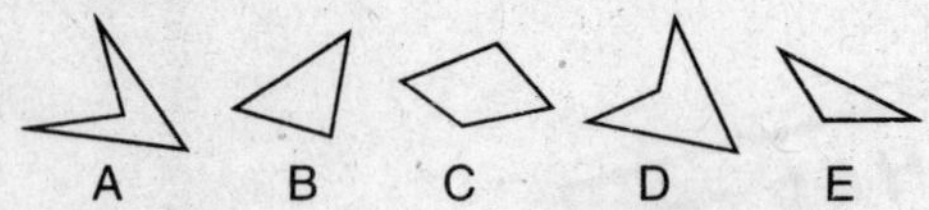

A B C D E

(a) ABD (b) ACD
(c) BDE (d) CDE

15.

A B C D E

(a) ABC (b) ACE
(c) BDE (d) CDE

Directions (Qs. 16-20) : *In each of the following questions five diagrams A, B, C, D and E have been given. Three of these diagrams make a complete square which have been given as one of the four alternatives under it. Find the correct alternative in each case.*

16.

A B C D E

(a) ABC (b) BDE
(c) CDE (d) BCD

17.

A B C D E

(a) ACD (b) BDE
(c) BCE (d) CDE

18.

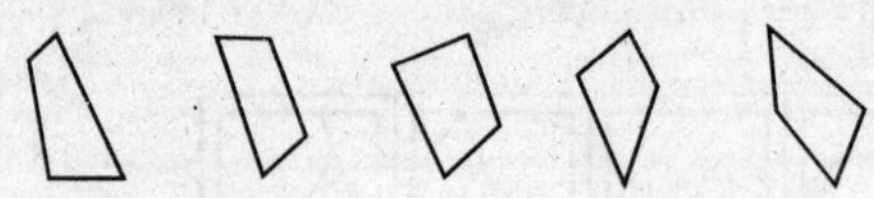

A B C D E

(a) ACD (b) BCD
(c) ACE (d) CDE

19.

A B C D E

(a) ABC (b) ACE
(c) ADE (d) CDE

20.

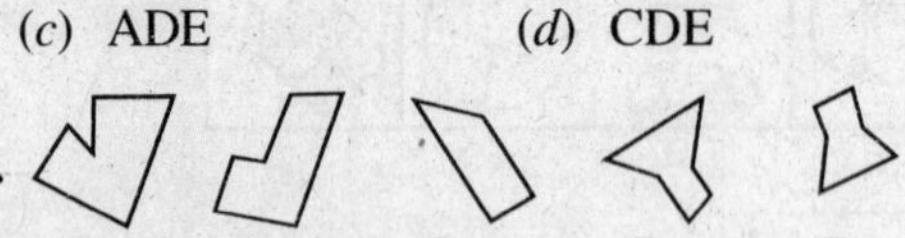

A B C D E

(a) BDE (b) ABC
(c) ACD (d) BCD

ANSWERS

1	2	3	4	5	6	7	8	9	10
(b)	(d)	(c)	(a)	(b)	(b)	(c)	(a)	(d)	(c)
11	**12**	**13**	**14**	**15**	**16**	**17**	**18**	**19**	**20**
(c)	(d)	(d)	(b)	(b)	(d)	(b)	(c)	(c)	(d)

CHAPTER

5

Space Visualization

In these type of questions, a template or a layout of a cube, dice or a box is given, which can be folded to produce different patterns. To solve these questions what is required is a clear study of the given layout and the selection of one figure, from the alternative patterns which can be made from the given layout. To attempt such problems understand the unfolded patterns given below:

Layout 1. 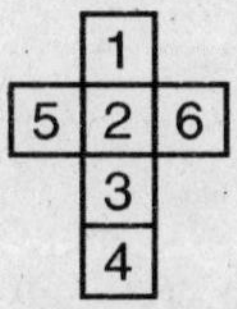 or 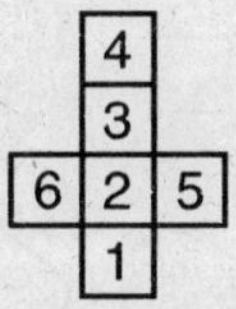

The opposite sides are :
1—3, 2 — 4 and 5 — 6

Layout 2. 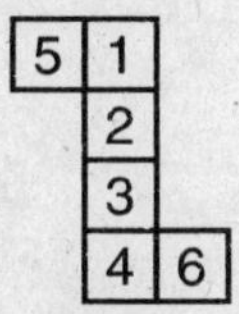 or 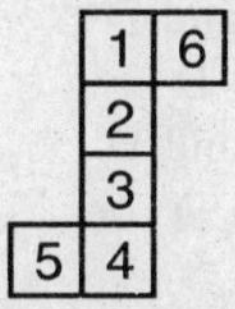

The opposite sides are :
1 — 3, 2 — 4 and 5 — 6

Layout 3. 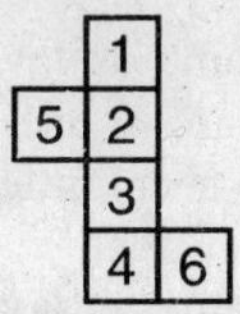 or 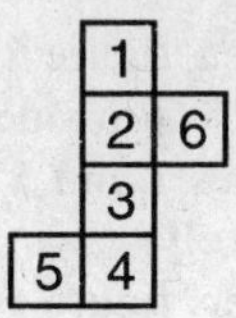

The opposite sides are :
1 — 3, 2 — 4 and 5 — 6.

Layout 4. 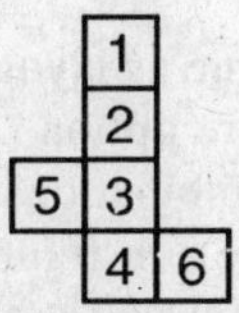 or 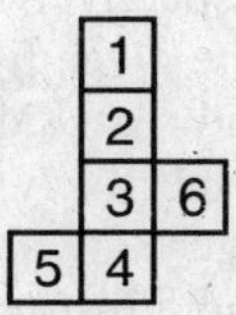

The opposite sides are :
1 — 3, 2 — 4 and 5 — 6

Layout 5. 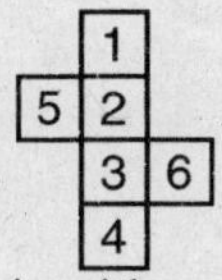 or 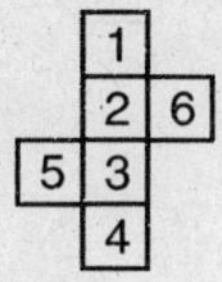

The opposite sides are :
1 — 3, 2 — 4 and 5 — 6

Layout 6. 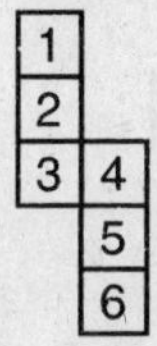 or 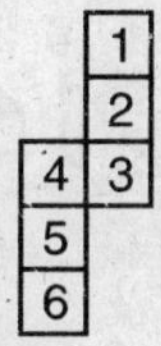

The opposite sides are :
1 — 3, 2 — 5 and 4 — 6

Layout 7. 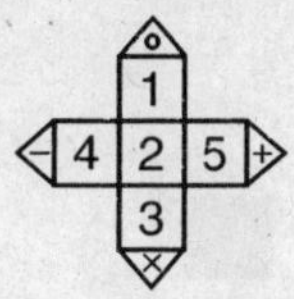

The opposite sides are :

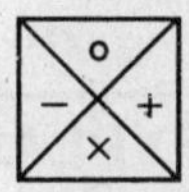 — 2, 1 — 3 and 4 — 5. Here, side 6 is divided into four parts

Layout 8. 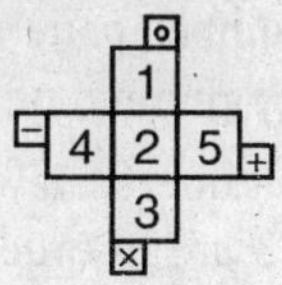

The opposite sides are

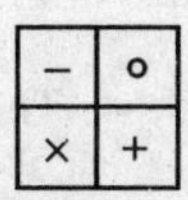 — 2, 1 — 3 and 4 — 5. Here, side 6 is divided into four parts.

Observe from the above layouts that all sides except the opposite side are adjacent sides. Also keep in mind that the three visible sides of the option figures are one of the opposite sides of each opposite pair.

MULTIPLE CHOICE QUESTIONS

Directions : *The figure is folded to produce different box patterns. Study the pattern to know if they can be produced from given figure and select the answer from the alternatives.*

1.

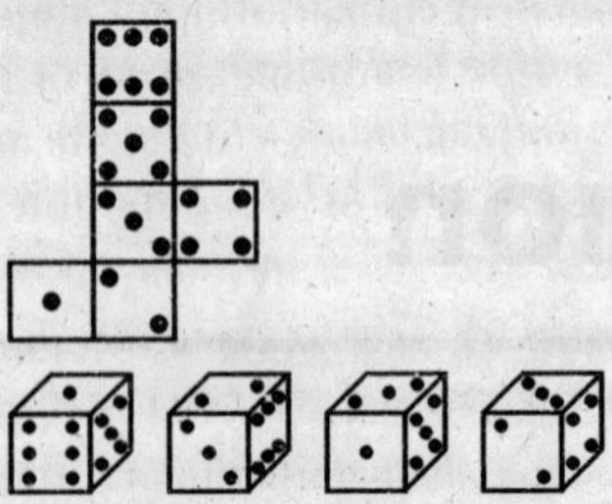

(*a*) (*b*) (*c*) (*d*)

2.

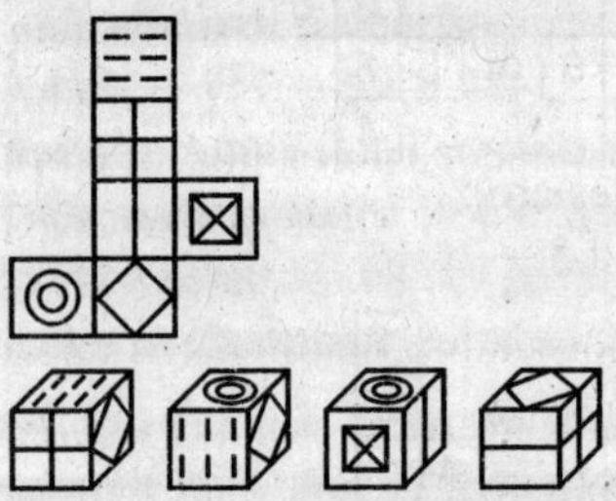

(*a*) (*b*) (*c*) (*d*)

3.

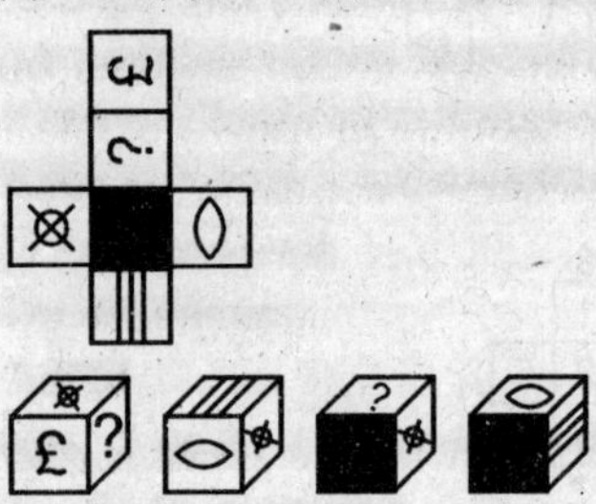

(*a*) (*b*) (*c*) (*d*)

4.

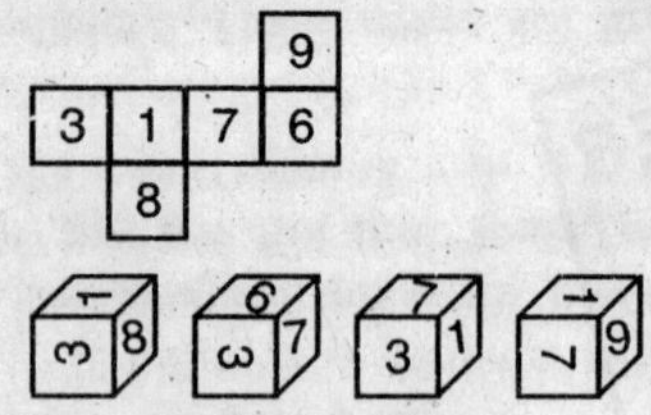

(*a*) (*b*) (*c*) (*d*)

5.

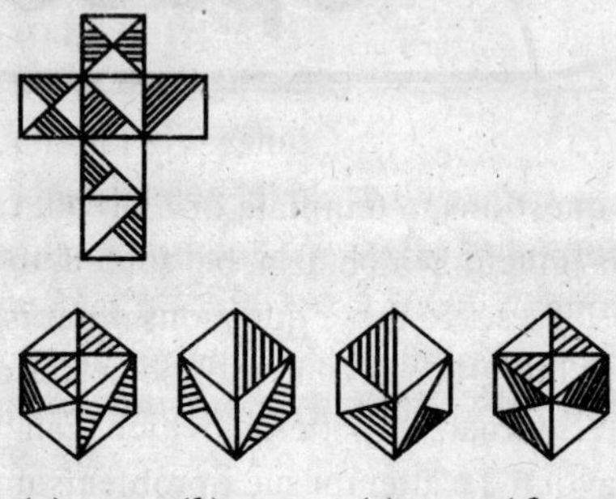

(*a*) (*b*) (*c*) (*d*)

6.

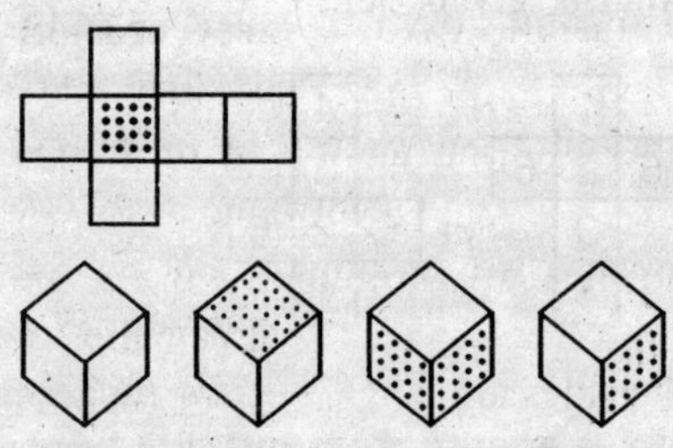

A B C D

(*a*) A, B and D
(*b*) B and D
(*c*) B, C and D
(*d*) A and D

EXPLANATORY ANSWERS

(All answers are based on number pattern of the sides as in the layout given in the beginning of this section)

1. (*d*) : The given figure is same as layout 4. The sides adjacent to top side 3 are in order 2, 5, 4, 6 — of these sides, 4 and 6 are seen on left and right sides respectively.

2. (*b*) : The given figure is same as layout 4. The sides adjacent to top side 5 are in order 4, 3, 2, 1 —of these sides 1 and 4 are seen on left and right sides respectively.

3. (*d*) : The given figure is same as layout 1. The sides adjacent to top side 5 are in order 4, 3, 2, 1 — of these sides 2 and 1 are seen on left and right sides respectively.

4. (*a*) : The given figure is same as layout 3. The sides adjacent to top side 2 are in order 1, 5, 3, 6 — of these sides 1 and 5 are seen on left and right sides respectively.

5. (*c*) : The given figure is same as layout 1. The sides adjacent to top side 6 are in order 1, 2, 3, 4 — of these sides 2 and 3 are seen on left and right sides respectively.

6. (*a*) : The given figure is same as layout 1. The top, left and right sides in figure option (a) are 1, 4 and 5 respectively (other combinations of sides for this figure are also possible); in figure option (b) 2, 1 and 5 respectively (other combination of sides for this figure are also possible; and in figure option (d) 1, 5 and 2 respectively (other combinations of sides for this figure are also possible).

CHAPTER 6 Pinch Hole/Paper Folding & Unfolding

These type of questions are based on a piece of paper which is folded and cut or punched in a particular manner. One of the option figures either resembles the pattern that would be formed when the paper is unfolded or resembles the form in which the paper is folded and cut or punched.

MULTIPLE CHOICE QUESTIONS

Directions (Qs. 1-5) : *In each one of the following problems, a square transparent sheet with a pattern is given. Figure out from amongst the four alternatives as to how the pattern would appear when the transparent sheet is folded at the dotted line.*

1. 

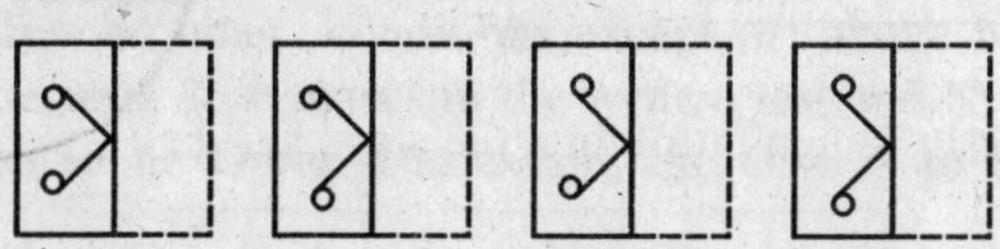

(a) (b) (c) (d)

2. 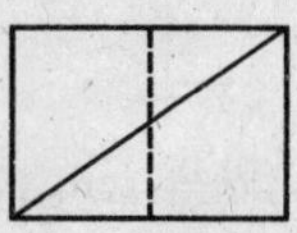

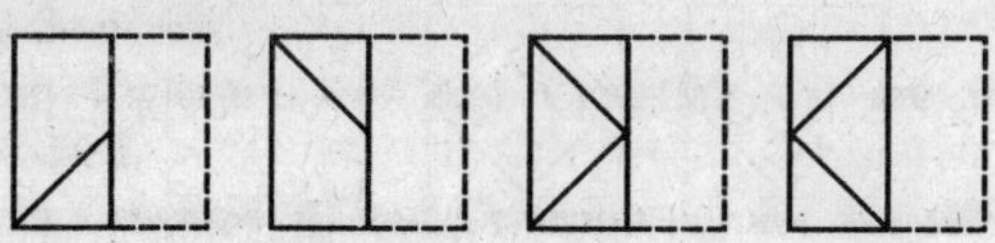

(a) (b) (c) (d)

3. 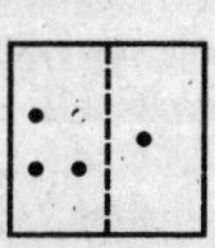

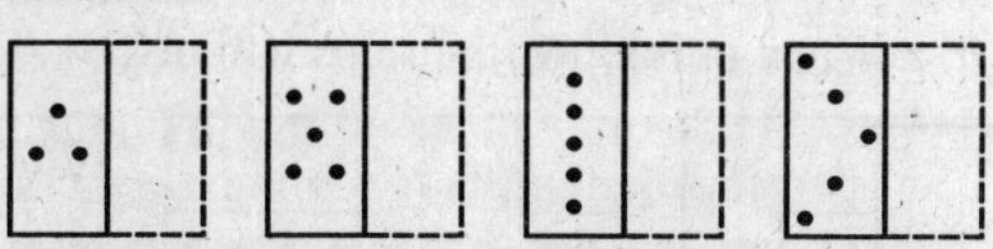

(a) (b) (c) (d)

4. 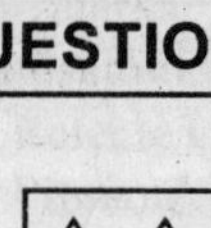

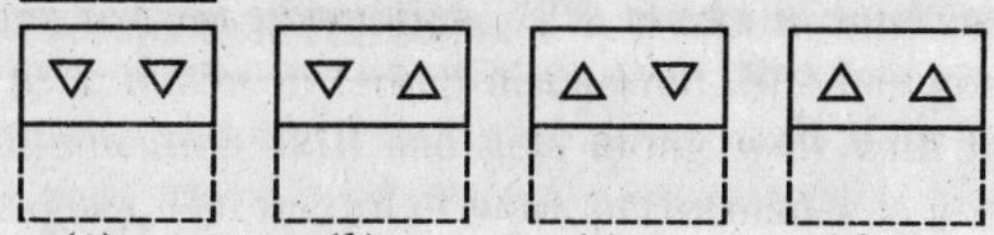

(a) (b) (c) (d)

5. 

(a) (b) (c) (d)

Directions (Qs. 6-13) : *In each of the following questions a piece of paper has been folded and then punched. From the given options figure out the correct response which shows how it will appear when opened.*

6. 

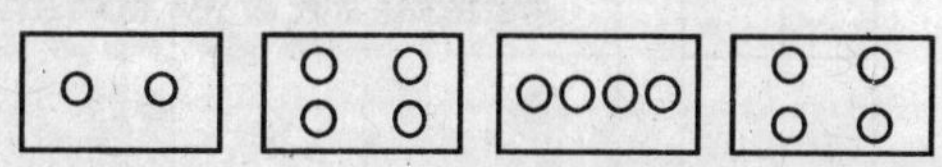

(a) (b) (c) (d)

7. 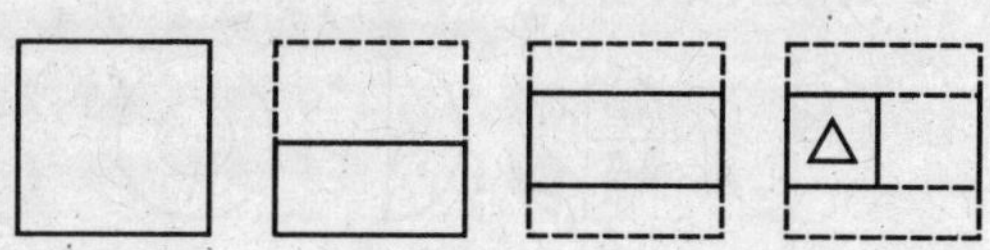

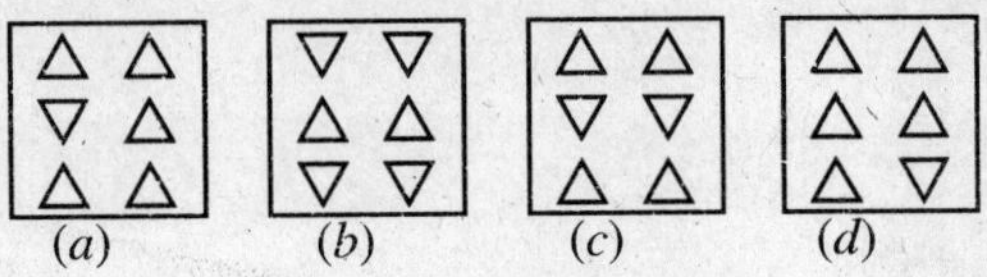

8.

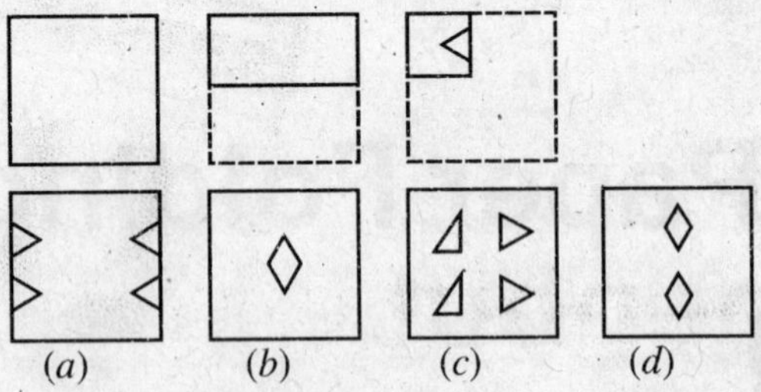

9.

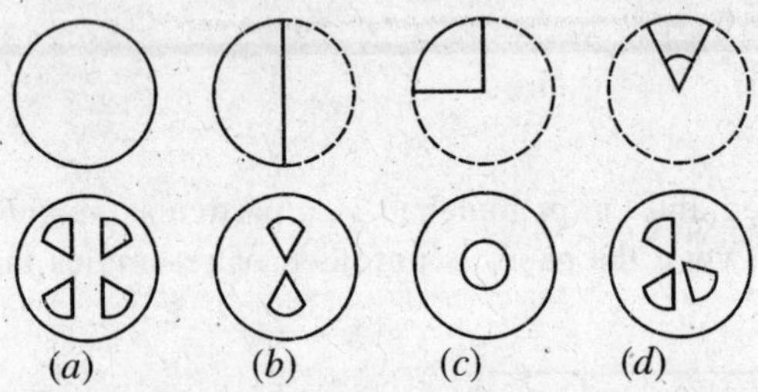

10.

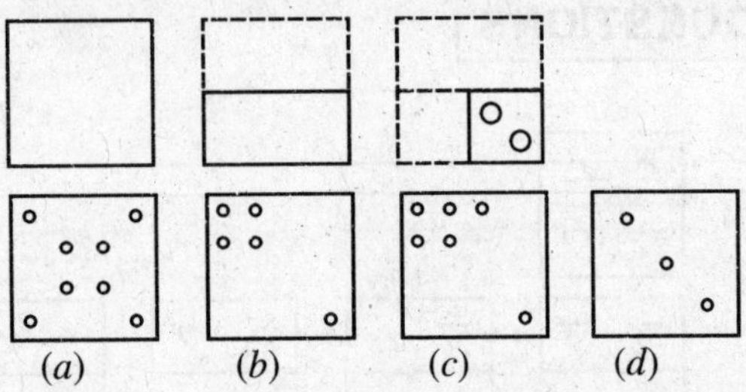

11.

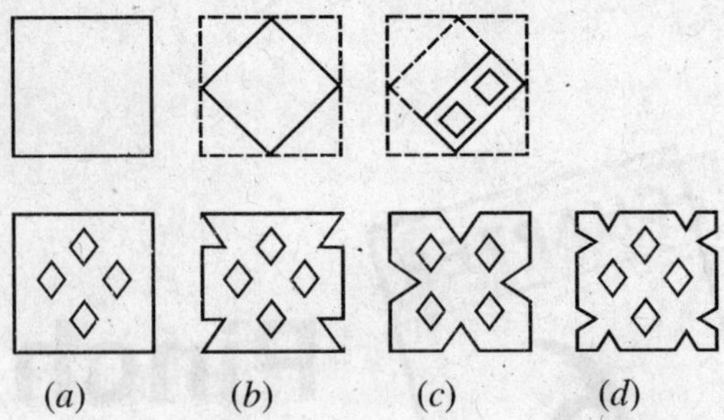

12.

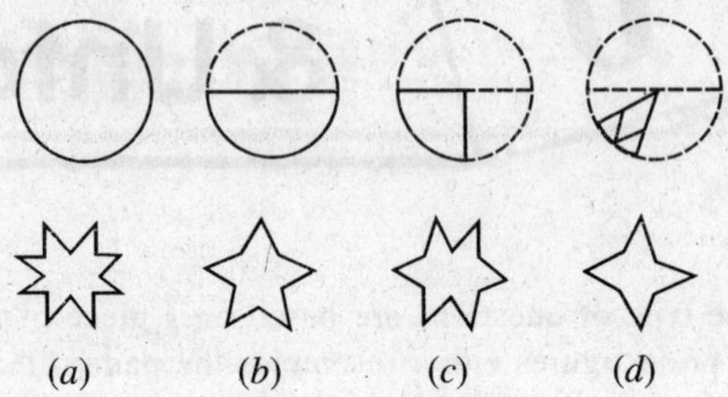

13.

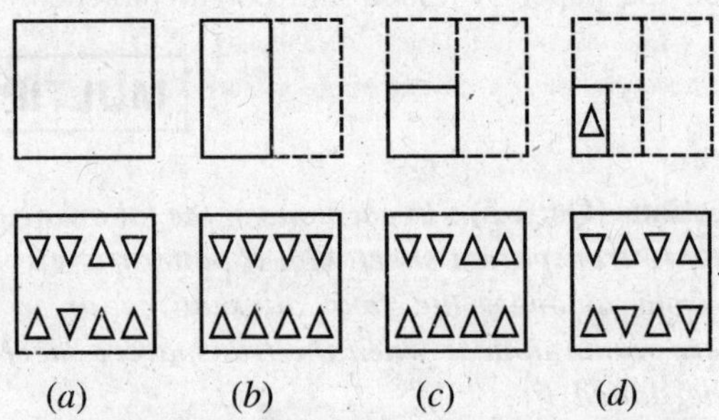

EXPLANATORY ANSWERS

1. (*d*)

2. (*c*)

3. (*b*)

4. (*d*)

5. (*b*)

6. (*c*) **:** When unfolding, the steps will be :

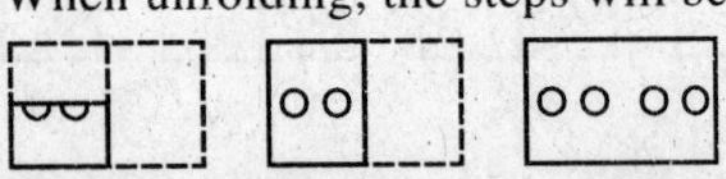

7. (*b*) **:** When unfolding, the steps will be :

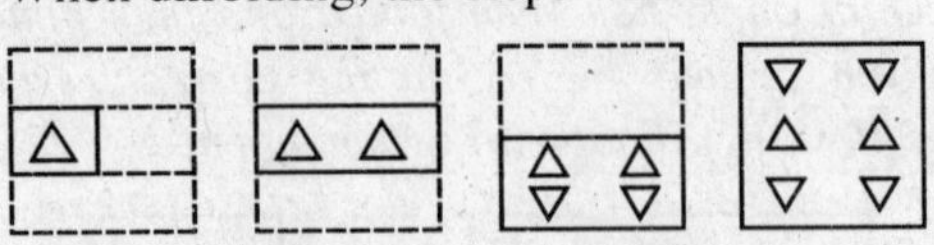

8. (*d*) **:** When unfolding, the steps will be :

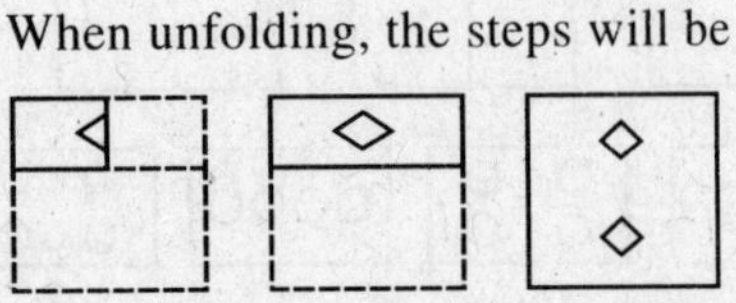

9. (*c*) **:** When unfolding, the steps will be :

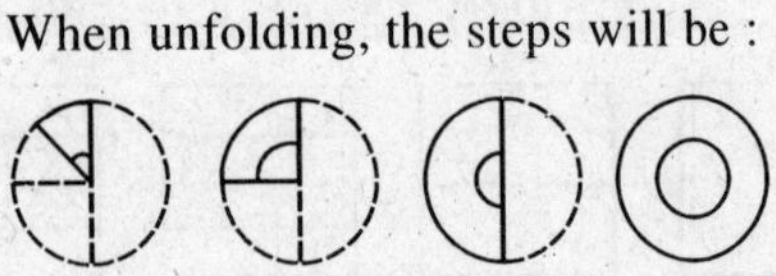

10. (*a*) **:** When unfolding, the steps will be :

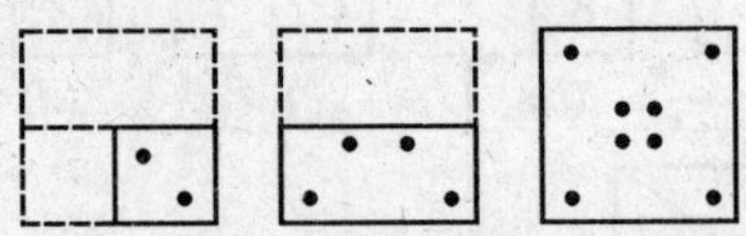

11. (*d*) **:** When unfolding, the steps will be :

12. (*a*) **:** When unfolding, the steps will be :

13. (*b*) **:** When unfolding, the steps will be :

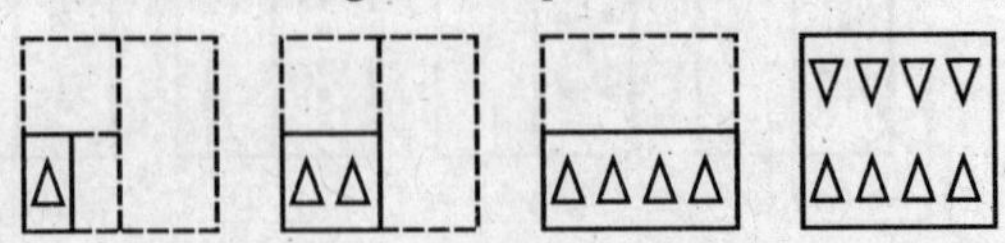

CHAPTER 7

Figural Pattern Folding and Completion

In these type of questions an incomplete figure pattern is given followed by alternative figures of which one will complete the given figure pattern. These figure patterns are mainly based on symmetries.

MULTIPLE CHOICE QUESTIONS

Directions : *In each question, which one of the alternative figures will complete the given figure pattern?*

1. **Pattern** 

Alternative figures

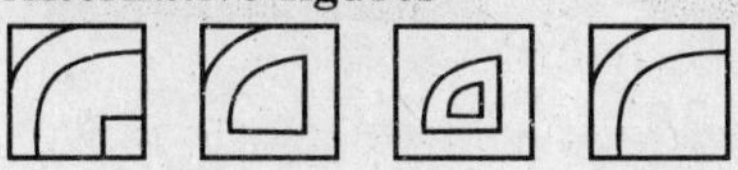

(*a*) (*b*) (*c*) (*d*)

2. **Pattern** 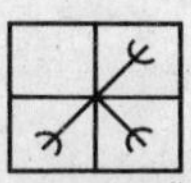

Alternative figures

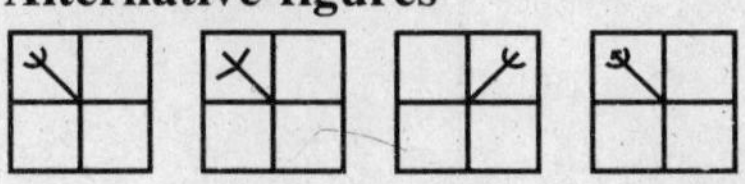

(*a*) (*b*) (*c*) (*d*)

3. **Pattern** 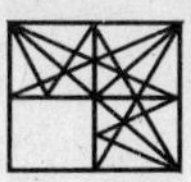

Alternative figures

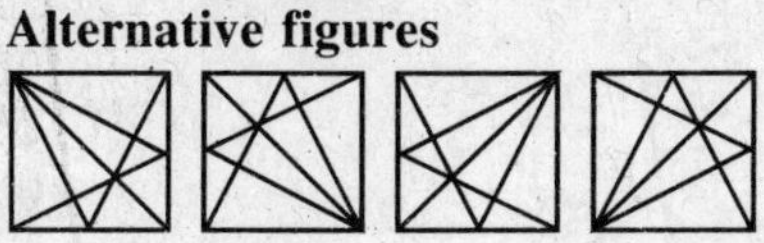

(*a*) (*b*) (*c*) (*d*)

4. **Pattern** 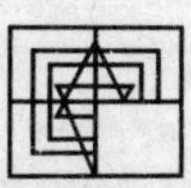

Alternative figures

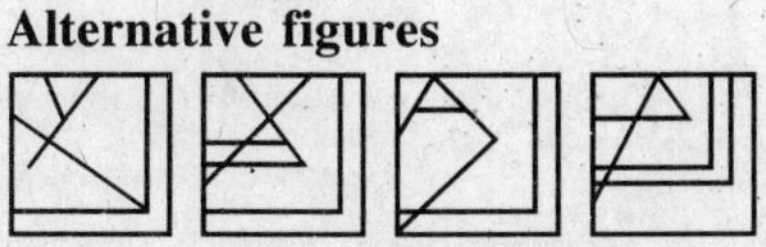

(*a*) (*b*) (*c*) (*d*)

5. **Pattern** 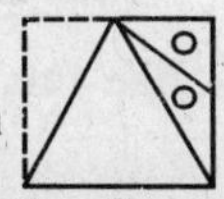

Alternative figures

(*a*) (*b*) (*c*) (*d*)

6. **Pattern** 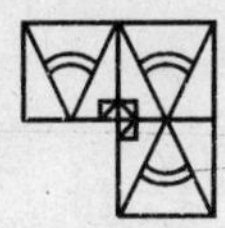

Alternative figures

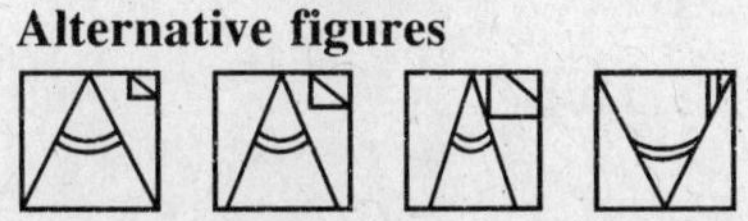

(*a*) (*b*) (*c*) (*d*)

7. **Pattern** 

Alternative figures

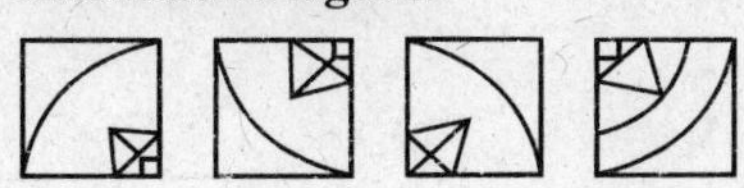

(*a*) (*b*) (*c*) (*d*)

8. **Pattern** 

Alternative figures

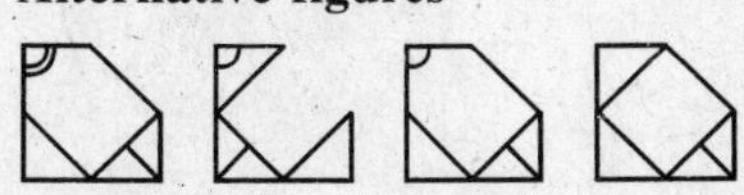

(*a*) (*b*) (*c*) (*d*)

9. **Pattern** 

Alternative figures

(a) (b) (c) (d)

10. **Pattern** 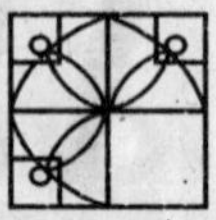

Alternative figures

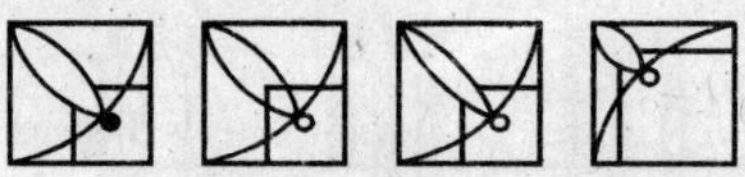

(a) (b) (c) (d)

11. **Pattern** 

Alternative figures

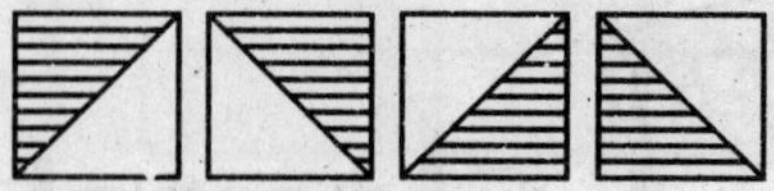

(a) (b) (c) (d)

12. **Pattern** 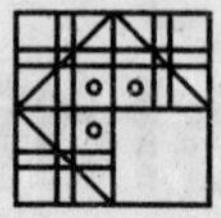

Alternative figures

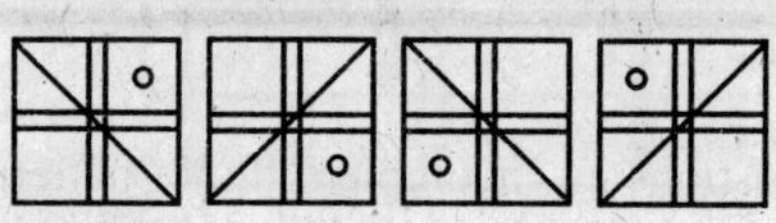

(a) (b) (c) (d)

EXPLANATORY ANSWERS

All the completed figures will look like this:

1. (b) : 

2. (a) : 

3. (d) : 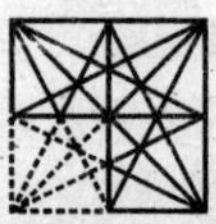

4. (d) : 

5. (a) : 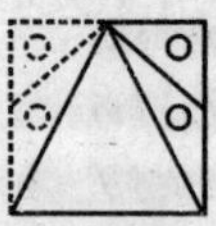

6. (a) : 

7. (b) : 

8. (c) : 

9. (a) : 

10. (b) : 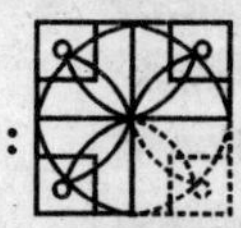

11. (a) : 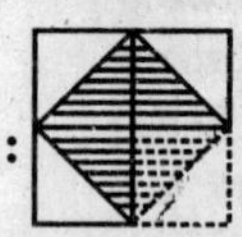

12. (d) : 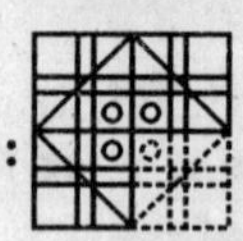

CHAPTER 8

Visual Memory

These type of problems are based on the mirror images or reflections of number, letters and figures. While attempting such questions one must be able to visualise clearly the questioned reflections, be they on vertical plane or on horizontal plane. Study the chart and information given below. The visualisation of letters and numbers is easier than the visualisation of figures for the simple reason that the figures have many forms and all cannot be summed up.

Horizontal Mirror Images (HMI) of Numbers

Number	*HMI*	*Number*	*HMI*
0	0	5	ꙅ
1	1	6	ꓭ
2	ς	7	⌐
3	Ɛ	8	8
4	ㄣ	9	୧

Note : HMI of 0 and 8 remain unchanged

Vertical Mirror Images (VMI) of Numbers

Numbers :	0	1	2	3	4	5	6	7	8	9
VMI :	0	Ɩ	ᘔ	3	ᔭ	ဌ	9	ㄥ	8	6

Note : VMI of 0, 3 and 8 remain unchanged.

Exceptions in style need caution. Example 3 will be 3, or 8 will be 8.

Horizontal Mirror Images of Capital Letters

Letter	HMI	Letter	HMI	H letter	HMI
A	A	J	Ⴑ	S	Ƨ
B	ᗺ	K	ꓘ	T	T
C	Ɔ	L	⅃	U	U
D	ᗡ	M	M	V	V
E	Ǝ	N	И	W	W
F	ꟻ	O	O	X	X
G	Ә	P	ꟼ	Y	Y
H	H	Q	Ϙ	Z	Ƨ
I	I	R	Я		

Note : HMI of A, H, I, M, O, T, U, V, W, X and Y remain unchanged.

Exceptions in style need caution. Example : A will be A, or X will be X.

Vertical Mirror Images of Capital Letters

Letters :	A	B	C	D	E	F	G	H	I	J	K	L	M
VMI :	∀	B	C	D	E	Ⅎ	⅁	H	I	ſ	K	Γ	W

Letters :	N	O	P	Q	R	S	T	U	V	W	X	Y	Z
VMI :	N	O	Ь	Ό	ᴚ	S	⊥	∩	Λ	M	X	⅄	Z

Note : VMI of C, D, E, H, I, K, O and X remain unchanged.

Horizontal Mirror Images of Small Letters

Letter	HMI	Letter	HMI	Letter	HMI
a	ɒ	j	ɈI	s	ƨ
b	d	k	ʞ	t	ɟ
c	ɔ	l	l	u	u
d	b	m	m	v	v
e	ɘ	n	n	w	w
f	ɟ	o	o	x	x
g	ǫ	p	q	y	y
h	ʜ	q	p	z	ƨ
i	i	r	ɿ		

Note : HMI of o, v, w and x remain unchanged.

Vertical Mirror Images of Small Letters

Letter :	a	b	c	d	e	f	g	h	i	j	k	l	m
VMI :	ɐ	p	c	q	ə	ɟ	ƃ	ɥ	!	ɾ	ʞ	l	ɯ

Letter :	n	o	p	q	r	s	t	u	v	w	x	y	z
VMI :	u	o	b	d	ɹ	s	ʇ	n	ʌ	ʍ	x	ʎ	z

Note : VMI of c, o and x remain unchanged. Letter 1 has exceptions: if it is a straight vertical line – 1 then it remains unchanged.

MULTIPLE CHOICE QUESTIONS

Directions (Qs. 1 to 15) : *In each question below which is the exact horizontal mirror image?*

1. DuST
(a) DuSꓕ (b) TSnD
(c) TSuD (d) ᗡuST

2. CHAIR
(a) ꓛHAIꓤ (b) CHAIꓤ
(c) ꓤIAHC (d) ƆHAIЯ

3. WHOM
(a) MOHW (b) WOHM
(c) ʍHOM (d) ʍOHM

4. plaque
(a) ənbɐld (b) ənbblp
(c) qlapue (d) ənbɐlp

5. brows
(a) dꓤows (b) drows
(c) ꙅword (d) sword

6. flying
(a) ƃuiʎlɟ (b) gnilyf
(c) gniylf (d) gnilyf

7. 4379
(a) 4379 (b) 4379
(c) 9734 (d) 4376

8. 57182
(a) 57182 (b) 57182
(c) 57182 (d) 57182

9. 69430
(a) 69430 (b) 69430
(c) 69430 (d) 69430

10. 2JKS
(a) 2JKS (b) 2JKS
(c) 2JKS (d) 2JKS

11. P9Yf3
(a) P9Yf3 (b) P9Yf3
(c) P9Yf3 (d) P9Yf3

12. GZ5QRh
(a) GZ5QRh (b) GZ5QRh
(c) GZ5QRh (d) GZ5QRh

13. 2$%CH
(a) 2$%CH (b) 2$%CH
(c) 2$%CH (d) 2$%CH

14. 7↑FN8
(a) 7↑FN8 (b) 7↑FN8
(c) 7↑FN8 (d) 7↑FN8

15. yk19G
(a) yk19G (b) yk19G
(c) yk19G (d) yk19G

ANSWERS

1	2	3	4	5	6	7	8	9	10
(c)	(b)	(a)	(a)	(c)	(d)	(b)	(a)	(d)	(c)
11	**12**	**13**	**14**	**15**					
(d)	(b)	(c)	(a)	(d)					

CHAPTER 9

Discrimination

In these problems one has to count the geometrical figures in a given complex figure. A little bit of systematic approach is needed to get the correct number of the asked figure. The shapes of all geometrical figures must be clear in mind.

MULTIPLE CHOICE QUESTIONS

1. How many triangles are there in the figure given below?

(*a*) 24 (*b*) 27
(*c*) 25 (*d*) 26

2. How many parallelograms are there in this figure?

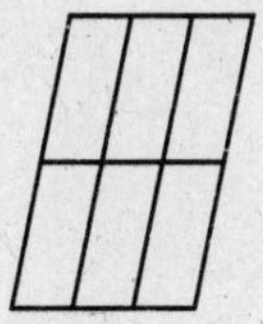

(*a*) 9 (*b*) 13
(*c*) 15 (*d*) 18

3. How many triangles are there in this figure?

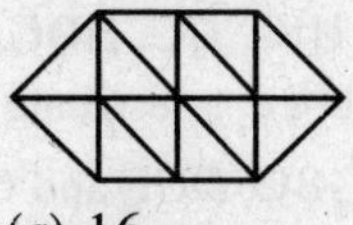

(*a*) 16 (*b*) 17
(*c*) 18 (*d*) 19

4. The number of rectangles in this figure are.

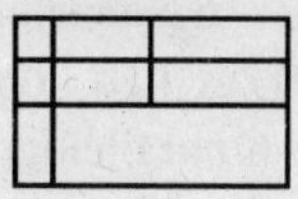

(*a*) 21 (*b*) 24
(*c*) 23 (*d*) 25

5. How many squares are hidden in this figure?

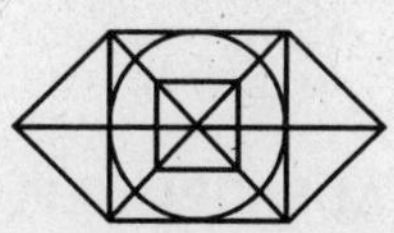

(*a*) 7 (*b*) 8
(*c*) 9 (*d*) 10

6. The number of triangles in this figure are.

(*a*) 19 (*b*) 16
(*c*) 21 (*d*) 15

EXPLANATORY ANSWERS

1. (*a*) :

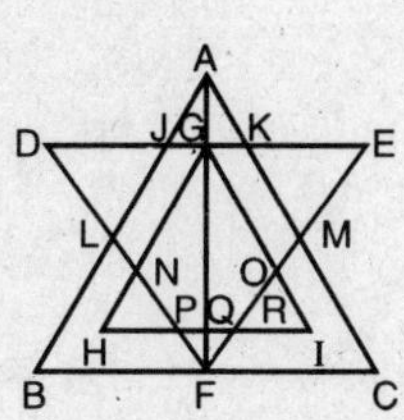

- The main triangles making the figure are ABC, DEF and GHI *i.e.*, – 3 triangles
- The simplest triangles are AJG, AGK, KEM, DJL, NHP, PQF, QFR and ORI *i.e.*, – 8 triangles

(2253) (GI)—9

- The triangles formed by the bisecting line AF are ABF, AFC, GHQ, GQI, DGF and GFE *i.e.,* – 6 triangles
- The triangles formed inbetween the three triangles AJK, ALF, AMF, DGN, DGF, LBF, MFC, GEO, GNF and GOF – *i.e.,* 10 triangles
- So, the total number of triangles is 3 + 8 + 6 + 10 = 27

2. (*d*) :

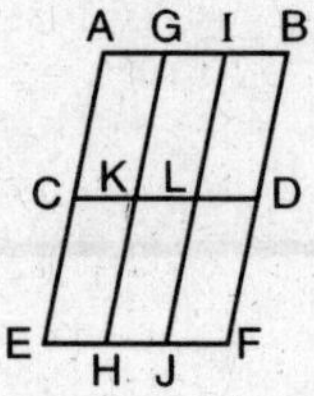

- The main parallelogram is ABEF *i.e.,* 1 parallelogram
- When divided into half by line CD the main figure has ABCD and CDEF *i.e.,* 2 parallelograms
- When further lines GH and IJ are drawn, the parallelograms are AGEH, GIJH and IBJF *i.e.,* – 3 parallelograms.
- The simplest parallelogram are AGCK, CKEH, GIKL, KLHJ, IBLD and LDJF *i.e.* – 6 parallelograms

Other parallelograms are AICL, CLEJ, GBKD, KDHF, AIEJ and GBHF – *i.e.,* 6 parallelograms

So, the total number of parallelograms is 1 + 2 + 3 + 6 + 6 = 18

3. (*a*) :

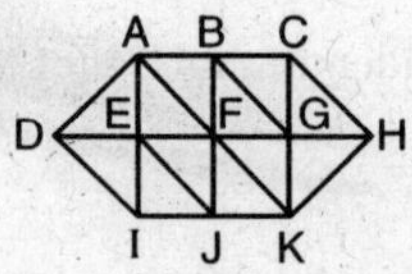

The simplest triangles are ADE, DEI, AEF, ABF, EIJ, EFJ, BFG, BCG, FJK, FGK, CGH and GHK – *i.e.,* – 12 triangles

The bisected triangles are ADI and CHK – *i.e.* – 2 triangles

Other triangles are AIK and ACK *i.e.,* – 2 triangles

So, the total number of triangles is 12 + 2 + 2 = 16

4. (*c*) :

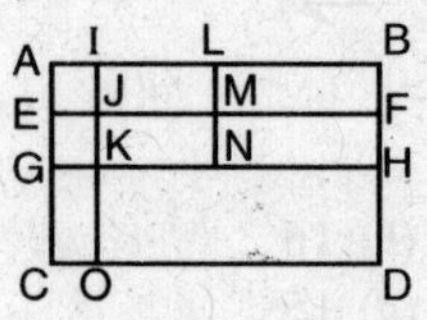

The main rectangle is ABCD – *i.e.,* – 1 rectangle

The simplest rectangles are AIEJ, ILJM, LBMF, EJGK, JMKN, MFNH, GKCO and KHOD *i.e.* – 8 rectangles.

The rectangles which have two parts are ALEM, IBJF, EMGN, JFKH, AIGK, IKLN, LBNH, EJCO and GHCD *i.e.* – 9 rectangles.

The rectangles which have three parts are AICO, ABEF and EFGH *i.e.* – 3 rectangles

The rectangles which have four parts are ALGN and IBKH *i.e.* – 2 rectangles

So, the total number of rectangles 1 + 8 + 9 + 3 + 2 = 23

5. (*d*) :

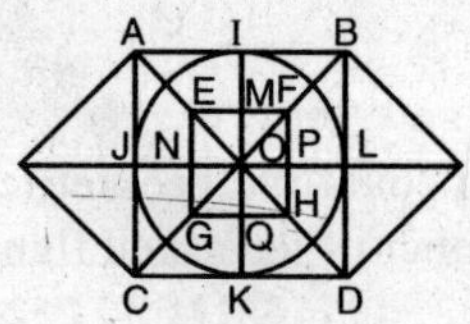

The main squares are ABCD and EFGH *i.e.,* – 2 squares

The simplest outer squares are AIJO, IBOL, JOCK and OLKD *i.e.,* – 4 squares

The simplest inner square are EMNO, NOGQ, MFOP and OPQH *i.e.,* – 4 squares

There are no other squares formed in the figure

So, the total number of squares is 2 + 4 + 4 = 10

6. (*b*) :

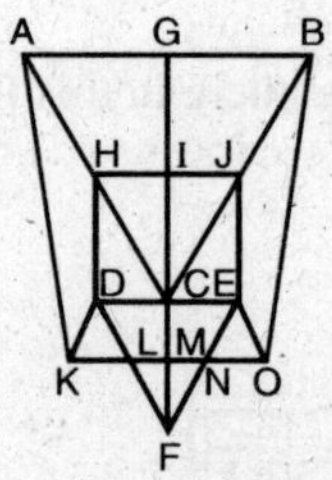

The main triangles are : ABC, DEF, LNF, and HJC *i.e.* 4 triangles

The simplest triangles are : HIC, IJC, HDC, JCE, DKL, LMF, MFN and NOE *i.e.* – 8 triangles

Other triangles are : AGC, GBC, DCF and CEF – *i.e.* 4 triangles

So, the total number of triangles is 4 + 8 + 4 = 16

CHAPTER 10

Embedded Figures

In these type of questions a figure form is given followed by alternative figures. In one of these figure options the given form is embedded. Practice of visualisation comes handy in attempting such easy questions.

MULTIPLE CHOICE QUESTIONS

Directions (Qs. 1 to 6) : *In the questions given below a figure is given. From the given alternatives select the one in which the given figure is embedded.*

1.

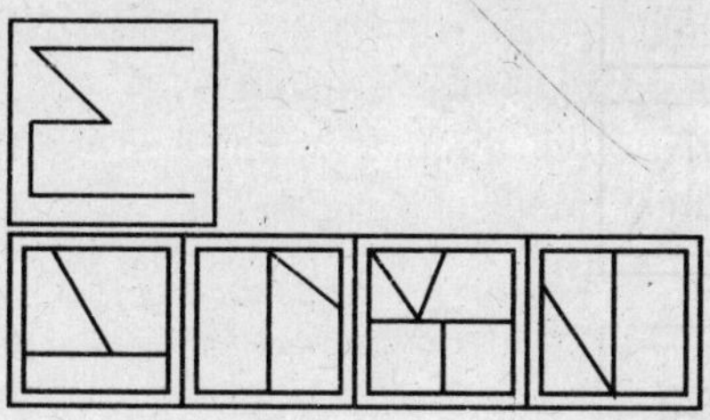

(*a*) (*b*) (*c*) (*d*)

2.

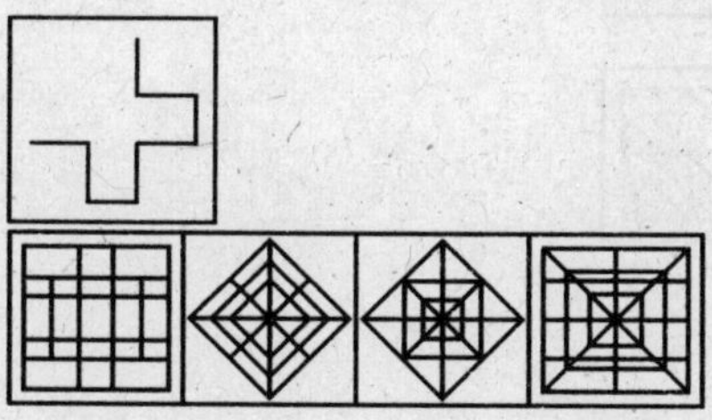

(*a*) (*b*) (*c*) (*d*)

3.

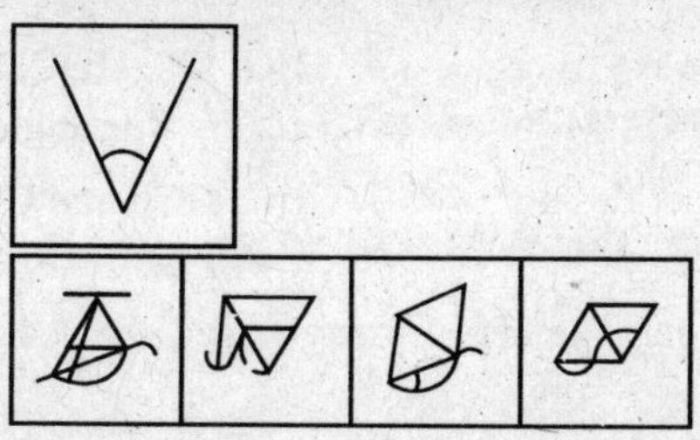

(*a*) (*b*) (*c*) (*d*)

4.

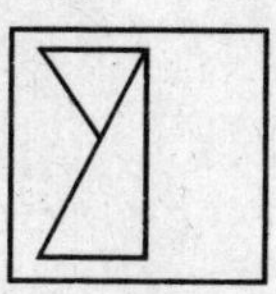

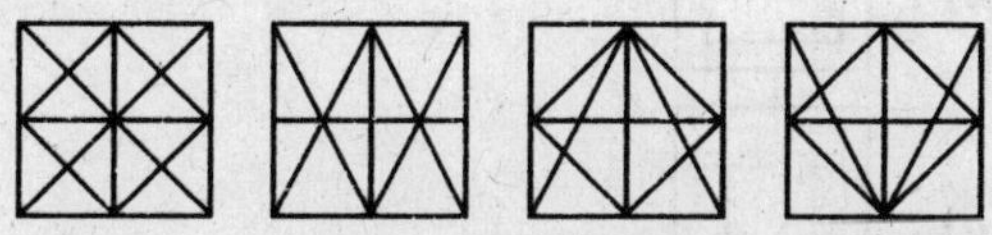

(*a*) (*b*) (*c*) (*d*)

5.

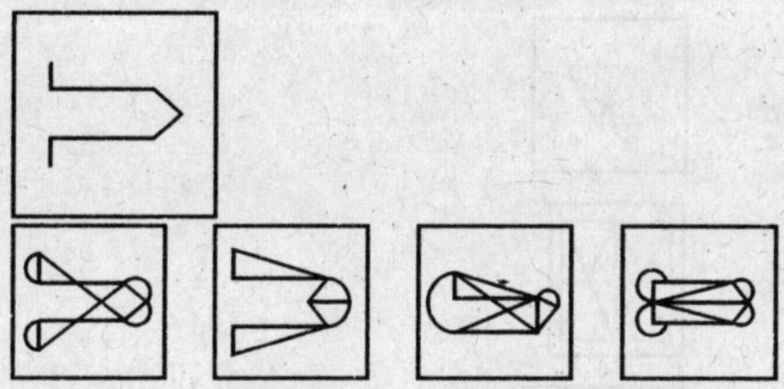

(*a*) (*b*) (*c*) (*d*)

6.

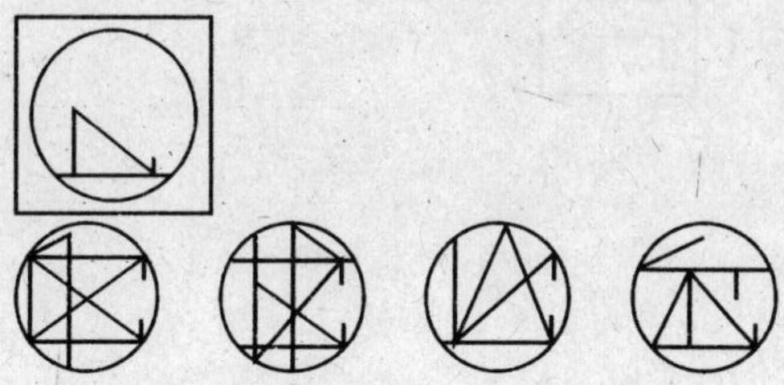

(*a*) (*b*) (*c*) (*d*)

Directions (Qs. 7 to 10) : *In each question given below find the figure form which is embedded in the given pattern.*

7.

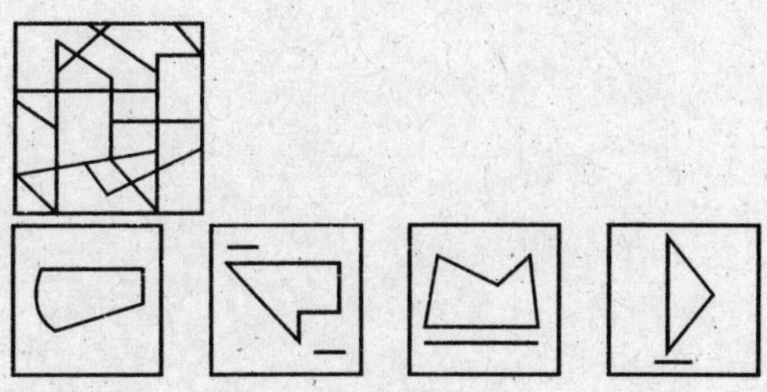

(*a*) (*b*) (*c*) (*d*)

8. 

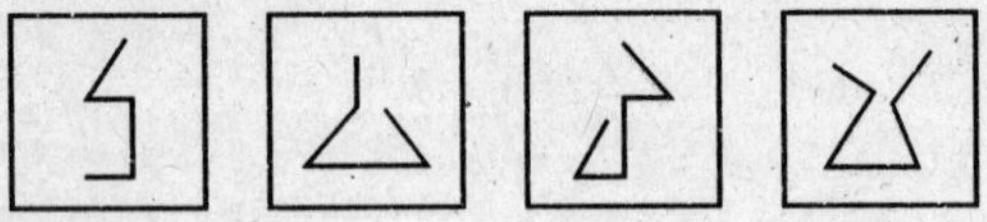

(*a*) (*b*) (*c*) (*d*)

9. 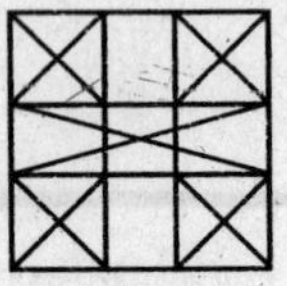

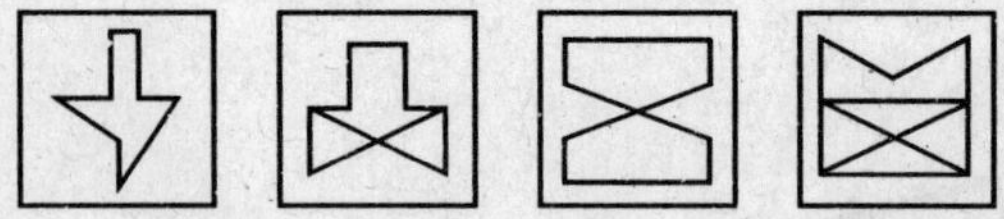

(*a*) (*b*) (*c*) (*d*)

10. 

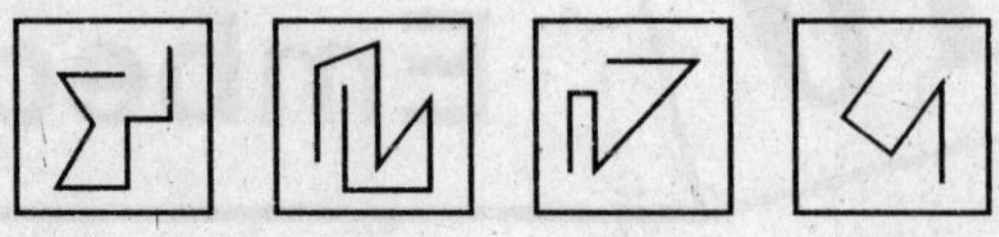

(*a*) (*b*) (*c*) (*d*)

EXPLANATORY ANSWERS

1. (*a*) : 

2. (*a*) : 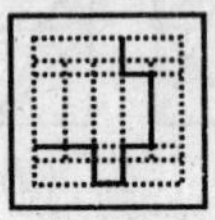

3. (*d*) : 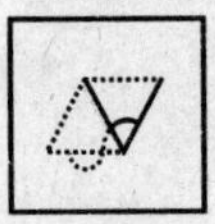

4. (*b*) : 

5. (*a*) : 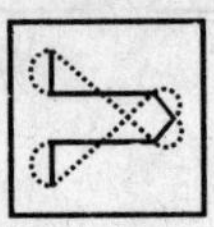

6. (*b*) : 

7. (*d*) : 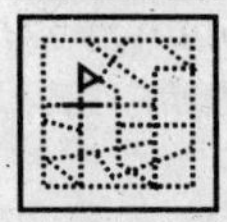

8. (*b*) : 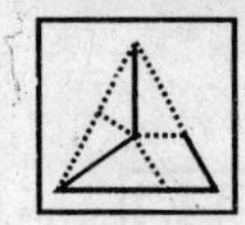

9. (*c*) : 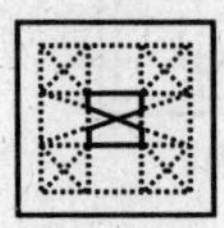

10. (*d*) : 

GENERAL STUDIES

1

Indian History

ANCIENT INDIA

INDUS VALLEY CIVILISATION
(2500-1750 BC)

- The earliest excavations in the Indus valley were done at Harappa in the West Punjab and Mohenjodaro in Sindh. Both places are now in Pakistan.

Important Sites

- The most important sites are Kot Diji in Sindh, Kalibangan in Rajasthan, Ropar in the Punjab, Banawali in Haryana, Lothal, Surkotada and Dhaulavira, all the three in Gujarat.
- Mohenjodaro is the largest of all the Indus cities and it is estimated to have spread over an area of 200 hectares.

Indus Valley Civilisation : An Objective Study

Major Sites	*Excavators*	*Year*	*River*	*Location*	*Important Findings*
1. Harappa	D.R. Sahni	1921	Ravi	West Punjab (Pakistan)	Granaries, Virgin Goddess, Cemetery, Stone symbol of Lingam and Yoni
2. Mohenjodaro	R.D. Banerjee	1922	Indus	Sindh (Pakistan)	Great Bath, Great Granary, Assembly Hall, Proto-Shiva, Brick Kilns, Mesopotamian seals
3. Chanhudaro	N.G. Mazumdar	1931	Indus	Sindh (Pakistan)	Bronze toy cart, Ink-pot, Lipstick, City without a citadel
4. Kalibangan	B.B. Lal & B.K. Thapar	1953	Ghaggar	Ganganagar (Rajasthan)	Decorated bricks, ploughed field surface, Firealtars
5. Lothal	S.R. Rao	1957	Bhogwa	Ahmedabad (Gujarat)	Dockyard, Rice husk, Fire altars, Double burial
6. Banawali	R.S. Bist	1973	Ghaggar	Hissar (Haryana)	Toy plough, Gridiron pattern of Town planning.
7. Dholavira	R.S. Bist	1990	Luni	Kutchh (Gujarat)	A Large well & a bath, A stadium
8. Surkotada	J. Joshi	1964	—	Gujarat	Bones of Horse, Pot burials

Salient Features of the Harappan Culture

- The Harappan Civilization was primarily Urban.
- Mohenjodaro and Harappa were the planned cities.
- The large-scale use of burnt bricks in almost all kinds of constructions are the important characteristics of the Harappan culture.
- Another remarkable feature was the underground drainage system connecting all houses to the street drains which were covered by stone slabs or bricks.
- The most important public place of Mohenjodaro is the Great Bath measuring 39 feet length, 23 feet breadth and 8 feet depth.
- Agriculture was the most important occupation. In the fertile soils, farmers cultivated two crops a year. They were the first who had grown paddy.
- Wheat and barley were the main crops grown besides sesame, mustard and cotton.
- Animals like sheep, goats and buffalo were domesticated. The use of horse is not yet firmly established.
- Bronze and copper vessels are the outstanding examples of the Harappan metal craft.
- A large number of seals numbering more than 2000 have been discovered.

Social Life

- Jewelleries such as bangles, bracelets, fillets, girdles, anklets, ear-rings and finger rings were worn by women. These ornaments were made of gold, silver, copper, bronze and semi precious stones.
- Fishing was a regular occupation while hunting and bull fighting were other pastimes.

- Manufacture of terracotta (burnt clay) was a major industry of the people.
- Figures of animals such as sacred bull and dove were discovered. The figures of Mother Goddesses were used for religious purposes.
- Most of the inscriptions were engraved on seals. It is interesting to note that the Indus script has not yet been deciphered.
- The Pipal tree was used as a religious symbol.
- The origin of the '*Swastika*' symbol can be traced to the Harrapan Civilization.
- The chief male deity was Pasupati, (proto-Siva) represented in seals as sitting in a yogic posture with three faces and two horns.

THE VEDIC PERIOD

RIG VEDIC AGE (1500 - 1000 B.C.)

- The Early Vedic period is known from the *Rig Veda*.
- The *Rig Veda* refers to Saptasindhu or the land of seven rivers. This includes the five rivers of the Punjab, namely, Jhelum, Chenab, Ravi, Beas and Sutlej along with the Indus and Saraswati.
- Historians view that the Aryans came from Central Asia. They entered India through the Khyber pass between 2000 B.C. and 1500 B.C. They first settled in seven places in the Punjab region which they called Sapta Sindhu. Slowly, they moved towards the Gangetic Valley.
- The Aryan Civilisation was a rural civilisation.

Vedic Literature

- The word 'Veda' is derived from the root 'vid', which means to know and signifies 'superior knowledge'.
- The Vedic literature consists of the four Vedas – Rig, Yajur, Sama and Atharva.
- The *Rig Veda* is the earliest of the four Vedas divided into 10 mandalas and it consists of 1028 hymns. The hymns were sung by *Hotri* in praise of various gods.
- The *Yajur Veda* consists of various details of rules to be observed at the time of sacrifice. Its hymns were recited by *Adharvayus*.
- The *Sama Veda* is set to tune for the purpose of chanting during sacrifice. It is called the book of chants and the origins of Indian music are traced in it. Its hymns were recited by *Udgatri*.
- The *Atharva Veda* contains details of rituals.
- Besides the Vedas, there are other sacred works like the Brahmanas, the Aranyakas, the Upanishads, and the epics Ramayana and Mahabharata.

Political Organisation

- During this period, the kingdom was tribal in character. Each tribe formed a separate kingdom.
- The basic unit of political organisation was *kula* or family.
- The highest political unit was called *jana* or tribe.
- There were several tribal kingdoms during the Rig Vedic period such as Bharatas, Matsyas, Yadus and Purus. The head of the kingdom was called as *rajan* or king.
- There were two popular bodies called the *Sabha* and *Samiti*. The former seems to have been a council of elders and the latter, a general assembly of the entire people.

Social Life

- Family was the basis of the society.
- The head of the family was known as *grihapathi*.

Economic Condition

- The Rig Vedic Aryans were pastoral people and their main occupation was cattle rearing. Their wealth was estimated in terms of their cattle.
- Carpentry was another important profession.

RELIGION

- The important Rig Vedic gods were Prithvi (Earth), Agni (Fire), Vayu (Wind), Varuna (Rain) and Indra (Thunder).
- Indra was the most popular among them during the early Vedic period.
- There were also female gods like Aditi and Ushas. There were no temples and no idol worship during the early Vedic period.

Rigvedic Rivers

River	Name in Rigveda
Indus	Sindhu
Jhelum	Vitasta
Chenab	Asikni
Ravi	Parushini
Beas	Vipasa
Sutlej	Sutudri
Gomati	Gomal
Saraswati	Sarasvati
Ghaggar	Prishadavati

LATER VEDIC PERIOD (1000–600 B.C.)

- This age is also called as the Epic Age because the two great epics the Ramayana and Mahabharata were written during this period.
- The Sama, Yajur, Atharva Vedas, Brahmanas, Aranyakas, Upanishads and the two epics are the sources of information for this period.

Political Organisation

- Larger kingdoms were formed during the later Vedic period.
- The king performed various rituals and sacrifices to strengthen his position.

- They include Rajasuya (consecration ceremony), Asvamedha (horse sacrifice) and Vajpeya (chariot race).
- Kingship became hereditary.
- Kings assumed titles like Ekrat, Samrat and Sarvabhauma.

Economic Condition

- Iron was used extensively in this period and this enabled the people to clear forests and to bring more land under cultivation. Agriculture became the chief occupation.
- Taxes like Bali, Sulk and Bhaga were collected from the people.
- Wealth was calculated in terms of cows.

Social Life

- The four divisions of society (Brahmins, Kshatriyas, Vaisyas and Sudras) or the Varna system was thoroughly established during the Later Vedic period.
- The Ashrama system was formed to attain 4 purusharthas. They were *Dharma*, *Artha*, *Kama* and *Moksha*.

Religion

- Gods of the Early Vedic period like Indra and Agni lost their importance. Prajapathi (the creator), Vishnu (the protector) and Rudra (the destroyer) became prominent during the Later Vedic period.

JAINISM AND BUDDHISM

JAINISM

- Jainism originated in the 6th century B.C. It rejected Vedic religion and avoided its rituals.
- Founded by Rishabha Deva. Rishabha Deva was succeeded by 23 Thirthankaras (prophets). Mahavira was the 24th Thirthankara.

Vardhamana Mahavira (540-468 B.C.)

- Vardhamana was born in a village called Kundagrama near Vaishali in Bihar.
- His father was *Siddhartha*. He was the head of a famous Kshatriya clan.
- His mother was *Trisala*. She was a princess of the Lichchhavi clan. She was the sister of the ruler of Vaishali.
- Vardhamana was married to *Yasoda*, a princess. They had a daughter.
- At the age of 30, he left his home and family. He became an ascetic (monk). He wandered from place-to-place in search of truth for 12 years.
- In the 13th year of his penance, he attained the highest spiritual knowledge called Kevalya or Jnana. Thereafter, he was called Mahavira and Jina. His followers were called Jains and his religion Jainism.
- He died at the age of 72 in 468 B.C. at a place called Pavapuri near modern Rajgir in Bihar.

Teachings of Jainism

- The three principles of Jainism, also known as Triratnas (three gems), are:
  1. right faith.
  2. right knowledge.
  3. right conduct.
- Mahavira preached his disciples to follow the five principles. They are:
  1. Ahimsa—not to injure any living beings
  2. Satya—to speak the truth
  3. Asteya—not to steal
  4. Tyag—not to own property
  5. Brahmacharia—to lead a virtuous life.

Spread of Jainism

- Mahavira preached his religion in Prakrit language which was the language of the masses.
- Chandragupta Maurya, Kharavela of Kalinga and the royal dynasties of south India such as the Gangas, the Kadambas, the Chalukyas and the Rashtrakutas patronised Jainism.
- Jainism was divided into two sects after Vallabhi Council, namely *Svetambaras* (wearing white dresses) under Sthulbhadra and *Digambaras* (naked) under Bhadrabahu.
- The first Jain Council was convened at Pataliputra by Sthulabahu, the leader of the *Digambaras*, in the beginning of the 3rd century B.C.
- The second Jain Council was held at Vallabhi in 5th century A.D. The final compilation of Jain literature called *Twelve Angas* was completed in this council.

BUDDHISM

Gautama Buddha (563-483 B.C.)

- Buddha's original name was *Siddhartha*.
- Siddhartha was born in the Lumbini Garden near Kapilavastu in Nepal. His father was Suddhodana. He was a Sakya chief of Kapilavastu. His mother, Mayadevi, died when Siddhartha was only seven days old. He was brought up by his step mother Mahaprajapati Gauthami.
- At the age of sixteen Siddhartha, married Yasodhara and gave birth to a son, Rahul.
- The sight of an old man, a diseased man, a corpse and an ascetic turned him away from worldly life. He left home at the age of twenty-nine in search of Truth.
- He wandered for seven years and at last, he sat under a bodhi tree at Bodh Gaya in Bihar and did intense penance, after which he got Enlightenment (Nirvana) at the age of thirty-five. Since then, he became known as the Buddha or 'the Enlightened One'.
- Buddha delivered his first sermon at Sarnath near Banaras (now Varanasi).
- He died at the age of 80 in 483 B.C. at Kushinagar in Uttar Pradesh.

Teachings of Buddha

- The Four Noble Truths of Buddha are:
  1. The world is full of suffering.
  2. The cause of suffering is desire.
  3. If desires are get rid off, suffering can be removed.
  4. This can be done by following the Eightfold Path.
- The Eightfold Path consists of:
  1. Right Thought.
  2. Right Belief.
  3. Right Speech.
  4. Right Action.
  5. Right Living.
  6. Right Efforts.
  7. Right Knowledge.
  8. Right Meditation.

Buddhist Literature

- In Pali language.
- Buddhist scriptures in Pali are commonly referred to as *Tripitakas, i.e.*, 'Three Baskets'.
- ***Vinaya Pitaka:*** Rules of discipline in Buddhist monasteries.
- ***Sutta Pitaka:*** Largest, contains collection of Buddha's sermons.
- ***Abidhamma Pitaka:*** Explanation of the philosophical principles of the Buddhist religion.

Main Buddhist Councils

Buddhist Council	Time	Place	Chairman	Patron
First	483 BC	Rajagriha	Mahakashyapa	Ajatasatru
Second	383 BC	Vaishali	Sabakamuni	Kalashoka
Third	250 BC	Patliputra	Moggaliputta Tissa	Ashoka
Fourth	AD 72	Kundalvana	Vasumitra, Ashwaghosa	Kanishka

The Mahajanapadas

Mahajanapadas	Capital
1. Kashi	Varanasi
2. Kosala	Shravasti
3. Anga	Champanagri
4. Magadh	Girivraj or Rajgriha
5. Vajji	Vaishali
6. Malla	Kushinagar and Pavapuri
7. Chedi	Shuktimati
8. Vatsa	Kaushambi
9. Kuru	Hastinapur, Indraprastha and Isukara
10. Panchal	Ahichhatra and Kampilya
11. Matsya	Viratnagar
12. Surasen	Mathura
13. Asmaka	Paudanya
14. Avanti	Ujjaini
15. Gandhara	Taxila
16. Kamboj	Rajpur (Hatak)

DYNASTIES OF ANCIENT INDIA

HARYANKA DYNASTY

- Bimbisara was the founder of Haryanka Dynasty.
- He was a contemporary of both Vardhamana Mahavira and Gautama Buddha.
- During his rule, Darius I, the Achaemenian emperor, conquered the Indus Valley area.
- Ajatasatru imprisoned his father Bimbisara.
- The first Buddhist Council was convened by Ajatasatru at Rajgir.
- The immediate successor of Ajatasatru was Udayin.
- Udayin laid the foundation of the new capital at Pataliputra situated at the confluence of the two rivers, the Ganges and the Sone.
- Shishunaga was the founder of Shishunaga dynasty.
- After Shishunaga, the mighty empire began to collapse. His successor was Kakavarman or Kalasoka. During his reign, the second Buddhist Council was held at Vaishali.
- Kalasoka was killed by the founder of the Nanda dynasty.

NANDAS

- The fame of Magadha scaled new heights under the Nanda dynasty.
- Mahapadmananda was the founder of Nanda rule in Magadha.
- The last Nanda ruler was Dhana Nanda. Alexander invaded India during his rule.

MAURYAN EMPIRE

CHANDRAGUPTA MAURYA (322–298 B.C.)

- Chandragupta Maurya was the founder of the Mauryan Empire. He overthrew Nanda dynasty with the help of Chanakya.
- Chandragupta defeated Seleukos Nikator, the Greek general of Alexander, in a battle in 305 B.C.
- Seleukos sent Megasthenes as Greek Ambassador to the Court of Chandragupta. Megasthenes wrote *Indica*.

- Chandragupta was a follower of Jainism.
- He came to Sravana Belgola, near Mysore with a Jain monk called Bhadrabahu. The hill in which he lived until his death is called Chandragiri.
- Chanakya served as prime minister during the reigns of Chandragupta and Bindusara.

BINDUSARA (298–273 B.C.)

- Chandragupta Maurya was succeeded by his son Bindusara.
- Bindusara was called by the Greeks as "*Amitraghatha*" meaning, slayer of enemies.

ASHOKA (273–232 B.C.)

- Ashoka was the most famous ruler of the Mauryan dynasty.
- The most important event of Ashoka's reign was his victorious war with Kalinga in 261 B.C.
- Ashoka convened the Third Buddhist Council at Pataliputra around 250 B.C. in order to strengthen the *Sangha*. It was presided over by Moggaliputta Tissa.
- Ashoka's edicts and inscriptions were deciphered by James Prinsep in 1837.
- The last Mauryan king, Brahadratha was killed by his minister Pushyamitra Sunga. It put an end to the Mauryan Empire.

SUNGAS

- The founder of the Sunga dynasty was *Pushyamitra Sunga*, who was the commander-in-chief under the Mauryas.
- He ascended the throne of Magadha in 185 B.C.
- Pushyamitra was a staunch follower of Brahmanism. He performed two asvamedha sacrifices.
- After the death of Pushyamitra, his son Agnimitra became the ruler.
- Agnimitra was a great conqueror. He was also the hero of the play *Malavikagnimitram* written by Kalidasa.

KANVA

- The last Sunga ruler was Devabhuti, who was murdered by his minister Vasudeva Kanva, the founder of the *Kanva dynasty*.
- The Kanva dynasty ruled for 45 years. After the fall of the Kanvas, the history of Magadha was a blank until the establishment of the Gupta dynasty.

SATAVAHANAS

- The founder of the Satavahana dynasty was Simuka.
- The greatest ruler of the Satavahana dynasty was *Gautamiputra Satakarni*.
- The greatest port of the Satavahanas was Kalyani on the west Deccan. Gandakasela and Ganjam on the east coast were the other important seaports.
- The fine painting at Amaravathi and Nagarjunakonda caves belong to this period.

SANGAM AGE (300 B.C. TO A.D. 300)

- The Sangam Age constitutes an important chapter in the history of South India.
- According to Tamil legends, there existed three Sangams (Academy of Tamil poets) in ancient Tamil Nadu popularly called Muchchangam. These Sangams flourished under the royal patronage of the Pandyas.
- *The first Sangam*, held at then Madurai, chaired by Agastya.
- *The second Sangam* was held at Kapadapuram, chaired by Tolkappiyar.
- *The third Sangam* at Madurai was founded by Mudathirumaran.

Political History

- The Tamil country was ruled by three dynasties namely the Chera, Chola and Pandyas during the Sangam Age.

CHERAS

- The Cheras ruled over parts of modern Kerala. Their capital was Vanji and their important seaports were Tondi and Musiris.
- The greatest Chera King was *Senguttuvan*.

CHOLAS

- The Chola kingdom of the Sangam period extended from modern Tiruchi district to southern Andhra Pradesh.
- Their capital was first located at Uraiyur and then shifted to Puhar. Kaveripattinam served as their port.

GUPTA PERIOD

- The Gupta period is considered as the *Golden Age* in the history of India because this period witnessed all round developments in Religion, Literature, Science, Art and Architecture.

CHANDRAGUPTA I (320-334 A.D.)

- In the beginning of the 4th Century A.D., Sri Gupta established a small Kingdom at Pataliputra. He is considered as the founder of the Gupta dynasty.
- The first notable ruler of the Gupta dynasty was Chandragupta I. He assumed the title *Maharajadhiraja*. The Meherauli Iron Pillar inscription mentions his extensive conquests.
- Chandragupta I is considered to be the founder of the Gupta era which starts with his accession in A.D. 320.

SAMUDRAGUPTA (335-380 A.D.)

- Samudragupta was the greatest of the rulers of the Gupta dynasty. The Allahabad Pillar inscription provides a detailed account of his reign.

- Because of his military achievements, Samudragupta was hailed as '*Indian Napoleon*'.

CHANDRAGUPTA II (380-414 A.D.)

- Samudragupta was succeeded by his son Chandragupta II Vikramaditya.
- The greatest of the military achievements of Chandragupta II was his war against the Saka *satraps* of western India.
- The famous Chinese pilgrim, Fahien visited India (A.D. 399 - A.D. 414) during the reign of Chandragupta II.

SUCCESSORS OF CHANDRAGUPTA II

- Kumaragupta (415-455) was the son and successor of Chandragupta II. His reign was marked by general peace and prosperity.
- Kumaragupta was the founder of the Nalanda University.
- Kumaragupta was followed by *Skandagupta* who ruled from A.D. 456 to A.D. 468.
- After Skandagupta's death, many of his successors like Purugupta, Narasimhagupta, Buddhagupta and Baladitya could not save the Gupta empire from the Huns. Ultimately, the Gupta power totally disappeared due to the Hun invasions and later by the rise of Yasodharman in Malwa.

PUSHYABHUTI DYNASTY (600 - 647 A.D.)

- The greatest king was *Harshavardhana*, son of Prabhakar Vardhana of Thaneshwar. He shifted the capital to *Kannauj*.
- *Hieun Tsang* visited during his reign.
- He established a large monastery at Nalanda. Banabhata adorned his court, wrote Harshacharita and Kadambari. Harsha himself wrote three plays–Priyadarshika, Ratnawali and Nagananda.

PALLAVAS

- The Pallavas established their kingdom in Tondaimandalam by Simhavishnu with its capital at Kanchipuram.
- Other great Pallava rulers were Mahendravarman I, Narasimhavarman I, and Narasimhavarman II.
- The *Kailasanatha temple* at Kanchipuram is the greatest architectural masterpiece of the Pallava art.

CHALUKYAS (543-755 A.D.)

- Pulakesin I was the founder of the Chalukya dynasty. He established a small kingdom with Vatapi or Badami as its capital.
- The structural temples of the Chalukyas exist at Aihole, Badami and Pattadakal (Virupaksha temple). Cave temple architecture was also famous under the Chalukyas. Their cave temples are found in Ajanta, Ellora and Nasik.

RASHTRAKUTAS (755-975 A.D.)

- The art and architecture of the Rashtrakutas were found at Ellora and Elephanta.

CHOLAS

- Cholas became prominent in the ninth century and established an empire comprising the major portion of South India. Their capital was Tanjore.
- The founder of the Chola kingdom was Vijayalaya.
- Rajaraja Chola built the famous Brihadeeswara temple at Tanjore.
- *Dancing Figure of Shiva* (Nataraja) belong to Chola period.

MEDIEVAL INDIA

ARAB CONQUEST OF SIND

- In 712 A.D., Muhammad bin Quasim invaded Sind. Quasim defeated Dahir, the ruler of Sind and killed him in a well-contested battle.

Mahmud of Ghazni

- In 1024, Mahmud marched from Multan across Rajaputana, defeated the Solanki King Bhimadeva I, plundered Anhilwada and sacked the famous temple of Somanatha. This was his last campaign in India. Mahmud died in 1030 A.D.
- Mahmud patronized art and literature. *Firdausi* was the poet-laureate in the court of Mahmud.

Muhammad Ghori

- Prithviraj Chauhan defeated Ghori in the first battle of Tarain near Delhi in 1191 A.D.
- In the Second Battle of Tarain in 1192, Muhammad Ghori thoroughly routed the army of Prithiviraj, who was captured and killed.
- After his brilliant victory over Prithviraj at Tarain, Muhammad Ghori returned to Ghazni leaving behind his favourite general Qutb-ud-din Aibak to make further conquests in India.

SULTANATE PERIOD

SLAVE DYNASTY (1206-1290)

- The Slave dynasty was also called Mamluk dynasty. Mamluk was the Quranic term for slave.

Qutb-ud-din Aibak

- Qutb-ud-din Aibak was a slave of Muhammad Ghori, who made him the Governor of his Indian possessions.

- After the death of Ghori in 1206, Aibak declared his independence. He assumed the title Sultan and made Lahore his capital.
- Muslim writers call Aibak Lakh Baksh or giver of lakhs because he gave liberal donations to them.
- He built the famous Quwat-Ul-Islam mosque at Delhi. He began the construction of the famous Qutb Minar at Delhi but did not live long to complete it. It was later completed by Iltutmish.

Iltutmish (1210-1236 A.D.)

- Iltutmish belonged to the Ilbari tribe and hence his dynasty was named as Ilbari dynasty.
- He shifted his capital from Lahore to Delhi.
- He organised the *Iqta system* and introduced reforms in civil administration and army.

Raziya (1236-1240 A.D.)

- She appointed an Abyssinian slave Yakuth as Master of the Royal Horses.
- In 1240, Altunia, the governor of Bhatinda revolted against her. She went in personally to suppress the revolt but Altunia killed Yakuth and took Raziya prisoner.
- Bahram Shah, son of Iltutmish killed her.

Balban (1266-1286 A.D.)

- Balban introduced rigorous court discipline and new customs such as prostration and kissing the Sultan's feet to prove his superiority over the nobles.
- He also introduced the Persian festival of *Nauroz* to impress the nobles and people with his wealth and power.
- He established a separate military department - *diwan-i-arz* – and reorganized the army.

KHILJI DYNASTY (1290-1320 A.D.)

- The founder of the Khilji dynasty was Jalaluddin Khilji.
- Ala-ud-din Khilji was the greatest ruler of the Khilji Dynasty.
- He was the first Muslim ruler to extend his empire right upto Rameshwaram in the South.
- The Sultan had built a new city called Siri near Delhi.
- Amir Khusrau the great Persian poet, patronised by Balban, continued to live in Ala-ud-din Khilji's court also.
- He introduced the system of *dagh* (branding of horses) and prepared *huliya* (descriptive list of soldiers).
- Ala-ud-din Khilji maintained a large permanent standing army and paid them in cash from the royal treasury.

TUGHLAQ DYNASTY

- Ghiyas-ud-din Tughlaq was the founder of the Tughlaq dynasty.
- To have the capital at the centre of the empire and safe from the Mongol raids, Tughlaq chose Devagiri as his new capital in A.D. 1327. The Sultan renamed the new capital Daulatabad.
- In 1329-30, Muhammad-bin-Tughlaq introduced a token currency.
- Firoz Shah Tughlaq became Sultan after the death of Muhammad-bin-Tughlaq in A.D. 1351.
- He was the first Sultan to impose irrigation tax.
- He had built new towns of Firozabad, Jaunpur, Hissar and Firozpur.
- Timur—Mongol leader of Central Asia, ordered general massacre in Delhi (AD 1398) at the time of Nasiruddin Mahmud (later Tughlaq king).

SAYYID DYNASTY

- Before his departure from India, Timur appointed Khizr Khan as governor of Multan. He captured Delhi and founded the Sayyid dynasty in 1414.
- Mubarak Shah, Mohammed Shah and Alam Shah were some of the other important noteworthy rulers of Sayyid Dynasty.

LODHI DYNASTY

- The Lodhis were Afghans.
- Bahlol Lodhi was the first Afghan ruler while his predecessors were all Turks. He died in 1489 and was succeeded by his son, Sikandar Lodhi.
- In 1504, Sikandar Lodhi founded the city of Agra and transferred his capital from Delhi to Agra.
- Babar marched against Delhi and defeated and killed Ibrahim Lodhi in the first battle of Panipat (1526).

BAHMANI AND VIJAYANAGAR KINGDOMS

- The break up of the Delhi Sultanate provided an opportunity for the rise of a number of kingdoms in the Deccan.
- After the decline of the Tughlaqs, there arose two important kingdoms in the Deccan. They were the Bahmani and Vijayanagar kingdoms.

VIJAYANAGAR EMPIRE

- The Vijayanagar Kingdom was set up in A.D. 1336. Its aim was to check the spread of Muslim power and protect Hindu Dharma in South India.
- Four dynasties – Sangama, Saluva, Tuluva and Aravidu – ruled Vijayanagar from A.D. 1336 to 1672.
- Vijayanagar was founded in 1336 by Harihara and Bukka of the Sangama dynasty.
- The Moroccan traveller, Ibn Batuta, Venetian traveller Nicolo de Conti, Persian traveller Abdur Razzak and the Portuguese traveller Domingo Paes were among them who left valuable accounts on the socio-economic conditions of the Vijayanagar Empire.

- The Hampi ruins and other monuments of Vijayanagar provide information on the cultural contributions of the Vijayanagar rulers.

KRISHNA DEVA RAYA (1509-1530)

- The Tuluva dynasty was founded by Vira Narasimha.
- The greatest of the Vijayanagar rulers, Krishna Deva Raya belonged to the Tuluva dynasty.
- Krishna Deva Raya himself authored a Telugu work, *Amukthamalyadha* and Sanskrit works, *Jambavati Kalyanam* and *Ushaparinayam*.
- He built the famous *Vittalaswamy* and *Hazara Ramaswamy* temples at Vijayanagar.
- Krishna Deva Raya renovated Virupaksha temple in A.D. 1510.
- After his death the enemies of Vijayanagar joined together and defeated the Vijayanagar ruler in the battle of Talaikota.

BAHMANI KINGDOM

- The founder of the Bahmani kingdom was Alauddin Bahman Shah also known as Hasan Gangu in 1347. Its capital was Gulbarga.
- Ahmad Wali Shah shifted the capital from Gulbarga to Bidar.
- *Gol Gumbaj* was built by *Muhammad Adil Shah*; it is famous for the so called '*Whispering Gallery*'.
- *Quli Qutub Shah* built the famous *Golcunda Fort*.

MUGHAL EMPIRE (1526-1707 AD)

BABAR (1526-1530 AD)

- Babar was the founder of the Mughal Empire in India.
- On 21st April, 1526 the first Battle of Panipat took place between Babar and Ibrahim Lodhi, who was killed in the battle.
- Babar was the first one to use guns or artillery in a battle on the Indian soil.
- Babar defeated Rana Sanga of Mewar in the battle of Kanwah in A.D. 1527.
- Babar was a soldier-scholar and wrote his own autobiography called Babar Nama in Turkish language.

HUMAYUN (1530-1556 AD)

- Sher Shah defeated Humayun at Chausa in A.D. 1539 and again at Kannauj in A.D. 1540.
- After losing his kingdom, Humayun became an exile for the next fifteen years.
- In 1555, Humayun defeated the Afghans and recovered the Mughal throne.
- After six months, he died in 1556 due to his fall from the staircase of his library.
- *Gulbadan Begum*, Humayun's half-sister wrote *Humayun-nama*.

SHER SHAH SURI

- The founder of the Sur dynasty was Sher Shah, whose original name was Farid.
- Sher Shah became the ruler of Delhi in 1540.
- Sher Shah organized a brilliant administrative system. The central government consisted of several departments.
- He built a new city on the banks of the river Yamuna near Delhi.
- Now the old fort called Purana Quila and its mosque is alone surviving.
- He built a Mausoleum at Sasaram, which is considered as one of the master pieces of Indian architecture.

AKBAR (1556-1605 AD)

- When Akbar ascended the throne in A.D. 1556 he was only 14 years old. His guardian Bairam Khan served him as a faithful minister and tutor.
- Bairam Khan, along with Akbar met Hemu in the second Battle of Panipat in 1556. Hemu was initially successful, but lost his consciousness after an arrow hit him. Akbar killed him.
- The Battle of Haldighati was fought between Rana Pratap of Mewar and Mughal army led by Man Singh and Asif Khan. Some historian say that this battle was indecisive but some say that Rana Pratap was defeated.
- Akbar abolished the pilgrim tax and in 1562, he abolished Jaziya.
- Akbar evolved a new faith called Din-i-Illahi or Divine Faith.

JAHANGIR (1605-1627 AD)

- When Akbar died, Prince Salim succeeded with the title Jahangir (Conqueror of World) in 1605.
- Jahangir's eldest son, Khusrau, rebelled against him. He was arrested and put into prison.
- *Guru Arjun Dev, the fifth Sikh Guru* was executed by Jahangir.
- In 1611, Jahangir married Mehrunnisa who was known as Nurjahan (Light of World).
- Jahangir died in A.D. 1627.

SHAHJAHAN (1628-1658 AD)

- The reign of Shahjahan is generally considered as the *Golden Age* of the Mughal period.
- Shahjahan is called as the *Prince of Builders*. He had built the Jama Masjid and Red Fort in Delhi and Taj Mahal in Agra.
- Fine arts like painting, music and literature reached high level of development during Shahjahan's time.

AURANGAZEB (1658-1707 AD)

- Aurangazeb was the last great Mughal ruler. He ascended the throne after killing his three brothers Dara, Shuja and Murad in a fratricidal war.
- Aurangazeb defeated Sikandar Shah of Bijapur and annexed his kingdom.
- Aurangazeb was against the Sikhs and he executed the ninth Sikh Guru Tegh Bahadur.
- He was called *Darvesh* or a *Zinda Pir*. He forbade *Sati*. Conquered Bijapur (AD 1686) and Golconda (AD 1687) and reimposed Jaziya and Pilgrim tax in AD 1679.
- He built *Biwi ka Makbara* on the tomb of his queen *Rabaud-Durani* at Aurangabad; *Moti Masjid* within Red Fort, Delhi; and the Jami or Badshahi Mosque at Lahore.
- Aurangazeb died in A.D. 1707.

LATER MUGHALS / FALL OF THE MUGHALS

Bahadur Shah (1707-1712)

- Assumed the title of *Shah Alam I.*

Jahandar Shah (1712-1713)

- First puppet Mughal emperor. He abolished *jaziya.*

Farrukhsiyar (1713-1719)

Mohammad Shah (1719-1748)

- Nadir Shah (*of Iran*) defeated him in the Battle of Karnal (1739) and took away *Peacock throne* and *Kohinoor diamond.*

Ahmad Shah (1748-1754)

Alamgir II (1754-1759),

Shah Alam II (1759-1806)

Akbar II (1806-1837)

- He gave Ram Mohan Roy the title '*Raja*'. He sent Raja Ram Mohan Roy to London to seek a raise in his allowance.

Bahadur Shah II (1837-1857)

- He was confined by the British to the Red Fort. During the revolt of 1857, he was proclaimed the Emperor by the rebels. He was deported to Rangoon after that.

Literature of Mughal Period

Author	Work
Babar	Tuzuk-i-Babari
Abul Fazal	Ain-i-Akbari, Akbarnamah
Jahangir	Tuzuk-i-Jahangiri
Hamid	Padshahnama
Darashikoh	Majm-ul-Bahrain
Mirza Md Qasim	Alamgirnama

THE MARATHAS

SHIVAJI (1627-1680 AD)

- Shivaji was born at Shivner in 1627. His father was Shahji Bhonsle and mother Jija Bai.
- His religious teacher was Samarth Ramdas and guardian was Dadaji Kondadev.
- In 1674, Shivaji crowned himself at Raigarh and assumed the title Chatrapathi.
- *Ashtapradhan* (eight ministers) helped in administration. These were Peshwas, Sar-i-Naubat (Military), Mazumdar or Amatya (Accounts); Waqenavis (Intelligence); Surnavis (Corres-pondence); *Dabir* or *Sumanta* (Ceremonies); *Nyayadhish* (Justice); and *Panditrao* (Charity).
- Successors of Shivaji were Shambhaji, Rajaram and *Shahu* (fought at Battle of Khed in AD 1708).

THE PESHWAS

- Balaji Vishwanath was the first Peshwa. He began his career as a small revenue official and became Peshwa in 1713. Baji Rao I was the eldest son of Balaji Vishwanath. He was considered as the "greatest exponent of guerilla tactics after Shivaji".
- It was during reign of Balaji Baji Rao (Nanasaheb) when the Marathas lost the Third Battle of Panipat.
- Baji Rao II (last Peshwa) was the first Maratha to have fled from the British attacks instead of fighting with them. Baji Rao II surrendered to Sir John Malcom.

THE SIKH

- Guru Nanak Dev was the founder of Sikhism, the religion that draws its elements from both Hinduism and Islam.
- Name of the ten Sikh Gurus and their works are given below:
  1. **Guru Nanak Dev (1469-1539AD):** The founder of Sikhism.
  2. **Guru Angad Dev (1504-1552AD):** Developed Gurmukhi.
  3. **Guru Amar Das (1479-1574AD):** Struggled against Sati system and Purdah system.
  4. **Guru Ram Das (1534-1581AD):** Founded Amritsar, the holy city of Sikhism.
  5. **Guru Arjun Dev (1563-1606AD):** He built the *Swarn Mandir* (Golden Temple).
  6. **Guru Hargobind (1595-1644 AD):** Established Akal Takht.
  7. **Guru Har Rai (1630-1661 AD)**
  8. **Guru Har Krishan (1656-1664 AD)**
  9. **Guru Tegh Bahadur (1621-1675 AD)**
  10. **Guru Gobind Singh (1666-1708 AD):** Founded the Khalsa and Sikh baptism, composed many poems, and nominated the Sikh sacred text as the final and enduring Guru.

MODERN INDIA

THE ADVENT OF THE EUROPEANS

THE PORTUGUESE

- Vasco-da-Gama, a Portuguese explorer, sailed through the route of Cape of Good Hope and reached near Calicut on 20th May 1498 A.D. during the reign of King Zamorin (Hindu King of Calicut).
- Vasco-da-Gama founded a factory at Cannanore on his second visit to India in 1501. In due course, Calicut, Cochin and Cannanore became the Portuguese trading centres.
- Francisco Almeida came to India in 1505. He was the first Governor of Portuguese possessions in India.
- The real founder of Portuguese power in India was *Alfonso de Albuquerque*. He captured Goa from the rulers of Bijapur in 1510. It was made their headquarters.

THE DUTCH

- The United East India Company of the Netherlands founded a factory at Masulipatnam in 1605.
- They built their first fort on the main land of India at Pulicut in 1609, near Madras (Chennai). They captured Nagapattinam from the Portuguese.
- They made Agra, Surat, Masulipatnam and Chinsura in Bengal as their trading centres.

THE DANES

- The Danish East India Company was established in 1616 in Denmark.
- They came to South India and founded a factory at Tranquebar (Tharangambadi) in 1620. They also made settlements at Serampore near Calcutta (Kolkata).

THE ENGLISH

- The English East India Company was formed in 1599 under a charter granted by Queen Elizabeth in 1600.
- The East India Company sent Sir William Hawkins to the court of the Mughal Emperor Jahangir in 1609 to obtain permission to erect a factory at Surat.
- In 1615, Sir Thomas Roe, another British merchant, came to Jahangir's court.
- He stayed for three years and succeeded in getting permission to set up their trading centres at Agra, Surat, Ahmedabad and Broach.
- In 1690, the British got permission from Aurangazeb to build a factory on the site of Calcutta. In 1696 a fort was built at that place. It was called Fort William.

THE FRENCH

- The French East India Company was established in 1664 under the inspiring and energetic leadership of Colbert, the economic adviser of the French King Louis XIV.
- In 1667, the first French factory was established at Surat by Francis Caron who was nominated as Director-General.
- French were defeated by English in the *Battle of Wandiwash* (1760).

EAST INDIA COMPANY

- After the Battle of Plassey in 1757 and the Battle of Buxar in 1764, the East India Company became a political power.
- India was under the East India Company's rule till 1858 when it came under the direct administration of the British Crown. Robert Clive was the first Governor of Fort William under the Company's rule.

GOVERNOR-GENERALS OF BENGAL

Warren Hastings (1772-85 AD)

- In 1772, the Company appointed Warren Hastings as the Governor of Fort William. The Dual System introduced by Robert Clive was abolished by Warren Hastings.
- Warren Hastings was known for his expansionist policy. His administration witnessed the Rohilla War, the First Anglo-Maratha War and the Second Anglo-Mysore War.
- Pitt's India Act (1784) was passed.

Lord Cornwallis (1786-93 AD)

- Cornwallis inaugurated the policy of making appointments mainly on the basis of merit thereby laying the foundation of the Indian Civil Service.
- Lord Cornwallis introduced Permanent Revenue Settlement.
- Tipu Sultan signed the Treaty of Srirangapatnam in 1792 with the British.

Sir John Shore (1793-98 AD)

- Played an important role in the introduction of Permanent Settlement.
- *Battle of Kharda* between the Nizams and the Marathas (1795).

Wellesley (1798-1805)

- Wellesley came to India with a determination to launch a forward policy that he adopted to achieve his object is known as the 'Subsidiary Alliance'.
- The Fourth Anglo-Mysore War started in 1799. The war was short and decisive. Tipu fought till his capital Srirangapatnam was captured and he himself was shot dead.
- Peshwa Baji Rao II signed the *Treaty* of *Bassein* with the British in 1802. It was a subsidiary treaty and the Peshwa was recognized as the head of the Maratha kingdom.
- The Treaty of Deogaon(1803) was signed between Bhonsle and Wellesley.

Lord Minto (1807-1813)

- Lord Minto concluded the Treaty of Amritsar with Ranjit Singh of Punjab in 1809.
- The Charter Act of 1813 was passed during this period.

Lord Hastings (1813-1823)

- Anglo Nepal War (1814-1816) and Treaty of Sugauli (1816).
- Third Maratha War (1817-18), dissolution of Maratha confederacy and creation of Bombay Presidency.
- He encouraged the freedom of the Press and abolished the censorship introduced in 1799.

GOVERNOR-GENERALS OF INDIA

Lord William Bentinck (1828-1835)

- Charter Act of 1833 was passed and he was made the first Governor-General of India. Before him, the designation was Governor-General of Bengal.
- The social reforms of William Bentinck made his name immortal in the history of British India. These include the abolition of *Sati*, the suppression of Thugs and the prevention of female infanticide.
- The Government Resolution in 1835 made English the official and literary language of India.

Lord Metcalfe (1835-36 AD)

- Known as liberator of press in India.

Lord Auckland (1836-42 AD)

- First Afghan War (1838-42), a disaster for the English.

Lord Ellenborough (1842-44 AD)

- Brought an end to Afghan war. War with Gwalior (1843), *Annexation of Sind* by Charles Napier (1843).

Lord Hardinge (1844-48 AD)

- First Anglo-Sikh War (1845-46) and Treaty of Lahore (1846). Gave preference to English educated persons in employment.

Lord Dalhousie (1848-1856)

- The Doctrine of Lapse was applied by Dalhousie.
- The first railway line connecting Bombay with Thane was opened in 1853.

VICEROYS OF INDIA

Lord Canning (1856-62 AD)

- Lord Canning became the first Viceroy of India in 1858.
- Revolt of 1857, Mutiny took place. Indian Penal Code 1860 was passed.

Lord Elgin (1862 AD)

- Wahabi Movement.

Lord John Lawrence (1864-69 AD)

- Established the *High Courts* at Calcutta, Bombay and Madras in 1865.
- Telegraphic communication was opened with Europe. Created the Indian Forest Department.

Lord Northbrooke (1872-76 AD)

- Kuka Rebellion in Punjab, Famine in Bihar.

Lord Lytton (1876-80)

- In 1878, the Vernacular Press Act was passed. This Act empowered a Magistrate to secure an undertaking from the editor, publisher and printer of a vernacular newspaper that nothing would be published against the English Government. This Act crushed the freedom of the Indian press. In 1878, the Arms Act was passed. This Act prevented the Indians to keep arms without appropriate license.
- Lord Lytton also held a Darbar at Delhi in 1877 in which Queen Victoria was declared as the Empress of India. This extravagant Darbar cost millions of ruppes.
- In 1878, the Statutory Civil Service was established exclusively for Indians.

Lord Ripon (1880-84 AD)

- Lord Ripon repealed the Vernacular Press Act and earned much popularity among Indians.
- Ripon appointed a Commission in 1882 under the chairmanship of Sir William Hunter.
- The Commission came to be known as the Hunter Commission. The Commission recommended for the expansion and improvement of the elementary education of the masses.
- Ripon was founder of local self-government in modern India.

Lord Dufferin (1884-88 AD)

- *Third Burmese War* (1885-86 AD). Establishment of the Indian National Congress in 1885.

Lord Lansdowne (1888-94 AD)

- Factory Act of 1891 granted weekly holiday and stipulated working hours for women and children.

Lord Elgin II (1894-99 AD)

- Southern uprisings of 1899. Great famine of 1896-1897 and Lyall Commission on famine was established.

Lord Curzon (1899-1905 AD)

- Curzon instituted in 1902, a Universities Commission to go into the entire question of university education in the country.
- On the basis of the findings and recommendations of the Commission, Curzon brought in the Indian Universities Act of 1904, which brought all the universities in India under the control of the government.

Lord Minto (1905-10 AD)

- Swadeshi Movement (1905-08); foundation of Muslim League (1906); Surat Session and split in the Congress (1907). Morley-Minto Reforms (1909).

Lord Hardinge (1910-16 AD)

- Capital shifted from Calcutta to Delhi (1911); Delhi Durbar; Partition of Bengal was cancelled.
- The Hindu Mahasabha was founded in 1915 by Pandit Madan Mohan Malaviya.

Lord Chelmsford (1916-21 AD)

- Gandhi returned to India (1915) and founded the Sabarmati Ashram (1916), Champaran Satyagraha, Satyagraha at Ahmedabad (1981), Kheda Satyagraha (1918).
- Rowlatt Act (March, 1919) and the Jallianwala Bagh Massacre (13th April, 1919).
- Khilafat Committee was formed and Khilafat Movement started (1919-20).
- Non-Cooperation Movement started (1920-22).

Lord Reading (1921-26)

- Moplah Rebellion (1921) took place. *Kakori Train* Robbery on 1st August, 1925.
- *Communal Riots* of 1923-25 in Multan, Amritsar, Delhi etc.

Lord Irwin (1926-31 AD)

- Lahore Session of Congress and *Poorna Swaraj* Declaration (1929).
- Simon Commission visited India in 1927.
- Dandi March (12th March, 1930). Civil Disobedience Movement (1930).
- First Round Table Conference was held in England in 1930. Gandhi-Irwin Pact.

Lord Willingdon (1931-36 AD)

- *Second Round Table Conference* in London in 1931 and *third* in 1932.

Lord Linlithgow (1936-43 AD)

- Congress Ministries resignation celebrated as '*Deliverance Day*' by the Muslim League (1939), the Lahore Resolution (23rd March, 1940) of the Muslim League demanding separate state for the Muslims. (It was at this session that Jinnah propounded his Two-Nation Theory). Outbreak of World War II in 1939. Cripps Mission in 1942. Quit India Movement (8th August, 1942).

Lord Wavell (1943-47 AD)

- Cabinet Mission Plan (16th May, 1946).
- First meeting of the Constituent Assembly was held on 9th December, 1946.
- Arranged the Shimla Conference on 25th June, 1945 with Indian National Congress and Muslim League but failed.

Lord Mountbatten (March to Aug, 1947)

- Last viceroy of British India and the first Governor-General of free India.
- Partition of India decided by the 3rd June Plan or Mountbatten Plan.

NATIONAL MOVEMENT (1885-1947)

INDIAN NATIONAL CONGRESS (1885)

- Allan Octavian Hume, a retired civil servant in the British Government took the initiative to form an all-India organization. Thus, the Indian National Congress was founded and its first session was held at Bombay in 1885. W.C. Banerjee was its first president. It was attended by 72 delegates from all over India.
- The second session was held in Calcutta in 1886 and the third in Madras in 1887. Between 1885 and 1905, the Congress leaders were moderates. The Moderates had faith in the British justice and goodwill. They were called moderates because they adopted peaceful and constitutional means to achieve their demands.
- In 1905, Gopal Krishna Gokhale founded the Servants of India Society to train Indians to dedicate their lives to the cause of the country.

Partition of Bengal (1905)

- By Lord Curzon on 16th October, 1905 through a royal proclamation, reducing the old province of Bengal in size by creating East Bengal and Assam out of the rest of Bengal.
- The partition of Bengal in 1905 provided a spark for the rise of extremism in the Indian National Movement.
- Curzon's real motives behind this partition were:
  - To break the growing strength of Bengali nationalism since Bengal was the base of Indian nationalism.
  - To divide the Hindus and Muslims in Bengal.
  - To show the enormous power of the British Government in doing whatever it liked.

Swadeshi Movement (1905)

- The Swadeshi Movement involved programmes like the boycott of government service, courts, schools and colleges and of foreign goods. It was both a political and economic movement.
- Lal, Bal, Pal and Aurobindo Ghosh played an important role.

Muslim League (1906)

- In December 1906, Muslim delegates from all over India met at Dacca for the Muslim Educational Conference.
- Taking advantage of this occasion, Nawab Salimullah of Dacca proposed the setting up of an organisation to look after the Muslim interests. The proposal was accepted.
- The All-India Muslim League was finally set up on December 30, 1906.

Minto Morley Reforms (1909)

- Minto, the Viceroy and Morley, the Secretary of State for India jointly proposed reforms to the Indian Councils. An Act, called the Indian Councils Act or the Minto-Morley Reforms Act was passed in 1909.
- A separate communal electorate was introduced for the Muslims.

The Lucknow Pact (1916)

- During the 1916 Congress session at Lucknow two major events occurred.
- The divided Congress became united. An understanding for joint action against the British was reached between the Congress and the Muslim League and it was called the Lucknow Pact.
- The signing of the Lucknow Pact by the Congress and the Muslim League in 1916 marked an important step in the Hindu-Muslim unity.

The Home Rule Movement (1916)

- Two Home Rule Leagues were established, one by B.G. Tilak at Poona in April 1916 and the other by Mrs. Annie Besant at Madras in September 1916.
- While Tilak's Movement concentrated on Maharashtra, Annie Besant's Movement covered the rest of the country.

August Declaration

- On 20 August, 1917, Montague, the Secretary of State in England, promised the gradual development of self-governing institutions in India.
- This August Declaration led to the end of the Home Rule Movement.

Rowlatt Act (1919)

- In 1917, a committee was set up under the presidentship of Sir Sydney Rowlatt to look into the militant Nationalist activities.
- On the basis of its report the Rowlatt Act was passed in March 1919 by the Central Legislative Council. As per this Act, any person could be arrested on the basis of suspicion. No appeal or petition could be filed against such arrests.
- This Act was called the Black Act and it was widely opposed. An all-India hartal was organized on 6 April, 1919.

Jallianwala Bagh Massacre (13 April, 1919)

- On 13th April, the Baisakhi day (harvest festival), a public meeting was organized at the Jallianwala Bagh (garden). Gen. Dyer marched in and without any warning opened fire on the crowd. The firing continued for about 10 to 15 minutes and it stopped only after the ammunition exhausted.
- According to official report 379 people were killed and 1137 wounded in the incident. There was a nationwide protest against this massacre and Rabindranath Tagore renounced his knighthood as a protest.

Khilafat Movement (1920)

- The chief cause of the Khilafat Movement was the defeat of Turkey in the First World War.
- The Muslims in India were upset over the British attitude against Turkey and launched the Khilafat Movement.
- Ali brothers, *Mohd Ali* and *Shaukat Ali* started this movement. It was jointly led by the Khilafat leaders and the Congress.

Non-Co-operation Movement (1920-22)

- Mahatma Gandhi announced his plan to begin Non-Cooperation with the government as a sequel to the Rowlatt Act, Jallianwala Bagh massacre and the Khilafat Movement.
- It was approved by the Indian National Congress at the Nagpur session in December, 1920.
- The Congress observed the Non-Co-operation movement in 1920. The main aim of this movement was to attain Swaraj through non-violent and peaceful means.
- The whole movement was abruptly called off on 11th February, 1922 by Gandhi following the Chauri-Chaura incident in the Gorakhpur district of U.P. Many top leaders of the country were stunned at this sudden suspension of the Non-Co-operation Movement.
- On 5th February an angry mob set fire to the police station at *Chauri-Chaura* and twenty two police men were burnt to death.

Swaraj Party

- Leaders like Motilal Nehru and Chittranjan Das formed a separate group within the Congress known as the Swaraj Party on 1 January, 1923.
- The Swarajists wanted to contest the council elections and wreck the government from within.

Simon Commission (1927)

- The Act of 1919 included a provision for its review after a lapse of ten years. However, the review commission under the chairmanship of Sir John Simon was appointed by the British Government two years earlier of its schedule in 1927.
- Indian leaders opposed the commission, as there were no Indians in it, they cried *Simon Go Back*.
- The government used brutal repression and at Lahore, *Lala Lajpat Rai* was severely beaten in lathi-charge.

Nehru Report (1928)

- The Secretary of State, Lord Birkenhead, challenged the Indians to produce a Constitution that would be acceptable to all. The challenge was accepted by the Congress, which convened an all party meeting on 28 February, 1928.
- A committee consisting of eight was constituted to draw up a blueprint for the future Constitution of India. It was headed by Motilal Nehru. The Report published by this Committee came to be known as the Nehru Report.

Lahore Session (1929)

- On Dec. 19, 1929, under the Presidentship of J.L. Nehru, the INC, as its Lahore session, declared Poorna Swaraj (Complete Independence) as its ultimate goal.
- On Dec. 31, 1929, the newly adopted tricolour flag was unfurled and Jan. 26, 1930 was fixed as the First Independence Day, which was to be celebrated every year.

Dandi March (1930)

- On 12th March, 1930, Gandhi began his famous March to Dandi with his chosen 79 followers to break the salt laws. He reached the coast of Dandi on 5 April, 1930 after marching a distance of 200 miles and on 6 April formally launched the Civil Disobedience Movement by breaking the salt laws.

Civil Disobedience Movement

- Countrywide mass participation by women.
- The Garhwal soldiers refused to fire on the people at Peshawar.

Round Table Conference

- The first Round Table Conference was held in November 1930 at London and it was boycotted by the Congress.
- On 8th March, 1931 the Gandhi-Irwin Pact was signed. As per this pact, Mahatma Gandhi agreed to suspend the Civil-Disobedience Movement and participate in the Second-Round Table Conference.
- In September 1931, the Second Round Table Conference was held at London. Mahatma Gandhi participated in the Conference but returned to India disappointed. In January 1932, the Civil-Disobedience Movement was resumed.

Poona Pact (1932)

- The idea of separate electorate for the depressed classes was abandoned, but seats reserved for them in the provincial legislature were increased.
- Thus, Poona Pact agreed upon a joint electorate for upper and lower castes.

Demand for Pakistan

- *Chaudhary Rehmat Ali* gave the term *Pakistan* in 1933.
- In March 1940, the Muslim League demanded the creation of Pakistan.

Cripps Mission (1942)

- The British Government in its effort to secure Indian co-operation in the Second World War sent Sir Stafford Cripps to India on 23 March, 1942. This is known as Cripps Mission. The main recommendations of Cripps was the promise of Dominion Status to India.
- Congress rejected it. Gandhi called Cripp's proposals as a "Post-dated Cheque".

Quit India Movement (1942-1944)

- The All India Congress Committee met at Bombay on 8th August, 1942 and passed the famous Quit India Resolution. On the same day, Gandhi gave his call of 'do or die'.
- On 8th and 9th August, 1942, the government arrested all the prominent leaders of the Congress. Mahatma Gandhi was kept in prison at Poona.
- Pandit Jawaharlal Nehru, Abul Kalam Azad, and other leaders were imprisoned in the Ahamednagar Fort. Quit India Movement was the final attempt for country's freedom.

Indian National Army (INA)

- On July 2, 1943, Subhash Chandra Bose reached Singapore and gave the rousing war cry of *'Dilli Chalo'*. He was made the President of Indian Independence League and soon became the supreme commander of the Indian National Army. He gave the country the slogan of *Jai Hind.*
- INA had three fighting brigades named after Gandhi, Azad and Nehru. Rani of Jhansi Brigade was an exclusive women force. INA headquarters were at Rangoon and Singapore.

Cabinet Mission (1946)

- The Cabinet Mission put forward a plan for solution of the constitutional problem. A proposal was envisaged for setting up an Interim Government, which would remain in office till a new government was elected on the basis of the new Constitution framed by the Constituent Assembly. Elections were held in July 1946 for the formation of a Constituent Assembly. Muslim league observed the *Direct Action Day* on 16 August, 1946.
- An Interim Government was formed under the leadership of Jawaharlal Nehru on 2 September, 1946.

Mountbatten Plan (1947)

- On 20 February 1947, Prime Minister Atlee announced in the House of Commons the definite intention of the British Government to transfer power to responsible Indian hands by a date not later than June 1948.
- Lord Mountbatten armed with vast powers became India's Viceroy on 24 March, 1947. The partition of India and the creation of Pakistan appeared inevitable to him.
- After extensive consultation Lord Mountbatten put forth the plan of partition of India on 3 June, 1947.
- The Congress and the Muslim League ultimately approved the Mountbatten Plan.

Indian Independence Act, 1947

- The salient features of this Act was the partition of the country into India and Pakistan would come into effect from 15 August, 1947.
- On 15th August, 1947 India, and on the 14th August Pakistan came into existence as two independent states.
- Lord Mountbatten was made the first Governor General of Independent India, whereas Mohammad Ali Jinnah became the first Governor General of Pakistan.
- C. Rajagopalachari became the first and last Indian Governor-General of India. When India became a Republic on 26 January, 1950 Dr. Rajendra Prasad became the first President of our country.

❑ ❑ ❑

2

Geography

WORLD GEOGRAPHY

THE UNIVERSE

- Existing matter and energy are together known as **Universe.**

GALAXY

- A galaxy is a huge system of billions of stars and clouds of dust and gases.
- Our solar system is a part of *Milky Way* galaxy.
- There are millions of galaxies that make the Universe.

STARS

- Stars account for 98 per cent of the matter in a galaxy. The stars nearest to the earth are *Proxima Centauri, Alpha Centauri, Barnard's Star, Sirius* and so on. Of these, *Sirius* is the brightest.

LIGHT YEAR

- Light year is the distance travelled by light in one year at a speed of 2,99,792.5 km. per second.

SOLAR SYSTEM

- The Sun, eight planets, satellites and some other celestial bodies known as asteroids and meteoroids form the solar system.

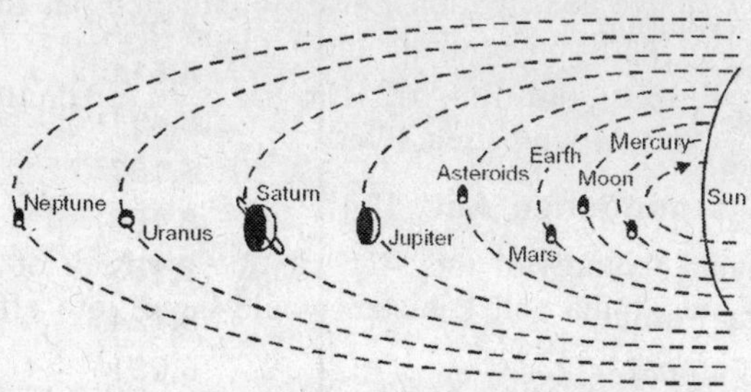

SUN

- The Sun is in the centre of the solar system.
- The Sun is a mixture of gases. It consists of 92% hydrogen, 7.8% helium and 0.2% other gases.
- The Sun is about 150 million km away from the earth.
- The sun is an ultimate source of energy for life on Earth.
- Sunlight takes 8 min 16.6 sec to reach earth.

Facts about Sun

Diameter	— 1.392×10^6 km
Volume	— 1.304 × 106 times the volume of earth
Temperature	— 6000°C at surface and 15 million degree C at the centre
Relative density	— 1.4
Gravitational Pull	— 28 times the gravitational pull of the earth

Facts about Planets

Closest to Sun	*Mercury*
Farthest from Sun	*Neptune*
Heaviest	*Jupiter*
Hottest	*Venus*
Inner	*Mercury, Venus, Earth, Mars*
Largest	*Jupiter*
Smallest	*Mercury*
Moons, None	*Mercury, Venus*
Moon; Largest	*Ganymede (Jupiter), larger than Mercury*
Nearest to Earth	*Venus*
Orbits; Order	*Mercury (closest to Sun), Venus, Earth, Mars, Jupiter, Saturn, Uranus, Neptune.*
Rings/largest number	*Saturn*
Spin; Backwards	*Venus (East to West)*

COMETS

- It has a head and a tail. Its tail originates only when it gets closer to the sun. The tail can be 20-30 million km long. It always point away from the sun because of the force exerted by solar wind and radiation on the cometory material.

THE EARTH

- The earth is the third nearest planet to the Sun.
- From the outer space, the earth appears blue because its two-thirds surface is covered by water. It is, therefore, called a blue planet. It is the densest of all planets.
- Rotation is the movement of the earth on its axis. Due to this rotation, day and night occur.
- The earth takes about 23 hours 56 minutes and 4 seconds to complete one rotation around its axis.
- Earth takes 365¼ days (one year) to revolve around the sun.

THE MOON

- Earth has only one satellite, that is, the moon.
- Its diameter is only one-quarter that of the earth. It is about 3,84,400 km away from us.
- The moon moves around the earth in about 27 days. It takes exactly the same time to complete one spin. As a result, only one side of the moon (only 59% of its surface) is visible to us on the earth.
- Moonlight takes 1.3 sec. to reach earth.

LATITUDE

- Imaginary lines drawn parallel to the equator. Measured as an angle whose apex is at the centre of the earth.
- The equator represents 0° latitude, while the North Pole is 90°N and the South Pole 90°S.
- 23½°N represents Tropic of Cancer while 23½°S represents Tropic of Capricorn.

LONGITUDE

- It is the angular distance measured from the centre of the earth. On the globe the lines of longitude are drawn as a series of semicircles that extend from the North Pole to the South Pole through the equator. They are also called meridians.
- The distance between any two meridians is not equal. At the equator, 1 degree = 111 km. At 30°N or S, it is 96.5 km. It goes on decreasing this way until it is zero at the poles.

INTERNATIONAL DATE LINE

- It is the 180° meridian running over the Pacific Ocean, deviating at Aleutian Islands, Fiji, Samoa and Gilbert Islands.
- Travellers crossing the Date Line from west to east repeat a day and travellers crossing it from east to west lose a day.

INDIAN STANDARD TIME (IST)

- Indian Standard Time is calculated on the basis of 82.5°E longitude which passes through Uttar Pradesh, Madhya Pradesh, Odisha, Chattisgarh and Andhra Pradesh.

EARTHQUAKES

- Earthquakes are a form of wave energy that is transferred through bedrock. It is transmitted from the point of the earthquake focus, as spherical seismic waves. They travel in all directions outward.
- The intensity of earthquake waves is recorded by *Seismograph*.

LANDFORMS

- There are three major landforms: mountains, plateaus and plains.

MOUNTAINS

- A mountain can be defined as an area of land that rises abruptly from the surrounding region.
- There are three types of mountains- *Fold Mountains, Block Mountains* and the ***Volcanic Mountains***.
- Himalayas, Alps, Andes, Rockies, Atlas, etc are examples of Fold Mountains. The Aravali range in India is one of the oldest **fold mountain** systems in the world.
- The Rhine valley and the Vosges mountain in Europe are examples of such mountain systems.
- Volcanic mountains are formed due to volcanic activity.
- Mt. Kilimanjaro in Africa and Mt. Fujiyama in Japan are examples of such mountains.

Major Mountain Ranges of the World

Range	Location	Highest Peak (m)	Length (km)
Andes	South America	6,960	7,200
Himalayas-Karakoram-Hindukush	South Central Asia	8,848	4,800
Rockies	North America	4,401	4,800
Great Dividing Range	East Australia	2,228	3,600
Western Ghat	Western India	2,637	1,610
Caucasus	Europe	5,642	1,200
Alaska	USA	6,194	1,130
Alps	Europe	4,808	1,050
Apennines	Europe	2,912	—
Ural	Asia	1,895	—
Atlas	North West Africa	—	1,930

PLATEAUS

- A plateau is an elevated flat land. It is a flat-topped table land standing above the surrounding area.

Principal Mountain Peaks of the World

Mountains	Height in Metres
1. Mount Everest	8,848
2. K-2 (Godwin Austen)	8,611
3. Kanchenjunga	8,597
4. Lhotse	8,511
5. Makalu I	8,481
6. Dhaulagiri I	8,167
7. Mansalu I	8,156
8. Chollyo	8,153
9. Nanga Parbat	8,124
10. Annapurna I	8,091
11. Gasherbrum I	8,068
12. Broad Peak I	8,047
13. Gasherbrum II	8,034
14. Shisha Pangma (Gosainthan)	8,014
15. Gasherbrum III	7,952

PLAINS

- A relatively low-lying and flat land surface with least difference between its highest and lowest points is called a Plain.

OCEANS

- Oceans of the world is classified into four groups: the Pacific, the Atlantic, the Arctic and the Indian.
- The Pacific is the largest ocean, being twice the size of the Atlantic. It covers about a third of the Earth's surface, and contains more than half the water on the planet.

Oceans of the World

Names	Area (Sq. Km.)	Greatest Depth
Pacific	166,240000	Mariana Trench
Atlantic	86,560000	Puerto Rico Trench
Indian	73430000	Java Trench
Arctic	13230000	—

Major Rivers of the World

River	Origin	Falls in	Length (Km.)
Nile	Victoria lake	Mediterranean Sea	6,650
Amazon	Andes (Peru)	Atlantic Ocean	6,428
Yangtze	Tibetan Kiang Plateau	China Sea	6,300
Mississippi Missouri	Itaska lake (USA)	Gulf of Mexico (USA)	6,275
Yenisei	Tannu-Ola Mts.	Arctic Ocean	5,539
Hoang Ho	Kunlun Mts.	Gulf of Chibli	5,464
Ob	Altai Mts., Russia	Gulf of Ob	5,410
Congo	Lualaba & Luapula rivers	Atlantic Ocean	4,700
Amur	Northeast China	Sea of Okhotsk	4,444
Lena	Baikal Mts	Laptev Sea	4,400
Mekong	Tibetan Highlands	South China Sea	4,350
Mackenzie	Great Slave Lake	Beaufort Sea	4,241
Niger	Guinea	Gulf of Guinea	4,200

Major Gulfs of the World

Names	Area (Sq. Km.)	Names	Areas (Sq. Km.)
Gulf of Mexico	15,44,000	Gulf of St. Lawrence	2,37,000
Gulf of Hudson	12,33,000	Gulf of California	1,62,000
Arabian Gulf	2,38,000	English Channel	89,900

Important Straits of the World

Straits	Water Bodies joined	Area
Bab-al-Mandeb	Red Sea & Arabian Sea	Arabia & Africa
Bering	Arctic Ocean & Bering Sea	Alaska & Asia
Bosphorus	Black Sea & Marmara Sea	Turkey.
Dover	North Sea & Atlantic Ocean	England & Europe
Florida	Gulf of Mexico & Atlantic Ocean	Florida & Bahamas Islands
Gibralter	Mediterranean Sea & Atlantic Ocean	Spain & Africa
Malacca	Java Sea & Bay of Bengal	India & Indonesia
Palk	Bay of Bengal & Indian Ocean	India & Sri Lanka
Magellan	South Pacific & South Atlantic Ocean	Chile
Sunda	Java Sea & Indian Ocean	Indonesia

Important Lakes of the World

Lake	Location	Area (Sq. Km.)
Caspian	Russia and CIS	371000
Superior	Canada and USA	82414
Victoria	Tanzania (Africa)	69485
Huron	Canada and USA	59596
Michigan	USA	58016
Tanganyika	Africa	32892

Lake	Location	Area (Sq. Km.)
Baikal	Russia (CIS)	31502
Great Bear	Canada	31080
Malawi	Malawi (Tanzania)	30044
Great Slave	Canada	28438

Highest Waterfalls of the World

Name(s) (Foreign)	Location
Angel (Salto Angel)	Canaima Nat'l Park, Venezuela
Tugela	Natal Nat'l Park, South Africa
Utigord (Utigordsfoss)	Norway
Monge (Mongefoss)	Marstein, Norway
Gocta Cataracts	Chachapoyas, Peru
Mutarazi (Mtarazi)	Nyanga Nat'l Park, Zimbabwe
Yosemite	Yosemite Nat'l Park, California, U.S.
Espelands (Espelandsfoss)	Hardanger Fjord, Norway
Lower Mar Valley (Ostra Mardolafoss)	Eikesdal, Norway
Tyssestrengene	Odda, Norway

Continents: Some Facts

Continent	Biggest Counrty	Highest Peak	Longest River
Asia	China	Mt. Everest (8848 m)	Yangtze Kiang
Africa	Algeria	Mt. Kilimanjaro (5895 m)	Nile
North America	Canada	Mt. Mckinley (6194 m)	Mississippi Missouri
South America	Brazil	Mt. Acancagua (6960 m)	Amazon
Europe	Russia	Mt. Elbrus (5642 m)	Ob
Australia	Australia	Mt. Coscuisco (2228 m)	Darling
Antarctica	—	Vinson Massif (5140 m)	—

INDIAN GEOGRAPHY

AREA AND LOCATION

- India is in the southern parts of the Asian continent. In the west of India lies the Arabian Peninsula while in the east lies the Indo-China Peninsula.
- India extends between 8°4' N and 37°6' N latitudes and between 68°7' E and 97°2' E longitudes.
- India, has a total geographic area of 32,87,263 sq. km. This is only 2.42 % of the total geographic area of the world but holds 17.5 per cent of the world's population.
- The 23½ºN, which is the Tropic of Cancer, runs across the country.
- India has a length of 3214 km from north to south and 2933 km from east to west. It has a land frontier of 15200 km.
- The total length of the coastline of the mainland, Lakshadweep Islands and Andaman and Nicobar Islands is 7,516.6 km.
- India ranks seventh among the countries of the world, in terms of the geographical extent.
- India is bordered on three sides by water and on one by land, it is also a peninsula.
- India shares its common border with Afghanistan and Pakistan in the north-west, China and Bhutan in the north, and Bangladesh in the east. In the south, Sri Lanka is separated from India by a strait, known as the Palk Strait.
- 82°30' E longitude is considered as the Indian Standard Meridian. The local time of this longitude is taken as the Indian Standard Time (IST). This is 5½ hours ahead of the Greenwich Mean Time.

THE INDIAN STATES/UT's ON INTERNATIONAL BOUNDARIES ARE:

- ***Bordering Pakistan:*** Jammu and Kashmir, Punjab, Rajasthan, Gujarat.

- ***Bordering China:*** Jammu and Kashmir, Ladakh, Himachal Pradesh, Uttarakhand, Sikkim, Arunachal Pradesh.
- ***Bordering Nepal:*** Bihar, Uttarakhand, UP, Sikkim, West Bengal.
- ***Bordering Bangladesh:*** West Bengal, Mizoram, Meghalaya, Tripura, Assam.
- ***Bordering Bhutan:*** West Bengal, Sikkim, Arunachal Pradesh, Assam.
- ***Bordering Myanmar:*** Arunachal Pradesh, Nagaland, Manipur, Mizoram.
- ***Bordering Afghanistan:*** Jammu and Kashmir (Pakistan-occupied area).

Important Passes

Jammu & Kashmir	Burzi-La
Himachal Pradesh	Bara La, Cha-La, Shipki-La
Uttarakhand	Niti-La, Lipu-Lekh-La
Sikkim	Jelep-La, Nathu-La
Arunachal Pradesh	Bomdi-La
Ladakh	Joji-La

Heighest Mountain Peaks of India

Peaks	Elevation• (in mts.)
Godwin Austin (K2)	8611*
Kanchenjunga	8598
Nanga Parvat	8126
Gasherbrum	8068*
Broad Peak	8047*
Dastegil	7885*
Masherbrum (East)	7821
Nanda Devi	7817
Masherbrum (West)	7806*
Rakoposhi	7788*
Kamet	7756
Saser Kangdi	7672

• *Above mean sea level in metres.*

* *Situated in Pak occupied Kashmir (PoK).*

Towns at River Banks

Town	River	Town	River
Agra	Yamuna	Varanasi	The Ganges
Ayodhya	Saryu	Kolkata	Hooghly
Cuttuck	Mahanadi	Delhi	Yamuna
Dibrugarh	Brahmaputra	Ferozepur	Satluj
Guwahati	Brahmaputra	Hardwar	The Ganges
Hyderabad	Musi	Jabalpur	Narmada
Kanpur	The Ganges	Kota	Chambal
Kurnool	Tungbhadra	Lucknow	Gomti
Ludhiana	Sutlej	Nasik	Godavari
Pandharpur	Bhima	Patna	The Ganges
Sambalpur	Mahanadi	Srinagar	Jhelum
Srirangapattam	Cauveri	Prayagraj	Confluence of the Ganges and the Yamuna
Surat	Tapti		
Vijaywada	Krishna		
Ahmedabad	Sabarmati		
Ferozpur	Sutlej	Raurkela	Brahmani
Jabaplpur	Narmada	Vadodara	Vishwamitri

Important Waterfalls of India

Waterfall	Hgt (Mt.)	River	State
Kunchikal	455	Varahi	Karnataka
Dudhsagar	310	Mandvi	Goa
Jog/Gersoppa	260	Sharavati	Karnataka
Rakim Kund	168	Gaighat	Bihar
Chachai	127	Bihad	Madhya Pradesh
Kevti	98	Mahanadi	Madhya Pradesh
Sivasamudram	90	Cauveri	Karnataka

Important Lakes of India

Name of lake	State/UT
Pulicat Lake	Tamil Nadu & Andhra Pradesh Border
Sambhar Lake	Rajasthan
Tso Moriri Lake	Jammu & Kashmir
Vembanad Lake	Kerala
Wular & Dal Lakes	Jammu and Kashmir
Chilka Lake	Odisha
Kolleru Lake	Andhra Pradesh
Loktak Lake	Manipur
Lonar Lake	Maharashtra
Pangong Lake	Ladakh

Rivers of India

Name	Originates From	Falls Into
Yamuna	Yamunotri	Ganga
Chambal	Singar Chouri Peak, Vindhyan escarpment	Yamuna
Ghaghara	Matsatung Glacier	Ganga
Kosi	Near Gosain Dham Peak	Ganga
Sabarmati	Aravalis	Gulf of Khambat
Krishna	Western Ghats	Bay of Bengal
Godavari	Nasik district in Maharashtra	Bay of Bengal
Caurey	Brahmagir Range of Western Ghats	Bay of Bengal

Name	Originates From	Falls Into
Tungabharda	Western Ghats	Krishna
Ganges	Combines Sources	Bay of Bengal
Sutlej	Mansarovar Rakas lakes	Chenab
Indus	Near Mansarovar Lake	Arabian Sea
Ravi	Kullu Hills near Rohtang Pass	Chenab
Beas	Near Rohtang Pass	Sutlej
Jhelum	Verinag in Kashmir	Chenab
Son	Amarkantak	Ganga
Brahmaputra	Near Mansarovar Lake	Bay of Bengal
Narmada	Amarkantak	Gulf of Khambat
Tapti	Betul District in Madhya Pradesh	Gulf of Khambat
Mahanadi	Raipur District in Chhattisgarh	Bay of Bengal
Luni	Aravallis	Rann of Kuchchh
Ghaggar	Himalayas	Near Fatehabad
Betwa	Vindhyanchal	Yamuna

Geographical Surnames

Bengal's Sorrow	Damodar River	City of Lakes	Srinagar
City of Palaces	Kolkata	Twin City	Hyderabad-Secunderabad
Gateway of India	Mumbai	City of Seven Islands	Mumbai
Pink City	Jaipur	Diamond Harbour	Kolkata
Paris of India	Jaipur	Switzerland of India	Kashmir
Manchester of India	Ahmedabad	Rice Bowl	Chhattisgarh
Kashmir of South	Kerala	Fruit Bowl	Himachal Pradesh
Son of Sea	Lakshadweep	Ganga of South	Cauvery
Queen of Mountains	Mussourie	Pitsburg of India	Jamshedpur
Iron City	Jamshedpur	City of Bridges	Srinagar
Hollywood of India	Mumbai	Residence of God	Allahabad
Scotland of East	Meghalaya	A Cross-road (Quadrivial) of National Highways	Kanpur
City of Nababs	Lucknow	Heart of India	Delhi
City of Temples & Ghats	Varanasi	Black River	Sharda
Land of Five Rivers	Punjab	City of Festivals	Madurai
City of Golden Temple	Amritsar	Queen of Deccan	Pune
Garden of India	Bangaluru	Sorrow of Bihar	Kosi River
Spice Garden of India	Kerala		

Major Indian Crops

Crops	Temp(°c)	Water(cm)	States where Produced
Wheat	15°-25°	60-90	Uttar Pradesh, Madhya Pradesh, Punjab
Rice	24°-26°	80-200	West Bengal, Uttar Pradesh, Punjab
Maize	18°-21°	50-60	Karnataka, Madhya Pradesh, Maharashtra
Jowar	20°-35°	40-60	Maharashtra, Madhya Pradesh, Karnataka
Soyabean	25°-27°	50-120	Maharashtra, Madhya Pradesh, Rajasthan
Cotton	20°-30°	80-150	Gujarat, Maharashtra, Telangana
Tobacco	20°-25°	75-80	Andhra Pradesh, Madhya Pradesh, Gujarat, Karnataka, Maharashtra, Uttar Pradesh
Tea	24°-30°	100-200	Assam, West Bengal, Kerala, Tamil Nadu, Uttar Pradesh
Ground Nut	15°-25°	60-130	Gujarat, Rajasthan, Tamil Nadu

❑❑❑

3

Indian Polity

INDIAN CONSTITUTION

- Demand for a Constituent Assembly composed of the people of India officially asserted by the Congress for the first time in 1935.
- The election for Indian Constitution Assembly held in 1946 according to the *Cabinet Mission Plan.*
- The first session of the Assembly was held in New Delhi on December 9, 1946. *Sachidanand Sinha* was elected provisional chairman of the session.
- On December 11, 1946, Dr. Rajendra Prasad was elected as the Permanent Chairman of the Constituent Assembly.
- The Constitution was framed by the Constituent Assembly of India, set-up in December 1946, in accordance with the Cabinet Mission Plan, under the Chairmanship of Sachidanand Sinha, initially.
- The total membership of Constituent Assembly after partition was 299, among them 70 were representatives from the Indian states and others from British India.
- The Chairman of the Drafting Committee was **Dr. BR Ambedkar**, also called the Father of the Constitution.
- The Constituent Assembly took 2 years, 11 months and 18 days to complete the Constitution.
- The Constitution, adopted on 8th November, 1949, contained 395 Articles and Schedules.
- The Constitution was delayed till 26th January because, in 1929, on this day Indian National Congress demanded Poorna Swaraj in Lahore Session under JL Nehru.
- Indian Constitution is a comprehensive document and it is the lengthiest written Constitution in the World.

THE PREAMBLE

- ***The Preamble of the Constitution:*** "We the people of India, having solemnly resolved to Constitute India into a Sovereign, Socialist, Secular Democratic Republic and to secure to all its citizen:

  Justice, Social, economic and political;

  Liberty of thought, expression, belief, faith and worship;

  Equality of status and of opportunity; and to promote among them all;

  Fraternity assuring the dignity of the individual and the unity and integrity of the nation;

  In our Constituent Assembly, this twenty-sixth day of November, 1949, do hereby adopt, enact and give to ourselves this constitution."

Foreign Sources of Indian Constitution

Foreign Sources	*Subject*
Britain	Parliamentary system, collective responsibilities of Cabinet
America	Fundamental right, Independent Judiciary, Judicial review
Canada	Division of powers
Ireland	Directive principles
Germany	Emergency provisions
Russia	Fundamental duties
Australia	Concurrent list

IMPORTANT ARTICLES

PART - I

UNION AND ITS TERRITORIES (ARTICLE 1 - 4)

- The Constitution says, "India, that is Bharat, shall be a Union of States".
- Parliament has the power to create any State, reduce it, change the name of boundaries of any State.

PART - II

CITIZENSHIP (ARTICLE 5 - 11)

- The Constitution provides for a single Citizenship.
- ***Indian Citizenship can be acquire:***
  1. by birth
  2. by descent
  3. by registration
  4. by naturalisation
  5. by incorporation of territory
- ***Indian Citizenship can be lost by:***
  1. renunciation;
  2. termination — it takes place if a citizen of India voluntary acquires the citizenship of another country; and
  3. deprivation — if the Government terminates the citizenship.

PART - III

FUNDAMENTAL RIGHTS (ARTICLE 12 - 35)

- Following fundamental rights are enjoyed by every Indian citizen, irrespective of caste, colour, creed and sex:
  1. ***Right to Equality:*** No special privileges, no distinction on grounds of religion, caste, creed and sex.
  2. ***Right to Freedom:*** The right to freedom of expression and speech, the right to choose one's own profession, the right to reside in any part of the Indian Union.
  3. ***Right to Freedom to Religion:*** Except when it is in the interest of public order, morality, health or other conditions, everybody has the right to profess, practice and propagate his religion freely.
  4. ***Cultural and Educational Rights:*** The Constitution provides that every community can run its own institutions to preserve its own culture and language.
  5. ***Right against Exploitation:*** Traffic in human beings and forced labour and the employment of children under 14 years in factories or mines, are punishable offences.
  6. ***Rights to Constitutional Remedies:*** When a citizen finds that any of his fundamental rights has been encroached upon, he can move the Supreme Court, which has been empowered to safeguard the fundamental rights of a citizen (Article 32).

PART - IV

DIRECTIVE PRINCIPLES OF STATE POLICY (ARTICLE 36 - 51)

- Directive principles are not enforceable through courts. Main aim of Directive principles is to provide social and economic base of a genuine democracy.

Some Important Directive Principles:

- Provisions for adequate means of livelihood for all citizens (Art. 39).
- Right to work (Art. 41).
- Right to human condition of work and maternity relief (Art. 42).
- Right to a living wage and condition of work ensuring decent standard of life of worker (Art. 43).
- Common Civil Code (Art. 44).
- Prohibit consumption of liquor (Art. 47).
- Prevent slaughter of useful cattle (Art. 48).
- Organise Panchayati Raj (Art. 40).
- Separate the judiciary from the executive (Art. 50).
- Protect and maintain places of historic monuments (Art. 49).
- International peace (Art. 51).

PART - IV A

FUNDAMENTAL DUTIES (ARTICLE 51A)

- The fundamental duties for the Indian citizens have been incorporated in the Constitution through the Constitution (42nd) Amendment Act, 1976. These duties are:
  1. to abide by the Constitution and respect its ideals and institutions, the National Flag and the National Anthem;
  2. to cherish and follow the noble deeds which inspired our national struggle for freedom;
  3. to uphold and protect the sovereignty, unity and integrity of India;
  4. to defend the country and render national service when called upon to do so;
  5. to promote harmony and the spirit of common brotherhood amongst all the people transcending religious, regional or sectional diversities and to renounce practices derogatory to the dignity of women;
  6. to value and preserve the rich heritage of our composite culture;
  7. to protect and improve natural environment including forests, lakes, rivers and wildlife, and to have compassion for living creatures;
  8. to develop the scientific temper, humanism and the spirit of inquiry and reform;
  9. to safeguard public property and to abjure violence;
  10. to strive towards excellence in all spheres of individual and collective activity so that the nation constantly rises to higher levels of endeavour and achievement.
  11. who is parent or guardian to provide opportunities for education to his child or, as the case may be, ward between age of six and fourteen years.

PART - V

UNION (ARTICLE 52 - 151)

The President

- The President is the Constitutional head of the Republic of India. He is more or less the titular head of the executive.
- He is the constitutional head but not the real executive. The real power is vested in the hands of the Council of Ministers.
- President is the first citizen of India.
- ***Qualifications:*** (i) Indian citizen, (ii) age not less than 35 years, (iii) should have qualification for election to Lok Sabha, (iv) should not hold any office of profit, (v) should not be a Member of Parliament or State Legislature.
- ***Election:*** Indirectly elected through Electoral College consisting of elected members of both the Houses of the

Parliament and elected members of the Legislative Assemblies of the States.

- According to the 70th Amendment Act, 1992, the expression 'States' include the National Capital Territory of Delhi and the Union Territory of Puducherry. Members of the Legislative Councils have no right to vote in the Presidential election.
- ***Powers:*** He makes appointments to all the constitutional posts.
- He can address either House of Parliament and dissolve Lok Sabha.
- All Bills passed by Parliament must receive his assent to become an Act.
- He issues ordinances when Parliament is not in session. No Money Bill can be introduced in Lok Sabha without his recommendation.
- He appoints 12 members of special repute in the Rajya Sabha.
- He has the power of *Pardon* to a criminal in special cases.
- The President holds the office for a period of five years. He is eligible for re-election.
- He is also entitled to rent free official residence called Rashtrapati Bhawan.

Vice-President

- ***Article 63*** of the Constitution stipulates a Vice-President for India.
- The Vice-President acts as the ex-officio Chairman of the Council of States (Rajya Sabha).
- He is elected by an electoral college consisting of the members of both Houses of Parliament in accordance with the system of proportional representation by means of the single transferable vote. He must be a citizen of India, not less than 35 years of age, and should be eligible for election as a member of the Council of States.
- Disputes in connection with election of a president or a vice-president are to be a dealt with in accordance with Article-71. Such disputes shall be decided by the Supreme Court.

Council of Ministers

- The Constitution of India provides for a parliament system of government under which the President is only Constitutional ruler and the real power is exercised by the Council of Ministers, headed by the Prime Minister.
- Council of Ministers is composed of all Union Ministers—the Prime Minister, Cabinet Ministers, Ministers of State and Deputy Ministers.
- The Council of Ministers is Collectively responsible to the Lok Sabha.
- The Prime Minister is a link between the President and the Council of Ministers.

Prime Minister

- The Prime Minister is the leader of the majority party in the Parliament.
- He is appointed by the President. Other Ministers are appointed by the president on his advice.
- The Prime Minister is the head of the Government and the head of the Council of Ministers.
- Jawaharlal Nehru was the first Prime Minister and the longest serving so far.

Union Legislature

- The Legislature of the Union, which is called 'Parliament' consists of the President and the two Houses of Parliament known as the Council of states (Rajya Sabha) and the House of the People (Lok Sabha).

RAJYA SABHA

- The Rajya Sabha is the Upper House of the Parliament and it is constituted of representatives from the States or the Constituent units of the Indian Union.
- It is a permanent body, one third of its members retiring after every two years.
- Its maximum strength is 250. Out of these, twelve members are nominated by the President from well-known personalities in the realm of Science, Art, Literature and Social Service. Rest of 238 representatives of the States and Union Territories are elected.
- Currently, the strength of the Rajya Sabha is 245.

LOK SABHA

- The Lok Sabha whose life is five years, is the Lower House of Parliament and comprises of members directly elected by the people.
- The House of the people (Lok Sabha) at present consists, 543 members directly elected from the states and Union Territories. By the 104th Constitutional amendment Act, 2019 the 2 Anglo-Indian reserved seats nominated by President in Lok Sabha are abolished.
- The House of the People shall continue for five years (unless sooner dissolved) from the date of its meeting and no longer and the expiry of the said period of 5 years shall operate as dissolution of the House.

Parliamentary Committees

- There are several Parliamentary Committees to assist the Parliament in its deliberations.
- These are appointed or elected by the respective Houses of Lok Sabha and Rajya Sabha on a motion made or are nominated by their presiding officers.
- Among the Standing Committees, three are financial Committees: (i) Public Account Committee; (ii) Estimate Committee; (iii) Public undertaking Committee.

Speaker of Lok Sabha

- Speaker is elected by the Lok Sabha from among its members.
- The Speaker will have the final power to maintain order within the House of the People and to interpret its rules of procedure.
- A Deputy-Speaker is also elected to officiate in absence of the Speaker.
- *G.V. Mavlankar* was the first Speaker of the Lok Sabha (1952-1956).

Supreme Court

- The Constitution provides for the Supreme Court, which consists of Chief Justice and 33 judges. They are appointed by the President of India.

QUALIFICATION AND TENURE

- Eligibility conditions for a judge of the Supreme Court are that he must be : (i) a citizen of India; (ii) a judge of a high court for a minimum period of 5 years; or (iii) an advocate of a high court for at least ten years or a distinguished jurist.
- Judges hold office till the age of 65.
- They can resign earlier or can be removed by the President on the recommendation of the two Houses of the Parliament by 2/3rd majority of the members present and voting.

Powers

- *Original jurisdiction:* Cases involving Government of India and the states or cases involving the enforcement of Fundamental Rights fall under original jurisdiction.
- *Appellate Jurisdiction:* In cases which are brought to it in the form of appeals against the judgement of the lower courts—It hears appeals in civil and criminal cases.
- *Advisory functions:* the Supreme Court advises the President on the constitutionality of a particular legal matter. However, its advice is not binding on the President.

Other Powers:

1. it is a court of record and can punish for contempt of itself;
2. it can make rules for regulating the practice and procedure of courts with the approval of the President; and
3. it can recommend to the President the removal of chairman and members of the UPSC. Supreme Court enjoys the power of judicial review (right of the court which declares as unconstitutional, the laws passed by the legislature and orders issued by executive) though it is not specifically mentioned in the Constitution.

- The first Chief Justice of India was H.J. Kania (1950-51).

COMPTROLLER AND AUDITOR GENERAL (CAG) (ARTICLE 148-151)

- The Comptroller and Auditor General of India is guardian of the public purse.
- It is his duty to see that not a *paisa* is spent out of consolidated fund of India or of a state without the authority of the appropriate legislature.
- He is appointed by President of India.
- A person with long administrative experience and knowledge of accounts is appointed.
- Holds office for 6 yrs or till 65 yrs of age.
- The President can remove him only on the recommendation of the 2 houses of Parliament (as in case of judge of Supreme Court).
- The CAG submits its reports to the President (in case of accounts relating to the Union Government) or to the State Governors (for State Government Accounts).
- The first CAG of India was *V Narahari Rao* (1948-1954).
- The CAG is not eligible for further office under the Union or State Governments. The expenses of the office of the CAG is charged to the Consolidated Fund of India.

ATTORNEY GENERAL OF INDIA

- The Attorney General of India is the first law officer of the Government of India.
- Though he is not a member of cabinet he has the right to speak in the House of Parliament, but he has no right to vote.
- The Attorney General of India shall be appointed by the President and shall hold office during his pleasure.
- His duty shall be to give advice on such legal matter from time-to-time as may be referred to him by the President.
- To be appointed as Attorney General, a candidate must be qualified to be appointed as a Judge of the Supreme Court.
- The Attorney General can participate in proceedings of the Parliament without the Right to Vote (Article 88).
- The first Attorney General of Independent India was MC Setalvad (1950-1963).

PART - VI

THE STATES (ARTICLE 152 - 237)

The Governor

- The Governor is appointed by the President and holds office during the pleasure of the President.
- Apart from the power to appoint the council of ministers, if the governor finds that the government of state cannot be carried on in accordance with the provisions of the

constitution (Art. 356), he may send his report to the President who may assume to himself the functions of the government of the state. (This is popularly known as 'President's Rule').

- Article 161 gives the Governor the power to grant pardons, reprieves, remission of punishment to persons convicted under the state law.
- Article 171 states that the States where Legislative Councils exists, the Governor can nominate some members from amongst those distinguished in literature, science, arts, cooperative movement and social service.

STATES LEGISLATURE (ARTICLE 168 - 212)

- The state legislature consists of Governor and legislative assembly.
- In some state like *Bihar, Maharashtra, Andhra Pradesh, Karnataka, Uttar Pradesh and Telangana* have a legislative council.
- The membership of the council should not be more than *one-third* of the legislative assembly but not less than 40.
- The legislative assembly of each state shall be composed of members chosen by direct election on the basis of adult suffrage and the number of members shall not be more than 500 or less than 60.
- The assembly of Sikkim, Goa, Puducherry and Mizoram have less than 60 members.

HIGH COURTS (ARTICLE 214-232)

- The High Court stands at the apex of the State Judiciary.
- As per the Constitution, there shall be a High Court in each State. But there may be a common High Court for two or more States and Union Territory, if it is provided by a law of the Parliament. For example, the Chennai High Court has its Jurisdiction over the State of Tamil Nadu and the Union Territory of Puducherry.
- The State Government has no control over it.
- There are 25 High Courts in India.
- The Calcutta High Court, established in 1862, is the oldest High Court in India.

THE PANCHAYATS (ARTICLE 243-243 O)

- Panchayati Raj was introduced in India with a view to associate the people with administration at grass-root level.
- It is a three-tier system as recommended by Balwant Rai Mehta Committee.
- Introduced by the 73rd Amendment Act, 1992 which envisaged a three tier system of local governance.

These are:

1. Gram Panchayat at the village level
2. Panchayat Samiti at the block level
3. Zila Parishad at the district level.

Jurisdiction and Seat of High Courts

Name	Year	Territorial Jurisdiction	Seat
Allahabad	1866	Uttar Pradesh	Prayagraj (Bench at Lucknow)
Andhra Pradesh	2019	Andhra Pradesh	Amaravati
Bombay	1862	Maharashtra, Goa, Dadar and Nagar Haveli and Daman and Diu	Mumbai (Benches at Nagpur, Panaji and Aurangabad)
Calcutta	1862	West Bengal and Andaman & Nicobar	Kolkata (Circuit Benches at Port Blair and Jalpaiguri)
Chhattisgarh	2000	Chhattisgarh	Bilaspur
Delhi	1966	Delhi	Delhi
Guwahati	1948	Assam, Nagaland, Mizoram and Arunachal Pradesh	Guwahati (Benches at Kohima, Aizawl and Itanagar)
Gujarat	1960	Gujarat	Ahmedabad
Himachal Pradesh	1971	Himachal Pradesh	Shimla
Jammu and Kashmir and Ladakh	1928	Jammu & Kashmir, Ladakh	Srinagar and Jammu
Jharkhand	2000	Jharkhand	Ranchi
Karnataka	1884	Karnataka	Bengaluru (Circuit Benches at Dharwar and Gulbarga)
Kerala	1958	Kerala & Lakshadweep	Ernakulam
Madhya Pradesh	1956	Madhya Pradesh	Jabalpur (Benches at Gwalior and Indore)
Madras	1862	Tamil Nadu & Puducherry	Chennai (Bench at Madurai)
Orissa	1948	Odisha	Cuttack
Patna	1916	Bihar	Patna
Punjab and Haryana	1966	Punjab, Haryana and Chandigarh	Chandigarh
Rajasthan	1949	Rajasthan	Jodhpur (Bench at Jaipur)
Sikkim	1975	Sikkim	Gangtok
Uttarakhand	2000	Uttarakhand	Nainital
Tripura	2013	Tripura	Agartala
Meghalaya	2013	Meghalaya	Shillong
Manipur	2013	Manipur	Imphal
Telangana	2019	Telangana	Hyderabad

THE MUNICIPALITIES (ARTICLE 243 P-243 ZG)

- Big cities have municipal corporations headed by the elected Mayor.
- For small towns there are elected boards or councils, in turn, elect their Presidents.
- Introduced by the 74th Amendment Act, 1993 which envisages three types of urban local bodies, namely, municipality (nagar palika), city council (nagar panchayat).
- Municipal governance in India was first introduced in Madras in 1688.

PART - XIII

(ARTICLE 301 - 307)

- In this part from Article 301-307 trade, commerce and intercourse within the territory of India are given.

PART - XIV

(ARTICLE 308 - 323)

- In this part services under the union and the states are given.
- ***Article 312:*** *All India Services* and ***Article 315:*** Public Service Commissions for the Union and for the States.
- The first Public Service Commission was set up in 1926, on the recommendations of the Lee Commission.

UNION PUBLIC SERVICE COMMISSION (UPSC)

- This Commission is responsible for:
  1. recruitment to all civil services and posts, under the Union Government by written examinations, interviews and promotions, and
  2. advising the Government on all matters relating to methods of recruitment, principles to be followed in making promotions and transfers. Its Chairman is appointed by the President.

STAFF SELECTION COMMISSION (SSC)

- The Union Government has constituted a Staff Selection Commission for recruitment to non-technical Class III posts in the central government and in subordinate offices.
- The Administrative Reforms Commission had recommended the setting up of such a Commission.
- The Commission has also been entrusted with the responsibility of making recruitment to Group 'B' services like Assistants' and Stenographers Grade 'C'.
- The Commission has a chairman and two members.

ELECTIONS (ARTICLE 324-329)

- The Constitution provides for an independent election commission to ensure free and fair election to the Parliament, the State legislature and the offices of President and Vice-President.
- Consists of Chief Election Commissioner +2 Election Commissioners. They all enjoy equal powers.
- The Chief Election Commissioner and other Election Commissioners are appointed by the President.
- Election Commissioners are appointed for a term of 5 yrs.
- They are not eligible for re-appointment. Also, they cannot hold any office of profit after their retirement.
- The Election Commission was established on 25th January, 1950 under Article 324 of the Constitution.
- The first Chief Election Commissioner was *Sukumar Sen.*

Functions

- Preparation of electoral rolls and keeping voters list updated.
- Recognition of various political parties and allotment of election symbols.

NITI AAYOG

- The Indian government has replaced Planing Commission with a new institution named **NITI Aayog (National Institution for Transforming India).**
- The Niti Aayog will comprise the following:
  1. Prime Minister of India as the Chairperson.
  2. Governing Council comprising the Chief Ministers of all the States and Lt. Governors of Territories.
  3. Regional Councils will be formed to address specific issues and contingencies impacting more than one state or a region. These will be formed for a specified tenure. The Regional Councils will be convened by the Prime Minister and will comprise of the Chief Ministers of States and Lt. Governors of Territories in the region. These will be chaired by the Chairperson of the NITI Aayog or his nominee.
  4. Experts, specialists and practitioners with relevant domain knowledge as special invitees nominated by the Prime Minister.
- The full-time organizational framework will comprise of, in addition to the Prime Minister as the Chairperson:
  1. Vice-Chairperson : To be appointed by the Prime Minister.
  2. Members : Full-time.
  3. Part-time members : Maximum of 2 from leading universities research organizations and other relevant institutions in an ex-officio capacity. Part time members will be on a rotational basis.
  4. Ex Officio members : Maximum of 4 members of the Council of Ministers to be nominated by the Prime Minister.
  5. Chief Executive Officer : To be appointed by the Prime Minister for a fixed tenure, in the rank of Secretary to the Government of India.
  6. Secretariat as deemed necessary.

FINANCE COMMISSION

- The constitution of the Finance Commission is laid down in Art. 280. The chairman must be a person having experience in public affairs; and the other four members also having wide experience in financial matters.
- It consists of Chairman and 4 other members.
- It shall be the duty of the Finance Commission to advice the President on matters such as the distribution between the Union and States of the net proceeds of taxes that is required to be shared.
- The Finance Commission is not a permanent body. It is dissolved after it has submitted its recommendations.

❒ ❒ ❒

4

Indian Economy

NATIONAL INCOME

- According to the National Income Committee (1949), "A national income estimate measures the volume of commodities and service turned out during a given period counted without duplication". Thus, national income measures the net value of goods and services produced in a country during a year and it also includes net earned foreign income. In other words, a total of national income measures the flow of goods and services in an economy.
- National income is a flow concept not a stock concept.
- In India, National income estimates are related with the financial year (April 1 to 31st March).
- The various concepts of national income are as follows:
  - *(i)* **GNP (Gross National Product):** GNP refers to the money value of total output or production of final goods and services produced by the nationals of a country during a given period of time, generally a year.
  - *(ii)* **NNP (Net National Product):** NNP is obtained by subtracting depreciation value from GNP. NNP can be calculated in two ways: (*a*) at market prices of goods and services and (*b*) at factor cost.
  - *(iii)* **National Income:** When NNP is obtained at factor cost, it is known as National Income. National Income is calculated by subtracting net indirect taxes from NNP at market prices. The obtained value is known as NNP at factor cost or National income.
  - *(iv)* **Personal Income:** Personal income is that income which is actually obtained by nationals. Personal income is obtained by subtracting corporate taxes and payments made for social securities provisions from national income and adding to it govern-ment transfer payments, business transfer payments and net interest paid by the government.

Methods of Measuring National Income

- According to Simon Kuznets, national income of a country is calculated by following mentioned three methods:
  - *(i)* **Product Method:** S. Kuznets gave a new name to this method, *i.e.*, product service method. In this method, net value of final goods and services produced in a country during a year is obtained and the total obtained value is called total final product.
  - *(ii)* **Income Method:** In this method, a total of net incomes earned by working people in different sectors and commercial enterprises is obtained.
  - *(iii)* **Consumption Method:** It is also called expenditure method. Income is either spent on consumption or saved. Hence, national income is the addition of total consumption and total savings.
- In India, a combination of production method and income method is used for measuring estimating national income.
- For measuring national income in India, in 1868, the first attempt was made by *Dada Bhai Nauroji*. He, in his book, *"Poverty and Un-British Rule in India"*, estimated Indian per capita annual income at a level of ₹ 20.
- After independence, the Government of India appointed the National Income Committee in August, 1949, under the Chairmanship of Prof. P.C. Mahalanobies, to compile authoritative estimates of national income.
- Estimation and publishing of National Income data by CSO (Central Statistical Organization) is done every year.
- National income includes the contribution of three sectors—primary sector, secondary sector, Tertiary sector.
- Under Primary Sector—Agriculture, Forest, Fisheries and allied sector are included.
- Under Secondary Sector—Manufacturing, Construction, Electricity, Gas and Water Supply are included.
- Under Teritiary Sector—Trade, Transport, Communication, Banking, Insurance, Real Estate, Community and Personal Services are included.
- The contribution of primary sector in GDP was 55.4% in 1950-1951. But now the share of primary sector in national income has come down. In 2022-23, the contribution of primary sector in GDP was 18.42%.
- The contribution of secondary sector has shown a steady increase from 15% in 1950-51 to 28.25% in 2022-23.
- The contribution of tertiary sector indicated a sharp improvement from 29.6% in 1950-51 to about 53.34% in 2022-23.
- At present estimation of national income is based on the base year of 2011-2012.

POPULATION

Census-2011: Population, Density, Decadal Growth Rate

S.N.	State/UTs	Population 2001	Population 2011	Density 2001	Density 2011	Decadal G. (%) 2001–2011
1.	J&K	10,143,700	1,25,41,302	100	124	23.6
2.	Himachal Pradesh	6,077,900	68,64,602	109	123	12.9
3.	Punjab	24,358,999	2,77,43,338	484	551	13.9
4.	Chandigarh	900,635	10,55,450	7,900	9258	17.2
5.	Uttarakhand	8,489,349	1,00,86,292	159	189	18.8
6.	Haryana	21,144,564	2,53,51,462	478	573	19.9
7.	Delhi	13,850,507	1,67,87,941	9,340	11320	21.2
8.	Rajasthan	56,507,188	6,85,48,437	165	200	21.3
9.	Uttar Pradesh	166,197,921	19,98,12,341	690	829	20.2
10.	Bihar	82,998,509	10,40,99,452	881	1106	25.4
11.	Sikkim	540,851	6,10,577	76	86	12.9
12.	Arunachal Pradesh	1,097,968	13,83,727	13	17	26.0
13.	Nagaland	1,990,036	19,78,502	120	119	–0.6
14.	Manipur	2,293,896	28,55,794	103	128	31.79
15.	Mizoram	888,573	10,97,206	42	52	23.5
16.	Tripura	3,199,203	36,73,917	305	350	14.8
17.	Meghalaya	2,318,822	29,66,889	103	132	27.9
18.	Assam	26,655,528	3,12,05,576	340	398	17.1
19.	West Bengal	80,176,197	9,12,76,115	903	1028	13.8
20.	Jharkhand	26,945,829	3,29,88,134	338	414	22.4
21.	Odisha	36,804,660	4,19,74,218	236	270	14.0
22.	Chhattisgarh	20,833,803	2,55,45,198	154	189	22.6
23.	Madhya Pradesh	60,348,023	7,26,26,809	196	236	20.3
24.	Gujarat	50,671,017	6,04,39,692	258	308	19.3
25.	Daman & Diu	158,204	2,43,247	1,413	2191	53.8
26.	Dadra & N. Haveli	220,490	3,43,709	449	700	55.9
27.	Maharashtra	96,878,627	11,23,74,333	315	365	16.0
28.	Andhra Pradesh	76,210,007	4,93,86,799	277	308	11.0
29.	Karnataka	52,850,562	6,10,95,297	276	319	15.6
30.	Goa	1,347,668	14,58,545	364	394	8.2
31.	Lakshadweep	60,650	64,473	1,895	2149	6.3
32.	Kerala	31,841,374	3,34,06,061	819	860	4.9
33.	Tamil Nadu	62,405,679	7,21,47,030	480	555	15.6
34.	Puducherry	974,345	12,47,953	2,030	2546	28.1
35.	Andaman & Nicobar Islands	356,152	3,80,581	43	46	6.9
36.	Telangana	—	3,51,93,978	—	307	13.58
	India	**1,028,737,436**	**1,21,08,54,977**	**325**	**382**	**17.7**

AGRICULTURE

- Agriculture is an important sector of the economy. Though the share of agriculture in national income has come down since the inception of planning era in the economy but still it has substantial share in GDP.
- In terms of composition, out of the total share of 14.65 per cent that agriculture and allied sector had in GDP in 2019-20.
- Agriculture in our country provides livelihood to about 49% of the population.
- Gross Capital Formation (GCF) in Agriculture and Allied sector relative to GVA in this sector has been snowing a fluctuating trent from 18.3 per cent in 2011-12 to 16.34 per cent in 2020-21.
- Agriculture provides raw materials to various industries and other agro-based industries. Cotton and Jute textile industries, Sugar, Vanaspati industry etc. are directly dependent on agriculture.
- India's foreign trade is deeply associated with Agriculture Sector. Value of agriculture exports to total exports of the country was 13.8 per cent in 2013. But the share of agriculture has come down in foreign trade at present. Share of agriculture in foreign trade was 11.76 per cent in 2018-19.

Various Crops and their producing states

Crops/Groups of Crops	Producing State (In Descending Order)
I. Foodgrains	
Rice	West Bengal, Uttar Pradesh, Punjab
Wheat	Uttar Pradesh, Madhya Pradesh, Punjab
Maize	Karnataka, Madhya Pradesh, Maharashtra
Total Nutri/ Coarse Cereals	Rajasthan, Karnataka, Maharashtra
Gram	Madhya Pradesh, Maharashtra, Rajasthan
Tur	Maharashtra, Karnataka, Telangana
Total Pulses	Madhya Pradesh, Rajasthan, Maharashtra
Total Food-grains	Uttar Pradesh, Madhya Pradesh, Punjab
II. Oilseeds	
Groundnut	Gujarat, Rajasthan, Tamil Nadu
Rapeseed & Mustard	Rajasthan, Madhya Pradesh, Haryana
Soyabean	Maharashtra, Madhya Pradesh, Rajasthan
Sunflower	Karnataka, Haryana, Odisha
Total Oilseeds	Rajasthan, Maharashtra, Madhya Pradesh
III. Other Cash Crops	
Sugarcane	Uttar Pradesh, Maharashtra, Karnataka
Cotton	Maharashtra, Gujarat, Telangana
Jute & Mesta	West Bengal, Bihar, Assam

Source: Economic Survey 2020-21

ECONOMIC PLANNING

☞ Five Year Plans in India

Plans	*Period*	*Investment (₹ Crore)*	*Objectives*
First Plan	April 1, 1951-March 31, 1956	1,960	Priority to agriculture, electricity and irrigation.
Second Plan	April 1, 1956—March 31, 1961	4,672	Development of basic and heavy industries.
Third Plan	April 1, 1961—March 31, 1966	8,577	Long term development of India's economy.
Annual Plan	April 1, 1966—March 31, 1967	2,137	
Annual Plan	April 1, 1967—March 31, 1968	2,205	
Annual Plan	April 1, 1968—March 31, 1969	2,283	
Fourth Plan	April 1, 1969—March 31, 1974	15,779	Enlarge the income of rural population and supply of goods of mass consumption.
Fifth Plan	April 1, 1974—March 31, 1979	39,426	Attain increased self-reliance and employment avenues.
Annual Plan	April 1, 1979—March 31, 1980	12,176	
Sixth Plan	April 1, 1980—March 31, 1985	1,09,292	Removal of unemployment
Seventh Plan	April 1, 1985—March 31, 1990	2,18,730	Food work and productivity were the basic priorities.
Eighth Plan	April, 1992—March 31, 1997	4,95,670	Raising employment
Ninth Plan	April 1, 1997—March 31, 2002	9,41,041	Agriculture and rural development
Tenth Plan	April 1, 2002—March 31, 2007	14,91,610	Growth rate 7.8 percent per annum.
Eleventh Plan	April 1, 2007—March 31, 2012	36,44,718	Literacy, Employment, Rural development & Transport development.
Twelfth Plan	April 1, 2012–March 31, 2017	43,30,000	Longterm development of India's economy.

15-YEAR VISION PLANE

With the end of the Twelfth Plan in March 2017 the era of five year plans came to an end. NITI Aayog has come forward with a draft 15-year vision plan to catapult the country's economy to more than three times as compared to the present day. The new plan is set to replace the centralised five-year plans the country has been following for decades. The new plan is accompanied by shorter sub-plan—a seven-year strategy for 2017-24, and a three-year 'Action Agenda' from 2017-18 to 2019-20. No less than 300 specific action points covering a wide range of sectors points covering a wide range of sectors have been drawn up as part of the 15-year vision.

MONEY AND BANKING

RESERVE BANK OF INDIA

- Reserve Bank of India (RBI) is the central bank of the country.
- Reserve Bank of India was established on April 1, 1935 under Reserve Bank of India Act, 1934 with a authorised capital of ₹ 5 crore.
- The Reserve Bank of India was nationalised on January 1, 1949.
- The general administration and direction of RBI is managed by a Central Board of Directors consisting of 20 members which includes 1 Governor and 4 Deputy Governors.
- The head office of the Reserve Bank of India is in Mumbai.

☞ **Establishment Years of Major Financial Institutions in India**

Imperial Bank of India	1921
Reserve Bank of India (Nationalisation of RBI took place on January 1, 1949)	April 1, 1935
Industrial Finance Corporation of India (IFCI)	1948
State Bank of India (SBI)	July 1, 1955
Unit Trust of India (UTI)	Feb. 1, 1964
IDBI	July 1964
NABARD	July 12, 1982
SIDBI	1990
EXIM Bank	January 1, 1982
National Housing Bank (NHB)	July 1988
Life Insurance Corporation (LIC)	Sept. 1956
General Insurance Corporation (GIC)	Nov. 1972
Regional Rural Banks (RRBs)	Oct. 2, 1975
Risk Capital and Technology Finance Corporation Ltd.	March 1975
Housing Development Finance Corporation Ltd. (HDFC)	1977

❒ ❒ ❒

5

General Science

IMPORTANT INVENTIONS

Name of Invention	*Inventor*	*Nationality*	*Year*
Aeroplane	Orville & Wilbur Wright	U.S.A.	1903
Ball-Point Pen	John J. Loud	U.S.A.	1888
Barometer	Evangelista Torricelli	Italy	1644
Bicycle	Kirkpatrick Macmillan	Britain	1839-40
Bifocal Lens	Benjamin Franklin	U.S.A.	1780
Car (Petrol)	Karl Benz	Germany	1888
Celluloid	Alexander Parkes	Britain	1861
Cinema	Nicolas & Jean Lumiere	France	1895
Clock (mechanical)	I-Hsing & Liang Ling-Tsan	China	1725
Diesel Engine	Rudolf Diesel	Germany	1895
Dynamo	Hypolite Pixii	France	1832
Electric Lamp	Thomas Alva Edison	U.S.A.	1879
Electric Motor (DC)	Zenobe Gramme	Belgium	1873
Electric Motor (AC)	Nikola Tesla	U.S.A.	1888
Electro-magnet	William Sturgeon	Britain	1824
Electronic Computer	Dr. Alan M. Turing	Britain	1943
Film (moving outlines)	Louis Prince	France	1885
Film (musical sound)	Dr. Le de Forest	U.S.A.	1923
Fountain Pen	Lewis E. Waterman	U.S.A.	1884
Gramophone	Thomas Alva Edison	U.S.A.	1878
Helicopter	Etienne Oehmichen	France	1924
Jet Engine	Sir Frank Whittle	Britain	1937
Laser	Charles H. Townes	U.S.A.	1960
Lift (Mechanical)	Elisha G. Otis	U.S.A.	1852
Locomotive	Richard Trevithick	Britain	1804
Machine Gun	James Puckle	Britain	1718
Microphone	Alexander Graham Bell	U.S.A.	1876
Microscope	Z. Janssen	Netherlands	1590
Motor Cycle	G. Daimler	Germany	1885
Photography (on film)	John Carbutt	U.S.A.	1888
Printing Press	Johann Gutenberg	Germany	c.1455
Razor (safety)	King C. Gillette	U.S.A.	1895
Refrigerator	James Harrison & Alexander Catlin	U.S.A.	1850
Safety Pin	Walter Hunt	U.S.A.	1849
Sewing machine	Barthelemy Thimmonnier	France	1829
Ship (steam)	J.C. Perier	France	1775
Ship (turbine)	Hon. Sir C. Parsons	Britain	1894
Skyscraper	W. Le Baron Jenny	U.S.A.	1882
Slide Rule	William Oughtred	Britain	1621
Steam Engine (condenser)	James Watt	Britain	1765
Steel Production	Henry Bessemer	Britain	1855
Steel (stainless)	Harry Brearley	Britain	1913
Submarine	David Bushnell	U.S.A.	1776

Name of Invention	*Inventor*	*Nationality*	*Year*
Tank	Sir Ernest Swinton	Britain	1914
Telegraph	M. Lammond	France	1787
Telegraph Code	Samuel F.B. Morse	U.S.A.	1837
Telephone (perfected)	Alexander Graham Bell	U.S.A.	1876
Television (mechanical)	John Logie Baird	Britain	1926
Television (electronic)	P.T. Farnsworth	U.S.A.	1927
Thermometer	Galileo Galilei	Italy	1593
Transformer	Michael Faraday	Britain	1831
Transistor	Bardeen, Shockley & Brattain	U.S.A.	1948
Washing Machine (elec.)	Hurley Machine Co.	U.S.A.	1907
Zip-Fastener	W.L. Judson	U.S.A.	1891

IMPORTANT DISCOVERIES

Discovery	*Discoverer*	*Nationality*	*Year*
Aluminium	Hans Christian Oerstedt	Denmark	1827
Atomic number	Henry Moseley	England	1913
Atomic structure of matter	John Dalton	England	1803
Chlorine	C.W. Scheele	Sweden	1774
Electromagnetic induction	Michael Faraday	England	1831
Electromagnetic waves	Heinrich Hertz	Germany	1886
Electromagnetism	Hans Christian Oersted	Denmark	1920
Electron	Sir Joseph Thomson	England	1897
General theory of relativity	Albert Einstein	Switzerland	1915
Hydrogen	Henry Cavendish	England	1766
Law of electric conduction	Georg Ohm	Germany	1827
Law of electromagnetism	Andre Ampere	France	1826
Law of falling bodies	Galileo	Italy	1590
Laws of gravitation & motion	Isaac Newton	England	1687
Laws of planetary motion	Johannes Kepler	Germany	1609-10
Magnesium	Sir Humphry Davy	England	1808
Neptune (Planet)	Johann Galle	Germany	1846
Neutron	James Chadwick	England	1932
Nickel	Axel Cronstedt	Sweden	1751
Nitrogen	Daniel Rutherford	England	1772
Oxygen	Joseph Priestly; C.W. Scheele	England; Sweden	1772
Ozone	Christian Schonbein	Germany	1839
Pluto (Planet)	Clyde Tombaugh	U.S.A	1930
Plutonium	G.T. Seaborg	U.S.A	1940
Proton	Ernest Rutherford	England	1919
Quantum Theory	Max Planck	Germany	1900
Radioactivity	Antoine Bacquerel	France	1896
Radium	Pierre & Marie Curie	France	1898
Silicon	Jons Berzelius	Sweden	1824
Special theory of relativity	Albert Einstein	Switzerland	1905
Sun as centre of solar system	Copernicus	Poland	1543
Uranium	Martin Klaproth	Germany	1789
Uranus (Planet)	William Herschel	England	1781
X-rays	Wilhelm Roentgen	Germany	1895

GEOGRAPHICAL EXPLORATIONS/DISCOVERIES

Place	*Explorer/Discoverer*	*Nationality*	*Year*
America	Christopher Columbus	Italy	1492
Hawaii Islands (Sandwich Islands)	Captain James Cook	England	1778
Newfoundland	John Cabot	England	1497
New Zealand	Abel Janszoon Tasman	Holland	1642
North Pole	Robert Peary	USA	1909
Sea Route to India (via Cape of Good Hope)	Vasco da Gama	Portugal	1498
South Pole	Roald Amundsen	Norway	1911

SCIENTIFIC INSTRUMENTS

Name of Instrument	*Used for*
Altimeter	measuring altitude
Ammeter	measuring strength of an electric current
Anemometer	measuring the velocity of wind
Audiometer	measuring level of hearing
Barometer	measuring atmospheric pressure
Callipers	measuring the internal and external diameters of tubes
Calorimeter	measuring quantity of heat
Compass	finding out direction
Dynamo	converting mechanical energy into electrical energy
Eudiometer	measuring volume changes during chemical reactions between gases
Galvanometer	detecting and determining the strength of small electric currents
Hydrometer	measuring specific gravity of a liquid
Hygrometer	measuring the humidity in the atmosphere
Lactometer	measuring the purity of milk
Manometer	measuring the gaseous pressure
Micrometer	measuring minute distances, angles, etc.
Microscope	seeing magnified view of very small objects
Photometer	measuring intensity of light from distant stars
Pyrometer	measuring high temperatures
Radar	detecting and finding the presence and location of moving objects like aircraft, missile, etc.
Radiometer	measuring the emission of radiant energy
Rain Gauge	measuring the amount of rainfall
Seismograph	measuring and recording the intensity and origin of earthquake shocks
Sextant	measuring altitude and angular distances between two objects or heavenly bodies
Spectrometer	measuring the refractive indices
Spherometer	measuring the curvature of spherical objects/surface
Sphygmomanometer	measuring blood pressure
Stethoscope	ascertaining the condition of heart and lungs by listening to their function
Stroboscope	viewing objects that are moving rapidly with a periodic motion as if they were at rest
Tachometer	measuring the rate of revolution or angular speed of a revolving shaft
Telescope	viewing magnified images of distant objects
Theodolite	measuring the horizontal and vertical angles
Thermocouple	measuring the temperature inside furnaces and jet engines
Thermometer	measuring human body temperature
Thermostat	regulating constant temperature
Ultrasonoscope	measuring utrasonic sounds
Viscometer	measuring the viscosity of a fluid
Voltmeter	measuring potential difference between two points.

DISEASES AND THE PARTS OF BODY THEY AFFECT

Disease	*Part of body affected*	*Disease*	*Part of body affected*
AIDS	Immune system of body	Jaundice	Liver
Arthritis	Inflammation of joints	Meningitis	Brain or spinal cord
Asthma	Lungs	Pleurisy	Pleura (inflammation of)
Cataract	Eyes	Polio	motor neurons
Conjunctivitis	Eyes	Pneumonia	Lungs
Diabetes	Pancreas	Pyorrhoea	Sockets of teeth
Diphtheria	Throat	Tuberculosis	Lungs
Glaucoma	Eyes	Typhoid	Intestine
Eczema	Skin	Malaria	Spleen
Goitre	Front of the neck (due to enlargement of thyroid gland)	Leukaemia	Blood
Gout	Joints of bone	Rickets	Bones

❐❐❐

6

Miscellaneous

CAPITAL & CURRENCIES

Country	Capital	Currency
* Afghanistan	Kabul	Afghani
* Algeria	Algiers	Dinar
* Angola	Luanda	New Kwanza
* Argentina	Buenos Aires	Peso
* Australia	Canberra	Dollar
* Austria	Vienna	Euro
* Azerbaijan	Baku	Manat
* Bahrain	Manama	Dinar
* Bangladesh	Dhaka	Taka
* Barbados	Bridgetown	Dollar
* Belarus	Minsk	Ruble
* Belgium	Brussels	Euro
* Bhutan	Thimphu	Ngultrum[1]
* Bolivia	La paz	Dollar
* Brazil	Brasilia	Real
* Bulgaria	Sofia	Lev
* Canada	Ottawa	Dollar
* Chile	Santiago	Peso
* China	Beijing	Yuan
* Colombia	Bogota	Peso
* Croatia	Zagreb	Kuna
* Cuba	Havana	Peso
* Cyprus	Nicosia	Euro
* Czech Republic	Prague	Koruna
* Denmark	Copenhagen	Krone
* Ecuador	Quito	Sucre
* Egypt	Cairo	Pound
* Ethiopia	Addis Ababa	Birr
* Fiji	Suva	Dollar
* Finland	Helsinki	Euro
* France	Paris	Euro
* Georgia	Tbilisi	Lari
* Germany	Berlin	Euro
* Ghana	Accra	Cedi
* Greece	Athens	Euro
* Guyana	George Town	Dollar
* Hungary	Budapest	Forint
* India	New Delhi	Rupee
* Indonesia	Jakarta	Rupiah

Country	Capital	Currency
* Iran	Teheran	Rial
* Iraq	Baghdad	Dinar
* Ireland	Dublin	Euro
* Israel	Jerusalem	Shekel
* Italy	Rome	Euro
* Japan	Tokyo	Yen
* Jordan	Amman	Dinar
* Kazakhstan	Akmola	Tenge
* Kenya	Nairobi	Shilling
* Korea (S)	Seoul	Won
* Korea (N)	Pyongyang	Won
* Kyrgyzstan	Bishkek	Som
* Kuwait	Kuwait City	Dinar
* Laos	Vientiane	Kip
* Lebanon	Beirut	Pound
* Liberia	Monrovia	Dollar
* Libya	Tripoli	Dinar
* Malaysia	Kuala Lumpur	Ringgit
* Maldives	Male	Rufiyaa
* Mali	Bamako	Franc
* Mauritius	Port Louis	Rupee
* Mexico	Mexico City	Peso
* Mongolia	Ulan Bator	Tugrik
* Morocco	Rabat	Dirham
* Myanmar (Burma)	Nay Pyi Taw	Kyat
* Namibia	Winohoek	Dollar
* Nepal	Kathmandu	Rupee
* Netherlands	Amsterdam	Euro
* New Zealand	Wellington	Dollar
* Nigeria	Abuja	Naira
* Norway	Oslo	Krone
* Oman	Muscat	Rial
* Pakistan	Islamabad	Rupee
* Panama	Panama City	Balboa
* Peru	Lima	New Sole
* Philippines	Manila	Peso
* Poland	Warsaw	Zloty
* Portugal	Lisbon	Euro
* Qatar	Doha	Riyal
* Russia	Moscow	Ruble

Country	Capital	Currency
✶ Saudi Arabia	Riyadh	Rial
✶ Slovakia	Bratislava	Euro
✶ Spain	Madrid	Euro
✶ Sri Lanka	Colombo	Rupee
✶ Sudan	Khartoum	Dinar
✶ Sweden	Stockholm	Krona
✶ Switzerland	Berne	Swiss Francs
✶ Syria	Damascus	Pound
✶ South Africa	Capetown (Legislative) Pretoria *(Administrative)*	Rand
✶ Tadzhikistan	Dushanbe	Ruble
✶ Taiwan	Taipei	Dollar
✶ Tanzania	Dodoma	Shilling
✶ Thailand	Bangkok	Baht
✶ Tunisia	Tunis	Dinar
✶ Turkiye	Ankara	Lira
✶ Ukraine	Kiev	Hyrvnia
✶ United Arab Emirates	Abu Dhabi	Dirham
✶ U.K.	London	Pound Sterling
✶ U.S.A.	Washington	Dollar
✶ Uruguay	Montevideo	Peso
✶ Uzbekistan	Tashkent	Som
✶ Venezuela	Caracas	Bolivar
✶ Vietnam	Hanoi	Dong
✶ Yemen	Sana'a	Rial
✶ Zimbabwe	Harare	Dollar
✶ Congo	Kinshasa	Franc
✶ Zambia	Lusaka	Kwacha

GEOGRAPHICAL EXPLORATIONS/DISCOVERIES

Place	Explorer/Discoverer	Nationality	Year
America	Christopher Columbus	Italy	1492
Hawaii Islands (Sandwich Islands)	Captain James Cook	England	1778
Newfoundland	John Cabot	England	1497
New Zealand	Abel Janszoon Tasman	Netherlands	1642
North Pole	Robert Peary	USA	1909
Sea Route to India (via Cape of Good Hope)	Vasco da Gama	Portugal	1498
South Pole	Roald Amundsen	Norway	1911

NATIONAL MONUMENTS OF SOME FAMOUS COUNTRIES

Monument	Country
Great Wall of China	China
Taj Mahal (Agra)	India
Emperial Palace (Tokyo)	Japan
Opera House (Sydney)	Australia
Eiffel Tower (Paris)	France
Pyramid (Giza)	Egypt
Kinder Disk	Denmark
Leaning Tower of Pisa	Italy
Statue of Liberty (New York)	USA
Kremlin (Moscow)	Russia

INTELLIGENCE AGENCIES OF SOME PROMINENT COUNTRIES

Country	Intelligence Agency
✶ India	*Research & Analysis Wing (RAW), Intelligence Bureau (I.B.), Central Bureau of Investigation (C.B.I.)*
✶ Pakistan	*Inter Service Intelligence (I.S.I.)*
✶ U.S.A.	*Central Intelligence Agency (CIA), Federal Bureau of Investigation (FBI)*
✶ Britain	*Military Intelligence (M.I.)-5 and 6, Special Branch, Ultra, Joint Intelligence Organisation*
✶ Israel	*Mosad*
✶ Egypt	*Mukhabarat*
✶ Japan	*Nicho*
✶ Russia	*K.G.B. (Komitel Gosudarstvennoy Bezopasnosty) (Committee for State Security)*
✶ Canada	*Security Intelligence Service (SIS)*
✶ S. Africa	*Bureau of State Security (BSS)*
✶ Iran	*Sabak*
✶ Iraq	*Al-Mukhabarat*
✶ Australia	*Australian Security and Intelligence Organisation (ASIO)*
✶ France	*S.D.E.C.E.*
✶ Spain	*C.E.S.I.D.*

MAJOR LANGUAGES OF THE WORLD AND THEIR SPEAKERS

Listing the languages spoken by approximately 1% of humankind (those spoken by more than 60,000,000 people), this table enumerates speakers of each tongue as a primary language.

Language	Speakers (millions)
∗ Chinese	1,322.8
∗ Spanish	471.4
∗ English	369.9
∗ Arabic	349.3
∗ Hindi	342.2
∗ Bengali	228.7
∗ Portuguese	232.4
∗ Russian	153.7
∗ Japanese	126.3
∗ Lahnda	99.6
∗ Marathi	83.1
∗ Telugu	82.6
∗ Turkish	82.2
∗ Malay	81.6
∗ Korean	81.5

Language	Speakers (millions)
∗ French	79.6
∗ Tamil	77.5
∗ Vietnamese	76.1
∗ German, Standard	76.5
∗ Urdu	69.0
∗ Javanese	68.3
∗ Persian	65.7
∗ Italian	64.8
∗ Gujarati	56.9
∗ Pushto	53.1
∗ Bhojpuri	52.3
∗ Hausa	48.6
∗ Kannada	43.6
∗ Yoruba	41.0
∗ Polish	40.0

***(Source:** The World Almanac-2022)*

NAME OF PARLIAMENTS OF SOME COUNTRIES

Country	Name of Parliament
Afghanistan	Shora
Argentina	National Congress
Australia	Federal Parliament
Austria	National Assembly
Bangladesh	Jatiya Sansad
India	Lok Sabha and Rajya Sabha
Bhutan	Tshogdu (National Assembly)
Britain	House of Commons and House of Lords
Canada	House of Commons and Senate
China	National People Congress
Denmark	Folketing
Iran	Majlis (Islamic Consultative Assembly)
Israel	Knesset
Japan	Diet
Myanmar	Pyithu Hluttaw (People's Assembly)
Nepal	Rashtriya Panchayat
The Netherlands	States-General

Country	Name of Parliament
Norway	Storting
Poland	Sejm
Russia	Federal Assembly (Council of the Federation and State Duma
South Africa	National Assembly and Senate
Spain	Cortes Generales
Sweden	Riksdag
Switzerland	Federal Assembly (Nationalrat and Standerat)
North Korea	Supreme People's Assembly
South Korea	National Assembly
U.S.A.	Congress (Senate and House of Representatives)
Ethiopia	Federal Council and House of Representatives
Iceland	Alpingi
Bulgaria	National Assembly
Cuba	National Assembly of People's Power

LARGEST AND SMALLEST COUNTRIES (Top 5)

Largest Country	Largest Country	Smallest Country	Smallest Country
(Area-wise)	(Population-wise)	(Area-wise)	(Population-wise)
Russia	China	Vatican City	Vatican City
Canada	India	Monaco	Tuvalu
China	USA	Nauru	Nauru
United States	Indonesia	Tuvalu	Palau
Brazil	Brazil	San Marino	San Marino

RELIGIONS OF THE WORLD

Religion	Member	Percentage	Religion	Member	Percentage
Christianity	2.5 billion	32.2%	Buddhism	545 million	6.9%
Islam	1.9 billion	24.7%	Sikhism	28 million	0.4%
Hinduism	1.07 billion	13.5%			

NATIONAL EMBLEMS OF IMPORTANT COUNTRIES

Country	National Emblem	Country	National Emblem
America	Golden Rod	Australia	Kangaroo
Ireland	Shamrock	Italy	White Lily
Israel	Candelabrum	Iran	Rose
Canada	White Lily	Great Britain	Rose
Chile	Candor and Huemul	Germany	Corn Flower
Japan	Chrysanthemum	Zimbabwe	Zimbabwe Bird
Denmark	Beach	Turkiye	Crescent and Star
The Netherlands	Lion	New Zealand	Kiwi, Fern Southern Cross
Norway	Lion	Nepal	Kukri
Pakistan	Crescent	Poland	Eagle
France	Lily	Belgium	Lion
Bangladesh	Water Lily	Mongolia	The Soyombo
Russia	Double headed eagle	Lebanon	Cedar Tree
Sudan	Secretary Bird	Syria	Eagle
India	Lioned Capital		

BOOKS AND AUTHORS

FOREIGN

Book	Author
∗ As You Like It	*William Shakespeare*
∗ A Tale of Two Cities	*Charles Dickens*
∗ Ben Hur	*Lewis Wallace*
∗ Das Kapital	*Karl Marx*
∗ David Copperfield	*Charles Dickens*
∗ Hamlet	*William Shakespeare*
∗ Iliad	*Homer*
∗ Inferno	*A. Dante*
∗ In Memoriam	*Lord Tennyson*
∗ Ivanhoe	*Walter Scott*
∗ Julius Caesar	*William Shakespeare*
∗ Lady Chatterley's Lover	*D.H. Lawrence*
∗ Lajja	*Taslima Nasreen*
∗ Les Miserable	*Victor Hugo*
∗ Leviathan	*Thomas Hobbes*
∗ Lolita	*V. Nobokov*
∗ Lycidas	*John Milton*
∗ Mein Kampf	*Adolf Hitler*
∗ Moor's Last Sigh	*Salman Rushdie*
∗ Mother	*Maxim Gorky*
∗ Mother India	*Katherine Mayo*
∗ Nana	*Emile Zola*
∗ Odyssey	*Homer*
∗ Origin of Species	*Charles Darwin*
∗ Othello	*William Shakespeare*
∗ Paradise Lost	*John Milton*
∗ Paradise Regained	*John Milton*
∗ Path to Power	*Margaret Thatcher*
∗ Pickwick Papers	*Charles Dickens*
∗ Razor's Edge	*Somerset Maugham*
∗ Republic	*Plato*
∗ The Tempest	*William Shakespeare*
∗ Time Machine	*H.G. Wells*
∗ Tom Sawyer	*Mark Twain*
∗ Treasure Island	*R.L. Stevenson*
∗ Twelfth Night	*William Shakespeare*
∗ Unto This Last	*John Ruskin*
∗ Utopia	*Thomas More*
∗ Wealth of Nations	*Adam Smith*
∗ Wonder that was India	*A.L. Basham*

INDIAN

Book	Author
✶ Ain-i-Akbari	*Abul Fazal*
✶ Anand Math	*Bankim Chandra Chatterjee*
✶ Arthashastra	*Kautilya*
✶ A Suitable Boy	*Vikram Seth*
✶ Bhagwat Gita	*Ved Vyas*
✶ Chidambara	*Sumitranandan Pant*
✶ Devdas	*Sarat Chandra Chatterjee*
✶ Discovery of India	*Jawaharlal Nehru*
✶ Ganadevata	*Tarashankar Bandopadhyaya*
✶ Geet Govind	*Jaya Dev*
✶ Geetanjali	*R. N. Tagore*
✶ Glimpses of World History	*Jawaharlal Nehru*
✶ Godaan	*Prem Chand*
✶ Gul-e-Nagma	*Firaq Gorakhpuri*
✶ Harsh Charita	*Bana Bhatta*
✶ India Divided	*Dr. Rajendra Prasad*
✶ Justice of Peace ke Aansu	Janardan Prasad Singh
✶ The Judgement	*Kuldip Nayyar*
✶ Kadambari	*Bana Bhatta*
✶ Kagaz Te Kanwas	*Amrita Pritam*
✶ Kamayani	*Jai Shankar Prasad*
✶ Kitni Nawon Mein Kitni Bar	*S. H. Vatsyayan*
✶ Kumar Sambhav	*Kalidas*
✶ Mahabharata	*Ved Vyas*
✶ Malgudi Days	*R.K. Narayan*
✶ Meghdoot	*Kalidas*
✶ Mritunjaya	*B.K. Bhattacharya*
✶ Mudrarakshasa	*Vishakhadatta*
✶ Prison Diary	*Jaya Prakash Narayan*
✶ Raghuvansha	*Kalidas*
✶ Rajtarangini	*Kalhana*
✶ Ramayana	*Balmiki*
✶ Ramcharit Manas	*Tulsidas*
✶ Rukh Te Rishi	*Harbhajan Singh*
✶ Satyarth Prakash	*Swami Dayanand*
✶ Sur Sagar	*Surdas*
✶ The Guide	*R.K. Narayan*

IMPORTANT DATES AND DAYS OF THE YEAR

✶ JANUARY

5-11 Road Safety Week
12 National Youth Day
15 Army Day
15-21 Pin Code Week
23 National Day of Patriotism
26 Republic Day
30 Martyr's Day

✶ FEBRUARY

1-14 Oil Conservation Fortnight
14 Valentine's Day

✶ MARCH

4 National Safety Day
8 International Women's Day
15 Consumers' Day
16 Immunisation Day
21 World Forest Day
22 World Day for Water
24 World Meteorological Day
1-7 Preservation of Blindness Week

✶ APRIL

7 World Health Day
7-13 Handloom Week
14-20 Fire Service Week
18 World Heritage Day
22 World Earth Day

✶ MAY

1 May Day
5 National Labour Day
8 World Red Cross Day
11 National Technology Day
15 International Day of the Family
17 World Telecommunication Day
24 Commonwealth Day
31 World No-Tobacco Day

✶ JUNE

5 World Environment Day
21 World Yoga Day
26 International Day against Drug Abuse and Illicit Trafficking

✶ JULY

11 World Population Day

✶ AUGUST

1-7 World Breast feeding Week
10 Sanskrit Divas
15 Independence Day
20 Sadbhavana Divas

✶ SEPTEMBER

1-7 National Nutrition Week
5 Teachers' Day
8 International Literary Day
14 Hindi Diwas

23 World Deaf Day
27 World Tourism Day

*** OCTOBER**

2 * Gandhi Jayanti
* International Day of Non Violence
* Anti-Leprosy Day
4 World Animal Day
6 World Habitat Day *(Ist Monday)*
8 Indian Air Force Day
14 World Standard Day
15 International Day of Rural Women
16 World Food Day
24 United Nations Day
27 Infantry Day
28 World Thrift Day
31 Anti-Terrorism Day

*** NOVEMBER**

2 All Saints Day
14 Children's Day
15-21 National Cooperative Week
19-25 Quami Ekta Week
20 Child Rights Day
26 Constitution Day

*** DECEMBER**

1 World AIDS Day
3 World Day for the Disabled
4 Naval Day
7 Flag Day
8 SMRC Day
10 Human Rights Day
14 National Energy Conservation Day

INDIAN DEFENCE

- The Supreme Command of the Armed Forces is vested in the hands of the President of the Country.
- The responsibility for national defence, however, rests with the Cabinet. All important questions having a bearing on defence are decided by the Cabinet Committee on Political Affairs, which is presided over by the Prime Minister.
- The Defence Minister is responsible to Parliament for all matters concerning the Defence Services.
- All the administrative and operational control of Armed Forces are exercised by the Ministry of Defence. The three services—Army, Navy and Air Force function through their respective service head-quarters headed by the chief of Staff. The post of Chief of Defence Staff (CDS) was created in 2019.

Indian Army Commands

Command	*HQ Location*
Eastern Command	Kolkata
Western Command	Chandigarh
Northern Command	Udhampur
Southern Command	Pune
Central Command	Lucknow
Training Command	Shimla
South-Western Command	Jaipur

Indian Air Force Commands

Command	*HQ Location*
Western Air Command	New Delhi
Sout-Western Air Command	Gandhinagar
Central Air Command	Prayagraj
Eastern Air Command	Shillong
Southern Air Command	Thiruvananthapuram
Training Command	Bengaluru

Indian Navy Commands

Command	*HQ Location*
Eastern Naval Command	Vishakhapatnam
Western Naval Command	Mumbai
Southern Naval Command	Kochi

Commissioned Ranks in Defence Services

Army	*Navy*	*Air Force*
General	Admiral	Air Chief Marshal
Lieutenant-General	Vice-Admiral	Air Marshal
Major-General	Rear-Admiral	Air Vice-Marshal
Brigadier	Commodor	Air Commodor
Colonel	Captain	Group Captain
Lieutenant-Colonel	Commander	Wing Commander
Major	Lt.Commander	Squadron Leader
Captain	Lieutenant	Flight Lieutenant
Lieutenant	Sub-Lieutenant	Flying Officer

INDIAN CULTURE

☛ Dance

India has a very rich tradition of tribal, folk and classical dances.

☛ Classical Dance

Dance	State	Famous Artists
• Bharat Natyam	Tamil Nadu	Yamini Krishnamurthy, Rukmini Devi Arundale, Swapna Sundari, Sonal Mansingh, Vaijanti Mala, Mrinalini Sarabhai, Chandralekha, Indrani, Ram Gopal, Bal Saraswati
• Kathakali	Kerala	Gopinath, K.K. Nayar, Kunju-Kurup, T.K. Chandu
• Kuchipudi	Andhra Pradesh	Sapna Sundari, Raja Reddy, Radha Reddy, Vedantam Satyanarayan, Vimpanti Chinna Satyam.
• Kathak	North India	Birju Maharaj, Gopi Krishna, Shambhu Maharaj, Sitara Devi, Vishnu Sharma, Durga Lal, Shobhana Narayan
• Odissi	Odisha	Kelucharan Mahapatra, Indrani Rehman, Madhavi Mudgal, Pratima Bedi, Samyukta Panigrahi, Sonal Mansingh, Debudas
• Manipuri	Manipur	Uday Shankar, Bipin Singh, Suryamukhi, Darohra Jhaveri

☛ Famous Folk-Dance

- Andhra Pradesh: *Dandari, Banjara*
- Asom: *Bihu, Keli Gopal, Sataria*
- Bihar: *Chhau, Magahi, Durga dance*
- W. Bengal: *Kirtan, Kalatri, Asweabadh, Brita, Kalidance*
- Chhattisgarh: *Saila, Karama, Bhagoria*
- Gujarat: *Garba, Rasalila, Tippani, Dandia,*
- Haryana: *Damyal, Lahoor*
- Himachal Pradesh: *Dussehra dance, Hikat, Notio*
- Jammu & Kashmir: *Dumhal*
- Jharkhand: *Jhau, Ghumakudia, Jadur, Sarhul, Soharai, Karama, Vaima, Loojhari, Jat-Jatin, Vidayat*
- Karnataka: *Yakshagan, Dolu Kunitha*
- Kerala: *Mohini Attam, Padayuni*
- Madhya Pradesh: *Lota Nritya, Jawara*
- Maharashtra: *Tamasha, Dahi Handi, Gof, Deepak Dindi*
- Manipur: *Dhol Cholam*
- Meghalaya: *Nongakarem*
- Nagaland: *Bamboo dance*
- Odisha: *Chhau, Maya Shabari, Dalachai*
- Punjab: *Gidda, Bhangra, Panihari*
- Rajasthan: *Ghumar, Kathaputali, Tera Tali*
- Tamil Nadu: *Terukalathu, Kabalatam, Kargam, Pulivesham*
- Tripura: *Hazagiri*
- Uttar Pradesh: *Rasalila, Nautanki, Thali, Huraka, Dhurang, Jhumela, Bol.*
- Uttarakhand: *Kajari, Karan*
- Goa: *Dhode Modini*

☛ Musical Instruments and Artists

- **Flute:** Hari Prasad Chaurasia, Panna Lal Ghosh, T.R. Mahalingam, N. Ramani, Vijaya Raghava Rao
- **Tabla:** Allah Rakha, Gudai Maharaj, Latif Khan, Zakir Hussain
- **Violin:** Lalgudi Jayaraman, L. Subramaniam, M.S. Gopal Krishnan, S. Subrahmaniam, V.G. Jog, N. Rajan
- **Shehnai:** Bismilla Khan, Imrat Khan
- **Sarod:** Ali Akbar Khan, Amjad Ali Khan, Alauddin Khan, Saren Rani, Brij Narayan
- **Sitar:** Pandit Ravishankar, Vilayat Khan
- **Santur:** Shiv Kumar Sharma
- **Rudraveena:** Zia Mohiuddin Dagar
- **Pakhawaj:** Govind Rao, Anokhe Lal, Kanthi Maharaj
- **Mridanga:** Palghat R. Raghu, U.S. Burman
- **Harmonium:** Purushottam Walawakar, M. Dhaulpuri
- **Guitar:** Pt. Vishnu Mohan Bhatt, Brij Bhushan Kalra
- **Ghatam:** T.H. Vinayakaram
- **Janjira:** V. Nagarajan
- **Symphony:** Jubin Mehta

WORLD HERITAGE SITES IN INDIA

A World Heritage Site is a place that is listed by UNESCO for its special cultural or physical significance. The list of World Heritage Sites is maintained by the international 'World Heritage Programme', administered by the UNESCO World Heritage Committee. The United Nations Educational, Scientific and Cultural Organization (UNESCO) seeks to encourage the identification, protection and preservation of cultural and natural heritage around the world considered to be of outstanding value to humanity. This is embodied in an international treaty called the Convention concerning the Protection of the World Cultural and Natural Heritage, adopted by UNESCO in 1972. India has 42 world heritage sites that include 34 Cultural properties, 7 Natural properties and 1 mixed site.

Cultural Sites in India

- ➨ Agra Fort (1983)
- ➨ Ajanta Caves (1983)

- Archaeological Site of Nalanda Mahavihara at Nalanda, Bihar (2016)
- Buddhist Monuments at Sanchi (1989)
- Champaner-Pavagadh Archaeological Park (2004)
- Chhatrapati Shivaji Terminus (formerly Victoria Terminus) (2004)
- Churches and Convents of Goa (1986)
- Elephanta Caves (1987)
- Ellora Caves (1983)
- Fatehpur Sikri (1986)
- Great Living Chola Temples (1987, 2004)
- Group of Monuments at Hampi (1986)
- Group of Monuments at Mahabalipuram (1984)
- Group of Monuments at Pattadakal (1987)
- Hill Forts of Rajasthan (2013)
- Historic City of Ahmedabad (2017)
- Humayun's Tomb, Delhi (1993)
- Jaipur City, Rajasthan (2019)
- Khajuraho Group of Monuments (1986)
- Mountain Railways of India (1999, 2005, 2008)
- Mahabodhi Temple Complex at Bodh Gaya (2002)
- Qutub Minar and its Monuments, Delhi (1993)
- Rani-ki-Vav (the Queen's Stepwell) at Patan, Gujarat (2014)
- Red Fort Complex (2007)
- Rock Shelters of Bhimbetka (2003)
- Sun Temple, Konarak (1984)
- Taj Mahal (1983)
- The Architectural Work of Le Corbusier (2016)
- Victorian Gothic and Art Deco Ensembles of Mumbai (2018)
- The Jantar Mantar, Jaipur (2010)
- Dholavira : a Harappan City (2021)
- Kakatiya Rudreshwara (Ramappa) Temple, Telangana (2021)
- Santiniketan, West Bengal (2023)
- Hoyasala Temples, Karnataka (2023)

Natural Sites in India

- Great Himalayan National Park Conservation Area (2014)
- Kaziranga National Park (1985)
- Keoladeo National Park (1985)
- Manas Wildlife Sanctuary (1985)
- Nanda Devi and Valley of Flowers National Parks (1988, 2005)
- Sundarban National Park (1987)
- Western Ghats (2012)

Mixed Site in India

- Khangchendzonga National Park (2016)

UNITED NATIONS (UN)

- The United Nations (UN) is an association of states which have pledged themselves to maintain international peace and security and cooperate in solving international political, economic, social cultural and humanitarian problems towards achieving this end.
- Trygve Lie of Norway (1946-52) was the first Secretary-General of the UN.
- ***Origin:*** UN Charter was signed by 50 members on June 26, 1945. Poland signed the charter later to become one of the original 51 member-states. It officially came into existence on October 24, 1945.
- ***UN Charter:*** The Charter is the Constitution of the UN and contains its aims and objectives and rules and regulations for its functioning.
- ***Aims and Objectives:*** They are security, welfare and human rights.
- ***Headquarters:*** New York.
- ***Flag:*** The flag is light blue in colour, and emblazoned in white, in its centre is the UN symbol—a polar map of world embraced by twin olive branches open at the top.
- ***Official Languages:*** The official languages of the UN are: English, French, Chinese, Russian, Arabic and Spanish. However, working languages are English and French only.
- ***Present Membership:*** At present 193 countries are members of the UN. South Sudan is the latest entrant to this world organisation.
- ***Main Organs of the UN:*** There are six main organs:
  1. General Assembly
  2. Security Council
  3. Economic and Social Council
  4. Trusteeship Council
  5. International Court of Justice, and
  6. Secretariat.

  1. *General Assembly:* It consists of representative of all members of the UN. Each member country has only one vote. It meets once a year and passes UN Budget. It is the main place for discussions and policy making in the UN.

2. *Security Council:* It is the Executive body of the UN and is mainly responsible for maintaining international peace and security. It has 15 members, 5 of which (USA, UK, France, Russia and China) are permanent members. The 10 non-permanent members are elected by General Assembly for two-year term and are not eligible for immediate re-election.
3. *Economic and Social Council:* It has 54 members elected by General Assembly.
4. *Trusteeship Council:* It looks after interest of the people in areas not yet independent and leads them towards self-government.
5. *International Court of Justice:* It has 15 judges, no two of whom may be nationals of the same state. They are elected by General Assembly and Security Council for a term of 9 years. The Court elects its President and Vice-President for a 3-year term.
6. *Secretariat:* It is the Secretariat of the UN and is headed by the Secretary General.

AWARDS AND HONOURS

NATIONAL AWARDS

BHARAT RATNA

- Bharat Ratna is India's highest Civilian Award. It was first awarded in 1954.
- The actual award is designed in the shape of a *peepal* leaf with Bharat Ratna inscribed in Devanagri script in the Sun Figure.
- This is India's highest civilian award. It is given for exceptional work on art, literature, science and recognition of public service of the highest order.
- The emblem, the Sun and the rim are of platinum. The inscriptions are in burnished bronze.
- Government servants are not eligible for it. The table shows the recipients of the award:

Bharat Ratna Award Winners

1.	Dr. S. Radhakrishnan	1954
2.	C. Rajagopalachari	1954
3.	Dr. C.V. Raman	1954
4.	Dr. Bhagwan Das	1955
5.	Dr. M. Visvesvaraya	1955
6.	Jawahar Lal Nehru	1955
7.	Govind Ballabh Pant	1957
8.	Dr. D.K. Karve	1958
9.	Dr. Bidhan Chandra Roy	1961
10.	Purushottam Das Tandon	1961
11.	Dr. Rajendra Prasad	1962
12.	Dr. Zakir Hussain	1963
13.	Dr. Pandurang Vaman Kane	1963
14.	Lal Bahadur Shastri	1966
15.	Indira Gandhi	1971
16.	V.V. Giri	1975
17.	K. Kamraj	1976
18.	Mother Teresa	1980
19.	Acharya Vinoba Bhave	1983
20.	Khan Abdul Ghaffar Khan	1987
21.	M.G. Ramachandran	1988
22.	Dr. B.R. Ambedkar	1990
23.	Dr. Nelson R. Mandela	1990
24.	Rajiv Gandhi	1991
25.	Sardar Vallabhbhai Patel	1991
26.	Morarji R. Desai	1991
27.	Maulana Abul Kalam Azad	1992
28.	Jehangir Ratanji Dadabhai Tata	1992
29.	Satyajit Roy	1992
30.	Shri Gulzari Lal Nanda	1997
31.	Mrs. Aruna Asaf Ali	1997
32.	Dr. A.P.J. Abdul Kalam	1997
33.	M.S. Subbalakshmi	1998
34.	C. Subramaniam	1998
35.	Jaya Prakash Narayan	1999
36.	Prof. Amartya Sen	1999
37.	Pt. Ravi Shankar	1999
38.	Gopinath Bardoloi	1999
39.	Lata Mangeshkar	2001
40.	Bismillah Khan	2001
41.	Bhimsen Joshi	2009
42.	C.N.R. Rao	2014
43.	Sachin Tendulkar	2014
44.	Pt. Madan Mohan Malaviya	2015
45.	Atal Bihari Vajpayee	2015
46.	Pranab Mukherjee	2019
47.	Nanaji Deshmukh	2019
48.	Bhupen Hazarika	2019
49.	Karpoori Thakur	2024
50.	L.K. Advani	2024
51.	Charan Singh	2024
52.	P.V. Narasimha Rao	2024
53.	M.S. Swaminathan	2024

REPUBLIC DAY AWARDS

Padma Awards

They fall in line after the Bharat Ratna. They are also discontinued in 1977 along with the Bharat Ratna and award was started again in 1980.

There are three Padma Awards:

- ***Padma Vibhushan:*** This award is given for exceptional and distinguished service in any field, including service rendered by Govt. servants.
- ***Padma Bhushan:*** This award is given for distinguished service of a high order in any field, including service rendered by Govt. servants.
- ***Padma Shri:*** This award is given for distinguished service in any field, including service rendered by Government servants.

Gallantry Awards

- ***Param Vir Chakra:*** The highest award for bravery or some daring and pre-eminent act of valour or self-sacrifice in the presence of the enemy, whether on land, at sea or in the air.
- ***Mahavir Chakra:*** It is the second highest decoration and is awarded for acts of conspicuous gallantry in the presence of the enemy, whether on land, at sea or in the air.
- ***Vir Chakra:*** It is the third in order of awards given for acts of gallantry in the presence of enemy, whether on land, at sea or in the air.
- ***Ashok Chakra:*** This medal is awarded for the most conspicuous bravery or some daring or pre-eminent act of valour or self-sacrifice on land, at sea or in the air but not in the presence of enemy.
- ***Vishishta Sewa Medal:*** It is awarded to personnel of all the three Services in class I, II and III in recognition of distinguished service of the "most exceptional" and "exceptional" and a "high" order respectively. Prefixes Parma and Ati are added before first two categories of medals respectively.
- ***Jeewan Raksha Padak:*** Awarded for meritorious acts or a series of acts of a human nature displayed in saving life from drowning, fire and rescue operations in mines etc.

OTHER NATIONAL AWARDS

SAHITYA AKADEMI AWARDS

- These prizes are awarded annually to the authors of the most outstanding books of literary merit published in each of the 22 languages which are specified in the Eighth Schedule of the Constitution.
- There are also two awards for Rajasthani and English. The award, in form of a casket containing an inscribed copper plate and a cheque of ₹ 1 lakh is given to the author or his/her heir.

DADA SAHEB PHALKE AWARD

- The award carries a cash prize of ₹ 15 lakh, a Shawl and Swarna Kamal. Mrs Devika Rani Roerich was the first person to receive Dadasaheb Phalke Award in 1969.
- The Award for 2021 has been given to Waheeda Rehman.

BHARATIYA JNANPITH AWARD

- Instituted in 22nd May, 1961, carries a cash prize of ₹ 11 lakh, a citation and a bronze replica of Vagdevi (Saraswati).
- Instituted by a literary organisation in India.

SARASWATI SAMMAN

- Given for outstanding literary works, value ₹ 15 lakh.

KALINGA PRIZE

- This award is given each year by the UNESCO and founded by former Odisha Chief Minister late Shri Biju Patnaik for popularisation of science.

INTERNATIONAL AWARDS

NOBEL PRIZES

- These Prizes were instituted in 1901 by a Swedish scientist, Dr. Alfred Nobel; the discoverer of Dynamite.
- Six prizes are awarded annually for (*i*) Chemistry, (*ii*) Physics, (*iii*) Medicine, (*iv*) Literature, (*v*) Peace and (*vi*) Economics—started since 1969.
- Five Indians so far have been awarded these Prizes, (*i*) Rabindranath Tagore for literature in 1913 for his work 'Gitanjali', (*ii*) C.V. Raman for Physics in 1930, (*iii*) Mother Teresa for Peace in 1979, (*iv*) Prof. Amartya Sen for Economics in 1998, (*v*) Kailash Satyarthi for Peace in 2014.
- In addition, four non-resident Indians have also been awarded the Nobel Prize. They are: (*i*) Hargobind Khurana for Medicine in 1968, (*ii*) Subramanian Chandrasekhar for Physics in 1983, (*iii*) Venkatraman Ramkrishnan for Chemistry in 2009, (iv) Abhijit Vinayak Banerjee for Economics in 2019.

GANDHI PEACE PRIZE

- The government instituted this ₹ 1 crore prize on the lines of the Nobel Peace Prize in 1995.
- It is the highest Civilian International award by the Govt. of India.

MAN BOOKER INTERNATIONAL AWARD

- The Man Booker International Prize was established in 2005, biannually rewarding an author for a body of work originally written in any language as long as it was widely available in English.
- From 2016, the prize became a translation prize, awarded annually for a single work of fiction, translated into English and published in the UK. Underlining the importance of translation, the £ 50,000 prize is divided equally between the author and the translator.

Highest Honours of Some Countries

Country	*Highest Honour*
India	Bharat Ratna
Pakistan	Nishan-e-Pakistan
Kuwait	Mubarak-Al-kabir Medal
Saudi Arabia	Shah Abdul Aziz Medal
Argentina	The Order of Sona Martin
Nicaragua	Augusto-Caesar Sandino Order
Vietnam	The Order of the Golden Star
Hungary	The Order of Banner
Britain	Member of British Empire, Victoria Cross
Japan	Order of Moulovenice Sun
Denmark	Order of Diana Brog
France	Legend of Honour
America	Presidential Medal of Freedom
Germany	Pore Lee Merit Iron Cross
The Netherlands	Netherlands Lion

SPORTS

OLYMPICS

- First of all these games were held by the Greeks in 776 B.C. on Mount Olympus in honour of the Greek God Zeus. In this way, the history of Olympic Games is about twenty eight hundred years old. These games continued to be held every four years until 394 A.D. when these games were stopped by a royal order of the emperor of Rome.
- The modern Olympic Games which started in Athens in 1896, are the result of the devotion and dedication of a French educator Baron Pierre de Coubertin and the first Olympic meet in the modern series was held in 1896 in Athens, the Capital of Greece. Since then, they are being held every four years except for breaks during world wars.
- The Olympic flag is white in colour with five coloured rings, each ring symbolic of a continent. Summer as well as Winter Olympics are held in the same year.
- The 2020 Olympic Games was held at Tokyo, Japan in 2021.
- The official Olympic Motto is *Citius, Altius, Swifter, Higher, Stronger*. The Head Office of International Olympic Committee (IOC) is at Lausanne (Switzerland).

COMMONWEALTH GAMES

- The Commonwealth Games are held every four years, in the year in which Asian Games are held. All the Commonwealth Countries (former colonies of Britain) can take part in it.
- The first Commonwealth Games were held in 1930 at Hamilton (Canada).
- There are currently 56 members of the Commonwealth of Nations, and 72 teams participated in the games.
- The 2022 Commonwealth Games, officially known as the XXII Commonwealth Games or Birmingham, 2022, held in Birmingham, England between 28 July to 8 August 2022.

ASIAN GAMES

- After the Second World War, most of the Asian Countries gained independence. On the lines of Olympic Games, Asian Games were planned every four years.
- India hosted the first Asian Games in 1951.

WORLD CUP CRICKET

- The first Cricket World Cup was organised in England in 1975. A separate women's Cricket World Cup has been held every 4 years since 1973.

List of Cricket World Cup

Year	Venue	Winner/Runner
1975	England	*West Indies beat Australia*
1979	England	*West Indies beat England*
1983	England	*India beat West Indies*
1987	India & Pakistan	*Australia beat England*
1992	Australia	*Pakistan beat England*
1996	India, Pakistan & Sri Lanka	*Sri Lanka beat Australia*
1999	England	*Australia beat Pakistan*
2003	South Africa	*Australia beat India*
2007	West Indies	*Australia beat Sri Lanka*
2011	India, Sri Lanka, Bangladesh	*India beat Sri Lanka*
2015	Australia, New Zealand	*Australia beat New Zealand*
2019	England	*England beat New Zealand*
2023	India	*Australia beat India*

HOCKEY WORLD CUP

- The first Hockey World Cup was organised in Barcelona (Spain) in 1971. Women's Hockey World Cup has been held since 1974.

FOOTBALL WORLD CUP

- The Football World Cup is organised by FIFA (Federation of International Football Association). The World Cup is called 'Jules Rimet Cup' named after the name of FIFA President Jules Rimet. The first Football World Cup was organised in Uruguay in 1930.
- In 1942 and 1946, the Football World Cup was not played due to World War II.
- Brazil is the only nation to have participated in every World Cup so far.

IMPORTANT CUPS & TROPHIES

International

- ∗ *American Cup* : Yacht Racing
- ∗ *Ashes* : Cricket
- ∗ *Davis Cup* : Lawn Tennis
- ∗ *Derby* : Horse Race
- ∗ *Grand National* : Horse Streple Chase Race
- ∗ *Jules Rimet Trophy* : World Soccer Cup
- ∗ *King's Cup* : Air Races
- ∗ *Merdeka Cup* : Football
- ∗ *Swaythling Cup* : Table Tennis (Men)
- ∗ *Ryder Cup* : Golf
- ∗ *Thomas Cup* : Badminton
- ∗ *U. Thant Cup* : Tennis
- ∗ *Walker Cup* : Golf
- ∗ *Wightman Cup* : Lawn Tennis
- ∗ *Rothman's Trophy* : Cricket
- ∗ *European Champions Cup* : Football
- ∗ *Grand Prix* : Table Tennis
- ∗ *Edgbaston Cup* : Lawn Tennis
- ∗ *Grand Prix* : Lawn Tennis

National

- *Agha Khan Cup* : Hockey
- *Beighton Cup* : Hockey
- *Bombay Gold Cup* : Hockey
- *C.K. Naydu Trophy* : Cricket
- *Deodhar Trophy* : Cricket
- *Duleep Trophy* : Cricket
- *Durand Cup* : Football
- *Dhyan Chand Trophy* : Hockey
- *Dr. B.C. Roy Trophy* : Football (Junior)
- *Ezra Cup* : Polo
- *Guru Nanak Cup* : Hockey
- *Holkar Trophy* : Bridge
- *Irani Trophy* : Cricket
- *Indira Gold Cup* : Hockey
- *Murugappa Gold Cup* : Hockey
- *Nehru Trophy* : Hockey
- *Nixan Gold Cup* : Football
- *Rani Jhansi Trophy* : Cricket
- *Ranji Trophy* : Cricket
- *Rangaswami Cup* : Hockey
- *Ramanujan Trophy* : Table Tennis
- *Rene Frank Trophy* : Hockey
- *Rohinton Baria Trophy* : Cricket
- *Rovers Cup* : Football
- *Santosh Trophy* : Football
- *Subroto Cup* : Football

SPORTS TERMS

- ***Badminton:*** Mixed doubles; Deuce; Drop; Smash; Let; Foot work; Setting.
- ***Base Ball:*** Pitcher; Put out, Strike; Home; Bunt.
- ***Billiards:*** Cue; Jigger; Pot; Break; In Baulk; In Off; Cannons.
- ***Boxing:*** Upper cut; Round; Punch; Bout; Knock down; Hitting below the belt; Ring.
- ***Bridge:*** Finesse; Dummy; Revoke; Grand Slam; Little Slam; No Trump; Rubber.
- ***Chess:*** Bishop, Gambit; Checkmate; Stalemate.
- ***Cricket:*** L.B.W. (leg before wicket); Creases, Popping-creases; Stumped; Bye; Leg-Bye; Googly; Hattrick; Maiden over; Drive; Bowling; Duck; Follow-on; No ball; Leg Break; Silly point; Cover point; Hit-wicket; Late-cut; Slip; Off-spinner; In-swing.
- ***Football:*** Off Side; Block; Drop-kick; Penalty-kick (or goal kick); Corner-kick; Free-kick; Dribble; Thrown-in; Foul.
- ***Golf:*** Boggy; Foursome; Stymic; Tee; Put; Hole; Niblic; Caddie; Links; The green; Bunker.
- ***Hockey:*** Carried; Short Corner; Bully; Sticks; Off side; Roll in; Striking Circle; Under-cutting; Dribble.
- ***Horse racing:*** Jockey; Punter.
- ***Polo:*** Bunker; Chukker; Mallet.
- ***Tennis:*** Back hand drive; Volley; Smash; Half-volley; Deuce; Service; Let; Grand Slam.

Stadiums and Places Associated with Sports

Name of Stadium	Sports	Place
Narendra Modi Stadium	Cricket	Ahmedabad
Arun Jaitley Stadium	Cricket	Delhi
Jawaharlal Nehru Stadium	Athletics	Delhi
Shivajee Stadium	Hockey	Delhi
National Stadium	Hockey etc.	Delhi
Ambedkar Stadium	Football	Delhi
Brabourne Stadium	Cricket	Mumbai
Wankhede Stadium	Cricket	Mumbai
National Stadium	Hockey etc.	Mumbai
Eden Garden	Cricket	Kolkata
Green Park Stadium	Cricket	Kanpur
Keenan Stadium	Cricket	Jamshedpur
Nehru (Chepauk) Stadium	Cricket	Chennai
Barabati Stadium	Cricket	Cuttack
Lords, Oval, Leeds	Cricket	Britain
Hedingle Manchester	Cricket	Britain
Black Heath	Rugby Football	London
Henley	Boat race	England
Wimbledon	Lawn Tennis	London
Wembley Stadium	Football	London
White City	Dog-race	England
Aintree	Horse-race	England
Tentbridge	Cricket	England
Patnee Martlake	Boat-race	England
Tibankham	Rugby Football	England
Sandy Lodge	Golf	Scotland
Forest Hill	Tennis	New York
Brooklyn	Baseball	New York
Melbourne	Cricket	Australia

Name of Playing Compound of Different Games

Name of Compound	Related Sports
Court	Lawn Tennis, Badminton, Netball, Hand ball, Volleyball, Squash, Kho-Kho, Kabaddi
Diamond	Baseball
Ring	Boxing, Skating, Wrestling, Circus, Riding display
Course	Golf
Board	Table Tennis
Pool	Swimming
Alley	Bowling
Mat	Judo, Karate II
Arena	Horse Riding
Vellodrum	Cycling
Field	Polo, Football, Hockey
Track	Athletics
Pitch	Cricket, Rugby
Rink	Ice Hockey

❑ ❑ ❑

7

Multiple Choice Questions

1. Match List-I with List-II and select the correct answer from the codes given below the lists:

List-I	List-II
(*a*) Napoleon Bonaparte	1. 'A history is contemporary history'
(*b*) Jean Jacques Rousseau	2. 'Liberty what crimes are committed in thy name'
(*c*) Croce	3. 'Man is born free but every-where he is in chains.'
(*d*) Madame Roland	4. 'I am the Child of Revolution'

Codes :

	(*a*)	(*b*)	(*c*)	(*d*)
A.	1	2	3	4
B.	4	3	1	2
C.	3	4	2	1
D.	3	4	1	2

2. Abraham Lincon was elected the President of United States in:
A. 1862 B. 1860
C. 1875 D. 1855

3. Who was known as the 'Prince of Humanists'?
A. Francisco Petrarch B. Dante
C. Boccacio D. Erasmus

4. D-Day is the day when:
A. Germany declared war on Britain
B. US dropped the atom bomb on Hiroshima.
C. Allied Troops landed in Normandy
D. Germany surrendered to the allies

5. Whose teachings inspired the French Revolution?
A. Locke B. Rousseau
C. Hegel D. Plato

6. At a time when empires in Europe were crumbling before the might of Napoleon which one of the following Governor-Generals kept the British flag flying high in India?
A. Warren Hastings B. Lord Cornwallis
C. Lord Wellesley D. Lord Hastings

7. Which one of the following statements regarding Fascism in Italy is *not* true?
A. The Fascists came to power as a result of popular uprising
B. In 1926, all political parties except Mussolini's party were banned
C. The Fascists suppressed the Socialist movement
D. The Fascists were hostile to the Communists

8. The fall of Czar Nicholas-II is known as:
A. Bloody Sunday
B. Bolshevik Revolution
C. February Revolution
D. October Revolution

9. Industrial Revolution took place first in:
A. France B. Germany
C. United Kingdom D. Japan

10. The British Prime Minister at the outbreak of World War II was :
A. Churchill B. Baldwin
C. Attlee D. Chemberlain

11. The 'Great Depression' (1929) economic crisis was met by adopting the policy of
A. Stimulus B. Marshall Plan
C. New Deal D. Open Door

12. The slogan "No taxation without representation" was raised during the:
A. American War of Independence
B. Russian Revolution
C. French Revolution
D. Indian Freedom struggle

13. In the nineteenth century the people of Europe started moving from the villages to the cities due to the impact of :
A. Epidemics
B. War
C. Industrialisation
D. Population explosion in villages

14. The important cause of the Civil War in America was:
A. Abolition of slavery
B. Quest for freedom
C. Industrialisation
D. Rebellion by the native Americans

15. Industrial Revolution could not have come about without:
A. Merchant capitalism
B. The Enclosure Movement
C. The services of the proletariat class
D. An agricultural revolution

16. Consider the following statements :
The French Revolution came about mainly due to the:
1. Extreme poverty of the people
2. Impact of the works of great writers
3. Cruelty of the rulers
4. Impact of impulsive reaction
Which of the above statements are correct?
A. 1, 2 and 4 B. 2 and 3
C. 1, 3 and 4 D. 1, 2, 3 and 4

17. Asia's oldest and largest Buddhist monastery is situated in :
A. Tawang (Arunachal Pardesh)
B. Lhasa (Tibet)
C. Trincomallee (Sri Lanka)
D. Ulan Bator (Mongolia)

18. Who was the main architect of the Russian Revolution?
A. Karl Marx B. Lenin
C. Stalin D. Tolstoy

19. V.I. Lenin is associated with :
A. Russian Revolution of 1917
B. Chinese Revolution of 1949
C. German Revolution
D. French Revolution of 1789

20. Which one of the following statements is *not* correct?
A. Voltaire believed in Natural Religion
B. Rousseau wrote *Social Contract*
C. Montesquieu authored *The Spirit of Laws*
D. Necker believed in 'General Will'

21. 6th April, 1930 is well known in the history of India because this date is associated with...........
A. Dandi March by Mahatma Gandhi
B. Quit India Movement
C. Partition of Bengal
D. Partition of India

22. Which ruler enforced the system of 'Price Control' in India?
A. Mohammad Tughlak B. Razia Begum
C. Alauddin Khilji D. Sher Shah Suri

23. The concept of 'Din-e-Elahi' was founded by which king?
A. Dara Shikoh B. Akbar
C. Sher Shah Suri D. Shahjahan

24. Who are supposed to be the earliest inhabi-tants of India? Where did they come from?
A. Aryans from Central Asia
B. Dravidians from Mediterranean
C. Negroids from Africa
D. Bhils and the Santhals from West Asia

25. The one chief characteristic of temple architecture of the Gupta Age was :
A. Absence of dome
B. Huge size
C. Beautiful carvings
D. absence of a covered courtyard for the gathering of worshippers

26. The Rigveda consists of :
A. 1000 hymns B. 2028 hymns
C. 1028 hymns D. 1038 hymns

27. The central point in Ashoka's dharma was :
A. royalty to kings B. peace and non-violence
C. respect to elders D. religious tolerance

28. The social evil which was conspicuously absent during ancient India was :
A. *Sati*-System B. *Devadasi*-System
C. Polygamy D. *Purdah*-System

29. Which, among the following, can be accepted as a novelty introduced by Mughal emperors to their buildings?
A. Domes B. Minarets
C. Arches D. Attached gardens

30. The first ruler of India who defeated Muhammud of Ghur was :
A. Mularaja II of Gujarat
B. Prithviraja Chauhan of Delhi
C. Jayachand of Kannauj
D. Parmaldeva of Bundelkhand

31. What important event happened in India in 1911?
A. Bengal was partitioned
B. Non-Cooperation movement was launched
C. India's capital was shifted from Calcutta to Delhi
D. Mahatma Gandhi presided over the Congress session

32. The first phase of the Congress Party (1885-1905) was characterized by its efforts to secure:
A. limited independence
B. complete freedom
C. Indianization of services
D. constitutional reforms

33. The Muslim League demanded a separate homeland for the Indian Muslims openly for the first time at its annual session held in Lahore in the year :
A. 1931 A.D. B. 1936 A.D.
C. 1940 A.D. D. 1941 A.D.

34. Under whose governorship did the East India Company secure the Diwani Rights in Bengal, Bihar and Odisha from Emperor Shah Alam?
A. Lord Cornwallis B. Lord William Bentinck
C. Lord Clive D. Lord Wellesley

35. The Simon Commission was generally boycotted by the Indian political parties. What was the reason for this general non-cooperation?
A. the Commission aimed at dividing the people
B. it was an 'all white' Commission
C. it came after the Jallianwala Bagh carnage
D. it was an eye wash

36. Aligarh Muslim University was founded by :
A. Dr. Saifuddin Kitchlu
B. Mohammad Ali Jinnah
C. Sir Syed Ahmed Khan
D. Maulana Mohammad Ali

37. Ibn Batutah was an African traveller visiting India during the time of :
A. Alivardi Khan
B. Ala-ud-din Khalji
C. Iltutmish
D. Mohammad-bin-Tughlaq

38. The battle of Wandiawash was fought in :
A. 1726 B. 1760
C. 1818 D. 1857

39. The abolition of *Sati* by government regulation was at the time of :
A. Warren Hastings B. Lord Wellesley
C. Lord Bentinck D. Lord Ahmerst

40. Pick out the wrong combination :
A. Dilwara Temple : Mt. Abu
B. Pashupati Temple : Kathmandu
C. Padmanabh Temple : Bangalore
D. Minakshi Temple : Madurai

41. Match the following:
(*a*) Chanhudaro (*b*) Kalibangan
(*c*) Lothal (*d*) Surkotada
1. Alleged discovery of the skeleton of horse.
2. Bead making.
3. Traces of a dock and ship on seal.
4. Evidence of ploughing the fields.
The Correct code is :

	(*a*)	(*b*)	(*c*)	(*d*)
A.	2	4	3	1
B.	2	1	3	4
C.	1	2	3	4
D.	2	1	4	3

42. Match the Harappan settlements with the banks of rivers on which they were located :
(*a*) Harappa 1. Ravi
(*b*) Mohenjodaro 2. Indus
(*c*) Ropar 3. Sutlej
(*d*) Kalibangan 4. Ghaggar
(*e*) Lothal 5. Bhogava
Codes :

	(*a*)	(*b*)	(*c*)	(*d*)	(*e*)
A.	1	2	3	4	5
B.	1	2	3	5	4
C.	2	1	3	5	4
D.	2	1	4	3	5

43. The Goddess 'Kannagi' whose many temples were erected during the 'Sangam Age' was the goddess of:
A. Chastity B. Love
C. Prowess D. Wisdom

44. The Jain goal of life is to attain deliverance from the fetters of mudane existence, the way to which lies through three jewels. Which one of the following was not included among the 'three jewels' of Jainism?
A. Right faith B. Right action
C. Right knowledge D. Right conduct

45. The most striking feature of the Ashokan pillar is polish. Name the Ashokan pillar which is considered to be the most graceful of all Ashokan pillars.
A. Sarnath B. Rampurva
C. Laurya-Nandangarh D. Rummindei

46. Which are the correct statements?
1. The land grants, started in Satavahana period, paved the way for feudal developments in India.
2. Silk and spices were the Chief Indian export articles of Indo-Roman trade.
3. The Guptas issued the largest number of gold coins in ancient India.
4. The first memorial of a 'SATI' dated 510 A.D. is found at Eran in Madhya Pradesh.
A. 1 and 2 B. 1, 3, and 4
C. 1 and 4 D. 1, 2, 3 and 4

47. Who among the following patronised the 'Gandhara' (Indo-Greek style) School of Art?
A. Ashoka, the Great
B. Harsha Vardhana
C. Kanishka
D. Chandragupta Vikramaditya

48. The Sultanate of Delhi had five ruling dynasties. The dynasty having longest and shortest period were :
A. Ilbari and Khalji B. Tughlaq and Khalji
C. Tughlaq and Sayyid D. Ilbari and Lodis

49. Which one of the following events took place at the last during reign of Muhammad-bin-Tughlaq?
A. Introduction of token currency
B. Increase of land-revenue in Doab
C. Transfer of Capital from Delhi to Devagiri.
D. Conquest of Khurasan and Iraq

50. The most learned medieval Muslim ruler who was well versed in various branches of learning including astronomy, mathematics and medicine was :
A. Jalaluddin Khilji B. Sikander Lodi
C. Ghiyasuddin Tughlaq D. Muhammad-bin-Tughlaq

51. The 'Sufis' had 12 silsilas. They propounded the idea of Union with God through:
A. Love B. Rituals
C. Fasts D. Prayers

52. Match the following:
(*a*) Peshwa 1. Foreign affairs
(*b*) Panditrao 2. Audit and accounts
(*c*) Amatya 3. Providing grants to scholars
(*d*) Sumant 4. General supervision
5. Military affairs

Select the correct code :

	(a)	(b)	(c)	(d)
A.	2	3	4	5
B.	4	1	2	3
C.	4	3	2	1
D.	3	1	4	2

53. The Regulating Act of 1773 can be regarded as the first measure to :
A. assert the right of British Parliament to legislate for India
B. separate the legislature from the executive
C. separate the judiciary from the executive
D. centralise law-making

54. What was the exact constitutional status of the Indian Republic on 26th January, 1950?
A. A Democratic Republic
B. A Sovereign, Democratic Republic
C. A Sovereign, Secular, Democratic Republic
D. A Sovereign, Socialist, Secular, Democratic Republic

55. When the British obtained the grant of Diwani of Bengal, Bihar and Odisha they acquired the right to:
A. maintain law and order in these territories
B. administer civil justice and collect revenue in these territories
C. collect revenue and establish revenue administration in these territories
D. militarily defend these territories

56. Which of the following were responsible for the growth of nationalism in India during the British rule?
1. Economic exploitation of India.
2. Impact of western education.
3. Role of the Press.
Select the correct answer using the codes given below :
Codes:
A. 1, 2 and 3 B. 1 and 2
C. 2 and 3 D. 1 and 3

57. Which one of the following nationalist leaders has been described as being radical in politics but conservative on social issues?
A. G.K. Gokhale B. B.G. Tilak
C. Lala Lajpat Rai D. Madan Mohan Malviya

58. Provincial Autonomy in British India was envisaged by the :
A. Act of 1909 B. Act of 1919
C. Act of 1935 D. Act of 1947

59. Dyarchy means :
A. double government
B. a government in which the centre is very powerful
C. a government based on division of power between centre and provinces
D. None of the above

60. The Indian National Congress observed 'Independence Day' for the first time on 26th January in :
A. 1920 B. 1925
C. 1930 D. 1947

61. ....is situated near the banks of Sabarmati River
A. Bhavnagar B. Aurangabad
C. Ahmedabad D. Rajkot

62. Sericulture is:
A. science of the various kinds of serum
B. artificial rearing of fish
C. art of silkworm breeding
D. study of various cultures of a community

63. The most abundant constituents of earth's crust are:
A. Igneous rocks B. Sedimentary rocks
C. Metamorphic rocks D. Granite

64. Indian Standard Time is based on:
A. 80°E longitude B. 82½°E longitude
C. 110°E longitude D. 25°E longitude

65. Tides in the oceans are caused by :
A. Gravitational pull of the moon on the earth's surface including sea water
B. Gravitational pull of the sun on the earth's surface only and not on the sea water
C. Gravitational pull of the moon and the sun on the earth's surface including the sea water
D. None of these

66. Nagarjunasagar Project is situated on the river:
A. Tungabhadra B. Cauvery
C. Krishna D. Godavari

67. The difference between the Indian Standard Time and the Greenwich Mean Time is:
A. – 3½ hours B. + 3½ hours
C. – 5½ hours D. + 5½ hours

68. Which of the following dams is not on Narmada river?
A. Indira-Sagar Project
B. Maheshwar Hydel Power Project
C. Jobat Project
D. Koyna Power Project

69. Which of the following statements is **not true** about the availability of water on the earth, the crisis for which is going to increase in the years to come?
A. About 97.5 per cent of the total volume of water available on the earth is salty
B. 80 per cent of the water available to us for use comes in bursts as monsoons
C. About 2.5 per cent of the total water available on the earth is polluted water and cannot be used for human activities
D. Possibility is that some big glaciers will melt in the coming ten-fifteen years and sea level will rise by 3-4 metres all over the earth

70. Which of the following is **not** a cash crop?
A. Jute B. Paddy
C. Cashewnut D. Sugarcane

71. Through which States does Cauvery River flow?
A. Gujarat, M.P., Tamil Nadu
B. Karnataka, Kerala, Tamil Nadu
C. Karnataka, Kerala, Andhra Pradesh
D. M.P., Maharashtra, Tamil Nadu

72. Indian Standard Time is the local time of 82½°E which passes through :
A. Guntur B. Delhi
C. Allahabad D. Kolkata

73. The 17th parallel defines the boundary between:
A. North and South Korea
B. USA and Canada
C. North and South Vietnam
D. China and Russia

74. During the period of south-west monsoon, Tamil Nadu remains dry because:
A. the winds do not reach this area
B. there are no mountains in this area
C. it lies in the rain shadow area
D. the temperature is too high to let the winds cool down

75. Which country does top in producing cocoa?
A. Ivory Coast B. Brazil
C. Ghana D. Nigeria

76. The biggest reserves of thorium are in :
A. India B. China
C. Russia D. U.S.A.

77. The Girnar Hills are situated in which of the following states?
A. Gujarat B. Karnataka
C. Madhya Pradesh D. Maharashtra

78. During December 22nd the sun is vertically over:
A. Tropic of Cancer B. Tropic of Capricorn
C. The Equator D. None of the above

79. Photosphere is described as the :
A. Lower layer of atmosphere
B. Visible surface of the sun from which radiation emanates
C. Wavelength of solar spectrum
D. None of the above

80. Broadly, there are three layers of the earth of the crust, the mantle and the core. The crust forms what percentage of the volume of the earth?
A. 0.5% B. 2.5%
C. 7.5% D. 12.5%

81. The grassland of Argentina is known as :
A. Pampas B. Campos
C. Savanna D. None of the above

82. Different seasons are formed because :
A. Sun is moving around the earth
B. of revolution of the earth around the Sun on its orbit
C. of rotation of the earth around its axis
D. All of the above

83. Eskers and Drumlins are features formed by:
A. underground water B. running water
C. the action of wind D. glacial action

84. Match List-I and List-II and select the correct answer using the codes given below the Lists :

List-I *(Rivers)*	List-II *(Towns)*
(*a*) Ghaghara	1. Lucknow
(*b*) Brahmaputra	2. Hoshangabad
(*c*) Narmada	3. Ahmedabad
(*d*) Sabarmati	4. Guwahati
	5. Ayodhya

Codes :

	(*a*)	(*b*)	(*c*)	(*d*)
A.	4	5	1	2
B.	5	4	2	3
C.	5	4	3	1
D.	3	5	2	1

85. Which of the statements as regards the consequences of the movement of the earth is not correct?
A. Revolution of the earth is the cause of the change of seasons.
B. Rotation of the earth is the cause of days and nights.
C. Rotation of the earth causes variation in the duration of days and nights.
D. Rotation of the earth effects the movement of winds and ocean currents.

86. The world is divided into :
A. 12 time zones B. 20 time zones
C. 24 time zones D. 36 time zones

87. The 'Kiel' canal links the :
A. Pacific and Atlantic Oceans
B. Mediterranean Sea and Red Sea
C. Mediterranean Sea and Black Sea
D. North Sea and Baltic Sea

88. Match the following :

List-I	List-II
(*a*) Himadri	1. Outer Himalayas
(*b*) Shivalik	2. Inner Himalayas
(*c*) Himanchal	3. Middle Himalayas
(*d*) Sahyadri	4. Western Ghats

Codes :

	(*a*)	(*b*)	(*c*)	(*d*)
A.	1	2	3	4
B.	4	2	3	1
C.	2	1	3	4
D.	1	2	3	4

89. The term 'Regur' refers to:
A. Laterite soils
B. Black Cotton soils
C. Red Soils
D. Deltaic Alluvial Soils

90. Location of sugar industry in India is shifting from north to south because of:
A. cheap labour
B. expanding regional market
C. cheap and abundant supply of power
D. high yield and high sugar content in sugarcane

91. Consider the following statements :
1. Ozone is found mostly in the Stratosphere.
2. Ozone layer lies 55-75 km above the surface of the earth.
3. Ozone absorbs ultraviolet radiation from the Sun.
4. Ozone layer has no significance for life on the earth.

Which of the above statements are correct?
A. 1 and 3 B. 2 and 4
C. 2 and 3 D. 1 and 4

92. Match List-I with List-II and select the correct answer using the codes given below the Lists :

List-I (Crops)	***List-II (Producer)***
(*a*) Banana	1. Brazil
(*b*) Cocoa	2. Ivory Coast
(*c*) Coffee	3. India
(*d*) Tea	4. China

Codes :

	(*a*)	(*b*)	(*c*)	(*d*)
A.	2	3	1	4
B.	3	2	1	4
C.	3	2	4	1
D.	2	3	4	1

93. Darjeeling and Dharamsala would be the right places to visit if one wanted to get a clear view respectively of :
A. Kanchanjunga and Dhauladhar ranges
B. Nandadevi and Dhauladhar ranges
C. Kanchanjunga and Nandadevi ranges
D. Nandadevi and Nanga Parvat

94. Atmosphere exists because:
A. The Gravitational force of the Earth
B. Revolution of the Earth
C. Rotation of the Earth
D. Weight of the gases of atmosphere

95. Victoria lake is located in the continent:
A. Africa B. Asia
C. North America D. South America

96. The famous Lagoon Lake of India is :
A. Dal Lake B. Chilka Lake
C. Pulicat Lake D. Mansarover

97. Where are most of the earth's active volcanoes concentrated?
A. Indian Ocean B. Pacific Ocean
C. Aral Sea D. Atlantic Ocean

98. Through which of the following states does the river Chambal flow?
A. U.P., M.P., Rajasthan B. M.P., Gujarat, U.P.
C. Rajasthan, M.P., Bihar D. Gujarat, M.P., U.P.

99. Which country is called the sugar bowl of the world?
A. Cuba B. India
C. Argentina D. USA

100. The area covered by forest in India is:
A. 46% B. 33%
C. 21.71% D. 23%

101. A closed economy is the one which :
A. does not permit emigration or immigration
B. permits emigration but no immigration
C. engages in no foreign trade
D. engages in no foreign and domestic trade or transit

102. In a developed economy the major share of employment originates in the :
A. primary sector B. tertiary sector
C. secondary sector D. any of the above

103. The Economic and Social Commission for Asia and Pacific (ESCAP) is located at :
A. Bangkok B. Kuala Lumpur
C. Manila D. Singapore

104. Commercial vehicles are not produced by which of the following companies in India?
A. TELCO B. Ashok Leyland
C. DCM Daewoo D. Birla Yamaha

105. What is 'Stagflation'?
A. Inflation with growth
B. Deflation with growth
C. Inflation after deflations
D. Inflation with depression

106. The main argument advanced in favour of small scale and cottage industries in India is that:
A. cost of production is low
B. they require small capital investment
C. they advance the goal of equitable distribution of wealth
D. they generate a large volume of employment

107. The most serious economic problems of India are:
A. Poverty and unemployment
B. Stagnation, not poverty
C. Unemployment, not poverty
D. Underdevelopment, not poverty

108. Which of the following is not one of the three central problems of an economy?
A. What to produce B. How to produce
C. When to produce D. For whom to produce

109. If saving exceeds investment, the national income will:
A. fall B. rise
C. fluctuate D. remain constant

110. In which of the following industries in India are the maximum number of workers employed?
A. Sugar B. Jute
C. Textiles D. Iron and Steel

111. Terrace Cultivation is practiced mostly:
A. in urban areas B. on slopes of mountains
C. on tops of hills D. in undulating tracts

112. Which of the following is a Selective Credit Control method?
A. Bank Rate B. RBI directives
C. Cash Reserve Ratio D. Open market operations

113. Which of the following taxes is not shared by the Central Government with the States?
A. Union excise duties B. Customs duty
C. Income tax D. Estate duty

114. ICICI is the name of a:
A. Financial Institution
B. Chemical Industry
C. Cotton Industry
D. Chamber of Commerce and Industry

115. Structural Unemployment arises due to
A. Deflationary conditions
B. Heavy industry bias
C. Shortage of raw material
D. Inadequate productive capacity

116. ECOMARC is a symbol related to:
A. Export goods
B. Import goods
C. Goods safe for environment
D. Best quality

117. The largest public sector bank in India is:
A. Central Bank of India B. Punjab National Bank
C. State Bank of India D. Indian Overseas Bank

118. Which of the following statements best explains the term contraband goods?
A. Goods produced only for exports
B. Goods produced in joint sector only
C. Goods for the trading of which licence is not required
D. Goods that are forbidden, from export, import or even possession, by law

119. Price in the market is fixed by:
A. Stock exchange rates
B. The demand and supply ruling in the market at a particular time
C. The Finance Minister
D. None of the above

120. Devaluation of currency helps to promote:
A. National Income B. Savings
C. Imports at lower cost D. Exports

121. Balanced economic growth can be achieved only if:
A. All the sectors of economy grow at the same rate
B. Population growth is arrested
C. All the inter dependent sectors grow in harmony
D. Basic and heavy industries are assigned highest priority

122. First share market in India was established in:
A. Mumbai B. Delhi
C. Kolkata D. Chennai

123. 'MODVAT' stands for:
A. Ad Valorem tax on output
B. Deduction of cost of inputs from the value of output
C. Reduction in import duties
D. Imposition of tax on professions

124. The headquarters of ILO is at:
A. Washington B. Geneva
C. The Hague D. Manila

125. The term 'devaluation' means:
A. Reducing the value of a currency in terms of another currency
B. Increasing the value of a currency
C. Revising the value of a currency
D. None of the above

126. Per capita net availability of pulses has shown a tendency of:
A. Increase over time
B. Decrease over time
C. Constant over time
D. First increase then decrease

127. National Income is the same as:
A. Net national product at market price
B. Net domestic product at market price
C. Net national product at factor cost
D. Net domestic product at factor cost

128. Which one of the following is not an example of indirect tax?
A. Sales tax B. Excise duty
C. Customs duty D. Expenditure tax

129. The major aim of devaluation is to:
A. encourage imports
B. encourage exports
C. encourage both exports and imports
D. discourage both exports and imports

130. Structural unemployment arises due to:
A. deflationary conditions
B. heavy industry bias
C. shortage of raw materials
D. inadequate productive capacity

131. When was the Family Planning Programme officially started in India?
A. 1950 B. 1952
C. 1956 D. 1962

132. When was the Reserve Bank of India nationalised?
A. 1947 B. 1949
C. 1950 D. 1951

133. Which of the following is *not* a feature of the Indian economy?
A. High rate of population growth
B. Disguised unemployment
C. Lowest rate of adult literacy
D. High rate of exports

134. The 'Relative Deprivation' approach for measuring poverty has been adopted by:
A. developing countries
B. developed countries
C. under-developed countries
D. None of the above

135. One of the main factors that led to rapid expansion of Indian exports is:
A. Imposition of import duties
B. Liberalisation of the economy
C. Recession in other countries
D. Diversification of exports

136. Sustainable economic development means an increase in the rate of growth of real:
A. total and per capita product
B. total and per capita product and level of literacy rate
C. total and per capita product and life expectancy at birth
D. total and per capita product, taking into account the cost of degradation of the quality of environment in this process

137. Functional unemployment occurs when:
A. unemployed have no qualification for job
B. people frequently change their job
C. people were thrown out from job due to recession
D. None of these

138. Which among the following does **not** have a 'free trade zone'?
A. Kandla B. Mumbai
C. Visakhapatnam D. Thiruvanantpuram

139. Sun Belt of USA is important for which one of the following industries?
A. Cotton textile B. Petrochemicals
C. Hi-tech electronics D. Food Processing

140. Commercial banking system in India is
A. unit banking B. branch banking
C. mixed banking D. None of the above

141. Who gives recognition to political parties in India?
A. Parliament
B. President
C. Supreme Court
D. Election Commission

142. The Quorum of the Legislative Council is :
A. one-fourth of its total membership
B. one-third of its membership
C. one-tenth of its membership
D. 25

143. The Indian Constitution is:
A. federal
B. unitary
C. a happy mixture of the federal and unitary
D. federal in normal times and unitary in times of emergency

144. Universal adult franchise implies a right to vote to all:
A. adult residents of the State
B. adult male citizens of the State
C. residents of the State
D. adult citizens of the State

145. When a resolution prefering a charge against the President has been passed by a specified majority in the House, it is sent to the other House for investigation. If, as a result of such an investigation, a resolution is passed through a specified majority by the other House, declaring that the charge has been sustained, the President shall leave his office. The specified special majority must not be less than :
A. two-third of the members present and voting
B. one-third of the members present and voting
C. three-fourth of the members present and voting and two-third of the total membership
D. two-third of the total membership

146. Which one of the following judicial powers of the President of India has been *wrongly* listed?
A. he appoints the Chief Justice and other judges of the Supreme Court
B. he can remove the judges of the Supreme Court on grounds of misconduct
C. he can consult the Supreme Court on any question of law or fact which is of public importance
D. he can grant pardon, reprieves and respites to persons punished under Union Law

147. The Vice-president of India can be removed from his office before the expiry of his term if :
A. the Rajya Sabha passes a resolution by a majority of its members and the Lok Sabha agrees with the resolution
B. if the Supreme Court of India recommends his removal
C. the President so desires
D. None of the above

148. The Chief Justice of a High Court in India is appointed by the :
A. Governor of the State
B. Prime Minister of India
C. Chief Justice of the Supreme Court
D. President of India

149. Which of the following statements is constitu-tionally not true about the passing of the Union Budgets, and Finance Bill in India?

1. Under the law, Finance Bill should be adopted by both the Houses of the Parliament within 45 days of its introduction.
2. If the Finance Bill is not adopted within specified period, the government loses its authority to levy the taxes proposed in the budgets.
3. In the absence of full budget, a vote-on-account gives the power to the government to spend.
4. Government cannot raise revenues without a proper approval of the Finance Bill

A. Only 2 B. Only 3
C. Only 4 D. Only 1, 2 and 3

150. Normally, on whose advice the President's Rule is imposed in a State?
A. Chief Minister
B. Legislative Assembly
C. Governor
D. Chief Justice of High Court

151. Which Article of the Indian Constitution deals with Amendment procedure?
A. Article 368 B. Article 358
C. Article 367 D. All of these

152. Government is the agency through which the will of:
A. the state is expressed
B. the people is expressed
C. the head of the state is expressed
D. the majority is expressed

153. In a unitary system of government :
A. The centre is all powerful
B. The centre is weaker than the states
C. The centre and states stand at par
D. The states and centre are supreme in their respective spheres

154. In Cabinet System of Government the real executive authority rests with :
A. The Council of Ministers
B. The Prime Minister
C. The Constitution
D. The Parliament

155. The Head of the State under a parliamentary government:
A. is an elected representative
B. is a hereditary person
C. is a nominated person
D. may be any one of the above

156. In the event of a ministerial proposal being defeated on the floor of the legislature, under the parliamentary system :
A. the government waits for a general no-confidence motion
B. the minister concerned is taken to task by the Prime Minister
C. the minister is forced to resign
D. the whole Council of Ministers resign

157. The "due process of law" is an essential characteristic of the judicial system of:
A. UK B. France
C. USA D. India

158. Under the Constitution it is :
A. obligatory for the President to accept the advice of the Council of Ministers but is not obliged to follow it
B. obligatory for the President to accept the advice of the Council of Ministers
C. not obligatory for the President to seek or accept the advice of the Council of Ministers
D. obligatory for the President to seek the advice of the Council of Ministers if his own party is in power

159. Which one of the following statements is correct?
A. the Presiding Officer of Rajya Sabha is elected every year
B. the Presiding Officer of Rajya Sabha is elected for a term of two years at a time
C. the Presiding Officer of Rajya Sabha is elected for a term of six years
D. the Vice-President of India is the ex-officio Presiding Officer of Rajya Sabha

160. The introduction of "no confidence" motion in the Lok Sabha requires the support of at least:
A. 50 members B. 70 members
C. 60 members D. 80 members

161. The High Court comes under :
A. State List B. Union List
C. Concurrent List D. None of the above

162. Which one of the following has been wrongly listed as a Fundamental Duty of the Indian citizens?
A. to develop scientific temper, humanism and spirit of inquiry and reform
B. to work for raising the prestige of the country in the international sphere
C. to protect and improve the natural environment
D. to strive towards excellence in all spheres of individual and collective activity

163. Which one of the following is not a Fundamental Duty as outlined in Article 51A of the Constitution?
A. to abide by the Constitution and respect its ideals
B. to defend the country and render national service when called upon to do so
C. to work for the moral upliftment of the weaker sections of society
D. to preserve the rich heritage

164. The main characteristics of the Directive Principles of State Policy given in the Indian Constitution are :
A. not enforceable by any court
B. fundamental in the governance of the country
C. 'Like instruments, instructions, political manifesto and a code of moral precepts which have to guide governors of the country'
D. no law can be passed, which is opposed to these principles

165. Of the following which are true?
A. In a State, the Legislative Council is dominant with regard to non-financial bills and the Legislative Assembly with regard to financial (money) bills
B. Vidhan Parishad can virtually block legisla-tion even if the same is passed by the Vidhan Sabha
C. In case of a tie between the two Houses, the Governor is duty-bound to call a joint session of the two Houses to have the issue settled on a majority verdict
D. If a Bill is twice approved by the Vidhan Sabha, it becomes law even if rejected by the Vidhan Parishad

166. Which one of the following types of emergency can be declared by the President?
A. Emergency due to threat of war and external aggresion
B. Emergency due to break-down of constitu-tional machinery in a State
C. Financial emergency on account of threat to the financial credit of India
D. all the three emergencies

167. The chairman of which of the following parliamentary committees is invariably from the members of ruling party?
A. Committee on public undertakings
B. Public accounts committee
C. Estimates committee
D. Committee on delegated legislation

168. Which of the following is not a formally prescribed device available to the members of parliament?
A. Question hour
B. Zero hour
C. Half-an-hour discussion
D. Short duration discussion

169. Which of the following is not a tool of executive control over public administration?
A. Power of appointment and removal
B. Line agencies
C. Appeal to public opinion
D. Civil services code

170. If the Speaker of the State Legislative Assembly decides to resign, he should submit his resignation to the:
A. Judges of the High Court
B. Deputy Speaker
C. Chief Minister
D. Finance Minister

171. Provision for free legal aid is mentioned in:
A. Fundamental Rights
B. Fundamental Duties
C. No Where
D. Directive principles of State policy

172. India is a Federal State because of:
A. dual judiciary
B. dual citizenship prevalent here
C. share of power between the Centre and the States
D. rigid Constitution

173. Residuary Subjects are those subjects which are:
A. contained in the State list
B. contained in the Union list
C. contained in the Concurrent list
D. not covered by any of the three lists

174. Which of the following writs can be issued, by the Supreme Court, to enforce Fundamental Rights?
A. Writ of Habeas Corpus
B. Writ of Mandamus
C. Writ of Quo Warranto
D. All of these

175. When the offices of both the President and the Vice-President of India are vacant, who will discharge their functions?
A. Prime Minister B. Home Minister
C. Chief Justice of India D. The Speaker

176. The Supreme Court tenders advice to the President of India on a matter of law or fact:
A. on its own
B. only when such advice is sought
C. only if the matter relates to some basic issue
D. only if the issue poses a threat to the unity and integrity of the country

177. Six months shall **not** intervene between two sessions of the Indian Parliament because :
A. it is the customary practice
B. it is the British convention followed in India
C. it is an obligation under the Constitution of India
D. None of the above

178. The States of the Indian Union can be recognised or their boundaries altered by:
A. the Union Parliament by a simple majority in the ordinary process of legislation
B. two-thirds majority of both the Houses of Parliament
C. two-thirds majority of both the Houses of Parliament and the consent of the legisla-tures of concerned States
D. an executive order of the Union government with the consent of the concerned State governments

179. The Basic Feature theory of the Constitution of India was propounded by the Supreme Court in the case of:
A. Minerva Mills Vs. Union of India
B. Golaknath Vs. State of Punjab
C. Maneka Gandhi Vs. Union of India
D. Keshavananda Vs. State of Kerala

180. Which one of the following writs is issued by a court in case of illegal detention of a person?
A. Habeas corpus B. Mandamus
C. Certiorari D. Quo-warranto

181. Name the instrument with the help of which a sailor in a submarine can see the objects on the surface of the sea.
A. Telescope B. Periscope
C. Gycroscope D. Stereoscope

182. 'Hemophillia' is the disease of ....
A. liver B. blood
C. brain D. bones

183. Vitamin A is abundantly found in ....
A. Brinjal B. Tomato
C. Carrot D. Cabbage

184. .... is not soluble in water.
A. Vitamin A B. Vitamin B
C. Vitamin C D. None of these

185. The blood vessels with the smallest diameter are called ....
A. capillaries B. arterioles
C. venules D. lymphatics

186. Out of the following .... has the greatest elasticity.
A. steel B. rubber
C. aluminium D. annealed copper

187. Cooking gas is a mixture of which of the following two gases?
A. Carbon Dioxide and Oxygen
B. Butane and Propane
C. Carbon Monoxide and Carbon Dioxide
D. Methane and Ethylene

188. The substance most commonly used as a food preservative is:
A. sodium carbonate B. tartaric acid
C. acetic acid D. benzoic acid

189. Normally, the substances that fight against diseases in human systems are known as:
A. dioxyribonucleic acids B. carbohydrates
C. enzymes D. antibodies

190. The SI unit of temperature is ....
A. Kelvin B. Celsius
C. Fahrenheit D. None of the above

191. One of the common fungal diseases of man is :
A. plague B. ringworm
C. cholera D. typhoid

192. A clear sky is blue because:
A. red light is scattered more than blue
B. ultraviolet light has been absorbed
C. blue light is scattered more than red
D. blue light has been absorbed

193. Jenner introduced the method of making people immune to :
A. small pox B. rabies
C. cholera D. polio

194. The largest cell in the human body is :
A. Nerve cell B. Live cell
C. Muscle cell D. Kidney cell

195. What is the device that steps up or steps down the voltage?
A. Dynamo B. Conductor
C. Inductor D. Transformer

196. The protein deficiency disease is known as :
A. Kwashiorker B. Cirrhosis
C. Eczema D. Clycoses

197. Iron deficiency causes :
A. rickets B. anaemia
C. cirrhosis D. goitre

198. Blood group of an individual is controlled by :
A. Haemoglobin B. Shape of RBC
C. Shape of WBC D. Genes

199. In a normal man the amount of blood pumped out by the heart per minute is about :
A. 1 litre B. 3 litres
C. 4 litres D. 5 litres

200. Red/green colour blindness in man is known as :
A. Protanopia B. Deutetanopia
C. Both A and B above D. Marfan's syndrome

201. The blue colour of the water in the sea is due to :
A. Reflection of the blue light by the impurities in sea water
B. Reflection of the blue sky by sea water and scattering of blue light by water molecules
C. Absorption of other colours by water molecules
D. None of the above

202. The image formed on the retina of the eye is:
A. upright and real B. larger than the object
C. small and inverted D. enlarged and real

203. Unit of loudness of sound is:
A. bel B. decibel
C. phon D. none of these

204. Oil rises up the wick in a lamp :
A. because oil is volatile
B. due to the capillary action phenomenon
C. due to the surface tension phenomenon
D. because oil is very light

205. The 'stones' formed in human kidney consist mostly of :
A. calcium oxalate
B. sodium acetate
C. magnesium sulphate
D. calcium

206. We hear the sound later, while the light is seen earlier:
A. because light's speed is more than that of sound
B. because lights travel in a straight direction while sound in a zigzag direction
C. because sound's frequency is lower than light
D. All of the above

207. Which part of an eye is transplanted?
A. Cornea B. Retina
C. Iris D. Sciera

208. The Universal donor group of blood is:
A. O B. A
C. B D. AB

209. The green colour of the leaf is due to :
A. Presence of Chloroplast
B. Presence of Chromium
C. Presence of Nicoplast
D. Presence of excess of oxygen

210. Voice of a child is more shrill than that of an elderly person because:
A. the pitch of the child's voice is higher than that of the person
B. the pitch is lower
C. the child is more energetic
D. None of the above

211. Camel uses its hump for :
A. storing water
B. storing fat
C. for balancing the body
D. temperature regulation

212. A man standing in a free falling lift releases a ball from his hand. The ball would be :
A. moving down B. moving up
C. stationary D. moving up and down

213. To change the quality of sound produced by an instrument we need to vary the:
A. pitch B. loudness
C. amplitude D. number of overtonnes

214. The disease caused by Asbestos is:
A. Emphysema B. Paralysis
C. Diarrhoea D. Dysentery

215. Sweetness of a sound depends upon its
A. wavelength
B. frequency
C. amplitude
D. periodicity and regularity

216. Bats can fly in the dark because :
A. they have a better vision in the dark
B. the pupils of their eyes are very big
C. they are guided by ultrasonic waves produced by them
D. any bird can do so

217. Blood is formed in the human adult by the :
A. heart B. spleen
C. kidney D. bone marrow

218. Pencil 'lead' is made up of:
A. graphite B. charcoal
C. lead oxide D. lampblack

219. The deficiency of which one of the following vitamins leads to bleeding of gums and loosening of teeth?
A. Vitamin D B. Vitamin C
C. Vitamin B D. Vitamin A

220. How much blood does a normal person have in his body?
A. 8 litres B. 4 to 5 litres
C. 10 litres D. 2 litres

221. Match List-I with List-II and select the correct answer using the codes given below the Lists :

List-I	***List-II***
(*a*) Visakhadatta	1. Mrichhakatika
(*b*) Shudraka	2. Ritusamhara
(*c*) Kalidasa	3. Kamasutra
(*d*) Vatsyayana	4. Devichandraguptam

Codes :

	(*a*)	(*b*)	(*c*)	(*d*)
A.	1	4	2	3
B.	4	1	3	2
C.	1	4	3	2
D.	4	1	2	3

222. In which one of the following langauges is the *Dalit* writing more conspicuous?
A. Punjabi B. Assamese
C. Marathi D. Odiya

223. The first writer to use Urdu as the medium of poetic expression was:
A. Amir Khusrau B. Mirza Ghalib
C. Bahadur Shah Zafar D. Faiz

224. The religious text of the Zoroastrians is named as:
A. Torah B. The Analects
C. Tripatika D. Zend Avesta

225. Name the music duo which composed music for Raj Kapoor's film 'Bobby'?
A. Laxmikant Pyarelal B. Shankar Jaikishen
C. Kalyanji Anandji D. Nadeem Shravan

226. Raja Harishchandra, an early Indian film, was produced by :
A. D.G. Phalke B. Ashok Kumar
C. Ardeshir Irani D. None of the above

227. All films are certified by .... before they are publicly exhibited.
A. Films Division
B. National Film Development Corporation (NFDC)
C. Directorate of Advertising and Visual Publicity (DAVP)
D. Central Board of Film Certificate (CBFC)

228. Who among the following was the director of the film 'Taal'?
A. Gulzar B. Shekhar Kapoor
C. Satish Shah D. Subhash Ghai

229. Who amongst the following actresses has played the leading role in the film Elizabeth?
A. Gwyneth Paltrow B. Cate Blanchett
C. Simi Garewal D. Kim Basinger

230. The film 'Train to Pakistan' is based on the novel of the same name, written by:
A. Bhishma Sahani B. Khushwant Singh
C. Amrita Pritam D. Khwaja Ahmed Abbas

231. Which of the following is a folk dance form of Jharkhand?
A. Pali B. Jhumar
C. Nati D. Chhau

232. The first feature film (talkie) to be produced in India was:
A. Hatimtai B. Alam Ara
C. Pundalik D. Raja Harishchandra

233. Who directed the film "Bombay"?
A. Shyam Benegal B. Meera Nair
C. Shekhar Kapoor D. Mani Ratnam

234. Late Pankaj Udhas was famous in which of the following fields?
A. Singing B. Acting
C. Music D. Literature

235. Who among the following is the director of the film 'Kaho Na Pyar Hai'?
A. Subhash Ghai B. Shekhar Kapoor
C. Ramesh Sippy D. Rakesh Roshan

236. The character played by Jim Carrey in the movie *Man on Moon* is based on:
A. Andy Kaufman B. Edwin Aldrin
C. John Glenn D. Neil Armstrong

237. A popular Hindi film-based on the famous Sanskrit play *Mrichhakatika*, was titled:
A. Meghadoot B. Amrapali
C. Utsav D. Shakuntala

238. Who composed the song 'Zara Yad Karo Kurbani'?
A. Javed Akhtar
B. Pradeep
C. Nusrat Fateh Ali Khan
D. Raghupati Sahay 'Firaq'

239. Who was the producer of the serial 'Mahabharat'?
A. Shyam Benegal B. B.R. Chopra
C. Ramanand Sagar D. Mani Ratnam

240. Which of the following is a folk dance of Rajasthan?
A. Garba B. Dandya
C. Jhumar D. Kathak

241. 'The Colonel' is the nickname of which Indian Test Cricketer?
A. Colonel C.K. Naidu B. Rahul Dravid
C. Mohinder Amarnath D. Dilip Vengsarkar

242. The term 'Grandmaster' is used in which of these games?
A. Judo B. Chess
C. Bridge D. Karate

243. The term "Derby" is related with which of the following?
A. Polo B. Swimming
C. Racing D. Horse Racing

244. With which game is Geet Sethi associated?
A. Basketball B. Chess
C. Snooker D. Tennis

245. Beighton Cup is related with which of the following?
A. Hockey B. Polo
C. Cricket D. Soccer

246. Match List-I with List-II and select the correct answer using the codes given below the Lists :

List-I	*List-II*
(*a*) Basketball	1. Lob
(*b*) Bridge	2. Revoke
(*c*) Golf	3. Pivot
(*d*) Tennis	4. Bunker

Codes :

	(*a*)	(*b*)	(*c*)	(*d*)
A.	2	3	1	4
B.	2	3	4	1
C.	3	2	1	4
D.	3	2	4	1

247. The head office of the International Cricket Council (ICC) is situated in :
A. Zimbabwe B. Australia
C. South Africa D. UAE

248. Match the following :

List-I	*List-II*
(*a*) Deodhar Trophy	1. Volleyball
(*b*) Durand Cup	2. Football
(*c*) Davis Cup	3. Cricket
	4. Tennis

Codes :

	(*a*)	(*b*)	(*c*)
A.	3	2	4
B.	3	1	4
C.	2	3	1
D.	1	2	4

249. Which of the following is called 'Grand Slam'?
A. Winning the highest number of medals in the Olympic games
B. Winning the men's singles title in Wimbledon Championship
C. Winning the Wimbledon Singles title successively for two years
D. Winning all the four championships Australian, French, Wimblendon and US

250. With which game is the term 'butterfly stroke' associated?
A. Swimming B. Cricket
C. Gliding D. Skiing

251. Who is the first Indian to win the 'International Grand Master' title in Chess?
A. Anupama Abhayankar
B. Bhagyashree Sathe Thipsay
C. Vishwanathan Anand
D. D.V. Prasad

252. The XXII Commonwealth Games were held in 2022 in:
A. Kuala Lumpur B. Bangkok
C. Victoria D. Birmingham

253. The term 'Tee' is associated with which of the following sports?
A. Golf B. Table Tennis
C. Polo D. Judo

254. The famous woman Tennis player who was stabbed during a match, is
A. Steffi Graf B. Monica Seles
C. Mary Pierce D. Martina Navratilova

255. The term 'Baseline' is related to which of the following?
A. Golf B. Hockey
C. Badminton D. Polo

256. In which Indian State did the game of Polo originate?
A. Manipur B. Rajasthan
C. Gujarat D. West Bengal

257. World Environment Day is Celebrated on :
A. June 9 B. June 11
C. June 5 D. June 13

258. Rafael Nadal is the well-known player associated with:
A. Hockey B. Cricket
C. Tennis D. Chess

259. Gagan Narang is the well-known player associated with :
A. Shooting B. Golf
C. Table Tennis D. Chess

260. Eden Garden, a famous Cricket stadium, is located in:
A. Kanpur B. Kolkata
C. Jamshedpur D. Pune

261. Maharaja Ranjit Singh Trophy is associated with :
A. Golf B. Hockey
C. Soccer D. Tennis

262. Neeraj Chopra is a distinguished athlete in which of the following games?
A. Swimming B. Weightlifting
C. Javelin Throw D. Archery

263. Cricket was an Olympic event at which of the following Olympics?
A. London, 1908 B. Amsterdam, 1928
C. Paris, 1900 D. Melbourne, 1956

264. WISPA competitions are associated with :
A. Squash B. Yatching
C. Boxing D. Billiards

265. Ryder Cup is the famous trophy of :
A. Golf B. Chess
C. Boxing D. Polo

266. Davis Cup is associated with the sport of :
A. Cricket B. Football
C. Tennis D. Hockey

267. 'Volley', 'Chop' and 'Drive Spine' are the term associated with :
A. Lawn Tennis B. Badminton
C. Table Tennis D. Golf

268. Lal Bahadur Shastri Stadium is located at :
A. Hyderabad B. Chennai
C. Ahmedabad D. Varanasi

269. The first winner of "Rajiv Khel Ratna Award" (Now Major Dhyanchand Khel Ratna Award) was :
A. Geet Sethi B. Sachin Tendulkar
C. Viswanathan Anand D. Karnam Malleswari

270. 2023 Cricket World Cup was held in :
A. India B. Sri Lanka
C. Bangladesh D. Australia

271. The first team event introduced in 1900 at Paris Olympics was :
A. Hockey B. Football
C. Cricket D. Baseball

272. Which of the following international tennis tournaments is held on grass court?
A. US Open B. French Open
C. Wimbledon D. Australian Open

273. Which cricketer is nicknamed as the pied piper of Punjab?
A. Yuvraj Singh B. Harbhajan Singh
C. Mohinder Amarnath D. Navjot Singh Sidhu

274. 'Merdeka Cup' is associated with ....
A. Golf B. Football
C. Squash D. Hockey

275. The first time athletes marched into the stadium behind their nation's flag in Olympics:
A. at St. Louis 1904 B. at London 1908
C. at Antwerp 1920 D. at Paris 1924

276. The "Dronacharya Award" is associated with:
A. Eminent Surgeons
B. Famous Sports Person
C. Sport Coaches
D. Expert Engineers

277. Which cricketer is nicknamed as 'Jumbo'?
A. Venkatesh Prasad B. Anil Kumble
C. Glenn McGrath D. Shane Warne

278. The first time the Olympic Games were organised by a private company at:
A. Montreal, 1976 B. Los Angeles, 1984
C. Atlanta, 1996 D. Rome, 1960

279. In which Asian Games Cricket was played first?
A. Guangzhou, 2010
B. Doha, 2006
C. Busan, 2002
D. Seoul, 1986

280. The term 'Penalty cick' is used in :
A. Hockey B. Football
C. Baseball D. Golf

281. "Green Revolution" began in India during the year:
A. 1972-73 B. 1977-78
C. 1980-81 D. 1967-68

282. Khmer Rouge is a dictatorial party of :
A. Cambodia B. Indonesia
C. Malaysia D. Thailand

283. Which country is not a member of SAARC?
A. Russia B. Bangladesh
C. Nepal D. Pakistan

284. The headquarters of WTO is located at :
A. Geneva B. Paris
C. The Hague D. Washington

285. The main function of the World Trade Organisation (WTO) is:
A. enforcing of Uruguay Round Agreements
B. facilitating multi-lateral trade relations of member countries and reviewing trade policies
C. administering trade dispute settlement procedures
D. None of the above

286. The Secretary-General of the UNO is appointed by the:
A. General Assembly B. Security Council
C. Trusteeship Council D. World Bank

287. The United Nations officially came into existence in 1945 on :
A. November 24 B. October 14
C. October 24 D. November 14

288. Which one of the following is true of the International Court of Justice?
A. The Judges of the Court are appointed according to the discretion of the Secretary General
B. No two Judges may belong to the same country
C. The Court consists of 20 Judges
D. The statute of the International Court of Justice is not an integral part of the UN Charter

289. Which of the following was not among the six founding countries of the European Community?
A. Belgium B. France
C. Germany D. UK

290. The smallest country in South America is:
A. Ecuador B. Guyana
C. Surinam D. Uruguay

291. In which year "Human Rights Resolution" was adopted by the U.N.?
A. 1945 B. 1946
C. 1947 D. 1948

292. Where is the headquarters of INTERPOL located?
A. Berlin B. California
C. Lyons D. Montreal

293. Parliament of which of the following countries is known as Great People's Khural?
A. Malaysia B. Mongolia
C. Thailand D. Indonesia

294. Numbers of major organs of United Nations are:
A. 3 B. 4
C. 5 D. 6

295. When is the UN Day celebrated?
A. October 24 B. January 24
C. June 24 D. September 24

296. Which one of the following organ of United Nations is known as the 'Policeman of the World'?
A. Security Council
B. International Court of Justice
C. The Secretariat
D. General Assembly

297. The members of the NAFTA include:
A. USA, Canada and Mexico
B. USA, Canada, Mexico and UK
C. USA, UK, Russia and Mexico
D. USA, Canada and Brazil

298. The sits of International Court of Justice is located at:
A. Vienna B. Paris
C. Hague D. New York

299. Which of the following is known as the Constitution of the UN?
A. UN Charter B. UN Assembly
C. UN Security Council D. UN Secretariat

300. The Headquarters of the Amnesty International is located at :
A. New York B. London
C. Geneva D. Addis-Ababa

ANSWERS

1	2	3	4	5	6	7	8	9	10
B	C	D	C	B	C	A	C	C	D
11	12	13	14	15	16	17	18	19	20
C	A	C	A	A	D	A	B	A	D
21	22	23	24	25	26	27	28	29	30
A	C	B	C	D	C	B	D	D	B
31	32	33	34	35	36	37	38	39	40
C	D	C	C	B	C	D	B	C	C
41	42	43	44	45	46	47	48	49	50
A	A	A	B	C	D	C	B	B	D
51	52	53	54	55	56	57	58	59	60
A	C	A	B	B	A	B	C	A	C
61	62	63	64	65	66	67	68	69	70
C	C	B	B	C	C	D	D	D	B
71	72	73	74	75	76	77	78	79	80
B	C	C	C	A	A	A	B	B	A
81	82	83	84	85	86	87	88	89	90
A	B	D	B	C	C	D	C	B	D
91	92	93	94	95	96	97	98	99	100
A	B	A	A	A	B	B	A	A	C
101	102	103	104	105	106	107	108	109	110
C	B	A	D	D	D	A	C	D	C
111	112	113	114	115	116	117	118	119	120
B	B	B	A	D	C	C	D	B	D
121	122	123	124	125	126	127	128	129	130
C	A	A	B	A	D	C	D	B	D
131	132	133	134	135	136	137	138	139	140
B	B	D	A	B	D	B	D	D	C
141	142	143	144	145	146	147	148	149	150
D	C	D	D	D	B	A	D	C	C
151	152	153	154	155	156	157	158	159	160
A	B	A	A	A	D	C	B	D	A
161	162	163	164	165	166	167	168	169	170
B	B	C	B	D	D	C	B	B	B
171	172	173	174	175	176	177	178	179	180
D	C	D	D	C	B	C	A	D	A
181	182	183	184	185	186	187	188	189	190
B	B	C	A	A	A	B	D	D	A
191	192	193	194	195	196	197	198	199	200
B	C	A	A	D	A	B	D	D	A
201	202	203	204	205	206	207	208	209	210
B	B	B	B	A	A	A	A	A	A

211	212	213	214	215	216	217	218	219	220
B	A	A	A	D	C	D	A	B	B
221	**222**	**223**	**224**	**225**	**226**	**227**	**228**	**229**	**230**
D	C	A	D	A	A	D	D	B	B
231	**232**	**233**	**234**	**235**	**236**	**237**	**238**	**239**	**240**
D	B	D	A	D	D	C	B	B	C
241	**242**	**243**	**244**	**245**	**246**	**247**	**248**	**249**	**250**
D	B	D	C	A	D	D	A	D	A
251	**252**	**253**	**254**	**255**	**256**	**257**	**258**	**259**	**260**
C	D	A	B	C	A	C	C	A	B
261	**262**	**263**	**264**	**265**	**266**	**267**	**268**	**269**	**270**
B	C	C	A	A	C	C	A	C	A
271	**272**	**273**	**274**	**275**	**276**	**277**	**278**	**279**	**280**
B	C	A	B	A	C	B	B	A	B
281	**282**	**283**	**284**	**285**	**286**	**287**	**288**	**289**	**290**
D	A	A	A	B	A	C	B	D	C
291	**292**	**293**	**294**	**295**	**296**	**297**	**298**	**299**	**300**
D	C	B	D	A	A	A	C	A	B

❐ ❐ ❐